THE AFRICANS W

Ancient Secrets Africa and

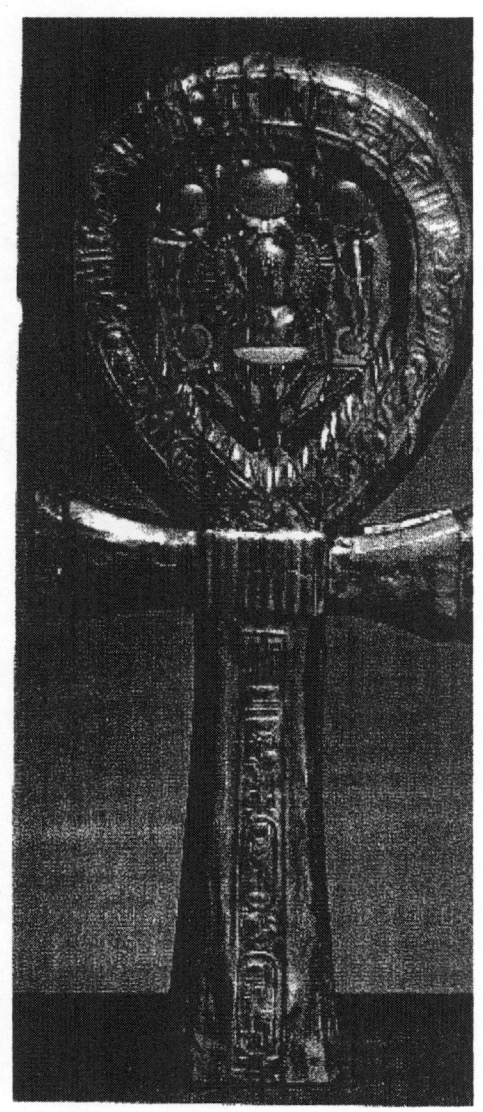

NANA BANCHIE DARKWAH

NKWA [ANKH]

This Ancient Egyptian cross is the earliest and most ancient sacred symbol of religion. Egyptologists that believe they have successfully deciphered Ancient Egyptian hieroglyphics say it is called the *ANKH,* meaning *LIFE.* The meaning is correct, however, that is not what the Ancient Egyptians called it. The original Ancient Egyptian word that Egyptologists tried to decipher was *NKWA.* The language from which this word originated is *Akan* and it actually means *LIFE.* This symbol was the Ancient Egyptian sacred religious symbol that reinforced the cross on which Jesus was crucified, as a sacred Christian symbol. How did this happen? The early Christian Church of Ancient Egypt adopted the *NKWA* symbol as the symbol of their Church and called it the *Crux Ansata.* From here, it was taken to Rome, and there it became a Christian symbol with only a slight variation in design. The symbol of *NKWA* below was excavated from the tomb of the *Akan* king *Tutu Ankoma,* the boy king of Ancient Egypt whose name Europeans have corrupted to Tutankhamun. He ruled from 1336-1327 B. C.

The Africans Who Wrote The Bible: Ancient Secrets Africa and
Christianity Have Never Told

Published by special arrangement with:
HBC Publications
Orlando FL

ISBN: 1-884631-06-1

PRINTED IN THE USA

CONTENTS

It is a strange fact that we have never known with certainty who produced the book that has played such a central role in our civilization. There are traditions concerning who wrote each of the biblical books – the five Books of Moses are supposed to be by Moses, the Book of Lamentations by the prophet Jeremiah, half the Psalms by King David – but how is one to know if these traditional ascriptions are correct?

Richard Elliot Friedman
In *Who Wrote The Bible*? 1987.

It is the strange authority granted to the Bible in our society, an acquiescence that pertains whether one is a Christian or not, together with the poverty of our knowledge and public discussions of the Bible, that is the stimulus of this book. Here we are with the Bible on our hands and we do not know how we got it, how it works, or what to make of it in public forum.

Burton Mack
In *Who Wrote The New Testament: The Making of the Christian Myth*, 1995.

How do we know, independent of the Bible, that Israel's presence in Egypt was preceded by an earlier presence in Palestine? Why is there no archaeological record of Israel or the Hebrew people prior to the thirteenth century B. C.? [The period of the so-called biblical Exodus]. Why is there no extrabiblical evidence linking any specific Semitic tribes to the Hebrew people? And why did the so-called ten lost tribes disappear without an archaeological trace of their existence?

Gary Greenberg
In *The Moses Mystery: The African Origin of the Jewish People*, 1996.

Though several nations had written records in the second, third, and fourth millennia B. C. from which modern historians can draw conclusions, there is no evidence that Israel was among them.

Gary Greenberg
In The Moses Mystery: The African Origin of the Jewish people, 1996.

In spite of their pretended intimacy with the Creator, the Jews never had great knowledge of things cosmic and metaphysical; they were but plagiarists culling mythic artifacts they did not understand.

Lloyd Graham
In *Deceptions and Myths of the Bible*, 1995.

If the Jewish people originated from Mesopotamia as the Bible claims, how did Tera, the name of the father of Abraham, the name of Abraham himself, the name of his son Isaac, and the names of his grandsons Esau and Jacob all come to be derived from African tribal words and names? From which African tribes in Mesopotamia did they originate for Jewish people to be carrying African tribal names? How did the earliest Jewish name for God, *Adonai* that became Adonis in Greek come to be derived from an African tribal word?

How did the name of the Jewish nation Israel come to be derived from an African tribal word with its African tribal meaning in the Bible?

How did millions of modern Jewish people come to have and still carry African tribal names?

How did the authors of the Old Testament documents Joshua, Samuel, Nehemiah, Isaiah, Jeremiah, Ezekiel, Daniel, Hosea, Amos, Obadiah, Jonah, Nahum, Habakkuk, Zephaniah, Haggai, Zechariah, Malachi come to have African tribal names?

Introduction

"Ex Africa semper aliquid novi," "there is always something new coming out of Africa."
Herodotus of Halicarnassus

Christianity has just entered its third millennium, and on Sunday, March 12, 2000, Pope John Paul II used his traditional Sunday Mass to apologize for the sins and atrocities of the Church against peoples and cultures around the world for the past two thousand years. From historical evidence, the sins of the Church are numerous. However, the worst lie and sin of the Church was the premeditated transformation of the racial and ethnic identities of Jesus Christ, his mother, and the entire people of the Bible from the black people they were to white people, to satisfy emerging European racist sentiments against black people. This made it possible for Christian Europe to perceive black people who created the concepts, doctrines, and sacramental practices that eventually became the foundations of Christianity as the cursed ones by the very God black people imagined, created, and personified. It made it possible for the Church to authorize Europeans to enslave black people because they were pagans. It made it possible for ignorant Europe to perceive black people as inferior and white people as superior. It also made it possible for Europeans to go to Church to worship a God that was created by black people and then come home to perpetrate the worst atrocities on black people that were their slaves. Worse of all, this made it possible for Christian Europe and Europeans to justify all the atrocities they were perpetrating against black people, the original people of the Bible, as ordained by God.

All these did not happen because the Church did not know that the original people of the Bible were black people. The Church has known this as long as it has known the mother of Jesus to be the Black Madonna of the Church since the past two thousand years. My point is the continued lie in Christianity about the black heritage of Jesus Christ and the people of the Bible has been the most atrocious and worst sin of the Church and Christianity in the past two thousand years.

The early apostolic fathers of Christianity and the Church knew of many things that they did not want Christian masses to know about the background history, content, and people of the Bible. As a result, the very design of Christianity was based upon protecting the Bible from the lay masses. Until the Reformation, therefore, the Bible was secretly guarded and its content was known to only a few in the Church. Because of the perceived need to protect the Bible from the masses, the earliest design and practice of Christianity was based upon placing a cadre of priests between the Bible and the people. These priests were secretly trained and taught to teach the Bible only in the manner prescribed by the Church. Even when the Bible became available to the masses, Christianity still argued that the Bible is so complex that the lay masses would not understand it so they still needed trained people to interpret the Bible to them. This was again intended to control the interpretation of the Bible based upon the secrets early apostolic fathers did not want the masses to know.

Because the development of Christianity was based upon many things that the apostolic fathers did not want the masses to know, interpretations of the Bible that began in Western Europe and was propagated around the world through Christianity have been based upon some serious falsehoods and false assumptions. Numerous European scholars have known and written about these falsehoods and false assumptions in the foundations of Christianity. For example, in Volume I of *The Natural Genesis: A Book of the Beginnings*, Gerald Massey (1883) called the story and practice of Christianity *the legendary lying lore*.

Among the falsehoods and false assumptions in the foundations of Christianity has been the belief that the Jewish people that followed the Bible into Europe actually wrote the documents of the Bible. Revelations of the African names of the authors of the Old Testament in this book will show that the Jewish people did not write the documents they compiled and edited for the Greeks for them to become the first Bible, the Greek Bible. Another assumption has been the false belief that the Jewish people were known as Jews and Hebrews where they originated before they went to Europe, but that was not so. The group of people that became the Jews and Hebrews had a different collective name derived from their racial, ethnic, and even tribal identities before they went to Europe to become Jews and Hebrews. Again, another assumption has been the false belief that the Jewish people were originally white people as we see them today. This has in turn led to the false assumption that the people of the Bible were also originally white like the Jewish people we see today, but that is all wrong. The discussion and revelation in this book will show that the people of the Bible were not white people and that Jews and Hebrews were not originally white people as we see them today.

Another false assumption that was derived from the deliberate deception in the Bible itself was the belief that the Jewish people originated from somewhere other than from the black African tribes that were the Ancient Egyptians. According to the Bible, the Jewish people went to Ancient Egypt as members of one family, the family of Jacob, sixty-six men in all (Genesis 46). However, the people supposedly left Ancient as several tribes. What does that tell you? The deception in the Bible's assertion that the Jewish people originated from Mesopotamia is revealed from the fact that historians, archaeologists, anthropologists, and geneticists have not be able to locate any other group of people from whom the Jewish people must have originated anywhere in the world, other than Africa. Again, the discussion and revelation in this book will show that racially, ethnically, historically, linguistically, culturally, genetically, and even biblically, the people that left Ancient Egypt into the so-called Exodus and later went to Europe to become the Jews and Hebrews originated from the African tribes that were the Ancient Egyptians.

Most people have heard the lingering and persisting rumor that Jesus Christ was a black man. However, nobody has ever heard of any evidence proving or disproving this assertion. Some people want to believe it but they do not have any basis for establishing such a belief, yet the rumor lingers in their minds. Two things make this rumor linger and continue to persist in the minds and imaginations of people. The first is the fact that the Jewish people claim that Jesus was a Jew. However, these Jewish people look like white people. Based upon the skin color of Jewish people today, the assumption has been that Jesus was white. Nevertheless, if Jesus was a white man and some one asserts that he was a black man, the Jewish people who claim Jesus was one of them should question and challenge such an assertion. Yet, they have been silent over this important issue for almost two hundred years since European scholars began revealing that the people of the Bible were actually black people, and that Jesus was truly a black man. This silence on the part of Jewish people is in itself a form of an admission that Jesus Christ was in fact a black man.

The second reason that keeps this assertion lingering in the minds of many people is the fact that Europeans designed Christianity around the life and teachings of Jesus Christ. Christianity has propagated the life and teachings of Jesus and portrayed him in all images around the world as a white man with blonde hair, blue eyes, and white skin. If anyone comes behind all these to assert that Jesus Christ was in fact a black man, this person is in fact calling Christian Europe and Christianity a lie. As a result, Christian Europe and Christianity should be able to question or challenge such an assertion in defense of their integrity. Yet, Christian Europe has also been silent over this issue just as the Jewish people have been. What is even more intriguing about this is that whereas Christian Europe's earliest portrayal of Jesus was the image of a black man, there is evidence that Christianity has quietly and slowly transformed this image into the image of a white man. That makes us suspect that there must be some truth in the assertion that Jesus was a black man, after all.

When people in the west read the Bible they come across stories of the lives of people from a different culture. That in itself has a fascinating appeal that makes them believe that everything they are reading is true. When we read the Bible in Africa, we wonder why Europeans

ii

have claimed the cultural traditions, religion, and lifestyle in the Bible for the Jews when we still live lives based upon traditions, religion, and lifestyle in Africa. For example, Jewish naming ceremonies and rituals have been *Ibo* naming ceremonies since these people lived in the Middle East and Egypt in ancient times.

Yet, according to the Bible, the supposed ancestors of the Jewish people originated from Ur of the Chaldees in Mesopotamia where there were no white people and there were no Arabs in this region at the time. There were only black people. Most of these people went on to live in Ancient Egypt where there were no white people but only black people. The Jewish people left Ancient Egypt and went to live in Canaan where again there were no white people and again they went to live amongst black people. From Canaan, these people went to Europe where they became known as Jews and Hebrews. Nevertheless, Christianity portrays Jesus Christ as a white man. As a result, Christianity should be able to tell the world how it came to know this Jesus to be a white man. It owes the world this clarification. However, all of these confirm that someone has been seeking to conceal something from Christian masses about the true racial and ethnic heritage of Jesus Christ, his mother Mary, and the people of the Bible.

Despite people's interest in knowing whether Jesus was a black man or not, this work did not set out to prove the racial and ethnic heritage of Jesus and the people of the Bible. It began from a disturbing revelation I came across in a related interest, and that interest was Ancient Egypt. In *A History of Ancient Egypt,* Nicolas Grimal revealed in his introduction that:

> It was not so long ago, however, that the combined influence of the Bible and Classical tradition conspired to produce a rather incoherent view of Egyptian civilization, and the great chronological disputes inherited from the nineteenth century are a continuing legacy (see Histoire de l'Egypte ancienne, translation by Ian Shaw, 1992.).

This was quite a profound revelation for me because I know of the classical efforts by Greek rulers and scholars to propagate the idea that the Greeks created the Ancient Egyptian civilization. I know of the work of Greek writers like Theocritus who asserted and propagated such a preposterous idea in his writings. I know of the work of Appolonius of Rhodes who wrote trying to blend Greek and Ancient Egyptian cultures to make the unfounded claims of the Greeks complete. I know that Ptolemy, a Greek ruler of Ancient Egypt after Alexander had conquered the Egyptians, asked Manetho to rewrite Ancient Egyptian history and convert the names of Ancient Egyptian kings into Greek. This was to make it possible for later Greek rulers of Egypt to fit their names onto the traditional kings' list and glorious history of Ancient Egypt.

I know that the classical tradition has had a classical reason to try to distort and destroy Ancient Egyptian history and civilization. However, what bothered me most about the above quotation was that I did not know why believers and protectors of the Bible would be involved in a conspiracy to distort and destroy Ancient Egyptian history and image. Why would believers of the Bible and the Christian faith be interested in making sure that some aspects of truths in Ancient Egyptian history are distorted or denied? In my ignorant mind, the question I asked myself was what has Ancient Egyptian history got to do with the Bible that is so important to make the biblical tradition also want to distort and destroy Ancient Egyptian history? Because of Grimal's observation, I became curious and interested to find out what Ancient Egypt had done to believers and protectors of the Bible to make them so much afraid of Ancient Egypt's true history.

This work, therefore, began from the curiosity and interest I developed in the history of Ancient Egypt and the Bible. These were immediately fuelled by my realization that I had the linguistic and cultural backgrounds to see into and understand the Ancient Egyptian story in ways western historians and Egyptologists have never known and understood before. I am not a historian and I am not an Egyptologist, but I found out that I have the ability to read and deeply understand the Ancient Egyptian story from a linguistic and cultural point of view that western historians and Egyptologists do not have.

From watching television documentaries and listening to comments made on Ancient Egypt, I became even more interested in the Ancient Egyptian story. I found out that my interest in this history was partly because some of the names of the kings, people, and places and aspects of the Ancient Egyptian story and culture sounded very familiar to me. They were very similar to the names and aspects of the modern lives of my people in Africa. I have heard the Ancient Egyptians were Africans but that was too general an association to mean anything to me.

With this interest, however, I ordered several Ancient Egyptian books, from a *Dictionary of Ancient Egypt* to the earliest western scholastic discussion of its culture. Again, within these books, I came across a most profound idea that opened my eyes and mind, and helped me to understand the Ancient Egyptian story even better. Perhaps more importantly, this idea helped me to firmly identify the specific African tribes that were the Ancient Egyptians. That is something western experts have not been able to do.

This profound idea was the revelation in one of the Ancient Egyptians books that the modern names of Ancient Egyptian kings, people, and places we hear and read about everyday are not the true and indigenous names of the kings, people, and places of Ancient Egypt. According to Joseph Kaster, the author of the Ancient Egyptian book I read, the original names of these ancient people and places were transposed from their original languages and cultures when the Ancient Egyptian story was first translated into the Greek language. What intrigued me most about this idea was the fact that some western scholars are still transposing these Ancient Egyptian names for reasons only known to them.

This revelation immediately opened my eyes and got me interested in the exercise of searching for the original Ancient Egyptian names that early Greek historians had transposed into Greek. I knew that finding these original names would lead me to the African tribes, languages, and cultures from which these people and names originated. This exercise was originally for my amusement and scholastic curiosity and little did I know that it was going to lead me into the discovery of secrets unknown and hidden for hundreds and in some cases thousands of years.

I am an African, specifically an *Akan*. As I began the exercise of trying to decipher the indigenous names of Ancient Egyptian kings, people, and places, I began to discover that most of these names were *Akan*. From a very distant mind, I began to understand why some of the names and aspects of the story of Ancient Egypt felt so familiar to me. I did not discover only *Akan* names in the Ancient Egyptian story, I also discovered *Ewe, Ibo, Yoruba, Ga-Adangme,* and *Hausa* names, especially in the Ancient Egyptian kings' list. It then dawned on me that I have discovered who the Ancient Egyptians really were from their indigenous African tribal names, languages, and cultures. It also dawned on me that though western scholars have written volumes about the Ancient Egyptians and some have even made elegant documentaries and comments about them, none has ever known the true African tribal origins and identities of these ancient magnificent people. These western scholars have never known what languages these people spoke in Ancient Egypt, and they have never known the true cultures of these ancient people. From this knowledge, I began a book entitled *Ancient Egypt: The Story Africa Has Never Told* to reveal my discoveries. Then I was side tracked.

With opened eyes and countless questions I could not answer in my mind, I began seeing transposed *Akan* and other African tribal names all around me everywhere I looked. I saw them at the end of movie credits and in books, especially in the bibliographies of books. I saw them in the names of businesses and in telephone books. I met people that carried transposed African names that did not even know that these names originated from African tribes. When I met real "white" people with transposed African tribal names, I became more fascinated about that than my discovery of the African tribal names of the Ancient Egyptians. The people I met were real humans and I wanted to tell a living story before going back to tell the ancient story. I met one man whose name fascinated me more than any other names. He is called *Sahene*. This is an *Akan* name meaning warlord. He spells his name just as we spell this word in *Akan* but he is influenced by European phonology so he pronounces it something like *Saheen*.

From books and the people I met, again I did not see only *Akan* tribal names but I saw *Ewe, Ga-Adangme, Hausa, Nzima,* and several other African tribal names. What perhaps fascinated me most was that these people looked white and the more I discovered their African tribal names, the more I became intrigued about them. When I inquired who these people were that carried transposed African tribal names, I was told that they were not Europeans. They were Jews.

I was never more confused because I never in my wildest dreams think that the Jewish people might have anything in common with black Africans. How did Jewish people come to carry African tribal names? I was even more confused to find out that the names these people carried were not from one African tribe but from several African tribes. The question that immediately came into my mind was how could "white" people that supposedly originated from biblical Canaan, far away from black African tribes, carry transposed African tribal names not from one tribe but from several black African tribes? Who are these people, and from where did they go to Europe? These were the questions that took me out of myself into searching for answers from the Ancient Egyptians through to the Jewish people, Africans, the Bible, and Christianity.

As the story began to unfold before me, I found *Akan* and other African tribal names in the history of Ancient Egypt and I also found *Akan* and other African tribal names among the Jewish people. Things were beginning to make sense. Ancient Egypt was closer to biblical Canaan than inner Africa, but I never put the two groups of people together in my wildest imaginations. After all one group was white and the other was black and I never imagined that any white people and black people could ever have a common racial origin. Nevertheless, the discovery I had made about these people never seized to haunt me.

I had discovered a linguistic and cultural relationship between the black African tribes that were the Ancient Egyptians and the Jewish people that were first Ancient Egyptians and then Canaanites and now Europeans through their common African tribal names, languages, and cultures. I wanted badly to find out the true story behind the linguistic and cultural relationship I had discovered between the Jewish people in Europe and the African tribal groups that were the Ancient Egyptians.

I found out that I did not know enough to be able to reveal or explain my discovery to anyone. I needed to learn more to be able to establish a credible link between these two groups of people that are continents apart before I could arrive at a conclusion about the possible racial and ethnic relationship between these two groups. For such information, I re-read Ancient Egyptian history. I concluded in my analysis that if the Jewish people have carried *Akan* and other African tribal names up till now, they must have some more evidence linking them to the *Akan* and other African tribes in their own history. I therefore read the history of Israel and Judea and found more *Akan* and other African tribal names in them. I even found the name of an *Akan* tribe in the history of the Jewish people. I was more convinced than ever that there was a definite racial, ethnic, linguistic, and cultural relationship between the *Akan* and other African tribes that were the Ancient Egyptians and the Jewish people that were also Ancient Egyptians before becoming Canaanites and later Europeans.

One well-known document that is always linked to the Jewish people around the world is the Bible. Not only were the Jewish people Ancient Egyptians, but also the documents of the Bible were originally compiled, edited, and translated into the Greek language in Ancient Egypt. When the Greeks first translated the Ancient Egyptian history into the Greek language, they transposed the *Akan* and other African tribal names of the Ancient Egyptians into the Greek language. It was therefore prudent for me to assume that in the translation of the documents of the Bible into the Greek language, the African tribal names of the people of the Bible would also be transposed into various renderings in Greek. I concluded further in my analysis that if there are

Akan and other African tribal names in the history of the Jewish people, there must also be some transposed *Akan* and other African tribal names in the Bible. As a result, I took to reading the Bible this time as a historical document. I have read several portions of the Bible before but this time, I was reading it with an open eye and mind for transposed *Akan* and other African tribal names of people and places. To my amazement, I found several of them. What shocked me most was my discovery of the transposed *Akan* and other African tribal names of the authors of the Books of the Old Testament. What was going on here, or better yet, what has gone on here?

For over two thousand years, people have read the names of the authors and people of the Bible and assumed that they were Hebrew names, but they were not. Believers in these biblical names and have even named themselves and their children after these authors and people in the Bible from the false assumption that these names were Jewish and therefore divine, but these names were indigenous African tribal names that were merely transposed into European languages.

The discovery of the *Akan* and other African tribal names among modern Jewish people and the discovery of these names in the names of the authors of the Old Testament Books revealed to me that the Jewish people did not write these documents as they claimed. Instead, people from *Akan* other African tribes wrote these document in Ancient Egypt as their names on these documents confirm. If Christianity were looking for divinity in these names, it has been fooled somewhere. How could these names be considered Hebrew names when they are plain *Akan* and other African tribal names? I did not know the answer to this question but that was enough to convince me further of the racial, ethnic, linguistic, and cultural relationship between the *Akan* and other African tribes that were the Ancient Egyptians and the Jewish people that were also Ancient Egyptians, then Canaanites, and now Europeans. I decided to explore the historical, biblical, linguistic, and cultural issues involved in this mystery. It was from the overwhelming revelations I came across that I chose the title of this book.

I was very sure that I have stumbled upon information that has never been known in biblical scholarship in Europe or for that matter anywhere in the world for over two thousand years. From a scholastic point of view, I wanted to be sure that this information has never been known anywhere before now. I therefore read the works of several biblical scholars. I needed to find out who the people that surrounded the region of Canaan in ancient times were. I therefore read the history of Babylon, and I identified an *Akan* tribe that was in ancient Babylon. I also read the history of Sumeria and found out that there were no ancient people called Sumerians. That was a fictitious name a western historian gave these unknown ancient people in 1850. I identified the two African tribes that were the Sumerians from the names and words these people left behind. From all these readings, I was more certain than ever that I have discovered what has never been known about the Bible before now.

I had found out that the *Akan* people were the most dominant group in Ancient Egypt and except in the history of the Sumerians, I had found more *Akan* names in all the sources I read than I found other African tribal names. As a result, I went back to Ghana in 1996 and 1998 to research into the broader history of the *Akan* people of West Africa. I wanted to find out the tribal relationship between the Jewish people in Europe and the *Akan* people in West Africa. I wanted to find out the reason the so-called people of the Bible have shared and continue to share the same tribal names and culture with *Akan* and other tribes in Africa.

The first question I had to answer was how could the history and identity of a possible black tribal group in Canaan have been related much less be found in the history and identities of black tribal groups in Africa? What was the racial, ethnic, historical, linguistic, and cultural relationship between these two groups of black people and where was this relationship before these groups parted ways? Another question that haunted me was if the Jewish people were from *Akan* and other African tribes, how did they become white?

From all these, I had more questions than answers and for the answers to my questions, I decided to search from three main sources. The first source was the biblical history of the racial and ethnic origin of the Jewish people. I found there was no complete answers there. The second source was the real history of the racial and ethnic origin of the Jewish people. Again, I found no complete answers there. The third source was Ancient Egyptian history and again I found no complete answers there either. However, I found that there were pieces of the answers to the puzzle in each of these sources and that all the sources put together provide the answers I was searching.

The Bible, however, gave me the most powerful answer in the biblical narrative in *Genesis 37-39* where the story of Jacob and his envious sons ended with the supposed sale of Joseph to Ishmaelites and Midianites. He ended up in slavery in Ancient Egypt. What is most intriguing in this biblical story is that there was no mention of any linguistic or cultural problems that any foreigner of a different racial, ethnic, linguistic, or cultural background should have encountered in Ancient Egypt. I also noticed that in the biblical story of Abraham and later Jacob and his entire family going to Ancient Egypt, there was no mention of any such linguistic and cultural problems that complete foreigners would have encountered among the African tribes of Ancient Egypt. The biblical narrative further states that Jacob and his family left Canaan and went to live in Ancient Egypt for four hundred and thirty years. Again, linguistic and cultural differences were no problems for these people. What do all these mean?

In fact, the Bible story states that Joseph rose to be like Pharaoh in all of Ancient Egypt not long after he had supposedly been there as a slave (see Genesis 44:18; 45:8). For Joseph to be appointed to such a high national office he needed to be related to the Ancient Egyptians racially, ethnically, linguistically, and culturally, but the biblical account did not mention any of these. The lack of any linguistic problems in the travels of Abraham, Joseph, and Jacob and his family to Ancient Egypt simply and clearly reveals that the so-called people of the Bible were of the same racial, ethnic, linguistic, and cultural heritage as the Ancient Egyptians to whom they supposedly went.

What is most intriguing about all these is that Abraham, the patriarch of the Jewish people and his descendants, from Isaac to Esau and Jacob, carried *Akan* names and names derived from *Akan* words before they supposedly went to the *Akan* people in Ancient Egypt. What was going on here and doesn't the fact that these people carried *Akan* names before they went to the *Akan* people of Ancient Egypt reveal their true racial and ethnic heritage? For me, everything was plain and the question therefore was not the racial, ethnic, linguistic, and cultural origin of these people but from which specific *Akan* tribe did Abraham originate for him and his descendants to be carrying *Akan* names? Even the name Joseph was derived from an *Akan* name. If the story of Joseph is believable than it was nothing more than the story of a black person from a black family somewhere in Canaan being sold into slavery to foreigners. These foreigners got to Ancient Egypt and found out that Joseph had the same language and cultural background as the Ancient Egyptians so they sold him to the Egyptians. What is interesting in this narrative is that Joseph felt so much at home among the Ancient Egyptians that he sent for his entire family to join him in Ancient Egypt. According to the Bible, it was this family that left Ancient Egypt to go to live in Canaan and later move to Europe. The Ancient Egyptians were black people so at this point it was becoming clear to me why believers and protectors of the Bible would want to distort and destroy Ancient Egyptian history.

As I have already pointed out, African tribal groups were the Ancient Egyptians and that means Jacob left Canaan to go to live among the African tribes that were the Ancient Egyptians. From this analysis, the historical picture of the relationship between the *Akan* and other African tribal groups that were the Ancient Egyptians and the Ancient Egyptian groups that moved to Canaan and then to Europe was slowly becoming clearer.

Through Ancient Egypt, I found the link and the racial and ethnic relationship between the black people that supposedly became the people of the Bible and the black people of Ancient Egypt that went into inner Africa to become the Africans. Were these people different or the same tribal groups of people? In my study, I found out that they were the same people belonging to the same race, tribes, languages, and cultures. The black tribal groups that ended up in Canaan and in Europe originated from the black tribal groups that were the Ancient Egyptians. This was how modern Jews and Hebrews in Europe came to share the same names and cultures with the *Akan* and several African tribal groups that were the Ancient Egyptians. This was also how the names of people and places in the Bible and in Jewish history came to be derived from *Akan* and other African tribal languages.

From the findings of this study, I say without hesitation or any reservation that the people of the Bible were black people. From the transposed *Akan* and other African tribal names of the authors of the Books of the Old Testament, I also say without hesitation or reservation that the black people who are now the Africans wrote the Bible. I qualify the Africans as the black people who are now the Africans because in ancient times the black people we see concentrated in Africa today did not live only in Africa. They lived from Africa to the Middle and Far East. There is even evidence of ancient black people in China and in Europe.

For over two thousand years, the Christian religion that developed from the teachings of the Bible has been content with the idea that the Jewish people created the documents and theosophical doctrines of the Bible and Christian religion. Christianity has in turn propagated this idea around the world. The question is why is it important for the world to know now that Africans wrote the Bible, and that the philosophy, laws, poetry, stories, and religious doctrines in the Bible were all ancient African people's ideas?

From my point of view as an African, there are several reasons the world must know that Africans wrote the Bible. For one thing, this is the very foundation of the history of all black people. It is the foundation from which black people derive their ancient identities and their modern humanity. It is therefore important for the world to know about this aspect of black identity and humanity. The very rise of Europeans from the Dark Ages through the Middle Ages into modern civilization was initiated from Bible. It is important to Africans for the world to know this and Europeans to acknowledge it. However, perhaps the first and the most important reason the world should know of the Africans who wrote the Bible is that ideas in the Bible were the bedrock upon which every aspect of European thinking, attitude, and action developed.

What was wrong in this development was that the foundations of these thoughts, attitudes, and actions were based upon certain false assumptions about the Bible. One of these assumptions was the idea that the Jewish people who claim to have written the biblical documents were racially and ethnically different from the African tribes from which they originated. Another assumption was that the Africans who wrote the Bible were pagans and they were the ones cursed in this Bible to be the slaves of Europeans. These and several misunderstandings from the Bible have immensely influenced and continue to influence our worldview in terms of how we see each other as humans, how we interpret daily events and phenomena in our lives, and how we even perceive ourselves beyond this life. For such an important role as the Bible has played in our lives, we all need to know its true source in terms of the people who actually wrote it.

Another reason we need to know of the Africans who wrote the Bible is that again the foundations of the canker of racism and racial prejudice were conceived and developed from the earliest false assumptions, misperceptions, and misinterpretations of the Bible. All of these were initiated and directed against black people in justification of slavery and exploitation of their resources in Africa. What is worse about this is that the canker of prejudice became so intense in Europe and Europeans became so obsessed with it that it turned in on Europeans themselves. The result has been the atrocities and never-ending wars in Europe and the European incited wars around the world. As I am writing, Catholics and Protestants, Jews and Muslims, and Christians and Jews are at each other's throats over African theosophical ideas whose origins they have never known. It is important for the world to know of the Africans who wrote the Bible so that the earliest false assumptions, misperceptions and misinterpretations that caused all these would be corrected.

Beyond the Africans and Europeans, European racism and racial prejudice spread onto all other non-Europeans. This Bible inspired racism is still going on and the world needs to know the truth about the Bible to help it change its thoughts, actions, and attitudes about all humans. These early canker and misinterpretations of the Bible continue to influence Christian perception and interpretation of the Bible even today. It is important therefore that modern Christians know who wrote the Bible so that they can understand and practice their faiths in the true racial, ethnic, and religious contexts the biblical documents and theosophical doctrines were designed. The irony in all these is that black people who invented religion and wrote the documents of the Bible have been at the brunt of the worst misinterpretations and the most atrocious actions because of the Bible. They have been the greatest sufferers from the racism and racial prejudice developed from the Bible and the continued ignorance and misinterpretations of it. It is important therefore that people get to know the truth about the Bible so that they can change the centuries old false assumptions, misperceptions, and misinterpretations they learned from the Bible.

From the influence of racism and racial prejudice developed through this Bible, European historians who undertook the writing of world history have practically relegated the Africans who laid the foundations of religion, civilization, and human history in every corner of this world to the position of a race that has never contributed anything to our humanity. Despite all that Africans have done for and throughout the world, western historians have credited nothing positive to Africa and African people. Africa's history and unparalleled historical achievements around the world have all been successfully denied, distorted, destroyed, and disparaged because of the misunderstood influence of this Bible.

Even where historical evidence unmistakably points to the black people in Africa, as the evidence in Ancient Egypt, western historians and Egyptologists most of who have been influenced by the Bible and most of who are Jewish scholars have refused to acknowledge it because some argue that biblical narrative and teachings do not support giving such credit to a supposedly devilish and cursed people that enslaved the Jews who are in Christian Europe view, God's children. As a result of all these, the Africans who created the foundations of everything we cherish in human civilization and development are now the ones who have, in the eyes of the west, contributed nothing to the world at all.

Knowing the Africans who wrote the Bible would not only release Africans and their history from the misunderstood and misinterpreted influences of the Bible, but it would also help the world understand the true foundations of its history and know the people that created these foundations. If ever people in this world were grateful for human civilization and development, they would then know who to thank for such developments for they were the Africans. Beyond all these, a basic need in our humanity is the need to place ourselves in time to help us construct our identities. We all need to see the past in our minds so that we can perceive and understand the thoughts and actions that brought us where we are today. This is what western historical scholarship has deprived Africans not because they deserve it but because believers and protectors of the Bible have wanted Africa to suffer indignities so that they could tell the Bible's story in the falsehoods they have imagined. It is time the reality of history is brought out and the history constructed from illusions to be corrected. I do believe that if John Locke had known that Africans wrote the Bible, his *Essays Concerning Human Understanding* would not have been so racist and prejudicial against black people, and his *Essay on the Reasonableness of Christianity* might have read differently. This is the effect of truth on perception and that is why the world should know about the Africans who wrote the Bible.

In reality, the revelation that black Africans wrote the Bible should not matter because all humans originated from black people, anyway (see Christopher Stringer, *African Exodus*, 1996, Jared Diamond, *Guns, Germs, and Steel*, 1997). However, the truth must be told. Nevertheless, this revelation is going to cause some people great concern and trepidation, and there are several reasons. Perhaps, the most personal one is the gradual realization that continuing education is a progressive discovery of ignorance, and not many of us feel comfortable knowing how ignorant we have been.

Dr. Charles Finch stated one of the reasons people are going to be comfortable with such revelations as are in this book in his introduction to *The Natural Genesis: A Book of the Beginnings* by Gerald Massey:

> In contemporary times, it is difficult for us to scan the past with a clear lens because the racial mythology imposed on the world over the last 500 years has obscured everything. Few, whether Jew or non-Jew are prepared to examine ancient Judaism in terms of its African origins. Insofar as the Hebrew Torah spawned both Christianity and Islam, such an examination would mean acknowledging that the religions of more than a third of the world's population are traceable in a direct line of descent to African sacred thought mediated through its codifier ancient Egypt. Experience shows that such is not an idea that many, of any faith, are prepared to contemplate with equanimity." (Dr. Charles S. Finch in *The Natural Genesis: A Book of the Beginnings* by Gerald Massey, Vol. 1, 1883).

Believers in the Bible who have developed their faiths from the traditional racist and prejudicial misperceptions and misinterpretations of the Bible would feel very uncomfortable knowing the revelation in this book. They would be uncomfortable from the fact that what I reveal in this book is not what they want things to be. They would be uncomfortable because they have long known that the truth can upset the cart. They will also be uncomfortable because the assertions in this book touch the innermost parts of their personalities, and these parts are their beliefs and perceptions. Most believers in the Bible who read this book would first be in psychological denial, and then their innate sense of self-preservation would kick in. They would begin looking for arguments to question the veracity of the revelations in the book. This would not be because what they read in this book is not true, but it would be because they would want to get back into the comfortable state of their beliefs and misperceptions even if these were developed from albeit lies.

The revelation in this book will also cause some people great discomfort and concern not because it is not true, but because for over two thousand years, Christian Europe has accepted and told Christians around the world that God-inspired Jewish priests wrote their holiest book, the Bible. Then, I come in over two thousand years later to change all that has been developed from this false idea by revealing that these so-called God-inspired Jewish priests were none other than *Akan* and other African tribes, and that their transposed names in the Bible confirm this. That can be understandably disconcerting but the truth must be told.

In my research, I found out that the Jewish people did not only carry   *Akan* and other African tribal names nut the first name they gave to the State they created in Canaan was an *Akan* name. When they changed this early name of their State, they gave it another *Akan* name. For over two thousand years, most Christians have assumed that the name of the State of Israel was Hebrew, but it was not. It was derived from an *Akan* word. I do believe that most Jews do not know the linguistic origin of this name either. The evidence and the original *Akan* meaning of this word is even in the Bible. For over two thousand years most believers have assumed and believed that the earliest name of the Jewish God, *Adonai* was Hebrew and that the name *Yahweh* that turned into the false name Jehovah in Europe was also Hebrew, but they were not. The question is if the Jewish people carried all these *Akan* names, what was the earliest language of these people for them to have named practically everything around them in the *Akan* language? These are the revelations the coming discussions in this book are about.

There is also discussion of the origin of the biblical documents in the book. I have already revealed that the names of the authors of the Books of the Old Testament are from *Akan* and other African tribal names. From this discussion, it becomes clear that Jewish people did not write the documents they compiled and translated into the Greek Bible. People from the black tribes from whom the Jewish people originated in Ancient Egypt wrote the documents of the

Bible. The evidence shows that the content of the documents did not originate from the Jews, they originated from Ancient Egyptian myths and the myths and legends of other lands.

As I have already pointed out, biblical narrative states that in their formative years, the Jewish people went to live in Ancient Egypt. Beyond the discovery of Ancient Egyptian documents in the Bible, a major important evidence that fully supports the fact that the Ancient Egyptians wrote a major part of the biblical documents is the fact that these people invented, documented, and practiced religion for thousands of years before the Jewish people supposedly went there. It was also thousands of years before the so-called Jewish people came back to Ancient Egypt after the Exodus to compile and translate the documents of the Bible for the Greeks. Moreover, Egyptologists have found exact Ancient Egypt documents in the Bible. What do all these mean to the true origin of the Bible?

What is fascinating about the revelations in this work is that the evidence can be found both in history and in the Bible, and it can be easily verified from the black tribes I introduce in the discussions. For those who know and have the necessary background to understand, the Bible gives us a clear picture of the close relationship amongst Ancient Egyptians, Jewish people, the Bible itself, Africans, and the Christian religion. Over the centuries, many western scholars have tried to explore and establish the veracity of this relationship, and the bold ones have concluded that religion, particularly the concepts of Christianity, originated from the minds and imaginations of the black people that were the Ancient Egyptians. Scholars like Gerald Massey went a step further to prove his assertion by identifying the Africanisms in the names and words that link Africans to the language and people of the Bible, and therefore to the origin of the Christian religion.

In more recent times, scholars of African descent have taken up where these early western scholars left off. These African scholars have tried to adduce evidence to confirm Africa's centrality in the creation of the religions of the world via Ancient Egypt. Unfortunately, most of the early works of these colleagues have all been based upon the same western false assumption. This assumption is the unspoken but lingering perception that the Ancient Egyptians are extinct. What makes this assumption even more preposterous is the fact that there are modern descendants of the ancient Jewish people that supposedly went to the Ancient Egyptians. If there are modern descendants of the Jewish people that went to Ancient Egypt, why then should there not be modern descendants of the Ancient Egyptians that received the Jewish people in Egypt? According to the Bible, the Jewish people supposedly went to Ancient Egypt because of hunger. If these ancient hungry people have survived up to today, what would have made the people that feed these hungry people disappear from the face of the earth? The Ancient Egyptians have not disappeared from the face of the earth because their modern descendants are alive and well, just as the modern descendants of the Ancient Egyptians that became the Jewish people are alive and well today in Europe.

Based upon the false assumption that the Ancient Egyptians are extinct, some scholars have tried to introduce the languages and religious beliefs of some black people as the original African languages and religious beliefs of the Ancient Egyptians. These scholars have used these introductions as proof of the religion of Ancient Egypt and the origin of religion in these ancient Africans. However, these colleagues have all failed to do two things. They have failed to link the people, languages, and religious beliefs they introduced in their stories to the story of religion as it is recorded in the Bible, and they have also failed to link the people they introduced in their stories to the central story of Ancient Egypt. Such a failure is unacceptable because Ancient Egypt was created and developed from the world's earliest religious thoughts, concepts, and sacramental practices. As a result, any group of people that any scholar introduces to prove the origin of religion in the African mind must not just be Africans but these Africans must be central in the Ancient Egyptian and biblical stories for such introduction to be credible. This is the reason earlier efforts to reveal the origin of religion in ancient African minds and imaginations have not received much scholastic attention beyond a few of us.

This revelation is going to take many by surprise and the reason is that Africans have not been vigorous participants in the scholastic discourse of issues of religion in the west. In fact, Africans have not even been vigorous participants in the telling of their own history. Western assumption over the centuries has been that Africa does not know anything and therefore has nothing to say or contribute, but that has been woefully wrong.

In the vacuum Africa has created by not telling her story to anyone, western scholars have raised themselves to the ranks of the experts and claimed the authority in telling Africa's story. Unfortunately, they have not done a good job of it because there are two sides to Africa and her story. There is the side that foreigners would be allowed to see and know, and there is the other side that even not all Africans are allowed to know unless they belong to certain royal houses. The side that outsiders are not allowed to know is the repository of the secrets and mysteries that Africa has been famous for since ancient times. As a result, it is clear that outsiders can never be the experts in telling Africa's story because they lack the basic elements that would let them fully understand what they are saying.

Why have western historians never found out the linguistic and cultural evidence of the Africans who wrote the Bible? There have been two major weaknesses in Europeans telling Africa's story. The first is the fact that western scholars who have sought to tell Africa's story have all lacked the necessary linguistic and cultural backgrounds to understand and interpret the story and its cultural settings appropriately. Even when they have the linguistic and cultural evidence before them, these scholars have not been able to see or link it to any specific group of humans in Africa. As a result, much of the stories western scholars tell about Africa have been shallow, speculative, and they have focussed on events instead of the people that created the events. Africa's story as told by western historians has therefore always lacked the human element in human history.

Knowing the language and the cultural setting in which a piece of history was created is extremely important for understanding that piece of history. How can anyone tell the story of a people one does not know, and how can anyone tell the story of a people whose language and culture one does not understand? History is a record of past human events and every past human event is created within a *culture*. Embedded in every culture is a *language* and this analysis shows that knowing the language and culture of any aspect of human history is important for understanding the human element in the story. Because Europeans who have sought to tell Africa's story do not have the necessary linguistic and cultural backgrounds, they have had to perceive and interpret Africa's story through the prism of European linguistic and cultural backgrounds, and the results have been woefully inadequate.

Because of these major linguistic and cultural limitations, ancient Greek scholars did not know and modern historians and Egyptologists still do not know that the names of the Ancient Egyptian kings, people, and places they have transposed into their tongues were originally African tribal names. For example, they do not know that the indigenous African tribal name of the boy king of Ancient Egypt was *Tutu Ankoma* and not *Tutankhamun*. They do not know that the royal dynasty of this boy king still exists in Africa, and that members of his tribe and royalty still carry the names *Tutu* and *Ankoma*. For the same reasons, the experts in this field have never been able to see and therefore they still do not know that the Ancient Egyptian king of the fourth dynasty who built the pyramid in the center was *Akuffu* and not *Khuffu*. Of course, they have never known or understood the linguistic evidence before them so they do not know that the name of the younger son of *Akuffu* was *Dade Afre* and not *Djedefra*, and his elder son was *Okyere Afre* and not *Chephren*. The most famous city of Ancient Egypt was Memphis, but western scholars have never known that Memphis was an ancient African city and it is still a modern African city called *Mamfe*. Those who want to see the modern city of *Mamfe* can go to the eastern region of Ghana to the *Akuapem* people. These are the people of Ancient Egyptian kings *Akuffu, Dade Afre,* and *Okyere Afre* and others

There is always something missing when one seeks to explain something from a tongue or culture one does not know. That is what has been happening in western attempts to explain aspects of history concerning Africa. I once listened quietly as one of my colleagues explained to me what the Ancient Egyptian word *Serekh* meant. This is a hieroglyphic symbol that used to be designed on the front doors of the kings and royal houses to show that they were the residences of royalty and power. This design can be traced to the Early Dynastic period and the Old Kingdom of Ancient Egypt. It was the image of the falcon standing on a rectangular frame with the king's spiritual name in the rectangle. It was in later times when another African tribe became the pharaohs of Ancient Egypt that the name *Serekh* was conferred onto this symbol, and that is what modern scholars know it to be.

My colleague was very knowledgeable about this symbol but I know the language from which this word originated. I know the meaning of the word. So in my mind, something was still missing. What was missing was the linking of this word to the Africans whose language it is to make the word a living symbol of a people and confirming that African tribes created the Ancient Egyptian civilization. The word *Serekh* is a corruption of the *Hausa* word *Sariki* meaning king. Notice how this word has been transposed into European orthography and phonology as *Serekh*. The *Hausa* people can be found today in Northern Nigeria. In the Middle and Late Periods of Ancient Egypt, *Hausa* royalty were also kings. The modern descendant of their ancient royal dynasty is now called the *Sadauna* of *Sokoto* and he can be found in Kano in Northern Nigeria. From such a detailed revelation, the word *Serekh* and the Ancient Egyptian story do not become part of an ancient history; it becomes the continuous story of a living people. This is the kind of linguistic and cultural link I expect scholars to make about the Ancient Egyptian story, religion and ancient Africans because it is there.

These are detailed aspects of Africa's history that outside scholars would never know unless Africans tell them. These secrets of Africa are revealed this early in the book to establish four main points. The first is the fact that without the necessary linguistic and cultural knowledge outsiders can never know these things about Africa. This is the main reason western scholars have never known the revelations I have just made about the Bible and the Jewish people. It is also the reason western scholars have never known the Africans that were the Ancient Egyptians. The second point is to establish the African origin of the Ancient Egyptian civilization by linking Ancient Egyptian history, language, and culture to living groups of people in Africa. The third reason is to use these names to reveal the specific African tribe that led the creation and development of the Ancient Egyptian civilization. The fourth reason is to establish direct racial, ethnic, linguistic, and cultural link between the *Akan* and African tribes that were the Ancient Egyptians and the other *Akan* and African tribal groups that left Ancient Egypt to Canaan and later to Europe to become the Jews and Hebrews.

What do these revelations mean? These names and the earlier names of the kings of Ancient Egypt linguistically and culturally confirm that the *Akan* people were the nucleus of the African tribes that created and developed the Ancient Egyptian civilization. The *Akan* people were the people to whom the Jewish people went in their formative years in Ancient Egypt. These were the people that invented religion in Ancient Egypt, and they were also the people out of whose minds and imaginations grew the foundations of our modern civilization.

For the first time in over five thousand years, Africa has now revealed her Ancient Egyptian identity. The world has never known who these Ancient Egyptians were, but it knows now. The Ancient Egyptians were black people whose modern descendants can still be found in Africa and in diaspora around the world.

Beyond their lack of linguistic and cultural knowledge, many western historians have never been able to see and tell Africa's story fully and truthfully because of their own prejudices. Most western scholars are so stuck on the traditional prejudices and negative perception of Africa that they cannot see and they have never seen anything positive about her, even in her culture.

Commenting on Catholic Father Cavazzi's negativism and condemnation of African dance in the Congo over three hundred years ago, Basil Davidson wrote:

> ... the fact is that Cavazzi was offering a true reflection of the profound contempt that white men have usually felt, then and long forward, for the moral and intellectual content of the black man's culture. Contempt grew into a conviction, later on, that the real trouble with Africans was that they had failed to "grow up" and were therefore lacking in some ingredient of the capacity to achieve a mastery over environment, which men have generally recognized as civilization (*Africa: The Face Behind the Mask* in The Light of the Past, 1967, p. 22).

These western sentiments have relegated Africa to a timeless primitive innocence and slumber from which no European thinks she would ever arise, and certainly just the other day, no European ever knew or would believe that Africa was the first to grow up and rise in culture, heritage, and civilization long before Europeans woke up. When some western scholars found out that our modern world and its so-called civilization rose this high from the shoulders and achievements of "primitive" and "barbarous" Africa, the discovery became a major embarrassment, so they decided to be quiet about it and let the traditional negative perceptions of Africa remain. However, the truth about Africa outside European sentiments is slowly emerging and in the words of some scholars, "it was unexpected." Basil Davidson summed it all up when wrote:

> Already we can trace an outline of an African "pageant of history" in which the protagonists, far from remaining "unmoved in primitive savagery," have manifestly traveled a long way from their starting point. We can find in traditional African thought, however, a prescientific maturity and sophistication that are emphatic in their projection of dynamic and coherent ideas about man and the universe. We can see in many of the arts of Africa, as a distinguished Italian ethnologist has lately written, the impulse of "ancient and elaborate traditions: not works of exuberant youth and still less childish inexperience, but products of conscious and thoughtful maturity." These conclusions rest on a large body of obscure and detailed work, much of which has been recorded only in specialist journals whose findings seldom reach a wide public (pp. 94-95).

From the sources I acquired the information for this book, it is clear that this has been a complex work that required knowledge from very different sources. I had to go through all that trouble because though this work is telling Africa's story, it is also a project of my own redemption from the negative pronouncements of the European missionaries of my childhood. These people did not know the source or understand the religious doctrines and ideas they were propagating, but they went around the world propagating them anyway. I am an African, and in the eyes of Christian Europe, I am a pagan condemned to the vigorous fire of damnation in Christian hell. How do I know this? Early Christians in Europe made that determination about all Africans. Later, Christians in Europe based their interpretation of the Bible on this and concluded that I am the cursed one. They used all of these to justify their consciences in the physical and mental enslavement of my people.

As if that was not enough, modern European missionaries and teachers from the former Basel Missionary Societies of Germany and Switzerland came to Africa to tell me that I am a pagan but they could save me from Christian hell. I did not know then that Christian hell was only in their imaginations, so like a fool, I believed them and submitted to be saved.

For my redemption and salvation from Christian Europe's imagined damnation of humanity, these European missionaries told me that I should for all intents and purposes cease to be African. In my ignorant mind, the very identity of being African was my natural default, so I spent half of my life running away from Africa trying to be "unAfrican" and "unpagan." The saddest part of this is that I almost succeeded. The western missionaries and teachers told me not to associate myself with anything African because it was pagan and uncivilized. They told me never to play African drums, sing, or dance to African songs because they were all pagan and uncivilized practices. Instead, they encouraged me to learn to dance the European waltz, slow foxtrot, and the rumba. They told me that those dances were Christian and more civilized practices and as a born again Christian, I deserved the best from Europe.

What hurts me today as I have seen through all these is the fact that in my ignorance, I believed these ignorant foreigners who did not have the linguistic and cultural backgrounds to know and understand who and what their Bibles were talking about. In their ignorance, these European missionaries assumed that the story of the Bible was about them, but now I know that it was from my people, and it was about me. From the pictures these missionaries showed us in Africa, most of us believed that God and Jesus were white. We believed that the biblical narrative was a European creation, and these European missionaries have come to share their God with us in Africa "out of the goodness of their Christian hearts." Now I know that these missionaries did not know and they still do not know that the biblical story was the story of my ancient ancestors and me.

Imagine how stupid I felt when I found out that what these missionaries and teachers were trying to teach me was not their own knowledge or creation. They were propagating a two thousand-year-old *legendary lying lore*, but they did not even have the historical, linguistic, and cultural backgrounds to know it. They had been propagating my ancestors' ancient theosophical ideas, but they did not know it because they have never cared to search for the source from where the religious knowledge they were propagating came. I did not know it then, either. They took advantage of my ignorance and they still do that to others in Africa. These are all part of the reasons the world should now know about the Africans who wrote the Bible.

These missionaries told me that I would be saved in the eyes of the Lord if I decided to forgo my African paganistic ways. They also told me that they came to the Gold Coast [Ghana] with the word of the *true God,* and that they came to save my people and me from the devil and his ways. By calling the Christian God the true God, the missionaries were again confirming that they came to us in Africa because we were pagans. Imagine my disappointment when I found out that these missionaries did not even know the origin of the God they professed to be their truer God than mine in Africa. Imagine my disappointment when I found out that it was the God of my ancestors and my people that Europeans adopted as the Christian God, and now they were using the same God to condemn me because they were as ignorant as I was.

European missionary teachers also told me that I had to be born anew because I was born a pagan and a sinner in the eyes of the Lord. For me to be born anew, they told me that I had to shed my indigenous identity. The first step in shedding my African identity was to give up my name. According to the missionaries, the name my people have carried for thousands of years and given to me in my turn to perpetuate the survival of our people was pagan. I believed them and submitted to be baptized and given a Christian name so the Lord would recognize me as one of his own, "on my way to Christian heaven." Again, I did not know then that Christian heaven was an adaptation of my people's ancient after-life imagination and concept. I thought it was real.

The missionary teachers told me that my name was pagan, so they gave me the name, Alexander. Whatever it meant or wherever the name came from I did not know, but I proudly went around the world introducing myself as Alexander. This name was not even a biblical name. It was later that I found out that these missionaries were not set on Christianizing me, but they were secretly Europeanizing me so I would never know about an African heritage and identity they did not want me to know and inherit. I did not know that a secret agenda to strip me of my identity and heritage was behind the early missionary activities and schooling. As a result, there was this situation in which the ignorant missionaries were leading me, an ignorant African to salvation. However, the advantage of the missionaries was that they had my ancestral story and a two thousand-year old legend of lies behind them as the truth. I did not know that my people's story is truer and that it is more than five thousand years old. What hurts me now is the fact that I believed everything these foreigners told me. I thought they knew what they were talking about.

European churches and their missionaries introduced education into my country. They called it western education, but I later found out that it was nothing but a modern adaptation of the knowledge and education my ancestors had created, developed, and practiced for thousands of years in Ancient Egypt (see Education in *The Dictionary of Ancient Egypt*, (ed.) Ian Shaw & Paul Nicholson, 1995).

I attended Presbyterian missionary schools from elementary school through my first college. I liked school. I was good in school. I loved my foreign missionary teachers because I believed then that they had come from *Aburokyire*, [Europe] to help save my people and me from the devil. What hurts me today is the fact that I grew up thinking what they said was the truth and everything they had in Europe was better than what I had in Africa. I grew up thinking that they knew more in Europe than we did in Africa. I did not know that everything they were then and whatever they think they are today were all from my ancient ancestral knowledge in Egypt.

My grandfather was worried that I had taken to my foreign teachers so much. When I was about eleven years old, the old man had an unforgettable conversation with me about school and my foreign missionaries and teachers. My grandfather said, "*Son. I hear Aburokyire is a very far place from here. Why would your missionary teachers come all the way from Aburokyire to teach and save us here*?" I ignorantly replied that the European missionaries came to us because they had been sent by God to come and teach and save us. "*Which God and from what have they come to save us?*" the old man asked. "*I hear that these people have not finished teaching and saving their own people in their homelands. Why would they leave their people and come here to teach and save us? If you had the power to save humans from something, son would you leave your people here and go to save people in foreign lands?* Grandpa asked me.

I did not know where this conversation was leading to and I was not interested because I wanted my grandfather to be saved with me. I also thought I knew it all from what my foreign teachers and missionaries had been telling me in school. I concluded in my logic that grandpa did not know and he did not understand because he did not get the opportunity to attend a Christian missionary school as I was attending. I was ignorantly proud of that and proud of myself. In anticipation of situations that may seek to challenge our Christian upbringing, our foreign teachers and missionaries warned us to beware because the devil would want to question our resolve to be Christians. I did not see Grandpa as a devil, but I began to see him differently from myself. I began to see him as the pagan my missionary teachers said all Africans were.

One day, the old man told me that he was worried about me because I was too gullible. I believed what the foreigners told me rather too easily, but I did not know any better. Then he gave me his final warning. "*These people are dangerous because they know what they are doing. They know what they are talking about is false but they want us to believe it anyway. For them to be successful in what they want to do, they need our future. They need our sons and daughters; they need our children. They need you and others like you because they work on minds. They take away minds. Son, I want you to go to school, but never give them your mind because a human body is like a snake's body. When one cuts off the snake's head, the rest is nothing but a rope. If you give these missionaries your head, you will never be like them, and the saddest part is you will never be yourself. You will never even know who you are.*" The old man was right.

What hurts me now is that I thought my grandpa did not know what he was talking about then so I believed my foreign teachers and missionaries instead. Now, I know that Grandpa was right. He knew something I did not know, but I was too young to be told my people's traditional secrets, and he was not ready to tell me yet. European missionaries came to Africa to find vanguards for the legendary lies they were carrying so that they could lead my people quietly into submission, and we submitted to them. Those of us who had been to school defended European and Christian lies before our own people and we were more credible than the Europeans. Later, I found out that was exactly what our European "saviors" and teachers wanted us to do. They wanted those of us they had schooled to defend their lies. For that they gave us certificates, diplomas, and degrees and we were walking around proud that we were the new generation of African Europeans. All of these could happen because of the introduction of African theosophical ideas to Europeans through the Bible. It is also one of the reasons the world should now know about the Africans who wrote the Bible.

One day, the old man asked me a question in frustration. *" Where were these people when our ancestors were creating wisdom?"* I had never heard that my ancestors ever created wisdom. The old people never told us in our rites of passage initiation. We have stories about *Ananse* the spider and wisdom, but I did not think it could refer to my ancestors. We have stories of *Ananse* the spider collecting and trying to hide all wisdom in the world somewhere, but I did not know that Europeans were going behind and digging my ancestors' past in search of this wisdom. My missionary teachers were taking credits for the knowledge my ancestors created, and I was also giving them the credit that was due me and mine. Instead of finding out when and where my ancestors created wisdom, I thought then that if wisdom were ever created, the ancestors of my missionary teachers must have created it because they were so wise in the things they were teaching us. What hurts me now is the fact that my grandpa did not live long enough for me to go back home to tell him that I have been to the home of my missionary teachers and found out the truth. My Ancient Egyptian ancestors created all the wisdom the missionary teachers came to teach me in Africa.

It hurts that the old man is not around for me to tell him that he was right in everything he thought and said. When my ancestors were creating wisdom thousands of years ago, the ancestors of my missionary teachers were still in the dark. After all, when the Roman Empire attacked and massacred almost a million people in Gaul as recently as 50 B. C., the Romans called the French people they massacred barbarians. As recently as 476 A. D. when Germanic tribes attacked and destroyed the Roman Empire, European history identified these Germanic tribes as barbarians from Western Europe. How do these people compare to my ancestors that invented religion, science, mathematics, astronomy, calendar, anatomy and physiology, medicine, hygiene, philosophy, art, music, architecture, painting, writing, and more thousands of years ago? Where were the ancestors of my missionary teachers more than five thousand years ago when my ancestors were actually creating religion, civilization, and wisdom? I found out that what my grandpa called wisdom was the religion and academic knowledge my missionary teachers came to propagate in our schools and Churches.

It was from this African background and upbringing in the hands of this old man that I started looking for knowledge about what my ancestors had done in ancient times. It was also from this background that I became interested in Ancient Egyptian history because I saw myself in it, but I did not know then that it was my ancestral history. It was through my interest in this ancestral story that I found out that the concepts and ideas from which the Bible and Christianity emerged were all my ancestral concepts and ideas. It was also through this interest that I found out that the people who actually wrote the documents that were used in designing the Christian Bible were my direct ancestors. I wonder why my missionary teachers did not tell me that I was an heir to all the religious and academic knowledge they came to propagate in Africa.

From my studies of Ancient Egypt and the Bible, I found out that no credible research or discussion of the Bible could bypass the African tribal groups that created and developed the Ancient Egyptian civilization. These were the people that created the concept of religion and the sacramental practices that became the Christian faith, beliefs, and practices in Europe. From the names of the authors of Books of the Old Testament, I also found the Africans who wrote the Bible and I even identified the tribes from which these ancient religious scholars originated. I did all these through linguistic and cultural analysis. The question is how credible is historical linguistics and cultural analysis? The answer is simple. Linguistic and cultural analysis of history is so valid and reliable that it is used to confirm modern genetic research.

For example, in a review of a recent article on *The Chinese Human Genome Diversity Project*, Cavalli-Sforza pointed out that one of the sources of information gathered for the project was the use of surnames, which are linguistic and cultural symbols. Cavalli-Sforza wrote that:

A China-U.S. Team has analyzed surnames from a 1/2,000 random sample of the Chinese population, by standard techniques of population genetics, and the picture [from the linguistic and cultural analysis] is largely superimposable on the genetic one. In fact, it is much more detailed given the magnitude of the sample and the number of the surnames *(Proceedings of National Academy of Science,* v. 95, #20, September 1998).

What this means is that historical linguistics and cultural analysis research can be as closely reliable as a genetic study. However, a major prerequisite for conducting such a study is still knowledge of the necessary linguistic and cultural backgrounds of the history that is being analyzed. This work is therefore very valid and reliable and the revelations of the phonologies, semantics, and etymologies of the names and words in the analysis are unimpeachable.

I know I had a lot of ancestral help in this enterprise because throughout the research, my mind kept going back to the last words the elders told us during our rites of passage initiation. Even in far away America, it was as if someone was right over my shoulder whispering those words in my ears for encouragement. *"Rise and never forget that beyond the elephant there is none greater, and you are the elephant."* Why have I not paid attention to this admonition since childhood? Perhaps it was because I thought my people did not know anything and instead my European missionaries and teachers knew it all.

After European missionaries and teachers had schooled me, I decided to educate myself and that was when I found out that it is not he who speaks first that speaks the truth. Europeans told the story of religion first and I thought they told the truth, but I was wrong. I also found out that my people in Africa have known more than they have cared to tell, and they have not been in a hurry to tell their story to anybody.

It was Gerald Massey who wrote that: *"It takes the latter half of all one's lifetime to unlearn the falsehood that was instilled into us during the earlier half. Generation after generation we learn, unlearn, and relearn the same lying legendary lore."* It is the cycle of this legendary lying lore in religion from Europeans who did not know and who still do not know what they have been propagating that I intend to break with this work. It took me over half of my lifetime to learn that like the rest of the world, I have been deceived by the "legendary lying lore."

It has not been an easy road from being a "pagan" in Africa to finding myself the modern descendant and heir to the great ones who created the concepts, philosophy, and documents that became the Christian Bible and a world religion. It is a soaring transformation that one has to experience to understand. I am not a pagan after all because my ancestors created the concepts, sacramental practices, and the Christian God. These are therefore already in me. It was my ancestors' creation that was linguistically dressed in foreign garbs, interpreted and embellished with fantastic stories, and brought back to my people and me, the descendants of the very people that created these ideas. Unfortunately, I believed what Europeans who thought they were saved in the eyes of the Lord told me. Now I know they said that to reaffirm their own senses of religious insecurities. I am the elephant and I know and understand it now.

This work is therefore dedicated to my Grandpa. It is also dedicated to all the modern elephants whose grandpas could not tell them how great they are. Because most grandpas could not tell their grandchildren how great these grandchildren are among humans, many grandchildren of the ancient elephants of Africa have been lost in foreign lands and in foreign indoctrination. Like me, they have lived their lives believing what foreign preachers and teachers have told them.

Fortunately, the ancestors from whose lives and achievements we acquired our greatness never cease to whisper into our ears. All we have to do is to stop and listen inside, and we will hear them say: *"Rise my children. We are the elephants. Beyond us, there is none greater."*

Most people have heard the lingering rumor that Jesus was a black man. If he were a black man, he must have come from a black tribe. The black tribes of Ancient Egypt and the Middle East are now located in Africa. That means these black tribes would know more about whether Jesus Christ was a black man or not, and if he were a black man they might even know the black tribe from which he must have originated. It is this broader view of the issue more than only Jesus being a black man that this work seeks to reveal.

The Bible is the ancestral religious story of my people and all black people. That is why the first Song of Songs in the Bible is about the pride of a black man and his ethnic heritage:

> I am black but comely,
> O ye daughters of Jerusalem,
> As the tents of Kedar
> As the curtains of Solomon.
> Look not upon me,
> Because I am black,
> Because the sun hath looked upon me. ...

> Song of Solomon, 1: 5-6
> King James Bible

In an era when much of the interaction between Europeans and Africans is based upon the color of each other's skin, I believe Christian Europe has long wished that the Song of Solomon had not revealed anything that pertains to the black ethnicity of the people of the Bible. This is one of the biblical evidence confirming that the people of the Bible were my people, black people. The Revised Standard Version (RSV) tones down the blackness by saying, *"I am dark, but comely."* This shows that Christian Europe has been aware of the revelation of the ethnicity of the people of the Bible in the Song of Solomon; and they have been quite uncomfortable with it. So they have chosen some euphemisms to cover up their discomfort.

The song of the celebrated King Solomon tells us that he was black and beautiful but there is something even more revealing in the Song. In the last line, the Song even seeks to explain why Solomon was black. In doing so, the song uses an explanation that Herodotus of Halicarnassus had used to explain the blackness of the Ancient Egyptians almost four hundred years before the Bible was compiled and translated into the Greek language in Ancient Egypt (see *The History of Herodotus*; translation by George Rawlinson, 1928. P. 88).

It is noteworthy that the Bible was compiled in Ancient Egypt, and a song in it uses the same explanation of the blackness of the Ancient Egyptians to explain the blackness of the people of the Bible. This means the compilers and translators of the biblical documents not only acknowledged the blackness of the Ancient Egyptians, but also they acknowledged the blackness of themselves and of the people of the Bible. In this regard, it is clear that they accepted the explanation of the blackness of the Egyptians as the same reason for the blackness of the biblical Solomon and his people. The Jewish people who now claim that the biblical story is their ancestral story went to live among the black people of Ancient Egypt for over four hundred years. All of these reveal that the Jewish people who look white now were also black people in ancient times.

This gives us one of the first biblical clues to the ethnicity of not only Solomon and the Jewish people but also of the people of the Bible in general. Solomon was a king over the Jewish people and if the ancient Jewish people were of any different ethnic background, a black king would not have ruled them. After all, no ethnic group of people would peaceably select their king from another ethnic group. All ethnic groups select their leaders from their own ethnicity. Solomon was therefore a black man who ruled over a kingdom of black people and these were the people of the Bible. By including this song and its explanation in the Bible, the Alexandrian Jewish scholars of the biblical documents also acknowledged their own black identities and heritage.

The use of Herodotus' classical explanation of the blackness of the Ancient Egyptians in a song in the Bible also confirms that the song originated from Ancient Egypt. Modern scholars have found that the Bible contains many original ancient Egyptian documents, and this is one of them. The Ancient Egyptian origin of this song is further confirmed in verse nine where the Song says: *"I have compared thee, O my love to a company of horses in Pharaohs chariots.* If this reference to the beauty of Pharaoh's horses were romantic, the romance in this comparison could only have been known and appreciated by Egyptians and not outsiders or foreigners in Canaan. This could only have been noticeable, romantic, and understood by Ancient Egyptian lovers who would be the only ones to know of the beauty of the horses in Pharaoh's stables. Who then would have written this romantic song other than an Ancient Egyptian lover that knew and appreciated the symbolism? This song, nevertheless, is said to be the Song of Solomon when he was the king of the Jewish people in Israel far away from Ancient Egypt and Pharaoh's horses. What does this reveal? It confirms what scholars have found out that the biblical documents were mostly Ancient Egyptian documents and stories. Yet, Christians have believed for over two thousand years that God-inspired Jewish prophets wrote the biblical documents when they were actually written by Ancient Egyptian priests and edited and rewritten by Jewish scholars.

To be able to reveal the identities of the Africans who wrote the Christian Bible, I must first reveal who the Jewish people were before they became Jewish to establish the foundation upon which to prove the fact that African people wrote the Bible. This becomes a revelation because apart from what is written in the Bible about the Jewish people, nobody knows who they are, where they came from to Europe, the language they spoke in ancient times, why some of them are black, and how they found religion before they came to Ancient Egypt.

In this discussion so far, I have revealed that the *Akan* people were the designers and developers of the Ancient Egyptian civilization, and this is confirmed by the fact that the names of the earliest kings from the earliest dynasty of Ancient Egypt are transposed *Akan* names. They are the *Akan* people that have held and kept the secret of the ethnic origin of the Jewish people for over three thousand years, and these people are ready to tell their story. The coming revelation of the African language the Jewish people spoke and from which they derived their ancient identity also reveals the original African tribal and ethnic origin of the Jewish people.

I decided at a point in time that if I were to produce a perfect work, I would never finish this book. As a result, the inadequacies in the book are reflections of me and they are all mine. I apologize for them. I would however like to thank my colleagues Paul Lake, Dr. Patricia McGraw, and Dr. Theman Taylor for their encouragement, reviews, and suggestions.

This book was written in far away America where I had very few *Akan* people to use as sounding boards. I would therefore like to thank my nephew Kwasi Aboagye and his wife Gloria Aboagye who were the only sounding boards when I wanted to clarify some aspects of *Akan* names, cultures, and traditions. The Sankofa Study Group of the Association for the Study of Classical African Civilizations and the people of the Imani Temple in Little Rock, Arkansas, were the first people to whom I revealed these ideas. I thank them fervently for their reception and encouragement. They made me feel that this information is something millions of people would want to know, so I kept chipping at it.

I think my wife and children were tired of hearing me preach these ideas and I thank them for their patience and encouragement. This is to Bertha, Kwasi, Amma, Kwadjo, and Adjoa for helping to create the environment and encouragement that made this work possible. I thank all the traditional custodians of the history of the *Akan* people in Ghana. With all my academic degrees, I still did not know, and I thank them for teaching me. More than anything else, these people taught me the folly in going out searching when what one is searching for is in one's own home. I wish I knew this before now.

There is something about the African and his history that is best said by W. E. Ward in his book *My Africa*. After living among the people of the Gold Coast and learning their ways for sixteen years, Ward wrote:

> The English and African attitudes to history are different. The Englishman is not interested in history; he prefers to forget it, to let bygones be bygones and to let sleeping dogs lie. But the African takes his history very seriously: even more seriously than the Irishman. He must, because an important part of his religion is the cult of his ancestral spirits – something more than reverence, perhaps not quite as much as worship (p. 37).

This quotation reveals the reason Africa has never forgotten her ancient history. Africa's ancient history is woven through her religion, and her religion is closely knit around her ancestors, the very foundation of her being. This is a foundation every African takes seriously and no one easily forgets.

Because of the heterogeneous nature of the intended audience of this book, choosing a writing style was not easy. I wanted the book to be as scholarly as possible but I did not want it to be directed solely towards the traditionally closed circles of scholars. I wanted the book to reach the broader audience of the millions who have accepted the Bible and its traditional interpretations without knowing where this book came from. Such people deserve to know who wrote the most favorite and "divine" book in their lives. I also had to take into consideration the fact that the ideas, language, and culture through which the discussions in this book are presented are African, and therefore foreign to western readers. For these reasons, I chose an informative, instructional, and explanatory writing style in which I emphasized and repeated important ideas to get my points across. After all, the biblical tradition has had a two-thousand year lead in teaching, preaching, propagating, emphasizing, and repeating the lies I am trying to expose, and the least I deserve, in this regard, is also repeating certain important ideas to make my point.

This work is about the Bible and the religion it spawned in Europe and spread around the world. This is not the story of an "extinct" group of people in the Bible with fictitious names like Amalekites, Jebusites, Perrizites, Amorites, Hivites, Hittites and so on. There were no such groups of people in the Bible with the same endings to their names like that. What is fascinating about these people with the same endings to their names is that they are all practically "extinct." There is something spurious about that. This, however, is the story of the living people from whose ancient minds and imaginations the concepts, doctrines, and documents of the Bible originated. It is, therefore, an ancestral story.

A s a result, an ancestral work like this would not be complete without dedicating it to the glorious life of our ancestors and the divine elements that give us life. This is to the earth and this is to the sky and everything in between. This is to the wind, fire, and water and the sustenance they give us. This is to life, and it is to health. This is to our ancient ancestors from whom we derive our greatness. This work is to these ancestors upon whom we rely to be granted all we need in this passage. This is to the recently departed who are on their way to joining the great ones as our ancestors. This is to Mom and Dad. This is to the sons and daughters of Africa spread around the world. This is to our children and the unborn children that will replace us in the circle of this life. Bertha, Kwasi, Amma, Kwadjo, and Adjoa, this is to you. This is to the prosperity of the circle of our lives and finally, this is to you, the reader.

Nana Banchie Darkwah.

March 15th, 2000

African Tribal Heritage of the People of the Bible

The time will come when our posterity will wonder at our ignorance of things so plain.
Seneca

In the future the so-called Dark Ages will perhaps be lengthened to include our own.
G. C. Lichtenberg

When ignorance gets started, it knows no bounds.
Will Rogers

Introduction

Before I discuss the African heritage of the people of the Bible, there is an important question to which I would like to draw readers' attention. For two thousand years, Christian Europe has taught us that the Jewish people wrote the Bible. From studies of the Jewish people, we find out that they are not Europeans, they went to Europe from somewhere else. The Bible claims that these people originated from and therefore went to Europe from Ur of the Chaldees in Mesopotamia. If we accept the Bible's claim, we again find out that the Jewish people did not originate from Europeans in Ur of the Chaldees because the people of Mesopotamia were not Europeans. Specifically, the Jewish people did not originate from English people. The question therefore is if the Jewish people are not Europeans or English people how did the authors of the New Testament come to be called by the English names Matthew, Mark, Luke, and John that are not Jewish names? How did the cousin of Jesus come to be called John the Baptist, an English name, when he was not a European and specifically when he was not an Englishman? How did the disciples of Jesus come to acquire English names like Simon, Peter, Andrew, Philip, Bartholomew, Thomas, Matthew, James, Judas and others when these people were not English men, and when these names were not Jewish names either?

Perhaps, the most important question here is why did the authors of the Old Testament documents show their indigenous African tribal names, and why did the authors and people of the New Testament come to acquire English names? By giving the people of the Bible these fictitious English names, Christian Europe sought to conceal something from us, the Christian masses. It is what Christian Europe has sought to conceal from the masses for over two thousand years that this book is about to reveal. There are some things we have been taught to believe in Christianity that were not so, and I want my readers to approach reading this book from the point of view of questioning obvious incongruenies like these in search of the truth.

This work is about the Bible and the religion that developed from it that has been spread around the world. It is something believers cannot explain but the philosophy of religion and the concept of God have had a huge mystical hold on the minds and imaginations of people around the world. Through the mystique of religious philosophy and the concept of God, the Christian Bible, believed to be a sacred book and the only book of religious truth, has acquired serious mystical dimensions to the extent that it has succeeded in even evoking some form of obsession in humans around the world. We have used this book and continue to use it to attribute and glorify the greatest of human achievements, but we have also used it and continue to use it to justify the most atrocious and inhuman acts in the history of our humanity.

The Bible imposes such an unquestioning soberness and obedience on its believers that most believers do not see where such a sacred and mystical book can be discussed academically. As a result, most of these people are not aware of scholastic biblical studies. To most believers, the only person with the "divine" authority to discuss the Bible is the preacher, and the only day such discussion can take place in "holiness" is Sunday. To these believers, bringing out logical and academic issues in the Bible makes them uncomfortable because the interpreting and controlling class of the Christian mind has told them that such discussions are "unbiblical" and even downright blasphemous. As a result of such teachings, the Bible has always been in the background of people's minds and imaginations in every discussion and undertaking. Currently, invoking the Bible seems to be the final word on social and moral issues in many societies in the Christian world. That is the magnitude of the control this book has had and continues to have over the lives of millions around the world.

In *Who Wrote the New Testament: The Making of the Christian Myth*, Burton Mack (1995) noted this in his prologue:

> It is the strange authority granted to the Bible in our society, an acquiescence that pertains whether one is a Christian or not, together with the poverty of our knowledge and public discussions of the bible, that is the stimulus for this book. Here we are with the Bible on our hands and we do not know how we got it, how it works, or what to make of it in public forum (p. 4).

This is a rather strange observation because the Bible itself tells us that the Jewish people wrote the documents of the Bible and gave them to the Greeks. However, historians and biblical scholars have found out that it is not true that the Jewish people wrote the Bible so we still do not know "how we got it," and we much less understand it. The making of the Christian myth that Burton Mack pointed out in the above quotation goes on daily. In a foreword to the Gideon New Testament, Psalms, and Proverbs, the producers wrote:

> The Bible contains the mind of God, the state of man, the way of salvation, the doom of sinners, and the happiness of believers. Its doctrines are holy, its precepts are binding, its histories are true, and its decisions are immutable. Read it to be wise, believe it to be safe, and practice it to be holy. It contains light to direct you, food to support you, and comfort to cheer you. It is the traveler's map, the pilgrim's staff, the pilot's compass, the soldier's sword, and the Christian's charter. Here Paradise is restored, Heaven opened, and the gates of hell disclosed."

I do know that the believers who wrote all these wrote them to glorify the Bible. However, the question that bothers me is how do people who do not know the origin of the biblical documents, people who do not know who wrote these documents, people who do not know where the book came from, and how the God of the Bible came to be know all these about the Bible? Or is the Bible such a great document that one does not have to know its origin or who wrote it to proclaim it in such theosophical highlights? This is an example of the making of the Christian myth. To believers in the Bible, it is sufficient to know that it is the "Book of God." Who this God is, and how he came to be does not matter. Because of the blind faith believers have in the Bible, the book has even been taken out of the minds and imaginations of humans from where it emerged, and given to God. Humans wrote the individual documents that were compiled into the Bible, and it is the revelation of the people who wrote these religious documents that the Greeks put together as the *Biblio* meaning the Book that this book is about.

The Bible without question is the greatest philosophy ever designed and written by man. It is no wonder that this Book humbles every human with whom it comes in contact, and it now has the attention of millions around the world. From centuries of carefully designed strategies to confer sacredness and divinity on the Bible, most Christians have come to believe that the Bible is the final authority on thinking, reasoning, and life. As a result, all thinking and reasoning stop for many people as soon as the Bible is invoked in any discussion. People do not know how to proceed in a discussion anymore once the Bible has been quoted in support of any debate.

People are almost frightened by the adulations that believing commentators shower on the Bible. In an Arts and Entertainment Network documentary on *Who Wrote the Bible*, the narrators pointed out that it is a book of sixty-six books with over eight hundred thousand words of enduring value. The narrator goes on to state that it is the cornerstone of our laws, ethics, moral code and the fountainhead of faith for over half the population of this earth. It is said to be the words of God and it has been translated into almost every language on earth. The Bible is perceived to be a book of inspiration, beauty, wisdom, and compassion.

The narrator concludes by pointing out that despite all these, the origins of the Bible are shrouded in the utmost obscurity and mystery. The Jewish people have claimed that their priests and inspired prophets wrote the documents of the Bible. If this is true, why should it be difficult for them to reveal the origin of this book? How can the origin of a book believed to be the greatest book of religious truth of over half the population of the world be kept a secret from the millions that believe in this book? What is going on here? Why has the origin and authors of the Bible been kept a secret for the past two thousand years? What made it necessary for such a secret to be kept? What is it that the traditional defenders of the Bible have been trying to hide from believers in this Bible?

The answers to all of these questions go back to the African origin of the people that became the Jews and Hebrews in Europe and the African origin of the authors and doctrines of the Bible and therefore Christianity. The Bible is in effect caught up in the comparative socio-political relationship between black and white people. Despite all these, even those who profess not to believe in the Bible still do not know how to respond once the Bible is invoked. The problem that has arisen from such reverence to the Bible is that in the grip of the Bible's unquestioning soberness, the world has come to accept contradictory and sometimes illogical ideas as part of our perception of religious truth. As Will Durant pointed out, the greatest snare of thinking is the uncritical acceptance of irrational assumptions and that is where the world is with the Bible, Christianity, and all other religions.

What amazes most scholars who study the Bible is the fact that no one dares to question where the Bible came from or who wrote it beyond the fallacy that the Jewish people wrote it. To most historians and biblical scholars, the question of who wrote the Bible has become a major area of scholastic inquiry. This area of research became even more important when biblical scholars found out that the people we have long known and believed wrote some documents of the Bible actually did not write those documents. In other words, some of the names the Bible itself gave us as the writers of some of the documents in it were false. This is the foundation upon which I am going to expose the traditional lies that have long been taught and preached about the Bible.

The Bible itself tells us that the Jewish people wrote the Bible. Early historians wrote and subordinated the histories of ancient civilizations of Egypt and the Middle East based upon this biblical assertion. Jewish history was carefully designed to complement this biblical assertion. Christianity has propagated this idea around the world for over two thousand years and yet modern research has shown that all of these were false. Historians, archaeologists, Egyptologists, and even Bible scholars have all found out that the people the Bible tells us that they wrote the documents of the Bible were not the authors of these documents. If the Jewish people wrote the Bible but the people they tell us wrote the documents of the Bible did not write these documents, should we still believe that the Jewish people wrote this Bible?

In 1987, Richard Elliot Friedman, one of the foremost scholars of the Bible wrote a book entitled *Who Wrote The Bible*? To write such a book one must be certain that the evidence in support of the traditional assertion of the authors of the Bible was false. In this book, Friedman used very cogent arguments to suggest the people who must have written the Bible. However, he pointed out before he began his speculation that:

> It is a strange fact that *we have never known with certainty* who produced the book that has played such a central role in our civilization. There are traditions concerning who wrote each of the biblical books – the Five Books of Moses are supposed to be by Moses, the book of Lamentations by the prophet Jeremiah, half the Psalms by King David – but how is one to know if these traditional ascriptions are correct? (p. 15, emphasis mine).

Here is one of the foremost Jewish biblical scholars revealing that authors the Bible claims wrote documents of the Bible did not write these documents. Unfortunately, such revelation about the true origin of the Bible is not the kind of information that is passed on to the believer on Sundays.

Discussions of the origin and the authors of the Bible have had their debating and controversial days. The *New York Times'* review of Friedman's book stated that it was "thought provoking" and would be "of interest to anyone who, aware of the unevenness and problems in the biblical text, seeks a sympathetic and perceptive guide." *U. S. News & World Report's* review pointed out that this book "promises to *rekindle* heated debate about the Good Book's origins." All of these go to confirm that western historical and biblical scholarship has never known with certainty who wrote the Bible despite the intense interdisciplinary effort that has been directed at this inquiry for centuries. The question that arises from the secrecy and mystery surrounding the origin and authors of the Bible is, what part of the Bible is the work of God and what part is the work of humans? This is a question most scholars who are confronted with the search for the origin and authors of the Bible ask themselves daily.

As I pointed out in the introduction, misquotations, misunderstandings, mistranslations, and misinterpretations of the documents of the Bible have caused the greatest controversies, confusion, and misery among humans. There is no literary work over which so many people have claimed knowledge and authority as the Bible. At the same time, there is no other literary work, whose narratives, intended meanings, and purposes have been so much speculated, misquoted, mistranslated, and misinterpreted.

The documents of the Bible were translated for the Greeks from who it traveled to entire Europe. It was in Europe that these documents first became a sacred book of religion. As a result, most of the controversies, confusion, and misery caused from the Bible originated in Europe. It is evident from this that Europeans have never understood the Bible because they have never known its place of origin, who wrote these documents, or the purpose it was intended to serve.

Western historians and biblical scholars have searched for the origin and the history behind the Bible but such scholastic search has been flawed by four main factors. The first of these factors is the fact that the leading scholars in biblical research have mostly been Jewish scholars who see the Bible as a record of their history and therefore cannot be known to outsiders. This gives them some kind of monopoly over biblical research. As a result, however, the focus of the search of these scholars has been on seeking and confirming what the Bible has said instead of searching for what might have been that the Bible did not say. From this focus, these scholars have narrowed their search for biblical information and the authors of the Bible within the context of the suggested geographical setting of the Bible and only around the history of Israel. In effect, there is some kind of conspiratorial protection from some biblical scholars to make sure that nothing is brought out to undermine Jewish people's place as the children of God in the eyes of Europeans.

Such conspiratorial protection of the Bible and the Jewish people must have been caused by the history of intimidation that has long surrounded scholastic search for the truth behind the Bible. Historical evidence shows that the early Church and most early biblical scholars were not tolerant and ready to accept any deviations from what they perceived as the "biblical truth." For example, Isaac ibn Yashush was among the early Jewish biblical scholars to find out that Moses did not write the first five books of the Bible as scholars of the biblical documents attributed to him. When he wrote to reveal the earliest reasons why Moses did not write the first five books of the Bible, he was perceived and called a heretic by his colleagues, especially Abraham ibn Ezra. There is also evidence that some early scholars who found out some truths that contradicted what has traditionally been accepted as biblical truths were urged to hide it and be quiet. In *Who Wrote The Bible?* Richard Elliot Friedman quoted ibn Ezra as having written to his fellow scholars almost threatening them that: "*And he who understands will keep silent*" (1987, p.19). This speaks volumes about the suspected conspiracy I have mentioned, and it seems to reflect a clear voice of intimidation from some Jewish scholars to hide the truth about the Bible. From such a historical background, I would say that the truth in Christianity would have been told more often if it were as safe to tell it as it is to hide it.

The second factor in the flaw of western scholastic search for the authors and history behind the biblical documents is the fact that most of the people that seek to find the authors of these documents are already believers in the teachings of these documents. They already believe these authors wrote these documents. As a result, the research visions of these scholars are also tunneled toward what would confirm their beliefs in these documents, and not any deviations that would perhaps undermine their beliefs or question the veracity of the Bible on some issues.

The third factor has been the early traditional power of the Catholic Church in condemning and thereby discouraging findings of any deviations from the normal religious beliefs in the Bible. For example, the Church rejected the work of Bonfils of Damascus and later deleted the passages in his work that questioned Moses' authorship of the first five books of the Bible. The Church relegated the work of Andreas van Maes on the same topic to the Catholic Index of Prohibited Books, the most powerful index of religious freedom censorship ever known. Later the Church also censored Isaac de la Peyrere's book suggesting that Moses did not write the biblical books attributed to him. De la Peyrere was arrested, jailed, and forced to recant. He did.

The Catholic Church and Judaism banded together and went after the Dutch philosopher Spinoza for revealing more evidence showing that Moses did not write the first five books of the Bible. Judaism excommunicated Spinoza, and the Church issued 37 edicts against his work. Some scholars believe that the later attempt on Spinoza's life was because of the powerful truths he tried to reveal. The Catholic Church burned almost all the books the French protestant, Richard Simon, wrote. As it can be seen, the Church's intimidation over centuries was enough to inform and warn scholars not to search or reveal anything that would question, disagree, and therefore undermine the veracity of the Bible. From these, it is clear that the foundations of the legendary lying lore in Christianity had the mighty hand of the Catholic Church behind it to ensure the continued survival and propagation of the Christian lying lore.

In this regard, the Church was very powerful, defensive, and protective of the Bible from being brought to "harm" through the revelation of truths behind the Book. The Catholic Church tried William Robertson Smith, the Scottish professor of the Old Testament and succeeded in removing him from his position as the Chair of a College in Aberdeen in Scotland. It is not difficult to understand why almost all the contemporary works out there have tended to support the biblical version of the stories and authors of the Bible, and why dissenting and revealing works have almost always been silenced in one way or another. For more discussion of this see Friedman, 1987, pp. 17-21.

The final flaw in western scholastic search for the people and authors of the Bible is in the fact that though the Bible gives a major clue, historical and biblical scholars have ignored it for almost two thousand years. By ignoring this clue, western scholarship has effectively turned its search off Ancient Egypt and her modern descendants, the black Africans. As a result, a revelation of the Africans who wrote the Bible would come as a major surprise to most believers, historians, and even biblical scholars who have for far too long believed that they have successfully speculated and therefore they know all the answers to the biblical riddle.

The difficulty of telling Africa's story in the west

This work is a revelation of the Africans who wrote the theosophical documents that became the Christian Bible of ancient Greece, Europe, and the world. For over two thousand years, the world has known and credited the Jewish people as the creators of the foundational concepts and documents that became the doctrines of Judaism for Jews, Christianity for Europeans, and Islam for the Arabs. However, few people have gone beyond this knowledge to verify whether it is true that the Jewish people created the foundational concepts, doctrines, and documents in the Bible or not. One of the most simple arguments supporting the fact that the

5

Jewish people did not write create the ideas or write the documents of the Bible is their inability to tell the world where and how these documents originated. Another is their inability to tell the world who truly wrote these documents beside the false authors they assigned to the documents. As a major part of the revelation in this work therefore, I will like to establish that the Jewish people did not create the foundational concepts or the theosophical documents that became the foundations of world religions. A larger ethnic group of black people from whom the Jewish people originated created the concepts of religion, the sacramental practices, and the religious documents that the Jewish people translated for the Greeks. This larger ethnic group of people is the modern descendants of Ancient Egyptians, and they can be found in Africa. This work will introduce the historical, biblical, linguistic, and cultural evidence to confirm this.

Before then, I would like to point out that Europeans have not known all the evidence I intend to introduce in this book, but they have known something about the African heritage of the Jewish people. They have long known that the Jewish people came to Europe from among a larger group of black people. However, they have never known the specific African tribal group from which the Jewish people originated. Much of what scholars have said about the ethnic origin of the Jewish people has usually been the generic statements pointing out that the Jewish people originated from Africa. Honestly, the Jewish people know that they originated from some black tribes, but they also do not specifically know which these tribes were.

Personally, I am aware that there was a time in the 1960s and 70s when the Jewish scholars were secretly traveling around Africa researching African tribes to find out where they must have originated. I do believe, however, that in these days when being associated with Africa is a denigration in Europe, they have stopped trying but the evidence in Africa has not gone away. I am personally aware that some Jewish scholars came to Ghana when I was there and studied *Akan* religion, especially the religion of the *Asante* people to find out if there were any similarities between that and Judaism or Christianity. To the Jewish people therefore, this work is going to be a major revelation of their roots because the work will reveal the larger ethnic group from which they originated and the tribes and ethnic groups that joined this larger group in the biblical Exodus.

This revelation is about what Africa knows, and revealing any positive truth about Africa today is not easy. As I have pointed out, over the centuries, the negative ideas that early western scholars wrote about Africa have now ossified in the minds and imaginations of people around the world. Most people do not want to shed their negative perceptions about Africa because keeping Africa down through these negative perceptions helps to keep them at a level on top, and that makes them feel psychologically good.

For example, there was a genetic study in America and China to try to find the origin of the Chinese people. This study was called the *Chinese Human Genome Project*. The study found out that the earliest Chinese people originated from Africa. In the review of this project in the *LA Times*, Li Jan, one of the researchers is reported to have said that his fellow Chinese scholars would be very upset because he revealed to the world that ancient Chinese people were Africans. This study was a well designed genetic study conducted by Chinese scholars in America and China. These scholars made this conclusion themselves but they never wanted it to be known that modern Chinese people originated from Africa. This is because the early negative ideas Europeans wrote and propagated about Africa have solidified in the minds and imaginations of people and it has made being African the worst of human flaws in this world. The Chinese scholars would be upset because they do not want to be associated with whatever Africa is in the eyes of the world.

For this reason, revealing a relationship between Africa, the Bible, and Christianity, as this book seeks to do, is even more difficult because in matters concerning religion, especially Christian religion, the truth is fervently guarded with a heavy armor of indoctrinated faith. A carefully designed propaganda and strategy to perpetuate the lies that early historians and apostolic fathers of Christianity told further protect this armor. As a result, not many people who

6

have adopted this religion know all they need to know about the religion they have adopted and devoted their lives. Because of this, when it comes to serious explorations into the Christian religion, one does not get to explore seriously with those who know the truth, instead one gets into discussing and sometimes debating with those who "do not know or understand, but believe." Unknowingly, these people have been the soldiers and the guardians of the *"legendary lying lore."*

The worst part of being involved in a discussion with such people is that their only source of religious and historical knowledge is the Bible and its interpretations. Unfortunately, these are rather too limited. What makes the only source of these people even more limited is the fact that they do not know, and they have never imagined that there might be eyewitnesses to the biblical story somewhere. The question is could all the people the Jewish people claim to have lived and interacted with and wrote about in the biblical narratives be extinct? The answer is an emphatic no. However, that is the impression the biblical neglect of these people seems to suggest.

From Christianity's deliberate silence about these people, most Christians do not know that in the past four hundred years, Christian Europe has been doing all it can to cut possible eyewitnesses off the biblical story. These eyewitnesses are the Africans who were the Ancient Egyptians. For example, most believers in the Bible as the book of God know that the Jewish people were in Ancient Egypt where they claim to have become a people. However, what these believers do not know is that the documents of the Bible were compiled, edited, and translated for the Greeks in Alexandria in Ancient Egypt. In much the same way, these believers have never imagined that there might be modern descendants of the Ancient Egyptians and therefore there might be descendants of eyewitnesses who might still know something that Christian Europe and believers around the world has never known about the Bible. What is worse is, most of these believers have never explored the role of the Ancient Egyptians in the Bible beyond what they have read and been told by the interpreters.

As a foundation for the continuation of this discussion, I would like to establish that the biblical story was a story about real humans, and their modern descendants continue to live on this earth. As a result, any historical discussion of the Bible that seeks to speculate, theorize, and restrict the discussion to only biblical references, or couch the discussion in inherent biblical fabrications to defend the faith is not enough. It is the human story behind the Bible that this book seeks to bring out so that those who believe would know and better understand what they believe. It may even help to strengthen and refine some believers' faiths. I must also point out that this work is not intended to question any Christian's faith. Instead the work is intended to tell the side of the biblical story that has never been told, or has been concealed from Christian masses, and that is Africa's side of the story. This is the background I would like readers to have to open their minds and prepare themselves for the revelations in this book.

Because western scholarship about Africa has mostly been based upon socio-political and negative anthropological sentiments and not the truth, Europeans have been the last people to know and understand any aspect of history about Africa. One of the most important aspects of African history that Europeans have failed to know and understand is the true story of the origin of religion, specifically the story of Europe's Christian religion. Among the peripheral evidence linking Africans to the documents of the Bible is geographical evidence. When we look at the Bible from a geographical point of view, we find out that geographically, the Jewish people became a people in Ancient Egypt not in Canaan. They became a people in Ancient Egypt before they moved to Canaan. The documents of the Bible were compiled and translated for the Greeks in Ancient Egypt. All of these suggest that the true story behind the Bible and Christianity can never be known and understood without knowing about the people that lived in Ancient Egypt and the Middle East in ancient times.

Our emerging knowledge
From the growth and development of knowledge in more recent times, Europeans continue to find out a close relationship amongst Ancient Egyptians, Africans, Jews, the Bible, and Christianity beyond what the Bible has stated or what the interpreters have said. In the formative years of Christianity, this relationship between Africans and the Bible did not matter. However, in more recent times since the relationship between Europeans and Africans has been based upon Europe's superiority and Africa's inferiority, it has become extremely important to Christian Europe that modern Europeans do not find out that the concepts and practices of Christianity were derived from ancient African theosophical concepts and sacramental practices. As a result, Christian Europe has long wished that the relationship amongst Ancient Egyptians, Africans, Jews, the Bible, and Christianity were never explored. Because of this, much of the true historical and archaeological information that tends to bring Ancient Egyptians and their modern descendants, the Africans, close to the origins of Christianity has always been either openly denied, or secretly suppressed.

Even information about Africa that is not about religion is either vehemently denied or quietly suppressed. Some western scholars have even made it their earnest duties to monitor what their fellow scholars write about Africa to make sure that these scholars do not reveal some of the deliberately hidden truths about this continent. In 1977, W. Y. Adams wrote a book entitled *Nubia: Corridor to Africa*. The title of the book scared many western historians and Egyptologists. Was Nubia the corridor through which African people went from inner Africa to become the Ancient Egyptians, or was it the corridor through which the Ancient Egyptians moved to inner Africa to become the Africans? Whichever way one looked at it, there seemed to be a link between the Africans and the Ancient Egyptians with Nubia as the corridor of passage. Linking Ancient Egypt to black Africans has been a relationship most western historians and Egyptologists have refused to accept or acknowledge. Consequently, some scholars had to monitor what Adams had to write closely.

In the introduction to his book, Adams acknowledged his frustration from the subtle control of truth about Africa and the intimidation of his colleagues when he wrote:

> "I did not originally set out to write this book for anthropologists, Egyptologists, or any of the scholarly specialists to whom the foregoing paragraphs are addressed. My intention was merely to make Nubian history known in an intelligible form to the general public, or at least to that part of it whose interest was kindled by the publicity given Abu Simbel and the High Dam salvage campaign. *Yet I found that, in the present state of our knowledge, I could not write a wholly popular book, knowing all the while that my professional colleagues would be looking over my shoulder.* For their sake (and sometimes at their insistence), I have introduced passages of discussion, debate, and sometimes downright quibbling which I had no original thought of including; as a result the lay reader may at times see more of the "dirty linen" of [western] historical scholarship than he wished to. ..." (1977, p. 9, emphasis mine).

The disdain in Adam's introductory paragraph clearly comes from his frustration in the assault on his conscience by colleagues who tried to intimidate him to hide whatever truth he must have found. The "dirty linen" of western historical scholarship about Africa, and the intimidation of some scholars to make sure that their colleagues do not reveal what early western scholarship has traditionally hidden is clearly evident in many modern scholastic works in history, anthropology, and science.

Early European knowledge of the black origin of Christianity
European scholars have long known about the African origin of the Jewish people, the Bible, and therefore the African origin of the religion Europeans call Christianity. This is about Africa and what European scholars have never known is the evidence from Africa that would confirm what they have long known about the Jewish people, the Bible, and Africans. It is the

evidence from Africa confirming the African heritage of the Jewish people, the Africa origin and authors of the doctrines of the Bible, and therefore the African origin of Christianity that this book intends to provide. The revelation in this book is therefore more specific and conclusive than has ever been attempted or revealed before now. However, that does not mean that Europeans have never known anything about the African heritage of the Jewish people. As a result, before I reveal anything about the ethnic origin of the Jewish people from what Africa knows, I will first explore what Europeans have known about the African origin of the Jewish people, and how they have reacted because of this knowledge.

In the introductory summary, I revealed that I have discovered the African tribes from which the Jewish people originated from the African tribal names they carry today. I linked the Jewish people to the African tribes that were the Ancient Egyptians. Proving the blackness of the African tribes that were the Ancient Egyptians is not difficult because they are still black. They still have a culture and tradition of kingship going back to Ancient Egypt. There is evidence of their royal dynasties originating from Ancient Egypt. Their kings still carry the royal names of their ancient ancestors and dynasties from Ancient Egypt. Their people also still carry the names of their ancestors that were the Ancient Egyptians and these modern descendants have rebuilt some of the ancient cities of their ancestors in Egypt and given these modern cities the same ancient names as they were in Egypt. In addition to all these, there is evidence of the blackness of the Ancient Egyptians in the images, wall paintings, and reliefs we have found in their ancient ruins in Egypt, and in museums around the world.

Proving that the Jewish people were originally black people is; however, more difficult than proving the blackness of the Ancient Egyptians because the Jewish people of today are white. To Europeans who were closer in time to the coming of the Jewish people to Europe, proving that the Jewish people were black people would not have been difficult. However, to modern generations that are far removed in time from the coming of the Jewish people to Europe it requires producing some of the evidence Christian Europe has sought to conceal in preservation of itself.

I have to prove the original black heritage of the Jewish people to validate my discovery of the black tribes from which they originated. It is important therefore for me to explain that among humans, it is the black skin color that changes to all the skin colors we have in the world. However, no mixture of humans can produce the black skin color except two black people. As a result, it is easier for black people to turn white as the Jewish people have done than it is for white people to turn black. This simply means it is at least possible for the original black people that became the Jews and Hebrews in Europe to turn white as they are today. For me to prove the black heritage of the Jewish people we must go to Europe where they have lived for over two thousand years to find out what Europeans have known about them.

Among the greatest of the hidden truths in Europe is the African origin and authors of the Bible and the concept of Christianity. Christian Europe has known this for over two thousand years. In its formative years, Christian Europe accepted the origin and authors of the doctrines of Christianity in the Africans without any hesitation or reservation. During this period, there is evidence that early Christian Churches in Europe worshipped black images of the people of the Bible for the sake of religious sanctimony and purity. Th e earliest black images of the people of the Bible in Christendom were therefore the earliest evidence of the African origin of the theosophical concepts and doctrines that became the documents of the Bible and the foundations of Christian doctrine in Europe.

Modern Europeans may not know this, or they may not want to know now, but the African origin of Christianity was common knowledge among western scholars and the early apostolic fathers of the Church long before Renaissance. It has been and it is still common knowledge through our modern times into this twenty-first century. In *The Aryan Myth: A History of Racist and Nationalistic Ideas in Europe*, Leon Poliakov revealed that knowledge of the people of the Bible as black people was common in Europe and in early European scholarship. In his chapter on *The Quest for the New Adam*, Leon Poliakov wrote:

> The scientists for their part were advancing even more remarkable hypothesis. James Cowles Prichard, by far the most popular anthropologist of the first half of the nineteenth century (who was a monogenist on the authority of the Scriptures, as he himself expressly admitted) had elaborated round about 1810, a kind of evolutionary theory according to which Adam and Eve were Blacks. It was only in the course of time that their descendants, as they became civilized and changed their way of life, had acquired a white colour (1996, p. 211, see also *Histoire Naturelle*, pp. 146-7, 151).

I would like to point out that the discussion of *The Quest for the New Adam* in Leon Poliakov's book is about Europe's search for a new and different source of origin when they determined that they could never have originated from the same [thus inferior] progenitor as black people. Do you think that from this background Europeans would acknowledge that the people of the Bible were black people?

In the introductory summary of this work, I revealed that I have discovered the African tribes from which the Jewish people originated. I discussed a few issues to show that the Jews were originally black people and here is evidence of such knowledge in Europe. Most early and modern European scholars have been influenced by the Bible to design their scholarship alongside what the Bible has said. What is most noteworthy in the work of this anthropologist, therefore, is that he freely admitted that he was a Christian, and he freely theorized that the people of the Bible beginning with Adam and Eve were black. Throughout Europe, statues, paintings, and all images of the people of the Bible have been portrayed as white people. What would make a Christian scholar assert that the people of the Bible were black in contradiction to the overt teachings and preaching of the Church? What would make a European scholar even assume that the people of the Bible were black people if he were not sure? What would make a European scholar and Christian risk being ostracized by his people and the Church to hypothesize that the people of the Bible were black people? This could only happen only if such a European scholar and Christian knew for sure that what he was talking about was the truth.

There is also a very important revelation in Prichard's assertion. From his European, Christian, and scholastic background, Prichard pointed out that white people originated from black people, and that they turned white only by changing their ways of life. This assertion may sound humorous today but modern science of the origin of humans has found it to be true. What would make a European, a Christian, and a scholar assert that Europeans were originally black people when the Church, Europeans, and most western scholars of the time were looking for ways to disassociate themselves from Africans? If Adam and Eve were black people then Europeans who look and claim to be different and superior to Africans because of their white skin color originated from black people. A branch of any tree cannot be superior to the stem from which it originates. Perhaps the most important point to bring out here is that if European anthropologists knew that Adam and Eve were black people then they admitted as late as the nineteenth century that the people of the Bible were black people. How then did Christian Europe come to have a white Jesus?

Prichard was not the only European scholar to point out that the people of the Bible were black. In 1933, Dr. John G. Jackson, an African American scholar wrote a book entitled *Was Jesus Christ A Negro? and The African Origin of the Myths and Legends of the Garden of Eden*. In this book, Dr. Jackson quoted the work of Sir Godfrey Higgins to support his assertion that Jesus was black.

In 1836, a knighted and renowned British orientalist, Sir Godfrey Higgins wrote *The Anaclypsis, or an Inquiry into the Origin of Languages, Nations, and Religions*. In this work, Sir Higgins also pointed out that the people of the Bible were black and that in all the early Catholic

Churches of Europe: *"the God Christ, as well as his mother, are described in their old pictures to be black [people]. The infant God in the arms of his black mother, his eyes and drapery white, is himself perfectly black"* (1836, p. 7, see also *Was Jesus Christ A Negro and The African Origin of the Myths and Legends of the Garden of Eden*, p. 14). What Sir Higgins also revealed indirectly was the fact that the doctrines of the Bible were originally black people's doctrines of religion and even the authors of our cherished Bible were black people. Arriving at this conclusion is rather simple. If Jesus were black and his people wrote his story, then the people that conceived and wrote this story must be also black. This confirms that the original people of God in the biblical story were black. It also reveals that the early Catholic Church knew, accepted, and acknowledged the black ethnicity of the people of the Bible by portraying the God Christ and his mother as the black people they originally were.

From his name Godfrey, Higgins must have been himself a Christian. Why would a Christian make such an assertion, if it were not true, in contradiction of what the Church has taught him to believe and what the Church itself has been propagating around the world?

Here is something else readers should consider in this analysis. The Jewish people sent the stories and documents of Christian doctrine to Europe as original Jewish people's stories and documents. They also told Europeans that the people of the Bible were their people. The question is if the people of the Bible and the Jewish people were not originally black people why would the Catholic Church, the foundation Church of Christian religion in Europe and around the world, portray Jesus and his mother as black people? What would have made it that necessary for the Church of white people to portray the most important personalities in Christianity as black people, and why? The answer is simple. The people of the early Christian Church did this based upon the blackness of the people they saw and called the Jewish people.

We must remember that early Catholic Church was closer in time to the coming of the Jews to Europe than any of the Renaissance painters that began to portray the people of the Bible as white people. Certainly, early apostolic fathers of the Church were closer to knowing the skin color of the Jewish people than leaders of our modern Churches. These early white apostolic fathers of the Church would have had no reason to portray Jesus and his mother as black people if they were not originally black. The early portrayal of Jesus and his mother as black people was therefore the gospel truth. That was why the Church portrayed Jesus and his mother in the original black images of the Jewish people at the time. This was how the earliest images of Jesus and his mother came to be black in the Catholic Churches of Europe.

On authority of the earliest Christian portrayals of the Jewish people as the people of the Bible, this piece of historical information reveals that the Jewish people who claim that the biblical story is their ancestral story were originally black people. If they were black people they must have originated from a larger tribal group of black people. It is this tribal group of black people that I am going to reveal to confirm the blackness of Jesus, his mother, and the people of the Bible, and also authenticate the revelation of the Africans who wrote the Bible.

Sir Higgins' revelation of the black ethnicity of Jesus, his mother, and the people of the Bible is very significant because the Catholic Church introduced Christianity to Western Europe. This revelation not only confirms that the Catholic Church has long known and acknowledged the African origin of Christianity, but also that Western Europeans have long known, accepted, and acknowledged the black heritage of Jesus, his mother, and her people. The acknowledgement of black people as the people of the Bible and the creators of the doctrines of Christianity began from the formative years of Christianity and lasted until racism and racial prejudice made it psychologically impossible and uncomfortable for Europeans to accept a black Jesus and his black mother, no matter how central and revered these people were in Christian doctrine and sacramental practices.

Sir Higgins anticipated that this revelation was not going to be received with equanimity among his people in Europe. He therefore armed himself with numerous irrefutable proofs. To prove his assertion, Sir Higgins did not theorize to give his fellow scholars and religious racists the opportunities to theorize alongside the racist "legendary lying lore" of Europe. Instead, he sent doubters of his assertion to places and Churches in Europe where such images of the *black Christ and his mother Mary* could be found. He sent his detractors to Cathedral-a-Moulins, the famous Chapel of the Virgin of Loretto where there was still an image of the black Jesus and his mother in that Church. He also sent unbelievers to the Church of Annunciata, the Church at St. Lazaro, and the Church of St. Stephen at Genoa where the black images of Jesus and his mother could also be found. Sir Higgins sent his challengers to the Church of St. Francisco at Pisa, to the Church at Brixen in Tyrol, and to the Church at Padua. Sir Higgins also sought to prove his assertion with churches closer to his readers in Western Europe. He therefore sent unbelievers in these places to the Catholic Cathedral at Augsburg, the Church of St. Theodore at Munich in Germany, and even to Rome and the Borghese chapel of Maria Maggiore.

Fig. 2: Bronze portrait of St. Peter at his Basilica in Rome today.

The big question is, if all these early Churches portrayed Jesus, the God Christ and his mother as black people what doubt should we have today about the origin and centrality of

Africans in the creation and development of the documents and doctrines of Christianity in Europe? The answer to this question is not about Christian Europe's doubt of the veracity of the black ethnicity of Jesus and his mother. The answer to this question is not even about religion. In the minds of Europeans, the real answer to this question was about acknowledging something about Africans that could raise Africans above Europeans. That was unacceptable even to Christian Europe. The issue therefore was whether accepting this truth erodes some aspects of Europe's self-conferred superiority over Africans or not. If it did, then this fact was simply unacceptable to "superior" Europeans. In other words, Europeans knew that Jesus, his mother, and the people of the Bible were all black people. However, they simply refused to accept it because it did not fit into Europe's comparative anthropological perception of itself and the black people who are now the Africans.

What I would like to point out to readers that may feel psychologically uncomfortable or socio-anthropologically insecure from knowing that Jesus, his mother, and the people of the Bible were black is a simple fact. The people of the Bible did not derive their racial and ethnic identities from European names, or Renaissance and other European paintings and artistic depictions of them. These people were real humans with a racial and ethnic heritage. The people of the Bible derived their black racial and ethnic heritage from the black people that were the Ancient Egyptians. These were the people some of who broke away from Ancient Egypt, went to live in Canaan, and later went to Europe to become the Jews and Hebrews. These Jews and Hebrews of Europe therefore derived their black racial and ethnic heritage from the black tribes from whom they originated in Ancient Egypt before they broke away into the biblical Exodus. The question of the racial and ethnic heritage of Jesus, his mother, and the people of the Bible is therefore not about the Christian religion or what European racial sentiments are willing to acknowledge. The racial and ethnic identity of Jesus, his mother, and the people of the Bible are about the true racial and ethnic heritage of the Jewish people and the people from whom they originated before they became the Jews and Hebrews in Europe.

What is interesting about all these is that the Jewish people who claim that they were the people of the Bible have not questioned or refuted the fact that the original people of the Bible were black people and that is how Jesus and his mother Mary came to be black. The Catholic Church also never questioned or refuted the veracity of the people of the Bible being black because it knew. However, the responsive action of the Church to all these revelations confirmed that the Church never wanted it to be known that the people of the Bible were black.

Sir Godfrey Higgins went on to point out that with the growth and development of European racism, many of the European Churches embarked upon concealing the truth of the blackness of the people of the Bible from the Christian masses and the European public. As a result, some of the Churches designed the propaganda to either explain why the earliest Christian images of Jesus and his mother were black, or deny entirely that these people were originally black. To make such denial and propaganda easy and plausible, most of the Churches removed the "black figurines" of Jesus and his mother from the Churches and European public view and replaced them with white images. The Church had worshiped the black images of Jesus and his mother in all Catholic Churches in Europe for over a thousand years therefore it could not question these revelations. Moreover, it was not the place of the Church to question the racial and ethnic background of the people of the Bible. As a result, the Church's action of quietly removing the black images of Jesus and his mother and replacing them with white images confirm that these revelations were true and unimpeachable.

Of course, such replacements became easy and well justified because by this time the Jewish people from whose blackness Europeans had known the people of the Bible looked white, and they were considered white in many European communities. What is interesting about this is that Sir Higgins also pointed out that the "black figurines" of Christ and his mother were not thrown away or destroyed. They were kept in secret basements and repositories where they are still held sacred by the few who know and believe in the religious purity, originality, and true spirit of Christianity (see *The Anaclypsis, Vol.1, Bk. IV, Chapt. 1*).

Despite these actions and propaganda by the Catholic Church, there are still some Churches in Europe that have retained the images of the black Jesus and his mother to this day. One of my students from Spain told me that some of the oldest Catholic Churches in Spain have not changed or concealed their ancient black figurines of Jesus and his mother to this day. This was confirmed in the History Channel's recent documentary on the *Inquisition*. In the discussion of the Inquisition in Spain, I saw at least one church in the video that still has its old black figurines of Jesus and his mother. In another recent History Channel documentary called the *Catacombs of Rome*, the earliest paintings of Jesus in Christian catacombs portrayed him as a black man with a lamb across his shoulders as Christ the Shepherd. In the Catacombs of St. Domitilla, another early Christian burial place underneath the city of Rome, there are several depictions of Jesus as a black man on the tombs of many of these early Christians. Again, we must remember that the Catholic Church was closer in time to the coming of the Jews to Rome so the artists in these catacombs depicted what they saw the earliest Jewish people were, and that was black.

I have personally lived and traveled far and wide in Europe. In one of our personal travels, my wife and I noticed that the statue of St. Peter outside St. Peter's Basilica in Rome was physically different from the one inside. The one inside was an image of a black man. I did not know why the same person would be depicted in two different racial images but I now know the reason for the difference. The one outside is for the pacification of European racial and prejudicial sentiments, and the one inside portraying a black man, is for the purity and sacredness of true Christian worship. Is the portrait of St. Peter above the portrait of a white person? Even today, some believers argue that the image of St. Peter in the Basilica was not originally black and that it is the bronze that was used in designing the statue that is turning black. Others also argue that the blackness of St. Peter in the Basilica is a miracle because St. Peter is turning into the black man he originally was.

Another question that has puzzled many believers in the Bible and biblical scholars is if the people of the Bible were not black, where did the Catholic Church come by the black Madonnas still in European Churches and Churches around the world? What is most fascinating about all these is that these black Madonnas are acknowledged and worshipped at the highest pinnacle of Christian worship.

On May 30, 1982. Mr. Ed Reiter wrote an article in the *New York Times* entitled *Medal Honors the 'Black Madonna.'* Below is the article:

> Life in Poland is bleak these days, but even in this time of lingering national trauma there are causes for celebration. One such occasion will take place this summer, when Polish Catholics mark the 600th anniversary of their "Black Madonna" shrine and a new medal, authorized by the Vatican, will enable people around the world to share in the observance – at least vicariously.
>
> The Black Madonna is a portrait of Mary, mother of Jesus Christ, said to have been painted by St. Luke on a plank from a table made by Jesus. The Roman Emperor Constantine is said to have carried the painting from Jerusalem to Constantinople. From there, centuries later, it passed into the hands of Prince Wladyslaw, founder of the monastery of Josna Gora, a Marian sanctuary in Czestochowa, Poland.
>
> Upon completion of the monastery in 1382, the Prince presented the painting to the Pauline Fathers there, and ever since then it has been an important object of veneration.
>
> Pope John Paul II, himself a son of Poland, has termed the Black Madonna, "the pulse of our nation within the heart of its mother." The shrine has helped unify Polish Catholics through recurrent periods of religious persecution and repression and millions of pilgrims visit it every year despite government efforts to discourage demonstrations of fervor. A counterpart shrine honoring Our Lady of Czestochowa has been erected in this country at Doylestown, Pa.

14

The 600th anniversary observance has prompted a number of special activities among Polish Catholics and other Catholics of Polish extraction. These will culminate Aug. 26 in a jubilee celebration at the shrine. Pope John Paul II is expected to attend if political conditions permit. The Pope did visit the shrine in 1979, shortly after becoming the first Polish pontiff in history, and offered a prayer at that time for justice and peace in a world "still under so terrible threats from many sides (quoted from Was Jesus Christ A Negro ... by Dr. Curtis Alexander, ed.).

This piece of information confirms that in the deepest recesses of the Catholic Church's knowledge, Jesus, his mother, and the people of the Bible were all black people. This particular piece of information is therefore extremely important for establishing the black and African heritage of the people of the Bible. The importance of this evidence is in the fact that the Catholic Church has tangible evidence of the ethnicity of the mother of Jesus Christ from an artistic portrayal from St. Luke. Without a doubt, the Catholic Church has known and portrayed Mary, the mother of Jesus, as a black woman for over two thousand years. Yet because of racism, this Church portrays Jesus as a blonde-haired, blue-eyed, thin-nosed, thin-lipped, white-skinned Son of God. What reveals the fallacy in this is the fact that this same Church continues to portray Mary, the mother of Jesus as the Black Madonna. How possible is it that the black woman, Mary, or for that matter, any black woman would have a blonde-haired, blue-eyed, white-skinned son with a black husband? Who else can this simple deception fool but Europeans who have never known the people and the story behind the Bible, anyway?

Despite Christian Europe's deceptive stories about the fatherhood of Jesus, we in Africa know that Jesus' real father was called *Osafo*, a carpenter. This was the indigenous *Akan* name that was transposed to *Joseph* in Greek and later in other European tongues. It was because of the calculated deception in the concealment of the ethnicity of Jesus Christ that Christianity began to claim that Jesus was the son of God. We in Africa know that Jesus was the son of *Osafo* before he became the son of the Christian God. This has also been the reason discussion of the brothers and sisters of Jesus have never come up anywhere in any Church. To most Christians, Jesus was an only child, the son of God, but that is part of the *legendary lying lore*.

From this analysis, the quiet and lingering assertions of the black ethnicity of Jesus, his mother, and the entire people of the Bible from the nineteenth century become unimpeachable. This revelation also confirms the idea that the Catholic Church and its Pope still acknowledge, honor, worship, and pray the mother of Jesus as the black woman she was. Why then are Jesus and his mother portrayed as white people in all the modern images of these people in Christianity when the Church has long known that they were black people?

The conspiracy in all these is that the Catholic and Protestant Churches of Europe came black people in Africa to introduce us to images of a white God, Jesus, and his mother Mary when they all knew that all these people were black. This has been the greatest lie in Christianity for the past two thousand years. However, Jesus and his mother alone could not have been the only black people in the Bible. They must have originated from a tribe of black people for them to be black and that confirms that the tribe and people of the Bible from whom they originated were all black people.

A major point that must be repeated from all these is that these black people of the Bible were not Jews, and they were not Hebrews. They originated from the black tribes that were the Ancient Egyptians. These were the tribes that moved south to become the Africans. In Africa, not only do we know that Jesus, his mother, and the people of the Bible were black people, but also we know the specific African tribes from which they originated. Notice that I have just pointed out that the Jewish people originated African tribes. This is because our knowledge reveals that the Jewish people did not originate from one black tribe. They originated from several black African tribes and the Exodus narrative in the Bible confirms this. A major question is, if these Jewish people did not originate from the black tribes that were the Ancient Egyptians, how did they come by and continue to carry the tribal and cultural names of these Ancient Egyptians?

15

How could the Jewish people have acquired such an African tribal and cultural identity without originating from an African tribe? What confirms the African tribal origin of the Jewish people beyond any shadow of a doubt is that, these people do not carry names from one African tribe. They carry names from several black African tribes thus confirming that they originated from several black tribes. Again, the question is from where did the Jewish originate that the names of all these black African tribes could be found?

The fact is the blackness of the people of the Bible has been a major thorn in the historical flesh of Christian Europe for over five hundred years now. As part of the effort to conceal the truth of the African origin of the Bible and Christianity, Christian Europe has fastened itself to the claim of the Jewish people that the documents and the theosophical ideas of Christianity were all Jewish people's creations. Again, what made it easy for Christian Europe to accept and portray the Jewish people as the creators of the concepts and doctrines of Christianity was the fact that at this time, Jewish people were accepted as white people because their skin color approximated white skin color. Moreover, accepting the Jewish people as the creators of the documents and ideas of Christian religion was more tolerable to European racial sentiments than acknowledging black people in Africa as the creators. Europeans have long suspected that the Jewish people did not create the biblical documents and religious doctrines they claim to have created. However, the acceptance of the Jewish people's story as the creators of the foundations of Christianity was necessary to cut off Africa's connection to the history, origin, concepts, and sacramental practices of Christianity.

In the introduction of this work, I revealed that from the transposed African names of the authors of the Books of the Old Testament, there is no doubt that Africans wrote the Bible. However, even if we accept the fallacy that the Jewish people created the documents and doctrines of the Bible, these documents and doctrines still originate from black people because the Jewish people originated from black African tribes. Again, if the Jewish people who supposedly created and introduced the concepts and documents of Christianity to Europeans were not black people why would the early Catholic Church of white people in the land of white people portray the most important people the Church worshipped as black people?

More evidence of black Jesus and his mother Mary

Revelation of the blackness of Jesus, his mother, and the people of the Bible was quite common in European scholarship of the nineteenth century. In the 1933 work of Dr. John G. Jackson, he also invoked the earlier work of Kersey Graves to support his assertion of the blackness of Jesus. In 1875, Kersey Graves also wrote a book entitled *The World's Sixteen Crucified Saviors*. In this book, Graves did not only identify the leitmotif of crucifixion in sixteen other religious and political figures around the world, but he also pointed out from evidence in Europe, that Jesus was black and the people of the Bible were originally black people. He wrote:

> There is as much evidence that the Christian Savior was a black man, or at least a dark man, as there is of his being the son of the Virgin Mary, or that he once lived and moved upon the earth. And that evidence is the testimony of his disciples, who had nearly as good an opportunity of knowing what his complexion was as the evangelists who omit to say anything about it. ... In the pictures and portraits of Christ by early Christians he is uniformly represented as being black (from *The World's Sixteen Crucified Saviors*, cited in *Was Jesus Christ A Negro* ... reprinted in 1987 by Curtis Alexander, ed.).

All of these confirm that my discovery of the black African tribes from which the Jewish people originated has some veracity in it. The people of the Bible originated from a black African heritage.

For Christian Europe and Europeans these revelations were not lies; they were simply unacceptable truths because acknowledging that the Jesus Europeans worship and the people of the Bible, their sacred book, were black people would definitely upset Europe's self-conferred superiority over black Africans. How could Christian Europe accept that the people of the Bible, the very black people Christianity claims are the cursed ones to be enslaved by Europeans, were black people? How could Christian Europe face the humiliation that the Africans they condemned as pagans were the very people that created the doctrines of Christian religion and wrote the documents that became the Christian Bible? From all that has happened in the history of the interaction between Europeans and Africans, how could Christian Europe acknowledge that the Jesus around whom they have designed the Christian religion was a black man?

It is clear that Christian Europe had reasons to refuse to acknowledge that the people of the Bible were black people. Early Christians in Europe knew all these but they covered it up. Today, this secret seems to have been so well hidden for so long that not only do modern Christians around the world not know the truth about the African origin of Christianity, but also these people have accepted the propaganda to deny and even challenge this truth. Nevertheless, this issue has kept coming up now and again for almost three hundred years. If it were not true, why would it keep coming up now and again over these centuries, and why has nobody questioned or disproved it?

As I have pointed out above, if any organization in Christendom knew of the original blackness of the Jewish people and therefore the original blackness of the people of the Bible, it would be the Roman Catholic Church. Perhaps, as a result of it, the Roman Catholic Church has had a tradition of not letting black people too close to its central organization and the hidden secrets of the Church about black people. As a result, it is an understatement for those who have experienced it to say that the Catholic Church is racist, and through history, the Church has done worse than that. In 1989, black Catholic priest, Archbishop George Augustus Stallings, Jr. was fed up with the Catholic Church's racism against black people in America so he broke away and formed the African-American Catholic Congregation (AACC). Seven months later, the Catholic Church in Rome excommunicated Archbishop Stallings. However, the American National Catholic Church (ANCC) that has often disagreed with some of the policies, teachings, and practices of the Catholic Church in Rome decided not to acknowledge the excommunication of Archbishop Stallings. Rev. Stallings was therefore still acknowledged and accepted as a Catholic priest in America. The American National Catholic Church elevated Stallings to the rank of a Bishop in the Catholic Church in 1990, and in 1991 made him an Archbishop.

Part of the reason for the excommunication of Archbishop Stallings from the Catholic Church was his propagation of the idea that Jesus was a black man. In an interview with *Emerge* in April 1995, Archbishop Stallings pointed out that the fact that Jesus was a black man is not new among black scholars and political leaders because a Black Nationalist called Robert Young pointed this out in 1829. In 1894, another black man called Henry McNeal Turner also brought it up. In the first half of the 20th century, Alexander McGuire and Marcus Garvey both brought it up. In the second half of the 20th century Rev. Albert B. Cleage, Jr. of the Pan-Africanist Orthodox Church and the Shrines of the Black Madonna in Detroit also preached and propagated this idea. In this 21st century, I am also bringing it up and finally producing Africa's evidence in support of all these people.

The first evidence Archbishop Stallings introduced to support his assertion that Jesus was a black man was in Matthew 1:1-17 where the 42 generations of Jesus are traced. Among these generations were four women, three of who were supposed to be Hittites or Canaanites. According to Archbishop Stallings, biblical scholars universally agree that these women, Tamar, Rahab, and Bathsheba, the wife of Uriah, were all black women. If these three women were black, what could have been the racial heritage of the rest of the people in the 42 generations of Jesus? Remember that during this period, there were no Europeans in or near the geographical region of Canaan, and the Arabs that live there today did not come there until after 600 A. D.

North Africa was one of the earliest centers of Christianity and three early Catholic Popes originated from there. Tradition says that the people of North Africa were converted to

Christianity with the assertion that Jesus, as a black man was one of them. Later, this assertion was changed to say that Jesus, the leader of the Christian religion walked among the people of North Africa when he was supposedly brought to hide in Ancient Egypt. So he was one of them. The New Testament states that Jesus was taken to Ancient Egypt in his infancy to hide him from the murderous intentions of King Herod (Matthew 2, 13: 15). Archbishop Stallings argues that if Jesus were white, he could not have been taken to Ancient Egypt to hide. The question Archbishop Stallings asked is "How could it have been possible for a blond-haired, blue-eyed, thin-nosed, thin-lipped, pale-faced baby to have been hidden among [a sea of black faces] in a land of black people in Ancient Egypt?" There are numerous questions that must be asked about this. The first and the most important question we have to ask here is why was infant Jesus taken to hide in Ancient Egypt and nowhere else in the entire geographical region of Canaan?

Archbishop Stallings also introduced the traditional evidence of the coin head of the Roman Emperor Justinian the Great to confirm that the earliest Roman portrayal of Jesus depicted him as a black man. This historical coin has been one of the earliest evidence of the portrayal of Jesus. On one side of this coin was Jesus with "kinky hair" and black features and on the other, a vast contrast from the physical features of Jesus, was Justinian, a European, with a straight hair, nose, and white features. Archbishop Stallings cited what Cambridge Ancient Encyclopaedia wrote about this:

"Whatever the fact, this coin," with the straight-haired Justinian on the obverse side, "places beyond doubt the belief that Jesus Christ was a Negro" (cited from Emerge, 1995, p. 24).

Archbishop Stallings continued that despite this "the image that we have seen Him portrayed in over 1 billion reproductions of Warner Sallman's rendition of the head of Christ" does not look like a black man. All of these are evidence of the traditional legendary lying lore in Christianity? · These are the foundations of the lies that have been accepted as the ultimate truths in Christianity today.

In addition to all these, Church historians do not forget the time when the Catholic Church acknowledged the true ethnicity of Jesus and the people of the Bible as black people. The Catholic Church itself does not forget the three black North African Popes in the early history of the Church. These people were Pope Victor I 189-199 A. D., Melchiades or Miltiades 311-314 A. D., and Gelasius 492-496 A. D. all of who are still honored in the Catholic Church as saints today (see J. A. Rogers, *World's Great Men of Color*, Vol. II, p. 5). This is a part of the early history of Christianity that most Church historians do not talk about. However, some historians point out that these black North Africans were made Popes in acknowledgement of the black heritage of Jesus and therefore Christianity itself.

What do all these mean? They mean Christian Europe has long known that the true Jesus that Christians are supposed to worship was a black man. Why then would Christian Europe change the black images of Jesus Christ, his mother, and the people of the Bible to white images? The answer is simple. The black images of Jesus and the people of the Bible were simply changed to white images to satisfy the emerging racism and racial prejudice of Christian Europe and Europeans against black people.

I must point out here that before Protestatism; there was no racism. Christian Europe used the Bible to create racism and racial prejudice against black people and therefore had to change the black image of Jesus to white to satisfy racism. Christian Europe achieved the change of the black image of Jesus Christ to a white image through four main processes. First, Christian Europe accepted slave traders' justification of their consciences and description of the Africans they were dehumanizing as inferior, uncivilized, and sub-humans. Secondly, Christian Europe determined that based upon its perception of black people, white and black people could not have originated from the same human origin. Thirdly, Christian Europe decided to search for the separate origin of Europeans and found it in the biblical narrative of Noah and the Flood. In its interpretation of this narrative, Christian Europe pronounced black people as the ones cursed by Noah to be the slaves of white people because black people are the descendants of Ham. Through these processes, it was no more acceptable for Europeans to worship the true image of the black Jesus when black people are supposedly cursed in the Bible. Finally, Renaissance artists and painters helped to change the images of the people of the Bible from black to white.

What this means is that modern worshipping of the white images of Jesus Christ, his mother, and the people of the Bible is a perpetuation of the racist sentiments of Christian Europe and Europeans. That is something modern Christianity that professes to be moving away from racism against black people should think about seriously and change the image of Jesus Christ back to the black person he was. Perhaps more importantly, this is something black Christians should think about seriously. I am not suggesting that black people should not help Europeans to perpetuate racism and racial prejudice against the black race. All I am saying is that there has been a major lie in the worship of a white Jesus in Christianity, and black people should think about it seriously in the name of religious purity.

Perhaps, what all Christians should first ask themselves is where the white Jesus Christ they worship originated in Europe. If Jesus did not originate anywhere in Europe, they should then find out if the people of Ancient Egypt where the Jewish people claim to have gone to live before moving to Canaan and Europe were Europeans. The fact is Christian Europe's white Jesus is nothing but a lie.

What is intriguing about all these is that most western scholars have also long known that Jesus Christ and the people of the Bible were all black people, but they have also kept it quiet. Nevertheless, European's knowledge of Jesus, his mother, and the people of the Bible as black people must have been the most widely known secret in Europe. This is because as late as September 27, 1999, a group of young British artists brought an impressionist realism art exhibition called *Sensations* from England to the Brooklyn Museum in New York. The art was very realistic, but the medium was repugnant to many people, to say the least. What caused the greatest sensation in this exhibition was one particular art piece called *The Holy Virgin Mary*. In this piece, Mary the mother of Jesus was portrayed as a black woman through the medium of dark elephant dung with portrayals of various parts of the human anatomy including the genitalia around her. This caused a great uproar among Catholics in America and especially the Catholics of New York. However, a spokesperson for the Catholic League was not so much upset by the fact that Mary had been portrayed as a black woman as the Virgin was portrayed in the medium of elephant dung and surrounded with genitalia.

This art piece seriously hit the Catholic Church's nerve. The Church has been doing everything it can for almost two thousand years to cover up the fact that the Holy Mary, Jesus, and the people of the Bible were black people. It has almost succeeded in distorting and destroying the foundations of this truth in Ancient Egyptian history and modern generations have never known this truth and then came this art exhibition that perhaps sought to reveal this secret to modern generations. The art piece was immediately seen by some Church leaders as seeking to reveal a truth that has been painstakingly concealed for a long time. The confusion over this art exhibition acquired socio-political dimensions as the then Mayor of New York, Rudolf Guliani, cut off about 7 million dollars of city funding from the Brooklyn Museum for exhibiting such art. Observers pointed out that secretly, the Mayor, who is a Catholic, was defending the thousands-year-old secret of the Church and its propaganda and denial that the people of the Bible were black.

Unfortunate for Christian Europe, the Jews were originally black people and that follows that Mary, the mother of Jesus was a black woman. Why should the Church fight it now through an innocent art exhibition? This is because the Church has long assumed that modern generations do not know this secret, so it had to continue to defend the centuries-old lies of the racial and ethnic origin of the people of the Bible. I believe this is the reason a work like this is needed to remind people of what was the truth because we have not come that far to forget how it was before. At least, not in Africa.

All of these revelations validate my discovery of the specific black African tribes from which the Jewish people originated. There should be no more generic talk about the black heritage or the African origin of the Jewish people because we can now place them in their tribes of origin in Africa

African tribal affinity of Jesus and John the Baptist

There is a lot of ethnic, linguistic, and cultural evidence of the black heritage of the Jewish people in the Bible and also in the history of the Jewish people that Europeans have never known. I do believe that modern Jewish people do not know the evidence of their African heritage in the Bible either, and they would never know unless Africans point these out to them. For example, here is a piece of linguistic and cultural evidence and revelation of the African tribal kinship of Jesus and John the Baptist.

Jewish history states that John the Baptist and Jesus had affinity to the *Essene* religious and political group of the Jews. This group was one of the four religious and political groups that emerged after 37 B. C. when the Romans defeated Antigonus, the last of the Hasmonean kings. The Romans left much of the decisions of ruling the Jewish people to local Jewish institutions that served in the Great Assembly and the Sanhedrin. The other three religious and political groups that emerged alongside the *Essenes* were the Pharisees, Sadducees, and Zealots. In the *Encyclopaedia Britannica*, scholars of Jewish history confirm the affinity of Jesus and John the Baptist to the *Essene* group by simply stating that:

It seems likely that both John the Baptist and Jesus had affinities with the Essenes (Britannica, 1996, P. 74).

The *Essenes* were a religious and political group of the Jewish people, but these people derived the name of this group from an African tribal identity, specifically they derived this name from the name of an *Akan* tribe. The *Akan* tribe from which the Jewish *Essenes* derived the name of their religious and political group was *Assin.* The *Assin* tribe is a tribe of black people, and the *Akan* tribal group of which the *Assin* people are members are also black, thus confirming the black racial and ethnic heritage of the ancient Jewish people before they went to become Jews and Hebrews in Europe. The *Assin* people can now be located in south central Ghana in West Africa. The following discussions would make it all very clear and later, I will reveal the so-called lost tribes of the Jewish people and show that the *Assin* tribe is one of them.

The conclusion here is if one of the lost tribes of the Jewish people is black then it follows that the rest would also be black and that should further confirm the African ethnic heritage of the Jewish people who claim to have originated from these lost tribes. The revelation of the kinship of Jesus and John the Baptist to a Jewish political group that carried an African tribal name not only adds to the evidence of the black racial and ethnic heritage of the Jewish people, but it also confirms what this discussion set out to do, and that is to go deeper into the African tribes that were the Ancient Egyptians to reveal the specific tribal groups from which the Jewish people originated.

African tribal composition of modern Jewish people

I have mentioned earlier that the Jewish people did not originate from one African tribe. People from several African tribes came together to become the Jewish people. This is one of the reasons the Jewish people have refused to reveal who they are because beyond the fact that they were originally black people, they do not have a single tribal identity. I found this out in the transposed African tribal names they have carried throughout their history and continue to carry even today. All of these should not surprise historians, the Jewish people, or Christians because the Bible tells us plainly in Exodus 12:37-38 that the people that went in the biblical Exodus were about six hundred thousand men on foot beside women and children. No biblical scholar or anyone who reasons beyond the Bible stories believes that these 600,000 men in the Exodus were the seventy men that supposedly went to Ancient Egypt, or even that these 600,000 men descended from the original seventy men in the family of Jacob that supposedly went to Ancient Egypt. Even if we accept that the seventy men from the family of Jacob went to Ancient Egypt from somewhere else, they could not have been the 600,000 men that left there in the Exodus. In addition to that, the Bible states that there was a "mixed multitude," a large number of people that did not belong to the House of Israel also in the Exodus. Who were these people and where are they now?

What does this analysis mean? It means the Bible itself reveals that the people that left Ancient Egypt into the Exodus to become the Jewish people did not originate from the family of Jacob, and neither did they originate from one tribe in Ancient Egypt. According to the Bible, these people may have come to Ancient Egypt as one family but they left as several tribes that could form a nation. How could that happen? This also reveals that the people that left Ancient Egypt into the biblical Exodus were Ancient Egyptians, thus they were black, and no other racial group or skin color. Jacob and his family of seventy men must have come to Ancient Egypt, but the people that left into the Exodus were more than one family, they were people from several different African tribes. This places the origin of the people that left in the biblical Exodus in Ancient Egypt. This idea is important because much of the exploration in this book is based upon this premise. At this point, I will reveal that the majority and dominant tribe that left Ancient Egypt into the biblical Exodus was from the *Akan* tribe. From the African tribal names they still carry, it evident that not all modern Jewish people originated from the *Akan* tribe. As a result, the mixed multitude that did not belong to the House of Israel was a multitude that was not from the *Akan* tribe. The biblical House of Israel was therefore the domain of the *Akan* people in the Exodus, and coming revelations of linguistic evidence will confirm this. What is fascinating about all these is that one of the biblical multitudes that did not belong to the *Akan* tribe has been found, as recently as 1999, to the Lemba tribe of Southeast Africa.

The revelation here is that the people that left Ancient Egypt in the biblical Exodus were mostly *Akan* people that were joined by groups of people from other African tribes. The names the Jewish people still carry confirm this. These people were all black. Moreover, as I will reveal later, the word *Israel* was derived from the *Akan* language, that was the language *Akan* people spoke in Ancient Egypt, and it was the language the people of the Exodus took to Canaan. In the Bible therefore, the House of Israel referred to the *Akan* people of Ancient Egypt, and the mixed multitude referred to people from the other black tribes of Ancient Egypt. We can still identify these tribes from the names modern Jewish people carry. This was the reason the *Akan* language became the language of the people that left Ancient Egypt into the Exodus. It was the reason, the people that left into the Exodus took an *Akan* name and identity, and it was also the reason these people gave *Akan* names to the places they went to live. Above all, this was also the reason modern Jewish people still carry *Akan* and other African tribal names.

Readers should look forward to further discussions of the reasons above because they are presented here as hints of what is yet to come. For those who know, these are not mere assertions. They are facts and nobody knows these facts better than the *Akan* people, modern descendants of the ancient black people that created the concepts and documents that the Jewish people passed on to the Greeks as their creations.

From this point of view, I consider this work a continuation and exculpation of the works of the Europeans who first sought to reveal the black ethnic heritage of Jesus, his mother, and the people of the Bible. In continuation and vindication of these earlier scholars, I will introduce evidence that has never been known in western scholarship or anywhere else, except in Africa. The evidence in this work will fulfill earlier European works by revealing Africa's evidence of the origin of Christianity. To this extent, this work will go deeper into the Bible to reveal the

African origin of the stories and names of the personalities around whom the biblical narrative and Christianity developed.

Evidence from both Europe and Africa should not only confirm the African origin of Christianity, but it should also put to rest European denials of the ethnic origin of Jesus, his mother, and the people of the Bible. I am aware that such a revelation is not something modern Europeans who have been raised in Europe's negative socio-political and anthropological sentiments toward Africa would want the world to know. Therefore, no matter how much evidence I produce from Africa, there would be some Europeans who would try to distort or deny it not because it is not true but because it makes them uncomfortable, and I am looking forward to discussing these ideas with such people.

European hatred of blacks and Jews and their common heritage

Beyond the open revelation and confirmation of the African origin of Christianity in pictures, paintings, sculptural depictions, figurines, and books in Europe, there is also evidence that European hatred of the Jew is because of his black heritage. However, Europeans dared not openly admit that they were persecuting and massacring the Jewish people because they come from a black heritage. Such an open admission would inadvertently be revealing the very secret Christian Europe has been seeking to conceal about black people and Africa's connection to the creation of religion, the documents of the Bible, and Christianity.

Christian Europe persecuted the Jewish people under the guise of competing religions between Christianity and Judaism. On the surface, that might be acceptable as a possible valid reason. However, what justification did European political leaders have for massacring blacks and Jews in the 1940s? The black heritage of the Jewish people was the real reason that made it possible for European political leaders who could not use the excuse of competing religions, to join in the persecution and massacre of black and Jewish people. However, revealing the true reason for this political persecution and massacre would again bring Africans into the center of the origin of Christianity, and that was the last thing Christianity and even the political leaders of Europe would want to reveal to the world.

It was within this atmosphere of European and Christianity's hatred for people from black heritage that European slave trade brought black Africans into Europe. This made it easy for Europeans to hate the blackness and African origin of their slaves. This has been the most dominant reason behind Europeans singling out Jews and black Africans [same people] as the people of their hatred. It all began from the introduction of the religious concepts and sacramental practices Africans had invented to Europeans.

Today, generations of Europeans have been raised to dislike and even hate blacks and Jews without knowing why because those who first knew the real reason never wanted the rest of the people to know. One of the ways in which those who first knew did not want others to know was the quiet removal of the original black images of Christendom from European public view and replacing them with white images.

Another traditional foundation of European hatred of blacks and Jews is also in the fact that Christianity has secretly accused the Jewish people of knowingly introducing Europeans to the African religious concepts and doctrines that became Europe's Christian religion. One major result of this introduction was that Europeans used these African theosophical concepts in the design of the foundations of their societies. This socio-political design became the Judeo-Christian foundations of European societal development. This means Europe's Judeo-Christian tradition is nothing more than African religious foundations of society building. It must be remembered that African religious foundations of society building was the bedrock of the development of the Ancient Egyptian civilization.

Because of the negative anthropological ideas of early European scholars against Africans, the knowledge that the Judeo-Christian foundations of Europe actually originated from African theosophy and philosophy has been a major source of socio-political embarrassment for

Europeans. This embarrassment is even worse because long before Europeans knew the origins of the religious ideas they had adopted, they condemned the African religious ideas and sacramental practices from which Christianity emerged as pagan. In other words, in the warped minds of extremists in Europe, the Jewish people had deliberately deceived Europeans so that the Jews would dominate Europe.

It was from this European background and belief in a conspiratorial deception of Europeans by the Jews that Hitler and his henchmen sought to be the heroes who would punish blacks and Jews by seeking to annihilate them. This is also the reason no credible reason has been given for the most atrocious massacre of blacks and Jews in human history, except that Hitler was demented. Even Hitler could not reveal the real reason for massacring millions of blacks and Jews. However, he left a hint that revealed that his hatred of these people was based more upon their ethnic heritage than any other reason. In Adolf Hitler's own book, *Mein Kampf*, he couched his true reasons for massacring blacks and Jews by stating that he hated the racial mixing of the Jew [the black African] and the [white] Aryan this way:

> The *black-haired* Jewish youth lies in wait for hours on end, satanically glaring at and spying on the unsuspicious girl whom he plans to seduce, *adulterating her blood* and removing her from the bosom of her own people. The Jew uses every means to undermine the racial foundations of a subjugated people. ... The Jews were responsible for *bringing Negroes* into the Rhineland, with the ultimate idea of *bastardizing the white race* which they hate and thus lowering its cultural and political level so the Jew might dominate (Mein Kampf, pp. 252-73, see translation by James Murphy, London, 1939; emphasis mine).

In Hitler's perception, the black hair of the Jew was his ethnic characteristic that was an indirect reference to the black origin of the Jew. The adulteration of the white girl's blood was in reference to the mixture of "pure: Aryan blood with "black" African blood. The bringing of the Negroes to Rhineland referred to the black slaves that the Jews brought to Germany, and the bastardizing of the white race was in reference to the feared mixing of the pure blood of Aryans with the impure and "black" blood of the African slaves and Jews. All of these can be best understood in the context of the comparative anthropological pronouncements that earlier, Renaissance, and later European scholars made against black people before and during the time of Hitler. All that Hitler said in this quotation was indirectly referring to the *Africanness* of the Jew and consequently the *Africanness* of the origins of Christianity since at least the Jewish people introduced the concepts and documents of Christianity to Europeans.

What is most intriguing about the Nazi massacre of blacks and Jews is that no one has dared to reveal that the Nazis also massacred black Africans alongside the massacre of the Jewish people. Have you ever heard that Hitler and his men also massacred black people? That part of the story is never told, and it is deliberately concealed because again it would link Africans to Jews and therefore Africans to Christianity. However, if Hitler accused and massacred millions of Jews because they brought Africans to Rhineland, what do you think he would do to the Africans these Jews brought to Rhineland? Why has the world never heard about the massacre of Africans in the holocaust? Again, this is because revealing that the Nazis massacred black people alongside Jews would leave a long trail of questions that could lead to the revelation of European hatred of the Jewish people for introducing the African theosophical concepts that became the Christian religion in Europe. The real dilemma of Europeans is that they have gone so irreversibly far with these African religious ideas and practices that they do not know what to do now but keep it going.

Another evidence that confirms that Europeans have long known about the African origin of the Jewish people, and that European interaction with Jews has always had the African origin of Jewish people undertone occurred after the Nazi massacre of blacks and Jews at the end of the 2nd World War. While most European leaders of the time openly condemned Hitler's approach to getting rid of Jews in Europe, these leaders also secretly sought other ways of getting rid of Jews in Europe. Even before the blood of the atrocious Nazi massacre of Jews could dry, European leaders were secretly planning how to get rid of the Jews in Europe without inviting world condemnation.

Fortunately these European leaders did not have to look far. They discovered the writings of Theodor Herzl, a Hungarian-born Jewish journalist in Austria. In 1896, Theodor Herzl wrote a book entitled *The Jewish State*. In this book, he argued for the establishment of a separate Jewish State outside Europe as the solution to "the Jewish question" and "remedy for European anti-Semitism." In Theodore Herzl's work, European leaders noticed that the Jewish people wanted their own State outside Europe. In this, European leaders found a way of getting rid of the Jewish people in Europe by helping to settle them elsewhere for them to create the State they wanted (see *Birth of Zionism* in *Britannica*, 1996, p. 82).

In 1947, these European leaders led by the British decided to help the Jewish people set up the State they had always wanted. These leaders decided to send the Jews [back] to Africa. Specifically, these European leaders decided to settle the Jews in Uganda in East Africa. The question is why would these European leaders decide to settle the Jewish people who looked more like Europeans than Africans in Africa? It was because they knew of the African origin of Jewish people. In addition to that, Uganda was then a British colony, and the British government believed then that it had the power to do whatever it pleased with its colonies without consideration of the people that originally lived in these lands.

As it was expected then, the Jewish people refused to be settled in Uganda much less anywhere in Africa. Theodore Herzl's ideas and the popularity of his suggestion of a Jewish State had galvanized the Jewish people into what had become a political Zionist movement, a Zionist World Congress, and the mouthpiece of Jews everywhere. Zionist leaders championed Jewish people's refusal to be settled in Africa; instead they asked to be "resettled" in Palestine the place their ancestors went to settle after the Exodus. As a result, European leaders helped them set up the Jewish State in Palestine and on May 14, 1948, David Ben Gurion proclaimed the declaration of independence of the State of Israel in Palestine. That was how Britain led European nations in the creation of the State of Israel in Palestine. It must be pointed out again that initial European leaders' idea to help the Jews set up their own State in Africa had the African heritage of Jewish people in mind.

From the growth of knowledge over the centuries, the evidence of Africa's connection to the origin and concepts of Christianity was becoming more known to scholars. From the fear of European masses finding this out, Europeans designed a new propaganda to forestall and counteract the spread of this knowledge. Europe's defensive propaganda was to attack and denigrate Africa. Europeans knew that the link between Africans, Jews, the Bible, and Christianity was Ancient Egypt. As a result, Europeans took the offensive to cut off Africa from Ancient Egypt. For this Europeans condemned Africans as a primitive race of people that could never have been capable of the great thoughts and imaginations that created religion, the foundations of knowledge, and the greatest human civilization on earth in Ancient Egypt. From this analysis, it becomes clear that the foundations of European hatred of the African were not laid from the fact that Africans are black or because they were enslaved. The foundations of continued European hatred for blacks and Jews go deeper into religion than most people know today.

As history continued into the revival of learning in Europe, the foundations of European hatred of blacks and Jews were eventually covered up by Renaissance scholarship that sought "justifiable scholastic" explanations for European hatred of blacks and Jews outside competing religions. They introduced race, skin color, brain size, and many other frivolous reasons to justify European hatred for blacks and Jewish people. This is the reason despite all that we know today condemning all the reasons of racism and racial prejudice, they still continue. That is because they are still secretly upheld in the misperception, beliefs, and misinterpretations of the Bible. All of these, however, confirm that Europeans have long known of the African heritage of the Jewish people. The question now is beyond what I have revealed, what else does Africa know?

African origin of the Jewish people.

Africa knows the African origin of the Jewish people. Africa is a large continent of several hundreds of tribes if not thousands and it would not be fair to leave readers on such a large continent without telling them where this story can be specifically found or verified. As a result, though this book seeks to reveal what Africa knows about the origin and authors of the documents of the Bible, it seeks also to be specific so that whatever is revealed in the book can be easily verifiable. I have already revealed that the majority and dominant group of the people of the Exodus was *Akan* people. From this point of view, perhaps, a more specific and more appropriate question that would better answer the coming revelation in this discussion is what do the *Akan* people know of the *Akan* origin of the Jewish people?

This part of the discussion is the story of the people who have held and kept the secrets of the people and the stories behind Christianity for over two thousand years. It is the story of the people who have held and kept the secrets of the true ethnic origin of the Jewish people for over three thousand years. Basically, it is story of the people who were the Ancient Egyptians to whom the Jewish people supposedly went over three thousand years ago. The biblical narrative reveals that the people that later became the Jews and Hebrews in Europe became a group of tribes in Ancient Egypt. Ancient Egyptians were therefore eyewitnesses to the formative years of the people that later became the Jews and Hebrews in Europe. They were also eyewitnesses to the foundations of the biblical story, so we would contact modern descendants of these Ancient Egyptians in Africa to prove the thesis of this book. These people have a story and theirs is part of the story Africa has never told for thousands of years until now.

As I pointed out earlier, the fact that Africa has never told her story does not mean there has been paucity in the number of outsiders who want to tell Africa's story. In the past four hundred years, there has never been a shortage, especially of western scholars who seek to tell Africa's story. As a result, many people in the west have grown to believe only what these scholars have written and said about Africa. This is because people in the west do not know that there is an African version of the stories their scholars have told about Africa. What is worse, people in the west do not have any means of verifying whether what their scholars have written and said about Africa is true or not.

Even some Africans have grown to believe what western scholars have written about Africa because they also do not have any means of verifying what these scholars have written and said other than the few western books that brought them the lies in the first place. Worse than that, many people in Africa do not know the prejudicial sentiments, from which some western scholars have written about Africa, so they have believed anything and everything these people have written as the ultimate truth. Unfortunately, these scholars do not know Africa's story. That is the reason they have still not been able to decode and dissect a plain story as the biblical story, to find out the people who wrote it, who they were writing about, why they wrote it, and what they were writing about.

In western scholarship, the Jewish people have claimed that the biblical story is their ancestral story of religion written by Jewish people, but that is not true. The people that wrote the biblical documents were not Jewish unless being Jewish meant being African and specifically *Akan*. Firstly, from the transposed *Akan* and other African names that the people that left Ancient Egypt in the biblical Exodus have carried up to today, these people were not Jewish. Secondly, from the transposed names of the people that supposedly wrote the documents of the Books of the Old Testament, it is evident that these people were from *Akan* and other African tribes. For over two thousand years, Christians and Bible scholars who have never known the linguistic and cultural origin of these names have assumed that they were Hebrew, but they were not. They were

Akan and other African tribal names. After I have revealed these names, they can be verified from the *Akan* people in Ghana and in Cote d' Ivoire in West Africa.

Beyond the linguistic and cultural evidence I present in this book, here is a simple historical evidence that also confirms that the people that supposedly wrote the biblical documents were not Jewish. Biblical scholars agree that the Exodus occurred in the 13th century B. C. During this period, the people that left Ancient Egypt in the Exodus were not Jews or Hebrews. They became Jews and Hebrews in Europe in the 2nd century B. C, almost eleven hundred years after they had left Ancient Egypt into the Exodus. According to the claims of Jewish scholars, their priests and prophets wrote the biblical documents long before the 2nd century B. C., and that was long before their people went to Europe to become Jews and Hebrews. This piece of history shows that the biblical documents were written long before part of the people of the Exodus went to Europe to become Jews and Hebrews. The question then is who were these people before they went to Europe to become Jews and Hebrews? Africa's revelation is about who these people were before they got to Europe over a thousand years after parting from their tribes of origin in Ancient Egypt. This revelation will also confirm that the people that went to Europe to become the Jews and Hebrews originated from African tribes, the dominant tribe of which was the *Akan* tribe.

To be able to reveal the racial and ethnic identities of the Africans who wrote the Bible, I must first reveal who the Jewish people were before they became Jewish people to establish the foundation upon which to prove that Africans wrote the Bible. This becomes a revelation because apart from what is written in the Bible about them, the Jewish people have failed to tell who they are. They have failed to reveal where they came from, the original language they spoke in their native land, and where and how they found the religion for which they supposedly wrote the documents of the Bible before they supposedly went to Ancient Egypt.

If the Jewish people supposedly went to live in Ancient Egypt for four hundred and thirty years as the Bible tells us then the people that left Ancient Egypt in the biblical Exodus were no more Jewish people. They were Ancient Egyptians and therefore black people. If the Jewish people were portrayed in the earliest images of Christendom as black people in Europe then they were black people. I do not believe even in these earliest times when this was not a major issue in Europe, Europeans would confuse the difference between black and white people. If the people that left Ancient Egypt in the biblical Exodus identified themselves with an *Akan* name then they were black people and specifically *Akan* people. If these people gave the nation they went to set up an *Akan* name then they were truly black people and specifically *Akan* people. Finally, if these people still carry *Akan* and African tribal names then they were originally Africans and we can trace them to their ancestral and African tribal roots among the black tribes in Africa as I have done. Such an exercise is easy because these tribes were the Ancient Egyptians. I have shown above that the ancient Jewish group called the *Essenes* derived their name and identity from the *Assin* tribe, one of the *Akan* tribal groups from which they originated. I have also revealed that the majority of the people that left Ancient Egypt in the biblical Exodus were *Akan*. People from other African tribal groups also joined the *Akan* majority into the Exodus. The biblical Exodus was, therefore, simply a movement of *Akan* and other African tribes from Ancient Egypt to Canaan where there were some more black African tribes.

Ancient African tribal name of the Jewish people

To be able to confirm all these, we must go back to the ancient times in the formative years of the people that left Ancient Egypt into the so-called Exodus and later went to Europe to become the Jews and Hebrews. We must go back to the times when these people had a name and identity but they were not known as Jewish people. We must go back to the times when the people that left Ancient Egypt had a collective African tribal name reflecting their African racial, ethnic, and linguistic identity. The Jewish people must have long forgotten this name, and I do not think many modern Jewish people know this ancient African name that carried their racial and ethnic identity before they went to become the Jews and Hebrews in Europe.

From the *Akan* and African tribal names of modern Jewish people, I knew immediately that they were related to *Akan* and other African tribes. From the *Akan* name of their nation, and the *Akan* names of their Gods, I knew that the people that left Ancient Egypt in the biblical Exodus originally spoke the *Akan* language. From the transposed *Akan* and other African tribal names of the people whose names are in the Bible as the authors of books in the Bible, I was more than certain that the people that left Ancient Egypt in the biblical Exodus were mostly *Akan*. The question that was left for me to answer was who were these people before they went to Europe to become the Jews and Hebrews? How did they identify themselves before they became Jews and Hebrews? How did they come by the *Akan* and other African tribal names they have carried to Europe after thousands of years? Were they African tribes before they became Jews and Hebrews, and what African tribes were they?

I found the answer to these questions in the history of the Jewish people. From this history, there is no doubt that the Jewish people have gone through numerous linguistic, social, and cultural transformations. The most obvious of these transformations, however, was the transformation of their skin color from black to fair, or white. Before these transformations, the people that left Ancient Egypt in the biblical Exodus were black people that had an African name of identity. The ancient racial, ethnic, and collective African name and identity by which the people that left Ancient Egypt into the biblical Exodus identified themselves, before they went to become Jews and Hebrews in Europe, was the name *Afrim*. The *Akan* people that these people left behind in Ancient Egypt called these people of the Exodus the *Afrim* people; and the people of the Exodus also called themselves *Afrim* people.

Beyond all the evidence presented in this discussion so far, the linguistic evidence of how the people that left Ancient Egypt into the biblical Exodus identified themselves before they went to become Jews and Hebrews in Europe is the most powerful evidence. This is the most conclusive evidence of the African origin and heritage of Jesus, his mother, and the all the so-called people of the Bible. It is the most conclusive evidence supporting the Catholic Church's earliest portrayal of the Jesus and his mother as black people, and it is also the most conclusive evidence that would reveal the African tribe or tribes from which the Jewish people originated.

Historically, the Jewish people have refused to reveal who they were before they went to Europe. What the revelation of their ancient name of racial and ethnic identity here simply means is that before these people became Jews and Hebrews in Europe, they were Africans and they identified themselves and had the collective African tribal name *Afrim* to prove it. This is a very important revelation that exposes the original racial, ethnic, linguistic, and cultural heritage of the people that left Ancient Egypt into the so-called biblical Exodus. From the word, *Afrim*, we can find out the African language and tribe that spoke that language in Ancient Egypt and conclude without any reservation that these people were from this tribe.

Linguistically, we trace the word *Afrim* to the *Akan* people, language, and cultural group. In the discussion of the *NKWA [ANKH]* symbol of Ancient Egypt, I revealed that the word *NKWA* was from the *Akan* language. In the *Akan* language, getting out of something is expressed as "*Fri mu.*" For example, getting out of this place is expressed in *Akan* as "*Fri ha*, and breaking away from a group or seceding, as the people of the so-called did is also expressed as "*Fri mu.*" The word *Afrim* therefore originates from the *Akan* words "*Fri mu.*" It has been contracted to "*Frim*" and the prefix "A" in *Afrim* indicates that some people performed the "*Frim*" action and *Afrim* refers to these people. This linguistic analysis should give readers some idea about the possible meaning of the word *Afrim* to the people that left Ancient Egypt in the Exodus and why they would identify themselves as such.

A major aspect of this revelation is the fact that looking at it from the Bible's perspective, the *Akan* people were the Ancient Egyptians to whom the Jewish people supposedly went in their formative years. It was also from these *Akan* people that the Jewish people supposedly left in the biblical Exodus. The fact is the biblical story about these people coming from somewhere to Ancient Egypt is even false. Beyond that, most Egyptologists and historians know that the Ancient Egyptians were the Africans but few have had the inclination to express it with the vigor this honor deserves.

Since western curiosity about Ancient Egypt developed into the academic study called Egyptology, scholars around the world have acknowledged three people as the top scholars in this field. From America, scholars have acknowledged James Henry Breasted. From England, scholars have acknowledged Sir Alan Gardiner, and from France, they have acknowledged Gaston Maspero. From the little I have read from the works of these people, I am convinced that they knew more about African origin of the Ancient Egyptian civilization than modern Egyptologists have been willing to acknowledge; and they were right. As late as the 1960's, Sir Gardiner acknowledged that the Ancient Egyptians were Africans and therefore they spoke an African language. In *Egypt of the Pharaohs*, Sir Alan Gardiner wrote:

> Since it is generally agreed that the oldest population of Egypt was of African race, it might be expected that their language should be African too (1961, p. 19).

This is another evidence of the African identity of the Ancient Egyptians. It is evident that I am not the only scholar to assert that the Ancient Egyptians are modern black Africans. Many scholars in Europe knew this long before me. In this discussion, not only do I show that the Ancient Egyptians were Africans, but also I go deep into Africa to reveal the specific African tribal groups that were in Ancient Egypt to confirm my assertion. The *Akan* tribe was the most dominant African tribal group in Ancient Egypt. It was the most dominant tribal group in the so-called biblical Exodus, and the African tribal language that Sir Gardiner expected these Africans would speak was the *Akan* language. This was the language the people that left Ancient Egypt in the biblical Exodus knew, spoke, and took to Canaan. This was the language modern history of the Jewish people call Classical Hebrew and it is the language claim they claim to have lost. That was why they identified themselves collectively as the *Afrim* people. That was also the reason they carried mostly *Akan* names and named their God and nation in the *Akan* language.

From this perspective, even if the people that left Ancient Egypt into the so-called biblical Exodus came to Egypt from somewhere else; they were black people that came to their fellow black people in Ancient Egypt. What is revealing here is that these people would not have taken an *Akan* name of identity, after leaving the *Akan* people in Ancient Egypt, if they were not *Akan* people themselves. They would not have carried mostly *Akan* names up to today if they did not originate from the *Akan* tribe. They would not have named their nation and God in the *Akan* language if they were not *Akan* people.

The *Akan* word *Afrim* in this context refers to people that broke away or seceded from people of the same tribal and ethnic origin. The biblical narrative of the Exodus confirms that the people of the Exodus broke away from the people of Ancient Egypt. What this biblical narrative sought to make us believe, however, was that the people of the Exodus were racially and ethnically different from the Ancient Egyptians, but that was a lie. From the ancient *Akan* name of the people that left in the Exodus, the word *Afrim* confirms that the majority of the people that left Ancient Egypt in the Exodus was Ancient Egyptian. Specifically, this majority was from the *Akan* linguistic and cultural group. From the ancient collective and modern individual names of the *Afrim* people, and from the names they gave to their God and nation, we discover the *Akan* language as the ancient language the *Afrim* people that left Ancient Egypt in the Exodus spoke. This was the African tribal language they spoke and their ancestors spoke long before modern Hebrew language, and even longer before they went to Europe to become the Jews and Hebrews.

What is most conclusive about the *Akan* name of identity of the people that left Ancient Egypt into the so-called biblical Exodus is that Jewish historians have also known of this ancient collective and ethnic name of the *Afrim* people before they went to become Jews and Hebrews in

Europe. Unfortunately, these historians might not have known the true origin of the Jewish people. They might not have been trained in linguistics and certainly, they might not have known of the *Akan* language and people in Ancient Egypt. As a result, it is evident that they do not know the language from which the word *Afrim* originated and meaning of the ancient name of identity of the *Afrim* people.

As with all the *Akan* and African words and names in the Bible, the *Akan* word *Afrim* has today been transposed into European orthography, and modern Europeans, biblical scholars, and Jewish historians have assumed that the word *Afrim* was originally Hebrew, but it was not. This word is extremely important in this discussion because it is a word referring to origin and language and these can easily lead to identifying the race and ethnicity of any people that spoke this language anywhere in the world. Not only have modern European and Jewish scholars assumed that the word was Hebrew, but also they have erroneously accepted and conferred a fictitious "Hebrew" meaning onto it. This "Hebrew" meaning was conferred onto this word to fit it into the false biblical narrative of the origin of the Jewish people in Mesopotamia. In an article on Jewish history in the *Encyclopaedia Britannica*, Jewish historians wrote that:

> In contact with foreigners, they [the people of the Exodus] called themselves *Ivrim* ("people from beyond the river), from which came Latin **Hebraeus**, the Old French **Hebreu** or **Ebreu**, and the English **Hebrew** used as an alternative for Jew (1996, p. 71).

The word *Ivrim* in this part of Jewish history is clearly an orthographic corruption of the *Akan* word *Afrim*. There is something in this quotation that suggests that the scholars of Jewish history that wrote this piece in the Britannica must have known that the word was not originally Hebrew. As a result, they included their meaning of this word in parenthesis to suggest covertly that this word is Hebrew, and they even know its meaning. However, if that was the intent, it is false. This falsehood is confirmed today by the failure of historians and archaeologists to find any evidence of artifacts or people in the geographical area of the suggested biblical origin of the Jewish people. The word is clearly from the language of the *Akan* people that were the Ancient Egyptians and every scholar that doubts this should verify it from the *Akan* people in Ghana in West Africa.

In the *Akan* language from which the word *Afrim* originated, it does not mean "people from beyond the river." This meaning is false because of several reasons. The most important among these reasons is the fact that despite intense search to find evidence to collaborate the biblical assertion of the origin of the Jewish people, no shred of historical, archaeological, or even anthropological evidence has been found to support the Bible's assertion of where the *Afrim* people originated anywhere in the entire Middle East. This directly supports my revelation of the African origin of the *Afrim* people that went to Europe to become the Jews and Hebrews.

In fact, the latest genetic evidence conducted by Jewish scholars has linked the Jewish people to an African tribe and not to any other tribes anywhere in the world including Semitic tribes. Again, this confirms my revelation that the people that left Ancient Egypt in the so-called biblical Exodus were not Jews and they were not Hebrews. They were mostly *Akan* people that were joined by several other black African tribes. Europeans and perhaps even the Jewish people themselves may not know this but I have found out that modern Jewish people carry more *Akan* names than other African tribal names, and as I pointed out, the names of the God of these people were also *Akan*. These and other reasons confirm that the people that left Ancient Egypt into the so-called Exodus were mostly *Akan* people that identified themselves in the *Akan* language before they went to Europe to become the Jews and Hebrews.

In the *Akan* language, the word refers to people that broke away from their original group of people, or people that seceded. It is important to point out that before these people supposedly went to Ancient Egypt and left there, the Jewish people never identified themselves anywhere in their real or biblical history as the *Afrim* or *Ivrim* people. The biblical narrative never identified

Abraham as an *Afrim* because he was not. The narrative never identified Isaac, Esau, or Jacob as *Afrim* people because they were not. This narrative never identified Joseph as an *Afrim* and it certainly never identified the supposed family of Jacob that went to Ancient Egypt at the request of Joseph as *Afrim* people either. It was only after these people had left Ancient Egypt in the so-called biblical Exodus that they began to identify themselves as the *Afrim* people. This is because the *Akan* word *Afrim* was the most perfect word that fitted and best described the historical circumstances of their leaving Ancient Egypt. They broke away from their tribes of origin. They were therefore in the *Akan* language *Afrim* people. This word was also the word that carried evidence of the racial, ethnic heritage, identity and closeness of the people of the Exodus to the Ancient Egyptians they left behind. Coming revelations of *Akan* names of people and places in the Bible and real history of the Jewish people will confirm all these.

Notice that the original *Akan* word is *Afrim*, and the orthographic corruption of this word that has falsely been believed to be Hebrew became *Ivrim*. Notice the phonological similarities even in this linguistic corruption. Not only does this discussion confirm that ancient Jewish people were black people, but also I have revealed the ancient racial, ethnic, linguistic and cultural name by which the people that left Ancient Egypt in the Exodus identified themselves before foreigners. They identified themselves collectively as *Akan* people with the *Akan* word, *Afrim*.

I must also point out that the people that left Ancient Egypt in the Exodus did not only identify themselves as the *Afrim* people, but also the name they gave to the nation they built in Canaan was also their *Akan* racial and ethnic identity, *Afrim*. The history of the Jewish people confirms that the first name of modern Israel was *Ephraim*. It is linguistically evident that this name was from the original *Akan* word *Afrim* that had been orthographically transposed to *Ivrim*, and it was this same *Akan* word that was further orthographically transposed to *Ephraim*. The direction of this linguistic corruption therefore began from the *Akan* word *Afrim* to *Ivrim,* and then to *Ephraim*. Phonologically, it is also evident that these words have a common root of origin.

The name *Ephraim* and its reference to the nation of the people that left Ancient Egypt in the Exodus is revealed in a story in Judges where it is written:

> Jephthah gathered together all the men of Gilead, and fought with Ephraim: and the men of Gilead smote Ephraim, because they said: Ye Gileadites are fugitives of Ephraim among the Ephraimites, and among the Manassites. And the Gileadites took the passages of Jordan before the Ephraimites: and it was so, that when those Ephraimites which were escaped said, Let me go over; that the men of Gilead said unto him, Art thou an Ephraimite? If he said, Nay then said they unto him, Say now Shiboleth: and he said Siboleth: for he could not frame to pronounce it right. Then they took him, and slew him at the passages of Jordan: and there fell at that time of the Ephraimites forty and two thousand (12:4-6).

This biblical narrative is very interesting because it reveals and conforms something about the black tribal identity of the *Afrim* people that Europeans, Christians, Bible scholars, historians, and even the Jewish people have never known. The biblical passage above reveals the identity of another black African tribe that lived and interacted with the *Afrim* people in this story. The narrative states that Gileadites that had rebelled against Jephthah escaped and sought refuge at *Ephraim* among the Manassites. Jephthah chased these people to *Ephraim* and defeated the *Ephraim* people in a war. After defeating the *Ephraim* people, the Gileadites began to differentiate and identify the rebels and refugees from the *Ephraim* people. In this exercise, the Gileadites asked men they encountered near the battlefield to pronounce the word *Shiboleth*. In this linguistic test, people that could not pronounce this word right were identified to be the Ephraimites that supported the Gileadite refugees against Jephthah and the Gileadites killed them.

What makes this biblical narrative even more revealing and interesting is the fact that it reveals that the Gileadites and the Ephraimites were of the same ethnic and racial heritage, but they were not of the same linguistic heritage. This means there were no physical distinguishing features between Gileadites and the Ephraimites. However, there was a linguistic difference. This linguistic difference was what the Gileadites used to distinguish the Ephraimites from the Gileadites in the narrative.

What Europeans, Christians, and Bible scholars have never known is that the biblical word *Shiboleth* was a corruption of an African word. The word *Shiboleth* is a linguistic corruption of words in the *Ga* language. The people and the language can be found today in southern Ghana in West Africa. This is the language of the people in Accra, the capital of Ghana. The *Ga* sentence that was corrupted into the biblical word *Shiboleth* was *"Ashi gbe le,"* meaning *Ashi killed him.* The Ga sentence *Ashi gbe le* was what was corrupted to *Shi gbe le* and then to the biblical *Shiboleth*. *Ashi* is a *Ga* male name, and the context in which this name and words were used as military passwords was semantically perfect.

The failure of the *Ephraimites* to pronounce these words correctly was due to the fact that the *Afrimites* spoke the *Akan* language. This language does not have the "sh" consonant combination as it is in the *Ga* language. This revelation shows that the people that were the biblical Gileadites spoke the *Ga* language, and therefore they were the *Ga* people. The *Ga* people are black and this also confirms that the *Afrimites* were also black people and this was the reason the Gileadites could not differentiate between the Ephraimites and the Gileadites except through differences in their languages.

Today, the *Ga* and *Akan* people live together in Ghana. There are no physical distinguishing features between them. The only difference that can be used even today to differentiate a Ga and an *Akan* in most cases is speech. From this analysis, it is prudent to assume that it was the tribal name *Ga* that was transposed to Gileadites to conceal its true linguistic identity. Both names begin with a "G" and when "I" is pronounced long, it produces the sound of a short "A." The history of Ancient Egypt also has numerous *Ga Adangme* names confirming that the *Ga* people were in that geographical region and also in Ancient Egypt. Beyond that, *Ga* names have been found among the modern names Jewish people carry. The most popular of the *Ga Adangme* names of modern Jewish people is the name of the former Prime Minister of Israel called *Netanyahu*. This name was derived from the two *Ga Adangme* names Netey and *Nyaho* – *Neteynyaho.*

By identifying themselves in ancient times as the *Afrim* people, it is clear that modern Jewish people were originally *Akan*. This is because the collective name of a group of people is an ethnic, linguistic, and cultural identity. The ancient *Akan* name of the people that left Ancient Egypt in the Exodus was therefore their ethnic, linguistic, and cultural identity before they became Jews and Hebrews in Europe.

I have already revealed that the *Akan* people were the nucleus of the African tribes that created and developed the Ancient Egyptian civilization. The *Akan* and other African tribes were therefore the Ancient Egyptians. The biblical story from *Genesis* to *Exodus* tells that Abraham and his family and Jacob and his family went to Ancient Egypt. As further discussions will show, these people were *Akan*. I will reveal the specific *Akan* tribe from which Abraham and his descendants originated in the discussion of the *Akan* people. The name of Joseph that is a European corruption of the *Akan* name *Osafo* also confirms that the Jewish patriarchs were originally *Akan* people. If the family of these *Akan* people went to Ancient Egypt then they went to fellow *Akan* people, and they left as *Akan* people in the *Exodus*. This was the reason the people that left Egypt in the Exodus identified themselves and their ethnicity and language in the *Akan* word the *Afrim*.

The word *Ivrim* is not even a cognate of the *Akan* word *Afrim*. It is the exact *Akan* word that has been simply Europeanized as western scholars have done to many more words in the biblical story. The only difference in the Jewish word *Ivrim* and the *Akan* word *Afrim* is that the "A" at the beginning of the original *Akan* word has been changed to "I" and then pronounced long to sound just like the original sound "Ah" in the *Akan* phonology.

31

From the revelation of the *Akan* and other African tribal origin of the Ancient Egyptians and the revelation of the ancient *Akan* name of ethnic identity of the Jewish people, three main conclusions can be drawn.

1. The first of these conclusions is that the Ancient Egyptians were originally *Akan* people that were joined by other African tribes in the course of the history of Ancient Egypt. This is confirmed by the fact that the earliest and most of the subsequent names of kings of Ancient Egypt are transposed *Akan* names. Not only that but also in religion, the most prominent names of the greatest deities of Ancient Egypt were Osiris and *Isis*. These names were Greek corruption and derivations from the names of the earliest *Akan* deities *Osoro* and *Asaase*. These two words are still *Akan* words with the same references to Heaven and Earth, the places where the ancient *Akan* people in Egypt believed these two deities resided respectively. It was from this ancient *Akan* designation of the abode of God that the world has come to believe that God resides in the sky or as Christians call it, heaven. In addition to all these, the rest of the names of Ancient Egyptian kings can also be traced to specific African tribes that still carry these names. I have shown earlier from the word *Serekh* that the *Hausa* people in Nigeria were also in Ancient Egypt. All of these people are black therefore the Jewish people who are supposedly the people of the Bible, could not have been white since they originated from these black people.

2. The second conclusion that must be drawn from these revelations is that though other African tribes that were also in Ancient Egypt joined in the biblical Exodus, the majority of the people that left in the Exodus were *Akan*. Most of the evidence of this has been revealed above but more evidence can also be found in the *Akan* and other African tribal names that modern Jewish people still carry. Not only have the *Akan* people and other African tribes that were in Ancient Egypt retained their ethnic and tribal names in Africa to this day, but also most Jewish people have retained their ethnic *Akan* and other African tribal names. From most of modern Jewish people's names, it is easy for people of *Akan* and other African tribal origin to identify the specific *African* tribes from which the ancient ancestors of these people originated.

Though most of these names have been transposed into foreign orthographies and phonologies, they are still discernible by Africans who know and are familiar with them. I would like to reiterate that the people that left Ancient Egypt in the biblical Exodus were mostly *Akan* people that were joined by other African tribal groups with no other racial group of people from anywhere amongst them. Again, this was the ethnic and cultural reason these people identified themselves and their ethnicity in the *Akan* language as the *Afrim*.

Scholars that wrote the Jewish history in the *Encyclopaedia Britannica* even showed that they did not believe the biblical story of the origin of the Jewish people. However, these scholars did not come out boldly stating that they know the biblical story of the origin of the Jewish people is false. Telling a truth that is different from what the Bible has said in a matter like this is almost like calling the biblical documents a lie. As a result, most western scholars who discover things that are different from what the Bible has said tend to tone down their presentation of the truth in order not to offend the Church.

In the *Britannica*, the scholars of Jewish history suggested that the biblical story of the origin of the Jewish people was a mere literary myth when they wrote:

> *Legendlike accounts* in the biblical book of Genesis *are the only direct source* for the origins of the Hebrews and the lives of their first ancestors, the *so-called Patriarchs* Abraham, Isaac, and Jacob (1996, p. 72, emphasis mine).

The Alexandrian Jewish scholars that compiled and translated the biblical story for the Greeks used the patriarchal story as the point of departure and separation of the group that went to Europe to become the Jews from their ancestral tribes and original black heritage. How they did this is revealed in the number of patriarchs they acknowledged as their ancestors. According to the Bible, the patriarchs began with Abraham, and then his son Isaac. Isaac had twin sons. The elder was known as Esau and the younger was Jacob. However, Esau is not mentioned as one of the patriarchs of the Jewish people. Why is Esau the elder son of Isaac not part of the biblical patriarchs of origin of modern Jewish people? The answer is because the inclusion of Esau would give away the *Akan* and African ethnic origin of the Jewish people as they sought to present it in the biblical chronology. More about this will be further revealed in the discussion of the biblical origin of the *Akan* people.

3. Meanwhile, the third conclusion from the revelations so far is the fact that the earliest language the people that left Ancient Egypt in the Exodus spoke was *Akan*. This is not just an extrapolation from logic, though logical extrapolation yields the same conclusion. Modern Jewish people claim that they have lost the original language they spoke from where they originated. Can this be true and if it is true what about the people they left behind, have they also lost that language? Who are the people they left behind in their place of origin?

Language experts acknowledge that language changes over time, but it does not just die or get lost when the people that speak it are alive. As a result, many scholars question how the language of a scholarly prolific group of people as the Jewish people could have been lost without a trace. For me therefore, losing the *Akan* language they spoke in ancient times was part of the strategy of the Jewish people to throw Europeans off their original racial and ethnic origin. What is interesting about this is that modern Jewish people do not know that their language is made up of evident transpositions of African tribal languages. For example when the Jewish people say: *Yeshua Ashi mi,* meaning *I am the Lord*, they are speaking Ga, the language of the biblical Gileadites I revealed above. The Ga people say *Yehua dzi mi* also meaning *I am the Lord*.

Jewish historians call their lost ancient language classical Hebrew, but it was not Hebrew. It was the *Akan* language. The evidence for this is not difficult to find by people that are familiar with the *Akan* language. The names of the biblical patriarchs are *Akan* names. The collective name and the ancient identity of the people that left in the biblical Exodus and later became the Jews in Europe was *Akan*. Both the ancient and modern names of Israel were both derived from the *Akan* language. In addition to that, there are numerous *Akan* names of important people, places, and deities in the biblical and real history of the Jewish people to confirm that the people that became the Jewish people in Europe originally spoke and made the so-called biblical history in the *Akan* language. Beyond it all, the names of the authors of the Bible are also *Akan*.

These are the major revelations for which this book is required to provide evidence and that is what readers should expect. The historians of *Britannica* also wrote, as it has been written in every history of the Jewish people, that:

> ... according to biblical tradition, the original home of the Hebrews was Mesopotamia, and Aramaic was their ancestral tongue (1996, p. 72).

These two assertions in Jewish history are both false. The people that left Ancient Egypt into the Exodus did not originate from Mesopotamia and they did not speak the ancient language Aramaic. They spoke the *Akan* language in their ancient formative years. What is most revealing about all these is that whereas I have revealed the tribes and languages from which the Jewish people originated, extensive scholarship in the search for their origin outside Ancient Egypt has not found any people or languages from which they must have originated in Mesopotamia and its surrounding region.

There is also something in the transformation of the names of the Jewish people from *Ivrim* to Jew and Hebrew that must be pointed out. Linguists have not supported the assertion that the names Jew and Hebrew originated from the word *Ivrim*. Scholars of language and linguistics that I consulted stated emphatically that the words Hebrew and Jew could not have been derived from the word *Ivrim*. This is because the words *Ivrim*, *Jew*, and *Hebrew* do not have any common linguistic, orthographic, or phonological foundations from which such derivations could be made even in linguistic corruption as would have been expected from European language speakers. These scholars confirm however, that the words *Ivrim* and *Afrim* have a common basic linguistic, orthographic, phonological and even a semantic foundation relating to origin suggesting that they must have originated from the same language.

What is of concern in this book is the fact that the original word *Afrim*, from which the ancestors of modern Jewish people got their ancient racial and ethnic identity, is an *Akan* word. This confirms the original African and specifically *Akan* heritage of the Jewish people, and it also gives us the first ethnic, linguistic, cultural, and historical clue to the true ethnicity and ancient language of the black people that later went to Europe to become the Jews and Hebrews.

Biblical patriarchs were not Jews or Hebrews

There is a major implication from the revelation of the *Akan* ethnicity and origin of the Jewish people that casts a totally different light on the patriarchal story and supposed origin of these people. Historically, the *Afrim* people did not become Jews or Hebrews until after the documents of the Bible were compiled, edited, and translated for the Greeks. That was when they followed the Bible to Europe where they got their names Jews and Hebrews. The earliest movement of the Jewish people to Europe began around the 2nd century B. C. when Jewish settlements began to emerge in Greece and Rome, and then Spain, France, and the Roman colonies of Western Europe. What this analysis means is that the biblical patriarchs from whom the Jewish people claim their "racial" and ethnic descent were not Jews or Hebrews because the people that left Ancient Egypt into the biblical Exodus did not become Jews and Hebrews till over one thousand years after these patriarchs.

In *Genesis* 14:13, Abraham is referred to as a Hebrew; and in 41:12, Joseph is also referred to as a Hebrew, but that is all false. Abraham was not a Hebrew or Jew and his son Isaac was not a Hebrew or Jew. The sons of Isaac, Esau, and Jacob were not Jews or Hebrews either, and so was Joseph the son of Jacob. These people were not even *Afrim* people because the *Afrim* people that later became Hebrews and Jews in Europe emerged after the Exodus, and that was over a thousand years after Abraham.

Ethnically and racially, the biblical patriarchs from whom Jewish people claim their descent were not Jews or Hebrews in the historical times they lived. The biblical reference to Abraham and Joseph as Hebrews in the Genesis story was therefore a late attempt to confer what a few group of *Afrim* people had gone to Europe to become on their ancestors and their so-called ancestral story. The biblical patriarch were at best Ancient Egyptians, thus *Akan*, and at worse *Afrim* also *Akan*. These patriarchs did not originate from Mesopotamia and they did not speak Aramaic. They had an original ethnic and tribal identity, and this book will reveal them.

An ethnic name is an identity and a heritage and what has puzzled some African scholars who know is why the *Afrim* people allowed Europeans to give them different ethnic names when they already had their ancient ethnic name and identity? Why would a whole people consent for their racial and ethnic identity and heritage to be changed by another group of people? How can an ethnic name be conferred on a people when it is acquired through natural relationships? Did the Jewish people accept these names because it helped to conceal their black heritage? Or was it their quiet accommodation to find a place to settle among Europeans?

The revelations I have presented in this discussion so far are profound. This is because they bring to light what has never been known to the world for over three thousand years. So far, I have revealed that the *Akan* people were the designers and developers of the Ancient Egyptian civilization and this is confirmed by the fact that the names of the earliest kings from the earliest dynasties of Ancient Egypt were transposed *Akan* names. The revelation of the ancient language from which ancient Jewish people derived their identity also reveals the original African tribal and ethnic origin of the Jewish people.

34

The story of the revelation of the Africans who wrote the Bible is therefore the story of ancient and modern *Akan* people and ancient and modern Jewish people. This is because modern *Akan* people are the descendants of the ancient *Akan* people of Ancient Egypt, and modern Jewish people are the descendants of the ancient *Afrim* people that left Ancient Egypt to Canaan and then to Europe. This work is therefore a living revelation of evidence from the ancient and modern descendants of these two groups of people.

As the reader must have already found out, this book is not concerned with generically proving that the ancient *Afrim* people were originally black people with an ethnic origin and heritage in the black tribes of Africa. From the above revelations, it is clear that the knowledge in this book goes far beyond the traditional generic linkage of ancient Jewish people to Africans. This work goes deeper into Africa to link modern Jewish people to the specific African tribes of their origin. That is what makes this work different.

The reason I had to do this to stand out from the rest is because several scholarly works in the west have already established the general African origin of the Jewish people. As a result, such a work by an African from an African background should be more informing than what has already been written in the west. One of the latest among the scholarly works that have established a generic link between Africans and Jewish people is called *The Moses Mystery: The African Origins of the Jewish People* by Gary Greenberg (1996). The title of this book says it all.

Beyond scholarly works of this nature, there is numerous biblical evidence of the African tribal origin of the *Afrim* people. However, Europeans have never known these because they do not have the necessary linguistic and cultural backgrounds to know and understand what is plainly stated in the Bible. For example, no Christian or biblical scholar in the west ever knew that the biblical word *Shiboleth* was a Ga word thus revealing that the Ga people who are now in Africa also lived and interacted with the ancient *Afrim* people that later went to Europe to become the Jews and Hebrews. This also confirms that the people of the Bible were black African tribes and black African tribes only.

What I have discussed and revealed so far is the basis of the coming revelations in this book. I did not set out to write a popular book. This is because I know that the secrets I have revealed here are secrets the early apostolic fathers, biblical scholars, and Churches in Christendom have sought to keep a secret forever. I know that Christian Europe would not want it to be revealed that for over two thousand years Europeans have been worshipping a God that was imagined, created, personified, and worshipped by black people for thousands of years before Europeans were introduced to this God.

I did not set out to write a popular book because I also know that Christian Europe would not want to know that the person they have called Jesus and worshipped for thousands of years, was a black man called *Ayesu*. This indigenous African tribal name that was corrupted to Jesus is still a common name among his people, the *Akan* people and other African tribal groups. I also know that Christian Europe would not want the world to know that Africans wrote the book that has become the greatest historical, poetic, philosophical, and holiest religious book in Europe and the world. The Bible spurned the foundation of modern Europe and it influenced and shaped the perception of the world of the earliest European thinkers. I do not think many Europeans would want such a credit to go to Africans because that would not fit into the centuries old European superiority and African inferiority perception of Europeans.

On the effects of Christianity on English civilization, for example, Albert C. Baugh and Thomas Cable wrote in *A History of the English Language* that the beginning of the effect of Christianity began around 669 A. D., when the Greek Bishop, Theodore Tarsus, was appointed the Archbishop of Canterbury. He went to England with Hadrian, "an African by birth." The Venerable Bede described Hadrian as "of the greatest skill in both Greek and Latin tongues." Today, I do not believe any English man would ever want to acknowledge that African thinking and imagination was part of the Christian thought and imagination that laid the foundations of English civilization. These foundations began through the building of churches, monasteries,

35

schools, and in the teaching of the Latin language to lay the foundations of modern western education. From their modern negative socio-political and anthropological sentiments, Europeans have lost the courage to acknowledge history, especially the part played by Africans in history. That is why a work like this that seeks to go back to reveal how it was before may not be popular with Europeans.

Nevertheless, I did not set out to write a popular book because I also know that most black people would not want the white Jesus they have grown to know and worship to be the African *Ayesu*. The image of God that Europeans introduced to us in Africa and around the world has been a white image, but that is at the heart of the legendary lying lore in Christianity. Nevertheless, that is what most Africans have grown to know. How can an African Jesus be the son of a white God? Some people would ask this question because they believe the God that was imagined and personified by black people is white. The answer to this question as it is revealed in this book may not make sense in the minds and imaginations of many black Christians because they have been taught lies for far too long. I wish they would find a new voice to sing a new song from these revelations.

Perhaps an interesting question should be asked here. If this black man Europeans call Jesus came back to earth, as Christian Europe has expectantly believed and propagated for over two thousand years, would Europeans give him the same pious reception as they had planned for the white Jesus in their minds and imaginations? Would black Christians accept and welcome him as their own after being deceived with a white Jesus for so long? This work is not intended to undermine the religious faiths of Christians. It is only intended to reveal a truth. Why would an African want to undermine the religious faiths of Christian Europe when Europeans have become so comfortable worshipping African theosophical ideas and personalities for thousands of years.

The little that I have revealed so far is a very serious revelation that must not be made lightly. A revelation of secrets that have been kept for thousands of years is not going to get by without people attempting to question and even challenge it. This is because we all grow to feel comfortable in what we think is our knowledge of truth. Moreover, there are a lot of people who have designed their entire lives around Europe's legendary lying lore because they were raised to believe it as the only truth. I am looking forward to people questioning and challenging the revelations in this work. I am looking forward to people asking me questions for further clarification where necessary.

I want African and western scholars who become interested in this work to continue the study of what I have presented here because half of Africa's story is yet to be told. This is a serious work that is going to make many people who wished it were not so very uncomfortable. As a result, I am going to make it easy for such people to contain their discomfort and try to disprove, not deny what I have stated in this book. I want those who feel uncomfortable with this truth to question and challenge the ideas presented in this work, but I implore such people not to question and challenge the work based upon their theories from the legendary lying lore we all studied in school.

To help my critics move away from theorizing in challenging the work, I will reveal for the first time, in over five thousand years, some more of the indigenous African names of Ancient Egyptian kings, people, and places. This may come as a surprise to many, but I will reveal the biblical evidence confirming that the so-called biblical patriarchs were *Akan* people, and that the *Akan* people in Africa also originated from the same bloodline of the so-called biblical patriarchs. I will also reveal some of the indigenous African tribal names that modern Jewish people still carry after thousands of years of separation from their *Akan* and other African tribes of origin in Ancient Egypt. To make it easy to check out these revelations, I will also reveal the places in Africa where these specific tribes can be located today.

I am writing this from the foundations of knowledge I acquired in Africa as a traditional African and a scholar, and the knowledge I acquired in the west also as a scholar. I therefore implore those who are interested in this work to check out the biblical sources, African tribes and

36

tribal names, people, languages, and cultures used in proving the thesis of this book before they set out to question or deny the revelations. Otherwise they will be criticizing and denying a comprehensive work from only half the knowledge that was used to create it and that would not be fair no matter how uncomfortable the revelations in this book might make such critics.

Throughout this chapter, I have invoked the black images of Jesus and his mother Mary in the earliest Catholic Churches of Europe as evidence that confirms the original racial heritage of modern Jewish people. In this regard, I introduced the nineteenth century work of Sir Godfrey Higgins. I also invoked the earliest black images of Jesus in the video documentary on the Inquisition and the Catacombs of Rome. I introduced my personal experiences of the two statues of St. Peter at the Basilica in Rome and presented a picture of the bronze image of St. Peter in the Basilica today. I also introduced Kersey Graves' work suggesting that Jesus was a black man. I showed that Adolf Hitler used indirect references of the black origin of the Jewish people in designing his hatred for blacks and Jewish people. Beyond that, the very first place Europeans sought to settle the Jewish people outside Europe was among black people in Uganda in East Africa.

I revealed the African name of the ancient people that became modern Jews in Europe. I linked this name specifically to the ancient *Akan* people that created and developed the Ancient Egyptian civilization. From this, I showed that the ancient *Afrim* people that became the Jews and Hebrews spoke the *Akan* language and that is why they took the *Akan* name *Afrim* as their ancient name and identity. These ancient *Afrim* people identified their earliest nation by the *Akan* name *Afrim* that was corrupted to Ephraim. In the discussion of Ephraim, I revealed the name and language of the ancient *Ga* people, another African tribal group with whom the ancient *Afrim* people came in contact in Canaan. The biblical narrative I quoted revealed that the *Ga* people and the *Afrim* people were of the same racial heritage and since the *Ga* people are still black, it confirms that the ancient *Afrim* people were also black. All of these further confirm that the early Catholic Church was not wrong when it portrayed Jesus and his mother as the black people they originally were.

Beyond all these, I introduced one of the most relevant modern works that confirm emphatically even in its title that modern Jewish people were originally black people (see Gary Greenberg, *The Moses Mystery: The African Origins of the Jewish People*, 1996). Gary Greenberg is himself a Jew. Finally, I also revealed that the Jewish people carried *Akan* and other African tribal names in ancient times and they still carry these names today. For example, I revealed that it was the *Akan* name *Osafo* that was originally transposed to Joseph in English and Josephus in Latin.

So far, I have not just asserted that the people of the Bible had a black heritage. I have revealed the specific black tribes from which they originated for them to acquire such a heritage. I have also revealed the language the people that left Ancient Egypt into the so-called biblical Exodus spoke thus confirming the black heritage from which they originated and more. The discussion so far has revealed that all of these revelations and discussions go back to Ancient Egypt. From these, I was beginning to understand why the biblical tradition would be interested in a conspiracy to distort and destroy Ancient Egyptian history. It was the biblical tradition's way of making sure that Christians in Europe did not get to know that the Jewish people, the so-called people of the Bible, were black people. This was also a way of denying the fact that the documents and doctrines of the Bible were created by black Africans, and it was also the ultimate way for Christian Europe to deny that Christianity originated from the minds and imaginations of black Africans.

What has happened to Christianity in the two thousand years of denying, conniving, and conspiring to hide the truth of its origin in the Africans is that Christianity that is propagated as the ultimate truth in world religions has become a lie. This is because Ancient Egypt was not only central to the formation of the Jewish people, but also it was central in the creation of the documents and doctrines of Christianity. Ancient Egypt was the beginning.

What I want readers to notice in this discussion is that I have not asserted and revealed the relationship among the Ancient Egyptians, the Africans, the *Afrim* people that went to Europe to become the Jews and Hebrews, the Bible, and Christianity in generalities. I have introduced real human and linguistic evidence to support this assertion. This is a living human story and I told it as such linking all of these to specific humans, histories, and languages that can be easily verified in Ancient Egyptian history, the Bible, Western Europe, and Africa.

2

In the Beginning... was Ancient Egypt

All great truths begin as blasphemies
George Bernard Shaw

Every now and then you meet a man whose ignorance is encyclopedic.
Stanislaw J. Lec

Introduction

"And Abraham journeyed, going on still toward the south. And there was famine in the land: and Abraham went down into Egypt to sojourn there; for the famine was grievous (Gen. 12:9). In the last chapter, I showed that the people that left Ancient Egypt to go to live in Canaan and later move to Europe to become the Jews and Hebrews originated from the African tribes that were the Ancient Egyptians. I showed the living tribes and languages from which these people originated. However, the biblical story that cannot be substantiated historically, archaeologically, anthropologically, and genetically suggests that the Jewish people originated from the line of Abraham outside Ancient Egypt, and yet there is no evidence in living humans, languages, or cultures anywhere in that region to support this.

From a close analysis of biblical narrative, some very revealing issues begin to emerge. What is intriguing about such revealing issues is that nobody has paid attention to most of them but these issues provide answers to the questions the Jewish people have sought to avoid and Christianity has failed to ask. These revealing issues also provide answers to the questions biblical scholars have failed to see. For example, according to the biblical narrative, why was there no other place in and around Canaan that Abraham and his family could have gone to escape from famine beside Ancient Egypt? Why was there no other place in and around Canaan that the patriarch could have traveled beside Ancient Egypt where religion had been developed and practiced for thousands of years? The Jewish people claim to have descended directly from Jacob. For this Jacob too, there was no other place he and his family could also have gone to escape from famine in Canaan, beside Ancient Egypt. There was no other place Jacob and his sons and family of seventy men could have gone to live and die beside Ancient Egypt. What do these mean? What are all these situations and supposed interactions with Ancient Egyptians trying to tell us about the Jewish people?

Why was there no other place that Jacob and his sons and family of seventy men could have gone to live for four hundred and thirty years and "grow" into several different tribes, except Ancient Egypt?" Much the same way, there was no other place the so-called "descendants" of Jacob could have claimed that they were enslaved in the building of magnificent creations as the pyramids, beside Ancient Egypt. There was no other place the single family of Jacob could have turned into a whole tribe of Jews and Hebrews of several different tribes, beside Ancient Egypt. Why was there no such other place for all these developments in the lives and history of the Jewish people beside Ancient Egypt? In ignorance, Christian Europe has interpreted all these to mean that it was because God wanted to use the Ancient Egyptians to reach his children, the Israelites. Because Europeans have never known where the Jewish people truly originated from this has been Christian Europe's proud answer to all these questions, and it has never known that all of these interactions mean something racial, something tribal, and something ethnic.

Weren't the Jewish people the people that the Bible claimed originated from Ur of the Chaldees? Why did their patriarchs not go "back home" to save themselves from famine? Weren't the Jewish people the people that the Bible claims God gave the land of Canaan? Why did this God not feed them in this land, and why did all the descendants of Abraham that supposedly became the Jewish people have to move to Ancient Egypt to survive famines? All of these seek to tell us something the Jewish scholars of the Bible refused to reveal and no one in Europe would ever know it unless Africa reveals it to them. Without knowledge of the racial and ethnic relationship between the biblical patriarchs and Ancient Egyptians, these biblical stories seem ordinary and that is just how Christianity has taken them.

Finally, why was there no other place that Jewish scholars could have gone to compile and translate the documents of the Bible they claim were their creations, beside Ancient Egypt? If the biblical documents were written by Jewish priests and prophets, why couldn't Jewish scholars translate these documents for the Greeks in Israel, but they had to do so in Ancient Egypt? If Jewish prophets and priest wrote the documents of the Bible who would have been the best custodians of these documents? Would it have been Hellenized Jews in Ancient Egypt or the priests and prophets of Israel for whom these documents were created? If Jewish prophets and priests created the biblical documents, why would these prophets not keep these documents in Israel but instead, they were found in Ancient Egyptian library?

Without a doubt, these documents would have been in Jerusalem in the custody of priests or somewhere in the archives of a temple in Israel, if Jewish prophets and priests wrote them. They would not have been in Ancient Egypt. This means if Hellenized Jewish scholars had to compile, edit, and translate these documents for the Greeks, they would have had to go to Israel to do so. Yet biblical tradition as presented in an Arts and Entertainment Network documentary on *Who Wrote The Bible* states that when Ptolemy, the then Greek ruler of Ancient Egypt, asked Hellenized Jewish scholars in Ancient Egypt to compile and translate the documents of the Bible into Greek, these scholars rather invited priests and scholars from Israel to Ancient Egypt to help them. Why did these scholars not go to the priests of Israel who would have been the custodians of these documents if Jewish priests and prophets actually created them?

Wouldn't it have been more prudent and courteous for Jewish scholars to go to the source and custodians of these documents in Israel? How could Ptolemy know that Jewish priests and prophets have written some religious documents he wanted translated into Greek for his people? The single answer to all these questions is that Jewish prophets and priests did not create the documents that became the Christian Bible. Ancient Egyptian priests and religious philosophers created these documents and therefore they were in Ancient Egypt. That was how Ptolemy got to know about them and wanted them translated into Greek for his people and that why the Jewish scholars that translated these documents had to bring priests and scholars from Israel to Ancient Egypt to help them and not go to Israel where the creators and custodians of these documents would have been. Perhaps, the most important question to ask in conclusion to this discussion is how did the authors of these documents come to have African tribal names?

Why did all these have to happen in Ancient Egypt, any way? What about the supposed biblical homeland of the Jewish people? These people claimed to have gone to Ancient Egypt from their original home in Mesopotamia, but they have been going around the world carrying African tribal names. They also claimed that God had given them the land of Canaan. This means these people belonged to both Mesopotamia and Canaan and yet Ancient Egypt was the place of their transformation from one family to a people of many tribes. There is no evidence of any tribe from which they originated in Mesopotamia. Ancient Egypt was the place their priests and scholars could compile the documents of the Bible for the Greeks. They claimed that Jerusalem was the center of their religion but the most important documents of their religion was found in Ancient Egypt. What is sad about al these is that Christian Europe has accepted all these as the gospel and simple truth but according to Oscar Wilde, the pure and simple truth is rarely pure and never simple.

Ancient Egypt was the beginning of the creation of the history of the Jewish people. There is no evidence of these people having any history anywhere before they supposedly went to Ancient Egypt or before they supposedly left there. Beside the biblical narrative that has been taken and propagated as the historical and gospel truth by Christianity, there is no other evidence of the Jewish people having created the documents that became the contents of the Bible anywhere. Beyond their claims, there is no evidence that the documents and doctrines of the Bible were known or practiced anywhere in Israel. Not only could the Jewish people not substantiate this claim but also historians and archaeologists have failed to find any evidence to support their claims. On the other hand, Africa has enough evidence to prove the origin of the Jewish people in African tribes, and Egyptologists have found abundant evidence to support the origin of the biblical documents in Ancient Egypt. These are areas Christianity does not know about. Ancient Egypt was the central setting of the biblical story from Abraham through Jacob to the creation of the Bible itself in Alexandria. In the beginning therefore, was Ancient Egypt.

The question then is what was it about "pagan" Ancient Egypt that made the so-called children of the Christian God like the place so much? If the Jewish people created the ideas and documents of the Bible as they claimed, why could these documents not have been compiled in Mesopotamia, Babylon, Canaan, or anywhere else but in Ancient Egypt? Again, don't all these seek to tell us something? They do and the early apostolic fathers knew it so they tried to interpret the Bible to conceal all these or they tried to neglect certain pasts of the Bible. It is one of the reasons Christianity focuses on the New Testament because they know the Old Testament is full of numerous historical inexactitudes. What is sad about all these is that historians, archaeologists, Egyptologists, and Bible scholars know a whole lot more about the Bible that ordinary believers in the Bible as a book of faith do not know. However, they are the believers that make the greatest noise about a book they know so little. What was the hidden significance of the centrality of Ancient Egypt in the story of both the Jewish people and the Bible? The evidence of the Ancient Egyptian origin of the Jewish people and the documents of the Bible are very clear in the Bible itself, yet Christian Europe sought to interpret them to fit into its socio-political sentiments. As a result, Christian Europe could not get the clues, and it still does not have any clue.

Despite all the evidence and some scholars say because of it, there is no aspect of human history that has been secretly denied and openly distorted as the history of Ancient Egypt. Doesn't anyone see here why the biblical tradition would not want western scholarship to acknowledge that the Ancient Egyptians were black people? Does anyone understand now why the biblical tradition would conspire with other forces to destroy and distort Ancient Egyptian history? There is no group of people on earth that the biblical tradition and false western scholarship have successfully pushed into oblivion as the Ancient Egyptians. Yet, there are modern descendants of Ancient Egyptians just as there are modern descendants of the ancient Jewish people that supposedly went to live in Ancient Egypt for over four hundred years. Isn't it obvious that these two groups are trying to conceal something about the Ancient Egyptians, and what is it?

For a reason only known to western scholarship on Ancient Egypt, the world does not even know who the Ancient Egyptians were. Historians and Egyptologists have quietly and almost nonchalantly pointed out that the Ancient Egyptians were the Africans but one cannot find such information presented anywhere for public knowledge except in a few specialized books, scholastic journals, and papers. In short, the majority of people that need to know this truth do not get to know about it. The evidence also shows that even most of those who get to know that the Ancient Egyptians were the Africans do not readily welcome or accept it. From all these, western scholarship has succeeded in telling the Ancient Egyptian story and continues to tell it as if these ancient magnificent people were extinct. Few people know that the Ancient Egyptians are the Africans and even fewer people know the specific African tribes that were the dominant tribal groups in Ancient Egypt.

The question is why would western scholarship do this to Africa and the world's greatest history of civilization and development? It is evident from all the sources that it is because of the towering magnificence of the Ancient Egyptians that western scholarship has pushed these ancient people into oblivion. This is to make way for the west to tell its story of civilization and development that were based upon the foundations of Ancient Egypt without acknowledging the superiority of the Africans in this regard. After all, compared to Ancient Egyptian history, development, and achievements there is no other human history of distinction and radiance in this world. In western perception, such credit of high superiority and achievement would have been credited to any other group of people on this earth except the Africans. The question is why?

Despite this, most scholars have known that modern descendants of Ancient Egyptians are the black people of Africa. As a result, the strategy of some European scholars have been that anyone that seeks to distort or destroy Ancient Egyptian civilization and history should also attack Africa for such distortion and destruction to be complete. As a result, some scholars have extended their efforts at pushing down the Ancient Egyptians onto the Africans so that they cannot rise to claim the magnificent Ancient Egyptian history that is theirs. In *A History of West Africa: An Introductory Survey*, J. D. Fage documented a necessary background for the understanding of whatever has been written by Europeans about Africa when he wrote:

> Most of those who, during the colonial period, sought to reconstruct the earliest history of Africa, were themselves outsiders, members of the colonizing nations of western Europe. They came from a society which technologically and materially was vastly more powerful than was late nineteenth century Africa, and which was therefore able to conquer, rule, dominate, and change Negro African societies in a most dramatic fashion. When these men began to discover the evidence for their earliest West African civilizations, they were therefore predisposed to think that these could not have been created by the Negro people they themselves have so easily conquered and come to rule. They believed, therefore, that they must have resulted from earlier invasions by alien conquerors comparable to themselves. ... By and large, nineteenth century Europeans had convinced themselves that "white"-skinned peoples represented a superior human type (1969, pp. 6-7).

This was the prevailing perception of Europeans about Africans long before the nineteenth century. As a result, even though ancient and modern Egypt are in Africa, western scholars have managed to portray it as a Near Eastern civilization, and they have also managed to argue that black Africans were not the creators of the Ancient Egyptian civilization. These are European scholars, and we in Africa have perhaps ignorantly expected them to know better than that. In fact, such European assertions have made us wonder whether these western scholars really know who and what they are talking about when they write about Ancient Egypt.

According to Montaigne: "There is a preschool ignorance that precedes knowledge and a postgraduate ignorance that follows it." In the case of knowledge about Africa and her history, the preschool ignorance of western scholarship has extended into postgraduate ignorance. Most western scholars think that the childhood of Africa began with their knowledge of Africa only a few hundred years ago. It is from this background that Ben Okri asked humbly: "How far back is our childhood? I think our childhood goes back thousands of years, farther than the memory of any race." In matters of history relating to Africa, readers will find out in this work that the memory and knowledge of Africa goes farther back than Europeans have ever known or can ever remember. One of the topics on which Africa's memory goes further back than the memory of Europeans is the topic of religion with Ancient Egypt as the origin. How far back is the childhood of European Christianity and where were the concepts and doctrines of European Christianity first conceived? The childhood of European Christianity goes farther back outside Europe among non-Europeans than Christian Europe has ever wanted Christians to know.

The Bible and Christianity are over two thousand years old, yet Christians around the world do not know where the ideas and sacramental practices of their religion originated, and the Catholic Church that has known the foundations of these has refused to tell them. Within this period, Christianity has accumulated an impressive corpus of literature as its history, but that history does not address issues of where Christian concept, doctrines, and sacramental practices of religion originated, where the documents of the Christian Bible came from, or who wrote these documents. As a result, the earliest documents of Church history simply claimed and sought to propagate ideas authors of these documents did not know their origin.

Among the body of documents that Christianity has accumulated as its history are the *First Epistle of Clement to the Corinthians* pleading with Christians that have rebelled against the Catholic Church to reconsider and submit to Church authority. Religious historians believe that Clement wrote this letter around 96 A. D. There is a second epistle to the Corinthians around 150 A. D. by an unknown author and religious scholars attribute this second letter to Clement. There is *The Epistle of Barnabas* written around 130 A. D. rejecting the assertions of Christian Jews that Christian Europe must also observe the Laws of Moses. In this letter, Barnabas argued that Jesus came to save man through his own laws and admonitions therefore man is no longer obligated to obey the Law of Moses. Note that Barnabas' letter was one of the earliest and most powerful letters in the foundation of European claim of Christian doctrines as their own and also it was one of the earliest documents that sought to separate the doctrines of Christianity from the Jews. In the records of Church history is also the document of *The Shepherd of Hermas* written around 150 A. D. Hermas is believed to be the brother of Bishop Pious of Rome. This work was an early attempt to recast the Book of Revelations into the realities of the 2nd century A. D.

Included in the historical documents of the Church are *The Epistle of Polycarp to the Philippians*, *The Martyrdom of Polycarp*, *The Writings of Ignatius*, *The Epistle of Mathetes to Diognetus*, *Origen*, *The Writings of Tertullian*, *The Writings of Cyprian*, *The Writings of Athanasius On Incarnation*, and the perhaps the most important documents, *The Writings of Augustine*. These could not be the foundation history of the concepts and doctrines that became the foundations of Christianity but that is what Christianity has claimed.

Religious historians consider Augustine the father of western theology because his ideas were instrumental in shaping the basic doctrines of Christianity. What is intriguing about all these Christian documents is that the earliest of these documents from the 1st century A. D. is almost a thousand years behind the creation of the ideas that became the foundations of the Christian Bible and converged into Christian doctrines. I am interested in where these concepts and doctrines originated before they got to Europe, but that has not been what Christian Europe has been interested in for a reason. The question Christian Europe has failed to ask is where these ideas originated before they got to Europe.

Where could Augustine have acquired such great insight into theology? What has been conveniently forgotten and therefore never revealed about the writings of Augustine is the fact that he wrote most of his influential works on Christianity while he was the Overseer of the Church at Hippo in North Africa. Augustine was in the same geographical area as Ancient Egypt where all the world's religious ideas and sacramental practices begun. What made the writings of Augustine from North Africa so influential on the Church and in Christian Europe? Did Augustine have access to the ancient religious ideas of Egypt, and could he also have been introducing Ancient Egyptian religious ideas to the Church without the Church not knowing the source from where these ideas came? For example, could his treatise on *Confessions* have been based on the same ideas in *The Ancient Egyptian Book of the Dead* where the dead had to confess before the gods of the underworld? Could this have been the same idea adopted by the Catholic Church in which members go to confess their wrongdoings to a seemingly underworld priests? These are questions most modern Christians would not ask because they have never been taught this aspect of the history of Christian religion alongside the history of Ancient Egyptian religion.

Origin of the concept of God, in the beginning ... was Ancient Egypt

Despite all the impressive historical documents the Church has compiled, there are some very fundamental issues that none of the Church's documents addressed. The Bible is the holiest book of Christian Europe and Christians around the world. It is the book upon whose principles and "practices" Europeans claim to have designed their societies, and they profess to live by it still. It is the book Europeans invoke to end all logic and reasoning in any discussion. It is also the book of spiritual strength for millions of Christians, and yet few people know where it came from, who wrote its content and even fewer have cared to find out where this book originated.

Most of the people I have questioned about the origin of the documents and ideas of the Bible say that God wrote them. Some say that God inspired ancient *Afrim* prophets to write them. In another way, others say that humans wrote the Bible, but God put words into their mouths. From these questions, I found out that most Christians do not want to be asked questions that would make them think beyond what the Bible wants them to know and believe. These people have been made to believe that thinking beyond the Bible to try to understand their own religions and faiths is blasphemous.

Unfortunately, most Christians around the world do not know that it has long been the strategy of the Church to make them accept only the ideas of the Bible and not look beyond it. This is because looking beyond the Bible into its surrounding history would expose Christians to the secrets that the Church has been concealing from them for the past two thousand years. Since the beginning of the growth of knowledge, what the early apostolic fathers of European Christianity have feared has been the introduction of new information that would reveal something Christianity has sought to conceal for thousands of years, like what this book is about to do.

What did the early apostolic fathers of Christianity seek to conceal from the Christian masses and why? The early apostolic fathers of the Church sought to conceal the fact that the concepts, document, and doctrines of the Christian faith were all black people's ideas and religious practices. Why would they want to do this? It was because even in those early times, these apostolic fathers felt that Europeans might not want to worship a God that was imagined, created, and personified by other people. If Christian masses knew this, the Church would be the loser, so the best way was to make sure that people did not get to know about the origin of the concepts, documents, and doctrines of Christianity in another land, especially Ancient Egypt.

So far, the strategy of the early apostolic fathers to make Christian masses ignorant of the truth, especially knowledge of the relationship among Ancient Egypt, the Bible, and Christianity has worked. It has worked so well that Christian masses do not even know where the concept of the God they worship originated. How did the concept of the Christian God begin? Most Christians do not know, and there is no Christian record that documents this. However, there is evidence of how the concept of God began in Ancient Egyptian records that documented the origin and form of God thousands of years before Christian Europe got to know and claim him.

In *Egyptian Religion*, Sir Wallis Budge wrote:

> The late Dr. H. Brugsch collected a number of epithets which applied to the gods, from texts of all [Ancient Egyptian] periods; and from these we may see that the ideas and beliefs of the Egyptians concerning God were almost identical with those of the Hebrews and Muhammadans at later periods [in history] (p. 37).

In early times when the world did not know much of its own history, when there was no archaeology, Egyptology, or even biblical scholarship, the Bible was the sole authority over every aspect of world and human affairs. It was unimpeachable because it was the only corpus of knowledge available and there was no other way of verifying whether its historical, archaeological, and even Egyptological knowledge was true or not. Today, things are different.

What makes the above quotation very significant is that it reveals where the concept of God in the three biggest religions of the world originated. It shows that the earliest concept of God was imagined in Ancient Egypt and that the concept of God of later religions is identical to this Ancient Egyptian concept. This was another way of nicely suggesting that the concept of God of later religions of the world originated from the earliest Ancient Egyptian concept. This quotation therefore reveals where the Jewish people took the concept of God, and it also shows where the Muslims got their concept of God. What makes this quotation even more significant is the fact that Ancient Egypt, Canaan, and the Middle East where Muslim religion originated are all in the same geographical vicinity. The Jewish people claim to have gone to live in the midst of the creators of the earliest concept of God, Ancient Egyptians, for over four hundred years. These Jewish people left Ancient Egypt and went to live in Canaan. So where could the religious ideas and beliefs of the Jewish people and Muslims have originated?

Most Christians and perhaps Muslims would not want to know this but early Egyptologists have already established that Christian and Muslim concepts of religion and God originated from the older and more ancient Egyptian concepts of religion and God. The only differences are the sacramental practices these religions have designed to support their perception of religion and God. Early Egyptologists have had access to the large depository of Ancient Egyptian religious literature now floating around in European Museums, and they have introduced more than enough evidence from this ancient literature to support their assertions.

Ancient literature beside the biblical documents

Most Christians do not know that there are other ancient religious documents other than their Bibles. Most do not know that there are other religious documents older than the biblical documents. Most of these religious documents that are older than the biblical documents and from which the biblical doctrines were taken are found in numerous Ancient Egyptian papyri tucked away in museums in Europe and around the world. Unfortunately, most Christians and even scholars outside the study of Ancient Egypt did not know that Ancient Egypt had a vast literature yet to be introduced to the world. At least, European scholars acknowledge that such Ancient Egyptian literature exists. As Sir Wallis Budge wrote in the *Egyptian Religion*:

> The literature of Egypt which deals with these subjects is large and as was to be expected, the product of different periods which, taken together, cover several thousands of years ... (p. 9).

Most Christians would never believe today that the concepts and ideas presented in the biblical documents belonged to the Ancient Egyptians or even that the biblical documents were compiled and translated for the Greeks in Ancient Egypt.

Origin of the concept of resurrection, in the beginning ...was Ancient Egypt

Many Christians must have heard of the concept of resurrection that has become the cornerstone of hope and faith in Christianity. They must have been taught to believe that they would die and resurrect and that Jesus would resurrect and come back to this world, but nobody would tell them that the concept of resurrection that Christians have conferred on Jesus is an Ancient Egyptian concept, perception, and practice of religion, life, and death. On the earliest concept of resurrection in religion, Sir Wallis Budge wrote further that:

> The chief source of our information concerning the doctrine of the resurrection and of the future life as held by the Egyptians is, of course, the great collection of religious texts generally known by the name of "Book of the Dead." The various recensions of these wonderful compositions cover a period of more than five thousand years, and they reflect faithfully not only the sublime beliefs, and the high ideals, and the noble aspirations of the educated Egyptians, but also the various superstitions and childish reverence for amulets, and magical rites, and charms, which they probably inherited from their pre-dynastic ancestors, and regarded as essentials for their salvation (p. 11, emphasis mine).

Notice from this quotation that the earliest greatest collection of religious texts were in Ancient Egypt and not in Israel. Because such documents were created in Ancient Egypt, archaeologists have found evidence of them in Ancient Egypt. Unfortunately, because the biblical documents were not created in Israel, no evidence of such documents have so far been found in Israel. From this knowledge, it becomes clear why the documents of the Bible had to be compiled and translated in Ancient Egypt and not in Israel. It also become clear why the Jewish scholars of Alexandria had to bring priests in Israel to Ancient Egypt to help them compile, edit, and translate the documents that became the first Bible, the Greek Bible.

From the above quotation, it also becomes clear that the concepts and practices of salvation and resurrection through religion were invented in Ancient Egypt, and they were major parts of Ancient Egyptian religion, beliefs, and practices for thousands of years before they became doctrines and beliefs in Christianity. Not only that, these concepts and doctrines of religion were documented in Ancient Egyptian literature thousands of years before the biblical documents were compiled from them and claimed by the Jewish scholars of Alexandria that these documents were their own. In the beginning was Ancient Egypt.

From Ancient Egyptian documents of religion into the Christian Bible
The Jewish scholars of Alexandria took the Ancient Egyptian perception and epithets of God, his form, and power and included them in the biblical narrative as exactly as the Ancient Egyptians conceived and verbalized them. How many Christians know this and how many that know would tell Christian masses about this? Sir Wallis Budge also presented a summary of Ancient Egyptian epithets pertaining to the most ancient concept of God and practice of religion long before these epithets and concepts got into the Christian and Muslim religions. Sir Budge wrote:

When classified, these Ancient Egyptian epithets read thus:

God is One and alone, and none other existeth with Him.

God is the One, the One who hath made all things

God is a spirit, a hidden spirit, the spirit of spirits, the Great Spirit of the Egyptians, the divine spirit.

God is from the beginning, and He hath been from the beginning; He hath existed from of old and was when nothing else had being.
He existed when nothing else existed, and what existeth He created after he had come into being.
He is the father of beginnings.

God is the eternal One, He is eternal and infinite; and endureth for ever and aye; He hath endured for countless ages, and He shall endure to all eternity.

God is the hidden Being, and no man hath known his Form. No man hath been able to seek out His likeness; He is hidden from gods and men, and He is a mystery unto His creatures.
No man knoweth how to know Him. His name remaineth hidden; His name is a mystery unto His children. His names are innumerable, they are manifold and none knoweth their number.

God is truth, and He liveth truth, and He feedeth thereon. He is the King of truth, He resteth upon truth, He fashioned truth, and He executeth truth throughout all the world.

God is life, and through Him only man liveth. He giveth life to man, and He breatheth the breath of life into his nostrils.

God is father and mother, the father of fathers, and the mother of mothers. He begetteth, but was never begotten; He produceth, but was never produced, He begat Himself and produced Himself. He createth, but was never created; he is maker of His own form, and the fashioner of His own body.

God Himself is existence, He liveth in all things, and liveth upon all things. He endureth without increase or diminution, He multiplieth Himself millions of times, and He possesseth multitudes of forms and multitudes of members.

God hath made the universe, and He created all that therein is: He is the Creator of what is in this world, of what was, of what is, and of what shall be. He is the creator of the world, and it was He Who fashioned it with His hands before there was any beginning; and He established it with that which went forth from Him. He is the Creator of the heavens and earth; the Creator of the heavens, and the earth, and the deep; the Creator of the heavens, and the earth, and the deep, and the waters, and the mountains. God hath stretched out the heavens and founded the earth. What his heart conceived came to pass straightway, and when He had spoken His word came to pass; and it shall endure for ever.

God is father of the gods, and the father of the father of all ideas. He made His voice to sound, and the deities came into being, and the gods sprang into existence after He had spoken with His mouth. He formed mankind and fashioned the gods. He is the great Master, the primeval Potter Who turned men and gods out of His hands, and He formed men and gods upon a potter's table.

The heavens rest upon His head, and the earth supporteth His feet; heaven hideth His spirit, the earth hideth His form, and the underworld shutteth up the mystery of Him within it. His body is like air, heaven resteth upon His head, and the new inundation [of the Nile] containeth His form.

God is merciful unto those who reverence Him, and He heareth him that calleth upon Him. He protecteth the weak against the strong, and He heareth the cry of him that is bound in fetters; He judgeth between the mighty and weak. God knoweth him that knoweth Him, He rewardeth him that serveth Him, and He protecteth him that followeth Him (Wallis Budge, *Egyptian Religion*, 1994, pp. 37-40, see also H. Brugsch, *Religion und Mythologie*, pp. 96-99).

These were some of the basic theosophical concepts and perceptions of God and religion that the Ancient Egyptians created and documented thousands of years before the Jewish scholars of Alexandria went to compile and translate these documents into the Christian Bible. Anyone who reads these Ancient Egyptian theosophical ideas today would think they came out of the Bible because they are exactly the same. Anyone who knows the Bible will immediately notice the striking similarities between this Ancient Egyptian and biblical documents pertaining to the concept of God. Does the fact that these concepts and documents already existed in Ancient Egypt before Jewish scholars went there to compile such documents for the Greeks suggest in any way that the biblical concepts and documents were taken from the older Ancient Egyptian concepts and documents? If your perceptions and beliefs in God in any religion are similar to any of these ideas, you must know that you are practicing Ancient Egyptian religion and perception of God, no matter what you may call it. You may now understand why biblical tradition has hated Ancient Egypt and done everything to make sure that such knowledge about Ancient Egypt does not come out. Could this be the reason Jewish scholars could not compile the biblical documents anywhere else but in Ancient Egypt? Is there any doubt that these Jewish scholars of Alexandria took the ideas of God, religion, and sacramental practices that became Christianity from the Ancient Egyptians?

Origin of the concept of a male God who lives in heaven

Christianity believes that God resides somewhere in the sky but when I ask Christians how they came to know that God lives in the sky, some say it is God that revealed his abode to humans. Here is an Ancient Egyptian epithet from the above quotation that placed God in heaven thousands of years before Christianity and other religions came to know and accept the abode of this God as the heavens.

> The heavens rest upon His head, and the earth supporteth His feet; heaven hideth His spirit, the earth hideth His form, and the underworld shutteth up the mystery of Him within it. His body is like air, heaven resteth upon His head, and the new inundation [of the Nile] containeth His form.

Beside the Christian God, the greatest elements in Christianity are the concepts of heaven and earth. Unfortunately, most Christians have been taught everything about heaven and earth except where the concepts of these two places originated. When I speak in places, I ask people if they have ever heard of Ancient Egyptian gods *Osiris* and *Isis* and most of them say no because they do not know the foundational history behind the religion they have adopted as theirs. The names *Osiris* and *Isis* were Greek linguistic corruption of the *Akan* words *Osoro* and *Asaase* meaning heaven and earth. Christians talk about heaven and earth, but they do not know how these two elements came to be at the center of their religion or where these two concepts originated. They got it from the Ancient Egyptians first through the *Akan* people that created these concepts in Ancient Egypt and then through the *Akan* and other African tribal groups that went to Europe to become the Jews and Hebrews.

In the earliest religion of Ancient Egypt that was the religion of the *Akan* people, *Osoro* was the abode and reference to the sky god, a male god; and *Asaase* was the abode and reference to the earth goddess. These Ancient Egyptian names for their gods and their abodes confirm that at least they had a god that lived in *Osoro*, the sky and he was the God upon whose head rested heaven.

How did all religions on earth come to believe that their Gods are all male? The Ancient Egyptian concept of a male God that lives in the sky was what was passed on into Christianity in Europe and religions around the world. Today, every religion's God is male. What is fascinating about this concept is that modern *Akan* people that created these ancient concepts still believe in *Osoro* and *Asaase* and pray to them. This belief can still be found in *Akan* prayer in the form of the pouring of libation to God.

Most Christians have been told that the *Afrim* people created the theosophical ideas of the Bible but they have never been told that these *Afrim* scholars compiled the biblical documents in Ancient Egypt. Moreover, most Christians have never been told that the foundations of the biblical ideas had already been created and documented in Ancient Egypt long before the *Afrim* scholars of the Bible came to compile the same documents and simply edit and translate them for the Greeks. Because most Christians do not know most of these, they have never been able to put it together that the *Afrim* people came from Ancient Egypt therefore they must have learned what they claim they knew from the Ancient Egyptians. However, the early apostolic fathers of Christianity knew this and that is why they conspired and connived to distort and destroy Ancient Egyptian history so that these ideas would never come out.

The creation of the earliest human concepts of religion in Ancient Egypt

This work is a revelation of the Africans who wrote the Christian Bible. To be able to do so, I need to establish a historical and geographical focal point where the Bible, Christianity,

Afrim people, and Africans interacted together. This work is therefore an attempt to weave together the related pieces of the stories of Ancient Egyptians, Africans, *Afrim* people, the Bible, and Christianity. As readers may already know, there are volumes of western literature on all of these topics. I therefore do not intend to recount what has long been written on these ideas. Moreover, most of these volumes were based upon the *legendary lying lore* and they are different from what I have to say anyway. As a result, I will provide only brief summaries where necessary and weave them into the single coherent story that they originally were. The thesis of the discussion in this chapter is that there is no idea, belief, or religious practice in Christianity and for that matter any religion in the world that cannot be traced to the ancient theosophical ideas of religion in Egypt. Even in the religions of the Far East that seems to be geographically far from Ancient Egypt, there is historical and cultural evidence that itinerant Ancient Egyptian priests went that far to propagate Egyptian religion and theosophical ideas.

As a result of all these, any discussion of the historical background to the creation of the Bible and Christianity cannot begin without first identifying the geographical location where the documents of the Bible were compiled, edited, and translated for the Greeks and all Europeans. As I keep pointing out, the documents of the Christian Bible were compiled, rewritten, and translated into the first Greek Bible in Ancient Egypt. Because of this, no prudent and unbiased scholarly discussion of the creation of Christianity can even begin anywhere without starting from Ancient Egypt, and there are several reasons for this.

Among these reasons is the fact that Ancient Egyptians were the first humans to conceive and develop sacramental practices of theosophy. According to the story of modern descendants of the Ancient Egyptians in Africa today, the concept of religion in Ancient Egypt developed from fear, superstition, and the human need to find answers and explanations for what these ancient people did not know and understand. To these ancient people, the need to find answers to what they feared and did not understand was a great need that satisfied a deeper "inner hollow" in the human quest for answers to the primordial questions of who we are, where we came from, and where we are going. The very first answers to these questions became the foundations of what is now known as religion. Religion as the medium for clothing humanity's inner spiritual nakedness, satisfying the deep "inner hollow," and answering the most fundamental human questions of humanity became the greatest psychological discovery humans have ever made about our humanity itself. This philosophy seemed to give meaning to life by pushing all our unanswered questions into death.

The philosophy of religion created by the Ancient Egyptians made a lot of sense, and since the "inner hollows" of human frailty and spiritual nakedness are universal, the concept of religion was accepted in every corner of the earth as satisfying and fulfilling a great human need. The Ancient Egyptians who are now the Africans were the first humans that thought of and designed the unique concept of religion. The greatest outcome of this creation was that these Africans used religion and its sacramental practices to bring out the best in our humanity by also imagining, building, and creating the greatest civilization on earth. That is the greatest and most remarkable evidence of the earliest origin and use of religion anywhere in the world. Everything these ancient Africans did in Egypt had a religious and cultural significance. The pyramids these people built had a religious and cultural meaning; the triangular shape of the pyramids had a religious and cultural meaning, and even the relief on the walls of the pyramids had their religious and cultural meanings.

The initial pondering of the primordial questions of our humanity and the answers that came to be the foundational concepts and ideas of religion came to the Ancient Egyptians from thousands of years of observation of the world and nature around them. From these observations, these ancient people realized that there were certain unchanging rules and principles that govern the universe, and therefore the lives of humans. Those who first tried to understand these principles were the earliest wise men of this ancient community and they became the earliest corps of our modern religious priesthood. Ancient Egyptian priesthood was a corpus of men that dedicated their lives to searching for answers and ways to understand and tap into the energies in nature's principles. Today, this Ancient Egyptian priesthood tradition can be found in every religion. The Catholic Church in particular sought to practice priesthood as closely as the Ancient Egyptians practiced it with celibacy, abstinence, and all.

Origin of the concepts of death, heaven, and hell

The ancient wise men of Egypt became obsessed with understanding the principles of the universe and finding ways to tap into the energies of these principles to enhance the quality of their lives on earth, and even have control over the direction and quality of their lives in death. Modern Christian concepts of dying and going to heaven or hell are mere adaptations of Ancient Egyptian imaginative perceptions of death, its relationship to the gods and religion, and doing good or evil in this life. Today, the doctrines and practices of most religions are based upon these ancient fundamental principles that acknowledge the roles of heaven, hell, earth, life, and death in religious thinking and practice. Almost all humans believe that the earth is this planet and there is a heaven above them somewhere in the sky, thanks to the earliest concepts of Ancient Egyptian religious thinking and sacramental practices. To find out about the earliest Ancient Egyptian thoughts on these doctrines see Dr. E Wallis Budge, *The Egyptian Book of the Dead*, 1895. Ancient Egyptians called this book *The Book of the Great Awakening* and what an awakening the concept of God and religion has been to all humanity.   •

Ancient Egyptians not only conceived the idea of theosophy; they designed the rituals and sacramental practices that went with this concept. On the back cover *of The Book of the Great Awakening,* Dr. Wallis wrote:

> *The Egyptian Book of the Dead is unquestionably one of the most influential books in history.* Embodying a ritual to be performed for the dead, with detailed instructions for the behavior of the disembodied spirit in the Land of the Gods, *it served as the most important repository of religious authority for some three thousand years.* Chapters were carved on the pyramids of the ancient 5th Dynasty, texts were written in papyrus, and selections were painted on mummy cases well into the Christian era. In a certain sense, it stood behind all Egyptian civilization (emphasis mine).

One of the greatest scholars of Ancient Egyptian studies called this Ancient Egyptian book on religion "one of the most influential books in history," yet few Christians have ever heard of this book or its influence on the religious doctrines and sacramental practices they go through everyday. The most important revelation in this quotation is that the most ancient and "the most important repository of religious authority" was in Ancient Egypt and not in Canaan or Israel. Christianity has just entered its third millennium, however, three millennia earlier and even longer before that "the most important repository of religious authority, and one of the most influential books in history," was this Ancient Egyptian book of religion. Then the *Afrim* people came in thousands of years later to introduce these ideas to Europeans and claim that these were their own ideas, and Europeans believed them. Europeans believed them so much they were willing to help distort and destroy the Ancient Egyptian sources that could reveal the truth. Notice that Sir Wallis Budge points out that this Ancient Egyptian book is "one of the most influential books in history." How could this and other Ancient Egyptian books of religion have been the most influential books in history without influencing the Jewish scholars that compiled, edited, and translated the documents of the Bible into Greek in Ancient Egypt?

Most Christians have been "indoctrinated" to accept the Bible as their only source of religious knowledge. As a result, most Christians have never heard of this book because the early apostolic fathers of Christianity have succeeded in making all Christians believe that the Bible is a source of itself and the only truth. What is most interesting about all these is that Christianity has never wanted its members and believers to find out the source from where the ideas and doctrines of their faith originated. As a result, it has succeeded in teaching these believers that anything beside the Bible is a lie. Nevertheless, that was only a clever way not to get people to search for the truth behind the faiths they have adopted and devoted their lives. For more information about Ancient Egyptian religious concepts and sacramental practices that became the foundations of Christian doctrine and sacramental practices, see Sir Wallis Budge: *Osiris & The Egyptian Resurrection,* Vols. I & II, London, 1911; Samuel Sharpe: *Egyptian Mythology and Egyptian Christianity,* London, 1863; Alexandre Moret, *Kings and Gods of Egypt,* New York, 1912.

In matters of religion, *The Egyptian Book of the Dead* is still the most influential book in history. It has influenced religious thought from the ancient times to the present. Ideas from this book still serve as the foundations for the creation of new religious knowledge and beliefs around the world. For example, in 1835, this was the book that the Englishman Michael Chandler sold along with some Ancient Egyptian mummies to early leaders of the Church of the Latter Day Saints in America. It was this book that Joseph Smith, the then leader of this Church, translated and proclaimed to his Church that it was a hitherto unknown holy work written by Abraham himself (see F. M. Brodie, *No Man Knows My History: The Life of Joseph Smith, the Mormon Prophet,* 1945). Joseph Smith's translation of this book is still influential in the Church of the Latter Day Saints, yet not many people in this Church would know or perhaps acknowledge today that this work was from the minds and imaginations of the black people that were the Ancient Egyptians.

I have stated and perhaps restated that in human history, no other group of humans ever developed the concept of theosophy to as high a spiritual and practical level as the Ancient Egyptians. Every modern religion including Christianity is nothing but an offshoot and adaptation of Ancient Egyptian concepts of theosophy and Godliness.

What then is theosophy? Theosophy was the foundational concept of religion. According to *Webster's Third New International Dictionary of the English Language Unabridged,* theosophy is " a body of doctrine relating to deity, cosmos, and self and held to rest on direct intuitions of supersensible reality by preternaturally perceptive individuals and to give wisdom superior to that of historical religion or empirical philosophy or science by which the initiate can master nature and guide his destiny." In terms of its practice, it is also "a system of often occult and esoteric thought presented as a means of individual salvation and sometimes associated with mysticism, pantheism, or magic." The works of scholars of Egyptology confirm that the earliest theosophical thoughts and practices were Ancient Egypt in origin. In the beginning therefore was Ancient Egypt.

The earliest preternaturally perceptive humans that first conceived a "body of doctrine relating to deity, cosmos, and self for the purpose of mastering nature and guiding their destinies" were the Ancient Egyptians. The earliest system of "occult and esoteric thought used as a means of salvation, and practiced through mysticism, pantheism, and magic" emerged in Ancient Egypt. It is a great irony how things have turned out today because just yesterday, a magician who was revealing some secrets of magic on television acknowledged the origin of magical practices in Ancient Egypt. As I have pointed out, it was from these foundations that the concepts of all religions emerged. The presence of Ancient Egypt in matters of the religions of the world can therefore not be denied, distorted, or avoided.

I believe this was the reason and perhaps the most powerful reason the *Afrim* scholars of the Bible in Alexandria admitted in the biblical documents that their ancestors had earlier gone to live in Ancient Egypt. I believe this admission was intended to give the concepts and documents they were passing on to the Greeks as their own some credibility. Otherwise, they would have done everything to avoid being related to Ancient Egypt in every way they could since they tried all kinds of ways to mask this relationship in the biblical narrative. It is for this reason that the Jewish people have refused up to today to reveal who they were before they became Jews and Hebrews, where they came from, and what language they spoke in their place of origin. Revealing any of these would easily give them away.

51

The *Afrim* scholars of the Bible also wanted the Greeks and Europeans to believe that the theosophical ideas and documents of the Bible were their original ideas and documents. This would have been difficult to believe since these same people claim that their ancestors went to live in Ancient Egypt for four hundred years. To make their claim of the creation of the biblical documents a little more credible, these scholars had to find a way to disassociate themselves from mainstream Ancient Egyptian religious ideas. So the scholars wrote that they lived in Ancient Egypt but they were not part of the mainstream of Ancient Egypt thought because they were slaves that lived in a separate geographical area from the rest of Ancient Egyptians, but that was not true. They were not slaves in Ancient Egypt, they were Ancient Egyptians.

The creation of religion and the concept of Gods in Ancient Egypt

Today, the name of God is a household word in every religion and language around the world. Even people that do not believe in God and religion have the concept of God in the recesses of their minds and disbeliefs. Most Christians do not know how this God came to be because the apostolic fathers of Christianity never wanted it to be known that the foundational concept of God was conceived by the black people that were the Ancient Egyptians.

Most European scholars have long known that black Africans created the concept of religion and God. However, not many have had the courage and honesty to credit these black Africans with such creation. At least, one scholar credited the Africans with creating the concept of religion and he did so powerfully. In the frontispiece to *Was Jesus Christ a Negro?* ... Dr Curtis Alexander quoted Peter Eckler as saying:

> That an *imaginative and superstitious race of black men* should have invented and founded, in the dim obscurity of past ages, a system of religious belief that still enthralls the minds and clouds the intellects of the leading representatives of modern theology – that still clings to the thoughts and tinges with it potential influence the literature and faith of the civilized and cultured nations of Europe and America, is indeed a strange illustration of the mad caprice of destiny, of the insignificant and apparently trivial causes that oft produce the most grave and momentous results – Peter Eckler (emphasis mine).

Peter Eckler points out that a group of ancient imaginative and superstitious people created a system of religion that still mystifies the greatest religious minds of the civilized world today. Guess who these ancient imaginative and superstitious people were? They were black people. What is worthy of note in this quotation is that Peter Eckler was a Jew. His are the people that have claimed before Europeans that they created the concepts of religion and Godliness for over two thousand years. However, he knew better. This quotation is therefore like a confession, as he wonders how such a great invention could have come to black people, a race of superstitious but imaginative people. However, it was because black people were superstitious and imaginative that they invented the concept of religion and Godliness. It was the foundational concept of religion that these superstitious and imaginative black people conceived, so it should mystify leading representatives of modern theology who acquired their foundational knowledge of theology from the foundational concept of these black people.

For religion and Godliness, the Ancient Egyptian did more. To bring the principles of the universe they had observed to human levels of reality, these Ancient Egyptians devised ways of humanizing, personifying, and representing these principles in physical realities. From the humanization of these principles emerged one supreme controller, a monotheist God the *Akan* people that created this concept in Ancient Egypt called *Onyame* [God]. Note this word carefully because later European scholars that went to Africa to research religion among the *Akan* people came out believing that the Christian word *Yahweh* was derived from a corruption of this *Akan* word for God.

Among modern *Akan* people, the descendants of the ancient people that first conceived this idea, the name *Onyame* for God was in reference to the one that filled his recipients with every form of satisfaction, an apt epithet for the earliest concept of God. This perception of God as one who satisfies those who receive him is still the perception and description of God in Christianity and many other religions. *Onyame* was the supreme Ancient Egyptian God that lived high above humans. Before this God came to live in the sky, he was first located on the pinnacle at the top of the pyramid to give him oversight advantage. The oversight advantage of this God was what eventually developed into the all-seeing all-knowing characteristic nature of the Christian God. From his abode atop the pyramid, this God became the *Osoro* God. Among the *Akan* people of Ancient Egypt, the mention of the word *Osoro* was a reference to the sky god. So this God came to be known as *Osoro* [Greek transposition - *Osiris*]. This was the perception and the abode of the God the *Afrim* people took away when they were leaving Ancient Egypt into the biblical Exodus. This was the reason Moses always saw and met this God on top of hills and in mountains in the desert where there were no pyramids. It was also the reason the Ten Commandments came from a mountain, Mount Sinai, not because it was a special holy mountain as we were taught in Sunday school in childhood (see *Exodus* 32, 33, 34).

Origin of angels and the hierarchy of the nature of Godliness

The Ancient Egyptians' perception of the supreme God was based upon their hierarchy of kingship in which there was a pharaoh below who were lower kings. Below these lower kings were chieftains, royal court advisors, helpers, and servants. The Ancient Egyptians reasoned that if the pharaoh, the representative of God on earth had such a supporting staff then the supreme God he represented must also have a supporting staff. This led to the imagination and creation of a divine supporting staff that came to include the "incorporeal beings that were lesser gods and messengers that fulfilled this supreme God's wishes and words." The Ancient Egyptians therefore humanized this God. Our modern belief in other participants in the reality of the Christian God and angels developed from this foundational perception of God and his divine and yet humanized supporting staff. This ancient pyramidal perception of a supreme God and other participants in the reality of this God also became the fundamental perception of God in Christianity and almost every religion, thanks to the Ancient Egyptians.

For example, in the practices and beliefs of Christianity, there is the concept of a supreme sky God that is derived from the same concept of the Ancient Egyptian god *Osoro* [*Osiris*]. The *Afrim* scholars of the Bible designed the supreme God of Christianity to fit into the same hierarchy as the supreme God of Ancient Egypt. It is important to note that the Ancient Egyptians did not have only a male sky God, they also had a female god called *Asaase* [*Isis*] to complement the male-female dichotomy, and also to complete their humanization of this God. With the male – female dichotomy in place, Ancient Egyptian Gods had "wives," and they produced children. It was through this Ancient Egyptian perception of God that the Christianity also came to have a God that could have a child.

Based upon the same Ancient Egyptian pyramidal perception of God, the Christian God was designed to have other gods or spirits [incorporeal beings] below him. Today, this imagined God is believed to have had a son, a real human called Jesus, who is perceived to be a participant in the reality of the perception of the Christian God. This Christian perception of the reality of God also includes a Holy Ghost, and there are angels [more incorporeal beings] that are all part of the reality of Christian "Godness." Alongside the Ancient Egyptian male-female dichotomy and perception of God, Christianity also had to have a woman in its perception of the Christian God. So the supposed mother of the Son of God became a part of the dimensional reality of the earliest Christian God. Why did the creation of a female participant in Christian Godness become necessary? The earliest introduction of a female God into the Christian reality of God was simply designed to complement the original Ancient Egyptian concept of *Osoro* [*Osiris*] and *Asaase* [*Isis*], the original male and female Gods that were created in Ancient Egypt. *Isis* was the wife of

53

Osiris and though the Christian God was not the husband of the mother of Jesus, he still had a child with her to fit him into the Ancient Egyptian reality of Godness. How did all these Ancient Egyptian ideas come to be the foundational ideas of Christianity? The answer is simple. The Greeks for whom the documents of the Bible were first translated knew of these ideas and perceptions of God and religion in Ancient Egypt. Therefore any deviation from these ideas and perceptions in translation would not have been acceptable to them so the Jewish scholars had to include all these Ancient Egyptian ideas to give the translation of the documents credibility.

All of these creations in Christianity were therefore nothing but variations and adaptations of Ancient Egyptian perceptions of this God in the form of a pyramidal polytheism. Unfortunately, Christians were not supposed to know this because the early apostolic fathers believed that the truth would undermine their faiths. The fact that Ancient Egypt was the fountainhead of religious thought and practice in this world was therefore not in doubt among early Christians. This was part of the reason the Catholic Church used to portray the God Christ and his mother in their real black ethnic and racial characteristics.

In modern scholarship, historians, Egyptologists, archaeologists, and even some biblical scholars have found that Ancient Egypt was the fountainhead of religion. Most scholars of Ancient Egyptian history have confirmed that the foundations of theosophy in this world originated from Ancient Egyptian thoughts and imagination. For some works of modern scholars whose works have confirmed the origin of religion in Ancient Egypt see Morenz, S. (1973): *Egyptian Religion*; Hornung, E. (1983): *Conceptions of God in Ancient Egypt: the one and the many*; Assman, J. (1984): *Theologie und Frommigkeit einer fruhen Hochkultur* (Theology and theosophy: An earlier high culture); Allen, J. P. (1991), *Religion and philosophy in Ancient Egypt*; Quirke, S. (1992) *Ancient Egyptian Religion*.

In *The Story of Civilization: Our Oriental Heritage*, Will Durant wrote this about Ancient Egypt and the foundations of religion showing that in Ancient Egypt, religion was everything:

> For beneath and beyond everything [in Ancient Egypt] was religion. We find it there in every stage and form from totemism to theology: We see its influence in literature, in government, in art, in everything except morality. ... We cannot understand the Ancient Egyptian – or man – until we study his gods (1935, p. 197).

European scholars who know and have the courage to tell the truth have also acknowledged that Ancient Egyptian religious concepts and sacramental practices were what the Jewish scholars passed on to the Greeks for them to become the foundations of Christian beliefs and practices. Durant stated further that:

> What distinguished this [Ancient Egyptian] religion above everything else was its emphasis on immortality. If Osiris, the Nile, and all vegetation might rise again so might man. The amazing preservation of the dead body in the dry soil of Egypt lent some encouragement to this belief, *which was to dominate Egyptian faith for thousands of years, and to pass from it, by its own resurrection, into Christianity* (1935, p. 202; see also earlier works like Briffault, R. 1927, v. 3, p. 205; Diodorus, Siculus, 1933, I, lxxxviii, 1-3; Howard, Clifford, 1933, p. 79; Tod, Lt. Col. Jas, 1894, p. 570, emphasis mine).

It is important to note in this quotation that Durant also pointed out that Ancient Egyptian concepts of religion, death, resurrection, and immortality were the same ideas that resurrected to become the foundational concepts of Christianity.

What is revealing here is that it was to this ancient nation of Egypt, that had developed theosophy to the highest degree on earth, that the *Afrim* people claim to have gone to live for four hundred and thirty years. Yet, they claim that they never learned anything about religion from the Ancient Egyptians and they never took any of the religious ideas they passed on to Europeans from Ancient Egypt. What is sad about this is that it has become the reality and truth of biblical study, but that is all part of the *legendary lying lore*.

Because the *Afrim* people supposedly first went to live in Ancient Egypt, left Egypt in the biblical Exodus, and then returned to Ancient Egypt to compile, rewrite, edit, and translate the documents that became the foundational documents of the Christian Bible and Christianity, it is imperative that we examine in detail where the *Afrim* people got their religious ideas.

Afrim people and the God of Christianity

Did the *Afrim* people know of the concept of God they passed on to the Greeks before they supposedly went to Ancient Egypt? Biblical writings do not fully support the assertion that these people knew of any concept of God before they went to Ancient Egypt. In some parts of the Bible, such an assertion is made but in other parts of the same Bible, such an assertion is refuted by the content of the narrative. Of course, the reality of knowing this God before going to Ancient Egypt was different from the reality of writing and claiming over a thousand years later that one's ancestors knew of this God before they went to Ancient Egypt. Even the reality of writing to claim that the ancestors of the *Afrim* people knew of God before they went to Ancient Egypt came to *Afrim* scholars of the Bible in Ancient Egypt.

In the first chapter, I revealed that the core groups of ancient *Afrim* people that later became the Jews and Hebrews in Europe were originally from *Akan* and other African tribes that were the Ancient Egyptians. What this means is that whichever way one looks at it, the concepts of the documents that became the foundations of the Bible and European Christianity were African. I have also pointed out that these concepts were specifically *Akan* in origin. What is most intriguing about the creation of the biblical documents in Ancient Egypt is that if the *Afrim* scholars of the Bible knew of these concepts and had supporting documents with them in their sojourn in other lands, they could have compiled, rewritten, and translated the documents of the Bible anywhere into any language before coming to Ancient Egypt to translated the documents they found there into Greek.

What do all these say about the origin of the documents of the Bible? Could the fact that Ancient Egypt had a long history of development of religious philosophy and a large repository of religious documents have been what made it possible for *Afrim* scholars to compile and translate the documents of the Bible in Egypt? Does this reveal that the documents the *Afrim* scholars compiled, rewrote, and translated into the Bible in Ancient Egypt were not original religious documents of the *Afrim* people? This may only be the foundation of the revelations in this book because there is more to come.

What seems to have thrown Europeans off the track of the origin of the Bible must have been the claim of the *Afrim* people that the God they introduced to the Greeks and Europeans was their God. They claimed that their ancestors had an intimate knowledge of and communication with this God before they went to Ancient Egypt, yet evidence in the Bible contradicts this claim.

There is evidence in the Bible to show that the *Afrim* people that supposedly left Egypt in the so-called biblical Exodus did not have any knowledge of and communication with this God before they went to Ancient Egypt. The most important evidence contradicting *Afrim* people' claim of having a God and an intimate knowledge of this God comes from the fact that they did not take this intimate knowledge of and communication with their God to Ancient Egypt. Why would they not? The answer is because they did not have such knowledge then. If they took this God and knowledge of him to Ancient Egypt, they would have had their knowledge of this God and communication with him still while leaving Ancient Egypt, but the evidence does not show such knowledge.

The Bible itself reveals that instead, they were the Ancient Egyptians that had a God and an intimate knowledge and communication with this God. For example, when this God supposedly wanted to deliver the *Afrim* people from the enslavement of the Ancient Egyptians, he did not ask an *Afrim* person. Why would a God of the *Afrim* people, a God they claimed to have had intimate knowledge and communication with not ask one of them to deliver his own people from bondage in Ancient Egypt? According to the Bible, this God supposedly appeared before an Ancient Egyptian called *Moses* and asked him to deliver the *Afrim* people from Ancient Egypt. Why would a God the *Afrim* people claim to have known before going to Ancient Egypt seek the deliverance of these people through an Ancient Egyptian this God supposedly did not know?

Is it not intriguing that throughout the supposed deliverance of the *Afrim* people from Ancient Egypt, this God never appeared before any of the *Afrim* people? He appeared only before Moses, the Ancient Egyptian. It was Moses that this God supposedly sent before Pharaoh. Why did this God not send an *Afrim* person? Here is another intriguing aspect of *Afrim* people's claim of having a God and knowing this God before they went to Ancient Egypt. Even when Moses told the *Afrim* people that this God had appeared to him and asked him to take them out of Ancient Egypt, the *Afrim* people did not believe him. This was because they did not have any knowledge of this God, they did not know of any God, and they had no intimate knowledge and communication with any God. In *Exodus* 2:14, the *Afrim* people asked Moses who made him the "prince and a judge" over them. Would a people that had a God and had an intimate knowledge of this God ask this question if a priest came to tell them that this God has asked him to save them from "slavery" and "bondage?" The question here is how did Moses know of this God but the people that later became the *Afrim* people did not know of him?

Throughout the Exodus narrative, this God appeared only before Moses. Why? In *Exodus* 33:11, the Bible says: "And the Lord spake unto Moses face by face, as a man speaketh unto his friend." How would Moses the Ancient Egyptian become the friend of the God of the *Afrim* people, a God they had known and had communication with before they went to Ancient Egypt? Who knew and was the friend of this God, was it the *Afrim* people or the Ancient Egyptians?

It was Moses alone that this God supposedly asked to meet on the mountain in the Sinai desert. In fact, this God did something that showed clearly that he did not know the *Afrim* people as they later claimed over one thousand years later. Not only did this God show that he did not know the *Afrim* people, but he also showed that he did not want the *Afrim* people near him. As a result, this God told Moses emphatically that: "And no man shall come up with thee, neither let any man be seen throughout the mount; neither let the flocks nor herds feed before that mount" (Exodus 34:3).

In this biblical verse, this God stated emphatically that he did not want any of the *Afrim* people near the mountain on which he was going to communicate with Moses. What is even more intriguing and revealing at the same time is that not only did this God not want any of the *Afrim* people near the mountain where he was going to meet Moses, but also this God did not even want the sheep, goats, and cows of the *Afrim* people grazing near that mountain at the time of his meeting with Moses. Why? Yet, these are the people that claimed to Europeans over a thousand years later that the God they introduced to them was their God and they had had an intimate knowledge and communication with this God since ancient times. They also told Europeans that they were the children of this God, and Europeans believed them. In support of all these, the early apostolic fathers designed stories and explanations of blind and unquestioning faith to support this *legendary lying lore*.

It was Moses and Moses alone that this God decided to give the Ten Commandments that were supposed to be the laws of living for his "children." What kind of father would not directly give his laws of living to his own "children," but would pass these laws through a supposed total stranger? Does this suggest truthfully that the *Afrim* people knew of this God, and does this confirm that they were the children of this God? Does it also show that these were the kind of people that could have written such elaborate dissertations about this God as they were presented in the biblical narrative? Readers would better understand this analysis when they find out that Moses was not a Jew.

Who was Moses?

One of the greatest assumptions in Christianity has been the fact that because Moses was supposedly chosen to deliver the Jewish people from Ancient Egypt, he must have been a Jew, but that was completely false. In support of this assumption, one of the greatest secrets kept in the *legendary lying lore* of the biblical story has been the fact that Moses was not a Jew. He must have been an *Afrim* because he supposedly left Ancient Egypt with the groups of people in the Exodus, but he was not a Jew. At this point, I must explain the difference between the *Akan* and other African tribes that left Ancient Egypt in the so-called Exodus and the group from these tribes that went to Europe to become the Jews and Hebrews.

Historians know that before the biblical Exodus, there were no humans known as Jews or Hebrews anywhere on earth. What happened is that after this group had gone to Europe to become the Jews and Hebrews, they turned round to confer their new names and identity onto the original *Akan* and other African tribal groups that left Ancient Egypt into the Exodus. This is the reason these people identify themselves as Jews but they still carry *Akan* and other African tribal names. From this revelation, it becomes clear that Moses was not a Jew because there were no Jews in his days, he did not originate from any Jewish tribe, and the people he led out of Ancient Egypt were not Jews or Hebrews either. These people were from the black people of Ancient Egypt that later moved into inner Africa to become the Africans.

From several pieces of writings, it is evident that most western scholars know about the *legendary lying lore* surrounding the Jewish people, the Bible, and Christianity. It is also evident that most of these scholars have tried not to reveal anything that would undermine the veracity of any of these, perhaps from fear of the power of the Church. In the *Encyclopaedia Britannica*, scholars of Jewish history wrote expressing their own doubts about what they were writing that:

> The central figure of the Exodus (13th century B. C.) and of the wandering in the desert is Moses, whose life story recorded in the Bible reads like an epic. In the consciousness of the Hebrews and the Jews at all times, Moses is the great liberator, leader, lawgiver, man of God, and "father of the prophets." Although no external evidence proves that such a man lived, the subsequent history of Israel cannot be conceived without Moses, and his existence must be taken as a fact (1996, p. 72).

This is an interesting quotation because it says in other words that there is no evidence that a man called Moses ever lived. However, the writers argue that we should believe that a man called Moses lived because he is in the consciousness of the Hebrew people and also because he is the central figure in the history of the Jewish people. In other words, without Moses, there will be no foundation to the history of the Hebrew people therefore we should acknowledge that such a man lived to make Hebrew history possible. Again in other words, the writers suggest that, because Moses has existed in the consciousness of the Hebrews and Jews, and because the real history of the Jewish people is woven around him, the fictional and epic-like stories of this man's life must be taken as facts. This, however, is understandable because Moses is the center of Jewish people's historical universe. However, there are fictional characters that have found their ways into the consciousness of millions around the world. Should we accept them as real characters too? There is no other group of people whose historical existence is entirely woven around one human as the story of Jewish people and Moses. The question is who was this Moses? What if the life of this Moses was fabricated to make the fabrication of the history of the Jewish people possible? Should we accept these also as facts?

Writing on the *Exodus* that made Moses "the central figure, leader, lawgiver, man of God, and the father of the prophets" of the Jewish people, the scholars of Jewish history further wrote in the *Britannica* that:

> Stripped of legendary embellishments, such as the Ten Plagues, the miraculous crossing of the Red Sea, and the Revelation in Mt. Sinai, the historicity of the Exodus is vouched for by the

psychological impress it left on the consciousness of the Hebrews and Jews. The Exodus became the cornerstone of Jewish history, religion, and nationhood (1996, p. 72).

This quotation is also quite interesting because if the *Afrim* people supposedly went to Ancient Egypt from Ur of the Chaldees, as the Bible claims then leaving Ancient Egypt should not have been the foundation of their history, religion, and nationhood. The foundation of their history, religion, and nationhood should have began from where they originated before they went to Ancient Egypt. All of these confirm my revelation of the true origin of the people that left Ancient Egypt to live in Canaan, and later went to Europe to become the Jews and Hebrews. According to their biblical claims of origin, these people should have had a history, religion, and a nation before they went to Ancient Egypt. They did not have any of these before they supposedly went to Ancient Egypt because they did not go to Ancient Egypt from anywhere. They were Ancient Egyptians. Because all of the biblical claims surrounding the origin of the *Afrim* people were lies, historians have found out that the *Afrim* people acquired the foundations of their history, religion, and nationhood from leaving Ancient Egypt and not before going there. In other words, the *Afrim* did not go to Ancient Egypt from anywhere before they left there.

In the quotation above, the scholars of *Britannica* were saying in the nicest way possible that the legend of the biblical Ten Plagues is just that, a myth. They also assert that the myth of the miraculous crossing of the Red Sea that Hollywood has propagated to the world more than the Bible has, was just fiction, and the so-called revelation and reception of the Ten Commandments on Mt. Sinai was also a hoax. However, because all of these were in the minds and imaginations of the *Afrim* people, the *Exodus* and its embellished legends led to the creation of the history, religion, and nation of the *Afrim* people. The question is if the Jewish scholars of the biblical documents could create such fantastic stories about plagues, crossing an entire sea, and receiving commandments from God, why should we accept the legend of Moses that "reads like an epic?" This is what western historians and biblical scholars have written about Moses and the Exodus. However, there is an African version that has never been known and that is what I have been seeking to tell from the beginning of this work.

The fact that these scholars point out that "the Exodus became the cornerstone of *Afrim* history, religion, and nationhood" has serious implications worth noting. It simply means that the people that left in the biblical Exodus had no history of their own before the Exodus. They had no religion of their own before the Exodus, and they had no nation of their own before the Exodus. How could a people that just left Ancient Egypt and supposedly originated from Ur of the Chaldees have no nation of their own? The answer is what I have stated above that they did not go to Ancient Egypt from anywhere. They were Ancient Egyptians from the *Akan* and other African tribes that were the Ancient Egyptians. All of these confirm that the people that left Ancient Egypt in the so-called biblical Exodus were Ancient Egyptians who had no separate history from Ancient Egyptian history. They had no different religion from the Ancient Egyptian religion they knew, and they had no other and belonged to no other nation than Ancient Egypt. Aren't these obvious? Otherwise, how could even the so-called patriarchs of the *Afrim* people have had *Akan* names? How could the so-called Jews and Hebrews that supposedly left in the biblical Exodus have named their God and nation in the *Akan* language? How could the people of the Exodus have carried *Akan* and other African tribal names to this day and not carry any evidence of their origin from any other place or tribes anywhere in the Middle East or for that matter anywhere else in the world?

I have already revealed that the people that left Ancient Egypt in the biblical Exodus were mostly *Akan* people joined by other African tribal groups. This confirms that the people that left in the so-called biblical Exodus were black Africans. However, it also means that the people that left in the Exodus were in tribes. Scholars of Jewish history in the *Britannica* also confirm the fact that people that the people that left Ancient Egypt into the Exodus were several different tribes. They point out that the tribal groups that left Ancient Egypt in the biblical Exodus fought and conquered "much of Canaan west of the Jordan." They wrote:

> Modern scholars believe that Canaan was conquered by tribal groups who made several independent and uncoordinated incursions during the 13th century B. C. (1996, p. 72).

Again here is something for interesting discussion. According to the biblical narrative, there is no evidence or mention that before the *Afrim* people supposedly went to Ancient Egypt they were made up of tribes. The only mention was that the family of Jacob numbering seventy men went to Egypt. The family of Jacob was not a tribe, it was just a family. This means this family must have belonged to a larger group of people that was the tribe. If these people were not tribes before they supposedly went to Ancient Egypt how, where, and when did they become the tribes that went into the Exodus to conquer Canaan? Who were these tribes, where did these tribes originate, and where are these tribes now? They were the *Akan* and other African tribes that I have already introduced. These tribes can be located mostly in West Africa. Apart from such a revelation that the Jewish people would not want the world to know, what would be the reason for the Jews and Hebrews to refuse to reveal where they originated, the tribes from which they originated, where these tribes can be located today, and the language these tribes spoke in ancient times or continue to speak today? The revelation of the *Akan* and African tribal names the Jewish people have carried with them until now will not only confirm all these but also it will reveal the particular African tribal groups that joined the dominant *Akan* group in the so-called biblical Exodus.

From what I know about Moses and the Exodus narrative, I do not believe the biblical story and its embellishments about him. However, I would like to discuss some pertinent issues in western scholastic analysis of the issues surrounding Moses only as an academic exercise. One of the greatest secrets Christianity has kept alongside the secret of the African racial and ethnic heritage of the *Afrim* people has been the racial and ethnic background of Moses. The impression the biblical documents and their interpretations have created is that the people that left Ancient Egypt in the Exodus were Jews and that Moses who supposedly led them into the Exodus was also a Jew, but that is all false. I have already explained that these people were some people before they became Jews and Hebrews in Europe, and that they were black people whose racial, ethnic, and tribal heritage is in the black tribes we find in Africa today.

Until most recently, western scholars did not discuss Moses for fear of revealing one of the greatest secrets the early apostolic fathers did not want Christian masses to know and thereby offending the Church. Since the Second World War, some more western scholars have shied away from discussing Moses and the truth behind the doctrines and practices of Christianity and Judaism for fear of being perceived as anti-Semites. I am not a Semite and I cannot be anti-Semite because I am of the same blood. As I have already pointed out, *Moses was not a Jew. Moses was an Ancient Egyptian.* Though most scholars have never wanted to discuss Moses openly, they have long known that he was not a Jew. The fact that Moses was not a Jew is very significant to the discussion of the Bible because the *Afrim* people derive their religious, historical, and national metamorphosis from who they were to who they became from Moses. Moses is the central personality in Judaism, and if he was not a Jew then the entire biblical story and its claims open up for serious discussion and questioning.

From what western scholars have known about Moses, the focus of discussion has not been on whether Moses was a Jew or not. The focus of scholastic discussion has been on finding out who he was since it has long been established among scholars who know that he was not a Jew. Among modern scholars to openly discuss the ethnic origin of Moses was C. O. Ward. In *Ancient Lowly*, Ward pointed out that the name Moses was Ancient Egyptian, and not an *Afrim* name. He hypothesized that the name might have been a shortened version of the Ancient Egyptian royal name *Ahmose* (see 1907, v. 2, p. 76).

Early Christians and most western scholars were never in doubt that Moses was not a Jew. In *The Natural Genesis: A Book of the Beginnings*, Gerald Massey revealed that the indigenous name of Moses was *Osarsiph*. Historians confirm that this name was first revealed by *Manetho,* an Ancient Egyptian priest of the 3rd century B. C. This name was taken up by Jewish historian Josephus, and through him and early Hellenized Jewish scholars, this indigenous name traveled to Europe. Early scholars accepted the ancient revelation of the ethnic name and identity of Moses and the fact that he was not a Jew. However, recently, Jewish scholars who have found out that without Moses their religious, historical, and biblical stories fall apart have sought to deny that he was not a Jew.

In an earlier discussion, I revealed that the name Joseph and Josephus were derived from the *Akan* name *Osafo.* I would also like to point out here that the indigenous name of Moses, *Osarsiph*, was also a Greek corruption of an indigenous *Akan* name. This *Akan* name was *Asaase* meaning earth. Even today, there are numerous *Akan* men and some men from the other African tribes that were with the *Akan* people in Ancient Egypt with the name *Asaase*. We first met this word in the discussion of the *Akan* Gods *Osoro* and *Asaase* in Ancient Egypt. We will meet the name in further discussions because this was also the *Akan* name of the goddess of Earth who was believed to have been born on Thursday. As a result, this earth Goddess was known and she is still known among the *Akan* people today as *Asaase Yaa.*

The name *Asaase* was not an unusual *Akan* name in Ancient Egypt because there were several Ancient Egyptian pharaohs whose names were *Asaase* or included the name *Asaase*. In Egyptology, it is the *Akan* name *Asaase* that has been orthographically transposed to *Isesi.* For example, the indigenous *Akan* name of the pharaoh *Djekara-Isesi* of the 5th dynasty is *Djakari Asaase*. This pharaoh and *Akenten* [Akhenaten] originated from the same royal line and tribe. Their modern descendants are the *Denkyira* people who can be found today in Ghana in West Africa.

Among modern scholars who spent a great deal of time and effort trying to find out who Moses was, was Sigmund Freud. The famous psychoanalyst spent part of his lifetime researching into the Moses mystery and how a supposed outsider came to be the social and political leader and religious fountainhead of the *Afrim* people. In his book *Moses and Monotheism,* Freud speculated that Moses must have been perhaps an Ancient Egyptian noble who followed the *Atenist* beliefs of *Akenten* [Akhenaten]. Again, what is interesting to note here is that Freud was a Jew who knew that Moses was not a Jew.

According to Gary Greenberg in The Moses Mystery... Freud equated *Akenten's* supposed worship of the *Aten* cult with *Adonai,* one of the earliest Hebrew names for God. I have already revealed that the people that left in the biblical Exodus were mostly *Akan* people joined by other African tribal groups and that they named no less an important character as their God in the *Akan* language. It is therefore interesting for me to reveal more in support of the revelations in this book that the word *Adonai* that western scholars have believed and claimed to be a Hebrew word was not originally Hebrew. This word got into the Greek language as *Adonis.* However, the word *Adonai* was derived from the *Akan* word *Adona* meaning the rare and lovable one. Semantically, that is an apt epithet for God.

What is interesting in Freud's equation of *Akenten's Aten* with the *Afrim* people's *Adonai* is that Freud acknowledged and traced the origin of the concept of monotheism to Ancient Egypt, specifically to *Akenten*, and not the *Afrim* people. Freud also discounted modern *Afrim* people's claims that it was God that chose Moses [an outsider] to lead the *Afrim* people by suggesting that Moses himself must have decided to lead the *Afrim* people out of his sympathy for their plight in Ancient Egypt.

The incredulity of the place of Moses as the spiritual leader of the Jewish people in the biblical story is also the focus of discussion in Gary Greenberg's *The Moses Mystery: The African Origin of the Jewish People.* In this book, Greenberg also perceived the biblical story through the prism of Ancient Egypt and found out what Christian Europe has always feared would come out one day as he pointed out that:

1. Moses served as chief priest in Akhenaten's cult and, after Akhenaten's death, had to flee Egypt to avoid execution.

2. Pharaoh Horemheb waged a bitter campaign to eradicate all vestiges of Akhenaten's heresy, eliminating the evidence stone by stone and word by word. As a result, Akhenaten remained lost to history until nineteenth century Egyptologists discovered ruins of his capital city.

3. When Horemheb died, Moses returned to Egypt, united his followers with other enemies of Egypt, and attempted to seize the throne of Ramesses I. The coup failed, but to avoid a civil war, Moses and his allies were allowed safe passage out of Egypt. This was the real Exodus (see 1996, summary on flap jacket).

The most important point in this discussion is that Moses was an Ancient Egyptian, may be a prince, or an important member of the royal family. That is how he could challenge the throne of Ramesses. An aspect of this explanation that seems to justify such an account could be possible is that from their names, it is clear that Moses and Ramesses were from different tribes, and as it was in Ancient Egyptian history, different tribal groups fought and took over power at different times creating the numerous historical differences and periods scholars have identified in Ancient Egyptian history. Moses was not an *Afrim,* and the people that left in the Exodus were Ancient Egyptians. That challenges and questions the two-thousand-year-old lore of the source from where the biblical documents originated. It is no accident that in all the analysis, the evidence points to Ancient Egypt.

Moses and the so-called Afrim people's God

The *Afrim* people that followed the Bible into Europe to become the Jews and Hebrews told Christian Europe that their religion and God were different from the Ancient Egyptian religion and God, and Europeans believed them. From this, Christian Europe turned around and classified Ancient Egyptian and black African religion and God as a pagan. This classification became Christian Europe's justification for the enslavement of Africans beginning in the 15th century. The question is were the God and religion the *Afrim* people passed on to Europeans different from the Ancient Egyptian God and religion that later became the African God and religion? Did the *Afrim* people even create this God and religion as they claimed before Europeans? There are numerous events and quotations in the biblical documents that confirm that it was the same God and religion of Ancient Egypt that the *Afrim* people simply passed on to the Greeks in Europe, and it was the same God and religion that the modern descendants of the Ancient Egyptians took to Africa.

Among these reasons, I have already pointed out that this God would not speak to or act through the very *Afrim* people who claimed later to have known him intimately. Why would *Afrim* people's God seek to communicate to them through a supposed pagan prince from Ancient Egypt? Though Exodus 33:11 contradicts 20-23, it was to Moses alone that God appeared and spoke to in the formative years of the Jewish people when they had "no history, religion, or nation." Why did the God the *Afrim* people claimed to have known so well never appear before them or speak to them during the Exodus? It is clear that it was not the *Afrim* people that knew this God. It was the Ancient Egyptians whose God he was that knew this God intimately and the biblical story of the Exodus confirms this. Without an Ancient Egyptian who knew and could communicate with this God, the *Afrim* people would never have been "saved" from "slavery" in Ancient Egypt.

Remember that these biblical stories were written over a thousand years after the events they described had supposedly happened. As a result, the Alexandrian Jewish scholars who rewrote and translated the documents of the Old Testament for the Greeks had the time to imagine and change the stories to embellish the historical foundations of the Jewish people instead of the Ancient Egyptians whose God and religion they really were.

Europeans have never known the biblical truth in over two thousand years; however, some modern African tribes have known this truth for over three. What do all these mean to the claim that the *Afrim* people are the children of God? If this were true, which father would only appear and speak to his children through a total stranger? In Africa, we know that the *Afrim* people are our people. We know the tribes from which they originated. We also know that if the *Afrim* people were the children of this God then we modern descendants of the people that created this God and had the earliest intimate knowledge and communication with this God would be his closest children.

The *Afrim* people do not deny that it was Moses that taught them everything they knew about this God. In Judaism, Moses is the Messiah and not Jesus because the *Afrim* people knew that the God they claim they knew intimately was the God of the people of Moses. Since they claim not to have originated from Ancient Egypt, this God could not have been their God. However, if it was Moses, the Ancient Egyptian that taught the *Afrim* people everything they knew about this God and religion then everything they knew originated from Ancient Egypt just as the *Afrim* people themselves originated from Ancient Egypt.

The Bible reveals that the God that the *Afrim* people later claimed to have known intimately from ancient times, was the God of the Ancient Egyptians and not the God of the *Afrim* people. Again, the fact that Moses was not a Jew becomes extremely significant here because it clarifies an equally extremely important issue about this God. Seeking a way to separate themselves from the Ancient Egyptian tribes from which they originated, the *Afrim* people claimed in the Bible that they originated from the line of Abraham through his son Isaac, and grandson Jacob. In this same Bible, God himself reveals that Moses was not one of the separatist *Afrim* people that later became Jews and Hebrews in Europe. If Moses were a Jew, God would have simply introduced himself to him as "the God of Abraham, the God of Isaac, and the God of Jacob" because Moses would also have been the descendant of Abraham as the *Afrim* people later claimed. However, when God introduced himself to Moses saying: "I am the God of thy father" (Exodus 3:6), this God was not referring to the father of a Jewish person because Moses was not a Jew. This God was referring to himself as the God of the father of Moses who was an Ancient Egyptian.

Everything the Jewish people claim to have known about religion was passed down to them through Moses their religious fountainhead. Yet, this God did not refer to himself even as the God of Moses. He referred to himself as the God of the father of Moses. In this biblical verse, God was revealing that he was first and foremost the God of the father of Moses who was an Ancient Egypt and not the God of the Jewish people. This was the reason the biblical narrative went on to add "the God of Abraham, God of Isaac, and the God of Jacob" thus separating Moses from the so-called patriarchs of the *Afrim* people. If Moses were a Jew, such an introduction separating the father of Moses from the patriarchs of the *Afrim* people would not have been necessary. This God would have simply introduced himself as "the God of Abraham, the God of Isaac, and the God of Jacob." However, because Moses was not a Jew this God had to include an addendum that specifically mentioned Abraham, Isaac, and Jacob. What is even more revealing in this biblical verse is that none other than God supposedly said this and that makes it the "absolute truth." However, these are all part of the lies in the *legendary lying lore* of Christianity.

More than anything else, Exodus 3: 6 confirms that the God Moses and the Jewish people were dealing with during the Exodus was first and foremost the God of the Ancient Egyptians before he supposedly became the God of the Jewish people through their patriarch and his descendants. Why would this God be first and foremost the God of the father of Moses, the

Ancient Egyptian? This is because the Ancient Egyptian were the first people to imagine, create, and personify the theosophical concept we have come to refer to as God.

However, this was not the only time this God revealed that he was not the God of the Jewish people. In Exodus 6: 2-3, again God told Moses that though he had appeared to Abraham, Isaac, and Jacob, he never revealed his real name to these people.

> "And God spoke unto Moses, and said unto him, I am the Lord: And I appeared unto Abraham, unto Isaac, and unto Jacob, by the name of God Almighty, but by my name JE-HO-VAH was I not known to them" (Exodus 6:2-3).

First we found out that this God did not select someone from the *Afrim* people to supposedly save these people from bondage in Ancient Egypt. This God selected an Ancient Egyptian called Moses. Then we also found out in the biblical narrative that this God would not let the *Afrim* people near him. Why? Then we also found out that this God would not even let the sheep, cattle, and herd of animals of the *Afrim* people near the mountain on which he was going to meet Moses. This then becomes the worst of ridicule when the God the Jewish people claim to have known intimately through Abraham, Isaac, and Jacob did not even reveal his real name to these patriarchs. However, he revealed his real name to Moses, the Ancient Egyptian and he supposedly met and spoke to him face to face as a friend.

The Jewish people first had to claim this God as their God for them to be able to pass him on to the Greeks successfully. However, evidence in the biblical narrative disproves the claim that this God was the God of the Jewish people. What this evidence reveals is that the God the Jewish people introduced to the Greeks for him to become the Christian God was the God of the Ancient Egyptians before he became the Christian God through the Jewish scholars of the Bible in Alexandria and not through the biblical patriarchs.

I have sat and listened to a lot of preachers and what I noticed was that some of them know about the fact that this God was the God of the father of Moses, the Ancient Egyptian. As a result today, most western preachers have quietly and cleverly cut off the part of the biblical narrative that refers to the father of Moses and the Ancient Egyptians. They proclaim this God is "the God of Abraham, the God of Isaac, and the God of Jacob," but that is not the entire biblical truth because these people did not have a God. According to Exodus 6:3, these people did not even know this God. These so-called patriarchs of the Jewish worshipped the Ancient Egyptian God about whom Abraham went to Ancient Egypt to learn. This God reveals in the verses quoted above that he did not know these people as well as he knew Moses and the Ancient Egyptians.

The latest evidence confirming that Moses was not a Jew but an Ancient Egyptian came in 1998. In December 1998, Disney released a full-length cartoon feature of the life of Moses. The title of this feature was *Prince of Egypt*. The question is if Moses were a Jew how could he have become an Ancient Egyptian prince? If he were a Jew, where was the Jewish kingdom from which he became a prince? He was an Ancient Egyptian prince and not a Jew and he could not have become a prince if he were a slave as the biblical narrative asserts that the Jewish people were in Ancient Egypt. Some people seek to confer the title of a prince on Moses because he was supposedly raised by the daughter and in the house of the pharaoh. I am a member of a royal family of the *Aduana* clan of the *Akan* people, and I know that being raised in the household of royalty does not make one a prince or royalty. I also know that many people did not know what that name of the Disney cartoon feature was seeking to reveal or confirm. Most Christians must have enjoyed this movie, but I do not think they knew what the title of this movie really meant to the story and origin of the foundations of Christianity.

All of these seemingly insignificant discussions add up to what some traditional people in Africa have long known to be the biggest lie ever told. In a conversation with an elder from the *Akim Abuakwa* royal house in Ghana, he asked me this question: "so do you say that the people of

Europe do not know all these that I am telling you? What then do they know?" He was much too surprised that Europeans did not know what we in Africa have known for so long.

The pyramidal foundations of the concept of monotheism

In the preceding pages, I have discussed the nature and character of Ancient Egyptian perception and creation of the concept of God and other "spiritual" beings as part of the reality of this God. Within their perception and creation of the concept of God, the Ancient Egyptians created monotheism. However today, they are not around to defend their creation, and the Africans, their modern descendants have never been vigorous participants in such discussions in the west. As a result, some scholars in the west have argued that that the Jewish people created theosophical monotheism. Despite the fact that all evidence suggests otherwise, this claim has started a major debate as to who created the concept of monotheism.

A major characteristic of the foundations of Ancient Egyptian religion that is still the foundational characteristic of every religion in this world is the fact that Ancient Egyptian monotheism was expressed in a pyramidal polytheism. This pyramidal polytheism began from lower gods [incorporeal beings] on earth to a supreme God in the sky. This was the original significance of the pyramid in Ancient Egyptian religion before it became an unsurpassed architectural feat.

One of the most important evidence speaking for the Ancient Egyptians in their absence is in the work of Sir Wallis Budge, the most renowned Egyptologist. In *Egyptian Religion*, Sir Wallis Budge pointed out that the original Ancient Egyptian concept of God was a monotheist God. He wrote:

> A study of ancient Egyptian religious texts will convince the reader that the Egyptians believed in One God, who was self-existent, immortal, invisible, eternal, omniscient, almighty, and inscrutable, the maker of heavens, earth, and underworld, the creator of the sky and the sea, men and women, animals, and birds, fish and creeping things, trees and plants, and the incorporeal beings who were the messengers that fulfilled his wish and word (p. 17).

It was not only this monotheist God of Ancient Egypt that the Jewish scholars of the Bible in Alexandria introduced to the Greeks and Europeans but also they introduced Ancient Egyptian sacramental practices of the religion and worship of this God into Christianity. For example, Ancient Egyptian conception of the resurrection of the spirit is also found in Christianity where this concept manifests itself in belief in the coming resurrection of Jesus Christ and the worship of an already risen "Holy" Ghost. The evidence that the Jewish people took the concept of religion, its inherent monotheism, pyramidal characteristics, and its polytheistic manifestations from the Ancient Egyptians can still be found in Christianity that has copied or modified all of these into its beliefs and practices.

Even the Bible acknowledges that the religious knowledge that the Jewish people claimed to have acquired originated from Ancient Egypt. In the *New Testament*, it is stated that Ancient Egypt was the source of all religious knowledge and wisdom. The Bible also points out that Moses, the religious fountainhead of the Jewish people, who is proclaimed by them to have created monotheism was in fact "instructed in all the wisdom of the [Ancient] Egyptians. "And Moses was learned in all the wisdom of the Egyptians, and was mighty in words and in deeds" (Acts 7: 22). Here then is the crux of the debate. The Jewish people do not claim to have invented religion or the concept of monotheism as a people. They claim however that their spiritual leader, Moses, was the one that invented the concept of monotheism. However, the Bible refutes this and reveals that everything Moses knew came from the Ancient Egyptians. That goes to reveal that the concept of theosophical monotheism was invented in Ancient Egypt. So where did the religious knowledge the Jewish people passed on to Europeans originate? It originated in Ancient Egypt.

In a quotation above, Gary Greenberg went even further to point out that "Moses was a priest in *Akenten's [Akhenaten's]* cult." He also pointed out that scholars have long held the Ancient Egyptian pharaoh *Akenten [Akhenaten]* as the creator of theosophical monotheism. He wrote:

> At first his [*Akenten's*] reputation soared. Historians hailed him as "the first individual," a religious reformer, a great thinker, witness to the truth, a magnificent poet, and artistic revolutionary, and even the forerunner of Moses. But even the most aggressive advocates of a link between Moses and *Akenten* still adhered to the Semitic model of Israel's roots (p. 5).

It is important to point out that Jewish ecclesiastics and biblical scholars figured out that crediting the creation of monotheism to an Ancient Egyptian pharaoh was rather too close to revealing the source from where they took the concept and documents of religion they passed on to the Greeks and Europeans. As a result, they had to do something to claim the creation of the concept of monotheism. To do this, they approach this with an *ad hominem* strategy. They could not attack the message so they had to do something about the reputation of *Akenten*, the Ancient Egyptian pharaoh that was threatening the foundations of a two thousand-year-old lie. As a result, from nowhere, the pharaoh all historians had hailed as the creator of monotheism was discredited and disgraced to protect the image of Moses and the *legendary lying lore*. Greenberg wrote:

> In recent years *Akenten's* [Akhenaten's] luster has worn thin. Today many Egyptologists dismiss him as a voluptuary, an intellectual lightweight, an atheist, and ultimately, a maniac. They sharply reject any connection between *Akenten* [Akhenaten] and Moses (p. 6).

It is clear from the two quotations above that the debate over who created monotheism is not between western scholars and Ancient Egypt. This debate is specifically between Jewish scholars of the Bible and Ancient Egyptians who are not around to defend their creation. Greenberg pointed out that most of these scholars "adhered to the Semitic model of Israel's roots." However, from what we know in Africa about the *Akan* origin of the *Afrim* people that went to Europe to become the Jews and Hebrews, there is no Semitic model of Israel's roots. If ever there were a model of the origin of the Jewish people, it would be an African tribal model and not a fictitious Semitic model. In the discussion above, it is clear that scholars know that *Akenten* created the concept of monotheism but other scholars that need that claim to support a traditional lie have sought to destroy the name and image of *Akenten* so that they can confer his creation on their Moses.

Despite all these, honest scholarship in Egyptology does not deny the fact that *Akenten* created the concept of theosophical monotheism. In *The Dictionary of Ancient Egypt*, Ian Shaw, Paul Nicholson, and the British Museum also wrote in support of the fact that *Akenten*; the Ancient Egyptian pharaoh was the creator of the concept of theosophical monotheism. They wrote:

> Attempts have occasionally been made to equate Moses with the pharaoh *Akenten* on the grounds that the latter introduced a peculiarly Egyptian form of monotheism, but there are no other aspects of this pharaoh's life, or indeed his cult *Aten* that remotely resemble the Biblical account of Moses (see 1995, under Biblical Connections, emphasis mine).

What needs to be pointed out in this quotation is that the authors admit that *Akenten* created the concept of monotheism. It is clear that these scholars have also been influenced by the biblical tradition, so they had to add that the monotheism of *Akenten* was different from the monotheism claimed by Jewish scholars for Moses. The concept of monotheism is a concept of monotheism without any differentiation or variation. I hope these scholars did not confuse the creation of the concept of monotheism with the development of different sacramental practices for the practice of this monotheism.

Considering the central role of Moses in *Afrim* people's claims that they invented and developed monotheism, the biblical statement revealing that Moses was not even a Jew is very significant. If Moses invented Jewish people's monotheism and he was an Ancient Egyptian instructed in Ancient Egyptian religious wisdom, words, and deeds, where then did Moses get his monotheistic ideas? Where did the *Afrim* people get their religious ideas, and how could they have invented the very ideas they learned from the Ancient Egyptians through Moses? Gary Greenberg answered these questions in the quotations I cited earlier in this chapter when he wrote:

1. The first Israelites were Egyptians, followers of Pharaoh Akhenaten [*Akenten*] whose [earliest] attempts to introduce monotheism into Egypt engendered rage among the religious establishment (emphasis mine).

2. Moses served as chief priest in Akhenaten's cult and, after Akhenaten's death, had to flee Egypt to avoid execution.

3. Pharaoh Horemheb waged a bitter campaign to eradicate all vestiges of Akhenaten's heresy, eliminating the evidence stone by stone and word by word. As a result, Akhenaten remained lost to history until nineteenth century Egyptologists discovered ruins of his capital city.

There are some interesting observations in these quotations that must be brought out. In the first place, there were no first, second, or third Israelites. Simply put, all the Israelites were Ancient Egyptians and they still have their Ancient Egyptian tribal identities to prove that. The next observation in the above quotation states unequivocally that monotheism, the core concept of religion that Christianity claims is its major differentiating characteristic, was an original Ancient Egyptian concept of religion first introduced by the pharaoh *Akenten*. Gary Greenberg points out that Moses was a chief priest of *Akenten* and that means Moses learned about monotheism from *Akenten* in Ancient Egypt. This shows that Moses did not invent or create monotheism as the *Afrim* people claim he did. According to Gary Greenberg, monotheism was an Ancient Egyptian concept of religion at the time the *Afrim* people were in Ancient Egypt, and Moses who supposedly delivered the *Afrim* people from Egypt was already a chief priest of the monotheistic ideas of Ancient Egypt.

The centrality of Moses in the religious development of the *Afrim* people can be found from *Exodus* through *Leviticus* into *Numbers* where it is claimed that God spoke to Moses. Not only do the historical facts betray *Afrim* people's claims of the invention and development of monotheism, even the biblical narrative also betrays their claims of religious knowledge and intimacy with a God they did not imagine, create, personify, or even worship before they supposedly went to Ancient Egypt. This again confirms that Ancient Egyptians invented the original religious knowledge the Jewish people took as their own after they were exposed to it by Moses. In *Deceptions and Myths of the Bible*, Lloyd Graham summed it all up poignantly when he wrote that the Jewish people "were but plagiarists culling mythic artifacts they did not understand" (p. 2).

From what most western scholars know now and from the similarities found between Ancient Egyptian and biblical literature, many Egyptologists now believe that the core concept of theosophical monotheism is more Ancient Egyptian than the creation of Moses or the *Afrim* people. To these scholars, the honor of the creation of the concept of monotheism goes to *Akenten* the Ancient Egyptian pharaoh and not to his chief priest Moses. For further discussion, see James Henry Breasted, *The Development of Religion and Thought in Ancient Egypt*.

Beyond all these, there is biblical evidence showing that the *Afrim* people were not monotheists (see *Exodus 32:15-24*). In this biblical story, when Moses went up Mount Sinai supposedly to receive the Ten Commandments from the "monotheist" God, the *Afrim* people felt religiously naked without him because he was the only one who knew and could communicate with this God. To satisfy their "inner hollows" in being left without a God, the *Afrim* people asked Aaron to make them a golden calf to worship. Aaron made them a golden calf and they worshipped it. Could this have been the behavior and actions of a people that intimately knew a monotheist God as they claimed over a thousand years later?

The controversy

Despite all the biblical and historical evidence showing that the *Afrim* people did not know anything about this God and despite all the evidence showing that instead they were the Ancient Egyptians that knew this God, there is modern controversy over who created the theosophical doctrines that became European Christianity. From the prompting and deliberate misdirection of *Afrim* scholars, western historical scholarship has written Ancient Egyptians and their modern descendants into extinction. This made it possible in western scholarship for *Afrim* scholars to become the sole authority over religion. They said that the *Afrim* people created monotheism and so that is what western scholars that knew otherwise not long ago had to accept as the "absolute truth." However, that is all in defense of the *legendary lying lore* ancient *Afrim* scholars have created for the *Afrim* people..

The question then is, if the Bible, history, early, and modern scholars have all confirmed that Ancient Egypt was the original place of the creation of the foundations of theosophy, why should it be a matter of debate now? The first reason is that Europeans have never been comfortable with Ancient Egyptians being the black people they were. Most of them have practically forgotten the black origin of the Jewish people because they now look white. For these people, acknowledging the Ancient Egyptian in this matter would have major serious religious and socio-political implications.

In the first place, that would confirm that the *Afrim* people that became the Jews and Hebrews in Europe were also originally black people. This would extend onto the line of Jesus to reveal that Jesus, his mother, and all the people of the Bible were black people. This would mean the Christian God that was imagined by these black people was a black God. This would also reveal that the so-called patriarchs claimed by the Jews and Hebrews were all black people. It would also mean that this God telling Moses that he was the God of Moses' father would mean that God was first and foremost the God of the black people of Ancient Egypt before he became the God of the supposedly "white" Abraham, Isaac, and Jacob.

Christian Europe would never want Europeans to know that it has been propagating and worshipping black people and the God of the black people of Ancient Egypt. As a result, Europeans believe that it is better to support the idea that the *Afrim* people that became the Jews and Hebrews were the creators of the concepts of Christianity than acknowledge the Africans of Ancient Egypt. That was seen to be more tolerable in Europe than to admit that black people of Ancient Egypt invented the theosophical ideas that were adopted in the creation of Europe's Christianity. From this point of view, Christian Europe began propagating the idea that the *Afrim* people invented the monotheist concept in Christian religion therefore they invented the doctrines of European Christianity. They encouraged the *Afrim* people to claim this honor though the *Afrim* people have long known that they are not who they say they are, and the honor of the creation of the doctrines of Christianity belongs to their distant tribes of origin in Africa.

The second reason there is controversy over who invented the theosophical concepts of Christianity is that though Europeans have found out that the concepts of Christianity originated from Ancient Egypt, they have refused to acknowledge Ancient Egyptians as the creators of religion. This is because that would bring black people too close to the center of the creation of Christianity. For two thousand years, therefore, Christianity has not been about the real truth. In more recent times, Europeans have sought to protect Christianity through racism, racial prejudice, deliberate misinterpretation of the Bible, and they have even sought to make Christianity their own creation.

This chapter is therefore intended to reassert the fact that Ancient Egypt was the original place of the invention of religion. Ancient Egyptian concepts and sacramental practices of religion were what the *Afrim* people passed on to Europeans as the foundational beliefs and sacramental practices of Christianity. In revealing such long kept secrets about the Christian religion, I have a daunting task. This is because people have been told and they have believed the *legendary lying lore* for so long that they now believe that whatever their Bibles tell them is the "absolute historical and religious truth," but that is not so. In this task, I will reveal some aspects of Ancient Egypt that have never been known anywhere in the world except in Africa. I will also seek to analyze the biblical story of the *Afrim* people, examine where these biblical stories compromise logic and truth and from there bring out what Africa knows about all these.

False and prejudicial beliefs of Christian Europe

I have pointed out that in Christian Europe, the *Afrim* people that introduced Ancient Egyptian theosophy to the Greeks have even succeeded in claiming the credit of the invention of this theosophy. The question is, if the concepts of Christianity were dominant Ancient Egyptian beliefs and practices for thousands of years before the *Afrim* people supposedly went to Ancient Egypt, then whose invention of theosophy did the *Afrim* people introduce to Europeans as Christianity? How can the *Afrim* people be the creators of Christian theosophy when they supposedly went to learn about religion from the Ancient Egyptians, and when it was an Ancient Egyptian that taught them everything they knew about God and religion? What has kept the myth of the *Afrim* people creating the theosophical concepts and doctrines of Christianity going is the fact that they have basically refused to reveal who they were before they went to Europe to become Jews and Hebrews. They claim to have originated from some tribes but they have refused to reveal these tribes, where these tribes can be located today, and what language they spoke at their place of origin. I do believe it is because of the African heritage in the answers to all of these questions that they have refused to reveal anything about themselves. However, Africa has no reason to conceal the facts anymore and that is why I am revealing them now.

There is no evidence of the *Afrim* people having left a mark of any religious concept and practices anywhere before they supposedly went to Ancient Egypt. There is historical evidence; however, to show that the *Afrim* people practiced Ancient Egyptian religion even after they left Egypt into the Exodus. If they had gone anywhere else other than Ancient Egypt, the story of the *Afrim* people having created monotheism and the concepts of Christian religion would have been somewhat acceptable. If they had compiled and translated the documents that later became the Christian Bible anywhere other than Ancient Egypt; perhaps their claims of having created these documents and invented monotheism would also have been sympathetically acceptable. Even if the biblical stories were the original stories of the *Afrim* people and did not include Ancient Egyptian myths, stories, and religious documents, perhaps their claim of having invented monotheism and the doctrines of Christianity would have been sympathetically acceptable. However, none of these is the case. Everything is centered on Ancient Egypt and yet because of black and white racial sentiments and prejudices, Europeans have failed to see through the Christian *legendary lying lore*. Remember that according to the Bible, *Afrim* people did not even write the first five books of the Bible. Supposedly, Moses, the Ancient Egyptian wrote these books.

All of these confirm that Ancient Egyptians created the concepts of the Christian Bible, and they invented the concept, rituals, and sacramental practices that became the Christian religion. They expressed all these in the pyramidal monotheism that became the basis of Christianity's perception and practice of religion and worship of God today. The points to be made here are simple. The people that left Ancient Egypt into the so-called biblical Exodus were not Jews. They were black people that originated from the *Akan* and other African tribes that were the Ancient Egyptians. These people that left Ancient Egypt into the Exodus did not create the concept of God or religion. The Ancient Egyptian tribes from which they originated created all these. The priests and prophets of the Jewish people did not create the theosophical documents that became the foundations of the Christian Bible. People from the *Akan* and other African tribes that were the Ancient Egyptians created these documents. The most fascinating aspect of all these is that the *Akan* and other African tribal names of the people that created the biblical documents are still evident after the two thousand year effort at transposing and concealing these names.

The very transformation of the *Afrim* people began in Ancient Egypt and their real history shows that they did not have a God from wherever they claim to have originated. There is even no historical or archaeological confirmation that they originated from anywhere before they came to Ancient Egypt. Their historical and biblical evidence show that they adopted Ancient Egyptian and other people's gods even after the Exodus. How credible is it then that Ancient Egyptians invented and practiced religion for thousands of years but the people that came later to live in Ancient Egypt would claim that they invented monotheism, the very foundation of Ancient Egyptian theosophy? Anyone who knows and understands Ancient Egyptian religion and knows and understands the traditional religion of her modern descendants knows that monotheism was the foundation of Ancient Egyptian and modern African religion.

The real cause of the debates and discussions that pitch *Afrim* people that became the Jews and Hebrews in Europe against Ancient Egypt in matters of religion is that most people do not know that there are Ancient Egyptian documents that refute every assertion the *Afrim* people have made about religion. As Sir Wallis Budge pointed out: " A study of ancient Egyptian texts will convince the reader that Egyptians believed in One God." If that is not monotheism, nothing in modern religion is.

Among the most important facts confirming that Ancient Egypt was the genesis of the theosophical ideas of Christianity is the fact that the Bible reveals that it was in Ancient Egypt that the *Afrim* people supposedly transformed from the family of Jacob into a people that are now claiming to be a different race. What is sad about this is that Christianity does not see that there is something wrong in such a ridiculous story. I have sat in Churches and heard many interpreters state that the Hebrews went to Ancient Egypt as a family but they left there as a nation. However, none of these interpreters have given thought to the fact that even f one tribe went into a foreign country and left there as several tribes that would make a nation, there is something fraudulent in the metamorphosis because no single tribe can become a nation as the *Afrim* people claim their one family became in Ancient Egypt. From all these however, even a discussion of the mysteries surrounding the ethnic and racial origins of the *Afrim* people begins from Ancient Egypt. This briefly was the story of Ancient Egypt before the *Afrim* people supposedly went there beginning from Abraham.

Abraham went to Ancient Egypt

There is a fundamental problem with Jewish people's claims of descendancy from the so-called biblical patriarchs. In *The Moses Mystery: The African origin of the Jewish People*, Gary Greenberg the President of the Biblical Archaeological Society of New York wrote in his analysis of the Bible's chronology that:

> This clearly shows that this portion of the Genesis chronology derives from Egyptian dynastic histyory, and that the Genesis author worked from reasonably accurate records in putting this history together (p. 81).

Because there is evidence that the biblical chronological story was fabricated from Ancient Egyptian dynastic history, there is the credibility question as to whether the names of the people in the chronology were real humans or the names of these people were manufactured out of thin air. What is interesting about these names is that most of them are African tribal names. For example, the supposed biblical name of the father of Abraham is *Tera* but it is clearly transposed from the *Akan* name *Tena*.

Nevertheless, the *Afrim* people claim that they knew of a God because their patriarch Abraham knew of this God. What is interesting about this is that just as these people went to Ancient Egypt so did their supposed patriarch. Another biblical evidence linking the *Afrim* people to Ancient Egypt and confirming that the *Afrim* people learned and took everything they knew about religion from Ancient Egypt can be found in these people's own legendary lore of coming and going out of Ancient Egypt beginning with their patriarch, Abraham. One question that needs to be asked here is if Abraham was from a different racial and ethnic background from the black African tribes of Ancient Egypt, how did he and his children and grandchildren get their names from *Akan* words and names? How did the father of Abraham come by the *Akan* name *Tena* that was transposed in the Bible as Tera?

Despite the numerous biblical attempts by the Jewish scholars of the Bible to separate the Jewish people from the black tribes from which they originated in Ancient Egypt, the evidence is enough to confirm that the Jewish people, beginning from their patriarch Abraham, learned the foundations of the doctrines of religion from the Ancient Egyptians. Abraham supposedly went to Ancient Egypt and the question is why Ancient Egypt and no where else in the entire geographical region of Canaan? The Bible tells us why, but most people have been too blinded by the *legendary lying lore* to see it.

Beyond this, there are numerous inconsistencies in the biblical narrative to arouse the suspicion of the most naive reader, yet most people do not get them. For example, the biblical story states that "the Lord appeared unto Abraham" (Genesis 12:7). However, Exodus 33:20-23 states that all claims of God having appeared to people are lies because God himself told Moses that: "Thou canst see my face: for there shall no man see me, and live." From biblical times, the scholars of the Bible have claimed that God spoke to some biblical personalities. Even today, some Christian capitalists claim to see and speak to God. I will reserve comment on that till I reveal the God they claim to see and speak to in the discussion of the *Akan* people.

If God appeared to Abraham, it means the people that later became the *Afrim* people had knowledge of God and religion from wherever they came to Ancient Egypt. If Abraham knew of any God before he went to Ancient Egypt it means he must have left his people somewhere that also must have known of this God. Yet, there is no evidence of any of these despite intense search and downright fabrication of truths to complement the Bible's "absolute truth." In the first place, there is no historical or archaeological evidence showing that the *Afrim* people that later went to Europe to become the Jews and Hebrews went to Ancient Egypt from anywhere. That in itself is enough to confirm that the *Afrim* people that later went to Europe were originally Ancient Egyptians. That should also be enough to confirm the *Akan* and African tribal origin that this work is set out to reveal. Beyond all these, there is no cultural evidence of the *Afrim* people having practiced or having left a legacy of religion anywhere they claim to have originated or even along the way to Ancient Egypt.

How did the *Afrim* people come in contact with Ancient Egyptian religious ideas? The answer to this question is what the *Afrim* people have been trying to deny and avoid for over two thousand years. Christian Europe has also been interested in Christians not knowing that *Afrim* people had close relationship with the Ancient Egyptians. To conceal the fact that the *Afrim* people belonged to the same ethnic group as the *Akan* and other African tribes of Ancient Egypt, the Jewish scholars of the Bible went to great lengths at fabricating historical and ethnic inexactitudes. They concocted stories making the *Afrim* people different from the Ancient Egyptians, especially from the *Akan* people.

To do this successfully, these scholars first had to cleverly cut off Esau from the line of patriarchs from whom the *Afrim* people claim to have descended. This means the descendants of Esau were not *Afrim* people but the descendants of Jacob his twin brother were. That is why we

70

read in the Bible that God is the God of only Abraham, Isaac, and Jacob and not his twin brother Esau.

According to the Bible's chronology, the *Akan* people that created and developed Ancient Egyptian civilization were part of the descendants of Esau. The *Afrim* scholars of the Bible knew of their origin from the *Akan* and other African tribes of Ancient Egypt so in their quest to separate themselves from these *Akan* and other African tribes in Ancient Egypt, they had to cut off Esau from the line of their patriarchy. Cutting Esau off the line of the patriarchs from whom the *Afrim* people supposedly descended was the surest way of cutting off the *Akan* people whose theosophical ideas these *Afrim* scholars took and gave to Europeans as their original ideas. It was a clever way of covering up their tracks of racial, ethnic, and religious origins.

When God said to Moses that: "I am the God of thy father, the God of Abraham, the God of Isaac, and the God of Jacob" did anybody realize that someone was deliberately left out in this declaration? Esau, the elder twin brother of Jacob was left out. Why did God supposedly leave him out from his relationship with the patriarchs of the *Afrim* people? Did God really leave out Esau or humans did, and why? Why was this God not also Esau's God as much as he was Jacob's God? Why should God be the God of Jacob who deceived Isaac and stole the blessing of Esau, and not the God of Esau who deserved to be blessed by Isaac in the first place?

There is biblical evidence showing that before the Ancient Egyptian God became the God of Abraham, the first biblical patriarch went to Ancient Egypt from where he took away with him Ancient Egyptian religious knowledge, sacramental, and cultural practices. The nature of the biblical narrative surrounding Abraham's trip to Ancient Egypt suggests that Abraham went to Ancient Egypt to join the Ancient Egyptian priesthood. This discussion is not intended to suggest that I believe the biblical story of *Afrim* people's origin from Ur of the Chaldees because my knowledge of the tribes from which they originated in Africa refutes their biblical origination. Nevertheless, I will base my discussion upon the biblical story and its interpretations because these are the only resources most Christians, religious scholars, and historians in the west have.

According to the biblical story, long before the descendants of Abraham supposedly became the *Afrim* people, Abraham went to Ancient Egypt (see *Genesis* 12). This part of the biblical narrative is very significant because the story of the *Afrim* people seeks to establish the beginnings of their supposed intimate knowledge of God through Abraham. Again, the biblical narrative states that God "appeared unto Abraham" before he went to Ancient Egypt though another section of the narrative suggests that it was a lie because no man would see God and live. Nevertheless, what this aspect of the biblical story seeks to reveal is that the Ancient Egyptians that later became the *Afrim* people first learned about God when Abraham went to Ancient Egypt.

Abraham's visit to Ancient Egypt establishes the close link of the very foundations of the *Afrim* people to Ancient Egypt, but Abraham's travel to Egypt was not the only *Afrim* link to Ancient Egypt. Remember that it was because they left Ancient Egypt that they became the *Afrim* people, an *Akan* name for a people that have broken away from a larger group. Beyond this name, there are several other biblical hints linking the *Afrim* people to Ancient Egypt, black people, and the origins of Christianity. The only reason such biblical hints are still in the Christian Bible is because Europeans have never known that they exist and that is because they do not have the linguistic or cultural backgrounds to identify them.

The biblical story of Abraham in Egypt

The are numerous hints of the racial and ethnic heritage of the *Afrim* people in the Bible. Unfortunately, one must have the linguistic, cultural, and African tribal knowledge to be able to identify and understand these hints. As a result, I will be drawing readers' attention to certain references in the Bible, discuss them, and ask some seemingly unimportant questions to draw readers' attention to them. Most of the discussions and questions are hints the reader should bear in mind because they will all come together after I have revealed the ultimate evidence to support them.

The supposed intimate knowledge of Abraham in the biblical narrative of the earliest interaction between this God and Abraham suggest something otherwise. It must be pointed out that it was not Abraham that supposedly decided to leave the Ur of the Chaldees, the supposed place of the origin of the *Afrim* people. It was Terah, Abraham's father that picked up his son Abraham, his grandson Lot, and daughter in law and left the place (see Genesis 11: 25-32). In this account, there was no mention of any God having asked Tera to move his family from Ur of the Chaldees to Haran. What is most interesting about the supposed travels of Terah and his family out of Ur of the Chaldees is that it was when they got closer to Ancient Egypt that Abraham supposedly came to know this God.

In Genesis 12:1, the narrative says that God asked Abraham to get out of his country, away from his family, and from his father's house in Haran for God to show him a land in Canaan. The Bible had already stated that Abraham and his family left Ur of the Chaldees their original home but here this same Bible is referring to Haran as the country of Abraham, the home of his family, and the house of his father. Why was Ur of the Chaldees not the country of Abraham, the home of his family, and where the house of his father would have been. Here is another biblical narrative that contradicts the claim of the origin of Abraham and therefore the *Afrim* people in Ur of the Chaldees. The reference to Abraham's country, his people, and his father's house here was Haran and not Ur of the Chaldees. How could Haran be the country of Abraham, the country of his family, and the country of his father's house and not be the country of origin of these people? This part of the biblical narrative is very remarkable because it supports the coming revelation of the *Akan* tribe that lived in the geographical vicinity of Haran. Abraham originated from this *Akan* tribe thus confirming that even the so-called patriarchs were Africans.

In the so-called formative years of the *Afrim* people, the patriarchal narrative in the Bible says that God told Abraham to leave Haran for God to show him a land he was going to give to Abraham and his descendants. Even in the earliest attempts of the *Afrim* scholars to create an impression of the *Afrim* people's intimate knowledge of this God through Abraham, there were some rather serious inconsistencies. The biblical story further states that under God's direction, Abraham and his family left Haran and came to Canaan where they found out that the land this God was going to give to Abraham and his descendants belonged to the Canaanites and they were already on this land (Genesis 12: 6). What is intriguing here is that this God did not know and so he did not tell Abraham that the land he was going to give him and his descendants already belonged to some other people. How credible is it that this God would give a land that belonged to other people to his supposed children? What would be the motive of this God for giving a land that belonged to other people to his so-called chosen children? How did this God choose these children, anyway? Did this God want his children to go to fight for this land and why? Logical analysis shows that this aspect of the biblical narrative leaves much to be desired.

However, this was not the only time in the biblical narrative that God supposedly gave the *Afrim* people land but they could not find or claim it. There is another story in Exodus in which God supposedly took the *Afrim* people from Ancient Egypt to a land in Canaan, but it took them forty years of wandering and searching in the desert for this land.

Christians are caught in the strangest of religious paradoxes. On the one hand, they are asked to confer the highest qualities of power, perfection, and omnipotence upon God, yet at the same time, they are asked to seek and accept explanations of the imperfection of this God to uphold their faiths. That is how these fallacies and inconsistencies became the foundations of Christian faith, belief, and "absolute truth."

The inconsistencies in the biblical story of Abraham and the appearance that God must have deceived him makes one wonder whether Abraham was dealing with the God that became the Christian God because in the beliefs of most religions, God supposedly does not fail his people. For example, in the foundational religious belief of the *Akan* people, *Onyame* [God] is *Oseadeeyo* meaning God is one who says and does it.

The biblical story goes on to say that because the land God gave to Abraham was already occupied by the Canaanites, Abraham and his family removed themselves from Canaan and went to live on a mountain between Bethel and Hai. The narrative continues that there was famine in the land where Abraham lived, so he and his family got up and traveled "south" to Ancient Egypt (Genesis 12: 9). Note here that God supposedly asked Abraham to leave his country and home in Haran, yet, in this part of the story, there is no mention of God warning Abraham of an impending famine, or asking him to go to Ancient Egypt for sustenance. How credible is it that the God we all have in our minds and imaginations would let famine overwhelm his supposed children and let them go looking for food in a completely foreign and supposedly "pagan" land? Beyond faith, this story fails to establish the intended impression of Abraham's intimate knowledge with this God and therefore *Afrim* people's intimate knowledge of this God through Abraham.

From where he was between Bethel and Hai, Abraham was closer to Haran and the Canaanites than he was to Ancient Egypt. Why did he not go back to Haran or even go to Canaan to ask for sustenance from the people that lived "on his land?" How credible is it that God asked Abraham to leave Haran to come to Canaan and not tell him there was going to be famine along the way? How credible is it that this God would lead his people into famine and not warn them or provide them with sustenance? If he was a total stranger to Ancient Egypt, how did Abraham know that there was food in Ancient Egypt and that he and his family would be fed when they got there? Did Abraham go to Ancient Egypt just for food, wealth, or religious knowledge? The biblical narrative shows that Abraham originally went to Ancient Egypt for religious knowledge and got wealth in addition.

The Bible suggests that Abraham went to Ancient Egypt on his own because there is no mention of God asking him to go there. From other parts of the biblical story, it is clear that Abraham went to Ancient Egypt not because he was hungry where he lived but because he went to learn from the Ancient Egyptian priesthood. How do we know this? The biblical narrative about Abraham going to Ancient Egypt reveals that.

For the sake of the purity of religious rituals, Ancient Egyptian priests were not allowed to marry, and women were not allowed in the priesthood. This was the origin of the celibate practice of the priesthood that passed into early Christianity in the design of the Catholic Church's priesthood. It was also from this Ancient Egyptian dogmatic perception of women and religious purity that Christianity long prevented women from joining the priesthood. Not only did Christianity learn the doctrines of religion from Ancient Egypt; it also learned religious sexism from Ancient Egyptians.

Abraham originally went to Ancient Egypt to join the priesthood. However, he was a married man so the Alexandrian *Afrim* scholars of the Bible had to create a fictitious story to conceal his marital status and his objective for going to Ancient Egypt. That was why Abraham supposedly told his wife that she was a very beautiful woman the Ancient Egyptians would kill for if they found out that she was his wife. As a result, Abraham asked his wife Sarai to lie about their marriage and declare herself single (see Genesis 12:11-15). For this, Abraham told his wife to forget that she was married and give herself to Ancient Egyptians so that he could do what he went to Ancient Egypt to do, and that was lie his way into Ancient Egyptian priesthood. The question is what was it that Abraham wanted to do in Ancient Egypt that was so important that he was willing to let his wife sacrifice herself and her marital dignity for it? It was the Ancient Egyptian priesthood.

Abraham was supposedly seventy-five years old when he left Haran, and his wife could not have been much younger. The fact that an almost seventy year old woman was so beautiful that the Ancient Egyptians would kill his seventy-five year old husband just to have her is simply farcical. However, such a lie would allow Abraham to get rid of his wife temporarily and enter into the Ancient Egyptian priesthood without anyone knowing that he was breaking the cardinal rule of this ancient priesthood. It is most likely that at the time, if the Ancient Egyptian priests found out that he was a married man, they would have killed him. However, the biblical narrative of Abraham going to Ancient Egypt makes more sense through his goal of going to join the Ancient Egyptian priesthood than his wife being just beautiful. The God Abraham went to learn about in this priesthood was the Ancient Egyptian God and that confirms the discussion above that whichever way one analyzes the Jewish people and their claims of the creation of the concept of God, religion, and the documents of the Bible, Ancient Egypt was the beginning.

The Ancient Egyptian God also became the God of Abraham after he was trained in the priesthood of Ancient Egypt. It was from this background that God supposedly introduced himself to Moses first as the God of his father the Ancient Egyptian, before he became the God of Abraham and then Isaac and Jacob.

Some Bible interpreters have argued that Terah took his son, grandson, and daughter-in-law out of Ur of the Chaldees in search of help for his barren daughter-in-law. However, Sarai's barrenness was important enough to seem that was the reason Terah supposedly took his family out of Ur of the Chaldees (see Genesis 11:30). At least this other evidence confirms that this family did not leave Ur of the Chaldees because some God asked them to do so. The biblical narrative shows, however, that Abraham's marriage to Sarai was not that important to him and therefore her barrenness could not have been the reason for their supposed movement from Ur of the Chaldees to Haran or Ancient Egypt.

Abraham and his wife's deception of Egyptian pharaoh

Questionable circumstances in the story of Abraham going to Ancient Egypt suggest that this biblical story was not the whole truth. It is not only the patriarchal story of the *Afrim* people that scholars have found to be untrue, but scholars have also found some inconsistencies in many parts of the biblical myth. For example, how can God be appearing to all these biblical personalities and this same God would say that no man shall see me and live?

In *The Moses Mystery: The African Origin of the Jewish People*, Gary Greenberg wrote about the disturbing inconsistencies in the biblical narrative when he stated that:

> (There is no extant portion of biblical text dated earlier than the third century B. C.) The final version attempted to weave a seamless narrative out of a diverse collection of *contradictory historical claims* that reflected clashing political philosophies and opposing religious doctrines. *The resulting compilation indicates numerous compromises of truth* (1996, p. 3, emphasis mine).

This confirms that historians and biblical scholars have compared original and biblical histories of the *Afrim* people and found that much of the biblical narrative is just not true. As Christians, we dare not think such thoughts because thinking such thoughts is blasphemous, but that is how the biblical tradition has cleverly succeeded in closing our minds to the truth for the past two thousand years. What is most intriguing about the patriarchal story of Abraham's trip to Ancient Egypt is the fact that though he was supposed to be a stranger going to Egypt for the first time, the biblical narrative shows that Abraham knew Ancient Egypt well before he went there for the first time. How could that be?

The crux of the story reveals that Abraham knew Ancient Egyptians so well that he even knew the morality of the people of Ancient Egypt around beautiful women like his wife. How credible is it that a total stranger would know the morality of a people he had never met before in a place he had never been before. The morality of a people is not something one can openly find out without any close acquaintanceship. Morality is something one can only find out through intimate knowledge of a people or a person. How did Abraham know of the supposed morality of the Ancient Egyptians before he went to Egypt for the first time? How did he know this so well that he could create a fictitious story around it? The answer is simple. It was not Abraham that knew the morality of Ancient Egyptians. Instead, they were the *Afrim* scholars of the Bible in

74

Ancient Egypt that knew this morality and they used it in creating their fictitious story about Abraham

The biblical story seeks to suggest that Abraham and his wife were strangers to Ancient Egypt, a supposed foreign and pagan land. One question that has bothered me is how did they overcome the language barrier of going into this supposed foreign land of foreign people, languages, and cultures? Everyone knows that anyone that goes into a completely foreign land would encounter language and cultural problems. As a result, it would take some time for such a traveler to fit into that foreign land. Yet the biblical narrative says that Sarai immediately ended up in the house of the great Pharaoh.

Could this part of Abraham's story be true? No. According to the traditions of the *Akan* people that were the earliest Ancient Egyptian tribes, this biblical story of Abraham in Ancient Egypt could not be true because even native Egyptian women did not have that easy access to the (king) pharaoh. Even today, among the *Akan* people, because of ancient traditions and beliefs surrounding menstruation and childbirth, women in general do not have that easy access to the king. In the tradition of kingship passed down from Ancient Egyptian kings to their modern descendants, especially the *Akan* in Africa, even the wives of the king do not have that easy access to being with the king. Certainly, this access would be even less for a supposed "foreign" woman, a stranger like Sarai who would not know the cultural practices of women around Ancient Egyptian kingship, or who might not even have spoken the language of the pharaoh.

Nevertheless, the biblical story continues that Sarai was taken to the house of pharaoh who later found out that Sarai was married to Abraham. The king asked Abraham why he and his wife had deceived him (see Genesis 12:18). Contrary to what Abraham told his wife, the king was very remorseful that Abraham and his wife had deceived him. He did not kill Abraham when he found out that he was the husband of Sarai. Instead, he and his people treated Abraham well and compensated him with sheep, oxen, he and she asses, men and maidservants, and camels (Genesis 12:16). This is where the story becomes even more suspicious.

The main outcome of this deception was that Abraham became rich from the compensations the Egyptians gave him and his family. The biblical story says " and Abraham was very rich in cattle, silver, and in gold" (Genesis 13:2). Why would Sarai agree not to tell Egyptians that she was the wife of Abraham and also agree to go to live in the house of the pharaoh when she knew she was a married woman? Today, that would be called prostitution. On the surface, it seems this was Abraham's plan to prostitute his wife in exchange for wealth considering that they came to Ancient Egypt poor and famished. However, this has been all part of the *legendary lying lore* of Christianity for the past two thousand years.

This part of the *Afrim* patriarchal story tends to reveal more than it might have been intended. It tends to reveal the common origin in the racial and ethnic background of Abraham and the Ancient Egyptians. How credible is it that any "foreign" beautiful woman coming into Ancient Egypt for the first time would so easily be taken to live in the house of none other than the pharaoh? How credible is it that a "foreign" woman supposedly from a different racial, ethnic, and linguistic background would so easily get to go to live with the pharaoh? It is not possible. Does this story reveal that Abraham's plan to get his wife in the house of pharaoh worked because there were no racial, ethnic, or linguistic barriers or differences between Abraham and his wife and the Ancient Egyptians?

Our kingship and royal dynasties in Africa descended directly from Ancient Egyptian dynasties. For example, the direct descendant of the Ancient Egyptian dynasty of *Gyakari Asaase* and Akenten is the *Denkyira* dynasty of *Oti Akenten*. Knowing our kings and the traditions surrounding our brand of kingship in Africa, it is unimaginable that a foreign woman would have access to the king when African women do not have that easy access to him. The conclusion of the biblical story states that because Sarai ended up in the house of the king as planned, this God punished and plagued the house of Pharaoh with many plagues. That was the first plague and it was not the last. Wasn't it Abraham and his wife that deceived the Ancient Egyptians and their

75

king? Wasn't it Abraham that needed to be punished in the eyes of this God for doing such a terrible thing? Again, here is a clear logical inconsistency in the biblical narrative. However, does what Abraham and his wife did reflect greed and the willingness to deceive or do anything for wealth? It appears so.

Here is another aspect of the biblical narrative that turns the entire narrative and the claims of the *Afrim* people upside down. I have stated that Abraham was not a Jew because the *Afrim* people that supposedly descended from Abraham did not become Jews and Hebrews over a thousand years after Abraham. The question is if Abraham from whom the Jewish people claim to have descended was not a Jew, how did his descendants become Jews? What was racial and ethnic background of Abraham before his descendants went to Europe to be called Jews and Hebrews? This patriarch acquired his name from *Akan* words and the names of his son and two twin grandsons were all *Akan* words and names. *Akan* people were not Jews or Hebrews. Abraham originated from an *Akan* tribe that I am going to reveal in a later chapter. However, some western scholars have also long known that Abraham was not a Jew. In the *Introduction* to *The Natural Genesis: A Book of the Beginnings* by Gerald Massey, Dr. Charles S. Finch wrote:

> It is necessary to point out, however, that Abraham was not himself Hebrew. ... and in any case, the Hebrew religion does not appear until Moses bestows the Law upon the Children of Israel at Sinai 700 years after Abraham (Massey, 1883, vol. 1).

Note this very carefully because I will be revealing the specific African tribe from which Abraham originated and the language and meaning of his name. The fact is becoming a Jew or Hebrew was a much later title and identity that was conferred upon the earliest small group of *Afrim* people that went to Europe. If Moses' reception of the Ten Commandments on Mount Sinai was seven hundred years after Abraham, then the Afrim people became Jews and Hebrews in Europe almost eighteen hundred years after Abraham. Again, the question that arises is what racial and ethnic identity were these people before they went to become Jews and Hebrews in Europe?

It is clear in the quotation above that Massey was also somewhat influenced by the biblical narrative because he assumed that the people that left in the Exodus acquired a different religion from the Ancient Egyptians through Moses, but that was false. It was the same Ancient Egyptian religion under the same God that Moses introduced to the *Afrim* people of the Exodus. However, the fact that Abraham was not an *Afrim* much less a Jew is another major revelation that shakes the biblical narrative, interpretations, and the claims of the *Afrim* people for the past two thousand years to the core. It suggests that Abraham's son Isaac could not have been a Jew and his children Esau and Jacob could not have been Jews either. The question then is who were Abraham, Jacob, and their families before they went to Ancient Egypt? What racial and ethic background were they before they went to Ancient Egypt? Where did they come from and why were these patriarchs named in the *Akan* language before they went to the *Akan* people in Ancient Egypt? This book will reveal the answers as part of the final revelations.

The fact that Abraham and his immediate descendants were not Jews also confirms that the people that supposedly went to Ancient Egypt [Jacob's family] were not Jews. They were not *Afrim* people either because it was their departure from Ancient Egypt into the Exodus that made them *Afrim* people. After staying in Ancient Egypt for four hundred and thirty years these people became Ancient Egyptians, and then they supposedly seceded to go to set up their own kingdoms. A major point that must be made here is that these people could not have lived in Ancient Egypt voluntarily for over four hundred years if they were not of the same racial, ethnic, linguistic, and cultural heritage as the Ancient Egyptians. I have shown that the Ancient Egyptians were black people and I have revealed some of the African tribes that were the Ancient Egyptians and this confirms what I have earlier revealed that the Jewish people originated from the *Akan* and other African tribes that were the Ancient Egyptians.

76

When they left the tribal groups from which they originated in Ancient Egypt, they became the *Afrim* people. They identified themselves as Afrim people to remind them of their original roots in Ancient Egypt and in the *Akan* and other African tribes from which they originated. According to Dr. Finch, these people became the *Afrim* people seven hundred years after Abraham. This means they lived and identified themselves as the *Afrim* people for about nine hundred years or more before they went back to Ancient Egypt and compiled, rewrote, and translated the religious documents of Ancient Egypt into the Old Testament Bible. It was after this time that they went to Europe and met Europeans who gave them the names Jews and Hebrews. This was almost two thousand years after Abraham and over a thousand years of living and identifying themselves as the *Afrim* people that originated from the *Akan* and other African tribes of Ancient Egypt.

Another biblical deception

Abraham's deception of the pharaoh and his people was the first biblical deception of the Ancient Egyptians by the biblical patriarchs, but it was not the last deception involving the descendants of Abraham. The same leitmotif of Jewish people supposedly coming to Ancient Egypt and God plaguing the Egyptians was later recycled with new characters and plagues in the time of Moses. In the second version of this story told in the *Exodus*, the Bible says that God did not want the Jewish people to leave Ancient Egypt into the Exodus empty-handed. According to the story, this God asked Jewish women to steal silver and gold jewels and clothing from their Ancient Egyptian neighbors and take these away with them into the Exodus (see Exodus 3:22).

Again, does this reflect greed and the willingness to deceive for wealth in the people that were leaving Ancient Egypt into the biblical Exodus? It appears so. Note that the biblical story states that the *Afrim* people were the slaves of Ancient Egyptians yet this part of the story shows that they were the neighbors and not slaves of the Ancient Egyptians. Otherwise, under what circumstances could a "foreign" slave woman borrow the silver and gold jewels of her mistress much less her neighbor? Does this suggest that the *Afrim* people were neither foreigners nor slaves in Ancient Egypt? This is an example of the contradictory claims that compromise the truth in the biblical narrative as Gary Greenberg pointed out. Which version of the biblical story is the truth? Were the *Afrim* people slaves or neighbors of the Ancient Egyptians? Could they have done what they did before leaving into the Exodus if they were foreigners or slaves?

Concerning the ethnicity of the Ancient Egyptians, we do have racial, ethnic, linguistic, and cultural evidence in Africa confirming that the Ancient Egyptians were the black tribes of modern Africa. Could Abraham have come from one of the black tribes that lived on the eastern borders of Ancient Egypt, or could he have been an Ancient Egyptian? How did he come to carry an *Akan* name before he went to the *Akan* people of Ancient Egypt? These are the real human aspects of the Bible story that Europeans have never known.

There are numerous gaps and inconsistencies in the patriarchal story and that makes one want to ask several questions. However, it is sufficient for the reader to simply note that the *Afrim* patriarchal story was centered on Ancient Egypt more than the land God supposedly gave to the *Afrim* people so Ancient Egypt must have been more to the *Afrim* people than the biblical story told. Since the *Afrim* patriarchal story is a story of origin, Ancient Egypt becomes a more credible place of their origin than Ur of the Chaldees, Haran, Canaan, or any other place. Even if they did not originate from Ancient Egypt, it is clear that they came to Ancient Egypt because they were of the same racial, ethnic, and linguistic background as the Ancient Egyptians, and the subsequent history of the *Afrim* people confirms this.

Jacob also went to Ancient Egypt

Incidentally, Abraham was not the only patriarch to go to Ancient Egypt. Again, there was famine in the land of Isaac just as there was famine in the land of his father Abraham. However, Isaac did not go to Ancient Egypt only because the biblical narrative says that this time

God told him not to go there (see Genesis 26:1-2). What was it about Ancient Egypt that made the patriarchs of the *Afrim* people keep going there? What was it about Ancient Egypt that made the place so important that God himself had to stop Isaac from going there? What were the Jewish scholars of the Bible trying to conceal about the Jewish people and Ancient Egypt? Why do modern Jewish people still carry the names of the African tribes that were the Ancient Egyptians?

From Isaac, the patriarchal travels to Ancient Egypt only skipped a generation because Jacob, the son of Isaac, and his family all went to live in Ancient Egypt. It was the family of Jacob composed of about seventy men that supposedly went to live in Ancient Egypt and supposedly metamorphosed to become the entire Jewish people after living there for four hundred and thirty years. It was in Ancient Egypt that the family of Jacob transformed from one family into the entire Jewish people that some western scholars have today even classified as a different race. It was in Ancient Egypt that the family of Jacob transformed into a people of several different tribes. What is intriguing about this is that the family of Jacob did not go to Ancient Egypt even as a tribe. It went there as a family.

There is a major difference between a family and tribe. A tribe is a larger family unit made up several families. One family is therefore a part of a tribe and not a tribe itself. Yet, this family supposedly went to Ancient Egypt and left there as a people of a nation made up of several tribes. How credible is it that a single family could transform into a nation of several tribes? This single family did not leave Ancient Egypt even as a single tribe, but it left there as several tribes. How could this happen? How could one family in a foreign land amongst foreign people transform into several different tribes? One family cannot turn into a different race of people in their own land much less in a "foreign" land. Analysis of the Bible's own story shows that something has been concealed about the true racial and ethnic origin of the people that left Ancient Egypt and later went to Europe to become the Jews and Hebrews.

The biblical metamorphosis of Jacob's family into a people was historically the Great Awakening of the Jewish people. What is most intriguing about this awakening was that the Jewish people did not awaken in their land of supposed origin. They did not awaken in the land God supposedly gave them, they awakened in the supposed foreign land of Ancient Egypt. Does this not expose the foundation of the lies in all these?

For the second time in their formative history, the Jewish people used hunger to explain their tarriance in Ancient Egypt. The biblical story states that Jacob and his family also went to Egypt to escape from famine in their land. For the second time in the formative years of the Jewish people, their God did not save his supposed children from famine so they had to go to a foreign and "pagan" land for sustenance. How logical is it that the Jewish people would always run to Ancient Egypt and nowhere else in the surrounding lands that were sometimes closer to them than Ancient Egypt was? Were the Jewish people the only people that were threatened by famine in the entire geographical area of Canaan, and why didn't any other group of people run to Ancient Egypt but them? The fact is, Ancient Egypt meant more to the racial, ethnic, and linguistic background and origin of the Jewish people than the biblical story told us. It is partly because of this that western scholars most of whom are Jewish have refused to acknowledge that Ancient Egypt was a black African civilization. This is because from such an acknowledgement, it becomes easy to conclude that the Jewish people were also originally black people.

It is clear at this time that Ancient Egypt was not only central to the metamorphosis of Jacob's family into the Jewish people, it was also the sanctuary for the Jewish people's survival. How credible is it that a people that claim to have originated from one land and was given another land by God would always go to a third and foreign land for their survival? What was it about Ancient Egypt that drew these people to her? What was it that the Jewish scholars of the Bible in Ancient Egypt could not tell but they could also not leave out of their narrative? Is it not strange that Abraham and his family and his grandson Jacob and his entire family would both face famine and go to "pagan" Egypt in the very formative years of their people's history? Why would this God send his supposed children to a pagan and foreign land for their sustenance? What do these mean in terms of the racial and ethnic relationships between the Jewish people and Ancient Egyptians? These people have refused to tell the world of their racial and ethnic origins so what does this strange part of the biblical story of their origins suggest about Ancient Egypt?

What is again intriguing in the biblical story of the formative years of the *Afrim* or Jewish people is that famine and the search for food were the same reasons the family of Jacob went to Ancient Egypt. Even when Joseph's brothers sold him to Midianite and Ishmaelite merchants, Joseph ended up in Ancient Egypt. Was the obvious central role of Ancient Egypt in the biblical story of the *Afrim* people intended to conceal something that they did not want to forget, but at the same time they did not want Europeans to know?

Neglecting the fallacies and compromises of truth and accepting the Bible's version of the origin of the Jewish people, the strange story of Abraham going to Ancient Egypt confirms that Ancient Egypt was not only central to the transformation of an *Afrim* family into a people, but it was also central to the creation of the Jewish people and the Christian religion. The *Afrim* people could not have gone to live in Ancient Egypt for four hundred years without learning about the ancient theosophical concepts and practices of Ancient Egyptian religion. If we temporarily accept the biblical story of their formative years as true, the *Afrim* people learned everything they knew about religion from the Ancient Egyptians. What is most interesting about all these is that beyond their ancient *Akan* name of identification, the *Afrim* people left several other cultural, linguistic, and historical clues about their racial and ethnic origin from the *Akan* people before they went to become the Jews and Hebrews in Europe.

From the family of Jacob to the Afrim people

One of the most incredulous aspects of the formative years of the *Afrim* people is their transformation from one family into almost a million people. For a people who claim to have come from a foreign land and be given another land by God, it seems very strange that every important thing that happened in the history of the *Afrim* people that became the Jews and Hebrews in Europe happened in Ancient Egypt. According to the Bible, the number of men that went to Ancient Egypt in the entourage of Jacob's family was seventy. While in Ancient Egypt, the biblical story suggests that this family was secluded, and they lived in a small area called Goshen. Here is another contradictory claim that compromises the truth. Why would the father and family of the Prime Minister of Egypt be secluded from mainstream Egyptian living when it was this Prime Minister Joseph that sent for them to join him in Ancient Egypt? Was it Joseph that arranged for his father and family to go to live in this area and why? The biblical narrative also states that these people were slaves in Ancient Egypt. What choice do slaves have to live in a different geographical area secluded from their supposed masters? If the *Afrim* people were slaves in Ancient Egypt, would it not have been the norm for them to live with and amongst their slave masters? How could they have been the slaves of Egyptians if they lived in their own geographical area in Goshen?

Historians and Bible scholars agree that the *Afrim* people were in Ancient Egypt for four hundred and thirty years. Nevertheless, before the Exodus, Jacob, Joseph and brothers, and the seventy males that originally came to Egypt had long died in Ancient Egypt. However, the Bible says their descendants had supposedly grown in number from the original seventy to 600,000 males. How credible is this? Who would believe that this number was made up of only the family of Jacob? Nevertheless, there is more. The Bible says that there were 600,000 males "on foot beside children," plus an unspecified number of females, and a "mixed multitude" that did not belong to the house of Israel (see *Exodus* 12: 37, 38). This shows that the number of Ancient Egyptians that left in the biblical Exodus were more than the number of the supposed family of Jacob.

The larger Ancient Egyptian composition of the people of the Exodus is also confirmed by the Bible's own revelation that the people of the Exodus were composed of several different tribes. I have already revealed the real human, linguistic, and cultural evidence that the Ancient

Egyptians were made up of *Akan* and other African tribes. This means the people of the Exodus were made up of Akan and other African tribes. Major evidence in support of this revelation is that the Jewish people still carry the African linguistic and cultural names their African tribal ancestors acquired from their tribes of origin in Ancient Egypt.

From the biblical account, there must have been as many as a million people or more in the Exodus. Where did these people come from? Under what prolific circumstances could a family of seventy males blossom to 600,000 in four hundred years? In the four hundred and thirty years that the family of Jacob supposedly blossomed from seventy males to 600,000, were the people still the family of Jacob after eleven generations or they were now Ancient Egyptians. Did Jacob's family live and marry within itself or they mingled and married with the Ancient Egyptians? Do the figures of the Exodus suggest that Jacob's family was now Ancient Egyptians or at the least they were of the same ethnic origin as the Ancient Egyptians? The biblical facts and figures show that the seventy males that supposedly went to Ancient Egypt were absorbed as Ancient Egyptians and that could not have been possible if the so-called house of Jacob did not come from the same black racial and ethnic heritage as the Ancient Egyptians.

In his *Introduction* to *The Natural Genesis: A Book of the Beginnings* by Gerald Massey, Dr. Charles S. Finch again noted that:

> *"In Massey's mind, the original Children of Israel actually were [Ancient] Egyptian in language, religion, and ethnicity.* Doubtless, he first arrived at this conclusion after becoming acquainted with the testimony of Josephus who, in his essay *Against Apion* paraphrases the Egyptian annalists' explanation of the Exodus, indicating that the people who so departed Egypt were themselves Egyptian, though outcasts (1883, v. 1, Introduction, emphasis mine)."

Dr Finch continued to point out that:

> The very least that can be said is that even if the progenitors of the Children of Israel, i.e., Jacob and his clan, immigrated into Egypt from outside it, in a matter of two or three generations, they would have become fully Egyptianized by race, language, and culture. After 430 years, it would have been an Egyptian multitude that departed Egypt, led by the Temple priest Moses, whom the Egyptians called Osar-siph. Fully trained in priestcraft, Moses the Egyptian would have literally "laid the law down" on the foundation of Egyptian models (1883, v. 1, Introduction, emphasis mine)."

Also in Exodus 12:37, 38, the Bible reveals that there were many people [a mixed multitude] in the Exodus that did not belong to the house Israel and that suggests on the surface that there were more Ancient Egyptians than people from the house of Jacob. However, there is a deeper ethnic meaning to that statement. In the Bible, God also revealed that he considered the people in the Exodus Ancient Egyptians more than people from the house of Jacob. In Exodus 3:6 when God first revealed his identity to Moses, he told Moses that he was the God of his father, the Ancient Egyptian. In Exodus 3:15 when God asked Moses to send his message to the people in the Exodus he asked him to tell them that: "The Lord of your fathers ... sent me unto you..."

In this message, God was introducing himself as the God of the fathers of the Ancient Egyptians in the multitude. Again, God was referring to himself as first and foremost the God of the fathers of the Ancient Egyptians in the multitude before this God continued to say that he was also "the God of Abraham, the God of Isaac, and the God of Jacob."

In Exodus 4:5, God again identified himself as the Lord God of their fathers before he mentioned Abraham, Isaac, and Jacob. What do all these revelations mean? They reveal that there were more Ancient Egyptians in the Exodus than there were people from the single house of Jacob. From this point of view, the 600,000 men on foot beside children would make sense because they could not all have come from the family of Jacob.

Doesn't the supposed growth of the *Afrim* people from 70 to 600,00 males hint at the sameness of the racial and ethnic origins of the Ancient Egyptians and the Jewish people? If we accept the biblical story, the Jewish people must have come to Ancient Egypt from a different place but they left as Ancient Egyptians. That is the reason they have refused to reveal their racial and ethnic identities especially since they knew long before Europeans found out that the Ancient Egyptians were black people, the people that can now be found in Africa.

Here is another intrigue. If the people of the Exodus were not Ancient Egyptians, how credible would it be that Ancient Egyptians would get up and follow their "foreign slaves" into some kind of freedom when they were free in their own land? How credible would it be that these Ancient Egyptians would get up and follow their "foreign slaves" when they knew that these "foreign slaves" did not have any land anywhere to which they were returning? Does the fact that an Ancient Egyptian multitude supposedly went with the Jewish people into the Exodus also hint that the *Afrim* people and the Ancient Egyptians were of the same ethnicity? Remember that these people were not Jewish people yet. Does this mean that the *Afrim* people might not have been strangers in Ancient Egypt as part of the story of Abraham almost revealed? Who really are the *Afrim* people? Is there something in the *Afrim* people's relationship to Ancient Egypt that they failed to reveal in the Bible? No, they revealed everything about their ethnic origins in Ancient Egypt in the Bible, but Europeans have never known them and the *Afrim* people have simply refused to reveal these to them.

Is the blackness of the Ancient Egyptians the reason the *Afrim* people have refused to reveal their racial identities for over two thousand years? Have the *Afrim* people been ashamed of having had a black heritage or they are ashamed of being white today? Is it because of the ethnic relationship between Ancient Egyptians and the *Afrim* people that some western scholars (including *Afrim* scholars) have refused to acknowledge Ancient Egypt as an African civilization?

Whatever the reasons are, some important facts are clearly established in the biblical story of the origins of the *Afrim* people. The first of these is the fact that the *Afrim* people came to Egypt as a single family and left as a people almost a million in number. That figure reveals something about the true ethnic origin of the *Afrim* people that later went to become the Jews and Hebrews in Europe. The second fact is that the people that left Ancient Egypt into the so-called biblical Exodus were not Jewish or Hebrews when they were in Ancient Egypt. They became the Jewish people over a thousand years later in Europe; and that says a lot about their true origins, their assertions to be a different race of people, and their claims of the creation of the monotheist religious concepts and practices that they passed into Christianity in Europe.

This discussion has so far taken us from when Abraham first went to Ancient Egypt to when the family of Jacob went to Egypt and then left Egypt in an Exodus. In this analysis, it is clear that in the lives of the Jewish people from Abraham through Jacob, Ancient Egypt was the beginning. Even the history of the *Afrim* people after they left Ancient Egypt shows that they had a special, unrevealed, and unexplained attachment to Ancient Egypt. This attachment could not have been anything less than the sameness of racial, ethnic, linguist, and cultural origins.

Reasons for the Exodus?

Until my research into the racial and ethnic backgrounds of the people who wrote the documents of the Christian Bible, I did not know that there were other explanations for the Exodus other than the one given in the Bible. To most people like me, the biblical story has been the only resource we have had, and we have been made to believe that it is the truth, "the whole truth, and nothing but the truth." Here is another version of the biblical story of *Exodus* that few Christians know about, and those who first found this out made sure that the Christian masses never got to know about it. The Jewish historian Josephus wrote that *Omane Anto* had written in his 3rd century B. C. history of Ancient Egypt that the so-called Jewish people's Exodus was the result of the Ancient Egyptians throwing these people out of the country.

81

This according to *Omane Anto* was to protect the Egyptians from the plague of leprosy that had broken out among the poor and enslaved Jewish people. *Omane Anto* was the indigenous *Akan* name that was corrupted and transposed to Manetho by Greek historians. *Omane Anto* also wrote that Moses was the Ancient Egyptian priest that went with the Jewish people as a missionary to teach them the religious laws of cleanliness based upon Ancient Egyptian priestly model and laws of cleanliness (see Josephus, *Works*, ii, p. 466; *Contra Apion*, vol. I). Again, here is another source that confirms that Moses was an Ancient Egyptian. These people were not Hebrews or Jews when they were leaving Ancient Egypt. I have revealed that they were from the *Akan* and other African tribes that were the Ancient Egyptians. If they were not from these tribes, who were they?

According to the above explanation of the so-called biblical Exodus, the Jewish people were lepers that were thrown out of Ancient Egypt from the fear of their leprosy spreading among the Ancient Egyptians. Josephus being a Jew naturally did not accept *Omane Anto*'s seemingly denigrating version of the reason for the Exodus. He believed that *Omane Anto* had confused the Jewish people with another group of Ancient Egyptians that were banished from Egypt because of leprosy. Josephus believed in the more dignified assumption that the ancient Jewish people were the *Hyksos* whose eventual expulsion from Egypt became the Exodus.

In his *Geography*, Strabo reported the *Omane Anto*'s story as the reasons for the Exodus (see Strabo, XVI, ii, p. 35). Later Tacitus also reported this same story in his work (see *Histories*, V, iii, translation by Murphy, 1930). The earliest works of these early scholars suggest that there must have been some truth to this version of the reason for the biblical Exodus. Beyond devotional and blind faith, here are three historical versions of a story that agree with each other and contradict the biblical version of the same story. Which version of these stories should we believe? However, if these stories were true then the Afrim people must have had a motive and malicious intent to steal the theosophical ideas of the Ancient Egyptians and make them their own as a form of revenge.

Here is a fourth story about the Exodus. The custodians of history in some of the *Akan* royal houses in West Africa have a story about some *Akan* princes that seceded to go to establish their own kingdoms elsewhere, and the *Akan* people have never heard from them since. The *Akan* people's story seems to fit into the part of the biblical story where the *Afrim* people asked Moses who made him a prince and a judge over them. The *Akan* people were the Ancient Egyptians and it also fits into the reality that the people that left in the Exodus were Ancient Egyptians.

The question is could the revelation of the leprosy of the people that left Ancient Egypt into the so-called biblical Exodus have been the reason the scholars of the biblical documents sought to disassociate themselves from their Ancient Egyptian tribes of origin. Could this have been the motive for them to fabricate a story of their origin from a place they did not originate?

Jesus also went to Ancient Egypt

From my knowledge and background as an African, and specifically an *Akan*, I know that the biblical story of the origin of the *Afrim* people is only a literary fabrication. The *Afrim* people were racially and ethnically Ancient Egyptians. We know their tribes of origin and every aspect of their biblical story of origin, development, and transformation confirms this. The entire biblical story of the *Afrim* people and their relationship to Ancient Egypt is so suggestive and plain that it is a wonder how Christian Europe has missed the fact that the religious doctrines and documents the *Afrim* people compiled, rewrote, and translated for them were Ancient Egyptian in origin.

From the discussion so far, we have found out that Abraham, the so-called patriarch of the *Afrim* people went to Ancient Egypt. Supposedly, God told Abraham's son Isaac not to go to Ancient Egypt (see Genesis 26:8). If God himself had to stop Isaac from also going to Ancient Egypt then going to Ancient Egypt must have been very important to the so-called patriarchs of the Jewish people. The question is why? Nevertheless, Jacob the son of Isaac and the grandson of Abraham and his entire family moved from Canaan to go to live in Ancient Egypt for four hundred and thirty years. Despite this and despite the fact that these so-called patriarchs carried *Akan* tribal names before they supposedly went to Ancient Egypt, the scholars of the Bible sought all kinds of ways to separate the black tribes of Ancient Egypt from whom they originated from the *Afrim* people.

Beyond all these, Jesus the central personality and object of worship in the Christian religion also went to Ancient Egypt. Again, the question is what was it specifically about the *Afrim* people and Ancient Egypt that the biblical scholars refused to tell us but could also not leave out? What is intriguing about the birth story of Jesus is that only Matthew wrote that Jesus was ever once in Ancient Egypt. Moreover, the time he was supposedly brought to Egypt, right after he was born, also casts some suspicion on the true origin of Jesus. In addition to this, the rest of the gospels did not touch this especially important aspect of Jesus' life. All of these suggest that there might perhaps have been something that the writers of the gospel did not want to tell and Matthew must have also failed to tell us the entire truth.

From Matthew's narrative, it is clear that he too was trying to hide some truth about Jesus and Ancient Egypt. For example, Matthew wrote emphasizing that Jesus was born in the land of Juda, and perhaps not in Ancient Egypt. Matthew wrote: "And thou Bethlehem, *in the land of Juda,* are not the least among the *princes of Juda:* for out of thee shall come a governor, that shall rule my people Israel" (2:6, emphasis mine). Was Jesus Christ born in Ancient Egypt? Was he an Ancient Egyptian? Why did the Jewish people not accept him as the Messiah as the Christians did? What did the early fathers of Judaism know about the Jesus story that we do not know now? Was it therefore a deliberate act on the parts of Mark, Luke, and John to conceal something about Jesus and Ancient Egypt? After all, disassociating the *Afrim* people of the Exodus from the Ancient Egyptian tribes from which they originated was the cardinal rule in the editing and translation of the documents that became the Christian Bible.

According to Matthew's narrative, Jesus was "born in Bethlehem of Judea in the days of Herod the King" (Matthew 2:1). What is interesting in this emphasis on where Jesus was born is that it seems the writer consciously felt that he had to provide a detailed description of where Jesus was supposedly born to deny his being born anywhere else. This suggests that perhaps the writer was afraid of someone asserting that Jesus was born somewhere other than Judea.

This introduction was followed by a story in which Jesus had to be taken as soon as he was born to Ancient Egypt (Matthew 2:13). The question is why was Jesus sent to Ancient Egypt and no where else in the entire geographical region of Canaan? Matthew points out that Jesus was in Ancient Egypt until Herod died. No one knows how long that was, but biblical historians and scholars all influenced by the same cardinal rule to disassociate Ancient Egypt from the so-called people of the Bible have managed to suggest that Herod died only two years after Jesus was sent to Ancient Egypt. This obviously was to suggest that Jesus was not in Ancient Egypt for long and this seems to have been heavily influenced by the idea of getting Jesus out of Ancient Egypt as early as possible to avoid the possible suggestion that either he was an Ancient Egyptian or he learned what he knew in Ancient Egypt.

According to the Bible, getting Jesus out of Ancient Egypt was so important that a prophet prophesied saying "Out of Egypt have I called my son." (Matthew 2:15). The very first observation we must make about this is that the gospels about Jesus were not written in Canaan. If Jesus was born in Bethlehem and he was taken to go hide in Ancient Egypt only for a short while, what would have made it necessary and prophetic for an infant to be called "out of Egypt?' Considering what the Bible claims Jesus Christ did, if he was called out of Egypt then it important. Who called this infant out of Egypt and what made it necessary for an infant that had been taken to hide to be called? Much of the life story of Jesus before he was thirty years old is shrouded in obscurity. What made it necessary for him to be called in infancy when he was supposedly taken to hide from being killed in his infancy by Herod? Was Jesus born in Ancient Egypt or was it his supposed short stay in Ancient Egypt that made it necessary for the prophet to prophesy that he would be called from Ancient Egypt? If Jesus' stay in Ancient Egypt was only temporary, then the prophet should have known it was not a big deal. Why then was it necessary to call him out of Egypt? Why did the rest of the gospels not touch the family of Jesus' escape to Egypt?

It is important to note three things about the story of Jesus in the Bible. In the first place, when the *Afrim* scholars of Alexandria found out that the Greeks believed the stories of the Old Testament whole hog, they decided to add some more stories to embellish themselves and reinforce the beliefs of the poor Greeks in them. As a result, some anonymous *Afrim* writers wrote the New Testament story as an addendum to the Old Testament the Greeks have believed to be from God. The second important thing to note is that the story of Jesus being taken in his infancy to hide in Ancient Egypt because King Herod wanted to kill him is just another clever literary explanation of something the biblical scholars did not want to reveal. This was intended to conceal the fact that like the legendary Abraham before him, Jesus also went to the *Akan* people in Ancient Egypt to study in the priesthood.

The indigenous *Akan* name of his father *Osafo* [Joseph] and the indigenous *Akan* name of *Ayesu* that was transposed to Jesus with the ornamental Greek suffix "s" confirm that Jesus was among his people, the *Akan* people in Ancient Egypt. The third point is that some scholars have suggested that the scholars of the New Testament deliberately created the story of Jesus to introduce a new Moses who would take the Jewish people into another land. In other words, the ancient *Afrim* people had Moses when they were leaving Ancient Egypt to go to live in Canaan. Again, these people were leaving Ancient Egypt and Canaan to Europe, and they needed a new spiritual leader, and that became the Jesus story. According to these scholars, it was the intent to design the story of Jesus as close as possible to the story of Moses that the birth of Jesus had to be linked to Ancient Egypt, and not that he was born in Ancient Egypt. However, considering the historical, racial, ethnic, and linguist lies that the biblical narrative has sought to tell, such an explanation of how the infancy of Jesus came to be linked to Ancient Egypt is spurious.

What is most intriguing about all these is this question: what was it about Ancient Egypt that the *Afrim* people began coming to and kept returning to even after they had left there in the famous Exodus? The answer is simple. Ancient Egypt was the place of their origin and therefore an ethnic sanctuary to the *Afrim* people even after God had supposedly saved them from slavery and bondage in Egypt. As Seneca pointed out: "posterity will wonder our ignorance of things so plain."

From biblical myths into historical reality

Beyond the biblical myths of the origin of the *Afrim* people, there are several events in the real history of these people that closely linked them to Ancient Egypt. As I pointed out earlier, most Christians may not know this but the Christian Bible was compiled, rewritten, edited, and translated in Ancient Egypt, and that is extremely important for understanding what the Bible is, who wrote its documents, and its origins. Could it have been a coincidence that the Bible was created in Ancient Egypt? Maybe, however, there is much in the history of the *Afrim* people to prove that right from their patriarchal times, they had an intense emotional attachment to Ancient Egypt more than foreigners to a place or the "slaves" of any place would ever have after they had supposedly been freed. It is important to point out that the *Afrim* people had this intense attachment to Ancient Egypt more than they had to Canaan, the land God supposedly gave them, or to Ur of the Chaldees where the Bible claims they originated.

According to western scholars, the theosophical ideas of the Jewish people were the foundations of the creation of the Christian and Muslim religions. However, history, archaeology, and Egyptology have all confirmed that these people acquired what they claimed they knew about theosophy from the Ancient Egyptians. Ancient Egypt must therefore be the starting point of discussion of any religion in the world. Nevertheless, some Europeans seeking to deny Ancient Egypt of this honor have always looked to the east for theosophical inspirations, and some have sought to proclaim that the religions of the east are the foundations of religion on earth. Even then, early European scholars' geographical demarcation of the theosophical east included Ancient Egypt until modern scholars found out that Ancient Egypt was a black African civilization. Since then some western scholars have sought to look for the foundations and origins of theosophical wisdom in the geographical east away from Ancient Egypt. In this quest, some western scholars have sought to make Brahma, Buddha, Confucius, Tao, and the rest the focus of their theosophical studies, but secretly they are only seeking to move away from acknowledging black people as the inventors of the theosophical wisdom they have adopted as their own. What is interesting about western scholars' search for the origins of theosophical wisdom in the east is that these scholars do have the evidence before them, but they cannot see that the black people they are seeking to avoid in Ancient Egypt and Africa are the same people that introduced their theosophical wisdom to the East before there was any religious thought in the East.

Evidence of black people in the ancient Far East

In my research, I have also identified linguistic and cultural evidence confirming that some African tribes lived in the Far East in ancient times. This finding was contrary to the accepted western view of the history and people of the East. It was also contrary to the western assertion that Africans have never moved to any other place other than where they evolved. As a result, I wondered for years how people in China and Japan came to have African tribal names, and people in Japan came to learn to play the same drums the *Akan* people call the *Fontonfrom*, the kind of drums that are carried with the drummer following and beating from behind. I also wondered who would believe me in the west if I revealed the linguistic and cultural evidence showing that black people who are now the Africans lived in the Far East in ancient times.

Fortunately, genetic studies emerged to give me the credible support I needed for my linguistic and cultural research. The most recent conclusive evidence confirming that black African tribes lived in the ancient Far East came from a genetic study that traced the racial and ethnic origin of ancient Chinese people to modern African tribes. I introduced this study and the comment of one of the researchers in the first chapter. This study was part of the result of *The Chinese Human Genome Diversity Project* published in the *Proceedings of the National Academy of Sciences* by Li Jin and his associates of genetic scientists. This work was published on Tuesday, September 29, 1998. The following day, Robert Lee Holtz of the *Los Angeles Times* announced the publication of this revealing genetic work to the world in a review. The title of Mr. Holtz' review in the *LA Times* was *Early Chinese from Africa, Study Confirms*.

What was perhaps most profound about this publication was the comment of Li Jin, the leading scientist, made to Mr. Holtz. Li Jin commented that the findings of his work would disappoint his fellow geneticists in China. The reason is obvious. It is not because the finding is not true, but because such a finding has been revealed for the world to know when almost all scholars around the world have joined the silent European tradition of never revealing anything positive or complimentary about Africa and black people. Publicizing the results of the study would therefore be disappointing to some Chinese scholars and people because they do not want to be associated with any part of Africa and black people though they also still carry African tribal names, physical features, linguistic, and cultural heritage, but they do not know that. The history of the Chinese people is full of African names but they do not know it. The name of one of the scientists in the study, S. Q. Kuang, is only a western orthographic variation of the indigenous *Akan* name *Kwan* or *Okwan*. How revealing!

In my linguistic and cultural studies of the Far East, I also found that the original name of *Confucius* that was *Kungfu Tse* could be traced *to Komfo Tse* and the language of the *Ga* people in West Africa. In the discussion above, I showed that these people were also in the Bible. Remember the biblical Gileadites that asked the *Afrim* people to say the word "Shiboleth"?

The *Ga* language and people can be found in southern Ghana in West Africa. What is revealing here is that in the *Ga* language, *Komfo Tse* means *father priest*, exactly was Confucius was.

85

In addition to the original name of Cofuscius originating from the *Ga* language, the name of the 1st century AD Chinese Confucius scholar *Kea Kwei* was also a linguistic corruption of the *Ga* royal name *Okai Kwei* (see Durant, *The Story of Civilization: Our Oriental Heritage*, p. 665). In Ghana in West Africa, *Okai Kwei* was the name of the sixth *Ga Mantse* [king] who died in 1666. British historians know about this king in the history of Ghana (see The Early History of Accra in *Short History of the Gold Coast*, W. E. Ward, 1935, p. 9). The name of *Hsia Kuei,* the Chinese artist from 1180-1230, is also a corruption of the *Ga* name *Ashia Kwei,* and there are more Chinese and Japanese names that originated from the names of the African tribes that were the original people in these places in ancient times.

There is modern evidence of an African tribe leaving its culture and fashion among the Buddhist priests of Tibet. These priests wear their outer cloths over their shirts across one shoulder just as ancient *Akan* male priests wore theirs, and modern *Akan* males still wear their clothing in West Africa. Statues of Buddha in temples in Thailand show Buddha wearing a cloth over his right shoulder just as *Akan* males do today. What is interesting about this is that elderly Tibetan women also wear their upper clothing across both shoulders just as elderly and venerable *Akan* women do today. This kind of cultural fashion among Tibetan women can be traced to the *Asante* people in Ghana. How else could the Chinese and Japanese people have acquire African tribal names and physical features, and how else could Tibetan priests wear their religious clothing just as ancient *Akan* priests wore theirs in Ancient Egypt. All of these confirm that before they became Africans, black people lived in the Far East in ancient times and they introduced their theosophical wisdom across the entire geographical region. Despite the obvious African physical features of the image of Buddha, who would believe in the west that the African name *Oboda* meaning the creator of the day could be the origin of the name of Buddha?

This is ancient evidence that is being revealed here for the first time to confirm two points. The first of these is the fact that ancient black people who are modern Africans invented theosophy and propagated their concepts and sacramental practices of religion to the Far East. The second point is the fact that in ancient times, only black people occupied the vast region from Africa through the Middle to the Far East. Beyond the genetic evidence found in *The Chinese Human Genome Project*, further evidence is in the pockets of black people in the region from India to China and beyond, and the black physical features that most people in this region still carry. This is also initial historical evidence to confirm that wherever they claim they must have come from in the east, modern Jewish people were black people that originated from black tribes. The coming revelation of the specific Akan tribal group from which the Jewish people originated only confirms this.

However, the evidence in the brief discussion above shows that the black people that were the Ancient Egyptians and now the Africans traveled to these far places and left evidence of their religious wisdom and culture there. This was part of the long, wide, and ancient history of the foundations of the theosophical wisdom that came to be centered in Ancient Egypt before the *Afrim* people supposedly went there much later to proclaim to Europeans that did not know then that these ideas were their inventions.

Ancient Egypt in the creation of the Muslim religion

Beyond Christianity, the other major world religion that also directly sprung out of Ancient Egyptian descedancy and theosophical ideas was the Muslim religion. The Bible tells us that there is an Ancient Egyptian connection in the creation of the Muslim religion among the Arabs. This biblical narrative suggests that Arabs descended from the child of Abraham and his Ancient Egyptian maidservant who was supposedly given to him when he traveled to Ancient Egypt (see *Genesis* 16). In the discussion above, I showed that Abraham got his knowledge of God and religion from Ancient Egypt though the biblical narrative unsuccessfully sought to conceal this. The maidservant Hagar who Abraham impregnated was an Ancient Egyptian and she got her knowledge of religion and God from her home in Ancient Egypt. This shows that from whoever one traces the origin of the Muslim religion, there is an Ancient Egyptian connection and therefore a black African connection.

The circumstances surrounding Abraham's impregnation of Hagar also reveals something about the common ethnicity of Abraham, Sarai, and Hagar. According to the Bible, Abraham's wife Sarai could not bear children so she asked Abraham to sleep with Hagar for "it may be that I may obtain children by her" (see *Genesis* 16: 2). In this particular biblical narrative, Sarai seeks and claims the children of her Ancient Egyptian slave because Sarai, Abraham, and Hagar were all the same people from the same racial and ethnic backgrounds. The maid was an Ancient Egyptian and that means she was black. The name of Hagar even sounds like a name I have heard amongst the *Ewe* tribe in Ghana before. This, however, in turn reveals that Abraham and his family were of the same ethnicity as the Ancient Egyptians. All of these are simple hints about the true origins of the *Afrim* people that went to Europe to become the Jews and Hebrews. Christian Europe has either overlooked such analyses or never paid attention to them because the conclusion would involve revealing something Europeans do not want the world to know about black people.

Whatever the situation, the discussion above shows that Ancient Egypt was the place and beginning of not only religion but also the beginning of the formation of the people that later went to Europe to become the Jews and Hebrews. In the biblical and formative history of the *Afrim* people, this beginning goes as far back to Abraham, Joseph, Jacob and his family, and to Jesus. This beginning also includes the compilation, rewriting, editing, and translation of the documents that became the Christian Bible in Ancient Egypt. Coming discussions revealing that the Jewish scholars of the Bible in Ancient Egypt took Ancient Egyptian theosophical documents, myths, and folk stories, rewrote and edited them as their own, and made them part of the documents of the Bible will show that Ancient Egypt was really the foundation of Europe's Christian religion and all that we call religion everywhere.

3

Historical Background to the Creation of the Bible

I think it is one of the scars in our culture that we have too high an opinion of ourselves. We align ourselves
with the angels instead of higher primates.
Angela Carter

Western perception of the documents of the Bible

In Christianity, myth and legend have acquired immense historical values and because
they have been told often and for too long, they have been given a glowing badge of truth and
credibility. For two thousand years, the Bible has been the source book of inspiration, faith, hope,
and spirituality for millions around the world. The Bible has taught us about life, death, and
eternal life, but not many of us know about the Bible itself. One of the most important ideas
Christian Europe and Christians around the world have least known about is the story behind the
creation of the Bible. From the discussion in the last two chapters, it is evident that they were the
Africans that created the foundations of religion and knowledge upon which our world lives
today. What happened after this was that in the past five hundred years, European politicians,
scholars, and religious leaders have used the knowledge and religion these Africans created to
shape human knowledge, perception, and view of the world. In this endeavor, what Europeans
have forgotten or conveniently overlooked is that it was the Bible the Africans wrote that laid the
foundations, directions, and justification for the courage that Europeans needed to do all the
positive and negative things they have done in human history. While not detracting from
European achievements in this regard, few Europeans have had the courage to acknowledge that
the Bible was the source book that opened the minds and imaginations of early and modern
Europeans and therefore Africans must be credited for this ancient creation. Even fewer
Europeans would admit today that it was the philosophical doctrines of the Bible and religion that
drifted Europeans towards what they now call civilization, just as religion and these same ideals
did for the Africans in Ancient Egypt over five thousand years before ago.

In *The Story of Civilization: Our Oriental Heritage,* Will Durant acknowledged the
centrality of the Bible in the emergence of European thought and imagination when he wrote:

> The conception of history promulgated by the Prophets and the priestly authors of the Pentateuch
> survived a thousand years of Greece and Rome to become the world view of European thinkers
> from Boethius to Bossuet (1935, p. 340).

Of course, Durant pointed this out as a credit to the Jewish people that Europeans have accepted
as having created the documents of the Bible. I am not sure that any European or for that matter a
Jewish historian would give such a credit to Africans even if he knew what I have revealed so far,
and what I am about to reveal next.

To this day, the history of the world is still perceived, designed, and interpreted in the
west from the ancient biblical perception of the world though growth of knowledge has taught us
that the childhood of our humanity goes back thousands of years before the Bible. The growth of
knowledge has also taught us that the childhood of the concept, doctrines, and practices of
religion that we have grown to think were biblical in origin also go back thousands of years
before the Bible. Nevertheless, our responsive growth in the knowledge of our selves has been
woefully disturbed and thwarted by biblical perception.

In Europe where the Bible was first hailed as the greatest book ever produced by God and man, there is today a dual perception of the documents of the Bible. There is the scholastic perception held by those who have delved deep into the history behind the documents of the Bible. These scholars have found out that the people, the history, and the documents of the Bible are not as sacred as the conspiracies of the priesthood have made them to be over the past two thousand years. What is sad about these findings is that they are not exposed to the public as mainstream knowledge about the Bible. Such a perception of the Bible of most western scholars is represented by what Will Durant wrote:

> The Old Testament is not only law; it is history, poetry and philosophy of the highest order. After making every deduction for primitive legend and pious fraud, after admitting that the historical books are not quite as accurate or as ancient as our forefathers supposed, we find in them, nevertheless, not merely some of the oldest historical writing known to us, but some of the best (1935, p. 339).

This perception points out plainly that the foundations of the documents of the Bible originate from primitive legends and myths. They are theosophically fraudulent and historically inaccurate. Moreover, the documents of the Bible are not as old as Christian Europe has made them to be. There were older documents. Nevertheless, these are not what the custodians of the Bible would like the masses to know.

Of course, Christians who still believe that these documents were written with the spiritual guidance of God counter this perception. There is therefore the divine perception of the biblical documents that holds that the Bible is the most sacred religious documents ever written for the salvation of humans. This interpretive perception was originally created by the Catholic Church in its quest for religious and political domination of Europe. This perception gave the Church the right of dictatorship with the inherent right to extort, ex-communicate, and kill by the most atrocious means ever conceived by man. Unfortunately, this perception is still fervently guarded by the supposed religious mandates of the powerful Christians who stand to benefit most in wealth and power from the ignorance of the masses. The saddest part of the Christian argument is that they do not even know the origin of the God to whom they attribute the biblical documents and such fervency.

Behind this perceptual duality has been a serious dilemma in Christian Europe. Should Christian Europe admit the myths, legends, pious fraud, and historical inaccuracies in the Bible thereby admitting its African origin, or deny the historical truth behind the Bible, deny the African origin of the Bible, and accept the pious fraud, historical inaccuracies, and logical inconsistencies therein? Most western religious scholars have never been able to deny the origin of religion in Ancient Egypt, but they have also never been able to bring themselves to accept Ancient Egypt as the origin of the theosophical doctrines that became the foundational concepts of Christianity. This dilemma became even thornier when Europeans found out that the Ancient Egyptian civilization was a black African civilization.

Some biblical scholars have long claimed and supported the idea that Jewish scholars wrote the documents of the Old Testament. However, this assertion is completely wrong, and it arises from the fact that most western scholars have never known who the Jewish people really are. How do we know that the claim that the Jewish people wrote the documents of the Old Testament is wrong? Th answer is simple. The writers of the documents of the Old Testament left their indigenous *Akan* and other African tribal names on these documents. Unfortunately, Christian Europe without the historical, linguistic, and cultural tare African. Not only do we know that these biblical names are African but we even know the specific African tribes to which these names and the names of modern Jewish people belong.

What is interesting and revealing about all these is that the African tribes to which these biblical names belong can still identify and discern them after three thousand years of corruption and transposition of African names and languages in both Ancient Egyptian history and the Bible. How could it have happened that Jews and Hebrews would write "their" religious documents and attribute them to authors with transposed African names? How could a supposedly different racial and ethnic group of people called Jews have supposedly written any document at all and assigned the author to an African? The answer is simple and it is what I have already pointed out that the people that left Ancient Egypt into the so-called biblical Exodus were not Jews or Hebrews. They were black people from the black tribes of Ancient Egypt. These were the black tribes that later moved into inner Africa to become the Africans. The Jewish people were therefore originally Africans, and specifically most of them were from the *Akan* tribe. I have pointed out that the Jewish scholars that compiled, edited, and translated the biblical documents into Greek did not acquire these documents from Israel. These were documents that were written by *Akan* and other African tribal authors in Ancient Egyptian religious archives or library. The Jewish scholars simply took these documents and transposed the original names of these authors into Greek. That was how the authors of the documents of the Old Testament came to carry mostly *Akan* and other African tribal names, and not Jewish names.

In this discussion, I have pointed out that the Jewish people of the Exodus were black people and they originated from the black tribes that were the Ancient Egyptians. As I have stated earlier, the Jewish scholars of the Bible at Alexandria did not have any body of religious documents ready to translate for the Greeks. There is no historical, biblical, or literary evidence of when, where, and how the authors of the Old Testament beginning from Moses wrote the books attributed to them. Remember that what these people supposedly wrote were not pieces of articles. They are considered books in the Bible. If Jewish prophets and priests created the books in the Old Testament, these books could not have been the only books created by these authors, and there should have been some evidence as to when, where, and how these authors created these and other books. Yet, there is no evidence of such nature. What does it mean? It means the Jewish scholars of the Bible in Ancient Egypt did not have any body of Jewish religious documents from which the biblical documents could have been simply translated for the Greeks.

The body of religious documents, from which the biblical documents were compiled, edited, and translated were Ancient Egyptian documents. These documents were what the Jewish scholars of Ancient Egypt took and claimed as their own before the Greeks, but it was a lie. As a result, all that the Jewish scholars of the Bible did in Alexandria was to compile, rewrite, edit, and translate Ancient Egyptian religious documents that were available to them into Greek, and that became the Old Testament Bible. As the Jewish scholars took these Ancient Egyptian documents that were written mostly by the *Akan* people of Ancient Egypt, they simply transposed the *Akan* and other African tribal names of the original authors into Greek, and these names are still discernible.

I would like to emphatically state again that the concepts, doctrines, and documents that the Jewish scholars compiled into the Old Testament were not original Jewish religious concepts, doctrines, and documents. These concepts and documents were Ancient Egyptian in origin created by the *Akan* and other African tribes from which the Jewish people originated.

The Jewish scholars of the biblical documents were largely right in their calculations of the effectiveness of the foundations of their deception. These scholars knew that their deception would work because they were passing these documents on to people of a foreign land. In reality, these deceptions have worked because they have gone undiscovered in these foreign lands for the past two thousand years. How do we know all these? Again, the transposed African tribal names of the authors of the Old Testament reveal what must have happened for such African names to appear in the biblical documents, and the revelation of the Africans who wrote the Bible in the last chapter would finally confirm it all.

The names of the authors of the Old Testament books are also found in the history of the Jewish people. How then did the names of these authors come to be part of the biblical and real history of the *Afrim* people that went to Europe to become the Jews and Hebrews? Again, the answer is simple. The history of the Jewish people was first written and woven into the Ancient Egyptian documents that became the Christian Bible. In *The Moses Mystery: The African Origin of the Jewish People,* Greenberg showed that the biblical chronology was based upon the exact Ancient Egyptian chronology of kings. This is how the Jewish scholars of the Bible in Ancient Egypt began to create Jewish history and religion alongside Ancient Egyptian historical and religious documents.

The Jewish scholars of the Bible first wrote a fictitious biblical history of the Jewish people around the African tribal authors whose documents they chose as biblical documents. The Old Testament is therefore more about the history of the Jewish people woven around the religion espoused by the authors of the Old Testament Books. With the Old Testament history of the Jewish people in place and accepted as the absolute truth in Europe, Jewish historians began to extract their history from the biblical account, and early western historians also began to write every history around this biblical account. Through the Old Testament therefore Jewish scholars, Christianity, and historians simply claimed the authors of the Old Testament and their works as Jewish.

As I pointed out in a quotation by Richard Elliot Friedman in an earlier chapter, the traditional myth surrounding the authors of some documents of the Old Testament is slowly changing. What is very significant about this gradually changing story and tradition surrounding the people we have been told wrote the documents of the Old Testament is that historians, archaeologists, and biblical scholars are beginning to find out that some of the people we have believed wrote some biblical documents did not write the documents attributed to them in the Bible. For example, Christians around the world, biblical scholars, and the Jewish people themselves have long asserted that Moses wrote the *Pentateuch*, the first five books of the Bible: Genesis, Exodus, Leviticus, Numbers, and Deuteronomy. Today, biblical scholars have found out that Moses did not write these documents. The battle to propagate such a discovery however, is a battle between historical facts and blind devotional faith.

These are discoveries that seriously undermine the blind devotional faith of Christianity. As a result, some biblical scholars tone down the religious impact of these undermining discoveries, perhaps from reverence to the Bible, by stating that Moses did not write *all* of the first Five Books of the Bible. Unfortunately, these scholars have never been able to determine which documents Moses supposedly wrote, which documents he did not write, and who wrote the rest of the documents he did not write. These scholars have also not been able to answer why the Jewish scholars of the Bible attributed these Books to Moses when they knew he did not write them.

Biblical scholars and researchers have also discovered that King David who we have long been taught wrote the Psalms did not write the biblical Psalms. Again, some scholars tone down the religious impact of this discovery by stating that King David wrote only half of the Psalms in the Bible. These scholars also cannot determine which half of the Psalms King David did write, which half he did not write, and who wrote the other half King David did not write. Again, these scholars and researchers have not been able to answer why the Jewish scholars of the Bible attributed the Psalms to David when they knew he did not write them. These revelations pose some very serious questions about the true origin and authors of the documents of the Old Testament. If the documents of the Old Testament were truly created by Jewish prophets and priests, why would Jewish scholars not know the authors and why would they attribute them to false authors? From this action, there is a clear sense of an attempt to conceal something borne from a willful attempt to deceive.

What did the Jewish scholars of the Bible in Ancient Egypt seek to conceal by attributing false authors to the documents of the Bible? They sought to conceal the Ancient Egyptian origin of the documents of the Bible. Such deceptions and several other circumstances surrounding the creation of the biblical documents in Ancient Egypt confirm that Jewish priests, prophets, kings, or scholars did not create the original documents of the Old Testament. These also confirm that

Bible scholars and researchers have already found out that there is some deception in the biblical narrative, but they have not been able to find out the real truth that could expose this deception. This is because scholars involved in these revelations in the west do not have the linguistic and cultural backgrounds to help them expose these deceptions by linking them to a specific history or group of people. They are these deceptions and their relationship to the history and African tribes of Ancient Egypt that this work is intended to expose.

What do these discoveries say about the origination of the documents of the Bible? Most of the biblical scholars that have found these disturbing discoveries about the Bible have not followed up to find out where these documents truly originated. Of course most Christians, biblical scholars, and historians do not even know that there were Ancient Egyptian sources from which the biblical documents could have been taken. A major factor that has helped these deceptions continue to survive is the seeming success of Christian Europe in disassociating the study of Ancient Egypt, the place and source of the biblical ideas and documents, from the study of the Bible. Because of this, most believers in the Bible have never thought of any relationship between Ancient Egypt and the Bible; and even less have ever thought of any relationship between the so-called people of the Bible and the Ancient Egyptians.

Most believers in the Bible have never seen or much less studied Ancient Egyptian history or religious literature so they have never known that there was a source in Ancient Egypt from which the biblical documents could have been taken. Moreover, the study of Ancient Egypt is considered a different discipline that is more historical than religious and therefore not common knowledge to the public much less Christians. Only a few scholars around the world are involved in Ancient Egyptian studies and much of what they find out is not disseminated to the public at large. What is worse, much of what scholars of Ancient Egypt know and find out is tucked away in libraries and museums where most Christians never look for religious explanations, clarifications, or enlightenment. However, even if we accept that Moses wrote the first five books of the Bible (which he did not), these documents could not have been original Jewish religious documents because as we have discussed earlier, Moses was not a Jew. Like most of the people that left Ancient Egypt to go to live in Canaan and later went to Europe to become the Jews and Hebrews, Moses was from the *Akan* tribe in Ancient Egypt.

Christian Europe has never bothered much to find out where the documents of the Bible came from, or who wrote them. However, some scholars have found out that Christian Europe does not want to know the source of the book it has proclaimed to be its "holiest book" for the fear that it might turn out to be not all that "holy" at all. This work is, however, not intended to challenge or question Christian Europe's perception of the Bible as a sacred book. This work is only intended to reveal the facts Europeans have tried to conceal and that is reveal that Africans wrote the documents of the Old Testament and produce the evidence for it. Fortunately, the Jewish scholars that compiled and translated the documents of the Old Testament did not hide or completely destroy the African names of the authors of the Books of the Bible and these names do not hide the African tribal groups from which these authors originated either. The linguistic and cultural evidence to all these are very plain in the Bible.

From the old documents to the new

I have focussed on the African tribal names of the authors of the Old Testament because there is evidence that the names of the authors of the New Testament were clearly and deliberately concealed to forestall any future revelation as I am doing about the Old Testament. The Old Testament Bible introduced the foundations, concept, and practice of Christianity in Europe before *anonymous* writers wrote the New Testament. Here is an intriguing question about the Bible that exposes the pervading intent to deceive in the Bible. Why did scholars of the Old Testament include the real tribal [albeit transposed] names of the authors but the writers of the New Testament concealed their names? What made this necessary? Jewish scholars that compiled and translated the documents of the Old Testament into Greek convinced the Greeks that God-inspired ancient Jewish prophets and priests wrote the documents of the Bible. As a result, the Old Testament acquired a canonical credibility for having been Godly and true because ancient God-inspired prophets wrote it. The foundations of Christianity therefore began from the premise that it was God that inspired Jewish prophets to write the documents of the Old Testament. The question is did God inspire Moses to write Ancient Egyptian religious ideas, myths, and folk tales as they are found in the First Five Books of the Bible, or were these Ancient Egyptian religious documents that the scholars of the Bible plagiarized? What about the documents of the New Testament? Who did God inspire to write those and why have we never known the true identities of the authors?

Historians and religious scholars agree that the New Testament was definitely not written by God-inspired prophets, but by contemporary Hellenized Jews in Ancient Egypt or Greece. Christianity as a religious doctrine and practice had already started from the Old Testament documents and the appearance of a new set of documents purported to be equally Godly and religious documents of the *Afrim* people became a major source of apprehension in early Christendom. The early Church did not want to risk the growing credibility in its assertion that the Old Testament is the word and the work of God to bring in new documents that were surely written by contemporary scholars. So the names of the authors of the New Testament had to be concealed to make it possible to confer some of the growing credibility of the Old Testament onto the New Testament documents.

What is least pointed out about the New Testament is that Jewish priests and religious scholars found the New Testament to be the worst form of religious deception of the Greeks and later Europeans. As a result, Judaism never accepted the documents of the New Testament as part of its traditionally divine religious truths. That was enough to warn the Greeks that the New Testament documents must have been designed to commit a pious fraud as Judaism saw them. Nevertheless, these new documents became the spiritual inspiration and direction for the design of a new form of religion based upon the New Testament. Today, Christians around the world still do not know where these documents came from but they believe it, and they attribute the writers of the New Testament gospels to some fictitious Matthew, Mark, Luke, and John. However, nobody knows who these authors were and most Christians know that these were not their real names, but it does not matter to them. This is because these documents have also been woven into to the devotional faith of Christianity as holy and God-inspired documents.

The compilers and translators of the Old Testament documents that became the foundations of the Christian Bible claimed that ancient Jewish prophets wrote these documents. That was clever because it effectively made it impossible to verify who the authors of these documents really were or the authenticity of the sources of these documents. As if that was not enough deception, the names of the contemporary authors who had just written the New Testament gospels were also concealed to thwart verification of the authenticity of the authors, their sources, and their stories. Could these have been the foundations of the deception that Europeans later claimed and used in the hatred and decimation of blacks and Jews? Where did the writers of the New Testament get their information and why did the early Church have to hide their names? Perhaps, the more intriguing question is, who was this Jesus and how did he come by the indigenous African tribal name that was transposed to Jesus in Greek?

Today Christians are not supposed to ask such questions because Christianity has taught us that such questions undermine Christian faiths. As a result, most professed and perplexed Christians do not want to show that the growth of knowledge, reality, and reason are leading them to find answers beyond the biblical documents, interpretations, and faiths. Nevertheless, many modern Christians have found that there must have been something in ancient religions that they are missing today, so they are moving away from Christianity in search of "what and how it was" before Christianity. After all, we have not come that far to forget how it was before.

In search of the biblical context

Every literature has a historical, geographical, linguistic, cultural, and even a political context. Because of these contexts, literature cannot be easily lost or stolen. They are these various contexts that interest many scholars who study the Bible. My personal interest in the Bible is in the human element in the creation of the faith and philosophy that has been spread as the ultimate truth through Christianity. This interest is not a new or even an original perception in the search for the story behind Christianity. In the 18th century, German philosopher Immanuel Kant and those who followed his ideas of religion sought to explore and understand the events and personalities in the Bible through its historical contexts. Kant and his followers believed that the events stated in the Bible actually happened, and if these events happened then they must have a historical, linguistic, cultural, geographical, and even a political context. Kant and his followers therefore argued that knowing these contexts can help Christian Europe understand the stories of the Bible better, so the Kantian School of philosophy set out in search of the history behind the creation of the Bible.

Consequently, theologians of the Kantian school of thought engaged in a century long quest for the historical Jesus, from Europe. Unfortunately, they did not succeed because events in the Bible that could have led these researchers to the historical Jesus had been taken out of their geographical, historical, social, and linguistic contexts, and these philosophers did not know these contexts. In addition to that, Christian Europe had wrestled the Bible and the faith created from this Bible out of the hands of the Jewish people who introduced the documents of the Bible and knew the historical, linguistic, and cultural sources and contexts of the Christian doctrine. Because the Jews were pushed to the peripheral of the Christian communities of Europe, they also refused to tell where the documents of the Bible originated.

So how can modern scholars search for the historical contexts of the biblical story to find out those who created them? Those who know and have the background to see the evidence before them in the Bible, history, languages, and cultures involved in the creation of the Bible should not have any problems. For those who do not have any of these backgrounds, the answer is in this conundrum. The Jewish people claim that they have lost ten of their original tribes. This means ten of their original tribes must be somewhere. However, where there are twelve tribes, the two that break away are the lost ones, not the ten that stay together. This means if we locate the tribes of the Jewish people that stayed together, we would find the answer to the creation of the biblical documents and who created them. The tribes that the Jewish people claim to have lost are still together in Africa. This simply means that anyone searching for the historical, linguistic, cultural, and even political contexts of the documents of the Christian Bible can find them by simply looking for the tribes that stayed together and are now in Africa.

For those interested in this search, here is a hint: the Jewish people were not the only participants or eyewitnesses to the history, geography, language, and even the political context of the documents and personalities of the Bible. The *Akan* people and the African tribes that were the Ancient Egyptians know more than it was ever recorded in the creation of the Bible.

Events leading to the creation of the Christian Bible

Historical records of the Jewish people confirm that the early documents of the Christian Bible were not edited until after the 7th century B. C., or perhaps much later. These records also confirm that the documents of the Christian Bible were not compiled, rewritten, edited, or translated in Israel or Judea, but in Ancient Egypt. Not only did the ancient foundations of the *Afrim* people begin in Ancient Egypt, but also the end of their ancient story in the east ended in Ancient Egypt. Remember that during this period, the people that left Ancient Egypt into the Exodus still identified themselves as *Afrim* people and not Jews or Hebrews.

In 722 B. C., about six hundred years after the Exodus, the Assyrians conquered the Northern Kingdom of Israel and forcibly resettled the *Afrim* people of this kingdom among the Babylonians and Assyrians on the eastern border of the Assyrian Empire. The history of the *Afrim* people states that it was from the forced intermingling of the *Afrim* people with the Babylonians and Assyrians that a new group of *Afrim* people called the Samaritans emerged. From the historical, linguistic, religious, and cultural evidence of the people of Assyria and Babylon, it is evident that these people were all black people at least eleven hundred years before modern Arabs came to settle in these places.

However, what is least known among Christians is the fact that when the *Afrim* people that left Ancient Egypt in the so-called biblical Exodus, were attacked, conquered, and displaced in Canaan by the Assyrians, most returned to Ancient Egypt. A large community of these people of the biblical Exodus escaped and returned to settle on the Nile Island of Elephantine in Ancient Egypt. According to historical traditions, the people of the Exodus that returned to Ancient Egypt returned with the Ark of the Covenant to Egypt. Modern scholars who have been searching for the biblical Ark of the Covenant claim that the *Afrim* people that returned to Elephantine in Ancient Egypt brought the Ark with them and from there it was mysteriously sent to Axum in Ethiopia where it is believed to be today.

Throughout their history, the most important religious artifact the *Afrim* people claim to have ever had was the biblical Ark of the Covenant. Again, the *Afrim* people selected Ancient Egypt to play another major role in their religious history. This time as a safe haven for themselves and their most important and divine religious artifact. Why did these people not leave the Ark with the group of *Afrim* people that lived in other nations? Why did the generation of the *Afrim* people that needed a shelter come back to Ancient Egypt after their ancestors had claimed to have been enslaved and tortured by the Ancient Egyptians? This is because regardless of what had happened, the *Afrim* people felt safer among their own racial, ethnic, and tribal groups in Ancient Egypt than anywhere else.

Though all of these happened before the documents of the Bible were compiled and translated for the Greeks, the scholars of the Bible never remotely mentioned that the ancestors of the people that left Ancient Egypt in the so-called biblical Exodus returned to Ancient Egypt. Neither did they mention that they compiled, edited, and translated the documents of the Bible in Ancient Egypt. These were because mentioning any of these would undermine the veracity and significance of the Exodus and entire biblical story. These revelations would also undermine the *Afrim* people's quest for a separate identity from their racial, tribal, and ethnic groups of Ancient Egypt.

According to the traditional story behind the Exodus, the *Afrim* people moved away from Ancient Egypt into the biblical Exodus to go to find a place to create their own kingdoms like the Ancient Egyptians. They went, tried it, and failed and they quietly moved back to their people in Ancient Egypt. Throughout the history of the *Afrim* people, Ancient Egypt was the place and the only place they went to in times of hunger, threat from outside, conquest, and desperation. Again, the question is why? Why did they not take their Ark to Ur of the Chaldees, the supposed place of their origin?

Many Christians do not know that despite the Biblical Exodus and the tone of antagonism the story sought to create between Ancient Egyptians and the *Afrim* people, these people began returning quietly to Ancient Egypt as far back as 722 B. C. The realities of *Afrim* people's history after the so-called Exodus make many scholars question whether the story of the Exodus ever happened at all. How can we logically reconcile the purported atrocities of the Ancient Egyptians toward the *Afrim* people and the return of these same people to their place of oppression hundreds of years later? If God came "to deliver them out of the hands of the Egyptians, and to bring them up out of that land unto a good land and a large, unto a land flowing with milk and honey" (Exodus 3:8), wouldn't the return of these people to Ancient Egypt be a major violation of God's will and even a sin against God? Nevertheless, the return of the *Afrim* people to Ancient Egypt was not considered a sin against God because it was a return to their racial, ethnic, and tribal roots.

In Exodus 14:13, Moses supposedly told the *Afrim* people that

Fear ye not, stand still, and see the salvation of the Lord, which he will shew to you today: for the Egyptians whom ye have seen today, ye shall see them again no more for ever.

This was the supposed prophecy of Moses as he was preparing the *Afrim* people for the so-called Exodus, but it turned out to be untrue because the *Afrim* people returned to Ancient Egypt in droves when the Northern Kingdom of Israel was defeated. How credible then are the biblical stories of the *Afrim* people and their supposed intimate knowledge of God, if this God delivered them from the hands of their Egyptian taskmasters but they came back in violation of this God's actions and their prophets' prophecy? Is this the reason the Bible never said anything about the return of the *Afrim* people to Ancient Egypt? Here is one of the situations in which the realities of the history of the *Afrim* people do not match the myth they created for themselves in the Bible. Here is another situation in which the fabrication of the origin of the *Afrim* people did not match the realities of their history when they were hungry, desperate, displaced, or threatened.

Defeat of the Southern Kingdom
The southern *Afrim* kingdom that was known as Judah escaped aggression from foreign empires for about 136 years after the destruction of the north. In 597 B. C., the king of Babylon conquered Judah and made Zedekiah [African name *Zedeki*] the puppet king for ten years from 596 to 586 B. C. During this period, the prophet Jeremiah supposedly warned the *Afrim* people that the safety of Judah lay in compromise and obedience to the king of Babylon. However, Zedekiah sought alliance with Ancient Egyptian King Hophra and revolted against the Babylonians hoping the Egyptians would come to help them ward off a Babylonian attack. The African indigenous name of Ancient Egyptian king Hophra was *Opra*. It is an *Akan* name. Today, this name has been shortened to *Pra*.

Again, it is remarkable to point out that even after God had delivered them from the Ancient Egyptians, the *Afrim* people still relied on Ancient Egypt while they were in far away Canaan. What happened in the alliance between Judea and Ancient Egypt was not clear but one thing that was clear was that the *Afrim* people had political affiliations with Ancient Egyptians even after the Egyptians had supposedly "enslaved and oppressed them." That contradicts an aspect of the entire slavery and Exodus narrative.

In 586 B. C., the Babylonians attacked Judah and captured Jerusalem. The Babylonians sent many of the Judeans to Babylon. This is how the *Afrim* people were introduced to Babylon and the east. As part of the strategy to disassociate themselves from Ancient Egyptians because of circumstances of history, the *Afrim* scholars of the Bible began to assert that their patriarchs, that is their ancestors, originated from Ur of the Chaldees. Because the claims of the origin of the *Afrim* people in Ur of the Chaldees was controversial even among various *Afrim* tribal groups, the writers and translators of the documents of the Bible had to give this claim acceptance and credibility to make *Afrim* people accept and believe it. As a result, they created a situation that suggested that Abraham did not know where he came from and that it was God that told Abraham that he and his people originated from Ur of the Chaldees (see *Genesis* 15, 7).

What is even more intriguing about the relationship of the *Afrim* people to Ancient Egypt is that before they were sent into Babylonian "captivity," many Judeans also escaped to Ancient Egypt supposedly bringing with them the prophet Jeremiah who was very old at this time. Despite the biblical story of the Exodus suggesting that the *Afrim* people left Ancient Egypt as slaves and under antagonistic conditions and rituals, a large population of *Afrim* people returned to Ancient Egypt as early as the 6th century B. C. Most of them continued to live in Egypt from the 6th century B. C. until the State of Israel was created before they began to move to Israel between 1948 and 1970. Some are still in modern Egypt.

Again, some questions need to be asked here. Didn't the prophet Jeremiah know that God delivered the *Afrim* people from Ancient Egypt therefore returning to Egypt was a blatant violation of God's will and a sin against God? Or was the biblical story of God's deliverance of the *Afrim* people from Ancient Egypt another part of the *legendary lying lore?*

Persia over Egypt
In the discussion so far, a later generation of most of the people that left Ancient Egypt in the Exodus were back in Ancient Egypt so it is necessary to explore a little bit of the history of Ancient Egypt when these people returned. In this brief discussion of the history of Ancient Egypt, I will reveal more of the original and indigenous African tribal names of Ancient Egyptian kings, people, and places. This revelation is the first true revelation of the names of these Ancient Egyptians in over five thousands years. It is also the very first revelation from modern descendants of the Ancient Egyptians in Africa. This revelation does not only confirm that modern descendants of the Ancient Egyptians are the black people of Africa, but it also shows that there are modern descendants of the Ancient Egyptians in the biblical story.

Just as the *Afrim* people returned to Ancient Egypt because of political changes in the land "God had given them," so were political and historical circumstances changing in Ancient Egypt. The rising power of Persia led to Persian conquest of Ancient Egypt in 525 B. C. As a result, Ancient Egyptians grew politically closer to the Greek City states and the Greek mercenaries they knew and had hired once before.

Earlier in Ancient Egyptian history, the Ancient Egyptian king known *as Asamoa Ateko I* had entrusted the defense of Ancient Egypt to mercenaries from Greek City States, so the Ancient Egyptians felt naturally closer to the Greeks than to the Persians who had just conquered them. *Asamoa Ateko I* was the original and indigenous *Akan* name of the Ancient Egyptian king who is now known in Egyptology as *Psammetichus I.* Even in muddle of this linguistic corruption, the indigenous *Akan* name of this king is discernible and evident.

After the death of Persian king Xerxes I, there was a period of political unrest in Ancient Egypt when the next Persian king, Darius, came to power. In 405 B. C., Darius died and his successor Amytaios seized power again in Ancient Egypt. Eventually, the Macedonian Greeks under Alexander the Great conquered the Persians and brought Egypt under Greek rule. Before Alexander the Great conquered Ancient Egypt, some *Afrim* people were still scattered in Babylon, Persia, and Asia Minor. After Alexander's conquest of Egypt, again another large group of *Afrim* people from all these places returned to Ancient Egypt. Again, the question is why would the *Afrim* people choose Ancient Egypt over every other place else including the land God had supposedly given them? Why did they not go to their supposed biblical home in Ur of the Chaldees, but always run to Ancient Egypt?

If God supposedly told Abraham that he came from Ur of the Chaldees, and his descendants had known and believed in this God, why have they never returned to their "home" in Ur of the Chaldees throughout their entire history? There is a difference between writing a fictitious history to claim one's origin in a place and living one's life to reveal where one truly originates. I have cited that in *The Moses Mystery: The African Origin of the Jewish People*, Gary Greenberg pointed out that: The first Israelites were [Ancient] Egyptians, followers of Pharaoh *Akhenaten,* whose attempts to introduce monotheism into Egypt engendered rage among the religious establishment (see 1996, flap jacket)). By their actions, the *Afrim* people discredited the story of their origin in the Exodus narrative and showed in every way that they originated and belonged to Ancient Egypt more than they belonged to Ur of the Chaldees or even the land God had supposedly given them in Canaan. As a result, it is more prudent to search for the tribal and cultural origins of the *Afrim* people in Africa via Ancient Egypt than search for them anywhere else.

Tribal problems of the Afrim people after their return to Ancient Egypt
The *Afrim* people had two major problems when they returned to Ancient Egypt after the Exodus. When they came back, not only did the generation of the returned *Afrim* population not

know their tribes of origin among the Ancient Egyptians, but also they had gone to intermingle with people of other lands. They were physically, linguistically, and culturally not the same as the tribesmen from which they originated. Some could no more claim to belong to the African tribes of Ancient Egypt because they were different. Because of this, the *Afrim* people that returned to Ancient Egypt grew closer to the Greeks who they were beginning to look more like than their Ancient Egyptian tribesmen. What was left for the returned *Afrim* people to do was to find a story of origin that would match their changed circumstances. They found several stories in Ancient Egypt and the foreign lands they had lived. Thus began the fabricated stories of creation, the claiming of legendary patriarchs, and a fantastic story of the *Afrim* peoples' political and spiritual development that could never leave out Ancient Egypt.

What is most revealing in all these is that while historical, archaeological, and anthropological search for the origin of the Jews in the Middle East did not yield any positive results, the latest genetic search for the origin of Jews linked them to an African tribe thus confirming the racial, ethnic, and original black heritage of the *Afrim* people. This genetic evidence was found in one of the *Afrim* tribal groups that refused to intermarry with the people in the land to which they were sent. This land is now the area around modern Yemen. This group retained their original racial characteristics therefore they could easily join the Ancient Egyptians in the Exodus from Ancient Egypt into inner Africa. The group is now called the **Lemba** tribe that can be found today in southeastern Africa. Dr. Tudor Parfitt in England will soon publish the story of the Lemba people. The title of the coming book is *Journey to the Vanished City*. There was a review of this genetic study in the New York Times on May 9th and 10th. However, this genetic study confirms that the *Afrim* people were originally black people.

Creating the Bible in Ancient Egypt

After Alexander's conquest of the East, Greek language became the lingua franca of the entire region around the Mediterranean basin. Around this time, there was a sizeable colony of Greek-speaking *Afrim* or Hellenized Jews, as their history identifies, them in Ancient Egypt. Among these Greek-speaking Jews in Ancient Egypt was the Jewish community of Alexandria that flourished and produced several Greek and Jewish literatures including the works of Philo of Alexandria. The question is why could these scholars not produce these literatures anywhere else in the lands they had been before they returned to Ancient Egypt? It was because the repository of the documents that made the creation of these literatures possible could be found in the Great Library of Ancient Egypt, and no where else.

In collaboration with Greek scholars, the Jewish scholars of the Bible in Alexandria began to compile, rewrite, edit, and translate the documents that were eventually put together by the Greeks as the Book or the Bible. Traditional history suggests that the compilation and translation of the documents of the Old Testament took over one hundred years because tradition again says that Jewish scholastic tradition required that each of the twelve tribes of Jacob [Israel] contributed six scholars for the translation. A deception that took a hundred years and more than two generations of scholars to plan should be a clever one; and this one has deceived millions of people around the world for over two thousand years.

Mathematically, there were supposed to be seventy-two Jewish scholars on the biblical project but there were only seventy. So the first Greek version of the documents that became the Christian Bible was known as the "Seventy" or the *Septuagint* in Greek.

However, if the compilation and translation of the biblical documents into Greek took one hundred years and it required six scholars from each of the supposed twelve tribes of the Jewish people then some very important issues should be brought out. The first issue is that the *Afrim* people claim that the Old Testament documents were original ancient documents of Judaism but that is part of the legendary lying lore. There was no body of documents of Jewish people's religion before the documents of the Christian Bible were compiled. The process of compiling and translating the documents of the Old Testament into Greek therefore was not a simple process of compiling and translating some documents that were already available. It was a process of slowly and secretly acquiring and compiling Ancient Egyptian documents and that was the reason the search and compilation of the documents of the Old Testament took a century to complete. This also means that the scholars that began this work were not the same people that completed it, and that would account for the doublets and numerous compromises of the truth in the Bible.

The second issue, and perhaps an even more important point for understanding the origin of the Jewish people is that if the Jewish tradition requiring each tribe to contribute six scholars for the translation of the biblical documents into Greek were true, it means that at least in the 3rd century B. C. when the documents of the Bible were being compiled and translated for the Greeks, the twelve tribes of the Jewish people were together somewhere. Otherwise where did they find the seventy scholars that supposedly undertook the biblical project? If these tribes were somewhere around the 3rd century B. C., what could have happened to ten of the tribes for them to disappear without a trace, without anybody noticing, and without any historical or archaeological record? Gary Greenberg stated that "The Twelve Tribes of Israel never existed" but these tribes not only existed, they still exist. Unfortunately, this is an example of some of the conclusions that come easy to scholars that do not have the linguistic and cultural backgrounds to the biblical story.

Around the time these supposed ten tribes disappeared, *Afrim* historical scholarship was far advanced enough for someone to have recorded what happened to these tribes, yet there is no record of even their existence. Is that possible, and what is being concealed here? I would like to reiterate that where there are twelve tribes, the two tribes that break away are the lost ones not the ten that stay together. The ten tribes were not lost, they are the two tribes that broke away and found themselves in Europe that were lost. The rest of the tribes are in Africa, and they are at the center of the revelation of this work.

Origin of the biblical documents

In the last chapter, I introduced these quotations from *Egyptian Religion* and pointed out that these concepts of God, religion, and documents existed in Ancient Egypt where the Jewish scholars went to compile, edit, and translate the biblical documents for the Greeks. Are there any similarities between these Ancient Egyptian and biblical documents?

"God is One and alone, and none other existeth with Him; God is the One, the One Who hath made all things."

"God is from the beginning, and He hath been from the beginning; He hath existed from old and was when nothing had being. He existed when nothing else had existed, and what existeth He created after He had come into being. He is the father of beginnings."

"God is the eternal One, He is eternal and infinite; and endureth for ever and aye; He hath endured for countless ages, and he shall endure all eternity."

"God is life, and through Him only man liveth. He giveth life to man, and he breatheth the breath of life into his nostrils."

"God himself is existence, He liveth in all things and liveth upon all things. He endureth without increase or diminution, He multiplieth Himself millions of times, and he possesseth multitudes of forms and multitudes of memebers."

"God hath made the universe, and he hath created all that therein is: He is the Creator of what is in this world, of what was, of what is, and of what shall be. He is the Creator of the world and it was He who fashioned it with His hands before there was any beginning; and he established it with that which went forth from Him. He is the Creator of the heavens, and the earth, and the deep, and the waters, and the mountains. God had stretched out the heavens and founded the earth. What His heart conceived came to pass straightway, and when He had spoken His words came to pass, and it shall endure for ever (See Sir Wallis Budge, 1959, pp. 37-40)."

Until now, nobody has performed a comparative analysis of Ancient Egyptian and biblical documents to reveal the true source of the documents of the Christian Bible. The Ancient Egyptian idea and document stating that *"God is from the beginning"* was what became the biblical introduction of *"In the beginning."* The Ancient Egyptian idea that *"God hath made the universe ... He is the creator of what is in this world"* was what the Jewish scholars took for it to become the biblical version *"God created heaven and earth."* Is it not interesting that the Ancient Egyptians began their document with the conception of a God who was *"from the beginning, and He had been from the beginning,"* and the biblical document also began with, *"In the beginning...?"*

Further comparative analysis of the Ancient Egyptian document above and the biblical documents reveal something else that has never been pointed out in support of Ancient Egyptian origin of the doctrines and documents of Christianity. It is clear that the Ancient Egyptian document above begins with the imagination and personification of the concept of God. This is because logically one cannot have a God creating everything in this world without first establishing how this God came to be. Because the Ancient Egyptians had to create the concept of religion from its very foundations, they began with how God came to be. However, the biblical documents do not begin with how this God came to be because the Ancient Egyptians had already created and personified him. Because the Jewish scholars of the Bible simply took the God the Ancient Egyptians had imagined and personified in their beliefs, the biblical document begins with a God seemingly from no where creating heaven and earth. The logic of the biblical God from nowhere did not become an issue for the Jewish scholars of the biblical documents because they were simply taking what the Ancient Egyptian had already established in concept, doctrines, documents, and sacramental practices. For such an enterprise, the Jewish scholars of the Bible did not have to go back to the beginning of the imagination and personification of this God, as the Ancient Egyptian had to do.

Is it not interesting that the Ancient Egyptian document that existed before the Bible began with a God that was the *"Creator of heavens and earth,"* and the biblical document also began with *"God created the heaven and earth?"* Is it not interesting that the Ancient Egyptian document began with *a God that created man and gave him life by breathing into his nostrils,* and the biblical documents also told the story of *a God that created man and "breathed into his nostrils the breath of life?"* Is it not interesting that the Ancient Egyptian document began with the imagination and conception of a God, His form, and capabilities, and the biblical document began with a God from nowhere? Could the scholars of the biblical documents have begun with a Christian God from nowhere because this God had already been imagined and personified by the Ancient Egyptians? Otherwise wouldn't it have been more prudent for the Jewish scholars of the Bible to begin the biblical documents from the conception and personification of this God just as the Ancient Egyptians had done?

Anyone who knows the beginning documents of the Bible would think the Ancient Egyptian excerpts above are excerpts from the Bible, but they are not. These were the writings of Ancient Egyptian perception of God and religion thousands of years before the documents of the Bible came to be compiled, edited, rewritten, and translated in Ancient Egypt. Why would a modern Christian think these are biblical excerpts? It is because these are the exact foundations, concepts, and perceptions of God that the Bible propagates as Christianity today. Can you now guess where the biblical ideas of God and the story of creation must have originated from these few excerpts? We now know that what Christianity has long asserted, as the Hebrew God is a lie.

This was the God the black people of Ancient Egypt had imagined and personified. The Jewish scholars of the Bible simply took and made this God their own before the Greeks and later Europeans.

Not only did the concept of God and the doctrines and sacramental practices of modern Christianity originate from Ancient Egypt but archaeologists and Egyptologists have found numerous actual Ancient Egyptian documents that they believe were the original sources of the biblical documents. Biblical scholars have also found numerous documents in the Bible whose sources they have never been able to identify. Because the work of biblical scholars is independent of the work of historical archaeologists and Egyptologists, biblical scholars have not been able to put together the idea that the sources of the biblical documents they cannot identify must have been Ancient Egyptian in origin. After all, we do have evidence of Ancient Egyptian stories and documents in the Bible.

What is interesting about the biblical documents for which scholars cannot find sources is that these biblical scholars most of who are Jews do not attribute the sources of these documents to the Jewish people either. However, because they have not yet supposedly found any Ancient Egyptian evidence relating to these documents, they do not attribute them to Ancient Egypt either. So not only do we have a Bible whose real authors Christians and biblical scholars do not know, but also we have a Bible whose archival sources we do not know.

Nevertheless, some biblical historians and scholars believe that the documents whose sources they cannot identify must all have originated from Ancient Egypt because there is evidence that the biblical scholars of Alexandria took and included numerous Ancient Egyptian documents in the creation of the Bible. Even if we find one Ancient Egyptian document in the Bible – and there are several - that should be enough to conclude that if the Jewish scholars of the biblical documents took one Ancient Egypt document, they could have taken and they took several more. However, thanks to the African names of the authors of the Old Testament documents, we now know that Jewish people's assertion that they created the biblical documents is totally false.

Ancient Egyptian evidence of the origin of the concepts and doctrines in the biblical documents can be found today in museums across Europe and around the world. The problems with these documents is that they are stuck in the discipline of Egyptology where Egyptologists are still deciphering most of them. Only a few people get to see or read what has been deciphered, and even fewer still have been interested in them. If Ancient Egyptian historical and religious documents of thousands of years ago have survived to be deciphered in modern times, then Jewish documents of later times from which they supposedly created the biblical documents must also be available for the record. Where is the evidence of the foundation documents from which the Jewish people claim they created the biblical documents?

How could the Ancient Egyptian evidence of the origin of the biblical documents be available in museums in Europe and the Jewish evidence of the origin of these documents be lost in history? Did such Jewish documents ever exist? According to Jewish history, the original documents from which the Jewish scholars claim they created the documents of the Bible are also lost. The search for the verification of Jewish people's claims of the origin of the biblical documents is thwarted by a simple loss without any one knowing what happened to these important documents in the center of the religious and historical lives of the Jewish people. Beyond the intrigue in Jewish people's claims of the loss of ten of their tribes, there is also much intrigue in the story surrounding the supposed loss of Jewish origins of the documents of the Bible. From where did the documents that were compiled and translated into Greek as foundations of the Christian Bible originate? This question and the names of the authors of these documents are central to determining who actually wrote these biblical documents and not the people that compiled and translated them into the Greek language or people that simply told foreigners that these documents were originally theirs.

It is evident in the Bible that the *Afrim* people that left Ancient Egypt into the so-called biblical Exodus had designs to steal and they actually stole from the Ancient Egyptians (see Exodus 3:21-22). Otherwise, why would the Jewish scholars of the biblical documents include such disparaging acts of their ancestors over a thousand years later into a so-called religious book they were compiling and translating for foreign people? Did their God really ask them to steal from the Ancient Egyptians as it is stated in the Exodus narrative? Does this reveal that perhaps the people that were leaving in the so-called biblical Exodus were not leaving Ancient Egypt willingly and that they wanted to do something to hurt the Ancient Egyptians before they left? However, these people did not steal only silver, gold, and clothes from the Ancient Egyptians, they also took with them some Ancient Egyptian religious documents. Some of these were the documents that they later attributed to Moses. From this point of view, how difficult would it have been for Afrim scholars of the Bible to further steal Ancient Egyptian religious ideas and documents.

In claiming the biblical doctrines, documents, and sacramental practices of religion they passed on to the Greeks as their own, the Jewish people asserted that these documents were original documents from their *Torah*, but again historical evidence refutes this. I have pointed out elsewhere that before the biblical documents were compiled in Ancient Egypt and translated for the Greeks, the *Afrim* people had no existing body of religious documents from which to compile the documents of the Bible. Remember that before the documents of the Bible were written for these people to follow these documents to Europe, they were still known as the *Afrim* people. They were not Jews or Hebrews yet. Remember also that, according to Jewish history, the name Judah from which Judaism was later derived, referred only to members of the tribe of Judah. From this analysis, it becomes clear that before the documents of the Bible were compiled and translated for the Greeks, the religion of Judaism for which they claimed the *Torah* had not been developed yet. The history of Jewish people confirms that Judaism was developed after 200 A. D. Scholars of Jewish history in the Britannica wrote:

> The "sages" (rabbis), whose teachings were collected in the *Mishnah* (about 200 A. D.) and in the Talmud, were Pharisees, *whose influence on the development* of Judaism was decisive (1996, p. 74, emphasis mine).

According to this quotation, it was in 200 A. D. that the religious documents that were used in the development of the *Torah* and Judaism were compiled. This is interesting because it was around the 3rd century B. C. that the documents of the Christian Bible were compiled and translated into the first Bible for the Greeks. This means the documents of the Bible could not have come out of the documents of the *Torah*. Instead, since the documents of the Old Testament are exactly as the documents in the *Torah*, one could argue that the documents of the *Torah* were taken out of the documents of the Old Testament, and therefore they both originated from Ancient Egypt. This should not be too far an argument because the people that compiled and translated these documents also originated from the African tribes that were the Ancient Egyptians.

All of these revelations are concealed by a simple story of loss. The mystery surrounding the true origin of the biblical documents began with the supposed translation of the first five books of the *Torah* from what is now called Classical Hebrew into the Aramaic language. This work was known as the *Targums*. Here is another example of the intended deception of the Jewish scholars of the Bible to transpose the names of people, places, and languages to conceal their origins and true identities. There was no language in Canaan called *Aramaic* in ancient times. The language that the scholars of the Bible transposed to conceal its true identity was *Ahmaric*, a language that is still spoken in Ethiopia.

The question is what was the Classic Hebrew language and what was the *Aramaic* language? Interestingly, Jewish history also claims that not only are the original religious documents they supposedly translated into *Aramaic* lost, but the Classical Hebrew language that they translated into *Aramaic* is also lost. If Jewish people have lost all these and they do not have any idea of what or where these languages are, I would like to reveal to them that Classical Hebrew was the *Akan* language of Ancient Egypt, and *Aramaic* was the Ethiopian language, *Ahmaric*. According to this history, the original documents and the original language that would provide the ultimate proof or disproof that the Jewish people created the documents of the Bible are all lost. Jewish historians asserted all of these losses without knowledge of the characteristics of language. No language can be lost when the people that speak it are still living. The *Akan* language of Ancient Egypt can still be found among the *Akan* people in West Africa, and the *Ahmaric* language can be found among the *Ahmaric* people in Ethiopia.

The fact is, Modern Hebrew was never an original language spoken by any group of people anywhere in the world. This is the reason we have never found any other groups of people anywhere that speak Hebrew apart from the Jewish people. Modern Jewish people may not know this but Modern Hebrew language emerged from a conglomerate of the African languages that were spoken by the people from the African tribes that went into the so-called biblical Exodus. What Jewish historians call Classical Hebrew was therefore an African language, specifically the *Akan* language.

Is it not evident that this aspect of Jewish history, the loss of Classical Hebrew, and the loss of the supposed original documents of the Bible are all fabricated to conceal something? What scholars that made this incredulous assertion forgot was that before Classical Hebrew was supposedly lost, the people that went into the Exodus carried names from this supposedly lost language and these people also named their God and the new places they settled in this supposed lost language. That is how we know that the ancient *Afrim* name for God, *Adonai* was derived from the *Akan* epithet for God, *Adona*. Most of the names of these people and places have been transposed but their etymologies in African languages are still evident. This means tracing the linguistic and cultural origin of the names of people and places of the Jewish people would reveal what Classical Hebrew was and the people that still speak it.

There is biblical, historical, linguistic, and cultural evidence to confirm that Classical Hebrew was the *Akan* language. For example, why would people that did not know or speak the *Akan* language collectively identify themselves in the *Akan* language as *Afrim*? Was Classical Hebrew created from *Akan* and other African languages? There is evidence in Modern Hebrew language also to confirm this. Remember that if the indigenous *Akan* name of Moses was *Asaase* then Moses was an *Akan* and he would have spoken and written in the *Akan* language. This means what is now called the lost classical Hebrew language was none other than the *Akan* language. I have already pointed out that the people that left Ancient Egypt into the Exodus were not Jews. The majority of them were *Akan* people joined by people from other African tribes. As a result, it should not be surprising when I reveal more evidence confirming that Classical Hebrew or the *Akan* language, was the dominant language of the Exodus.

As I have pointed out above, it was the mixture of *Akan* and other African tribal languages that became the Modern Hebrew language. For example, in Modern Hebrew, the Jewish people say: *Yeshua [A] shimi* meaning *I am the Lord*, and the *Ga* people that I have revealed were the biblical Gileadites also say *Yehoa dzi mi* also meaning *I am the Lord*. As far apart as the speakers of the two languages are today, the syntactic, phonological, and semantic similarities between the two phrases and languages are evident.

Another issue that comes into this discussion is the deception in the transposition of the *Ahmaric* language to *Aramaic*. Are there any phonological similarities between the names of these two languages and is it not intriguing that they are both languages? Doesn't the fact that there are black people in Ethiopia that identify themselves as Jews confirm that ancient *Aramaic* was the modern *Ahmaric* language of Ethiopia? Look at the two words: *Ahmaric* and *Aramaic*. Could the word *Ahmaric* be the original word that was cleverly transposed to *Aramaic* to conceal the true location and identity of this language? From the historical lies we have found in the Bible, this is entirely possible.

Such a clever transposition of the word *Ahmaric* to *Aramaic* could be deliberate because the story of *Afrim* people says that after the *Torah* was supposedly translated from classical *Afrim* language into *Aramaic*, the original classical *Afrim* documents got lost and they have since been lost in history. To some biblical scholars, the classical loss of the supposed original documents of the Bible effectively concealed what the original documents of the *Afrim Torah* were, and it also concealed forever, the original language and linguistic contexts that could have confirmed the racial and ethnic heritage of the Jewish people and also the true source of the documents of the Bible. Fortunately, the African tribal names of the authors who wrote the documents of the Bible do not only reveal the tribes of these authors but they also reveal the language in which these authors must have written the original religious documents that became the Old Testament Bible in Europe. As a result of this, we can still find out what Classical Hebrew was and we can also find out the racial and ethnic origin of the Jewish people that spoke this language.

Some religious scholars and historians also point out that the supposed loss of the original documents of the *Torah* was the beginning of a series of losses that culminated in the loss of not one but ten tribes of the *Afrim* people thus also helping to conceal the racial and ethnic identities of these people. However, the *Afrim* people left us a clue that they were in tribes so we can go out searching for the lost tribes among tribes that were in the geographical location of the biblical story. How credible is it that a scholarly prolific group of people like the Jewish people could recount their supposed ancestral story dating back to Abraham but they could not keep any historical record of the existence and movement of ten of their own tribes?

Western religious scholars and historians also point out that what is most intriguing about the supposed losses of the *Afrim* people is the fact that they all relate pertinently to issues of origination of the documents of the Bible and the racial and ethnic origin of the Jewish people. Could these losses be calculated attempts by the *Afrim* people to conceal some things they did not want Europeans to know about themselves and the sources of the documents of the Bible? That is the general perception.

Linguistic corruption of African names in the biblical documents
The quest for the source of the documents that were compiled and translated into the Christian Bible has intrigued numerous European scholars. The fact that these documents were compiled and translated in Ancient Egypt has, however, provided some western scholars with a definite geographical setting from where to look for the true source of these documents. Fortunately, these scholars were not wrong in their geographical search because they have uncovered many Ancient Egyptian documents that they believe were the original sources of the documents in the Bible. I will introduce these documents in the discussion of the *Akan,* the people whose documents they were.

However, from discoveries of the close Ancient Egyptian connection to the documents of the Bible, the geographical setting of the compilation and translation of these documents in Ancient Egypt has been extremely important for two main reasons. The first reason is the fact that this explains the nature and source of the transliteration and corruption of the African words and names of places in the Bible and the names of the authors of the Old Testament. Western scholars would not know this because again it requires linguistic and cultural knowledge they do not have. Africans, especially the *Akan* on the other hand, can easily see the corruption of the African names of people and places in the Bible into western orthography and languages.

Such corruption and transposition of African names of people and places in the Bible was not the first time in the history of the interaction between Europeans and Ancient Egyptians. The first biblical documents were translated for the Greeks, and in matters of historical transliteration and corruption of African names, the Greeks were masters. They started this in the 5th century B. C. with the coming of earliest Greek scholars to Ancient Egypt.

In the 5th century B. C., Herodotus of Halicarnassus (c. 484-420) was one of the first Greeks to travel and record the history of Ancient Egypt for his people in Greece. His work has since become the most credible source book of Ancient Egyptian history for Europeans for over two thousand years. Because Greek language and culture and Ancient Egyptian languages and cultures were completely different from each other, the Greeks made a horrendous linguistic job of rendering Ancient Egyptian names of people and places into the Greek language. Since then, Ancient Egyptian history as the Greeks recorded and told it has become a complete linguistic and cultural disaster. It is partially because of Greek linguistic and cultural distortion of the languages and cultures of Ancient Egypt that Europeans have succeeded in denying Africans the credit for the creation of this magnificent civilization.

From such a historical background, it is prudent to expect that Greek and Jewish scholars of the biblical documents in Alexandria would again transpose and corrupt the African names in the Bible in their translation of these documents into the Greek language. Many well-meaning scholars have been aware of the terrible effects such linguistic and cultural distortions have had on every aspect of Ancient Egyptian studies. In *The Wisdom of Ancient Egypt*, Joseph Kaster pointed this out when he wrote:

> Much sympathy is to be extended to the many interested persons who, in their various readings in [Ancient] Egyptian history, religion, and related subjects have been utterly confused by the wide disparity in the transliteration of [Ancient] Egyptian words and proper nouns. ... We have a number of royal names rendered into Greek in various Greek writings dating from the late period. *The Greeks had quite a cavalier attitude to all foreign names and absolutely "murdered" them* (1968, pp. xii-xiii, emphasis mine).

My sympathy also goes to Christian Europe that has been led into worshipping a God that was imagined and personified by the black people of Ancient Egypt. My sympathy goes to Christian Europe for assuming and believing that in the hands of black people in Africa, this same God is pagan. The worst part of this is that Christianity does not know how the Christian God came to be. My sympathy further goes to Christian Europe for worshipping African personalities in the Bible without knowing it until now. However, as a result of Greek cavalier attitude toward other people's names, languages, and cultures, the original African tribal names of Ancient Egyptian kings, people, and places were transliterated into the Greek language. This made it almost impossible for even Africans to identify the names and ethnic identities of these Ancient Egyptians. It has also made it difficult to link modern descendants of Ancient Egypt in Africa to the Ancient Egyptians, until now.

Since the discussion now requires that I establish the African identity of Ancient Egypt, I will reveal the specific tribal origin of the indigenous African tribal names of some Ancient Egyptians to make my point. I began such a revelation in the previous chapters and I will reveal some more. For example, the Greeks transposed the indigenous African tribal name of the Ancient Egyptian priest who wrote the history of Ancient Egypt for the Ptolemys from its indigenous *Akan* name of *Omane Anto* to *Manetho*. This means the indigenous African name of the Ancient Egyptian personality we call *Manetho*, was not **Manetho**. It was *Omane Anto*. This is an *Akan* name, but it is specifically the name of the *Akuapem* and *Kwahu* tribes of the *Akan group*. This name in *Akan* simply means *Omane* the posthumous child.

The Greeks also transposed the indigenous and very important *Akan* name of Ancient Egyptian sky God from *Osoro Kantamanto* to *Osiris Khentimentiu*. It was also through Greek transposition of Ancient Egyptian names that the indigenous *Akan* name of the Ancient Egyptian sot known as *Gyasi Kraseneboo* became *Djesekaraseneb*. It was through Greek linguistic corruption and transposition of Ancient Egyptian names that the indigenous *Akan* name of the popular boy king *Tutu Ankoma* became *Tutankhamun*, *Akuffu* became *Khuffu*, the ancient *Akan* city of *Mamfe* became *Memphis*, *Dade Afre* became *Djedefra*, and *Okyere Afre* became *Chephren*. The entire history of Ancient Egypt was transposed into the Greek language in the same corrupt manner. That was exactly what was done to the original and indigenous African tribal names of the Africans who wrote the Bible. In the case of the Bible, the transposition of the African names of the authors got worse as the Bible was introduced to more European tongues. For further revelation of the African names of Ancient Egyptian people and places, see *Ancient Egypt: The Story Africa Has Never Told*, a soon to be published manuscript also by this author. I would also like to point out for the benefit of those who would like to verify the revelation of the *Akan* and other African names of the authors that wrote the Bible that the *Akan* people who still carry these names are in Ghana.

Abraham's tribe, the Kwahu people

As part of the early revelation of the African origin of the philosophy of religion and the origin of the ancient Afrim people that went to Europe to become the Jews, I would like to reveal the African tribe from which Abraham originated. In doing so, I would also like to introduce a particular tribal group of the *Akan* people. The introduction of this tribal group is important to the biblical patriarchal story. This Akan tribe is the *Kwahu* tribe and the *Kwahu* people. These people can be found today in the eastern mountains of Ghana, but that is not where they lived in ancient times. Historical records show that these people used to live in the region of the Upper Tigris River in modern day Iraq. Western historians identified them in history as the people of *Adiabene* after the name of their royal house. Western historians have written that *Adiabene* was a vassal kingdom of the Parthian Empire. Guess what, the word *Adiabene* is an *Akan* word meaning one has inherited *Abene*. Modern *Kwahu* people in Ghana have rebuilt a new tribal capital and given it the same ancient name *Abene*. Whoever goes to verify these revelations from the *Kwahu* people in Ghana should ask them what language *Adiabene* is, what it means, and whether they know of any modern town called *Abene*.

According to Jewish history, the name of ancient *Kwahu* people that lived in the Upper Tigris River appear in Jewish history because Jewish people went to *Adiabene* to convert the royal family and people of *Adiabene* to Judaism. The importance of the people of *Adiabene* to Jewish people's history therefore is that not long after they were converted to Judaism, the people of *Adiabene* converted to Christianity. Why was the conversion of the king and people of *Adiabene* to Judaism so important that it is still recorded in Jewish history (see *Britannica, 1996,* Jews, p. 75)? After all, according to Jewish people's history, during the Roman Empire, Jewish religious values attracted many people in many lands. As a result, Jewish people succeeded in converting many people in many l ands to Judaism. Why then was the conversion of the people of *Adiabene* so important to the Jewish people? The answer is simple and it is about the true origin of the so-called biblical patriarchs.

Tera and his son, the biblical patriarch Abraham, did not move to Haran from Ur of the Chaldees as God supposedly told Abraham in the Bible. This God got his geography wrong. The biblical patriarch and his father originated from among the *Adiabene* people that lived in the Upper Tigris Valley in ancient times. This is a serious assertion and how do we know this? Today, *Akan* people basically share all names but within the *Akan* cultural tradition and among the *Akan* people we know that certain names originated from and are indigenous to certain *Akan* tribes. For example, every *Akan* knows that the name *Akuffu*, the name of the 4th dynasty king of Ancient Egypt, originated from the *Akuapem* tribe. Every Akan knows that the names *Osei* and *Tutu* originated from the Asante tribe. From this therefore it is easy to know that the name of the boy king of Ancient Egypt, *Tutu Ankoma* was an *Asante* name. In the same way, there is some linguistic and cultural evidence in the names of the patriarchs that link them directly to the *Akan* language and tribe. Specifically, these linguistic and cultural clues link the biblical patriarchs to the ancient *Adiabene* people that were in the Tigris and Euphrates valley. As I have pointed out, the ancient people of *Adiabene* were and they are still *Akan* people. They speak the *Akan* language and they have retained their *Akan* traditional names and identities from ancient times up today. The success of this research depended in part on the fact the Africans that were in Ancient

106

Egypt and in the Middle East in ancient times have all retained the ancient names of the people, places, and things.

I have revealed that the name of the father of Abraham was *Tena* and not Tera as it was transposed in the Bible. It was an *Akan* name and the names of the so-called patriarchs of the Jewish people: *Abre ham* [Abraham], *Sakyi* [Isaac], *Gyakabo* [Jacob], and *Sau* [Esau] all originated from *Akan* words and names. They are *Akan* names because the *Akan* people carried these names in ancient times and they still carry these names from their ancient past. Not only did the patriarchs of the *Afrim* people carry these *Akan* names, but also these names can still be traced to the *Akan* language and names of modern *Kwahu* or ancient *Adiabene* people. For example, anyone who lands in Ghana today looking for a man named *Sau* will be told to go to look for him among the *Kwahu* people. This is because the name *Sau* that was transposed to *Esau* in the Bible is specifically *Kwahu* in origin. This revelation exposes the fact that whether one perceives the Jewish people as Ancient Egyptians or one sees them as descendants from the line of Abraham, they were all black people, specifically from the *Akan* tribe. This was the reason the so-called biblical patriarchs went to the *Akan* people in Ancient Egypt, and it was also the reason the majority of the people in the Exodus were Akan people. This was also the reason, the people of the Exodus initially spoke the *Akan* language, the so-called Classical Hebrew, carried *Akan* names, and named their God and places in Canaan in the *Akan* language. These patriarchs originated from a black tribe, they were *Akan* people, they spoke the *Akan* language, and specifically, they originated from the *Kwahu* tribe that was the vassal kingdom of the Parthian Empire in ancient times.

Interestingly, the Tigris and Euphrates valley is closer to Haran, the biblical country of Abraham and his people, than Ur of the Chaldees. These patriarchs and their descendants were *Akan* and that is why they felt at home among the *Akan* and other African tribes in Ancient Egypt. These were the racial and ethnic reasons these people and later *Afrim* people kept coming and going from Ancient Egypt. This was also the reason the Bible did not mention any linguistic and cultural problems encountered by these people when they supposedly traveled to Ancient Egypt.

As I have already pointed out, the people that left Ancient Egypt into the biblical Exodus were mostly *Akan* the people of Jacob that supposedly went to live in Ancient Egypt were also *Akan* people. Look at the indigenous *Akan* name *Gyakabo* [Jakabo] that was transposed into *Jacob* in European languages. This was the reason the ancient names of Jewish people, places, and even the earliest names of "their" God were *Akan* names. It was all because these people were the same black people from the same black tribes. These tribes were the people whose modern descendants can be found today in Africa and in Diaspora around the world.

Spread of the corruption of African names in the Bible

From Greek transliteration of the names of the Africans who wrote the Bible, the linguistic corruption and distortion of these names became worse because the transliteration of the biblical documents did not end with the Greek language. The Greek documents were used as the sourcebook in the foundation of the Christian religion throughout Europe and later around the world. As the religion of the early biblical documents spread throughout the Greek-speaking world, early Christians adopted the *Septuagint* as the first Christian Bible. In due course, the *Septuagint* and new documents called the *New Testament* were combined and written in Greek and Aramaic and that became the foundational design of the Bible we have today.

The spread of Christian religion made it necessary to further translate the Greek Bible into different languages thus worsening the original Greek distortion and corruption of the African names of the people, places, and authors in the biblical documents. The Bible's philosophy was so well received in Europe that every nation and language in Europe wanted its own version of the Bible. As a result, a universal linguistic corruption of the names of people and places in the Bible began and it included the African names of the authors of the Old Testament.

107

In the 2nd century A. D., what was then the Greek Bible was translated into Latin and Syrian, and in the 3rd century, it was translated into Coptic the then language of what was left of the glory of Ancient Egypt. In the 4th century A. D., the Bible was translated into Ethiopian, Gothic, and Georgian, and it was translated into Armenian in the 5th century. The importance of the tracing of the translation of the Bible into these various languages is that every language sought to impose its own linguistic and orthographical characteristics on the Bible in attempts to make the book its own. In so doing, the phonology and etymology of the African names of the people who wrote the Bible became even more corrupted under these foreign tongues. What saved the corruption and transposition of some of the biblical names from worsening was that some of the early translators of the Bible tried as best as they could to retain the original orthographies and phonologies of the biblical names for the sake of authenticity and religious purity. This was the same reason that made the early Catholic Church portray Jesus and his mother in their true black heritage.

Perhaps, the most enduring translation of the Bible occurred in the 6th century A. D. when St. Jerome finished combining and translating the original *Septuagint* and the Latin Bible into what became known as the Latin *Vulgate*. This was what was brought to Western Europe. Despite numerous errors and linguistic corruption in the *Vulgate*, it became the standard sourcebook for the propagation of Christianity in Western Europe for over one thousand years. From this moment on, St. Jerome's translation with its errors and linguistic corruption became the source from which later translations into other European languages and versions of the Bible were made. As if the corruption and transposition of the African words and names in the Bible were not enough, the errors and linguistic corruption of St. Jerome added to the problem and spread throughout Europe.

The Latin *Vulgate* became the basis of the Douai-Reims Version of the Bible, and this was the version all Catholics were authorized to read until around the beginning of the 20th century. In the 6th century A. D., the Bible was translated into Nubian language, and it was translated into Arabic in the 7th century. It was translated into Anglo-Saxon in the 8th century and as Christianity spread into more lands in Western Europe, the Bible was translated into German, Slavonic, and Frankish in the 9th century. It was translated into French in the 12th century, and Spanish, Italian, Dutch, Polish, and Icelandic in the 13th century. All of these translations and the variety of the languages involved should give the reader an idea of the magnitude of the systematic linguistic corruption of the African names of the people and places in the Bible, including the names of the Africans who wrote the Old Testament. Among the last Western European languages into which the Bible was translated were English, Czech, and Danish in the 14th century. There was no European country in which the people wanted their own version of the Bible as in England. King James himself wanted one for his people. This is rather interesting and very ironic because the English people colonized the Gold Coast in Africa where they acted as if they wrote and owned the Bible. European missionaries acted in Africa as if they had known the philosophy of the Bible since the beginning of time and that Africans have never known anything about this philosophy.

During the Renaissance, the revival of the study of ancient Greek led to the rediscovery of some supposed original Greek biblical texts and that resulted in the resurgence of fresh translations of the Bible. Among these new translations was the translation of Dutch humanist Desiderius Erasmus who published a version of the New Testament containing the original Greek translation from Hebrew alongside his own translation of the text into Latin in 1516. Eight years after the Reformation, Martin Luther translated the original Greek and Hebrew texts of the New Testament and published them in German in 1522. In 1534, he published the complete Bible containing the Old and New Testaments. This became the official Bible of German Protestantism and the document from which later protestant European translations were made.

Today, the Bible in the English language is the most popular book throughout the world but English was one of the last European languages into which the book was translated. The first

English Bible is believed to have been copied by John Wycliffe and his Christian followers. However, it was the work of William Tyndale that became the accepted basis for subsequent translations of the Bible into English. Tyndale translated the New Testament and part of the Old Testament and these early English translations of the Bible were put together as the King James or the Authorized Version in 1611. Before it became the King James Version, the English Bible was redesigned into a new rhetorical style that replaced the literalisms in the original Jewish texts and Greek translations. The English designers adopted a new style of using synonyms to convey intended biblical ideas and meanings. These early European attempts to change the original rhetorical style of the Bible paved the way for the many false translations and interpretations of the biblical texts today.

Around the time of the invention of printing in 1450, the Bible had been translated into only 33 European languages. In the nineteenth century, this number rose to 71, and by the twentieth century, the complete Bible had been translated into more than 250 languages with portions translated into almost 1400 languages. As if the translations of the Bible that began in classical times were not enough, new translations described as revisions emerged in the twentieth century. Some of these revisions were intended to delete language that would be offensive to modern European socio-political sentiments. For example, where King Solomon said, "I am black and handsome," in the Song of Solomon, the new version said: "I am dark and comely." This should confirm to the reader that there was a conscious linguistic and artistic attempt to change the language of the Bible and the images of Jesus, his mother, and the people of the Bible from black to white.

There has since been a revision of King James Version. The *Revised Standard Version* appeared around the middle of the twentieth century and the *New English Bible* was introduced in the 1960s. The *New Revised Standard Version* appeared in 1989. This version is strictly American because it is the version commonly used and accepted by American Protestants. Why have these revisions been so necessary in Christianity? These revisions have been necessary to redesign the Bible to satisfy the racial and socio-political sentiments of our time. They have been necessary to conceal some aspects of the revealing ethnic references that Christian Europe believes would be offensive to Europeans.

The Catholic Church has also revised its Bible. Among the Catholic revisions was the revision and translation of Ronald Cox between 1945 and 1949. The *Catholic Jerusalem Bible* appeared in 1966, and the *New American Bible* appeared in 1970. From all these, it is prudent to expect that the phonologies and etymologies of the African names of the people who wrote the Old Testament should have been deeply buried under the ruble of corrupt foreign tongues. However, these names are still discernible because of the uniqueness of the African languages and cultures from which the names originated.

As I have pointed out, these numerous revisions were influenced by European socio-political and anthropological sentiments. It was in these revisionist attempts that some editors sought to change words and story lines to cover up references to the black ethnicity and origin of the Bible.

Effect of the Bible on the emergence of Western Europe
Earlier in this chapter, I cited Will Durant's observation of the effect of the Bible on the growth and emergence of Europe. Durant pointed out that the Bible became the world-view of European thinkers from Boethius to Bossuet. The Bible has meant a lot to the emergence of Western Europe. However, as much as Europeans have been proud of the Bible, the secret knowledge that the Bible is an African theosophical book embarrasses them. The importance of the Bible to Europeans was obvious from how every European country sought to create its own linguistic version of this book.

Around the 2nd century B. C., the ideas and concepts that later became the Bible began to spread throughout Europe, and the Jewish people claiming to be the creators and authors of these ideas followed them to Greece, Rome, Spain, France, and other Roman colonies in Western Europe. The Bible introduced a concept of God and a nature of humanity and life into western European thinking. Through the ways these ideas were expressed, the Bible became the foundation of western societal thinking and intellectualism. For example, inspired by the chronological concept of the Bible, Galen, the Greek physician began in the 2nd century A. D. to compile bibliographies of scholastic works of his time. In the 4th century A. D., St. Jerome compiled stories of famous men in his *De viris illustribus.*

The introduction of the earliest concept of history to the English people and the very development of the earliest European identity were closely linked to the Bible. For example, one of the earliest scholastic works in the English language by the Venerable Bede in 731 A. D. was based upon biblical perception and thinking, and it was aptly called the *Ecclesiastical History of the English People.* These and other works were among the earliest foundations of western intellectual development. Not only the English people but almost all Europeans began the search for their various individual and national identities and histories through the Bible. That was how Europeans supposedly came to originate from Noah's son Japheth and the Africans from Ham.

The classical translation of the Old Testament into Greek became the foundation that made it possible for the New Testament and Christian theology and liturgy to be articulated and propagated. The translation of the Bible into Latin and its introduction to the rest of Western Europe after the fall of the Roman Empire shaped western living and thinking for over a thousand years. The need for the translation of the Bible into several European and non-European languages led to the development of writing systems in many European and later foreign languages. Martin Luther's 1534 translation of the Bible was considered the foundation text for the development of modern German language, and the Authorized Version of 1611 also became the foundation text for the development and propagation of modern English language. Modern spread and domination of the English language as a world language became possible through the Bible and the propagation of the Christian religion it gave birth.

Beside the development of national identities and languages, the Bible did more for Europeans than introduce them to Godliness and scholasticism. The Bible was the foundation of western civilization and societal development. This foundation was what developed into what is now called the Judeo-Christian tradition based upon the Christian belief that the biblical documents originated from the Jewish people. The Bible gave the west a developmental identity. Through the help and leadership of the Catholic Church, the western world was designed upon religious foundations in which religion, or specifically the Bible's tradition of religion became the fountainhead of societal organization and values.

Today, even Europeans who are not Christians live by some basic societal assumptions and presuppositions that were derived from the Bible. In other words, the legitimacy and respectability of the west was derived from the Bible, and all of the west's societal values and issues derive their foundations of thought and discussion from the Bible. From this point of view, the western world itself took its place in history in direct reference to the Bible. Christianity propagated the place of Western Europeans among humans through the Bible and once Europeans found their place, the Bible became the cornerstone of everything in Europe.

As scholars of biblical literature wrote in the *Britannica* (1996):

> "It would be impossible to calculate the effect of such presuppositions on the changing ideas and attitudes of Western People with regard to the nature and purpose of government, social institutions, and economic theories. ... In theory, the West has moved from the divine right of kings to the divinely given rights of every citizen, from slavery through serfdom to the intrinsic worth of every person, from freedom to own property to freedom for everyone from the penalties of hopeless poverty. Though there is a wide difference between the ideal and the actual, biblical literature continues to pronounce its judgement and assert that what ought to be can still be" (p. 905).

In short, the Bible brought the concept of what is the ideal in human nature and interaction to Western Europe and that is what Western Europeans continue to strive for today. In America, violence in schools and among teenagers has been so bad that some people have advocated posting the Ten Commandments in schools and in all public places to remind young children of the Bible's morality. For all these, Europeans should have been grateful to the Africans who wrote this book. Instead, they embarked upon concealing the fact that Africans wrote the book that has been and meant so much to them.

Europeans did not even do well in accepting the Jewish people that introduced the Bible and the foundations of religion and modern scholastic thought to Europe. How Europeans treated the Jewish people was not how one is supposed to treat a benefactor. In the beginning, the Jewish people were welcomed as the people that wrote the Bible and introduced Europeans to Christianity. However, when Europeans found out that there have been some lies in the whole enterprise, they eventually wrestled the foundations and practice of Christianity from the hands of the Jewish people and sought to make it a European instead of a Jewish or foreign creation. To do so, Europeans pushed the Jewish people to the margins of Western European reality and societies. They practically forced them out of Christendom, the kingdom of Christianity.

As a result, in the 6th century A. D., Jewish scholars of the Talmudic schools in Palestine and Babylon decided to reassemble and compile the old Jewish scriptural documents from which they claimed the Christian Bible and religion were supposedly derived. However, there are numerous questions about that because there is something about this claim that is not supported by their historical documents. This part of the history of the Jewish people states that Jewish scholars finished compiling the documents of their scriptures now called the Masoretic version in about ten years, and Judaism was revived. How could it take the Jewish people of the 6th century A. D. ten years to "reassemble" and "compile" the scriptural documents of the Masoretic version and it would take Jewish scholars of Alexandria a hundred years to compile and translate the biblical documents into Greek? What is significant about the supposed compiling and reassembling of Jewish people's old scriptural documents in the 6th century A. D., is that this confirms that there was no specific body of Jewish people's scriptural documents the scholars of Alexandria could have translated into the documents of the Bible. This was the reason these scholars took Ancient Egyptian documents and tried to make them their own.

Ancient Egyptian documents in biblical literature

Perhaps the more important reason the compilation and translation of the documents of the Bible in Ancient Egypt is very significant in this discussion is the fact that historians, Egyptologists, and biblical scholars have all found what they call numerous similarities between Ancient Egyptian and biblical literature. However, these scholars who were all raised in the biblical perception of things have never had the courage to state clearly and unequivocally that the Jewish scholars of the Bible in Alexandria took Ancient Egyptian documents and translated them for the Greeks as their own. Their findings however, confirm two main issues; either the biblical stories were taken directly from Ancient Egyptian literature or they were rewritten alongside existing Ancient Egyptian stories. One fact stands out clearly in the analysis of some of the documents of the Bible, and that fact is they were not original Jewish people's documents.

How does an anthology of other peoples' myths, legends, and religious stories become a holy book to another group of people? This can only happen out of ignorance of the sources of the documents. It must be pointed out here that most of the stories and events that were attributed to God-inspired Jewish prophets had supposedly taken place several hundreds of years before they were compiled and translated into the Greek language. It is therefore not inconceivable that the Jewish compilers and translators of these documents would want to weave their translations alongside established and existing stories of Ancient Egypt and other lands to make their

111

translations more credible, or modify the Ancient Egyptian stories and seek to make them their own.

Inconsistencies in the documents of the Bible

One very important evidence that confirms that the stories and documents that were translated into the Old Testament were not from original Jewish sources comes from the suggestion that it took the Alexandrian scholars one hundred years to compile, edit, rewrite, and translate these documents into the Greek language. Bigger and more complex books with equally more complex information have taken less time to translate. Why would a book of folk stories like the Bible take a hundred years to translate? The answer is because the Jewish scholars that translated these documents did not have the documents. They translated as they acquired them. They were Ancient Egyptian documents and they were not readily available to outsiders as the Jewish people were at this point in their history.

Another major evidence confirming that the documents of the Bible were not the original creations of the Jewish people can also be found in the confusion and inconsistencies in the stories of the Bible beginning from *The Book of Genesis* in the Creation story. The editors of the creation story could not figure out how to adapt the Ancient Egyptian story of creation to make it acceptable and credible even to the generations of Alexandrian Jewish scholars who compiled and translated the documents. As a result, there are today two different versions of the story of Creation in the Bible. There is the old Ancient Egyptian myth of creation and there is its adaptation, editing, and rewriting by the Jewish scholars of Alexandria. These are what many people have accepted as the word of God and the words of truth. Which version is the truth, which is the old myth, and which of the two is the word of God? Which God are we talking about here? Is it the transformed pagan *Yahweh* whose story was embellished to deceive the Greeks?

In the 17th and 18th centuries, western scholars became aware of the numerous inconsistencies and "double-speak" in the biblical narrative. Such inconsistencies and doublets would not occur if the scholars of the Bible had specific documents of their own to translate for the Greeks. An existing body of religious documents would have been authoritative and would not have been so inconsistent and compromising of the truth. These would have long been ironed out if they were Jewish priestly and prophetic documents that had existed before such a translation project.

Biblical double-speak is seen in parts of the Bible where the same story is told and retold with only minor changes in details. For example, scholars have found two versions of the Creation story. One version created man after the creation of plants and wild life (see Genesis 1). In the second version, man was created before plants and wildlife (see Genesis 2). Scholars have also found out that there are two versions of situations in which Abraham had to lie to foreign kings that Sarah, his wife, was his sister. For an unexplained reason, Abraham named his son Isaac twice, and there are also two versions of stories recounting the number of animals Noah took into the Ark. If these were existing Jewish people's religious documents such situations would not have happened but they were new documents found in Ancient Egypt and the Jewish scholars could not agree which versions to include in the Bible. It seems every Jewish scholar of the Bible in Ancient Egypt had his own idea of how the stories should be edited and retold.

Western historical and biblical scholars have long known about this biblical incongruity and more but they seem to have adopted a strategy of making sure that the Christian masses did not get to know about them. This is because that could undermine the credibility of the Bible and the faith that has been created around it.

Nevertheless, scholars have found great biblical confusion in the telling of the creation story. The final document became an attempt of Jewish scholars to fuse together two different versions of myths and legends in the *Genesis* narrative. The different myths and legends in the Genesis account are now known as the "J" and the "E" narratives. These names are given to the two different versions of the creation account because in one version, God was referred to by the name *Jehovah* derived from the name of the god, *Yahweh*.

Even the name *Jehovah* that Christians have given God is false. According to Durant:

> In Hebrew *Yahweh* is written as *Jhvh*; this was erroneously translated into Jehovah because the vowels *a–o–a* has been placed over *Jhvh* in the original, to indicate that *Adonai* was to be pronounced in place of *Yahweh*; and the theologians of the Renaissance and the Reformation wrongly supposed that these vowels were to be placed between the consonants *Jhvh* (see Durant, 1935, p. 332, Encyclopaedia Brit., 11th ed, xv; Jewish Encyclopaedia, vii, p. 88).

In another version of the creation story, God is referred to by a more common name as *Elohim*. If this God already existed in the lives and imaginations of the Jewish people, they would not have been confused about what his name was supposed to be. However, because this God did not exist in the lives and imaginations of the Jewish people, their scholars had to quibble over what name to identify this God and that was the reason for the two versions of the same account giving God different names. It is apparent that the scholars that supposedly compiled, edited, and translated the documents of the Bible into Greek did not agree on how to present the stories, myths, and legends upon which they had laid their hands. It is also clear in the Bible that this must have been a major confusion with factions wanting to tell the story one way and others wanting to tell it another way. It is prudent to assume therefore that there must have been two powerful factions of Jewish scholars that did not agree on how to present the information they had found in Ancient Egypt.

Early religious scholars used to believe that the *Yahvist* version of the creation story was written in Judea while the *Elohist* version was written in *Ephraim*, later known as *Israel*. However, that was one of the earliest assumptions scholars and preachers used to try to explain the embarrassing confusion and inconsistencies in the Bible.

According to Will Durant, Jean Astruc was the first scholar to point out the differences in the Genesis stories of creation in 1753. Since then, later historians and biblical scholars have asserted that the Bible combined not just the two "J" and "E" documents but four different documents. In their analysis of the "E" version of the Genesis creation story, biblical scholars have found that the *Elohist* version was derived from a third document that dealt mostly with priestly order and laws. This third document was therefore named the "P," or the Priestly Code. Biblical scholars have also determined that the fourth source from where the documents of the Bible were taken is known as the "D" or the Deuteronomic Code. According to these scholars, the foundations and sources of the documents that became the Old Testament were derived from these sources. I must point out that the priestly code and the deuteronomic code were all part of Ancient Egyptian religious foundations for thousands of years before the Jewish people supposedly went there, and even longer before the biblical documents were translated into Greek in Ancient Egypt.

The discovery of these sources also shed light on the nature and variety of the sources from where the documents of the Bible were derived. This shows that these sources must have originated from a highly advanced and sophisticated civilization of religion. Such a highly advanced and sophisticated civilization of religion was Ancient Egypt and not Israel or Judea. Among the reasons it was Ancient Egypt that had such a unified, advanced, and sophisticated concept of religion is the fact that the Bible presents a unified concept of God, doctrines, and sacramental practices for the worship of this God. However, historical evidence shows that the people that left Ancient Egypt into the Exodus had no such unified concept of God and religion in Canaan. As a result, these people could never have produced such a highly advanced treatise on religion and there are several reasons for this.

Among these reasons is the fact that these people were not the kind of settled, peaceful, and stable people to have produced as advanced thoughts of theosophy as we find in the biblical documents. As early as they found a place to settle in Canaan, the people that left Ancient Egypt into the Exodus were beset with inter tribal squabbles, wars, and divisions. Scholars of Jewish history in the Encyclopaedia Britannica pointed out these intertribal squabbles when they wrote:

> Following Solomon's death, *dissatisfaction among the northern tribes of Israel* led to their secession from the house of David and the establishment of the kingdom of Israel. From that time the Davidic dynasty ruled only the kingdom of Judah in the south (1996, p. 73, emphasis mine)

It must be pointed out here that just as the people that left Ancient Egypt into the Exodus broke away from Egypt, so did the tribes that left in the Exodus also break away from and fight each other. For over two hundred years, there was a divided monarchy among the *Afrim* people as Israel and Judah fought each other intermittently.

The various tribal groups also disagreed over their own religious beliefs, doctrines, and sacramental practices and they fought over them. These were the major reasons that led to the dynastic divisions and the creation of the two kingdoms of Israel and Judah. These serious religious divisions among the people of the Exodus also led to the formation of religious and political sects known as the Pharisees, Sadducees, Zealots, and Essenes in Judea.

The Pharisees believed in the adaptation of the old Mosaic laws to new situations. They believed in resurrection of the dead, religious reward and punishment in a world hereafter, and the divine origin of the Mosaic Law and even its interpretations. They introduced worshipping in the synagogues and emphasized the study and reverence of the Mosaic Law.

The Sadducees opposed the Pharisees in every way. They were a highly conservative sect made up of priests, aristocrats, and wealthy merchants. They believed seriously in the cult of sacrifice for the atonement of sins. These people did not acknowledge the validity of the Oral Law, and believed that human affairs were not God's business. This sect was formed around 200 B. C.

The Zealots were fanatic partisan devotees but they were different from the Sadducees. The Essenes was a seemingly but not actually monastic order. They believed in ritual purity and the exclusion of women in the sacramental practices of religion. The point is these people did not have a unified concept of religion and practice for them to be able to produce a unified perception of God and religion as we see in the Bible?

All of these divisions and internal wars weakened and opened the *Afrim* people for external aggressions, defeats, destruction, and captivity. These people were therefore not the kind of peacefully settled people for them to create such advanced and sophisticated works of religion as the "J," "E," "P," and "D" documents that biblical scholars believe were the sources of the documents of the Bible. How could people that did not have a unified perception of God, religion, and its sacramental practices in their homeland suddenly acquire a unified perception of all these in Ancient Egypt for these to become the biblical documents? The only source left then for these people to acquire such a unified perception of all these was Ancient Egyptian library resources. That was where such sophisticated and advanced religious documents could be found. How could the priests and prophets of a people that disagreed so intensely over their own religious concepts, doctrines, and practices have created such a unified concept of religion from which the documents of the Bible could have been derived? The production of such a work requires a long period of stability and theosophical development and the people of the Exodus did not have that. The divided opinions of their prophets and priest over religion shows that Jewish prophets and priests could not have created the documents of the Bible as they later claimed. Jewish scholars of the biblical documents in Ancient Egypt transferred all their people's historical divisions over religion onto the Bible, hence the inconsistencies, doublets, double-speak, and numerous compromises of truth in the Bible today

Elohist and Jehovist versions of the story of creation

It is apparent that the religious disagreement and confusion of the *Afrim* people in Canaan even influenced their scholars' presentation of the stories in the biblical documents in Ancient Egypt. They could still not agree and that was the cause of the doublets, in which different people wrote and included their own versions of the stories with only slight variations. The first version of the biblical story of creation is known as the *Elohist* version. Passages in the Bible that scholars have attributed to Elohist creation can be found in Genesis 11: 10-32; 20:1-17; 21: 8-32; 22: 1-14; 60-63; 65; Exodus 28: 20-23; 20-22; 33: 7-11; Numbers 12; 22-24 etc (see *Britannica*, iii, p. 502). The second version of the biblical story of creation is known as the Jehovist version. Passages that scholars have attributed to Jehovist creation can be found in Genesis 2:4 to 3: 24, 4; 6-8; 11: 1-9; 12; 13; 18; 19; 24; 27: 1-45; 32; 63, 64; Exodus 4; 5; 8:20 to 9: 7; 10; 11; 33: 12 to 34: 26; Numbers 10: 29-36; 11, etc.

Perhaps the most important difference in the inconsistency and confusion in the Bible right from the *Genesis* narrative is the fact that the two versions had different names for God, the creator. Why would these versions have different names for the same God? This was because this concept of God was new to the Jewish scholars that found themselves thrust into the middle of compiling Ancient Egyptian religious documents and translating them for the Greeks. In the first version, the Jewish word for the Creator was *Elohim* referring to *The Gods*. The concept and reference to Gods was Ancient Egyptian in origin thus confirming that the biblical creation story was the Ancient Egyptian myth of creation.

In *Egyptian Religion*, Sir Wallis Budge explained the Ancient Egyptian concept of Gods when he wrote:

> ... mention must be made of the *neteru*; *i. e.*, the beings or existences, which in some way partake of the nature or character of God, and are usually called "gods" (p. 29).

Sir Wallis Budge continued that:

> The early nations that came in contact with the Egyptians usually misunderstood the nature of these beings, and several modern Western writers have done the same. When we examine these "gods" closely, they are found to be nothing more or less than forms, or manifestations, or phases, or attributes, of one god, that being Ra the Sun-god, who it must be remembered was the type and symbol of God (1994, p. 29).

This quotation explains the confusion in the use of Gods in the Creation story. Because the myth of the creation story was not an original Jewish story, the scholars of the biblical documents took the name of Gods just as it was in the Ancient Egyptian document they came across. Biblical scholars point out that this original reference to Gods was changed in our modern Bible to a singular God. However, the evidence that the original biblical story began from reference to several Gods and not one embellished God can also be seen in the creation of man in Genesis 1:26 where the editors of the documents of the Old Testament wrote:

> "And God said, Let *us* make man in *our* image, after *our* likeness: and *let them have* dominion over ..."

This God was speaking to other Gods. Who were *"us"* in the creation story, and who did *"our"* refer to in the first version of the biblical story of creation? Do these pronoun and reflective pronoun refer to one God or several Gods?

In the second version of the creation story, evidence of reference to several Gods is still seen in the use of the Jewish words *Jehovah Elohim* that also referred to *God of Gods*. Again, this means to the editors and translators of the biblical documents, there were several Gods but one was supreme. This reference to *God of Gods* again reveals the influence of the Ancient Egyptian perception of Gods and its pyramidal monotheism. Again, in the second version of the creation story, reference to Gods was changed to refer to one God over several Gods. Who was this God and who were the other Gods? It is in Ancient Egyptian records and practice of religion that reference to God and Gods appear. Again, this confusion confirms that the biblical story of creation was an Ancient Egyptian story.

Beyond Ancient Egypt, modern history and biblical scholars have found out that what is now known as the biblical myth of creation was not an unknown myth around the world at the time of the creation of the documents of the Old Testament. According to scholars, this myth was also told in various versions in Nubia, Phoenicia, Chaldea, Babylonia, Assyria, India, Persia, Etruria, China, and even across the Atlantic in far away Mexico long before the Jewish people sought to make this myth their own in the Bible. The question here is, how could God have inspired Jewish prophets to create this story when it was already the legend of many lands and peoples some of which the Jewish people had been to and knew?

Reference to several Gods in the biblical story is not only in the creation story. There are other instances in which God himself refers to several of his colleagues. Again in *Genesis*, God supposedly spoke as if he was speaking to someone else:

> And the Lord came down to see the city and the tower, which the children of men builded. And the Lord said, Behold, the people is one, and they have all one language; and this they begin to do: and now nothing will be restrained from them, which they have imagined to do. *Go to let us go down,* and there confound their language, that they may not understand one another's speech (11:5-7, emphasis mine).

This passage in the Genesis account was intended to explain why the people in the Exodus had different languages. Why was this God surprised that the people had one language? It was because the people were composed of several different tribal groups that spoke several different tribal languages. When these people came to live together they began to adopt one language. This aspect of the biblical story also confirms that the fictitious Tower of Babel story was an African story involving the coming together of several tribal groups to make the building of the pyramids in Ancient Egypt possible.

What is also intriguing is that this God could not see what the children of men were doing from wherever he was, so he had to come down to earth with his colleague or colleagues for them to see clearly what humans were doing on this earth. When he came, he could not believe his eyes so he had to seek confirmation from other Gods perhaps by asking them to see what the children of men had been doing. Then he told his fellow Gods to go down with him to confound the languages of the children of men. Is this a monotheist God as Christian Europe proclaims today or a pyramidal polytheist God as it was in Ancient Egypt where Jewish scholars compiled and translated the biblical documents? Again, this biblical passage refers to Gods and this was the Ancient Egyptian concept of God and Gods.

Several western scholars who have found contradictions and confusion in the biblical narrative have been quite about them. That is why it was remarkable that a Bishop of the Church would so openly reveal some of the biblical contradictions and confusion. In *The Pentateuch and Book of Joshua Critically Examined*, Anglican Bishop John William Colenso of South Africa brought out the most disturbing details of the confusion, contradictions, and inconsistencies in the biblical story of creation. According to Bishop Colenso:

> The following are the most noticeable points of differences between the two cosmogonies:
>   In the first, the earth emerges from the waters, and is, therefore *Saturated With Moisture.* In the second, the whole face of the ground requires to be moistened.
>   In the first, the birds and the beasts are created before man. In the second, man is created before the birds and the beasts.

In the first, all fowls that fly are made out of the waters. In the second, the fowls of the air are made out of the ground.

In the first, man is created in the image of God[s]. In the second, man is made out of dust of the ground and merely animated with the breath of life; and it is only after his eating the forbidden fruit that the Lord said, "Behold, the man has become as one of us, to know good and evil."

In the first, man is made lord of the Whole Earth, in the second, he is merely placed in the garden of Eden, To Dress It, And Keep It.

In the first, the man and the woman are Created Together as the closing and completing work of the whole creation; created also, as is evidently implied in the same kind of way, to be the complement of one another and, thus created, they are blessed together. In the second, the beasts and birds are created Between the man and the woman. First, the man is made of the dust of the ground, he is placed by himself in the garden and charged with a solemn command and threatened with a curse if he breaks it; Then Th Beasts And Birds Are made and the man gives names to them; lastly, after all this, the woman is made out one of his ribs, but merely as a helpmate for the man (1863, Vol. 1, pp. 171-3).

Again, two important observations can be made out of the contradictions and confusion in the biblical story of creation. The first is that two different groups of *Afrim* scholars who did not agree on how to adapt these ancient stories decided to include both versions into the Christian Bible. The second observation is that the story of creation was not an original *Afrim* people's story else there would not have been so much confusion in simply telling it. The question again is which version of the story of creation is the word of God and which is the myth of man? Both of them are works of man. *Cambridge Ancient History* suggested that the *Afrim* scholars must have learned of some of the ancient myths of creation while they were in captivity in Babylon (v. iii, p. 481).

Perhaps, the weirdest part of the creation story is the fact that Jewish scholars of the Bible did not know whether God should create a man, a woman, or a man and a woman in one person. As a result, the earliest creation of man made him/her a hemaphrodite. Will Durant wrote:

The Persian and the Talmudic forms of the Creation myth represent God as first making a two-sexed being – a male and a female joined at the back like Siamese twins – and then dividing it as an afterthought. We are reminded of a strange sentence in Genesis 5:2: *"Male and female created he them, and blessed them, and called their name Adam": i.e. our first parent was originally both male and female* – which seems to have escaped all theologians except Aristophanes (see Durant, 1935, p. 329; see also Plato's *Symposium*).

The idea of God creating a male and female human first appears in Genesis 1:27 where it is stated: *"So God created man in his own image, in the image of God created he him; male and female created he them."* If the God that was introduced to Europeans in the biblical documents were the God of the Hebrew people and if Jewish prophets and priests wrote the Bible's creation story why would their scholars be so confused as to what kind of human "their" God created? Even if the Bible's creation story were Jewish people's story, why would their scholars have so much difficulty in simply telling it?

All of these reflect the kind of confusion one would encounter in adapting other people's concepts of religion and perception of God without understanding them. In this case, the confusion arose from the *Afrim* scholars of the Bible seeking to adapt and claim Ancient Egyptian concepts and ideas of God as their own. How could the terrible mistake of God creating one person that was both male and female and calling him Adam occur?

Here is another evidence confirming that the Jewish scholars of the biblical documents in Alexandria compiled, edited, and translated Ancient Egyptian theosophical documents and they were highly influenced by Ancient Egyptian concepts and perceptions of God. The Ancient Egyptians that created the concept of God based the creation of this concept upon the normal male and female dichotomy. As a result, the Ancient Egyptians did not have one male God but every male God had his female counterpart. For example there were *Osoro* and *Asaase*, [Osiris and Isis]. Beyond that the *Akan* people that created the concept of God and religion in Ancient Egypt had a god and goddess for everyday of the week. This was how the concept of God and Gods came to be found in the creation story. As a result, the concept of Gods that the *Afrim* scholars were editing and translating for the Greeks was a concept of male and female. The Jewish scholars of the Bible that compiled, edited, and translated Ancient Egyptian theosophical documents for the Greeks misunderstood this Ancient Egyptian concept of God. As a result, they sought to present man as having both male and female characteristics from the nature of the dichotomy of male and female Gods in the Ancient Egyptian documents they were translating.

Archaeologists have also found evidence confirming that many of the biblical stories were not Jewish in origin and that these stories and myths have also been found in places other than Ancient Egypt. In *The Chaldean Account of Genesis*, George Smith of the British Department of Oriental Antiquity found Assyrian clay tablets in Mesopotamia between 1873-74. Readers should remember that what scholars have determined to be Assyrian clay tablets might not have been Assyrian in origin because there is evidence that there were black people living in Mesopotamia in ancient times long before the Assyrians. This could be the reason the people of Mesopotamia and Ancient Egypt shared such common theosophical legends and myths.

The tablets George Smith found were believed to have been created between 1500 to 2000 BC. In these tablets, Smith found the Chaldean story of creation and the fall of man as they were narrated exactly in the Bible. This was almost 1700 years before the documents of the Bible were compiled in Ancient Egypt. Smith and other scholars also found the myths of Paradise, the Flood, and the Tower of Babel in the ancient folklore of Egypt, India, Tibet, Babylonia, Persia, even Greece, Polynesia, Mexico, and several other places.

What is fascinating about these findings is that in almost all these ancient myths, there was man as the protagonist and a serpent or a dragon as the antagonist seeking to steal the immortality of man from him. In almost all these stories, there were forbidden trees as the instrument of man's fall. From all these, how true then is it that it was God or Gods that inspired Jewish priests and prophets to create these stories as religious stories? It is important to point out here that while western historians and archaeologists have found evidence of these ancient myths and legends in several different lands, these scholars have never found any evidence of such myths and legends in Israel. These are some of the scholastic revelations that Christian Europe has long wished were never made, and it has also wished Christians would never get to know them.

Scholars have also found that the "Sumerians" perhaps had the earliest version of the story of the flood. In *Our Oriental Heritage: The Story of Civilization,* Will Durant wrote:

> When their civilization was already old – about 2300 B. C. – the poets and scholars of Sumeria tried to reconstruct its ancient history. The poets wrote legends of a creation, a primitive Paradise and a terrible flood that engulfed and destroyed it because of the sin of an ancient king. This flood passed down into Babylonian and Hebrew tradition, and became part of the Christian creed. (see also Cambridge Ancient History, I, p. 456).

Durant also pointed out that in 1929, Professor Wolley found some evidence of the so-called biblical flood. He dug up an area in Ur and found a layer of silt and clay that he believed were deposited during a catastrophic overflow of the Euphrates River and that lingered in the memories of later generations as the flood. Notice how western scholars have long been influenced into searching for confirmation of biblical documents in the Middle East. This is because they have believed the biblical narrative is the truth and nothing but the truth. This 1929 finding seeks to confirm that there was no biblical flood as it was recorded and embellished in the Bible with a drunken character who saved the world from extinction. The biblical story of the flood was an existing story also taken by the *Afrim* scholars of the Old Testament from some other people. If these stories were all plagiarized then the question again is which of these were the words of God or Gods and which of these were plain plagiarism of other people's myths and legends?

It is important to point out that all these western scholars were looking for answers to their biblical questions beyond Ancient Egypt. This is because they had been influenced by the biblical tradition into believing that Ancient Egypt was even a devilish nation and that the story of God could never have originated from there. In reality, the biblical tradition was destroying Ancient Egypt's image to make sure that the truth in the origin of all the religious ideas of Christianity was never exposed.

Where scholars have not been able to determine the source of a biblical story, they have tried to determine its veracity and found that most of the stories had been too much embellished to compromise the truth. *In The Story of Civilization: Our Oriental Heritage,* Will Durant pointed out that the story of Jonathan and David, for example, were "merely masterpieces of literary creation like the jolly story of Samson, who burned the crops of Philistines by letting loose in them three hundred foxes with torches tied to their tails, and in the manner of some orators, slew a thousand men with the jawbone of an ass" (1935, p. 304-5). Such scholastic observations of fantasy in the Bible create a major problem because the Bible is supposed to be a sacred and true account of events that actually happened through the Christian God or Gods.

Durant also pointed out that the Jewish people even took the idea of the creation of the Ten Commandments, the Mosaic Law, and the conferring of divine origin onto it from other people. This is because long before the creation and conferring of divine origin unto the Mosaic Law by the *Afrim* people, many people in the geographical region of Canaan had done the same thing and that the *Afrim* people must have copied this from them. Durant wrote:

> It was the usual thing for ancient law-codes to be of divine origin. We have seen how the laws of Egypt were given it by the god Thoth, and how the sun god Shamash begot the Hammurabi's code. In like manner a deity gave to King Minos on Mt. Dicta the laws that were to govern Crete; the Greeks represented Dionysius, whom they also called "The Lawgiver," with two tablets of stone on which laws were inscribed; and the pious Persians tell how, one day, as Zoroaster prayed on a high mountain, Ahuraa-Mazda appeared to him amid thunder and lightning, and delivered to him "The Book of the Law." They did all this, says Diodorus Silicus, "because they believed that a conception which would help humanity was marvelous and wholly divine; or because they held that the common crowd would be more likely to obey the laws if their gaze were directed towards the majesty and power of those to whom their laws were ascribed (see Durant, p. 331, see also Diodorus Silicus I xciv, p. 1-2, Doane, T. W., *Bible Myths and their Parallels in other Religions,* 1882, pp. 59-60).

It was from this same leitmotif and along these same lines that *Afrim* scholars of the Bible created the story of Moses going up Mount Sinai to receive two Tablets of the Law from God. What do all these mean to the biblical documents, their veracity as God-inspired documents, and their sources? At least, this should make us aware that these biblical stories were plagiarized stories from other people and lands and that they are therefore not as divine as ignorance of all these has made them to be in the past two thousand years.

Science and the Book of Genesis

In the *Moses Mystery: The African Origin of the Jewish People,* Gary Greenberg pointed out that the emergence of the *Documentary Hypothesis* and science began to cast doubt on the Genesis narrative. Specifically, the emergence of the theory of evolution seriously challenged the narrative of the creation, the flood, and other aspects of the biblical story. In addition to these, the growth of the discipline of archaeology into a science that seeks to confirm history has led to the discovery and continued discovery of evidence and many ideas that contradict the biblical narrative. In his conclusion to this discussion, Greenberg wrote:

The convergence of these academic streams overflowed the banks of fundamentalist biblical inerrancy, consigning much of Genesis to the realm of myth, including the Genesis chronology. Ironically, recent advances in Egyptian archaeology enable us to demonstrate that the Genesis chronology is derived from a historically accurate chronology of Egyptian dynasties (1996, p. 30).

Here is one of the few scholars who have been bold enough to reveal that the Genesis chronology was directly "derived from a historically accurate chronology of Egyptian dynasties." Why would the Jewish scholars of the biblical documents in Alexandria develop a chronology based directly upon Ancient Egyptian chronology of kings? That was because these scholars were compiling, editing, adapting, and translating Ancient Egyptian theosophical documents that were based upon the chronology of their kings. To make the stealing of the Ancient Egyptians documents easy and credible, the Jewish scholars of the Bible in Alexandria also had to design and base their adaptation upon a chronology. That was why they developed a biblical chronology based exactly upon the Ancient Egyptian chronology to make consequent editing and adaptation of the Ancient Egyptian stories possible and credible. The question here is if the Genesis chronology was taken directly from Ancient Egyptian chronology of kings, what other parts of the Genesis and the entire biblical narrative could not have been taken along with the chronology? After all, the biblical chronology was designed from the Ancient Egyptian king's lists to make it possible to fit the adaptation of the rest of the Ancient Egyptian theosophical documents exactly onto it.

Unfortunately, the *Book of Genesis* is the most important book in the entire Bible because it seeks to establish the supremacy of the Christian God over man and the universe. It seeks to establish the relationship between humans and the Christian God and it also seeks to settle the question of the creation and origin of humans. Perhaps more importantly for the Christian religion, the *Book of Genesis* also seeks to establish an intimate relationship between the Jewish people and a God or Gods. However, if the attempt to establish all these foundations through the *Book of Genesis* is fictitious, how much credence should we give to the rest of the biblical stories that are nothing but plagiarized "pagan" stories from other people and other lands? Perhaps the most important question then is to what extent are the biblical stories the works of God or even the works of God-inspired men if Jewish prophets did not create the content of these works?

In comparative history, all these religious ideas can be traced to one origin and that origin is Ancient Egypt. Since the documents of the Bible were compiled and translated in Ancient Egypt, there is no doubt that the biblical documents also contain numerous Ancient Egyptian religious myths.

The linguistic corruption of Kpotufe to Potifar in the Bible

Historians, archeologists, and Egyptologists have unearthed numerous Ancient Egyptian documents. From these documents, these scholars have found the sources of many of the biblical documents but because they have all been raised and influenced in the biblical tradition, they have simply stated that they have found what they call great similarities between Ancient Egyptian and biblical documents. These scholars have found that the greatest similarities between Ancient Egyptian and biblical literature can be found in the stories of Joseph and Moses. Remember that the name Joseph was derived from the *Akan* name *Osafo* and Moses was also derived from the *Akan* name *Asaase*. Remember that the story of Joseph in Ancient Egypt occurred in a period when there supposedly were no Jews in Ancient Egypt except Joseph. There if this story were important to be recorded, it would have been recorded by Ancient Egyptian scribes and not Jewish scholars. What this means is that for the story of Joseph in Ancient Egypt to be included in the biblical narrative, it had to be taken from Ancient Egyptian sources.

In much the same way, the story of Moses occurred in mainstream Ancient Egypt involving the Pharaoh and his daughter raising Moses in the palace. During this period, the Bible says the Jewish people lived elsewhere in the land of Goshen and they would not have known anything about the story of Moses. As a result, if this story were important to be recorded in history, it would have been recorded by Ancient Egyptian scribes and not Jewish scholars. After all Moses was not a Jew, and why would Jewish scholars have been interested in the story of his infancy? Again, what this means is that for the Jewish scholars of the Bible to have included this story in the biblical documents, they should have taken it from Ancient Egyptian sources. Modern scholars have excavated these original Ancient Egyptian sources and that is the reason scholars have found what they call great similarities between these biblical stories and Ancient Egyptian stories. Actually, what these scholars have found are not similarities between these two documents, instead they have found the original Ancient Egyptian documents from which these biblical stories were derived. The stories of Joseph and Moses could not have originated from anywhere other than Ancient Egypt. After all the stories of both Joseph and Moses were set in Ancient Egypt, anyway.

Egyptologist have found that the story of Joseph being seduced by the wife of *Potifar* is very similar in names and detail to the Ancient Egyptian story known as the *Tale of the Two Brothers* (see Simpson, Faulkner, & Kelly, *The Literature of Ancient Egypt: An anthology of stories, instructions, and poetry*, 1972, pp. 92-107; Joseph Kaster, *The Wisdom of Ancient Egypt: Writings from the time of the Pharaohs*, 1968, pp. 270-281). As Kaster summarized it:

> ... this story has as its underlying motif that of the married woman who is carnally attracted to a youth serving in her household. She attempts to seduce him, but he remains adamantly chaste out of loyalty to his master and refuses to succumb to her wiles. Then, with all the "fury of a woman scorned," she accuses the youth to her husband of having attempted to rape her, and the expected violent consequences ensue (1968, p. 270).

This is a story based upon dream interpretation by a young man who had supposedly been sold into slavery to foreigners, yet he ended up in Ancient Egypt. From my knowledge of the source of the biblical story of Joseph and what we have discussed about the myth of the stories of creation, the flood, and the Tower of Babel, it is evident that the Jewish scholars of the Bible in Alexandria also took and adapted this Ancient Egyptian story to make it their own. In their fashion to make every story they took their own, the Alexandrian scholars of the Bible made Joseph the great dream interpreter extraordinary. They sought to create Joseph's story to make it sound like the Ancient Egyptians had never known of dream interpretation before Joseph supposedly went there. However, scholars have found out that dream interpretation was also an original an Ancient Egyptian religious and cultural practice for thousand of years and that the biblical story of Joseph was a literal translation of an Ancient Egyptian story. Not only was the story Ancient Egyptian but also the original contexts in which dream interpretation became a religious and cultural practice were all Ancient Egypt. Is it a wonder that Christian Europe and some Jewish scholars have all sought to push Ancient Egypt down or control what is revealed about her to continue covering up their *legendary lying lore*?

On *The Interpretation of Dreams* and the biblical story of Joseph, Joseph Kaster also wrote:

> The ancient Egyptians placed much importance on dream interpretation. The extent to which it permeated popular culture can be discerned in the Joseph narrative of the Bible; *the entire episode has a completely authentic Egyptian background, and is shot through with Egyptianisms – literal translations into Hebrew* (p. 153, emphasis mine).

In this quotation Kaster, an Ancient Egyptian scholar, pointed out emphatically that the biblical story of Joseph was an authentic Ancient Egyptian story. He pointed out that the entire story has an authentic Egyptian background and the rhetoric of the story reflects Egyptianisms. Since we have all been taught that God-inspired Jewish prophets and priests wrote the documents of the Bible, the question is at what point did God inspire these prophets and priests to write this

Ancient Egyptian story as their religious document? About now, readers should begin to understand why the Biblical tradition has conspired to destroy and distort Ancient Egyptian history and deny the Africans of its creation.

The practice of dream interpretation in Ancient Egypt was much older, but even this record as presented by Joseph Kaster was over twelve hundred years older than the biblical account of Joseph and his dream interpretation. Among the more ancient records of dream interpretation found in Egypt is a papyrus from the 19th Dynasty, that is around the 13th century B. C., the very period believe the *Afrim* people left Ancient Egypt into the Exodus.

Sir Alan Gardiner edited and published an Ancient Egyptian Dream book in 1935. The book is known as *The Hieratic Papyrus Chester Beatty III: Hieratic Papyri in the British Museum*, 3rd Series. Sir Gardiner showed in this work that the papyrus was derived from an even older text from around 2000-1800 B. C.

Scholars have long known that the story of Joseph was an original Ancient Egyptian story. Simpson, Faulkner, & Kelly have even suggested that the story was based upon a myth that concerned two gods of the Seventeenth Nome of Middle Egypt. If all of these biblical writings can be traced to sources outside Jewish priests, prophets, scholars, and divine creation then what should we make of the faith that has been created out of the stories of the Bible?

On the Ancient Egyptian papyrus that scholars have found, the indigenous African name of the man whose wife sought to seduce his brother was not Joseph. It was *Anubi*. Interestingly, in the traditional story of the *Ewe* people, the indigenous African tribal name of the man whose wife sought to seduce his brother was *Kpotufe*. This was the original indigenous African tribal name that the Jewish scholars of the Old Testament simply transposed to *Potifar*. The Jewish scholars of the Bible in Ancient Egypt simply took the *Ewe* name *Kpotufe* and transposed it to *Potifar* in the Bible. Note the remnants of the etymology and phonology of the original name *Kpotufe* in the transposed name *Potifar*. This is still an indigenous name of the *Ewe* people who can be found today in the Volta Region of Ghana in West Africa. The interesting question is at what point in the religious lives of the Jewish people did God inspire their priests and prophets to write an ancient *Ewe* folklore as their religious story? Beyond the fact that *Kpotufe* was transposed to *Potifar*, and the fact that the *Ewe* people still tell this folklore, what other evidence shows that the *Ewe* people were in Ancient Egypt or anywhere near the geographical region of the creation of the biblical documents? Are the *Ewe* people mentioned anywhere else in the biblical narrative or anywhere else relating to religion? Yes, they are mentioned in the Bible and also in scholastic works.

In *The Folklore of the Old Testament*, Sir J. G. Frazer who helped establish Achimota College in the Gold Coast [Ghana] pointed out that before it became the belief of Christians, the belief that man was created from the dust of the earth was a popular religious belief around the world. According to Sir Frazer, the Ewe people have believed this from ancient times and "The *Ewe* speaking people of Togoland in West Africa think that God still makes men of clay" (1923, p. 11). Again, according to Sir Frazer, even the myth that God created man from the dust of the earth was not an original Jewish people's myth. It was a popular supposedly "pagan" belief long before it became a Christian story and belief.

What is noteworthy in this discussion is that not only are we discovering that most of the theosophical ideas that the Jewish scholars of the Bible passed on to Europeans were not original Jewish people's ideas, but also these ideas became the foundations of Christianity. How could it be that this would be the creation of God-inspired Jewish prophets if the idea that God created humans from the dust of the earth were already a popular supposedly "pagan" belief around the world before Jewish scholars included this in the Bible for it to become a Christian belief?

The real reason these stories became the foundations of Christian faith was that the Greeks and Europeans to whom these stories were introduced were ignorant of the true sources of origin of the stories, and perhaps the Jewish scholars of the biblical documents were counting on that. What makes all of these embarrassing to Christian Europe today is that without searching for the sources of Christian doctrines, documents, and beliefs, Christian Europe turned around and proclaimed that the people that first imagined, believed, and from whom these ideas evolved, were all pagans. When it found out the truth, Christian Europe had no choice but seek to destroy Ancient Egyptian history and also seek to conceal these truths from the Christian masses.

It is significant to point out here that Sir Frazer, a European scholar who worked in the Gold Coast [Ghana] found the ancient religious beliefs of a supposedly pagan people in Africa to be the same as the modern beliefs of Christianity in Europe. How could this happen? This could happen because some of the *Afrim* people originated from and were in contact with the *Ewe* people in Ancient Egypt long before they went to Europe to become Jews and Hebrews. In fact, part of the "mixed multitude" that left Ancient Egypt in the so-called Exodus was from the *Ewe* tribe. How do we know this? We know this from the fact that modern some Jewish people still carry *Ewe* tribal names as the linguistic and cultural marks of their true racial and ethnic identities, though they may not know this. To understand how the *Afrim* people had contact with the *Ewe* people in ancient times, let us explore where Togoland is and who the *Ewe* people are today.

The name Togoland, now shortened to Togo is a country in West Africa east of Ghana. It was a German colony until the end of the 2nd World War. With the defeat of Germany after the 2nd World War, this colony was separated into two by a League of Nations plebiscite in 1951. Part of Togoland was added to the then British colony of Gold Coast and the other was made the French colony of Togo. As a result, the *Ewe* speaking people can now be found in both Ghana and Togo. However, these places are their modern places of residence but they lived in places far from Ghana and Togo in ancient times.

Ewe people in ancient times

How could the ancient *Afrim* people have come in contact with the *Ewe* tribe in West Africa? The two groups of people did not come in contact in West Africa or Europe. Around 2700 B. C., the *Ewe* people were among the African tribes that lived in the region of modern Syria stretching down to the estuary of the Tigris and Euphrates. In *Civilization Before Greece and Rome*, H. W. F. Saggs stated that:

> Egyptian documents mentioned a major international power in north Syria called Kheta, and the cuneiform inscriptions knew of a land of Hatti linked to Carchemish on the Euphrates in north Syria. Hatti and Kheta were evidently the same name... (1989, p. 10).

Before I discuss the *Ewe* people from this quotation, I would like to point out that the ancient name *Carchemish* on the Euphrates River in north Syria reveals that another African tribe other than the *Ewe* tribe also lived in this region. This was the Ga tribe from whose language the name of the *Carchemish* was derived. The name *Carchemish* is derived from the *Ga* words *Kaa Kee Mi* meaning do not tell me. Notice how "Mi" in the *Ga* language is the same semantically and phonologically as the English word "Me." The *Ga* and *Ewe* people can be found today in the same geographical location in West Africa.

Concerning the *Ewe* tribe, there are several clues that reveal who this major international power was in the above quotation. How do we know that the ancient international power that was in the region of north Syria were the *Ewe* people? We know this because they left their language. The words and names *Hatti* and *Kheta* are from the *Ewe* language. They are names that are still used by the *Ewe* people. Ancient *Kheta* was a geographical location of a place of the *Ewe* people and these people have built a modern city and named it *Keta* after their ancient settlement in North Syria. This modern city also called *Keta* is located in the Volta Region of Ghana. The city of *Keta* was built on a lagoon that is also named after the ancient city of *Kheta* as the Keta Lagoon. Anyone who lands in Ghana should ask of Keta on the Keta Lagoon, and he/she will be directed to the *Ewe* people.

123

In 1876, British orientalist Archibald Sayce suggested that the cultural artifacts found in north Syria must have been created by the Hittites mentioned in the Bible, but he was wrong. The artifacts belonged to the *Ewe* people that lived there in ancient times. They might have been named the Hittites in the Bible because most of the biblical names were transliterated in a way as if it was done deliberately to conceal their ethnic and tribal identities. An example is the *Kpotufe* and *Potifar* corruption. Even modern *Ewe* people whose names are still *Kpotufe* would find it difficult to identify *Potifar* as a corruption of their traditional name *Kpotufe*.

The *Ewe* people were later in Ancient Egypt where they were also kings. They were linked to the El Amarna Letters found in 1887 in modern Egypt. These letters are believed to have been the correspondence between *Amenofe III* [an Ewe name] and his son *Akenten* from 1370-1349 B. C. The name *Amenophis* is the Greek corruption of the modern *Ewe* name *Amenofe* (ending pronounced with an aspirant p). Among the El Amarna letters was also a letter from the king of Hatti himself. When *Akenten* became king of Ancient Egypt, the king of Hatti sent him a congratulatory letter. This shows that the Ancient Egyptians and the kingdom of Hatti were on good international relations. The *Ewe* people were therefore not only established in the region of the Tigris and Euphrates Rivers, they were also established in Ancient Egypt and their story was part of Ancient Egyptian history, literature, and folklore. It was from there that their story also became a part of the biblical story.

What makes the story of Joseph a complete Ancient Egyptian and therefore an African story is the fact that even the name Joseph is a transposition of the *Akan* name *Osafo*. Would you be surprised to know that some Jewish people still carry the *Akan* name *Osafo* or *Saffo* after over three thousand years of separation from the *Akan* and other African tribes in Ancient Egypt? There is a popular and renowned Jewish scholar at the California Institute for the Future called *Paul Saffo*. His ancestors of three thousand years ago were *Akan*. That is a major revelation, isn't it?

What is of historical interest to those who know about these revelations is that the African tribes I have mentioned in this discussion lived together in the same geographical area in ancient times, and they still live together in the same geographical area in West Africa. The fact is these people are all black and that confirms the original black identity of the ancient Jewish people who took these people's stories and tried to make them their own.

The literary and linguistic similarities between this Ancient Egyptian story and the biblical story of Joseph cannot be coincidental especially since the phonology and etymology of *Potifar* is still evident in the original name *Kpotufe*. From the point of view of Greek corruption of Ancient Egyptian names, it is clear that *Kpotufe* was the original name that was transposed into the Greek language as *Potifar*. The story is originally Ancient Egyptian and specifically, it was the folklore of the *Ewe* people.

Biblical Psalms and Proverbs

What I have discussed in this chapter so far should be enough to convince the reader that the Jewish scholars of the Bible in Alexandria simply took and translated Ancient Egyptian documents for the Greeks. However, there is more. Another plagiarism that scholars have found between Ancient Egyptian and biblical literature can be found between the works of *Akenten* and other Ancient Egyptians and some passages in the Bible. Scholars have found that the songs of *Akenten* known in Egyptology as the *Hymn to the Aten* is strongly similar to biblical Psalm 104.

In an earlier discussion, I pointed out that historians and biblical scholars have now found out that King David did not write the biblical Psalms. In Elliott Friedman's Who Wrote The Bible, he pointed that scholars believe that David wrote only "half of the Psalms" (1987, p. 15). Egyptologists have found an Ancient Egyptian papyrus that has the same prayers and supplications as biblical Psalm 104. How could it happen that Egyptologists would find an Ancient Egyptian papyrus with biblical Psalm 104 on it when this papyrus is much older than the creation of the biblical documents in Ancient Egypt? It could happen only if the Jewish scholars of the Bible took this Psalm from the repository of Ancient Egyptian prayers and supplications, and the evidence shows that they did just that. If these biblical scholars of Alexandria took Psalm 104 from an Ancient Egyptian source, what would prevent them from taking the entire Psalms from the same source? Isn't that the reason biblical scholars have now found out that King David did not write the Psalms, at least not half of them?

Further analysis of Ancient Egyptian and biblical literature has also revealed that the Book of Proverbs in the Old Testament is very similar to an Ancient Egyptian late period wisdom text of admonition called *Instruction of Amenemipet son of Kanakht*. In all these, remember that most western scholars have been raised in and influenced by the biblical tradition. As a result, they do not feel comfortable exposing any lies in the Bible. However, some scholars that have the courage to say so have openly proclaimed that the Book of the Proverbs attributed to King Solomon was not the work of King Solomon. These scholars state that the source of the Proverbs is Ancient Egyptian. In *The Story of Civilization: Our Oriental Heritage*, Will Durant pointed this out in a footnote that:

> The Proverbs, of course, are not the work of Solomon, though several of them may have come from him; they owe something to Egyptian literature and Greek philosophy, and were probably put together in the 3rd or 2nd century B. C. by some Hellenized Alexandrian Jew (1935, p. 342, emphasis mine).

What is sad about these revelations is that biblical scholars have long known all these but they have chosen to be quiet and let Christianity wallow in its ignorance.

Much of the discussion so far has concentrated on what western scholars have found in Europe. However, the evidence western scholars have found in Africa also shows that the Proverbs were taken from African tribes, especially from the *Akan* people that invented religion and created and developed the Ancient Egyptian civilization. Perhaps, out of courtesy to the Bible, most western scholars who have found such similarities between Ancient Egyptian and biblical literature do not come out boldly accusing the Jewish scholars who claim these documents of plagiarism. They state it mildly by suggesting strongly however, that the authors of the Proverbs and other biblical stories might have been strongly influenced by the original Ancient Egyptian texts of *Amenemipet* known as the *Instruction of Amenemipet* and the *Hymn to the Aten*.

From all these, it is clear that biblical literature was not just translated into Greek in Ancient Egypt, but the Jewish scholars of Alexandria took Ancient Egyptian documents and made them major parts of the documents of the Christian Bible. For the scholastic discussion of Ancient Egyptian documents in the Bible see John A. Wilson in James B Pritchard (ed.), *Ancient Near Eastern Texts Relating to the Old Testament*, Princeton University Press, 1950).

For the most recent works of Egyptologists who have found similarities between Ancient Egyptian and biblical literature see P. Montet, *Egypt and the Bible* (1968); D. B. Redford, *A Study of the Biblical Story of Joseph – Genesis 37-50* (1970); D. B. Redford, *Egypt, Canaan, and Israel* (1992); S. Groll, *Pharaonic Egypt, the Bible and Christianity* (1985); A. F. Rainey, *Egypt, Israel, Sinai – archaeological and historical relationships in the Biblical period* (1987).

In his most recent writings however, D. B. Redford who is now the Director of the *Akenten* Temple in Egypt has succumbed to pressures to acknowledge the Jewish people as the creators of monotheism. Unfortunately, this director may not even know that he is the director of a temple built by *Akenten* of the *Dankyira* tribe and that the ancient dynasty of the king over whose temple he is the director can still be found in Africa.

Ancient Egypt, Abraham, and a Covenant with God

In an earlier discussion of the Jewish people, I mentioned that what is most intriguing about the foundations of these people is that even their so-called patriarch Abraham came to

Ancient Egypt before he supposedly went to sign a pact with God on behalf of his people. The biblical story of Abraham going to Ancient Egypt sought to present a story that clearly had numerous gaps that compromised modern logic and truth. What makes Abraham's journey to Ancient Egypt very significant is the fact that he went there to study religion, godliness, and priesthood. After his study, the God of the Ancient Egyptians became his God and that transferred onto his son Isaac and his grandson Jacob. What God supposedly told Moses in Exodus 3:6 confirms this.

The Alexandrian scholars of the Old Testament also took an aspect of Ancient Egyptian religious culture and practice and tried to make them the creation of the Jewish people through the story of their patriarch, Abraham. In this biblical narrative, Abraham took an aspect of Ancient Egyptian religious culture and sought to make it the original culture of the Jewish people by claiming that God told him and his descendants to practice that culture. The biblical story also shows that the supposed intimacy of the Jewish people with this God did not begin until after Abraham had gone to study priesthood in Ancient Egypt.

According to the biblical narrative, when God gave the land of Canaan to Abraham and his descendants, he did not ask for anything in return. However, after Abraham returned from Egypt, where he had seen circumcision as part of Ancient Egyptian a religious and cultural practice, the biblical story states that this God decided to make a circumcision covenant with Abraham and his descendants (see *Genesis* 17: 6-14). Throughout the biblical narrative until Abraham returned from Ancient Egypt, there was no mention of circumcision as a religious ritual in the life of Abraham or his people. What made this cultural and religious practice of the Ancient Egyptians a cultural and religious practice of Abraham and his people all of a sudden?

Abraham was not circumcised until he was ninety-nine years old, and he was circumcised on the same day with his son Isaac. If circumcision were original religious and cultural practices of Abraham and his people, he would not have waited to be circumcised at ninety years old. He would also have circumcised his son earlier than the age he was circumcised. This fact and the circumcision covenant with God therefore confirm that circumcision was not a religious or cultural practice of Abraham or his people before he went to Ancient Egypt. It also shows that Abraham and his people did not know anything about circumcision because it was not their religious or cultural practice. If the religious and cultural practice of circumcision was that important to the relationship between God and the Jewish people why did God not introduce the covenant earlier but waited after Abraham had returned from Ancient Egypt where he had seen it practiced? Incidentally, the religious and cultural practice of circumcision claimed to have been introduced by this God in a covenant with Abraham and his descendants was not a new cultural or religious practice in Ancient Egypt. It was a long-standing religious and cultural ritual of Ancient Egyptian priests and males for thousands of years before Abraham supposedly went to Ancient Egypt.

Why did the Jewish scholars of the Bible seek to make circumcision the original culture and religious practice of the Jewish people when they did not invent anything but instead took everything from the Ancient Egyptians? My only guess is that they thought at the time that nobody would ever find it out, but scholars have found this out now.

There is scholastic evidence of the ancient practice of circumcision in Egypt long before Abraham went there. An Ancient Egyptian stele of the First Intermediate Period dating from 2181-2055 BC over a thousand years before Abraham supposedly went to Ancient Egypt mentions that 120 Ancient Egyptian boys were circumcised at one time. A 6th dynasty (c. 2300 BC) relief of the mastaba tomb of the vizier *Ankhmahor* at Saqqara shows a scene in which the actual practice of circumcision was taking place in Ancient Egypt. As a side-note, the Ancient Egyptian name *Ankhmahor* is a derivation from the *Ewe* name *Ankama and* the *Akan* name *Ankoma*.

The cultural and religious practice of circumcision in Ancient Egypt was one of the first things Herodotus noted about the Ancient Egyptians. In his history of Ancient Egypt, Herodotus wrote about the priests of Ancient Egypt and their practice of circumcision as a clean and pure religious ritual. He stated:

> They are of all men the most attentive to the worship of god, and observe the following ceremonies. ... They are circumcised for the sake of cleanliness, thinking it better to be clean than handsome. They shave their whole body every third day that neither lice nor any other impurity may be found upon them. ... They wash themselves in cold water twice every day and twice every night (see Herodotus, Histories II, 37; Durant, p. 200).

The cultural practice of circumcision was not an original practice of the people of Abraham until he went to see it practiced in Ancient Egypt and he decided to make his people do the same as part of the religious and cultural practices he had learned in Ancient Egyptian priesthood. The ancient Roman writer Strabo even mentioned that there was female circumcision in Ancient Egypt. In modern times, female circumcision in Africa has been the subject of controversy. It is interesting to note that this practice is still found only in Africa where people claim it has been their ancient religious and traditional ritual for thousands of years. This tradition confirms Africans as the Ancient Egyptians and also confirms the *Afrim* people that left Ancient Egypt into the Exodus as the descendants of the African tribes that were the Ancient Egyptians. For modern scholastic works on Ancient Egypt and circumcision see O. Bardis, *Circumcision in Ancient Egypt,* 1967; F. Joncjheere, *La circoncision des anciens Egyptiens,* 1951; E. Strouhal, *Life in Ancient Egypt,* 1992.

It is rather interesting to note that it was after Abraham had left Ancient Egypt where saw circumcision as a religious practice and ritual that his God supposedly asked that circumcision must be a covenant between him, his male descendants, and this God.

I have already revealed that Abraham came to Ancient Egypt from the *Akan* tribe at *Adiabene* that was the vassal kingdom of the Parthian Empire in the Tigris and Euphrates Valley. These people were black and they are still black people in West Africa. In 40 B. C., this Parthian Empire helped Antigonus, the last of the Hasmonean kings to reestablish his authority and independence in Judea. The people of the Parthian Empire must therefore have been black because the people of their vassal kingdom at *Adiabene* were black and they willingly helped the black people of Judea to regain their independence. What would have made it that easy for Abraham to prescribe an Ancient Egyptian cultural practice for his people. Culture is tied to ethnicity and that means people do not just adopt other people's cultures unless there has been a period of cultural interaction and a vigorous effort at cultural transfer from one group to the other. On the other hand, culture is easily transferable amongst groups of the same racial and ethnic origin. What does Abraham taking the cultural practice of circumcision from Ancient Egypt suggest about the ethnicity of the Ancient Egyptians and Abraham and his people?

The discussion so far has shown that not only did the Jewish scholars of the Bible take and adapt Ancient Egyptian stories, but also they took some aspects of Ancient Egyptian culture and sought to make them their own. This was made possible by the fact that the Jewish scholars of the biblical documents must have anticipated that their own people would not believe the logic in the presentation of these stories outside their original contexts, so they designed a rhetorical pattern in which they attributed whatever they wanted to say or do to the Gods. If the Gods said it, then it is unimpeachable. This clever approach was to make people believe the biblical documents through [blind] faith. The *Afrim* scholars of the Old Testament even took the personification of God and the rhetorical pattern of making God speak through humans from the Ancient Egyptians who were the first humans to conceive and personify this God.

The greatest secret revealing that the Jewish people were part of the African tribes of Ancient Egypt is yet to come. This secret is the single most important reason western scholars led mostly by Jewish scholars have refused to acknowledge that the Ancient Egyptians were black people.

127

Beyond the similarities and connections found between Ancient Egyptian and biblical culture and literature, there is verifiable historical evidence linking Ancient Egypt to the Bible. Among the evidence is the fact that in the 8th century B. C., Hosea, the prophet and ruler of Samaria once requested military assistance from Ancient Egypt to ward off the advance of the Assyrians. Incidentally, the indigenous *Akan* name of the prophet Hosea was *Osee* without any silent 'H" in front. However, this historical evidence shows that the Jewish people were in good political and military relationships with Ancient Egypt even after they claimed to have been enslaved by the Ancient Egyptians and delivered from "slavery" by a God through Moses.

Akenten, Moses, and Monotheism

Despite all the revelations supporting Ancient Egyptian origin of the biblical documents, some Jewish scholars still claim that the Jewish people created monotheism. The very beginning of the biblical documents they claim as theirs reveals that these people knew of Gods and God of Gods and not a single God. That is not monotheism. Fortunately, some western historians, Egyptologists, and biblical scholars have gone beyond the biblical story of Moses, the historical account of the Exodus, and Jewish people's claims of their creation of monotheism in search of the truth. These scholars have found and therefore concluded that Ancient Egyptians created the religious concept of monotheism and that the Ancient Egyptian king whose indigenous *Akan* name was *Akenten* was the one who invented the concept of monotheism, and not Moses or the *Afrim* people.

The fraudulent argument that the Jewish people created monotheism is still possible today because the Bible and its assertions and interpretations are in front of millions of people around the world. On the other hand, Ancient Egyptian documents that contradict the biblical claims and reveal the veracity of the biblical documents, their interpretations, and explanations are hidden in museums and introduced in trickles only in scholastic journals that the majority of people around the world do not get to see.

I would like to quote again a passage I have already quoted to confirm that Ancient Egyptian religion was a monotheistic religion from its foundations thousands of years before the family of Jacob supposedly went to Egypt. Here is the quotation:

> A study of ancient Egyptian religious texts will convince the reader that the Egyptians believed in One God, who was self-existent, immortal, invisible, eternal, omniscient, almighty, and inscrutable; the maker of the heavens, earth, and underworld; the creator of the sky and the sea, men and women, animals and birds, fish and creeping things, trees and plants, and the incorporeal beings who were the messengers that fulfilled his wish and word (Sir Wallis Budge, *Egyptian Religion*, 1994, p. 17).

Why is it that no scholar, not even Jewish scholars of the Bible, have written such glorious lines in support of Jewish people's claims of the creation of monotheism? The answer is because the Jewish people were not monotheists. The evidence of this is in the biblical story about Moses, Aaron, the Ten Commandments, and the Afrim people's worship of the Calf.

Sir Wallis Budge went on to point out that at no time in the history of the Ancient Egyptian did these people stray from this concept of one God. He wrote further:

> It is necessary to place this definition of the first part of the belief of the Egyptian at the beginning of the first chapter of this brief account of the principal religious ideas which he held, for the whole of his theology and religion was based upon it; and it is also necessary to add that, however far back we follow his literature, we never seem to approach a time when he was without this remarkable belief (p. 17).

So why are some scholars still arguing today that the *Afrim* people that later went to Europe to become the Jews and Hebrews created religious monotheism? The first reason is that Ancient

Egyptians have not been around to speak and question these fraudulent scholars, and the second reason is that this claim is intended to move Christianity away from the foundational concepts of Ancient Egypt from where these concepts originated as much as possible. In other words, this argument is in support of the *legendary lying lore* in Christianity.

In *The Moses Mystery: The African Origin of the Jewish People*, Gary Greenberg suggested that Moses learned the concept of monotheism from the Ancient Egyptian monotheist *Akenten*. As I have already pointed out *Akenten* was the indigenous *Akan* name of the Ancient Egyptian king whose name was transposed into the Greek language as *Akhenaten*. Today this *Akan* royal name is stuck in western scholarship of Ancient Egypt as *Akhenaten*, but the indigenous tribal name is *Akenten*. The phonology and etymology confirming that the *Denkyira* [*Akan*] royal name *Akenten* was what was transposed to *Akhenaten* in Egyptology is still evident even in *Akhenaten*. When one pronounces the "a" in *Akhenaten* long, it sounds closer to the original phonology of the indigenous *Akan* name *Akenten* because it then sounds like "Akheneten." For more information about him see Aldred Cyril, *Akhenaten, Pharaoh of Egypt: A New Study*, London, 1968.

Ancient Egyptian monotheism in the Atenist movement

Because the name of *Akenten* was wrongly transposed into the Greek language as *Akhenaten*, some Egyptologists in their speculative imaginations have taken the suffix *Aten* out of *Akhenaten* and suggested that *Akenten* created monotheism, but his brand of monotheism was a cult known as *Aten*. These scholars had to call *Akenten's* brand of monotheism a cult so as to differentiate it from the cult of Christian monotheism but again, that is all part of the *legendary lying lore*. What these scholars claim is false because the name from which this so-called cult was derived is completely wrong. Such wrong interpretations of the Ancient Egyptian story are nothing but subtle attempts to find fault with *Akenten's* concept of monotheism so as to make Moses and the Jewish people the creators of monotheism. However, the evidence shows that Moses learned monotheism from *Akenten*. All of these lies have been possible in support of Christianity because modern descendants of Ancient Egyptians now in Africa have not been a vigorous part of western scholastic discussion about Ancient Egypt, otherwise they could reveal to western scholars a few things about Ancient Egypt.

In recent support of the Jewish people's claim of the creation of universal monotheism, some Egyptologists have also argued that the object of *Akenten's* worship was the sun disc, but that is also wrong. *Akenten* introduced a form of monotheism in which the God that was to be worshipped above every other God was the God in the sky where the sun resides. The fact is western scholastic interpretation of the history and culture of Ancient Egypt has been greatly influenced more by these scholars' Judeo-Christian upbringing and influence and how they want knowledge to fit into this Judeo-Christian perception than what the reality was in ancient times.

Akenten's sun disc was a symbol of the sky-God. *Akenten* is an **Akan** name and the *Akan* language of reference to the monotheist God was, has been, and is still *Onyame a owo soro*, the God of the sky. The *Akan* word for sky is *Osoro* and this was the name of the sky-God the Greeks transposed into their language as *Osiris*. In the *Akan* language, *Osoro* means the sky not the sun. Apparently, the misinterpretation of *Akenten's* concept and symbol of monotheism led early Greeks, Romans, and later western Europeans to worship the sun god but that was not what *Akenten* worshipped or intended to be worshipped.

It is evident that western scholars' modern claims that the Jewish people created monotheism are modern socio-political attempts to take another glory away from Africa. This is because there are more records of early European historians, biblical scholars, and Egyptologists acknowledging Ancient Egyptian religion as the original foundation of monotheism than there are acknowledging the Jewish people created it. This was the state of the knowledge of western historical scholarship until it became necessary to conceal or distort the truth because later scholars found out that the Ancient Egyptians are the modern black people in Africa. The logic of some western scholars in this is, if the Ancient Egyptians were not black people then their religion was the origin of monotheism. However, since they were black people, Europeans cannot accept black people as the inventors of the concept of their religion so the honor of the creation of monotheism must go to the Jewish people. Unfortunately, these people must never have known that the people that left Ancient Egypt into the Exodus were originally known as the *Afrim* people that originated from the black tribes of Ancient Egypt. These scholars must have never known that these *Afrim* people were the people that went to Europe to become the Jews and Hebrews. All of these confirm that the ideas of religion that became European Christianity originated from black people.

Early European evidence in support of monotheist Egypt

Evidence of early European acknowledgement of Ancient Egyptians as the inventors and creators of the concept and practice of monotheism is overwhelming. In the *Natural Genesis ...,* Gerald Massey pointed out that Iamblichus:

> "... represented the Egyptians as worshippers of the one God, uncreated, unique, omnipotent, and universal. He starts with this as their starting point, and affirms that all other gods of the Pantheon are nothing more than the various attributes and powers of the Supreme Personified. In short, he makes Monotheism the foundation instead of the summit of the Egyptian religion (1883, Book 1, Section 1, p. 1).

Massey continued to show that the perception of Ancient Egyptian religion as monotheist in origin had been the dominant view of most European scholars for a long time. For example, Champollion-Figeac wrote that:

> A few words will suffice to give a true and complete idea of Egyptian religion. It was purely monotheistic, and manifested itself by a symbolical Polytheism (1883, Book 1, Section 1, p. 1).

De Rouge stated that one idea pervaded the cult of Ancient Egyptian religion: *"that of a single primordial God"* (Massey, p. 1).

Gaston Maspero, the renowned French Egyptologist, was of the opinion that *"all the forms and names of the innumerable gods [of Ancient Egypt] were for the worshipper only so many terms and forms of the one God."* (Massey, p. 2).

M. Chabas also pointed out that " *all the gods and goddesses [of Ancient Egypt] are but different aspects and attributes of the one sole God who existed before everything"* (Massey, p. 2).

Beyond all these, the biblical story of the Jewish people shows that if they ever were monotheists, they became monotheists from the leadership and direction of Moses, the Ancient Egyptian priest. How then can they claim to have invented monotheism? This makes it clear that ethical monotheism could not have been the original idea of the Jewish people. They took that also from Ancient Egyptians and have since tried to make it their original creation to support other false claims in the Old Testament.

In support of all these, I would like to restate what I have already revealed that the ancient *Afrim* people that went to Europe to become modern Jewish people were Africans because they originated from the African tribes of Ancient Egypt. Specifically, the dominant tribe of modern Jewish people was the *Akan* tribe that was joined in the Exodus by other African tribes. It has been a shame that western scholars, especially Jewish scholars would claim to have invented monotheism when Ancient Egyptians are not around to tell their side of the story.

Nevertheless, modern scholarship has done enough to tell Ancient Egypt's side of the religious story and the evidence is clear that every aspect of religious knowledge the Jewish people acquired from the ancient to modern times originated from Ancient Egypt.

Even the Bible reveals that the God that Jewish people claim to be their God was first the God of Ancient Egyptians. The question is if the ancient *Afrim* people were not black people where did they come by and adopt the black African names for their God, for themselves, and their ancient and modern nation, Israel? Or do they not know that the ancient names for their God, themselves, and their nation Israel were all in the *Akan* language?

Secrets revealed

One of the secrets the early apostolic fathers of Christianity have been able to conceal from the Christian community for over two thousand years is the fact that the Old Testament document, the foundations of the Christian Bible, is not a religious record of the Jewish people. The Old Testament document is a composite of Ancient Egyptian theosophical myths, legends, practices, and culture edited to make it look like it is the original record of the Jewish people. The God that the Jewish scholars of the Old Testament introduced to the Greeks and subsequently to entire Europe was the Ancient Egyptian God, and not the God of the Jewish people. They did not have a God of their own until they went to Ancient Egypt where they adopted Ancient Egyptian Gods; and their history shows that even after they left Ancient Egypt, these people worshipped Ancient Egyptian Gods. The real history of the Jewish people shows that they did not have a God of their own even after they left in the Exodus. The Jewish people never imagined or created a God of their own. It was the *Akan* God of Ancient Egypt that all the nearby lands adopted and worshipped and the Jewish people also adopted and worshipped this God too. It was this God that they introduced to the Greeks and subsequently to Europeans. In *Exodus*, God never stopped reminding Moses for him to tell the Ancient Egyptians in the Exodus that he was the God of their fathers before he became the God of Abraham, Isaac, and Jacob.

Documents of Biblical Literature

From all the findings of similarities between Ancient Egypt and the Old Testament in literature, culture, rhetoric, and thought, there is only one question to ask. Where did the documents that were compiled into the Old Testament come from? As I keep pointing out, the original documents that were compiled into the Old Testament were Ancient Egyptian religious documents. The Jewish scholars of the Bible simply took these documents and tried to make them their own perhaps to deceive or impress the Greeks. Perhaps, they did this with impunity because they were aware that what was Ancient Egyptian also belonged to the Jewish people because of their true racial and ethnic origin.

Throughout this discussion, I have pointed what biblical scholars have known and found out in their research and I have also pointed out what scholars of Ancient Egyptian history and Egyptologists have known and found out through their research. Though these two kinds of scholars seem to be researching the same geographical area and around the same topics, they never seem to have collaborated in their research. What is regrettable about this is that the work of Egyptologists based upon an enormous quantity of obscure and detailed work have been presented only in specialist journals and documents whose findings reach only a handful of the public that needs to know. Much of what Egyptologists have found has revealed some truths behind the biblical documents and contradicted most of the claims in Christianity.

Biblical scholars have claimed that about forty different authors wrote the biblical documents of the Old Testament over a period of about 1500 years or more. If this were true, when and where did Jewish priests and prophets find 1500 years in their history to write the biblical documents? However, we know today that this statement is spurious because the authors the Jewish scholars of the biblical documents assigned to some of the documents did not write these documents. The statement that the authors of the biblical documents wrote the documents

131

over a period of 1500 years is also false. It is only intended to support the claim that the Jewish people have known and worshipped God and have produced these documents over the long period of time they have known and worshipped this God, but that is a lie. It also suggests that the Jewish people had these documents before and during their sojourn in Ancient Egypt, but that is also false. Evidence in Jewish history shows that they had no nation or history much less a unified religious perception even after the Exodus. Historians suggest that the *Afrim* people left Ancient Egypt in 1300 B. C. into the Exodus. Historical records also show that it was around the 2nd century B. C. that the biblical scholars of Alexandria compiled, rewrote, edited, and translated the documents of the Old Testament for the Greeks. That is an eleven hundred-year difference that makes that these documents were written over a period of 1500 years mathematically dubious. Beyond all that the historical circumstances of the Jewish people does not support the claim that they wrote these documents. The discovery of Ancient Egyptian documents in the Bible also reveal that the claims that the Jewish people created these documents over a period of 1500 years are all lies. Nevertheless, the final documents of the Old Testament became 39 different documents supposedly from a selection of several hundreds.

The New Testament was created from 27 different documents also supposedly from a selection of several hundreds. The question is where did the extra documents come from and where are they now? Another intrigue about the contents of the Bible is that biblical scholars and historians have determined that the documents of the Old Testament were never intended to be added or related to any other documents of religion. This is because the writers of the Old Testament and the readers of the time believed that the doctrines of religion that were propagated through the Old Testament were the ultimate and only true knowledge and religion. Biblical scholars therefore point out that the last document of the Old Testament written by Malachi was written more than 400 years before Jesus was born, and the New Testament documents about Jesus and the writings of Malachi were never supposed to be related or put together in any religion.

I may be the first African scholar to trace the Bible to its African tribal, linguistic, and cultural origin. However, I am by no means the first scholar to do so. A European beat me to this linguistic approach in the nineteenth century. What is fascinating about such a trace is that European scholars of the nineteenth century were so much convinced of the African origin of the Bible and Christianity that some set out in search of the African linguistic evidence in the Bible to prove their assertions.

Among such European scholars, the work that stands out most is the work of Gerald Massey. In *The Natural Genesis: A Book of the Beginnings,* Gerald Massey traced some of the most important names in the Bible to their African linguistic roots in 1883. Massey revealed the African tribal names and languages from which the name of Eve originated. He found out that this name existed as *Efe* in the Bibi language, *Efe* in Ihewe [Ewe], and in Oloma. He went on to reveal that the name *Adam* meaning father could be found as *Adam* in Yala, Opanda, and Igu [Igbo] languages. This name is also known as *Adama* and *Adamu* in Yasgua. It is also found as *Odam* in Koro, *Dame* or *Dami* in Esitako, *Atami* in Dsuku, *Atami* in Igala, *Itame* in Bini, *Etame* in Ihewe, *Itame* in Oloma, *Etemi* in Anan, and *Tamo* in the Bute language (1883, vol. 2, p. 16). I would like to add that there is also *Afi* a female name in the *Ewe* language and there is *Odame* a male name in the *Akan* language. There is also *Adom*, an *Akan* male name meaning providence. This is mostly probably the name that was transposed into Greek and other European languages as Adam. Remember that the *Akan* word *Adom* was already the name of a geographical place in Canaan – Adomea [*Idumea*].

In the 19th century, Gerald Massey also showed that variations of the name *Eden* meaning an enclosure, house, or home could be found in many African languages including the *Akan* word *Edan* meaning house (vol. 2, p. 19). For a European who did not know these African languages as well as I do, Gerald Massey's study was near perfect. The issue here is, if Africans wrote the documents of the Bible as this book asserts then they must have written them in an African language. This means we would find African words or their transposed variations in the Bible, and there are numerous. For the sake of this particular discussion however, I must reveal here that the name *Eden*, the first biblical home of man, was derived from the *Akan* word *Edan* meaning house or home.

The abode of the biblical Adam and Eve was a home. Africans and the *Akan* in particular do not have a tradition of growing gardens around their homes. Later European translators of the biblical documents added the concept of a garden to the word *Edan* as part of Christian Europe's subtle attempts to make the biblical context more European and more acceptable to Europeans. In the revelation of the African tribal word from which the biblical word Eden was derived, I revealed the African tribal group that wrote the Bible and the language in which the biblical documents were originally first written. Th e group was the *Akan* tribe and the language was *Akan*. Jews or Hebrews did not write the biblical documents and the people of the Bible were not Jews or Hebrews. They were from *Akan* and other black African tribes before they went to Europe to become Jews and Hebrews. All of these go to confirm the thesis of this book, that Africans wrote the religious documents that became the Christian Bible in Europe.

From what we have discussed in terms of the origin of the biblical documents, it is evident that the biblical documents that were attributed to long dead Jewish prophets were all Ancient Egyptian religious and socio-political documents. A major testimony to this is the fact that most of the names of the authors of the Old Testament are African and specifically *Akan* names. What makes this revelation even more fascinating is that the *Akan* people in West Africa still carry the same names as the authors of the Old Testament Books.

The Old Testament alone was used to establish the foundations of the Christian religion over a hundred years before the New Testament was introduced as part of the documents of Christianity. That was the reason the New Testament was never written or translated into the Hebrew or Aramaic languages, and it was also the reason Judaism did not accept or acknowledge the New Testament or Jesus as a participant in the reality, conception, and personification of God.

The fact that the Jewish people do not acknowledge Jesus as part of the conception and reality of God is also interesting. If the story of Jesus as it was told in the New Testament truly happened, then it is prudent to assume that the Jewish people must have been closest to this story and events than any other group of people. This means that the *Afrim* people knew more of the story of Jesus' religious importance than Europeans. The question therefore is, if the *Afrim* people whose story the story of Jesus was supposed to be do not accept Jesus as a Messiah or the son of God, how can Europeans proclaim Jesus to be the Messiah and son of God? Christianity claims that Jesus was human. How can a human be the son of an imagined and personified God? Was it because this God was so effectively personified by the Ancient Egyptian creators of the concept of God? Isn't it because he is an imaginary God that the editors of the biblical narrative created a fictitious conception between this God and Mary, the mother of Jesus?

How can an imagined and personified character impregnate a woman? Biologically, how can a human or for that matter any living thing be created without the combination of male and female union? In the era of ignorance, this was believable as spiritual but today, we know more than what people knew in the formative years of Christianity. Do not forget that as Christians, we are not supposed to question, we are only supposed to believe.

In the Apocrypha, there is an *Ecclesiaticus*; or *The Wisdom of Jesu, the Son of Sirahch* [*Saara*]. Is there another story of a Jesu that many people do not know and Christianity does not want them to know? Note the slight difference in the spelling of the name of Jesus in the Apocrypha. The spelling of the name of Jesus in the Apocrypha approximates the indigenous *Akan* name *Ayesu* that was transposed into Greek as Jesu and then the Greek ornamental suffix "s" was added to make it Jesus.

The prophets who wrote the Bible

Today, the Christian world believes that Jewish prophets wrote the documents that became the Old Testament and the Christian Bible because that is what they have been told and made to believe for over two thousand years. People around the world have been made to believe the lies in Christianity as the truth to the extent that most would find it difficult to believe that there is any other truth beside what they have been made to believe. Supposedly, most of the early prophets of the Jewish people left no writings. Why? Only the later prophets left some writings. Among the first supposed Jewish prophets whose writings were included in the Bible were Amos, Hosea, Micah, and Isaiah. What is interesting about these prophets is that their names are transposed African tribal names. According to biblical scholars, these prophets were supposedly social priests whose works and denunciations of the Jewish people were aimed at the sins of the Jewish society of the time more than a religious world. A shift in Jewish people's claim of the creation of monotheism is that they now claim these priests propagated what they now call "universal ethical monotheism." However, this is only intended to by-pass Moses because of the problem he creates by not being a Jew.

The Jewish prophets also propagated the concept of sin and a judgement day, but again these were older Ancient Egyptian religious concepts as it can be easily found in the Ancient Egyptian *Book of the Dead*. Did any Catholic know that *The Purging of Guilt* or *Confession* is an old Ancient Egyptian religious and death ritual? Those interested in finding out about this can read *Ancient Egyptian Book of the Dead*, Chpt. 125.

They are the ancient works of such African religious writers that have been proclaimed to be the works of God by many gullible souls. As Lloyd Graham put it, who but the gullible would accept the life story of a "fratricidal Cain, a drunken Noah, a jealous and dishonest Jacob, and murderous Moses and Joshua" as the words of God? Who but the ignorant would believe that humans did not conceive a human but he was conceived in a union between an imaginary God and a human? Who knew for sure that this imagined God was a male to make this conception possible and acceptable anyway? Does any Christian know that the God that the Jewish people worshipped after the Exodus was a female God? Her name was merely changed to a male God. I will reveal the name of this female God and the change from a female to a male name in the coming discussion of the ethnic origin of the Jewish people.

The more one studies the biblical documents alongside Jewish and Ancient Egyptian histories, the more intrigued one becomes. The Bible is supposed to be about God and man. We know about the Christian God, his son, the mother of his son, the angels that serve them, and even a [Holy] Ghost. Unfortunately, Christian Europe knows more about God than they know about the Bible and the Jewish people that introduced the documents and concept of God to them. If the Bible is truly the book of God, why is there so much secrecy about the humans surrounding it, particularly about the racial and ethnic identity of the people who claim to have written it? Why is there so much secrecy about the original language of the documents that became the foundations of the Christian Bible? Would anyone believe that the original language of the documents of the Bible was *Akan*? Who are the *Akan* people? Why is there so much secrecy about the rest of the black tribes of the Jewish people? Is it because the Jewish people are now "white" and the tribes from which they originated are still black? Are these tribes also not "the children of God" as the Jewish people claim they are? Why the secrecy about the more contemporary writers of the New Testament? Why have the Jewish people never admitted that they were black people who have simply turned "white" by intermingling and intermarrying with white races?

During the so-called Babylonian exile of the *Afrim* people, another group of priests arose to sustain the spirits and unite the oppressed *Afrim* people in Babylon. According to Jewish history, these priests also left writings that were included in the Old Testament. These later priests were Zephaniah, Nahum, Habakkuk, Hezekiah, Josiah, Jeremiah, and Ezekiel. All of these names are transpositions of African names into the Greek language, and the indigenous African tribal names from which these names were derived will be revealed later.

Differences in the documents and versions of the Bible

Throughout the centuries of translations of the biblical documents from one language into another, some parts of the Bible were rejected by some religious denominations for their own religious, social, and political reasons. As a result, the documents of the Bible began to lose their original content, context, and rhetoric. In some places in Western Europe, the Bible was redesigned to suit emerging nationalistic ideals, and the interpretations given to biblical texts were also manufactured to fit into social, political, economic, and nationalistic perceptions. Today, the book that is purported to be the foundation of Christian worship of a universal God is different for different groups of Christians.

Below are the tables of contents of the Old Testament that was the primary document of the Jewish, Christian Protestants, and Catholic Bibles. Note the differences:

Afrim	Protestant	Catholic
Torah ("The Law")	Old Testament	
Genesis	Genesis - 1st Book of Moses	The Book of Genesis
Exodus	Exodus - 2nd Book of Moses	The Book of Exodus
Leviticus	Leviticus - 3rd Book of Moses	The Book of Leviticus
Numbers	Numbers - 4th Book of Moses	The Book of Numbers
Deuteronomy	Deuteronomy	Book of Deuteronomy
	The Book of Joshua	The Book of Josue
Nevi'im ("The Prophets")	The Book of Judges	The Book of Judges
Joshua	The Book of Ruth	The Book of Ruth
Judges	1st Book of Samuel	1st Book of Kings
1st Samuel	2nd Book of Samuel	2nd Book of Kings
2nd Samuel	1st Book of Kings	3rd Book of Kings
1st Kings	2nd Book of Kings	4th Book of Kings
2nd Kings	1st Book of Chronicles	1st Book of Paralipomenon
Isaiah	2nd Book of Chronicles	2nd Book of Paralipomenon
Jeremiah	The Book of Ezra	1st Book of Esdras
Ezekiel	The Book of Nehemiah	2nd Book of Esdras
Hosea		The Book of Tobias
Joel		The Book of Judith
Amos	The Book of Esther	The Book of Esther
Obadiah	The Book of Job	The Book of Job
Jonah	The Psalms	The Book of Psalms
Micah	The Proverbs	The Book of Proverbs
Nahum	Ecclesiastes	Ecclesiastes
Habakkuk	The Song of Solomon	Solomon's Canticle of Canticles
Zephaniah		The Book of Wisdom
Haggai		Ecclestiasticus
Malachi	The Book of Isaiah	The Prophecy of Isaias
	The Book of Jeremiah	The Prophecy of Jeremias
Ketuvim ("The Writings")	The Lamentations of Jeremiah	The Lamentations of Jeremias
Psalms	The Book of Ezekiel	The Prophecy of Ezechiel
Proverbs	The Book of Daniel	The Prophecy of Daniel
Job	The Book of Hosea	The Prophecy of Osee
The Songs of Songs	The Book of Joel	The Prophecy of Joel

135

Ruth	The Book of Amos	The Prophecy of Amos
Lamentations	The Book of Obadiah	The Prophecy of Abdias
Ecclesiastes	The Book of Jonah	The Prophecy of Jonas
Esther	The Book of Micah	The Prophecy of Micheas
Daniel	The Book of Nahum	The Prophecy of Nahum
Ezra	The Book of Habakkuk	The Prophecy of Habacuc
Nehemiah	The Book of Zephaniah	The Prophecy of Sophonias
1st Chronicles	The Book of Haggai	The Prophecy of Aggeus
2nd Chronicles	The Book of Zechariah	The Prophecy of Zacharias
	The Book of Malachi	The Prophecy of Malachias
		1st Book of Machabees
		2nd Book of Machabees

Note the orthographic differences between the Protestant and Catholic documents and imagine how these differences would lead to phonological differences that would in turn contribute to further corruption of the names of the authors of these documents. Did you know that the word *Machabee* is *Akan*? The indigenous *Akan* words are <u>*Ma ka bi*</u> meaning I have also had my say.

The New Testament
The canonical credibility of the documents of the Old Testament haunted the documents of the New Testament. In *Who Wrote the New Testament: The Making of the Christian Myth*, Burton Mack summarizes the story of the New Testament by pointing out that contrary to widely held beliefs, Christian gospels are not historical accounts of a single set of events that complement each other. The gospels came out of the early history of different and divergent Christian communities whose "anonymous" writers wrote different episodes for special purposes and people. Documents that were selected and compiled as the New Testament were therefore selected from a large body of literature written by various Christian communities over a period of more than one hundred years. This is the reason no two writings in the New Testament ever agree on several issues and despite centuries of editing, they still do not agree. It is also the reason the names of the authors had to be concealed. Burton Mack also pointed out that:

> … with the exception of seven letters by Paul and the Revelation to an otherwise unknown John, the writings selected for inclusion in the New Testament were not written by those whose names are attached to them" (p. 6).

In addition to the documents we know today as the New Testament, there were earlier gospels that sought to teach about Jesus but these were suppressed and not included in the New Testament. Perhaps, the best known of these earlier gospels are the *Sayings Gospel Q* and the *Gospel of Thomas*.

As it was with the Old Testament, there is also an Ancient Egyptian connection to the documents of the New Testament. Three fragments of Ancient Egyptian papyri found to be the twenty-sixth chapter of the Gospel of Matthew were excavated in modern Egypt in 1901. These papyri contained partial lines from ten scattered verses throughout the chapter. Scholars have determined that these documents came from a 2nd century papyri that were bound into a book. There is something interesting from this excavation. Matthew was the only author of the synoptic gospels that sought to tell us that Jesus was sent to Ancient Egypt as soon as he was born to hide from King Herod. Was Matthew trying to tell us something about the Ancient Egyptian birth and heritage of Jesus Christ? If Jesus was even a political leader of the Jewish people, why did his story and activities not appear anywhere in Jewish history? How did his story come to be written in Ancient Egypt and not in Canaan, Israel, or Judea?

The fact that there are Ancient Egyptian papyri of parts of the New Testament shows that the New Testament documents were also written in Ancient Egypt. However, there are questions to be asked here. Could the New Testament documents about Jesus also have been Ancient Egyptian religious documents that the Jewish scholars took and simply adapted with the name of a new character?

It is obvious that the New Testament documents were not written in Europe. Specifically, they were not written in England. It is also obvious that these documents were not about Europeans; specifically, they were not about English people. If the name Jesus was derived from an African tribal name, then his story is an African tribal story and it could not have been written by Europeans that were not anywhere near the place and time this story was written. The question then is how did the authors of the New Testament documents come to be called English names like Matthew, Mark, Luke, John, Peter, James, Timothy and others when these authors were not English men? What is interesting about this is that we in Africa know that Christian Europe has deceived Europeans and Christians around the world, but Europeans have never figured this out. What is sad about it all is that all of these deceptions were undertaken to support European racism and racial prejudice against black people whose story it was. Otherwise, how could the authors of the Old Testament carry African tribal names and the authors of the New Testament carry fictitious English names?

The documents of the Old Testament inaugurated the Christian faith. Why was it necessary for communities of the early Christian Church to add other documents to the foundation of the Bible's faith? It must be pointed out that what are presented in the Bible, as the gospels are not true historical accounts but the story of a recollection of the sayings and activities of Jesus. These recollections were ostensibly intended to confer part of the sacredness of the emerging Christian faith on a Jewish personality because that had its social and political advantages at the time.

In more ways than one, the creation of the Christian faith around the personality of Jesus with the support of Jewish scholars was an act of religious secession, revolution, and betrayal of the beliefs of the Jewish people. This is part of the reason Judaism, the traditional Jewish faith, whose object of worship is God and its central personality of faith is Moses, does not acknowledge Jesus as a true participant in the concept and reality of God. As a result, there is no New Testament in the Hebrew Bible. It can be found only in the Protestant and Catholic Bibles. Why?

The documents that were compiled into the New Testament were mostly letters and private documents that were supposedly put together about 35 years after the death of Jesus. From the beginning, there were even Christians that doubted the veracity of the stories about Jesus and failed to accept him as part of the sanctity and reality of God. The inclusion of Jesus as part of God challenged the very foundations of the claims of Christian monotheism. Other Christians believed that the writings about Jesus were nothing more than reflections of Jewish and Greek perceptions of God and Jesus. This was because the story of Jesus was told through the experiences of people most of who never saw him.

Below are the contents of the New Testament in the Protestant and Catholic Bibles. Among Christians in Europe as a whole and especially among Protestants and Catholics, there has been and there is still an attempt to be different from each other. This struggle to be different from each other has affected all other religions, and it has even affected the content of the Bible that Churches use, though it is supposed to be about the same God or Gods. Note the attempts to give the same contents different titles in both Bibles.

Protestant Bible	*Catholic Bible*
Gospel According to Matthew	Gospel of Jesus Christ According to Matthew
Gospel According to Mark	Gospel of Jesus Christ According to Mark
Gospel According to Luke	Gospel of Jesus Christ According to Luke
Gospel According to John	Gospel of Jesus Christ According to John
Acts of the Apostles	Acts of the Apostles
Letter of Paul to the Romans	Epistle of St. Paul the Apostle to the Romans
1st Letter of Paul to the Corinthians	1st Epistle of St. Paul the Apostle to the Corinthians
2nd Letter of Paul to the Corinthians	2nd Epistle of St. Paul the Apostle to the Corinthians
Letter of Paul to the Galatians	Epistle of St. Paul the Apostle to the Galatians
Letter of Paul to the Ephesians	Epistle of St. Paul the Apostle to the Ephesians
Letter of Paul to the Philippians	Epistle of St. Paul the Apostle to the Philippians
Letter of Paul to the Colossians	Epistle of St. Paul the Apostle to the Colossians
1st Letter of Paul to the Thessalonians	1st Epistle of St. Paul the Apostle to the Thessalonians
2nd Letter of Paul to the Thessalonians	2nd Epistle of St. Paul the Apostle to the Thessalonians
1st Letter of Paul to Timothy	1st Epistle of St. Paul the Apostle to Timothy
2nd Letter of Paul to Timothy	2nd Epistle of St. Paul the Apostle to Timothy
Letter of Paul to Titus	Epistle of St. Paul the Apostle to Titus
Letter of Paul to Philemon	Epistle of St. Paul the Apostle to Philemon
Letter of Paul to the Hebrews	Epistle of St. Paul the Apostle to the Hebrews
Letter of James	Epistle of St. James the Apostle
1st Letter of Peter	1st Epistle of St. Peter the Apostle
2nd Letter of Peter	2nd Epistle of St. Peter the Apostle
1st Letter of John	1st letter of St. John the Apostle
2nd Letter of John	2nd Epistle of St. John the Apostle
3rd Letter of John	3rd Epistle of St. John the Apostle
Letter of Jude	Epistle of St. Jude the Apostle
Revelation to John	Apocalypse of St. John the Apostle.

The Apocrypha

The Old and New Testaments are not the only religious documents of Christianity. In the early years of Christianity, many religious scholars who knew the sources of the biblical documents also wanted to add their ideas to the Bible. As a result, many documents of dubious authenticity floated around early Christian communities and very strange circumstances began to surround the early years of the creation of the Bible. This is also one of the reasons the names of the authors of the New Testament had to be concealed. However, the Christian community finally found out that some of the writings they believed to have been written from the ordination of God were downright fictitious.

Among the supposed fictitious Christian writings were the documents that were compiled into what is now called the *Apocrypha*. Among the synonyms of the Greek word *Apocrypha* are "doubtful authenticity, disputed, fraudulent, spurious, fictitious, and fake." These synonyms show that there were numerous fictitious documents claiming to be Christian documents and that the documents of the *Apocrypha* were not religious books worthy to be included in the documents of the Bible of early Christian communities. Early Christian leaders determined what document was fictitious and what was not. They determined what documents to include in the New Testament and what to exclude. From this, the assumption has been that what were included in the Bible were gospels and gospel truths, but they were not. The question is how did the early Christian leaders differentiate writings from the ordination of God from the so-called fictitious ones? The answer is it was arbitrary. However, we have accepted them all as the truth today.

Nevertheless, Christianity grew out of the documents compiled by Greek-speaking Jewish scholars in Alexandria in Ancient Egypt and the early converts into Christianity were mostly Greeks in Egypt, Greeks on the mainland, and people from the lands that were ruled by the Greeks at that time. The Greek Bible from Alexandria was therefore the first official Bible of Christianity, and references and quotations from this original Bible in the New Testament confirm that the Bible from Alexandria was the original. Within this Alexandrian Bible, scholars of religion have found some books whose origins no one knows and therefore their acceptance and canonical statuses have been a matter of great controversy among various Christian denominations and communities. Again, if the Bible is a book of God why is there so much confusion over the acceptance of some documents and the rejection of others. Why the secrecy around some of the writings supposed to be the words of God?

The New Testament does not directly refer to the documents of the *Apocrypha* but there is evidence in it to show that the writers of the New Testament knew of the *Apocrypha,* and the early apostolic fathers of the 1st and 2nd centuries also knew of it. Throughout the history of the creation and re-creation of the Bible, some Christian groups have accepted the *Apocrypha* and versions of their Bibles have included the *Apocrypha* while others have excluded it. Even those who have excluded the *Apocrypha* in their versions of the Bible have tended to use the documents freely in their religious discussions and writings. Synods of early leaders and councils of the African Church held at Hippo in 393 and Carthage in 397 and 419 A. D. accepted the *Apocrypha* as sacred scriptures. However, today most Christians do not accept it as such. Below are the contents of the *Apocrypha*:

The First Book of Esdras
The Second Book of Esdras
Tobit
Judith
Additions to the Book of Esther
The Wisdom of Solomon
Ecclesiaticus; or The Wisdom of Jesu the Son of Sirahch
Baruch
The Letter of Jeremiah
The Prayer of Azariah and the Song of the Three Young Men
Sussanna
Bel and the Dragon
The Prayer of Manasseh
The First Book of Maccabees
The Second Book of Maccabees

Note the Ecclesiasticus; or the Wisdom of Jesu, the Son of Sirahch in the *Apocrypha*. The Old Testament books of Ezra and Nehemia are the first and second books of Esdras in the Catholic Bible. The Catholic Bible also puts the two books of Esdras together as the third book of Esdras yet they are not considered part of the Protestant or Catholic Bibles. Eastern Orthodox Churches accepted and included all the books of the *Apocrypha* including Third Esdras in their Old Testament. The Prayer of Manasseh was included only in an appendix to the Latin Vulgate.

It has been over two thousand years since Europeans were introduced to the concepts of Christianity. The outward perception has been that Europeans still do not know the true source of the concepts and documents they accepted and adopted as their religion. However, the evidence shows that though historians and biblical scholars may not know the details I am revealing here, they have known the general outline of the racial and ethnic relationships in the story of Ancient Egyptians, Africans, Jews, the Bible, and Christianity. This evidence also shows that they have been doing everything they can to deny, distort, and destroy evidence of this relationship. More than that, the evidence also shows that Christian Europe has been doing everything over these two thousand years to make sure that this information does not become public knowledge.

The fact still remains that Ancient Egyptians created and practiced the concept of religion thousands of years before Christianity emerged out of this creation. Research of Europeans in Africa among the modern descendants of Ancient Egyptians has confirmed that some of these Africans still have the earliest foundations of Christian thought and practice in their so-called "pagan" religions, culture, and traditions. From the discussion so far, I have established that every aspect of the foundation of Christian thought and practice, from the people that claim to have created the concepts and documents of the Bible to the actual creation of the Bible originated from Ancient Egypt.

Early apostolic leaders and religious scholars knew of the difficulty of making Christianity, its beliefs, and practices, a European creation with the imposing figure of Ancient Egypt in the background. As a result, these people embarked upon bringing down the name and image of Ancient Egypt so as to bolster the name and the image of Christianity. In Christianity, this practice was practically overt. As Nicolas Grimal stated in his introduction to *A History of Ancient Egypt:*

> It was not so long ago, however, that the combined influence of the Bible and the Classical tradition *conspired* to produce a rather incoherent view of [Ancient] Egyptian civilization. ... (1992, emphasis mine).

The question is why would the Bible and Classical tradition conspire to distort Ancient Egyptian civilization and history? What would the Bible gain and what would the classical tradition also gain from such conspiracy? The answer is simple. The distortion of Ancient Egyptian civilization and history would help the Bible and Christianity cut off their origins from Ancient Egypt. In other words, the Bible gains in such conspiracy by being able to continue to deny that the biblical documents and the foundation doctrines of Christianity originated from Ancient Egypt. For the classical tradition, there is an even greater gain for itself and entire Europe. Ancient Egyptians invented the foundations of modern civilization. They invented religion, Gods, monotheism, agriculture, mining, manufacturing, engineering, transportation, postal service, commerce, finance, education, schools of government, paper and ink, writing system, books, libraries, alchemy, science, mathematics, astronomy, calendar, anatomy, physiology, medicine, surgery, hygiene, architecture, painting, music, art, sculpture, philosophy, and every possible concept that has made our modern civilization possible. In our era of racism and racial prejudice, Western Europe in particular cannot concede such great achievements to Ancient Egyptians and therefore Africans. As a result, Western Europe has insisted that its civilization came from Greece and the Greek civilization did not come out of Ancient Egypt. This lie, however, has been more and more difficult to uphold with the growth of knowledge. Therefore, the easiest approach to upholding this lie has been to distort Ancient Egyptian civilization and history to make it inferior to Greek civilization and help to uphold Western superiority over Africans.

For example, what western professor of literature would tell his students that the concept of Carpe Diem – seize the day – by Kafka, was first written in a poem in Ancient Egypt around 2200 B. C.? That would credit this idea to the Ancient Egyptians and therefore the Africans. Yet, the Ancient Egyptian papyrus of this poem is now held in Leyden Museum. What professor of medicine would tell his students that "the glory of Egyptian science was medicine"? As Durant wrote:

> From such depths we rise in Egypt to great physicians, surgeons, and specialists, who acknowledge an ethical code that passed down into the famous Hippocratic oath (1935, p. 182, see also Garrison, *History of Medicine*, p. 57).

Notice how Ancient Egyptian ethical code of medicine was passed down for it to become the Hippocratic oath and the modern creation of the Greeks. All of these have been about concealing, distorting, and denying Ancient Egyptian achievements so others can claim the honor and the glory in these achievements in eyes of the modern world.

Grimal is right about the conspiracy of Christianity and the classical tradition to distort and deny Ancient Egypt's enviable place in the religions of the world, especially the Christian religion. The statement however, sounds as if the conspiracy against Ancient Egypt and modern descendants of Ancient Egyptians has stopped, but it has not. It is still going on in even more subtle ways in western historical scholarship and even in Egyptology.

For example, many scholars of African descent and even some European scholars who cannot be deceived have never understood why despite the overwhelming evidence, European historians and Egyptologists still refuse to acknowledge that Ancient Egyptian civilization was a black African civilization. The reason is simple. The early apostolic fathers of Christianity have long known that what they call Christianity today is nothing more than a reincarnation of Ancient Egyptian religious doctrines and practices of faith. If they acknowledge that Ancient Egypt was a black civilization, it would mean they also have to acknowledge that the concepts and doctrines of Christianity are ancient black African creations.

Christian Europe knows that despite professing to the Christian religion and God, most Europeans do not want to know that the concepts and doctrines of Christianity are ancient African creations. This is because it would be inconsistent with early Christian leaders' pronouncement of African religion as "pagan," and it would also be inconsistent with European socio-political perception of itself as the superior one and Africans as the inferior ones. How would it sound to hear that Christian Europe adopted "pagan" Africa's concepts and doctrines of religion, or superior and civilized Europe merely redesigned inferior and primitive Africa's ancient civilization into modern civilization?

Despite public scholastic denials, Europeans know that all of these originated from Ancient Egyptian thoughts of religion and civilization. Secretly, Christian Europe has been fighting off the name and image of Ancient Egypt that have loomed rather too largely over the history and practice of Christianity for over two thousand years. This is the reason the influence of the Bible and classical tradition have long conspired to distort the true history of Ancient Egypt as a basis for the denial of the Bible and Christianity's relationship with Ancient Egypt and the African people. Nevertheless, Ancient Egyptians and their modern descendants in Africa have been in the middle of whatever has happened in this world through religion and they cannot be pushed aside now.

141

4

Effects of Christianity on Europeans, Ancient Egyptians, and their Modern Descendants in Africa.

> The great snare of thought is uncritical acceptance of irrational assumptions.
> Will Durant

> If you want to see man at his worst, observe what he does to fellow men in the name of God.

> Realism is a corruption of reality
> Wallace Stevens

Introduction

I showed in the last chapter that the documents of the Christian Bible originated from Ancient Egyptian religious documents and that the Jewish scholars that had to translate these documents for the Greeks merely claimed them as their own. However, perhaps revealing the origin of the biblical documents is not as important as the effects of the introduction of these documents to the Greeks and Europeans on Europeans themselves, the Ancient Egyptians, and their modern descendants in Africa. The importance of the revelation of these effects is that like other issues concerning religion, Christian Europe and historians have almost swept them under the rug and where they are mentioned they are not mentioned as the effects of the introduction of the philosophy of religion to Europeans.

Traditionally, historians, archaeologists, Egyptologist, and even paleontologists have perceived, imagined, and woven a world history of events as if historical events have no causes or ripple effects. These scholars have told much of the story of ancient civilizations as if the people that created these ancient stories are extinct and there are no modern descendants of these ancient people. All of these have been caused by the influence of the Bible in which all other groups of people were made to disappear except the Jewish people. For example, the biblical story states that Abraham, Jacob, and their families went to Ancient Egypt. The descendants of these people supposedly became the Jewish people in Europe. These people are still living and can be found in places around the world. If the descendants of these people that supposedly went to Ancient Egypt because of hunger are still living then the Ancient Egyptians that received and fed them must also be living somewhere, but nobody has ever heard or even thought of them.

Perhaps worse than this, western historians have told much of the history of the world through speculative imagination. That is, where they did not know what was, and they did not have any way of finding it out, they imagined and speculated names and parts of the historical events to keep their versions, perspectives, and history of the world going. For example, in the study of ancient civilizations, we all studied the civilization of the *Sumerians*. What the historians never told us is the fact that there were no ancient people called the *Sumerians*? So how did western historians come by the name *Sumerians*? Someone just pulled it out of thin air.

In their speculative imaginations and from biblical influence, western historians assumed that the *Afrim* people invented the cuneiform writings that archaeologists had found in the region where the so-called *Sumerians* lived in ancient times. However, in 1850, Hincks found out that the *Afrim* people did not invent the cuneiform writing that were used in Semitic languages of the east. Instead, he found out that the *Afrim* people learned cuneiform writing from an earlier group of people that were not Semites at all, and nobody knew who these people were, or where they are now. Nevertheless, historians needed to name these people to keep the fabrication of their story of human civilization going, so Oppert gave these unknown people the hypothetical name *"Sumerians."* Today not many people know that there were no ancient people called the *Sumerians* (see Durant, 1935, p. 118, footnote), and perhaps no body knows that these so-called Sumerians were the *Nzima* and *Ahanta* people that can be found in West Africa. We all went to school to learn the *legendary lying lore* of history and we still learn prevarications as truths.

Another major flaw in western historical scholarship is that it tells the story of the world in isolated chunks as if none of the events that happened five or three thousand years ago have any relationship to what happened a thousand years ago or what is happening now. Western historians have told the story of the world in geographical isolation as if what happened in Europe had nothing to do with what later happened in Africa, or elsewhere around the world. Today we know that is wrong because history is the ripple effects of human thoughts and actions through time. As a result, history must look at what is happening today as the results of the thoughts and actions of the people of yesterday. However, western strategy of perceiving history in isolated geographical chunks has served the west well. It has made it conveniently possible for them to include the aspects of history that are complimentary to the west's socio-political perception of itself, and exclude aspects that are uncomplimentary to this perception. This approach to history has also made it conveniently possible for western historians to compromise the truth and even manufacture the trend of historical events based upon their socio-cultural perception of what they think should have been and also based on their socio-anthropological perception of who the story is about.

Most western historians and biblical scholars have known this but they would not tell that the introduction of Ancient Egyptian and therefore black people's concepts of religion to Europeans have had the most terrible consequences on Europeans and the Ancient Egyptians and their modern descendants in Africa. In Europe, the consequences of the introduction of black people's religion through Ancient Egyptian documents were direct. There were the Inquisition, and several religious wars that could be tied directly to religion. Unfortunately, many historians have never linked the historical circumstances that led to the terrible consequences on Ancient Egyptians and Africans to European Christianity. This is because many events occurred in the interim to push Christianity that started the circumstances of these terrible consequences to the background. Christian Europe started the historical circumstances that led to the enslavement of Africans and the subsequent plunder of their human and mineral resources. This is not an accusation; it is a historical fact that is confirmed in both European and African histories. Of course, the Catholic Church, the Christian power of these times, did not know then that in its condemnation and negative pronouncements on Africans, it was dealing with the modern descendants of the Ancient Egyptians that created the theosophical doctrines out of which Catholic Christianity grew.

Religion in African and European interaction

Most Egyptologists do not deny that Ancient Egyptians created the concept of religion and the ritualistic beliefs and sacramental practices that are seen in most religions around the world today. The modern descendants of these Ancient Egyptians became the Africans. According to the biblical story of the origin of the *Afrim* people, the *Afrim* people supposedly went to Ancient Egypt where they learned about religion. They took what they had learned into the Exodus and later returned to Ancient Egypt to pass this same concept of religion on to the Greeks and entire Europe. The irony in this trend of historical events is that much of the story of African and European interaction and the woes of Africans from this interaction was caused by European misunderstanding of the religious doctrines that the *Afrim* people had passed on to them. Some western historians and almost all historians of African descent have attributed the history of negative interaction between Europeans and Africans to the inhumanity and greed of Europeans. However, Christianity and specifically the Catholic Church was in the forefront of the

143

creation of the atrocious historical circumstances that led Europeans to this inhumanity, greed, and the woes of Ancient Egyptians and their modern descendants in Africa.

The terrible consequences of the introduction of a deeper philosophy of religion to Europeans are still affecting Africans and people of African descent around the world today. Even the *Afrim* people that introduced Ancient Egyptian religious concepts and practices to Europeans have suffered greatly because of that. That is why it is important that this aspect of history is told to bridge what Europeans think the story was and what Africa knows the true story to be. Another great irony in all these is that, the theosophical doctrines Ancient Egyptians invented were the very ideas that Europeans used to destroy the last vestiges of Ancient Egyptian religion and subjugate modern descendants of the Ancient Egyptians in far away Africa.

In the last chapter, I discussed the centrality of Ancient Egypt in the religions of the world. Specifically, I sought to bring out the relationship amongst the Ancient Egyptians, *Afrim* people, modern Africans, the Bible, and Christianity. I qualify Africans as the modern Africans because in ancient times, the black people that are concentrated in Africa today lived and were spread all the way from Africa through the Middle to the Far East. Black people lived from inner Africa to China in ancient times. The genetic, linguistic, and cultural revelation in this work shows that some black tribes lived as far as China in ancient times and that is why there are still black people in parts of China.

This discussion is intended to show that Christian Europe led by the Catholic Church had a greater self-interest in creating the historical events that led to the woes of Ancient Egyptians and Africans more than any single socio-political institution in Europe at the time. The discussion will also show that Christian Europe had a greater self-interest in distorting and denying Ancient Egyptian history. It also had the greatest self-interest in European scholars refusing to acknowledge that the Ancient Egyptians were modern black Africans because that would immediately reflect on the *Afrim* people and ultimately reveal the black identity and origin of the Bible and Christianity.

The translation of the theosophical documents that became the Christian Bible into Greek began around the 3rd century B. C. in Ancient Egypt. This was a cross-linguistic translation from the language of the Ancient Egyptians to the then language of the *Afrim* people and then into the Greek language. It is important to remember that at this period in their history, the *Afrim* people were not Jews or Hebrews. They became Jews and Hebrews after the Bible was completed and the foundations of Christianity had begun in Greece and Rome. Before this time, they still identified themselves by their African racial, ethnic, and tribal identity as the *Afrim* people.

The *Afrim* people followed the Bible and Christianity into Europe where they were given the names Jews and Hebrews. Because the Bible was translated into Greek in Ancient Egypt, early Greek Christians knew and accepted the origin of the biblical documents in Ancient Egypt without any reservations. The early Greek Orthodox Church had no rivalry or racial sentiments against Ancient Egypt perhaps out of respect for the fact that the Greeks knew that whatever they had become came from Ancient Egypt.

Unfortunately, the Romans that sought to take over religion from the Greeks did not know about the foundations of Christian thought and religion in Ancient Egypt. These people did not know or understand the origins of the theosophical doctrines they were copying from the Greeks and since then religious diversity and tolerance has never been the same.

Earliest European religious intolerance

In 176 B. C., the Romans conquered the Greeks and took literacy, knowledge, and the foundations and documents of Christianity back with them to Rome. The Roman Empire moved to grab the eastern lands that Alexander the Great had conquered for the Greeks. These lands included Ancient Egypt. Soon Roman politicians realized that the source of all the knowledge they had taken from the Greeks came from Ancient Egypt. As a result, most of these politicians sought to go to Egypt, the source of all knowledge at the time to see things for themselves. As Nicolas Grimal observed in *A History of Ancient Egypt*:

> Even the Romans' appreciation of Egypt was not solely due to the country's wealth, although this was clearly the main attraction for Mark Anthony, Julius Caesar, Germanicus, Hadrian, Severus and the rest. ... ***Egypt was regarded as a place of great scholarly achievement*** by such disciples of Aristotle as Theophratus, and it served to assuage Rome's thirst for eastern values (1994, p. 2, emphasis mine).

As early as the Romans acquired the eastern lands of Alexander the Great, the powerful religious influences of these lands, especially Ancient Egypt began to affect Roman religious values. The Romans began to discard their old religious beliefs and practices in favor of the Ancient Egyptian concepts of religion and sacramental practices. In *Egypt of the Pharaohs*, Sir Alan Gardiner pointed this out when he wrote that:

> With the decay of belief in the old gods of Olympus, the populations of Rome and the provinces fell easy victims to whatever Oriental faith was dangled before their eyes. The cult of Isis spread into every corner of the {Roman] Empire, though even those who most greatly honoured the goddess were at a loss to know what to make of her (1964, p. 8).

Notice how the two scholars quoted above commit a serious geographical blunder by referring to Ancient Egypt as *eastern* and *oriental*. It is deliberate. This blunder began from the tradition of western scholars not even acknowledging that geographically, Ancient Egypt was in Africa, for fear that it would bring black people too close to the creation of human civilization and the concepts and doctrines of European Christianity.

Just as Europeans later did with Christianity, the Romans adopted Ancient Egyptian cults and pantheons, but they did not understand the religious values of these cults and they did not even know the appropriate ritualistic practices for the cults they had adopted as their own. Nevertheless, the Romans were so fascinated and influenced by Ancient Egyptian religious ideas and sacramental practices that many Roman leaders and citizens became concerned. Roman leaders saw this as a corruption and pollution of Roman religious and moral values. As a result, in the 2nd century B. C., Cato led the Roman Senate to decree against the practice of Bacchanalian religious rituals that they believed were nothing but *foreign pagan religious cults*. For the people's fascination with Ancient Egyptian religious values and practices, Romans leaders blamed Ancient Egypt and they sought to discredit and destroy her image from early times.

In *Fontes Historiae Religionis Aegypticae,* Thomas Hopfner presented some parts of the writings of Juvenal (47-127 A. D) who was one of the earliest Romans to write to discredit Ancient Egyptian religious ideas and practices. Unfortunately, the Romans who had taken to these foreign religious ideas and practices were not convinced that these ideas were no good pagan cults. Consequently, the Roman public refused to abandon their newfound religions or their fascination with them. At the same time, Roman political leaders were determined to save the empire from corruption and pollution from foreign religious influences. These leaders were not ready to let foreign religious thoughts influence and dominate the religious lives and thinking of the Roman public. As a result, the Roman leaders sought to crack down on their people and their fascination with "pagan" cults, and the people were also ready to defend this fascination. So a civil war broke out in Rome over what was the first ever-religious war of intolerance in the world. It was a violent clash between the Roman people and their leaders. As Grimal put it nonchalantly:

> At the cost of a few thousand [Roman] lives, traditional Roman values were thus temporarily saved from the uncontrollable spread of the East (p. 2).

This civil war is very important in the history and propagation of religion in Europe and later around the world because it seemed to be the precursor of things to come. The religious intolerance that led to the civil war in Rome prognosticated the extent to which Roman leaders would go to save their political ambitions and the Empire from the influence of *foreign and pagan religious ideas*. It was from this aspect of Roman history of religious intolerance that the Catholic Church later took stance against different religious views, beliefs, and practices and the Church sought to dominate and eliminate them all. The Church's later history of religious persecutions, massacres, Inquisition, and religious wars originated from this early aspect of the history of religion in Rome.

In Ancient Egypt, the marriage of Caesar to Cleopatra who was erroneously believed to be the last descendant of the Ancient Egyptian Pharaohs effectively sealed Roman domination of Ancient Egypt. Nevertheless, Egypt still retained its ancient mystique and image as a center of religious wisdom and learning, and this image eventually got to Rome through Roman travelers who had visited Ancient Egypt. The foundations of what turned out to be a two thousand-year secret war between the Catholic Church and Christian Europe against Ancient Egypt began with what Nicolas Grimal pointed out as the "orientalization" of religion in Europe. According to Grimal, with the coming of the Romans to Egypt:

> Two images of [Ancient] Egypt were then superimposed on one another. The first was that of the Hellenistic [claim of] civilization of Egypt, which was recorded in the works of such writers as Theocritus. The cultures of the Greeks and the Egyptians were blended successfully both in the works of Appolonius of Rhodes and in the general currents of Alexandrian thought. The second image of Egypt was based on a tradition that can already be described as "orientalizing," illustrated by the writings of Apuleius or Heliodorus of Emesa. *The orientalizing tradition continued to emphasize the mysteries of the ancient civilization, while progressing along the same lines as the contemporary schools of philosophy.* ... This movement toward esotericism was encouraged by the spread of Egyptian cults throughout the Roman Empire. Through the figures of Osiris, Isis, and Anubis, the cults popularized the suffering of the archetypal Egyptian sovereign, perceived as one of the models for life and death (p. 3, emphasis mine).

Notice how some early Greek writers like Theocritus sought to propagate the false idea that the Greeks civilized Ancient Egypt instead of the other way round. This was because at that time, Ancient Egypt was a colony of Greece, and the Greeks sought to blend their history with Ancient Egypt so as to make Greece the creator of the Ancient Egyptian civilization. As it has been said, "history is the polemics of the victor" and that was exactly what some ancient Greek writers of early times sought to do, to create history to suit them, the victors. They were fabricating history to fit into their socio-political sentiments.

However, the most important reason later Greek historians sought to reverse the comparative histories of Greece and Ancient Egypt was that the Greeks were looking for ways to insert themselves into the center of the more glorious history of civilization and achievements of Ancient Egypt. This was the reason Ptolemy asked the Ancient Egyptian priest *Omane Anto* to write the history of Ancient Egypt and transpose the names of the Ancient Egyptian Pharaohs into Greek. This was to make it easy and possible for the Greek rulers of Egypt to fit their names onto the list of names of the then world-famous Ancient Egyptian pharaohs. The African names of these pharaohs were too linguistically and culturally different for the names of the Greek rulers to be fitted onto them so these African names had to be first transposed into Greek and that was what *Omane Anto* did for the Greeks. It was also from this background that Cleopatra sought to proclaim herself a direct descendant of an Ancient Egyptian Pharaoh. These are some of the shameful historical reasons some western historians and Egyptologists have never had the courage to acknowledge that the Ancient Egyptians were black people.

Catholic persecution of Ancient Egyptians

Today, most western scholars after digging the dead bodies and ruins of Ancient Egypt and finding no hidden mysteries claim that Ancient Egypt was not as mysterious as early people made her to be. In *Egypt of the Pharaohs*, Sir Alan Gardiner wrote:

> As the Greek and later Roman influence fastened its grip on the land of the Pharaohs, the traditional native lore was withdrawn more and more into the hands of the priesthood, in whose interest it lay to insist upon and to over-emphasize the profound wisdom and mysterious knowledge of their ancestors (1964, p. 8).

This sentiments of this quotation is also a modern western perception to make the interpretation of this ancient story fit into the socio-political sentiments of our time. The quotation above seems to suggest that Ancient Egyptian priests invented the story of the arcane religious wisdom and pristine knowledge of the Ancient Egyptians. However, many people of the time knew better and they believed more in what they saw and heard about Ancient Egypt, and not what religious fanatics or scholastic propaganda wanted them to believe.

From the knowledge of early Romans that Ancient Egypt was the foundation of religious wisdom and learning, some early western historians and biblical scholars began to assert and propagate the idea that true religion and divine knowledge could be found in the mysteries of Ancient Egypt and not in corrupt western European churches. This was bad for Ancient Egypt because western scholars that believed in her were pitching Ancient Egypt against the power of European Christianity, then the Catholic Church. Nevertheless, this idea was propagated right into Rome, the heart of the Roman Empire, through the writings of some early Roman scholars. This was a great insult, humiliation, and threat to the growth and development of early Christianity. The Catholic Church knew how Roman leaders had dealt with the competition of foreign religious ideas. Learning from Roman politicians, the Church refused to accept such humiliation in people's comparisons of Ancient Egypt and the Catholic Church just as Cato refused to allow "pagan" Baccahanalian rituals in his Republic. Romans ruled Ancient Egypt, and the Church declared a secret war on Ancient Egypt to destroy and distort Egypt's image and at the same time save and bolster the acceptability and credibility of the doctrines of the then budding Christian religion.

The Church's war on Ancient Egypt and efforts to uphold the Church over Ancient Egyptian civilization and knowledge began as Christianized Roman leaders of Ancient Egypt started a secret war on the then crumbling ancient civilization. In 356 A. D., Roman Emperor Constantius II began attacking and closing down Ancient Egyptian temples to try to destroy the foundations of Ancient Egyptian religious mystique. However, the actions of Constantius were not enough to destroy the beliefs of Ancient Egyptians in their religion or even the beliefs of Europeans in Ancient Egyptian religious mystique.

Fourteen years later in 380 A. D., Roman Emperor Theodosius decreed that Catholic Christianity was to be the sole State religion of Ancient Egypt and that meant all indigenous *pagan cults* were to be abolished and destroyed. The irony in this decree was that Theodosius ignorantly perceived Ancient Egyptian religion as pagan religion without ever knowing that the so-called pagan cults of Ancient Egypt were the very foundations from which European Christianity emerged. Notice how the ignorance of Europeans that received black people's theosophical ideas as their Christianity condemned black people's religion as pagan. This condemnation was not derived from the superiority or inferiority of the European or African God. It was clearly borne out of Christian Europe's earliest socio-political and socio-anthropological sentiments toward black people. Evidence of this can also be deduced from the earliest anti-Jewish edicts that church councils issued against Jews in 312 and 325 A. D.

From this point of view however, Christianity is no different from any other form of religion on earth; they all originated from the so-called *pagan* theosophical foundations. As these

147

so-called *pagan* ideas and practices went to foreign lands, they were simply described in foreign tongues and given elegant foreign names and descriptions, but they were all from the single so-called *pagan* imagination and thought that were conceived by Ancient Egyptians.

The threat of Ancient Egypt to early Catholic Christendom was so great that eleven years later in 391 A. D., Theodosius decided to deliver the *coup de grace* by ordering the massacre of the last of the Serapeum priests at *Mamfe*. This massacre of the last of the Ancient Egyptian priests was to make sure that Ancient Egypt; the then greatest religious rival of the Catholic Church was annihilated.

As terrible as it may sound today, the Catholic Church also had its secret reasons of revenge in the massacre of the Ancient Egyptians. The Church felt that pagans in Europe had persecuted Christians for far too long and that it was time for Christians to turn the tide and massacre pagans in return. So it came to do this in Ancient Egypt against black people. According to the Catholic Church's line of thinking, the massacre of the Ancient Egyptian priests was Christian revenge for their persecution and massacre in Europe. Nicolas Grimal noticed and commented on this when he wrote:

> The Christians gained revenge for their persecution at the hands of the "idolaters" by destroying pagan temples and libraries and by massacring the intellectual elite of Alexandria, Mamfe [Memphis], and the Theban region. ... From the mid-sixth century AD onwards, after the final closure of the temple of Isis at Philae, a veil of silence was drawn over necropolises and temples ... (Grimal, p. 3).

Notice how the early introduction of the doctrines of Christianity to Europe resulted in Christian persecution and massacres that did not begin in Europe but in Ancient Egypt. This trend of religious intolerance and persecution has been everywhere European Christianity has been introduced.

The threat of Ancient Egypt to the biblical tradition did not end with the massacre of the Ancient Egyptian priests and the closing down of the world's most ancient religious temples. This was because the reality and centrality of Ancient Egypt in religious wisdom and knowledge was so overwhelming that western scholars kept finding more and more evidence of the supremacy of Ancient Egyptian religious wisdom over European Christianity. This seriously threatened early Church leaders and made them even more insecure in their attempts to develop the Church into what can be described today as a modern religious corporation. The Church was therefore forced to take the defense of its image against Ancient Egypt into Europe where this defense resulted in the massacre and persecution of Europeans for over one thousand years.

Ancient Egyptian religious wisdom over the Catholic Church

The greatest threat of Ancient Egypt to the biblical tradition was Ancient Egypt's own towering mystique and surrounding aura as the original place of arcane religious wisdom. In an essay entitled *Egyptology, Ancient Egypt, and the American Imagination*, Bruce Trigger traced some of the historical circumstances in the threat of Ancient Egypt to Christianity (see Bruce Trigger in *The American Discovery of Ancient Egypt*, 1995).

The last of the Ancient Egyptian priests was massacred in 391 A. D. and their temples were closed down, but the mystique of Ancient Egypt as a place of arcane religious wisdom has persisted and continued to persist even up to today. In his essay, Bruce Trigger pointed out that as early as the 5th century AD, one of the earliest propagators of the arcane religious wisdom of Ancient Egypt was Horapollon who wrote the *Hieroglyphica* acknowledging Ancient Egypt as the fountainhead of all religious knowledge and wisdom. In this work, Horapollon also suggested that Ancient Egyptians concealed their religious mysteries in their writings therefore there were divine religious secrets in the hieroglyphics.

148

Again, this revelation seriously threatened the Church that was afraid that new Ancient Egyptian religious ideas and practices might be discovered and introduced to Europeans to undermine the growing biblical tradition. This threat was even more serious because Horapollon's assertion led many historians and biblical scholars of the time into the romantic belief that the hieroglyphics were emblems of the repository of Ancient Egyptian secret wisdom and mysteries. Everybody would want to know a religious secret if there were one. As a result, European scholars of the time including historians, biblical scholars, and Church leaders went in search of ways of deciphering and understanding hieroglyphics in their quest for true religious wisdom. Christian Europe in the name of the Catholic Church was more threatened than ever.

In the next thousand years of the Church's control of Europe, the Church's response to its fears resulted in diseases and wars, the Crusades, Inquisition, witch hunting, burnings at the stake, massacres, and the ingrained prejudice and bigotry that Europeans are still struggling with today. A thousand years after the massacre of the Ancient Egyptian priests to destroy the threat of Ancient Egyptian rivalry in religion, the Church was even more threatened by Ancient Egypt's mystique than ever and this mystique was not going to die away soon.

Hieroglyphics and the arcane religious wisdom of Ancient Egyptians

As some Renaissance scholars were searching for ways to prove the subhumanity of the African during slavery, others were searching for the arcane religious wisdom the Africans left behind when they were the Ancient Egyptians. One thousand years after Horapollon had written his book, a whole new generation of European scholars, Renaissance scholars, discovered Horapollon's *Hieroglyphica* in the fifteenth century. That sent a new of generation of European scholars, religious leaders, and even agnostics in search of ways to decipher Ancient Egyptian hieroglyphics to gain access to the hidden wisdom in them.

This was the reason the deciphering of the hieroglyphics became such a major pre-occupation of some European scholars. It was also the reason the supposed decipherment of the hieroglyphics by Jean-Francois Champollion in the nineteenth century was considered to be such a great break-through and major achievement in western learning. Unfortunately, Champollion's decipherment of the hieroglyphics was based upon the wrong premise that Ancient Egypt was a monolingual nation just as most modern European nations are today. However, that premise is false. Ancient Egypt was as multilingual nation as we see on the African continent today. Ancient Egyptian writings were therefore not in one tribal language. As a result, deciphering one language could not give western scholars the orthographic clues to the numerous documents that were written in other tribal languages. This is the reason less than a tenth of the supposed recovered papyri from Ancient Egypt have been successfully deciphered up to date. The deciphering formula that Champollion left behind does not fit all the languages of all the papyri Egyptologists and archaeologists have recovered from Ancient Egypt. What is worse, most of these scholars do not even know that they are dealing with different African languages.

As late as the nineteenth century, the supposed decipherment of hieroglyphics helped to spur many western scholars in search of the lost religious wisdom of the Ancient Egyptians. The Catholic Church was still threatened by Egyptian mystique more than ever as many scholars and even religious leaders drifted toward Ancient Egyptian civilization and its mysteries. The Church knew that the scholars could easily undermine the Judeo-Christian tradition it had successfully created in Europe so it designed ways of fighting back. One of these ways was to silence the truth.

Neoplatonism

Also in the fifteenth century, Renaissance scholars rediscovered what they called *Neoplatonism* in their discovery of a set of philosophical writings. These Renaissance scholars believed that these writings came directly from a god, *Hermes Trimegistus*, the Greek name for the Ancient Egyptian god, Thoth. Notice here how the Greeks took Ancient Egyptian gods, and gave them Greek names to make these gods look like they were the indigenous gods of the Greeks. That was what the Greeks did to Ancient Egyptian history and the biblical story.

The thirst of Europeans for the arcane religious wisdom of Egypt was unquenchable. As soon as the supposed writings of *Trimegistus* were discovered, some Renaissance scholars formed themselves into a hermetic body of scholars that studied the Neoplatonic documents in search of Ancient Egyptian secrets and mysteries. *Neoplatonism* led to the growth of philosophical writings known as the *Hermetic Corpus* and this movement led to the reintroduction and worship of Ancient Egyptian deities throughout Europe all over again.

Among the Renaissance humanists who helped to propagate Neoplatonic ideas of the primordial revelation of religion to the Ancient Egyptian god Thoth were Romans Marsilius Ficinus and Cosimo de' Medici. The more Renaissance scholars studied religion, the more they realized and therefore asserted that what the Jewish people brought to Europeans was not true religion because the Ancient Egyptians were the ones that had the true revelation of religion. The revelation of the Africans who wrote the Bible asserts that the theosophical concepts and doctrines that the Jewish passed on to the Greeks and Europeans originated from Ancient Egypt. However, over five hundred years ago Renaissance scholars were making the same assertions.

According to Renaissance humanists, Moses and Pythagoras simply stole ideas in the neo-platonic revelations to design their doctrines, but theirs were not the true doctrines. Renaissance humanists and Diderot's Encyclopaedists, especially Voltaire, asserted that long before Moses, the Ancient Egyptians possessed "a pristine revelation of divine wisdom" never revealed to the Hebrews, Greeks, and Romans. It is important to note here that in the hierarchy of the origination of religious wisdom, the Renaissance scholars and Encyclopaedists acknowledged and began from Ancient Egypt to the Hebrews, Greeks, before the Romans. All of these have already been said and written and European scholars have long known them. What I am doing in this work is to introduce the detail evidence that confirm the veracity of these early assertions.

Scholars of the Age of Enlightenment, especially Diderot's Encyclopaedists particularly Voltaire argued that:

> Moses was far from being the original source of religion and science, but had derived everything from Ancient Egyptians. The Jews had given nothing; they had stolen everything (see Leon Poliakov, *The History of Aryan Myth: A History of Racist Ideas in Europe*, 1996, p. 141).

Today, such Renaissance pronouncements have been described by some as anti-Semitic. However, they were true. Nevertheless, such pronouncements from most of the leading scholars of Europe did not help the position of the Church either. The propagation of such ideas among Renaissance scholars became an even greater threat to the Church as the ideas slowly became part of the foundations of the revolution against the Church known as the Reformation. The mystique of Ancient Egypt was shaping religious history in Europe over a thousand years after the last of the Ancient Egyptian priests had been massacred. More than ever, the very foundations of Christianity in Europe were threatened and the Catholic Church had to fight back.

As belief in the arcane religious wisdom of Ancient Egypt grew in Europe, numerous Renaissance scholars set out in search of this religious wisdom and they began to develop new concepts and foundations of religion based upon their findings. Some of the religious concepts that came out of Renaissance scholars' findings and beliefs in Ancient Egyptian wisdom included the idea that there is a divine power that animates the world and connects everything to each other. From this basis, they developed the belief that there is the "presence of All in even the smallest created thing" and there are "irrational and unseen forces throughout the world" (Bruce Trigger, *The American Discovery of Ancient Egypt*, 1995, p. 24). Today, these ideas are fast becoming the beliefs of new cults and religions around the world. Even modern "religion" of environmentalism has its roots in these Ancient Egyptian beliefs.

150

Ancient Egyptian Pope?
The design of the organization of the Catholic Church was based upon Ancient Egyptian hierarchy of kingship. The name of the Pope and most of the cultural practices of installing a new Pope were all derived from ancient Akan practices of kingship in Ancient Egypt. For example, the name Pope was derived from the *Akan* word *Papa*, a venerable name for an elderly *Akan* male. The way the Catholic Church carries a new Pope on a throne-like chair and parades him around is exactly as the Akan people introduced their kings to the public in Ancient Egypt, and exactly as these people continue to do today. The early Catholic Church therefore identified itself closely with Ancient Egypt and adopted most of its sacramental practices, from celibacy in the priesthood to monasticism in Ancient Egyptian religious practices. From this closeness, even leaders of the Catholic Church were being swayed into believing in the arcane religious wisdom of Ancient Egyptians. It was from this point of view that Pope Alexander VI claimed that he was the direct descendant of the Ancient Egyptian god *Osoro* and that was what qualified him most to be the Pope.

Such ignorant and shameful proclamations are seldom revealed in Western European narration of history. Pope Alexander VI could not have been the descendant of *Osoro* because, as I have pointed out, the word *Osiris* is a Greek corruption of the *Akan* word *Osoro*. *The Akan people whose language and god was Osoro are black people, and Pope Alexander could not have descended from them. I believe that if Pope Alexander knew this today, he would not have liked to have descend from them.* The *Akan* people still worship *Osoro* and *Asaase*. They were the first people to worship *Osoro* and *Asaase* and today almost all religions acknowledge this concept by speaking of heaven and earth. That belief is only one of the basic concepts of religion that passed from Ancient Egyptian religion into religions of the world.

Despite the great threat of Ancient Egyptian civilization, the greatest problem of the Catholic Church was its own internal corruption in which people were asked, for example, to pay money for the Church to forgive them their sins. This foundation of corruption in Christianity can still be found among Christian capitalists that seek to make their money through the Christian religion around the world.

Ancient Egypt and the formation of modern secret societies
The campaign against the propagation of the foundations of religion in Ancient Egyptian wisdom became a central concern for the Church. During the Church's counter offensive known in history as the Counter-Reformation, the Church's desire to stamp out beliefs in Ancient Egyptian religious wisdom led to the execution of Giordano Bruno. He had written that Ancient Egyptian religious concepts were older, purer, and therefore less corrupt than the Catholic Church and Christian Europe. That was a serious insult to the integrity of the Church so the Church ordered his execution, but it still had its eyes on Ancient Egypt itself.

As part of the Church's campaign to restore its integrity, Isaac Casaubon analyzed the Neoplatonic philosophies in 1614 and concluded that the Neoplatonic writings could not antedate Christian writings therefore they could not be purer than the writings of the Bible. Nevertheless, the yearning to go beyond the Christian religion in search of the original wisdom and rituals of religious practice in Ancient Egypt continued in Europe. Gradually, the Church was beginning to lose some of its leaders to Ancient Egyptian mystique and aura. Among one of the staunch researchers into the secrets of Ancient Egyptian religious wisdom was the seventeenth century Jesuit priest Athanasius Kircher who suggested that Ancient Egyptians had surpassed all modern ideas in everything. Such beliefs and pronouncements by leaders and members of the Church became even greater threats to the biblical tradition.

Consequently, the Church came out in a vigorous counter offensive in which it openly went after its critics. There came a time when it was dangerous to one's life to openly express ideas about the corruption of the Church and the purity and arcane religious wisdom of Ancient Egypt. The Church went on the offensive cracking down on scholars that believed and propagated the purer religious wisdom of Ancient Egypt. In the 17th century, the French Calvinist who wrote revealing that Moses did not write the first five books of the Bible was arrested and forced to recant before the Pope and the life of the Dutch philosopher Spinoza was also threatened over the same pronouncements.

Unfortunate for Ancient Egypt, the more the Church cracked down on believers in her arcane religious wisdom, the more curious people became and the more attracted they were to finding out what they believed the Church did not want them to know.

Even throughout the dangerous times when the Church persecuted scholars, Renaissance Hermetic ideas never died. They were passed underground into secret societies that believed in practicing religion and religious rituals supposedly according to how they believed the Ancient Egyptians practiced them. These Renaissance secret societies have lasted to this day in the secret teachings of the Oddfellows, Rosicrucians, Freemasons, White Brotherhood, and others. Through such secret propagation of ideas, western belief in Ancient Egypt as the original source of all religious wisdom and knowledge persisted into the nineteenth century, and it continues even today.

The final counter offensive in counter-reformation

Even during the Counter-Reformation, the Catholic Church and the biblical tradition were still seriously threatened by the scholastic propagation of the religious wisdom of the Ancient Egyptians. As a result, and as part of the Counter-Reformation, most of the religious documents that gave early European scholars ideas about Ancient Egypt were either destroyed or hidden from the Christian public. Consequently, ideas about Ancient Egypt began to die down and the Church went on an even greater offensive against Ancient Egypt. Many modern historians and religious scholars believe that the Roman Catholic Church's library at the Vatican in Rome still holds most of the historical and religious secrets the Church has never wanted Christians to know for almost two thousand years.

The Church sought to reinterpret and propagate biblical ideas to destroy the image and mystique of Ancient Egypt before its masses. In Christian perception and reinterpretation of the Bible, Ancient Egypt was no more the beginning and center of human history. Instead, the Church claimed that the beginning and center of human history was Palestine. Christian reinterpretation of religious history was based upon the idea that Palestine was above Ancient Egypt in matters relating to religion and that the Egyptians were only used by God to work out his relations with his chosen people, the *Afrim* people. Christian Europe did not know that the *Afrim* people that sought to place the center of religion of the world in Palestine were Ancient Egyptians themselves and that their religion was basically the Ancient Egyptian religion.

It was clear that Christian Europe did not even believe in the hypothesis of the foundations of history and the center of religion in Palestine because while it was seeking shelter from the assault of Ancient Egypt's image in the Jewish people, Christians were at the same time persecuting these people (see the anti-Jewish edicts of Elvira Spain in 312, and of Nicaea in 325 A. D.).

Christian reinterpretation of the Bible against Ancient Egypt also included the idea that it was because God only wanted to use the Ancient Egyptians to get to his people that no Ancient Egyptian king was mentioned by name in the Bible. Unfortunately, Christian Europe did not know then and it still does not know now. Nevertheless, it does not want to believe that the Bible itself acknowledges that the Christian God was an Ancient Egyptian God before he became the God of Abraham, Isaac, and Jacob. Moreover, western religious scholars did not know that if the Jewish scholars who compiled and translated the Bible had mentioned any Ancient Egyptian Pharaoh, they would have easily given themselves and the sources from where they were stealing the documents of the Bible away.

In Exodus, Christians who searched to reinterpret the Bible against Ancient Egypt found that Egypt had been portrayed as a paganistic and idolatrous civilization. As a result, Christians were charged to condemn and reject any ideas that were supposed to come out of Ancient Egypt. Christians were made to believe that Ancient Egyptians enslaved the Jewish people in the building of the pyramids. Though George Sandys had refuted this idea as far back as 1615, Ancient Egypt was still perceived and despised by Christian Europe as a land of slavery and oppression of God's people. As Will Rogers pointed out, "when ignorance gets started, it knows no bounds." Christians were charged to despise such pagan civilization and whatever religious ideas it might have had. All of these ideas originated from the false Christian notion that the Christian God was different from and better than the Ancient Egyptian God was. Christian Europe did not know that it was the one and the same God the Ancient Egyptians imagined created, personified, and worshipped for thousands of years before the Jewish people introduced this God to Europeans.

Christian Europe did not make any reference to Abraham prostituting his wife for wealth and knowledge in Ancient Egypt. However, the story of how the wife of *Kpotufe* [Potifar] tried to seduce *Osafo* [Joseph] was used to reinforce Christian stereotype of Ancient Egypt as a sexually promiscuous civilization that must be condemned by all in the eyes of God.

Modern revival of Ancient Egypt

Early in the twentieth century, one of the most popular writings that sparked the revival of Ancient Egypt in modern religious thought was the work of James Henry Breasted. In 1912 Breasted published the *Development of Religion and Thought in Ancient Egypt*. In this work, he traced the development of religion and philosophical concepts in Ancient Egypt from prehistoric times to the late Period. Also in this work, Breasted showed that wisdom literature of the New Kingdom of Ancient Egypt was the source of the documents of the Old Testament. Of course, the Church and Christians did not like that so the book was never very popular.

It is remarkable to note here that Dr. Breasted pointed out clearly that the Old Testament documents were Ancient Egyptian in origin. Here was a western scholar who had studied the development of religion and thought in Ancient Egypt pointing out connections between the ancient religious documents of Ancient Egypt and the Bible, but Christian Europe was neither impressed nor amused because of the Church's fears. On the question of who invented the theosophical concept of monotheism, Breasted portrayed the monotheist Ancient Egyptian King *Akenten* as the first Christian and Protestant before his time. Throughout all these, the greatest success of the Church against Ancient Egypt was the fact that the Church succeeded in condemning the truth in Ancient Egypt as lies and making the lies in the Bible the essence of Christian faith. Nevertheless, western belief in the arcane religious wisdom and knowledge of Ancient Egypt still persisted, and it persists in many religious circles even up to today.

Ancient Egypt in the foundations of America

In America, belief in the arcane wisdom and knowledge of Ancient Egypt was central in the foundations of the new nation under God, indivisible, with liberty, and justice for all. Towards the end of the eighteenth century, many of the founders of America's republic like Benjamin Franklin, Thomas Jefferson, and George Washington were all members of the secret religious society of Freemasonry in search of Ancient Egyptian wisdom and guidance in the building of this new nation.

There is the quiet talk among Freemasons that George Washington got to be the first President of America because he was selected by a group of his peers who were all Freemasons. It was through these early members of American Freemasonry that an unfinished Ancient Egyptian pyramid and an All-seeing eye came to occupy the center of the Great Seal of the United States. A Congress that consisted mostly of members of this secret organization approved this Seal in 1782. Most people know that the pyramid is definitely an Ancient Egyptian symbol, but few people know that the All-seeing eye is also an Ancient Egyptian symbol. It was from this symbol that the appellations of God as All-seeing, All-knowing, and Omnipotent evolved. These were Ancient Egyptian perceptions of God long before they became Christian acknowledgements of this God. Below is a symbol of the All-seeing eye in Ancient Egyptian jewelry.

Even the emerging literature of young America was influenced by belief in the arcane religious wisdom of the Ancient Egyptians. In the *American Hieroglyphics*, John Irwin pointed out that the works of famous American writers as Emerson, Melville, Poe, Thoreau, and Whitman acknowledged and interpreted what was happening in their times as hieroglyphic manifestations of God's will. In Edgar Alan Poe's *Some Words with a Mummy* (1845), an Ancient Egyptian mummy that had been restored to life through electrical shocks defended the preeminence of Ancient Egyptians in government, religion, and science over the modern world. This was Poe's way of resurrecting and popularizing some of the beliefs that had persisted about Ancient Egypt in his time.

At the beginning of the nineteenth century, the most popular children's book in America was the *Hieroglyphic Bible*, a book supposedly written in the emblems of the original religious wisdom of Ancient Egypt. Among several twentieth century artistic works based upon the theme of the arcane wisdom of the Ancient Egyptians was the 1933 movie *The Mummy* by Karl Freund and Norman Mailer's 1983 novel *Ancient Evenings*.

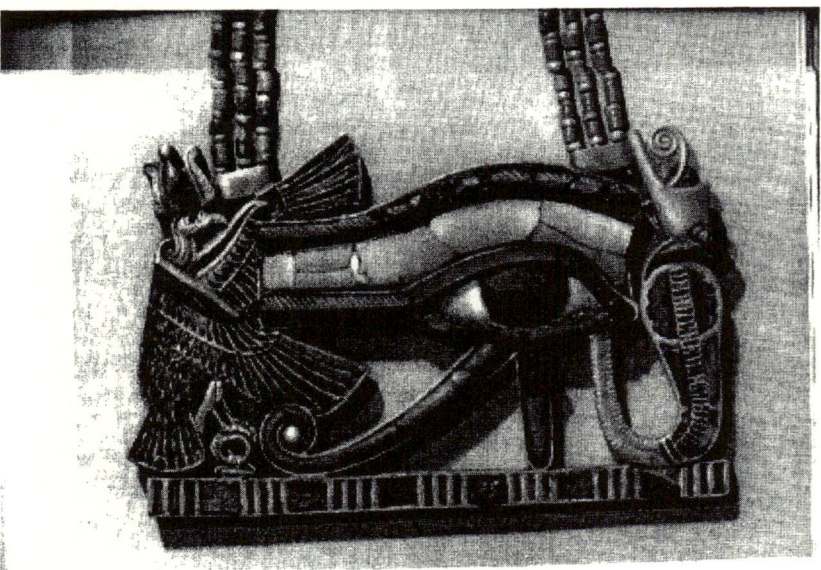

Fig. 3: The All-seeing eye as an Ancient Egyptian symbol before it became a Christian perception of God and symbol in the Seal of America.

Revival of fears of Ancient Egypt

Modern revival of Renaissance ideas has somehow revived the old fears of the biblical tradition of Ancient Egypt. In the twentieth century, the campaign to discredit Ancient Egypt was broadened to reach a wider audience through the silver screen in movies like *The Egyptian* (1954), *Land of the Pharaohs* (1955), *The Ten Commandments* (1956), and *Cleopatra* (1963). These films were designed to revive Judeo-Christian eminence and resentment against Ancient Egypt and at the same time strengthen Christianity's rejection of the possible infiltration of yet unrevealed ideas that might pose a threat to Christianity.

Most recently in the Fall of 1998, there was a revival of the secret Judeo-Christian war against Ancient Egypt in a cartoon feature that chronicled the life of Moses. The irony is that this movie was entitled *Prince of Egypt* thus confirming what religious scholars have known for a long time that Moses was not a Jew, but an Ancient Egyptian. The question is why would an Ancient Egyptian offer to lead supposed "slaves" out of Egypt to no definite place of destination? Nevertheless, the prestigious Time Magazine devoted the cover story of its December 14th edition to the Moses story. The problem with all these is that none of the stories surrounding Moses and the Jewish people has been proven or can be proven outside the Bible. What these latest features still failed to reveal to Christians around the world was the fact that Moses, the central figure in the Jewish religious story, was not a Jew therefore Christianity must rethink the veracity and their interpretation of this part of the biblical story.

Through Renaissance scholars, the Church was pitched strongly against Ancient Egyptian mystique, and the campaign to distort the history of Ancient Egypt continues today in the works of modern European scholars who do not even know that they are involved in an over two-thousand year old crusade against the creators of the theosophical doctrines of world religion in Ancient Egypt. What has scared the Church and Christian Europe most about Ancient Egypt is the fact that Christianity is not an indigenous European religion. This means Christian Europe does not have any control over any future revelations that might emerge to threaten the veracity of the story of Christianity, or reveal its true origin in the black people of Africa.

The Church's leadership hierarchy from Ancient Egypt

As I have pointed out, the irony in all these is that the leadership hierarchy of the Catholic Church and later all European Protestant Churches were designed after the Ancient Egyptian hierarchy of kingship. For example, the Pope in the Catholic system was made the equivalent of the Pharaoh. The Archbishop in the Anglican system was based upon the hierarchy of leadership of the Catholic system. The original Catholic leadership design was based upon the false idea that the Pope was a direct descendant of the gods of Ancient Egypt, or direct descendant of the Pharaohs. From this, the Catholic Church saw itself as the next religious power, replacement, and inheritor of Ancient Egyptian wisdom. Even the parading of a new Pope through Rome today, in a chair carried high, is exactly like the parading of the Pharaoh and it is practiced by modern *Akan* people that were the Ancient Egyptians.

The threat of Ancient Egypt to Christianity has been so multi-dimensional that despite all the efforts of the Church, Ancient Egypt is still perceived to be the repository of religious secrets modern humans have not yet known. Because of Ancient Egypt, there has been a revival of the quest for arcane religious wisdom in ancient civilizations. In North America, for example, some people go to ancient Mayan and Inca ritual sites in South America for inspiration. Many truth seekers in and around Europe go to Egypt for their inspiration. Christianity has not been able to convince most of such people. This is because most of the people that know a little of the history behind the Bible argue that in the first place, Ancient Egyptians invented the concept of religion and the Jewish people that Europeans believe invented the concepts of Christianity first went to Ancient Egypt. This means the Jewish people must have acquired the concepts of religion they passed on to Europeans from the Ancient Egyptians, and the Ancient Egyptians must have known something that the Jewish people did not know. As a result, people going to the Ancient Egyptians in search of the true wisdom of religion is the wisest thing to do. Moreover, these truth seekers argue that the Bible was translated into the Greek language in Ancient Egypt and that also means the Bible must have been created with Ancient Egyptian religious documents that were not necessarily Jewish documents, and they are correct.

Modern threats

The greatest threat to Christianity today, however, is the fear of the religious and socio-political implications from the revelation of the fact that the Ancient Egyptians were black people whose modern descendants are the Africans. What this means is that if Ancient Egyptians were the black Africans then the Jewish people would also be originally black people. Such a revelation would have far reaching implications because that would in turn mean that the people of the Bible were black and the doctrines of European Christianity are nothing but ancient African religious concepts and they are. Christians in Europe also know that Europeans would not want to know about the relationship amongst Ancient Egypt, the Jewish people, the Bible, Christianity and the people of Africa. This is because despite their professed Christianity, Europeans know that revealing that Ancient Egyptians were black people would undermine what Christian Europe has fought to establish in more than five hundred years; and that is the perpetuation of the superiority of Europeans and the subjugation of Africans through religion.

Perhaps more than that, Christian Europe knows that Europeans may not want to worship ancient African theosophical ideas if they found this out because of European racial sentiments towards Africans. For the Church's preservation therefore, the biblical tradition supported by Jewish scholars began a secret campaign of making sure that European scholars never revealed the simple and obvious truth that the Ancient Egyptians were black people. Those of us who know and have the evidence that we are modern descendants of Ancient Egyptians are still fighting this secret war to tell our story.

Despite the atrocious history created by the Church in Europe in a thousand years, very few western scholars link what happened in the past and even what is happening now in religions around the world to the earliest Catholic Church's negative handling of religious rivalry. The Church's teachings of religious intolerance was so thorough and effective that to Europeans, religious intolerance became the norm and Christian thing to do on behalf of God. From this background, intolerance of diversity and difference in any aspect of life became normal to Europeans. This intolerance was eventually extended onto our humanity and differences among humans became the greatest reason for hatred of each other. Today intolerance of each other is still ingrained in our religious practices.

Protestantism eventually emerged in response to all the evil things the Catholic Church had done and continued to do. Modern divisions and intolerance even among the Protestant Churches are still legacies from their tutelage by the Church. What is important to point out here is that the Catholic Church's ambitions and intolerance did not end in Europe. They became religious wars in the Middle East and eventually ended in the enslavement of Africans.

Consequences of Christian Europe's actions on Africans

The effects of the introduction of religion to Europe and the Catholic Church's early ambitions and attempts to dominate religion inside and outside Europe led to grave negative and terrible consequences on Africans, the modern descendants of Ancient Egyptians. Specifically, the greatest fall-out of the introduction fell on the modern descendants of the ancient *Akan* people, the very people whose ancient ancestors conceived the idea of theosophy and designed the first religion from which all religions of this world emerged.

In the discussion of the secret war of Christian Europe on Ancient Egypt, a major historical event that occurred in African and European interaction to help Christian Europe bring down Ancient Egypt and its modern descendants in far away Africa was slavery. Different versions of the story of the enslavement of Africans have been told by many historians in the west, but none has ever revealed that the Catholic Church was the cause and the political and spiritual power behind European enslavement of the African people beginning from the 15th century. How did this happen? It happened from distant religious and political events that had nothing to do with the Africans. Even these historical events did not look related in anyway, but they were.

In 476 AD, Germanic barbarians attacked and destroyed Rome and consequently the Roman Empire. Western historians believe this was the most predominant historical event that sent Europe into the Dark Ages. As Europe was coming out of the Dark Ages, she was faced with

156

political chaos, and Europeans were bitterly embroiled in wars with each other in search of their ethnic, political, and national identities and borders. Medieval Europe was, therefore, mostly a disorganized continent onto itself with rather very little contact with the outside world. Historically, the paths of Africans and the history of Europeans were never designed to cross, but these paths did cross through developing circumstances in Europe and the Middle East.

After the destruction of the Roman Empire, the Catholic Church stepped in the political and leadership vacuum that had been created in Europe. Evidence of the use of religion and the Catholic Church's role in laying the foundations of European social, economic, and political development can still be found in how western Europeans proudly describe their historical traditions within the context of religion as the Judeo-Christian tradition.

Before the Church could introduce the Judeo-Christian foundations of nationhood and society building to Europeans, it first had to bring peace to Europe. It therefore became the responsibility of the Church to bring peace and order into the chaos of Europe. The Church needed to do that to make it possible for the propagation of the gospel. In a calculated plan to bring peace among warring Europeans, the Catholic Church designed a strategy to introduce Europeans to an outside religious enemy instead of Europeans seeing each other as enemies. At the same time, the Church secretly sought to dominate religious thought inside and outside Europe by attacking and eliminating any rival religions that gave it the opportunity to do so and the Church's first opportunity came soon enough.

Spill-over from the Crusades onto Africans
In Palestine, Moslems had taken over Jerusalem and blocked Christian Europe's access to the so-called "holy-land." Christian Europe perceived Jerusalem as the center and capital of Christendom and that meant Christians in Europe could not concede their capital and "holiest" city to a rival religion. The Catholic Church therefore decided to shift the attention of Europeans from rivalry and wars among themselves to the Moslems. The Church decided that Christian Europe should go to fight to free its "holiest" city from Moslem control. The Church called for the First Religious Crusade (1096-99). For Christian Europe, going to fight to reclaim Jerusalem was seen as the highest act of religious sacrifice and redemption in the eyes of the Lord. Unfortunately, after almost a thousand years since the Catholic Church called for the Crusades, the war between Moslems and Christians is still going on in the same place over the same reasons.

The early success of the Crusade exposed Europeans to the outside world for the first time, and this introduction spurned new political and commercial ties with nations and people as far as India and the Middle and Far East. From the commerce that grew between Europeans and people of these foreign lands, Europe got gold, precious stones, silk, ivory, spices, and other items of trade. Europeans began to lay the foundations of their social and economic development. Europe's trade with the Far East was by land through Asia, and the Mongol Empire controlled these land routes. This Asian Empire was friendly to Christian Europe so European traders had free passage through the Asiatic lands. However, the history and politics of the Middle East and Asia began to change. As it dragged on, the Crusades eventually failed and after over two hundred years of fighting, Christian Europe lost all the lands it had earlier won from the Moslems.

The Moslems eventually won the Crusades but they were still not very secure from further attacks from Christian Europe. Towards the end of the 14th century, the Moslems turned their attention to the Mongol Empire that occupied the lands around them. These Moslems saw in the Mongols a possible threat to their true security from Christian Europe because the Mongols were still friendly to Christian Europe. As part of consolidating their security from Christian Europe, the Moslems under the Ottoman Empire attacked and defeated the Mongols and they blocked not only Christian Europe's access to Jerusalem but also access to all the land routes to India and the Far East. It is important to remember that all these historical events were happening because the Jewish people introduced African religious ideas to Europeans who did not know what these were or understand them, but they were willing to defend them with their lives.

The search for a sea route to India and the Far East

For some strange reason, the Africans who created the concept of theosophy had to be dragged into the middle of these Moslem and Christian religious wars, and Africa' woes in their interaction with Europeans began from these distant events in geo-political history. When the Moslems blocked the land routes to India and the Far East, Europeans decided to search for other ways around the Moslem land blockade to get to the East. They decided to do this by exploring a sea route along the shores and around Africa. That is how Western European and African history crossed paths over five hundred years ago. That is also how the terrible negative effects of the consequences of the introduction of religion to Europeans reached Africa.

The first Europeans to come in contact with Africans in the heart of the African continent were the Portuguese. At the southernmost point of Europe on the Atlantic shores, the Portuguese were closest to Africa and that gave them a geographical advantage in the search for a sea route along and around Africa's shores to India and the Far East. In 1418, Prince Henry sent the first Portuguese expedition with the goal of trying to reach Cape Bojador on the Moroccan coast. The ship was caught in a heavy storm that blew it off course. The crew, however, accidentally found themselves on the Madeira Islands. From this time onwards, Portugal kept sending ships to try to reach the Cape, and they eventually reached it in 1433. After Cape Bojador, the Portuguese sent more ships further south along the Atlantic shores of Africa every year. Some of the ships got lost, but others made it to the shores of northwest Africa.

In 1445, the Portuguese explorer Dinis Dias reached the estuary of the Senegal River on the southwestern verge of the Sahara desert. To the Portuguese, this was a great discovery because at the time, Christian Europe believed that the Senegal River was sacred. Christians believed then that the Senegal River flowed out of the Nile, which was considered one of the most glorious rivers from the "Garden of Eden." Note that even during this late relatively primitive period, Europeans knew that the biblical "Garden of Eden," the cradle of the creation of humanity was in Africa.

In 1455 and 1456, the Portuguese seafarers reached the estuary of the Gambia River and Cape Verde Islands. In 1460, Prince Henry died, but the expeditions did not stop. King John II who succeeded Henry approached the seafaring enterprise with his own motives. As the Portuguese got closer and closer to the West Coast of Africa, they heard from the Arabs about the magnificent civilized kingdoms of the people of West Africa especially the kingdom of the place called Ghana. The Portuguese therefore named the Atlantic Gulf through which they came to the people of Ghana, the Gulf of Guinea. This was a corruption of the indigenous name, Ghana. The fact that this gulf is still known by this Portuguese linguistic corruption is a testimony to the hundreds of years of linguistic corruption of African names of people and places by early Europeans.

Gold and the denigration of Africans

This is where the historical events that led to the denigration of black people and the subsequent events that led to Christian Europe not accepting a black Jesus anymore began. The Portuguese landed in the part of West Africa the British later named the Gold Coast in the 1460s. The irony in the first European contact with Africans is in the fact that the Portuguese landed among the *Akan* whose ancient ancestors invented the concepts of religion in Ancient Egypt. Remember that they were these concepts of religion the Ancient Egyptians created that brought Europeans to the Middle East to fight the Moslems and introduced Europeans to the outside world. It was from such an introduction to the outside world that European commerce with the Middle and Far East began, and it was in the protection of the gains from this commerce that Europeans decided to search for a sea route to the East around the Moslem land blockade.

158

These first Europeans in Africa landed among the *Fante* people. The *Fante* people are part of the *Akan* tribal groups found today in Ghana and Cote d'Ivoire. Note how cyclical history can be and how atrocious it can be in the hands of the wrong people.

When the Portuguese people landed in the Gold Coast, they saw that the Africans wore and even used gold in their religious rituals. The Portuguese came to the Gold Coast with guns, and using threat of torture and death, Portuguese sailors forced the *Fante* people to take them to where they got their gold. The *Fante* people showed the Portuguese a coastal hill that turned out to be very rich in gold. The Portuguese sailors immediately opened a gold mine in a coastal town called *Abrobi*, near modern *Kommenda* in modern Ghana.

The Portuguese had not reached the Far East but they had found plenty of gold along the way in a hitherto unknown place in Africa. Back in Portugal, the Portuguese had to manufacture a story to tell their people where they got such abundant gold. To the Portuguese people, the sailors who had been to Africa described the West Africans from whom they were stealing the gold as uncivilized sub-humans who did not even know the value of the gold they had. The portrayal of the people of the Gold Coast as uncivilized sub-humans who did not know the value of gold suggested to the Portuguese people that they were superior to the Africans because they the Portuguese were civilized, they were humans, and they knew the value of gold.

This false portrayal of the Africans in contrast to the Portuguese turned out to be what was accepted and used in Europe to justify European conscience in what later became the atrocious plunder of Africa's human and mineral resources by Europeans. It was this myth of comparative anthropology that crystallized into racism over the centuries as generations of Europeans in all fields of endeavor sought the elusive evidence of their civilization, superiority, and humanity over Africans. Some Europeans are still searching.

However, what this centuries old elusive search has succeeded in doing is that it has succeeded in brainwashing generations of Europeans into believing that they are superior to Africans so they have developed negative attitudes toward African people to match their false senses of superiority. European search for the elusive evidence of their civilization and anthropological superiority over Africans has also succeeded in influencing what some European scholars say and write about Africa and the African people today. In other words, some Western European scholars have resorted to lying and concealing the truth in their scholarship to uphold Europe's self-conferred superiority over Africans. To a great extent, there are even some European scholars who monitor what their colleagues say and write about Africa to make sure that traditional hidden truths about Africans are not revealed to upset Europe's centuries old assertions of civilization, superiority, and humanity over Africans.

What happened to Africans with the coming of the Europeans also happened to Native Americans when Europeans got to North America. In both situations, Europeans had to prop their consciences with false propaganda and misinformation about the people from whom they were stealing. In the *Invasion of America*, Francis Jennings made an observation that aptly applies to Africa too. He noted that in all European travels, plunder, and exploitation of foreign people, they had to justify their consciences on the inhuman and atrocious treatment of people in these foreign lands. As a result, they fabricated quantities of propaganda to counter attacks on their consciences by their fellow Europeans. Jennings stated that:

"The invaders also anticipated, correctly, that other Europeans would question the morality of their enterprise. They therefore [prepared] ... quantities of propaganda to overpower their own countrymen's scruples. The propaganda gradually took standard form as an ideology with conventional assumptions and semantics. We live with it still" (1975, p. vii).

This is the reason people in and outside the west should listen to and read information about Africa written by Europeans with a pinch of salt. In Europe, the greatest propaganda was the myth of the uncivilized and sub-human nature of the African. Again, this is historically ironic because the ancient ancestors of modern Africans created the civilization and religion that modern Europeans have adopted. For Europeans to turn around now to characterize the descendants of the creators of civilization and religion as uncivilized sub-humans is very ironic. Nevertheless, making African people uncivilized sub-humans became the foundation of the propaganda in Western Europe's interaction with the African people. This was also the foundation of the myth that later became European superiority over the African. Europeans still live by this and Africans still live with it.

Meanwhile, in Portugal, some Christians began to question the morality of the Portuguese enterprise of plundering the wealth of Africans. In their defense, Portuguese merchants and seafarers were forced to prove that African people were truly uncivilized sub-humans upon whom no Christian should confer pity or consideration. In their attempts to swing conscientious Christian criticisms to their side, Portuguese merchants and sailors also argued that *Africans were pagans and since pagans were considered the enemies of Christianity, the Africans did not deserve Christian sympathy.* Christianity that originated from paganism started all these historical events, and now the position of Christianity against pagans was being invoked to justify European greed and inhumanity towards Africans in the form of Portuguese plunder of the resources of the Gold Coast. Such were the reinforcements in the foundations of false European perceptions that later influenced and continue to influence European scholarship and thinking about Africa to this day.

The Portuguese and the foundations of slavery in Africa

To prove back in Portugal that the Africans were uncivilized sub-humans that did not deserve Christian or even human pity, Portuguese sailors kidnapped four *Fante* men who were mending their fishing nets on the Atlantic shore near the Portuguese gold mine at *Abrobi* in the Gold Coast. They took these poor men to Portugal. In Portugal, these kidnapped Africans were specially prepared to look awful, "uncivilized", and "sub-human" before the Portuguese public. These men were then put on display in Lisbon. When the Portuguese people first saw these black men, most of them became convinced that they were looking at tangible physical evidence of their own superiority. The Portuguese people were therefore the first Europeans to be successfully deceived into believing the propaganda of greed, and this helped to launch entire Europe's negative attitude toward Africans.

After the Portuguese seafarers finished displaying the four men they kidnapped from the Gold Coast, they gave the men as presents to their merchants and financiers. These Africans from the Gold Coast were the first to be introduced into European servitude, and soon African servants became prized possessions and symbols of affluence in wealthy Portuguese homes. To satisfy the demand for African servants in Portugal, the Portuguese sailors that went to the Gold Coast made it a habit of capturing and kidnapping more and more Africans in each expedition.

When the people surrounding the Portuguese gold mine noticed that more and more of their people were turning out missing everyday, they suspected the Portuguese must have something to do with them. Some of the Africans even suspected that the Europeans were cannibals that were eating the missing people. It turned out that these Europeans were worse. The local Chief complained of the missing people to the Portuguese Governor and the Portuguese people changed their strategy of acquiring their slaves. They no more captured the people along the coast for fear of antagonizing the coastal people among whom they lived.

First, they went inland and showed off European goods to people most of who had never seen such goods before. The Portuguese offered to give the goods to the families of people that volunteered to go to work in their gold mines on the coast. Numerous able-bodied people volunteered and parents believing that their children were going to work on the coast to bring back home wealth in the form of European goods also volunteered their able-bodied children. The Portuguese showered the families of these people with European goods and led their people to the coast. On the coast, the Portuguese offered these strangers shelter in the dungeons of their castle.

The dungeons opened out at the other end into the sea, and at night the people that were supposed to be brought to work in the gold mine were bound, gagged, and quietly sent into waiting boats behind the castle. The boats took these poor people onto waiting ships offshore, and the lives of these Africans began as slaves. This was a great trickery that went on for a long time because the people on the coast did not know much about the people that were brought from inland. At the same time, the people inland assumed that their relatives were working in a gold mine on the coast, and these people would one day come back home with European goods, but they never saw them again.

At a point in time, the Portuguese found out that they could not use trickery to acquire their merchandise anymore. They therefore brought enough soldiers to their post in the Gold Coast to support the slave trade. They began to use these soldiers and African guides to ransack villages and capture men, women, and children in the night and blame it on other villages. This started distrust and skirmishes among the Africans. Next, they supported one village against the other, gave the village they supported arms and ammunitions and set it to attack the other and bring the captured people to work in the Portuguese mine on the coast. Finally, they had the Africans fighting each other and bringing captured people on the coast to the Portuguese.

Portuguese settlement for slaves in the Gold Coast

About three decades after their arrival on the Gold Coast, the Portuguese decided to establish a place and settle in the West African community permanently. In 1481, they decided to annex the Gold Coast by establishing a permanent settlement with a garrison to protect it. A Portuguese fleet with more than a garrison of soldiers and prefabricated wood, pre-cut stones, and materials for building a castle landed on the Gold Coast on January 19th, 1482 near where the Portuguese gold mine had been established earlier.

Fig. 4: The Elmina Castle in Ghana, the holding cell and passage of no-return for millions of Africans that were carted into slavery in Europe and America.

161

The Portuguese claimed that the soldiers were brought there to protect Portuguese ships going and coming from the east, but that was a lie. Bartholomew Diaz was a captain of one of the ships in this fleet, and Christopher Columbus who discovered America a decade later was among them. It was in the Gold Coast that Columbus decided he could go to the east by traveling west because he saw two oriental dead bodies wash ashore where the Portuguese fleet had landed near Elmina. Reluctantly, the African king of the place the Portuguese landed showed the Portuguese sailors some land on the shore where they could build their castle. Because this place was near where they had established their gold mine, the Portuguese named their place of settlement *Elmina*, meaning the Mine. The castle still stands in Ghana. Above is the Elmina Caste today. Notice the back of the castle towards the sea. At high tide the sea comes directly behind the castle and rowing boats can dock directly behind the back opening of the castle.

When they felt they had successfully established a pipe line of supply of humans in their unconscionable dealings in the Gold Coast, the Portuguese decided to set up a permanent post where they had succeeded in setting up a semi-genuine gold trade and a clandestine slave trade. To keep this pipeline flowing, next they used their soldiers to force the Africans to bring them the people they needed and overtime, the Africans unwillingly became forced partners in the enslavement of their own people. From the capture of the first four men by the Portuguese sailors, the foundations of what later became a full-blown slave trade were laid in the Gold Coast. Of about thirty-three European slave forts and castles that later sprung up on the West Coast of Africa to support the slave trade, about twenty-nine were built in the Gold Coast where the unconscionable and atrocious trade began and flourished.

As a result, the millions of Africans that were eventually taken into slavery in Europe and later in America were taken initially from the Gold Coast. It was later after Europeans converged on the Gold Coast that the slave trade was expanded into surrounding countries of the Gold Coast. However, almost all these Africans were initially shipped through the Gold Coast where there were fortified forts and castles to hold the human cargoes till slave ships arrived.

The King of Portugal claimed to have annexed the area surrounding the *Elmina* Castle. He gave the Portuguese African settlement the name of St. George d"Elmina and conferred the rights and privileges of a Portuguese city onto it with Don Diego d'Azambuja as its first mayor. From the Portuguese settlement on the Gold Coast, the enslavement of the African people intensified and so was the denigration of Africans in Europe (see W. E. Ward, The Coming of the Europeans in *Short History of Gold Coast*, 1935).

Treaty of Tordesillas

In Europe, Portugal's neighbor, Spain also set out in search of foreign wealth and that brought Spain into the Americas. After Columbus' discovery of America, the Spaniards continued to search for a sea route to India and the Far East through the west. Soon, Portuguese and Spanish sailors met on the Spice Islands in the east, and the earliest European conflict on a foreign soil began to brew. It must be pointed out that Portugal and Spain were both Catholic nations and the Catholic Church benefited greatly from the foreign plunder and exploitations of these two countries. It was in the interest of the Church therefore to make sure that these two countries did not fight each other to dominate the foreign lands.

In an arbitration initiated by the Catholic Church, the rulers of Portugal and Spain came together in 1494 to sign a non-aggression and non-interference treaty called the *Treaty of Tordesillas*. This treaty was designed to protect Portuguese and Spaniards' territories abroad from each other's intrusion. By this treaty, Portugal and Spain divided the rest of the *non-Christian* world between themselves with an imaginary line in the Atlantic Ocean, about 1300 miles west of Cape Verde Islands. Every land to the west of this demarcation was for the Spaniards, and all land east of the demarcation was for the Portuguese. Notice how the atrocities of the Portuguese and Spaniards towards the people whose wealth they were stealing were justified in terms of Christianity and paganism. Religion was at the center of it all. What was wrong was the fact that to Europeans, this religion was the medium and justification of the perpetration of inhumanity on other people, and to the Africans who created the concept, it was untold misery.

The demarcation of the pagan world had, however, left out the rest of Western European countries and that started a revolution by itself. Note the role the Church was playing in all these historical circumstances. Spain and Portugal had convinced the Catholic Church that their enterprises abroad were also intended to introduce pagans in "their" foreign lands to Christianity. Because of this, the open exploitation of "pagans" in foreign lands by Christians from Spain and Portugal was fully endorsed by the Catholic Church. What this meant was that the so-called pagans in these foreign lands were religiously different from Christians therefore they deserved the Church's intolerance, brutality, and atrocity as a way of teaching them a lesson. However, these two countries alone could not supply all the manufactured goods needed in the trade with their "colonies." As a result, other European countries also took to the sea in search of foreign trade and wealth; and they sometimes infiltrated into Spanish and Portuguese territories in these foreign lands. The Catholic Church perceived the rest of western European countries as going to these foreign lands because of greed, while Portugal and Spain were perceived as going to these lands to Christianize pagans. So Portugal and Spain became the favorites of the Catholic Church.

Catholic Church's approval of the enslavement of Africans

Most of the rest of Western Europe's infiltration into these foreign pagan lands was on Portuguese "properties." The Catholic Church stepped in to protect its interests in Portuguese plunder and exploitation of foreign lands by protecting the Portuguese from Western European incursions into Portuguese foreign territories. In 1514, Pope Leo X issued a papal bull forbidding all Western European countries from interfering in Portuguese foreign lands. *Pope Leo X also gave the Portuguese merchants the Catholic Church's formal permission to openly take Africans as slaves because they were pagans.* An issue I have never understood is how could the religious practice of the Africans that imagined and created the concept of God be paganism and the practice of the worship of this same God by Europeans would be Christianity that is supposed to be better? The fact is it was this same God and sacramental practices of worshipping this God that the Jewish people introduced to the Greeks and Europeans. The differentiation of the God of the Africans from the God of Christian Europe was based upon early European racist perception of themselves as everything about them being civilized and superior and everything about the African being uncivilized and inferior. This racist mentality had taken such great hold on European comparative anthropological thinking that Christianity had to come up with an inferior God for Africans and a superior God for Europeans. The God of Christianity is the same God the black people of Ancient Egypt that have now moved into inner Africa imagined, personified and worshipped for thousands of years before the Jewish people that went to Europe to become the Jews and Hebrews introduced this God and his worship to Europeans.

The Catholic Church therefore did not condemn or look the other way in the enslavement of Africans; the Church authorized it and it owes Africans a special apology for its role in this most terrible aspect of African history. Somehow, the Church might think the Africans do not know it, but we do. The issue here is if Africans were pagans, the most logical thing for the Church to do was ask that the Africans be Christianized. Why should they be enslaved? Nevertheless, what began as a clandestine slave trade now had open support from the highest seat of European Christendom and political power, and this intensified Portuguese atrocities and inhumanities in the Gold Coast. With European intensification of atrocities and inhumanities on the Africans also grew more denigratory propaganda about the uncivilized nature and sub-humanity of the Africans.

Notice how the Catholic Church started all of these historical circumstances and moved into the background to enjoy its rewards from the countries it supported. The permission by the Catholic Church for the Portuguese to openly take the people of the Gold Coast slaves has been perceived by some religious scholars as the greatest irony in the history of Christianity. The

Ancient Egyptians whose modern descendants are the *Akan* people and the other tribes of the Gold Coast invented the philosophy of religion and its original sacramental practices. The irony therefore is in how the religion the ancestors of the *Akan* people invented was used to enslave their descendants and strip them of their humanity by a religious body that emerged from the very theosophical doctrines the ancestors of these people created.

Africa's gold and humans in Europe's Religious Reformation

When Pope Leo X ordered that no Western European countries should interfere with Portuguese foreign lands in the papal bull of 1514, the rest of Christian Europe protested to the Church to rescind its decision on such a prohibition. The Church did not want the benefits it got from the Portuguese and Spaniards to spread across all Europe so it refused to let in the rest of Western Europeans. After three years of negotiations in which the Catholic Church refused to change its mind, the rest of Western Europe decided to break away from the Catholic Church for the freedom to pursue its own religious and economic agenda. This break away is known today in European history as the Reformation of 1517. Notice how Pope Leo X issued his papal bull in 1514 against the rest of Western Europe and how three years later Western Europeans broke away from the Catholic Church.

The history of the circumstances that led to the Reformation has been told from the perspective of Europe and western historians have told this story as a glorious religious revolution. However, there was nothing religious or glorious about the real causes of the Reformation. The Reformation ended in the break away of Western Europeans from the Catholic Church but the religious aspect of the story was nothing but a façade to conceal the real economic reasons behind the Reformation. What is least revealed is the fact that the Reformation was secretly and deeply motivated by economic greed closely linked to the plunder of gold and the enslavement of the Africans in the Gold Coast.

Fig. 5: Picture of some of the European cannons that enforced slavery and protected slave dealers from other intruding Europeans.

Breaking away from the Church was the only way the rest of Western Europe could get around the Catholic Church's political and economic favoritism of Portugal and Spain. The Reformation almost covered the tracks of the Catholic Church's involvement in the plunder of the resources and enslavement of the African people. However, the Church had already done enough to be permanently linked and remembered in the history of slavery by those who know and have the courage to tell the truth. That is very ironic.

The Reformation and the scramble for Africa

Looking at the history of the Reformation in Europe alone, historians have told the world that the Reformation was a glorious religious revolution. However, looking at the Reformation from its subsequent history and spillover into Africa, the Reformation was nothing but a revolution to give Western Europeans the freedom to join in the plunder of Africa's human and mineral resources.

The Reformation gave Western Europeans the religious and political freedom to pursue their economic motives; and it also opened the way for them to rush into foreign lands, especially to the Gold Coast where the plunder of gold and slaves in Africa had begun. The deep economic motive of the Reformation can be seen in the historical fact that right after the Reformation, almost every Western European nation rushed to the Gold Coast and sought to be a part or even control the trades in gold and humans. At one time or another, there were the Portuguese, Dutch, French, English, German, Danes, and Swedes in the Gold Coast, all searching for gold and slaves.

As more and more Europeans became involved in the exploitation of Africa's human and natural resources, the propaganda against the African people in Europe to justify European atrocities and inhumanities in Africa grew. European rivalry of the Dark Ages and the economic greed thereafter descended upon Africa as these foreigners did not fight against the Africans for settlement, but they fought among themselves for the control of the wealth in gold and slaves. European cannons of slave trade and colonization still stand the sentry they stood five hundred years ago in the Gold Coast [Ghana]. Notice above that these cannons did not point to the Africans inland. They were not the threats. The cannons pointed to other Europeans that "intruded" from across the ocean.

It was from this convergence and over-crowding that the Europeans decided to spread the slave trade to the immediate lands surrounding the Gold Coast. Again, alongside all these historical events, Western European propaganda against Africans intensified and spread throughout Europe.

As more and more Africans were taken to Europe as slaves, they became the worst pinches on European consciences. Two main problems arose with the introduction of Africans into European communities and households. When most Europeans had never seen Africans before, they readily accepted their sailors' and merchants' propaganda of European superiority over Africans. Through slavery, African men and women were planted in almost every European household. From the pride and dignity with which these Africans carried themselves even in slavery, most Europeans of conscience could not find any evidence or justification of African inferiority, continuation of the enslavement of Africans, or even European superiority. The question of the morality of slavery therefore soon became a vigorous European household and societal debate.

The Bible in the search for the morality of slavery

The first problem the slave trade and the plunder of Africa's wealth and resources posed in Western Europe was the problem of Christian morality. Christianity created all these problems for the Africans and now Christianity was called upon to decide if it was morally right for these problems to continue. The question was whether it was morally Christian to engage in perpetrating such inhumanity, misery, and plunder on the African people. Christian Europe was forced to respond to the question of the morality of slave trade, and for that they had to use the only resource they had, *The Bible*. This is where the foundations of racism and racial prejudice against black people began. The irony is, the religious documents that African people had created in Ancient Egypt were now the documents Europeans were using to justify or condemn the enslavement of the descendants of the people that wrote them. Would the Bible, Africa's own religious document, come to the rescue of Africans?

To most Christians, European inhumanity and racism were definitely against Christian and biblical principles of morality, but the economic gains through the plunder of Africa's wealth and the free labor of African slaves were perceived to be good for Europe's economic development and survival. As a result, Christians in Europe were forced to make a choice between their religious morality and economic greed, and they chose to reinterpret the Bible to justify their morality and greed at the same time. To do so, Christian Europe had to prove through the Bible that Africans were pagans and truly inferior sub-humans therefore enslaving them did not violate Christian or human morality.

Proving that the African was pagan was easy. However, proving that he was inferior and sub-human was more difficult because in the biblical story of creation, Christianity professes the equality of all humans through the Adamite or the Theory of Monogenesis. The Adamite or Theory of Monogenesis suggests that all humans are equal because we came from the same ancestors, Adam and Eve. In an earlier discussion, I showed that scholars have found that even these names of our earliest biblical ancestors have African origins. To be able to prove that Africans were inferior and sub-human, Christian Europe first had to reject the biblical theory of human origins, and it did.

The religious freedom that came to Western Europe through the Reformation opened the door for Western Europeans to redesign their own religions, moralities, and sacramental practices. Even the Bible was rewritten in many countries, and it is believed that many parts in the original biblical documents were modified, censored, or omitted to suit European sentiments of the time. King James of England, for example, made his own version of the Bible. From all these, the little traditional morality from fundamental religious beliefs that Europeans had learned under the Catholic Church were mostly thrown overboard. Western Europeans were now free not only to reinvent their own brands of Christianity, but also to question and reinterpret the Bible any way they pleased.

What is most interesting is that Western European scholars also began to base the emerging scholarship of the time upon the false assertions of the Bible and Christianity. Almost all of them supported the Bible's views on these issues as Bory de Saint-Vincent, one of the most vocal anthropologists and the strongest proponents of the Christian theory of polygenism asserted that:

"Revelation ... nowhere prescribes that we are to believe exclusively in Adam and Eve ... (see Leon Poliakov, *The History of Aryan Myth: A History of Racist Ideas in Europe*, 1996, p. 220).

In all these, the influence of economic greed in the reinterpretation of the Bible became obvious as Christians in Europe agreed and asserted that Africans were sub-humans who did not deserve Christian pity or consideration. It was the Catholic Church that authorized that Africans should be taken as slaves, and though Western Europeans had broken away from the Church, the Protestant Churches that emerged also supported the Church's mandate to take Africans as slaves. This was because Africans were pagans but more importantly, they were economically profitable pagans.

The earliest justification of slavery and European inhumanity towards Africans was based upon Portuguese assertions that African s were pagans and uncivilized sub-humans. All these assertions were made without any proof but now Europeans needed proof of the sub-humanity and uncivilized nature of the Africans. Again, Christian Europe sprang into the forefront of the quest for this proof. To prove this assertion, Christian Europe not only had to reject the theory of Monogenesis and prove that Africans were sub-humans, but they also had to search for another explanation of human origins to give Europeans a different and more superior origin from the biblical origin of humans.

The popular Noah's curse

Christians in Europe claimed to have found the "evidence" of European superiority and the biblical mandate for Europeans to enslave Africans in their interpretation of the so-called Noah's Curse in *Genesis* 9:20 - 26. From a rather far-fetched interpretation of a biblical story Europeans never understood or knew its origin, Christian Europe used the story of a drunken Noah whose son Ham saw his nakedness but did not cover him. Noah's sons Shem and Japheth went and covered their drunken father's nakedness. As a result, when drunken Noah woke up, he decided to bless the two sons who covered his shame and curse instead his grandson from the son who refused to cover his shame. What is most intriguing about this story is that Noah did not curse his son Ham who had offended him directly, but he cursed Canaan, his grandson and the son of Ham instead. Other than a drunken man's logic, how logical is this? Why would Noah curse his grandson instead of the son who offended him? Who but a drunken man would think this way and do such a thing? Nevertheless, Noah is said to have blessed his other sons Japheth and Shem to enslave the descendants of their brother Ham for failing to cover his drunken father's shame. What is interesting about this story is that Christians believed that this curse was true and Christian Europe believed its God supported this logic and curse.

Without any understanding or knowledge of the source of this story, Christian Europe conferred the so-called blessings of drunken Noah on themselves and the curse of Canaan on black people, the Africans. That was not difficult to do because Africans were already enslaved in Europe so Christian Europe conveniently interpreted this biblical story to mean that the descendants of Ham were the Africans who were already enslaved in fulfillment of the so-called Noah's curse.

However, this same Bible reveals that black people are not the descendants of Ham but because Europeans do not have the linguistic, cultural, and tribal background to understand the biblical stories, they have never known this for almost two thousand years. That is a long time to wallow in biblical ignorance. The revelation of the fact that black people are not the descendants of Ham is part of the revelation of this work, and it will be presented in coming discussions. However, who would today accept the curse, blessing, and story of a drunken character as the religious truth other than people who do not know where the story came from in the first place? Nevertheless, all of these fabrications were slowly reinforcing, shaping, and influencing early Western European thinking and scholarship about Africa and Africans.

The Bible in the search of superior European origin

Next, Christian Europe had to show that Europeans and Africans did not come from the same human lineage as the Bible states because Europeans claim they came from a more superior stemma. For the proof, Christian Europe had to search for European superior origin in the Bible, and they found it. What they found was not what had been written in the Bible but their interpretation of what they wished should have been written in the Bible for them at the time.

Again, Christian Europe found its explanation of human differences and origins in their interpretation of the story of Noah and the biblical flood. According to Christian Europe's interpretation of the flood, the first humans on earth originated from Adam but these humans were all wiped out in the biblical flood thus making human equality through the Theory of Monogenesis obsolete. Christians in Europe argued that after the flood, a new group of humans with different lineages emerged. Who were in this new group of humans? Christian Europe claimed that this new group of humans originated from the sons of Noah. Were Noah and his sons not the descendants of Adam? They were, but the fact that this so-called new group of humans was also descendants of Adam and Eve did not matter to Christian Europe. In its twisted logic, Christian Europe did not see the origins of the children of Noah in Adam; all Christian Europe wanted was an exegesis to help disassociate superior Europeans from inferior Africans.

The Bible in Christian Europe's concept of polygenism

The new origin of humans was then found in the three sons of Noah, who Christian Europe believed peopled the earth after the flood (see *Genesis 9, 19*). Christians in Europe claimed that Europeans were different and more superior because they originated from Noah's son Japheth, while Asians originated from his son Shem, and Africans, the slaves and the cursed ones, were the descendants of Ham. Through this false interpretation of the Bible, Christian Europe laid the foundations out of which the modern anthropological theory of polygenesis later emerged. Though modern science has found and confirmed that all humans originated from the same stemma in Africa, there are some western scholars who still cling onto Christian Europe's invention of the theory of polygenism. These scholars refuse to accept the same origination of Europeans, Africans, and all other humans, and they devote much of their scholarship trying to prove that Europeans come from a different line from all other humans. It is important to realize that Christian Europe and the biblical tradition provided the entire initial arguments and fictitious "proofs" for what later became European racism.

Since then, most Europeans have tried to argue for the different origin of Europeans and Africans. In America, arguments of polygenism were and are still the most popular form of justification of the conscience of Christians who believed in slavery and now continue to live by racism. In the *African Exodus: The Origins of Modern Humanity*, Christopher Stringer & Robin McKie wrote emphatically:

> We [humans] emerged out of Africa less than 100,000 years ago and replaced all other human populations. Our genes betray this secret of common racial heritage; further, *the apparent racial distinctions of modern humans that have given rise to centuries of prejudice and inequality are shown to be merely geographical variants* (1996, summary on front flap cover, emphasis mine).

This is what modern science knows about human origins. However, during the Renaissance, new academic knowledge developed from the foundations of the false theological assertions and proclamations by the Churches.

Renaissance scholarship takes over from European Christianity

About the time Christian Europe was struggling with seeking proof of the sub-humanity and inferiority of Africans through the Bible, Western European Renaissance was beginning. This is the overlap in history that slowly helped to push the fundamental role of Christianity and the Church in the plunder and enslavement of Africans to the background. This is also the historical overlap that makes western historians and Africans blame Europeans in general for what happened to Africans. Most scholars do not know that Christianity, especially the Catholic and Protestant Churches, laid the foundations for all the racist perceptions Renaissance scholars came to propagate as scholarship. After all, it was Christian Europe that first asserted that black people were the descendants of Ham and therefore they were cursed for Europeans to enslave them.

This meant that it was all right for Christians in Europe to have African slaves because it was ordained in the Bible. It was Christian Europe that first asserted that Europeans and Africans did not come from the same human origins and that Europeans came from a more superior line of origin. By the time of Western European Renaissance, Christian Europe had laid all the necessary foundations for the growth and development of racism and racial prejudice. There was not much evidence in the Bible to prove all the intolerance and prejudice of Christian Europe. However, it had laid all the foundations of hatred, prejudice, intolerance, and racism. All Renaissance scholars had to do was search for the academic language and false academic justifications to support what everybody believed to have been ordained by God. In other words, it was the Christian duty of most Renaissance scholars to produce scholastic evidence in support of Christian Europe's theological fallacies.

168

Some early Renaissance scholars felt that Christian Europe's assertions of different European origin did not make sense and they tried to make a mockery of it by offering a new lineage of human origin that according to them "made more sense." It was from this perspective that in his *Spaccio della bestia triofante*, Giordano Bruno (1584) suggested that if Western Europeans wanted to be different from all other humans, they should accept human ancestry in Enoch, Leviathan, and Adam with the Jews being the only people to come from Adam. According to Bruno, if Europeans wanted to be different they should accept Enoch and Leviathan because they were far more removed from Adam than Noah's sons were. In other words, Bruno was telling Christian Europe that no matter how far removed Europeans were from Adam, all humans are equal because they all originated from one progenitor and that was Adam.

Western scholars, especially Renaissance scholars sought to expand the scholastic arena of assertions of European superiority over Africans to give it more "legitimacy." As a result, Renaissance scholastic quest for the justification of this false superiority passed from economics into religion, anthropology, science, sociology, anatomy, physiology, politics, history, and psychology. The academic quest for European superiority can still be found in these academic disciplines where some scholars conduct "research" and skew their interpretations to propagate an aspect of European superiority and African inferiority or the inferiority of other groups of people. From this point onward however, most European scholastic discussions about Africa began to deny and distort facts, and truths were concealed to uphold Europe's false and self-conferred superiority.

Some scholars suggest that it was around this period that the Catholic Church began removing the black images of Jesus and his mother in the Churches from public view. This paved the way for Renaissance artists to begin painting a white Jesus and his mother, and the entire biblical story was rendered in white characters, but that was only to support the lying lore that was beginning in Christianity.

I must point out, however, that not every western scholar of the Renaissance era used his scholarship to perpetrate racism against Africans. There were some that *saw* no inferiority or sub-humanity in the African, and there were those that *believed* in the *legendary lying lore* that Africans were sub-humans and inferior to Europeans. In the *Discours sur l'origine de l'inegalite parmi les hommes*, Jean-Jacques Rousseau chastised his European colleagues in their propagation of ignorance when he wrote:

> The whole world is inhabited by nations of which we only know the names and we presume to judge the human race (1755, j).

From his other works, however, Rousseau was not a saint either. In the *Cosmos*, Alexander von Humboldt wrote:

> "Whilst we maintain the unity of the human species, we at the same time repel the depressing assumption of superior and inferior races of men" (see translation by Otte, 1848, London, p. 368).

Johann-Gottfried von Herder (1774 - 1803) wrote in his *Outlines of Philosophy of the History of Mankind*:

> *The Negro has as much right to term his savage robbers albinoes and white devils ... as we have to deem him the emblem of evil, and descendant of Ham, branded by his father's curse* (Book VI, p. 260, emphasis mine).

Unfortunately, those who believed that the African was inferior were more prolific and therefore, they dominated the comparative anthropological discussion in Europe.

Western scholarship in support of racist biblical assertions

Among the earliest of Europe's prejudiced scholars against Africans was John Locke, the famous English philosopher. In *An Essay Concerning Human Understanding*, Locke (1490) argued that a black person was not a human being because:

> A [European] child having framed the idea of a man, such a complication of ideas in his understanding makes up a single complex idea which he calls man whereof white or flesh colour in England being one, because white colour was one of the constant simple ideas of the complex idea he calls man: and therefore he can demonstrate by principle, it is impossible for the same thing to be and not to be, that a Negro is not a man (Bk. IV, Chpt. VII, 16 - Instance in Man).

In this logic, the great English philosopher argued that the children of England, having known only white people would find it difficult to differentiate between the white people they have known and black people. To an English child therefore it is only the white man that is human and not the black man. This was the logic of someone Europeans have dubbed a great philosopher.

Wilhelm Gottfried Leibniz, the German mathematician and philosopher did not support European racism and inhumanity toward Africans. He wrote a special response to Locke in his essays entitled *New Essays Concerning Human Understanding*. In this, Leibniz wrote:

> It must be admitted that there are important matters in which the *barbarians* surpass us, especially in bodily vigour, and even so far as the soul itself is concerned. In certain respects one might say that their practical morality is better than ours since they have neither the avarice to hoard nor the ambition to domineer. ... With us there is more of the good and the bad than with them. A wicked European is worse than a savage is. He puts the finishing touches on evil (Bk. I, II, 20).

Scholastic racial classification

One of the most interesting aspects of looking back at early European scholarship on the races was that most of these scholars had direct African heritages with their African names to prove it, but they did not know. For example, J. Beddoe wrote a book entitled *The Races of Britain, A Contribution to the Anthropology of Western Europe*. The etymology of the name Beddoe is African; specifically it is an *Akan*. The *Akan* name from which this European version was derived was *Badu*, a name usually given to the tenth born in *Akan* culture. So it is clear that Europeans that originated from black people were denigrating black people to make themselves feel superior.

Christian Europe's perception of other humans as it saw it through its ignorant interpretations of the Bible was where most of Renaissance scholarship began. Especially, the discipline of anthropology began from Christian Europe's racist foundations against black people during slavery. It was no wonder therefore that several western disciplines took to the false "biblical" theory of polygenism. In 1684, the father of French anthropological racism, a philosopher and skeptic called Francois Bernier divided all humans on earth into four main races. According to Bernier, *the first human race was, of course, the Europeans in whose category were the Ancient Egyptians and Hindus*. In this original classification of humans into races, Bernier ignorantly classified Ancient Egyptians as Europeans and for over two centuries now many Europeans still believe that the noble Egyptians were their ancestors. This has been part of the reasons some western scholars have fought vehemently to deny that the Ancient Egyptians are the black Africans.

When Europeans believed that Ancient Egypt was their ancestral heritage they gave Egyptians every credit due them for the creation of the foundations of human civilization on this earth. Later when Europeans found out that the Ancient Egyptians were the black people of Africa they tried to deny and distort what they themselves had earlier said and written about the Ancient Egyptians. This, however, was the earliest among the numerous claims by Europeans asserting that Ancient Egyptians were Europeans. Europeans wanted the glory of Ancient

Egyptian ancestry for themselves and it is one of the jealous reasons western scholars have refused to acknowledge Africans as the creators of this magnificent ancient civilization. Unfortunately, the evidence these scholars have in Europe is nothing compared to the evidence we have in Africa.

In Bernier's classification of humans into races, the second race of humans was the African "whose skin color was necessary for this classification", and the third race was made up of the Chinese and Japanese people. Bernier stated that the fourth race was the Laplanders who he called "vile animals."

Leibniz also condemned Bernier's arbitrary racial classification of humans by stating that:

> All this is not reason for supposing that all men who inhabit the earth do not belong to the same race, as modified by different climates. ... (*see Otium Hanoveriana sive Miscellanea*, Leipzig, 1718, p. 37; quoted in *Edward Tyson*, M. D. F. R. S., by Ashley Montagu 1937, p. 397, Philadelphia).

Nevertheless, European anthropologists took up the classification of humans as their contribution toward upholding Christian Europe's assertion of the superiority of Europeans over the rest of the human race.

Christian Europe had taken the issue of slavery as far as the interpretation of the Bible would allow, and it was left to emerging scholars of the Renaissance to legitimize the racism and racial prejudice that emerged from all that. By now, the enslavement and denigration of the African people in Europe and America had gone on for several centuries. What began as history and myth to calm European consciences was now accepted and used by Renaissance and later European scholars as the foundation for the classification of human origins in introspective philosophy. Many Europeans still live by these biblical and scholastic fallacies and all Africans still live with it.

From all these do you think Christian Europe could look into the eyes of the true black Jesus, worship Him, and ask for His forgiveness? No, Christian Europe could no longer worship this black man. It therefore opted to change the image of Jesus Christ from black to white to satisfy racism rather than religious purity.

The Catholic Church and the Trans-Atlantic slave trade

Again, western historians have told the story of the Transatlantic Slave Trade as if it had nothing to do with Christianity or the Catholic Church. If the Catholic Church as the most powerful political, social, economic, and spiritual institution of Europe did not legitimize the slave trade, this unconscionable trade in humans could not have gone on for centuries. It would have died as soon as it started. Initially, European enslavement of the Africans was centered in Europe. Here is the involvement of the Catholic Church in the Transatlantic Slave Trade that brought millions of Africans into the plantations of misery in the Americas. Once again, the Catholic Church's involvement was instrumental in extending the enslavement of Africans from Europe to America.

In the 16th century, a Spanish slave merchant called Juan Spulveda argued that native Americans were barbarians and therefore they must be taken as slaves as Aristotle had written. However, the Catholic missionaries that had gone to settle among the native Americans did not agree that the pagans they were trying to Christianize should be taken slaves. So a Catholic Dominican called Bartolome de Las Casas argued powerfully that native Americans were humans who must be evangelized and treated as free men. The Catholic Church agreed. So in the papal bull *Sublimi Deus* of 1537, the Church proclaimed that native Americans could receive the Catholic faith and sacrament. This is evidence of how powerful the Church was in the historical events of the plunder and enslavement of human beings in foreign lands.

171

The Dominican Bartolome de Las Casas, while seeking to free native Americans from slavery, suggested to the Catholic Church that as free humans that were entitled to the Catholic faith and sacrament, native Americans could not be used as free labor in the new European plantations in the Americas. Instead, de Las Casas suggested that Africans should be brought and used as free labor in the Americas. The Church agreed and soon European slave traders found a new and expanded market for African slaves in the Americas. That was what blossomed into the infamous Trans-Atlantic Slave Trade in which millions of Africans were brought to the Americas.

From this time onward, deliberate discrimination against African people became open and evident. Black people became the butts of European denigration as they were accused of everything, from being cursed in the eyes of God to responsibilities for crimes of incest and castration. Generations of Western Europeans have since been born and educated into believing, accepting, living, and practicing the [im]morality of the denigration of the African. Most Western European scholars from Shakespeare, Poe, and Mellville took these false European perceptions of black people and used them in their literature thus further "academizing," legitimizing, and propagating these false ideas to the next and later generations.

In the free and open field of European assertions of superiority over Africans without proof or challenge, everything imaginable was fabricated as evidence of the African's inferiority and the European's superiority. As Leon Poliakov pointed out in his summary of the works of Professor W. D. Jordan:

"... when the most primitive [European] passions sought expression through pseudo-scientific generalizations, [even] travelers' tales were enough to transform fantasies about the bestiality of blacks into anthropological theories" (p. 136).

However, very few in our generation are aware that all of these began from the introduction of religion to Europe and European misunderstanding and misuse of the theosophical concepts that became Christianity.

From the Bible to academic racism

The passing of Christian Europe's racist misinterpretations of the Bible into academic knowledge and learning became necessary for the works of early academic scholars to be recognized and accepted by Christians in Europe. In 1666, Georgius Hornius, a Professor of Leyden University and the author of *Arca Noae sive historia imperiorum et regnorum* asserted that Christian Europe's biblical interpretation of the origins of Europeans in Noah's son Japheth was correct. I wonder how this professor would feel today if he found out what I am about to reveal and also the fact that the story of the biblical flood and the characters in it are all myths. Nevertheless, Professor Hornius asserted that in his "research", he had found out the evidence confirming that the descendants of Noah were divided into the Japhethites who became the white people, the Shemites who became the yellow people, and the Hamites who were the black people.

The writings of Hornius established and legitimized skin color as one of the criteria of inferiority and superiority. Blackness was perceived to be evil and whiteness was perceived as purity. Instantly, the African's dark skin color became his greatest mark of identity, inferiority, and denigration.

Not all European scholars were willing to follow the *legendary lying lore* to please the Church or their fellow Europeans. However, it was not easy for scholars who found out the truth about Africans to say it and certainly it was not easy for the few western scholars who knew that the assertions against black people were not true to speak out.

Against the denigration of the black skin, some scholars quietly asserted that black skin is the original color of human skin and therefore the black skin color was more superior to white skin. This assertion prompted Pierre-Louis de Maupertuis (1698-1759), the president of the Academy of Science of Berlin under Frederick II to respond to such scholars in his *Dissertation physique a l'occasion du Negre Blanc.* In this work, he argued that because black people occasionally have albinoes who may be considered white, white skin was the original color of humans and therefore white skin was more superior to black skin. He wrote:

> One might perhaps conclude, from these unexpected births of white children among black peoples that white is the primitive colour of mankind while black is only a variation which has become hereditary in the course of centuries but which has not entirely effaced the white colour, the latter tending always to reappear. For one never sees the contrary phenomenon; one never sees black children born of white ancestors. ... This would perhaps be sufficient to conclude that white is the colour of primitive man and that it is only due to some accident that black has become the hereditary colour of the great families which populate the torrid zone; amongst which nevertheless, the primitive colour is not so completely effaced that it does not occasionally reappear.
>
> This difficulty as to the origin of the Negroes, so often reiterated, and which some people would like to use to contradict the story taught by Genesis, that all the peoples of the earth issued from a single father and mother; this difficulty is removed if one admits an argument which is at least as worthy of credit as *all that which has so far been imagined to explain the problem of generation* (1757, Chpt. VI, emphasis mine).

The most important point in this quotation is the admission by Maupertuis that western scholars had been imagining all kinds of falsehoods to explain their wishes of origins and self-conferred superiority.

Georges-Louis Buffon

Georges-Louis Buffon, a scientist and philosopher, who was considered the precursor of Charles Darwin, was the first to be interested in the "scientific" study of man and animals. He drew rather interesting parallels between the two. In his *Natural History or Histoire naturelle generale et particuliere*, Buffon wrote that human color could not be used to determine humanity, sub-humanity, inferiority, or superiority because differences among humans do not translate into differences in our humanity. He wrote:

> Men vary in colour from white to black; some have double the height, girth, nimbleness, or strength of others. ... and in character they may be endowed with or they may lack all the qualities (Poliakov, p. 165).

In this same work, Buffon presented the most powerful argument yet against the dehumanization of the African by arguing that in nature, animals of different species can never procreate, and since black and white people can procreate together, black people are as humans as white people. He wrote:

> ... If it were not for the fact that White and Black can procreate together ... there would be two quite distinct species. The Negro would be to man what the donkey is to the horse, or rather, if the White was man, the Negro would no longer be man but an animal of another species like the ape. ... (Cited from Poliakov, p. 165).

This powerful argument of the African's humanity and equality to the European through procreation infuriated most European anthropologists and pseudo-scientists. Consequently, they set out not to prove the sub-humanity of the African but to prove that Africans were not humans at all. In many European societies, there was the societal move to stop any interracial union and consequently the procreation between black and white people. This is because Europeans argued that black people would use interracial marriages to seek to be humans and equal to white people. Christian Europe also argued that such unions were against God's will because if God wanted black people to be humans he would have created them white. Many European societies and so-called Christians still abhor interracial marriages for this reason. Christian Europe believed that it was doing the will of God by preventing such "unnatural" unions.

Pseudo science in support of racism

In another *Essay Concerning Human Understanding*, John Locke responded to scholars who supported black people's humanity and equality through procreation. He argued that the fact that white and black people can procreate does not prove that black people are humans. He tried to prove this assertion by stating that "he [Locke] had seen with his own eyes a creature which was the issue of a cat and a rat, and had the plain marks of both [animals] about it" (Bk. III, Chpt. VI. p. 23; also in Poliakov, p. 150). In other words, he had seen two animals of different species procreate, so procreation cannot be used to prove the African's humanity, much less his equality to the European. Buffon's assertion of the African's humanity and equality to the European through procreation was so powerful that much of 18th century pseudo "science" and anthropology were devoted to trying to disprove Buffon's *Equality of black people through procreation Hypothesis* just to prove that the African was not human at all. It was also intended to prove the superiority of the European.

The period after Buffon's assertions were devoted to "scientific" experimentation with crossbreeding. This early science of crossbreeding was not taken as seriously anywhere as in France where "scientists' reported numerous "successful" results in crossbreeding that sought to prove that procreation could not be used to establish the humanity of African people. In this, as in much of Western European scholarship of the time and even now, fabricating a lie with the motive of proving European superiority was the acceptable norm in comparative anthropology.

The scientific community of France was informed and it accepted the fabrication that *Reaumur had successfully crossed a chicken with a rabbit* (see "Reaumur embryologiste ..." in *Revue d'histoire des sciences, XI.* 1958, J. Rostand; see also Linnaeus, *Metamorphosis Planetarium,* 1755).

Maupertuis in his *Letter for the progress of the Sciences* called on all farmers to experiment with such "artificial unions," and there was no end to the responses that were reported. The French veterinarian Bourgelat claimed to have dissected a new breed of animal called a "jumart" which was the cross between a bull and a mare (see J. Rostand , 1958). Fortunio Licenti claimed that he had observed in his research that man can procreate with a cow, and even with a hen (see Poliakov, 150; Jacques Roger, *Les sciences de la vie dans la pensee francaise du XVIIe siecle,* Paris, 1963, pp. 31-4, 44, 83). It became clear that European scholars were willing to defend and preserve the European superiority they have grown to know even if they had to resort to fabrications in "scientific" and anthropological scholarship. This practice is still going on today.

During the Age of European Enlightenment, Voltaire sought to make a science of the theory of polygenism that emerged from Christian Europe's attempts to prove that Europeans were more superior to Africans and that both did not come from the same human tree.

From all these fabrications, the intended conclusion of European "scientists" and anthropologists was reached when Johann Fabricius claimed to have the proof that Negroes did not descend from the issue of two humans, but they descended from the cross between humans and apes. This conclusion was for many western scholars of the time enough proof that black people were not real humans. Fabricius' assertion and conclusion is still stuck in the minds and psyche of most Europeans to this day. Even today, some Europeans, including those who have been schooled believe that black people descended from apes. Unfortunately, these people do not know how or where Europeans originated, and they would hate to be told that white people originated from the albino [supposedly devilish] children black people discarded in evil forests in ancient times.

From the growth and development of knowledge, many western scholars began to find out that what they had been taught, as the truth was lies. Later, western scholars found out that modern Africans were the Ancient Egyptians, the magnificent people that laid the foundations of what the world is today. These scholars also found out that these ancient Africans were the inventors of theosophy and not the Jewish people. They also found out that the Bible was compiled and translated in Ancient Egypt and Ancient Egyptian religious documents and concepts were used in creating this Bible. These were truths that seriously undermined the biblical tradition and Europe's self-conferred superiority. The first instinct of Christian Europe was to deny these truths. However, Christianity has never ceased to be haunted by the fact that one day these truths might come out.

Christian Europe's inhumanity, brutality, atrocity, and seemingly unfeeling attitude towards Africans were possible because of seven main reasons:

1. Christian Europe and especially early Catholic Church did not know and most Christians still do not know that the Africans Christian Europe called pagans were the people that invented the concept of religion from which European Christianity and other world religions emerged.

2. Christian Europe and especially early the Catholic Church believed erroneously and they still believe that the Christian God is different from a pagan God because they have never known that Christianity grew out of paganism and that the Christian God is as much a pagan God as the so-called pagan Gods. To this extent, Christianity is nothing but a European word for ancient African paganism.

3. Christian Europe and especially early Catholic Church believed in its bigotry and prejudice that Africans were the enemies of Christians because they were pagans and that being inhuman, brutal, and atrocious to African people was a will of God all Christians should perform.

4. Christian Europe and especially early Catholic Church accepted and propagated the so-called uncivilized, pagan, and less than human nature of the African to justify Christian consciences in the enslavement of the African people.

5. Christian Europe and especially the Catholic Church falsely interpreted the Bible to justify bigotry and prejudice that eventually became a Christian moral duty in Europe.

6. Perhaps what led Christian Europe onto such ungodly paths was the deception that made them believe that the Bible is the utmost truth in world religion and that God-inspired Jewish prophets wrote the documents of the Bible therefore it is unimpeachable.

7. Christian Europe believed that the ancient *Afrim* people that became the Jews and Hebrews in Europe were a different people that did not originate from black heritage. So Jews were accepted in Europe as the children of God while the tribes from which they originated in Africa were condemned as the pagans and cursed ones.

As a result of all these, revealing that "pagan" Africans wrote the documents that the *Afrim* people compiled, edited, and translated into the Old Testament would seem a major act of blasphemy to many Christians because they have been made ignorant for far too long. If the *Afrim* people had told Europeans that they were originally black people, perhaps all of these would have taken a different historical turn. That is why it is important that the search for the Africans who wrote the documents of the Christian Bible should now begin from the revelation of who the ancient *Afrim* people really were before they went to Europe to become the Jews and Hebrews. It is also important at this point to reveal some facts in the real history of the Jewish people to prove that the biblical philosophy, doctrines, and documents they claimed were their creations could not have been theirs and the evidence is in their real history and not in the biblical lies.

5

Racial and ethnic origin of the ancient *Afrim* people that went to Europe to become the Jews and Hebrews

The Bible may be the truth, but it is not the whole truth and nothing but the truth.
Samuel Butler

Most people are bothered by those passages of Scripture they do not understand, but the passages that bother me are those I do understand
Mark Twain

It's been many and many a year since you and I were one person.
Edwin Schrock - Arthur, Illinois

Introduction

In preceding discussions, I have already revealed that the people that left Ancient Egypt into the Exodus were black people, and that these people were not Jews or Hebrews. These people were an amalgamation of people from the black tribes that were the Ancient Egyptians. These were the tribes that moved into inner Africa to become the Africans. I have also revealed that the dominant tribe of the people that went into the so-called biblical Exodus was the *Akan* tribe. We know this because these people of the Exodus identified themselves to foreigners as the *Afrim* people and that word is *Akan*. It was because the majority, of the people in the biblical Exodus, was *Akan* that the earliest name of the God of these people was an *Akan* name, and the ancient and modern names of their State Israel were also derived from the *Akan* language. That was also the reason many Jewish people still carry *Akan* and other African tribal names. In other words, the most important evidence of the origin of the Jewish people in the *Akan* and other African tribes that were the Ancient Egyptians is in the *Akan* and other African tribal names that these people have carried up to today, after over three thousand years of separation from these tribes. I have also mentioned elsewhere that African tribal names are unique and that they can lead one to the specific African tribe from which one originated. The names of modern Jewish people therefore reveal the composition of the tribes and people that left Ancient Egypt into the biblical Exodus. Beyond all these, the *Akan* people, their language, and culture are the most dominant features in the biblical narrative.

The above revelations are fascinating because as early as the Renaissance, European scholars found out that the biblical assertion of where Jewish people came from is false. What is intriguing about this is that for the past two thousand years since the *Afrim* people went to Europe to become Jews and Hebrews, they have refused to reveal who they were before they got to Europe, where they came from, the language they spoke in their place of origin, or the language that is spoken in the geographical region where they originated. Despite the Jewish people's strange refusal to reveal their racial and ethnic identities, Europeans were not curious to find out where these people came from until much later. These Europeans were more fascinated by the philosophy of the biblical documents than finding out where these people originated so as to find out where the fascinating philosophy of the Bible originated. Despite the fact that Europeans did not know who these people were, they still discriminated against and ostracized the Jewish people as early as the beginning of the 4th century. Why would Europeans do this to people they called the children of their God? It was because these people were different, and early Europeans that came in contact with them knew that they had a black heritage.

Christian Europe concealed the real reasons for early European discrimination against the Jewish people by accusing them of being the enemies of God, desecrating the Host, [anti-Christ] and killing Christian children for their blood in baking *matzot*. Since I have mentioned *matzot*, I have to reveal something about it that links the Jewish people to their tribes of origin in Africa. Most people in the west know that *matzot* is an indigenous Jewish religious and cultural food that is eaten only by the Jewish people. Throughout my travels, I have never heard of any other group of people that ate *matzot* other than the Jewish people. What people do not know about *matzot* is that it is not the original creation of the Jewish people. These people learned to make and eat *matzot* from the African tribes from which they originated in Ancient Egyptians. These tribes still make and eat matzot in West Africa. I loved it. We fry and not bake it. It is fascinating for me to know that despite three thousand years of the separation of the *Afrim* people from their African tribes of origin, we all still eat the same food. It is even more fascinating for me to know that we both have the same name for this food. We also call it *matsa*. Anyone who goes to Ghana and lands in Accra should ask for the *Zongo Lane*. At the *Zongo Lane* the person should ask for a place to buy *matsa* or one can see it being fried and sold by the roadside. It is a popular food. This is one of the unknown cultural links that tie the ancient *Afrim* people that went into the biblical Exodus and later went to Europe to become the Jews and Hebrews to their tribes of origin in Africa.

In searching for reasons why Christian Europe would discriminate and ostracize the very people that introduced Europeans to the concept and documents of Christianity, there is a question that must be asked about the *Afrim* people. Why would a people refuse to reveal who they are or where they come from, unless they have something to hide? What did the early Jewish people have to hide in Europe? It was their racial and ethnic heritage, and that made matters worse for them. A group of people refusing to reveal who they are or where they come from is suspicious, and Europeans suspected the Jews of the most atrocious and ridiculous crimes. However, it meant more to these Jewish people to be quiet and look ridiculous and suspicious in the eyes of Europeans than reveal anything that would undermine European acceptance and credibility in the biblical documents they had claimed as theirs. If the Jewish people had revealed to Europeans that they were from the black people of Ancient Egypt, I do believe that the course of human history would have been different.

However, the dignity of early Jews in Europe lay in European belief in the Bible and the belief that the Jewish people were the children of the God Europeans worshipped. That was enough for the early Jews in Europe and they were not ready to reveal anything that would undermine this belief. Revealing that the *Afrim* people were originally black could have undermined Europe's acceptance and credibility in the Bible. Revealing that the *Afrim* people were black people could also have exposed the hidden secrets of the Ancient Egyptian origin of the biblical documents. After all, Europeans have believed everything in the Bible in toto and held the Jewish people on a high religious pedestal. Why should the Jewish people reveal where they originated to change European's high and divine opinions about them?

Unfortunately, Europeans who do not know any of these truths have upheld and propagated the biblical falsehood of the *Afrim* people for over two thousand years. What is even more unfortunate about this is that this has been at the expense of the people that created the Ancient Egyptian civilization, the concept of God, religious doctrines, and the sacramental practices that the *Afrim* people introduced to the Greeks and later all Europeans. It is in support of the denial of the black people of Ancient Egypt their creations and achievements in both civilization and religion that the Jewish people have conveniently lost the ancient language they spoke, and supposedly lost ten of the tribes from which they originated. For Europeans who had no easy ways of finding out the truth, this was acceptable, but what about the tribes that are supposed to be lost? They know the truth, and they even know the biblical evidence in support of the truth. What the Jewish people and perhaps nobody in the west ever counted on is the fact that Africa would still know these things

Right from the beginning of this book, I revealed some very important ideas that laid the foundations for the revelation of who the ancient *Afrim* people were before they became the Jews and Hebrews in Europe. These ideas touched on who they were, where they came from, and the earliest language they spoke in ancient times. In this regard, I pointed out that:

1. Early Europeans in Greece and Rome, at least, knew that modern Jewish people came to Europe from among a group of black people, but they did not know from which specific group of black people the Jewish people originated. This was because at that time, these people did not know the tribal organization of black people and in fact they still do not know.

2. The Jewish people also knew then that they originated from among some black tribes but they did not specifically know who these tribes were or where they are today.

3. The Catholic Church has known of the black racial and ethnic heritage of the Jewish people and the people of the Bible since the beginning of Christianity. This was the reason the early Church openly portrayed the earliest images of Jesus and his mother as the black people they were.

4. Evidence of the earliest artistic portrayals of Jesus and his mother can be verified from books, and it can still be found in modern historical documentaries of the *Inquisition* and the *Catacombs of Rome* and Domitilla. In addition to this, the Catholic Church still has a black Madonna in Churches and Seminaries around the world. How else could the mother of the foundations of Christianity have been a black woman if the people of the Bible were not black people?

5. In my own travels to the Vatican in Rome, I noticed that St. Peter has been portrayed in two different racial features. The one inside the Basilica is black.

6. As late as September 1999, an impressionist art exhibition from England called *Sensations* came to the Brooklyn Museum in New York. An artist in this exhibition portrayed Mary, the mother of Jesus as a black woman. The Catholic Church in New York was upset about that. The Church argued that it was insulting for someone to portray an icon of another person's religion through the medium of elephant dung. However, the spokespersons of the Church refused to confront the issue of Mary being portrayed as a black woman because they did not want to reveal in a public debate what the Church has been trying to conceal for over two thousand years.

7. Around 37 B. C., after the Romans had conquered the Jewish people, one religious political party that emerged alongside the Pharisees, Sadducees, and Zealots was the *Essenes*. This name was derived from the ancient but still modern name of one of the supposed lost tribes of the Jewish people. This was the *Assini* tribe that can be found today in Ghana in West Africa. Scholars of Jewish history state that Jesus and John the Baptist belonged to the *Essene* group. The *Assini* people are still black. For a long time, there has been the speculation that Jesus was a black man. The revelation and introduction of the *Assini* people not only confirms that Jesus, John the Baptist, Mary, and the people of the Bible were black, but they also reveal the specific tribes of black people from which they originated.

179

8. In the book Hitler wrote, the black heritage of the Jewish people was the greatest reason for the Nazi massacre of blacks and Jews during the Second World War.

9. European leaders of post World War II knew that the Jewish people originated from black tribes. These tribes can now be found in Africa and that was the reason European leaders led by the British offered to settle the Jewish people in Uganda among their people in Africa.

10. The people that left Ancient Egypt in the biblical Exodus were Ancient Egyptians, and specifically, they were *Akan* because after they left Ancient Egypt, these people identified themselves in the foreign lands they traveled as the *Afrim* people.

11. The word *Afrim* is *Akan* referring to people that have seceded or broken away from a larger group of people. What is interesting about the *Akan* meaning of *Afrim* is that if the *Afrim* people were foreigners from somewhere else as the biblical narrative claimed almost one and half thousand years later, they would have had a name of their identity before coming to Ancient Egypt and they would not have identified themselves after leaving Ancient Egypt as the *Afrim* people. However, because they were Ancient Egyptians that have broken away from Ancient Egyptian tribes, *Afrim* was the perfect name for them to identify themselves in foreign lands. What is also interesting about the name *Afrim* is that its *Akan* meaning perfectly fits into the historical circumstances of the biblical Exodus. The *Akan* people are black and they can be found today in Ghana and Cote d'Ivoire in West Africa. This confirms that the people that broke away from them and called themselves the *Afrim* were also black people.

12. The revelation of the name *Afrim* comes from Africa's side of the story. However, scholars of Jewish history in the west also confirm that the people that left Ancient Egypt into the biblical Exodus referred to themselves as the *Ivrim* people. It was the *Akan* word *Afrim* that was transposed and presented in European orthography as *Ivrim*. Two European alphabetic and phonological systems came together to make the transposition of the *Akan* word *Afrim* to *Ivrim* possible. The first influence was the German alphabet. In German, the alphabet "v" is pronounced as the English "f." So that from German alphabetic influence the word *Ivrim* is actually pronounced as *Ifrim*. That brings the pronunciation of this word as closely as possible to its original *Akan* pronunciation. The second influence is from English alphabets. In English alphabets, the vowel "I" has two pronunciations. It can be pronounced as a long "I" as in "dime," or a short "I" as in "nickel." When the initial "I" in the word "*Ivrim*" is pronounced long in English with a German pronunciation of the "v," it approximates the original pronunciation of the word *Afrim* in the *Akan* language. Linguistically therefore, it is clear that it was the *Akan* word *Afrim* that has been transposed to *Ivrim*. The *Afrim* people of the Exodus also conferred this collective name onto their nation. The earliest name of the State of Israel was also the *Akan* word *Afrim*. Again, there was a western transposition of this *Akan* word when it referred to the nation of the *Afrim* people. Western historians and biblical scholars transposed the same *Akan* word *Afrim* into western orthography as *Ephraim*. The State of Israel's earliest and ancient name was also *Afrim*, this time spelled as Ephraim.

13. By identifying themselves with the *Akan* word *Afrim*, it is clear that the ancient *Afrim* people were originally *Akan* people, and therefore they were black.

14. The *Akan* people were the earliest Ancient Egyptians. They were the designers and developers of the Ancient Egyptian civilization. In support of this, I revealed the hitherto unknown indigenous names of the earliest kings of Ancient Egypt, the *Akan* kings, people, and places in Ancient Egyptian history.

15. The *Akan* people also created the concept of God, religion, and the sacramental practices that went with both in Ancient Egypt. I presented the evidence for this in the two oldest and most popular deities of Ancient Egypt that carried the *Akan* names *Osoro* and *Asaase* [Osiris and Isis].

16. By also identifying themselves with the *Akan* word *Afrim*, it is also clear that the ancient language of the people that left Ancient Egypt into the biblical Exodus was the *Akan* language. This is confirmed by the fact that the names of the biblical patriarchs of these people claim were from *Akan* words and names. In addition to this, most of the names of the people that wrote the Old Testament are *Akan* names. The indigenous tribal name of Jesus is *Akan*. Even today, millions of modern Jewish people still carry *Akan* and African tribal names. All of these do not only confirm the hundreds of years of speculation that Jesus was a black man and the Jewish people were originally black people but also they reveal the specific black tribes from which the *Afrim* people originated before they went to Europe to become Jews and Hebrews. They also reveal and confirm and the ancient language the people of the Exodus spoke before they acquired modern Hebrew..

17. Among the facts I introduced to show that the Jewish people were originally black people was the fact that the *Akan* people were not the only black people in the biblical narrative. The *Ga* people were also in the Bible (see Judges 12: 4-6). In these verses, I revealed that the original African language from which the biblical word *Shibboleth* was derived was the *Ga* language. The *Ga* people are black, and they can also be found today in Ghana in West Africa. What is revealing about the ethnic identity of the ancient *Afrim* people in this biblical quotation is that it reveals that the ancient *Afrim* people and the ancient *Ga* people were of the same racial and ethnic heritage. This was the reason the Gileadites had to use language and not physical features to differentiate themselves from the *Afrim* people. In the *Akan* language, the "sh" consonant combination is produced from the combination of "hy." On the other hand, the Gileadites spoke the *Ga* language in which there is the "sh" consonant combination. This was the reason, the Gileadite soldiers used a sentence in which there was an "sh" consonant combination to differentiate the Gileadite refugees from the *Afrim* people. That was why in this biblical narrative, *Jephthah* and the *Gileadites* who are believed to be the ancient *Ga* people asked the *Afrim* people to say some *Ga* words for them to determine whether they were *Gileadites* or not. In an earlier discussion of this passage, I revealed that the *Ga* sentence that was corrupted into the biblical *Shiboleth* was *"Ashi gbe le,"* meaning *Ashi killed him.*

18. This work is a very detailed revelation but it is not the only scholastic work to point out the fact that the ancient *Afrim* people that became the Jews and Hebrews in Europe were originally black people, and therefore Africans. One of the latest scholarly works that sought to establish a general link between modern Africans and the ancient *Afrim* people is *The Moses Mystery: The African Origins of the Jewish People* by Gary Greenberg (1996). The title of Greenberg's book establishes its

thesis, and it is significant that Greenberg who is also a Jew confirms that they originated from Africa

Genetic evidence of the African origin of the ancient Afrim people

Perhaps, the greatest evidence confirming that the ancient *Afrim* people that went to Europe to become the Jews and Hebrews were black people is the latest genetic evidence linking them to a black African tribe. It is important to point out that genetic evidence; perhaps the most recent powerful evidence of our humanity has linked the Jewish people to a black African tribe and not to any Semites or Europeans. The evidence is therefore conclusive.

For people whose so-called patriarchs in the Bible carried *Akan* tribal names, there is no more need to prove their racial and ethnic origin in the ancient *Akan* tribes of the Middle East, Ancient Egypt, and modern Ghana and Cote d'Ivoire in West Africa. For people that identified themselves in foreign lands in ancient times as the *Afrim* people, a name that originated from the *Akan* language, there is no more need to prove their racial and ethnic origin in the *Akan* tribe. For people that have retained their *Akan* and other African tribal names after separating themselves from these tribes for over three thousand years, it not necessary to show that they were Africans by any other means. For people whose God had the *Akan* names *Adonai* and *Yahweh* from the *Akan* words *Adona* meaning the rare and loveable one and *Yaw*, the ancient *Akan* God of Thursday, there is no need to prove their racial and ethnic affiliation to the *Akan* people. For people who lived in Ancient Egypt where the ancient *Akan* people were in ancient times, there is no need to prove that these people had *Akan* affiliation and heritage. Finally, for people whose real and biblical history is full of *Akan* and African tribal words and names, there is no more need to prove their origin in modern *Akan* and African tribes. The people that left Ancient Egypt in the biblical Exodus were not generic Africans because we do know the specific African tribes from which they originated from the names they have carried throughout all these years.

The evidence I have introduced and discussed in detail in the previous chapters should be enough, but there is more. The above revelation of the affiliation of the ancient *Afrim* people to the *Akan* and African tribes that were in Ancient Egypt should be enough to show that these people were originally black people from *Akan* and African tribes. However, there is more evidence confirming their origin in the black people that lived in Ancient Egypt and the Middle East in ancient times.

The biblical history of the origin of the people that went to Europe to become the Jews and Hebrews was deliberately written to deceive readers. The lie in this was written in search of a place of origin for the *Afrim* people instead of their origin in Ancient Egypt. The Jewish scholars of the Bible did their best to lie about their origin but they forgot the simple linguistic and cultural evidence that could betray them. Modern historical, archaeological, and anthropological search for the origin of the ancient *Afrim* people based upon the biblical directions have not provided any evidence of the origin of modern Jewish people in the Middle East. This is because scholars have been searching for the origin of these people in the wrong geographical direction. What has thrown most European scholars off the right track in their search for the origin of the ancient *Afrim* people is the fact that this false biblical narrative was intended to mislead. Secondly, these scholars have been so much influenced by the Bible and western prejudicial sentiments towards Ancient Egypt and Africa that they have never brought themselves to imagine that the *Afrim* people must have had racial and ethnic relationships with modern Africans that were the Ancient Egyptians.

Such a thought among European scholars is almost unimaginable to modern scholars because the Jewish people are now considered white people while Africans are still black. The changes in the skin color of the Jewish people have also helped to throw modern Europeans off the track of their true origins. Moreover, in European racist interpretation of the Bible, the Jewish people are the children of the God Europeans worship while this God supposedly cursed the Africans to be the slaves of Europeans. In the logic of Christian Europe's interpretation of the

Bible, the children of God could never have originated from the cursed ones of this God. From all these, it is clear that imagining and suggesting that the ancient *Afrim* people that went into the biblical Exodus and later went to Europe to become the Jews and Hebrews were originally black people would challenge European fundamental perception of the Bible. Beyond that it would completely overturn most of the false and racist interpretations Europeans have given to the biblical narrative. Worse than that for Europeans, such a suggestion would seriously question Europe's self-conferred superiority over Africans. It would also undermine the veracity of Christianity in the eyes of Europeans if it were found out that Christian Europe has been worshiping God in the doctrines and concepts created by the people who are supposed to be the cursed ones.

Despite all these, the most conclusive evidence confirming that the people that left Ancient Egypt into the biblical Exodus were originally black people comes from the fact that not all the tribal groups that left Ancient Egypt into the Exodus followed the Bible and the development of Christianity to Europe. Most of these people stayed in Canaan and modern surrounding countries. One of the African tribal groups that left Ancient Egypt into the Exodus but did not go to Europe to become Jews or Hebrews has been found in Africa. These people are still black like all the other African tribal groups from which they originated in Ancient Egypt and also like all the African tribal groups that left Ancient Egypt into the biblical Exodus. What makes the finding of these people even more conclusive is the fact that they were found through the latest and most powerful scientific study for identifying human origin and heritage.

This latest and most powerful scientific study for identifying human origin and heritage since the last couple of decades of the 20th century has been genetic studies. Some modern *Afrim* scholars know that their ancestors originated from among the tribal groups that live in Africa today but they do not know the specific tribal groups from which they originated. Just knowing that they originated from African tribes has not been enough for these scholars. Africa is a large continent with hundreds of tribes and almost a thousand languages. As a result, some *Afrim* scholars have quietly and almost secretly embarked upon a search for the specific African tribes from which their ancestors originated through genetic studies. It was one of such studies that found a tribe of ancient *Afrim* people that did not go to Europe to become Jews and Hebrews

I read in the *New York Times* on May 9th, 1999 that an extensive genetic research has found out that an African tribe known as the Lemba tribe has the same male chromosome of DNA sequences as are found among the *cohen*, the priestly family of the Jewish people. This study began from the curiosity of a medical doctor, Dr. Karl Skorecki, of the Technion-Israel Institute of Technology as he wondered whether he, a priest himself, was related to another priest that was coming to read the Torah. Jewish priestly family is believed to be the descendants of Aaron, the brother of Moses, and that Moses himself conferred the priesthood on the male descendants of his brother. From this curiosity, Dr. Skorecki contacted a human genetic population expert, Dr. Michael Hammer, of the University of Arizona. Dr. Hammer is an expert in tracing male populations through the Y or male chromosome. According to geneticists, the genetic materials on most chromosomes change through generations but the male chromosome does not change that drastically, and it is frequently passed on from father to son.

Genetic researchers also claim that the mutations on the male chromosomes are best suitable for tracing human population history because each generation has its own distinct pattern of mutation. In 1997, Drs. Skorecki, Hammer, and other colleagues began analyzing the Y-chromosomes among male Jewish populations, both priests and lay Jews. In this study, the researchers found a unique mutation pattern found only among the priestly family, the *Cohens*. The researchers found the same patterns of genetic markers in the *Ashkenazi* and *Sephardic* priestly populations. They found that 45 percent of *Ashkenazi* priests had this genetic marker while 56 percent of the *Sephardic* priests had it.

Based upon these genetic findings among Jewish populations, Neil Bradman, a business man and chairman of the Center for Genetic Anthropology at the University College of London, decided to extend the study to populations believed to be related to the Jewish people around the world. In this effort, Bradman sought the expertise of David B. Goldstein, a population geneticists at Oxford University. Goldstein identified an even more unique set of genetic patterns that could be found mostly among Jewish priests. These special mutations were not common in lay Jews, and they were practically non-existent in non-Jewish populations.

Armed with this unique Jewish priestly chromosome mutation, Goldstein tested the DNA samples of males from the Lemba tribe of Southeast Africa. Goldstein found out that in the Lemba population, 9 percent of the men carried the unique priestly Y-chromosome of Jewish priests. In a particular Lemba clan known as the Buba clan, 53 percent of the males carried this unique DNA signature of Jewish priests. Statistically, therefore, males from the Lemba tribe carried a higher incidence of the Jewish priestly DNA signature than the Ashkenazi population, and they were almost equal to the Sephardic population. Within the Lemba tribe as a whole, the incidence was 9 percent while it was only 3 to 5 percent among the entire Jewish population. It could therefore be said that statistically, the Lemba people are more Jewish than the Jewish people are. This study was reported in the American Journal of Human Genetics in 1999.

The question is who are these Lemba people? They are a tribe of Bantu–speaking people spread between the northern fringes of South Africa and Zimbabwe. They number about 50, 000 and are mostly Christians, but they practice Jewish traditions. They circumcise their males, keep one day of the week holy, and they do not eat pork or pork-like meat products. These people claim that they lived in Judea in ancient times, and were led out of Judea by a leader they call Buba. According to these people they came to Africa from the north, specifically from a place called Senna. They moved to Africa and rebuilt their ancient city Senna in their present location.

This story of the exodus of the Lemba people into Africa has also been researched and verified by Dr. Parfitt, Director of the Center for Jewish Studies at the School of Oriental and African Studies in London. Dr. Parfitt has studied the Lemba people for over a decade and he went out to verify their story of origin. He found it in modern Yemen and also found the Yemeni port of Sayhut through which the Lemba people must have traveled to Southeastern Africa. Dr. Parfitt's travels and findings in his search for the city of Senna was published in a book entitled *Journey to the Vanished City* published by Phoenix Publishing in London.

On May 9, 1999, the *New York Times* reviewed the works of Drs. Skorecki, Hammer, and Parfitt in an article entitled: ***Group in Africa Has Jewish Roots, DNA Indicates***. Nicholas Wade did this review. The relevance of the introduction of these research studies and findings is that they are an important and conclusive confirmation that the *Afrim* people that left Ancient Egypt into the biblical Exodus and later went to Europe to become the Jews and Hebrews were originally black people. The Lemba people are black, and the question people are asking is how did these people become black when the Jewish people from whom they probably originated look white? What is wrong with this question is that it perceives the relationship between the Jewish people and the black tribes from which they originated from top down, instead of perceiving it from bottom up, that is from the black tribes to the Jewish people.

The fact that the Lemba tribe, a Bantu-speaking black people now living in southern Africa once lived in biblical Judea is a major confirmation of the fact that the people that lived in Judea were black people. According to the Bible, the people that left Ancient Egypt into the Exodus were the people that built the northern and southern nations of Judea and Ephraim [Israel], and that confirms that the people of the Bible were all black people. This in turn confirms what I have revealed about the origin of the Jewish people in the black tribes that were the Ancient Egyptians.

What is most interesting about the genetic discovery of the relationship between the Jewish people and the *Lemba* tribe is that these people were also Jewish priests, according to this genetic revelation. Beyond the fact that the documents of the Old Testament were taken from Ancient Egyptian religious documents, the genetic revelation of the Lemba tribe also shows that the concepts, doctrines and documents that became the foundations of the Christian Bible originated from black people.

The question is how could a black Bantu tribe in southern Africa be linked and related to the descendants of the biblical Aaron, the elder brother of Moses? If the descendants of Aaron were black people, what was Aaron himself, and if Aaron was the elder brother of the great Moses, then what was Moses? All of these are questions that go to the heart of the true origin of the ancient *Afrim* people that went to Europe to become modern Jewish people. These questions prompt us to question and rethink the ancestry of these ancient *Afrim* people.

Traditional thinking influenced by the biblical narrative suggests that the *Afrim* people originated from somewhere other than among the black people of Ancient Egypt. As a result, anybody that is found today to be related to the Jewish people is perceived to be the one seeking to originate from the Jewish people and not the Jewish people that originated from these people. That direction of thinking has been woefully misguided.

Even the title of the New York Times article cited above shows the unquestioned and unverified influence of the Bible in the perception and interpretation of this genetic study. According to the title of the review, it is a tribal group in Africa that has been found to have Jewish roots and not the roots of the Jewish people that have been found in an African tribe. How can a black tribal group in Africa have the roots of white Jewish people in Europe if this tribe and the Jewish people were never related or supposed to have had any contacts anywhere? From the perception of the history of Ancient Egypt and the biblical and real history of the ancient *Afrim* people, they are the roots of the Jewish people that have been found in one of the black African tribes from which these Jewish people originated.

A question Mr. Wade posed in the review is very interesting because it reveals the biblical influence and general perception and direction of thinking on issues of the origin of the ancient *Afrim* people that went to Europe to become the Jews and Hebrews. The question was *how did Jewish priestly male chromosome come to be found in a black, Bantu-speaking people that look very much like its southern African neighbors?* In other words, how can the male chromosome of white Jewish people that supposedly had no relationship with black people in Africa be found in black Bantu-like speaking people in Africa today? It is obvious that Mr. Wade has been deceived by the white skin color of the Jewish people.

It is clear that the *Lemba* tribe in Africa did not originate from modern white Jewish tribe in Europe. Instead modern white Jewish people originated from the black *Lemba* tribe in Africa. This means the Jewish priestly chromosome that scholars have found was not originally a Jewish priestly chromosome. It was originally a *Lemba* tribal chromosome before it became a Jewish priestly chromosome when the Lemba tribal group among the ancient *Afrim* people went to Europe to become Jews and Hebrews.

From this point of view, the answer to Mr. Wade's question in his review is that white Jewish people can never turn black, but black Lemba people can turn white through several ways over a couple of thousands of years. From this point of view, the direction of the origin of the Jewish people is from Africa [black] to Europe [white] and not the other way round. This means that they are not the Lemba tribesmen in the Exodus that turned into black people. Instead, they are the Lemba tribesmen in the Exodus that went to Europe that turned into white people. This is a very important and conclusive scientific evidence revealing the racial and ethnic origin of the ancient black people that went into the biblical Exodus and later went to Europe to become the Jews and Hebrews. This analysis is simple but it has escaped many in the west because Africa is the last place anyone would even conjecture the origin of the Jewish people because of the falsehoods in the Bible and centuries of false biblical interpretations.

What is fascinating about all these is that Europeans have believed them so much that they are the ones defending these lies though they have never known whether these are true or false. In an unrelated discussion in his book entitled *A History of the Ancient Egyptians;* Nicholas

Grimal issued this warning to his European colleagues who have been blinded by the biblical and European perception of history and knowledge. He wrote:

> It is essential to remain cautious in this kind of assertion however, since the African side of the situation is still poorly known and the Egyptian evidence is itself far from complete (1994, p. 19).

Part of the African side of the biblical story that has been poorly known for thousands of years is what I am revealing in this work. So far the evidence shows that the biblical story that has shaped European perception of history and knowledge in this world is not the truth, the whole truth, and nothing but the truth. The *Afrim* scholars of the biblical documents in Alexandria designed the lies and Christian Europe took it over and interpreted and propagated around the world.

Nevertheless, the genetic discovery of the *Lemba* people and the tribal, linguistic, and cultural evidence and revelation I have presented so far confirm that the people that left in the biblical Exodus and later went to Europe to become the Jews and Hebrews were black people. These people originated from the black *Akan* and other African tribes that were in Ancient Egypt. From these black people originated Jesus, his mother Mary, St Peter, and there rest of the people of the Bible. That was the fact and the reason Jesus and his mother were portrayed as the black people they were by the early Catholic Church before the advent of European racism.

As I pointed out elsewhere, some Jewish scholars have quietly analyzed the Ancient Egyptian, biblical, and real history of the Jewish people and concluded that they originated from Africa. As a result, some of these scholars have made numerous and sometimes secret attempts to research their origins among African tribes. Because of this, the genetic finding that was reviewed in the *New York Times* was extremely important to Jewish people. As a result, the day after Mr. Wade had reviewed the genetic study, May 10, 1999; Mr. Wade's review was summarized and again published in the New York Times as special Jewish news. The title of this special republication was: *Jewish Studies News: Genes Show Lost Tribe of Israel is Black.* Note here that in this second review, the title suggests that it is Jewish studies news because it is important for Jewish scholars to know this.

However, there are some fundamental flaws in some of the conclusions drawn out of the studies by the *New York Times* review. Relating it to the biblical narrative, the *Lemba* people were part of the "mixed multitude" that went with the *Afrim* people in the so-called biblical Exodus but they are not one of the supposed ten lost tribes of Israel. The linguistic and cultural characteristics and requirements of the lost tribes are that they must be the same groups of people with a common linguistic and cultural heritage, and they still do. I will introduce them in the next chapter. The clue for the search for the so-called lost tribes is in the fact that the people that left Ancient Egypt in the Exodus identified themselves as *Akan* people through the *Akan* name *Afrim*. As a result, it is prudent to assume that the so-called lost tribes must all have *Akan* heritage.

The discovery and the conclusions of this genetic study support other revelations I have made. This also confirms that the ancient *Afrim* people that went to Europe to become the Jews and Hebrews were not white people before their relations went to Africa to become black people. That is impossible. They were black people from black African tribes before they went to Europe to become white. In addition to the Ancient Egyptian linguistic and cultural history I have revealed so far, this genetic study also confirms that the Ancient Egyptians were black people.

From the biblical, historical, and genetic study of the origin of the ancient *Afrim* people, not only have I established that they were black people but also I have revealed the particular dominant African tribe from which the ancient *Afrim* people originated. I have also revealed that this was the tribe in Ancient Egypt from where the biblical story began.

What is most puzzling about the origin of the *Afrim* people is what Gary Greenberg pointed out that there was no real history of the *Afrim* people before they went to Ancient Egypt and before they left into the Exodus. This also means there was no record and there is no record of the separate existence of the *Afrim* people from Ancient Egypt before they left into the biblical

Exodus. Not only is there no real or biblical history of the ancient *Afrim* people before the Exodus, but also there is no real or biblical evidence of any group of people among whom they originated in the Middle East, as the biblical narrative sought to suggest. All of these give credence to the revelation that the so-called ancestors of the ancient *Afrim* people did not go to Ancient Egypt from Ur of the Chaldees. They were Ancient Egyptians and belonged to the tribes of Ancient Egypt that seceded from their original black tribes, and that is why their history began from the Exodus. This was the reason the ancient *Afrim* people and modern Jewish people do not have any real history before they supposedly went to Ancient Egypt, and that was also the reason there was no evidence of any group of people from whom they originated anywhere in the Middle East.

Inadequacy of the biblical evidence

All that scholars know about the ancient *Afrim* before they went into the Exodus is from only the biblical narrative. To many scholars, that has not been adequate. However, historians have been able to piece together the history of the *Afrim* people after the Exodus. Today, the ancient *Afrim* people are not called *Afrim* people any more. They are Jews and Hebrews. These ancient black people from black African tribes are not black any more; they are considered white in most European communities. They claim that they wrote the theosophical documents that became the foundational documents of the Christian Bible, yet they do not have any evidence in their history to prove this either. Two fundamental questions any one would have to answer in such a proof is how Ancient Egyptian documents came to be part of the biblical documents and how the authors of the Old Testament documents came to carry indigenous though transposed *Akan* and other African tribal names.

What is worse, European scholars who did not set out in search of evidence of the origin of the biblical documents have found more of such evidence in Ancient Egyptian studies than they have found in the history of the ancient *Afrim* people. Some western scholars researching in Africa have even found more evidence relating to the biblical documents among the modern descendants of the Ancient Egyptians than they have found in Jewish history. The question is who were the ancient *Afrim* people that became modern Jews and Hebrews in Europe? What evidence do they have in their real history to support who they are today and confirm that they wrote the theosophical documents they passed on to the Greeks?

The revelation of the fact that the ancient *Afrim* people that became the Jews and Hebrews in Europe were black people has very serious implications for history and religion. In the first place, this would confirm that the Ancient Egyptians among whom they supposedly went to live for hundreds of years were black people. That would also confirm the revelation of the *Akan* and other African tribal presence in Ancient Egypt. In addition to the names and cultural evidence I have revealed, this also confirms the revelation that the *Akan* people were in Ancient Egypt and they were the creators of religion, the power behind the Ancient Egyptian civilization.

In religion, this revelation confirms that apart from the fact that the documents of the Bible were originally Ancient Egyptian religious documents, the people that supposedly wrote these documents were not Jews or Hebrews. If anything at all, these people were *Afrim* and not Jews or Hebrews because they were the ancestors of the people that went to Europe to become the Jews and Hebrews. They themselves did not originate from any Jewish or Hebrew ancestry. They were black people that originated from the black tribes whose modern descendants are the Africans. Moreover, the names of the people that wrote the Old Testament are not Jewish or Hebrew names. They are pure African tribal names that have been simply transposed into European languages, phonologies, and orthographies. These names can still be traced to the African tribes of their origin, and I will do that in the final chapter.

Again, all of these confirm that Jesus and his mother Mary were black people as the Catholic Church used to portray them in European Churches until racism made it difficult for Christian Europe to worship a black Jesus and his mother. What is sad about the effect of racism on Christianity is that in all their racist sentiments, superior Europeans could not imagine or create their own God, a Son of this God, or his Virgin Mother. They simply turned the black ones they had adopted and worshipped for centuries into white images to satisfy racism and racial prejudice through skin color. Truth has never influenced the bigot, but false learning and lies always have.

Who were the ancient Afrim that became the modern Jewish people of Europe?

In this discussion, I intend to discuss the over two thousand year old enigmatic questions of who the ancient *Afrim* people that went to Europe to become the Jews and Hebrews really were and where they came from. The enigma in these questions is compounded by the fact that modern *Afrim* people who are now the Hebrews and Jews in Europe claim to originate from the line of Abraham. Unfortunately, historians and biblical scholars have found that Abraham was not a Jew just as Moses was not a Jew, and they are right. Even if we accept the false biblical story that the ancient *Afrim* people that became modern Jews originated from Abraham, they would still not be Jews or Hebrews. This is because the name Abraham was derived from the *Akan* words *Abre ham*, meaning tired of wandering. How could Abraham have acquired a name from *Akan* words if he was not originally an *Akan*? How could the Jewish scholars of the Bible have given Abraham this name if they themselves did not know the Akan language or have Akan heritage?

If the ancient *Afrim* people that became the Jews in Europe came from the line of Abraham then they were not originally Jews. The issue becomes even more complex from the fact that if Abraham was not originally a Jew then his son Isaac was also not a Jew, and so were his grandsons Esau and Jacob from whom ancient *Afrim* people claim to have descended directly. What makes this revelation even more interesting is the fact that the names Isaac and Jacob were also derived from *Akan* name and words. When we examine the biblical ancestral origin of the Jewish people through the language and culture of the names of the so-called patriarchs, we find that these ancestors were not Jews, and if we look at Ancient Egyptian origin of these people we also find out that these people were not originally Jews or Hebrews. Again, the question then is who were these people before they became the ancient *Afrim* people and modern Jews and Hebrews in Europe?

The two histories of the ancient Afrim people

There are two versions of the history of the ancient *Afrim* or modern Jewish people. These two versions are like the noon clock and the siren. The noon clock chimes the noon and the siren yells it out loud. Whether the noon clock is fast or slow does not matter to the siren, whether the time the clock keeps is correct or not the siren will still yell out the noon. That is exactly what happened between the biblical and real history of the *Afrim* people. The Bible first made some historical assertions about the *Afrim* people and the historians of the *Afrim* history simply picked these up and propagated them as the historical truth. Otherwise, how could a group of tribes that were not yet a people, without a nation, and a history before the 13th century B. C. claim to have had a history of civilization dating back to 4000 years as their scholars wrote in *The Illustrated Atlas of Jewish Civilization: 4000 Years of Jewish History*?

The more popular version of the history of the *Afrim* people, however, is the biblical version that has been propagated as the truth to millions around the world for the past two thousand years. Supposedly, this version begins from the travel of Tera, the father of Abraham from Ur of the Chaldees and it continues into the travel of Abraham from Haran to Ancient Egypt. I have already revealed that the name of Abraham's father was transposed from the indigenous *Akan* name *Tena* to Tera. This shows that the family of Abraham was *Akan* before it went to the *Akan* people in Ancient Egypt. That has serious implications for the biblical story of the origin of the Jewish people. However, the biblical narrative continues about a century later into the family of Jacob going to Ancient Egypt and the transformation of this family in Ancient Egypt into the people that became the ancient *Afrim* and later the Jews in Europe. In the biblical version of their history, the religious history of the ancient *Afrim* people after the Exodus is carefully embellished with a romantic religious life and an intimate knowledge of a God that never happened in Canaan.

The other version of the history of the ancient *Afrim* people that became the Jews in Europe is the real history of a people that supposedly went to Ancient Egypt to be introduced to the concept of God and religion. These people were introduced to the Ancient Egyptian God. They learned the religion and sacramental practices of Ancient Egyptians, and went on from Egypt worshipping this God and practicing this religion. What is interesting about it is that these ancient *Afrim* people have worshipped this Ancient Egyptian God and practiced Ancient Egyptian religion up to today. They were these God and religious practices that they passed on to the Greeks for them to spread through entire Europe.

Though much of the real history of the *Afrim* people was derived from their biblical history, what is most intriguing about the two histories is that the biblical version and the real history do not match in many respects and they do not even support each other. The biblical narrative of the origin and life of the *Afrim* people is supposed to be their history. Every written history is supposed to have some basis in fact. Unfortunately, there is no independent historical or archaeological evidence to support the biblical narrative of the origin and life of the ancient *Afrim* people. This is not because scholars have not searched for such evidence. Numerous scholars have devoted their lives searching for some historical and archaeological evidence to support the biblical stories, but they have found nothing. There is the rumor that modern *Afrim* archaeologists in Israel have been burying artifacts and later unearthing them to try to establish some relationship of the ancient *Afrim* people to the lands around Israel. However, that rumor can not be substantiated though that scholastic deception has been done before in history and anthropology in Europe. For example, some scholars question the story of the discovery of the so-called Dead Sea Scrolls and the careful design in this discovery by an Arab and not a Jew.

Not only do the biblical story of their origin and real history of the *Afrim* people not support each other in many respects but also, there are serious discrepancies between the two versions. As a result, the biblical history that is perceived by many Christians as unimpeachable has been carefully and cleverly superimposed upon the real history that religious leaders do not want many people to know. This is to try to make the real history of the *Afrim* people also unimpeachable to those who believe in the biblical story. How many Christians know the true history of these ancient *Afrim* people?

The foundations of western historical, archaeological, and anthropological scholarship developed from the foundations of biblical thinking and the directions of biblical interpretations. For this reason, what has made an exploration into the real history of the *Afrim* people even more difficult is the fact that western historians and archaeologists have interpreted their historical and archaeological findings alongside the accepted and historically false biblical thinking and perception. As a result, the myth of the origins of the *Afrim* people has almost crystallized into the rock-hard truth of modern Christianity. Today, a cursory look at the biblical and real history of the *Afrim* people looks like they are one and the same story, but they are not.

This work is not intended to disprove the biblical or real history of the ancient *Afrim* people after they left Egypt. Instead, it is intended to reveal that there is a third version of the story that is not known anywhere except in Africa among the modern descendants of the Ancient Egyptians. These people were not only eyewitnesses, they were the central players in the biblical story. It is the story of these eyewitnesses and central players that I have been using to reveal identities, ethnic backgrounds, languages, cultures, and parts of the two versions of stories that have either been deliberately excluded or never been known.

Despite the great interest Christian Europe and biblical scholars have had in knowing who the *Afrim* people are, where they came from, and what language they spoke in their home-land, the *Afrim* people have refused to tell them anything. In fact, most of the attempts by the *Afrim* people to reveal any of these result in more questions than answers.

The real history behind the Bible

In their real history, the Jewish people have stated categorically that they are from a mixture of several races. How could a group of people originate from a mixture of several races? They are human races that mix therefore before any group of people could become a mixture of several races, that group must first belong to an original race for such a mixture to be possible. The question that the history of the *Afrim* people that went to Europe to become the Jews and Hebrews fails to ask is what was the original race of the *Afrim* people before they went to mix with other races? They could not have mixed with other races if they did not belong to a race.

This is nothing new to us in Africa because the true racial origin of the *Afrim* people is even established in the Exodus narrative. According to *Afrim* historians' explanation of this mixture of races, it occurred because the *Afrim* people took on the physical characteristics of the indigenous people among whom they went to live. However, that is false and not an adequate explanation. This explanation still does not tell us what the race of the *Afrim* people were before they went out to take on the physical characteristics of other races. As a result, nevertheless, the history of the *Afrim* people states that they belong to several racial groups ranging from fair to dark. This makes the historical account of the origin of the *Afrim* people extremely interesting because this history must explain the original color of the *Afrim* people before the variance in their skin colors began. Remember that the direction of changes in human skin color does not go from white into black. Instead, it goes from black into white so the explanation of the fair and dark skin color of the *Afrim* people should be very interesting.

In the *Encyclopaedia Britannica*, this is what scholars wrote about the *Afrim* peoples' story of race, ethnic origin, and physical characteristics.

> Some theorists have considered the Jews a distinct race, although this has no factual basis. In every country in which the Jews have lived for a considerable time, their physical traits came to approximate those of the indigenous people. Hence the Jews belong to several distinct racial types, ranging, for example, from fair to dark. Among the reasons for this phenomenon are voluntary or involuntary miscegenation and the conversion of Gentiles to Judaism (1996, p. 71).

This assertion is false and not an adequate explanation of how *Afrim* people became fair and dark. From the perspective of the black tribes from which they originated, the ancient *Afrim* people that went to become the Jews and Hebrews in Europe originated from several black tribes of the same race and not several races. The fact that they went to foreign lands to mix with other races does not neutralize their original race and ethnic heritage. I have to point out that the idea for the explanation of the race and ethnic origin of the *Afrim* people through their different physical characteristics was imagined in the scholastic studies of Jewish history in the early 20th century. In *The Jews – A Study of Race and Environment*, M. Fishberg wrote:

> Beginning with biblical evidence and traditions, it appears that even in the beginning of the formation of the tribe of Israel they were already composed of various racial elements. We find in Asia Minor, Syria, and Palestine at that time many races – the Amorites, who were blondes, dolichocephalic, and tall; the Hittites, a dark complexioned, probably of Mongoloid type; the Cushites, a negroid race; and many others. With all these the ancient Hebrews intermarried, as can be seen in many passages in the Bible (1911, p. 181).

It is clear that this study and conclusion were immensely influenced by the biblical account of the origin of the ancient *Afrim* people that became the Jews and Hebrews in Europe. The quotation says so itself. Any scholar who accepts that the beginning of the formation of Israel is the beginning history of the ancient *Afrim* people that became the Israelites and later the Jews and Hebrews in Europe is wrong. From what I have pointed out, this assertion is false. The assumption inherent in this assertion perceives the ancient *Afrim* as a people that suddenly

190

appeared from nowhere after the biblical Exodus of 13th century BC, but that is impossible and wrong because the *Afrim* were a people in Ancient Egypt before they went into the so-called Exodus. The most powerful evidence introduced to establish the true origin of the ancient *Afrim* or modern Jewish people is the linguistic and cultural evidence in this book. It is the most powerful because it does not draw the evidence from a hypothetical group of extinct ancient people. It does not draw its evidence from skin color or physical characteristics. It traces and draws its evidence from the ancient *Akan* and other African tribes that were the Ancient Egyptians, the ancient *Afrim* people that left Egypt into the Exodus in Canaan, modern *Akan* and other tribes in West Africa, and modern Jewish people in Europe. This evidence is therefore different from the biblical and any scholastic evidence ever produced to explain the true origin of the ancient *Afrim* people that became the Israelites and later the Jews and Hebrews in Europe.

The question that historians of Jewish history need to address is not the question of the several racial types the Jewish people have become from going to live among several races of people. The fundamental question that we all need to pose is, what was the original race of the Jewish people before they went to live among other races and took on the physical characteristics and traits of these races? A corollary question that might be easier to answer is what was the original race and ethnic background of the ancient *Afrim* people before they went to become the Jews and Hebrews in Europe? Who were the ancient *Afrim* people that left Egypt in the Exodus before they got to Asia Minor, Syria, and Palestine, and before the formation of the tribes of Israel? How did the social organization of the one family that supposedly went to Ancient Egypt become tribal just like the tribes they left in Ancient Egypt? How did the so-called patriarchs of the Jewish people come to carry *Akan* names even before Abraham got to the *Akan* people Ancient Egypt? The answer to all of these questions is that they were black people as all the evidence above has shown, and as I have already pointed out, ancient *Afrim* people who are modern Jewish people originated from several black tribes of the same race and not several races.

What is most interesting from the claims of the scholars of *Afrim* history is that they now range from fair to dark suggesting that they were not originally fair or dark. What were they then? The *Afrim* people may look white or fair now but we in Africa know that they originated from black African tribes, and we even know the specific tribes from which they originated just from the tribal names they still carry. What is also most interesting and most revealing about this aspect of *Afrim* people's history of origin is that both their biblical history and real history were made through African languages and culture. Moreover, they have carried linguistic and cultural elements of their African origin and heritage with them up to now, but I do not think they know these and I do not think they ever thought anybody else would know or remember this. However, the idea that some of the *Afrim* people are fair and some are dark is also interesting because it suggests some ideas that need to be explored.

For a people to be both fair and dark suggests racial mixing with fair and dark people as their history seems to suggest. The question is how did they become fair and how did they become dark? Evidence of racial mixing among all humans on earth has shown that the offspring of the union between a black person and any other race does not result in a naturally dark child. That is because dark skin color is the basic and original human skin color from which all other skin colors emerged through racial mixing and geographical variance. The evidence from race mixing shows that only two black people can produce a naturally dark offspring. The question then is what skin color were the ancient *Afrim* people before they became involved in the racial mixing that produced the dark people among them? Or which African people did they convert to Judaism and mix with and where did such mixing and conversion take place? Was it in Europe or Africa? The lie in this is that the real history of the *Afrim* people seeks to deny that they were originally black people. Again, if the *Afrim* people were originally not black people, with which dark people did they mix to produce the dark people among them, and where did that supposed racial mixing take place?

The fact is the original ancient *Afrim* people going back to their so-called patriarch Abraham and his descendants were all black people. How do we know this? I have already revealed that the name Abraham was derived from *Akan* words and the names of his son Isaac and his grandchildren Esau and Jacob were all also derived from *Akan* names and words. In addition, these names and words lead us to a particular ancient *Akan* tribe that was in the geographical region from where the Bible claims Abraham originated. For example, among the *Akan* people the *Akan* name *Sau* from which the biblical name *Esau* was derived is so unique that any *Akan* person can tell any foreigner the specific *Akan* tribe from which this name originates. The indigenous *Akan* name of Abraham's father, *Tena*, is also unique among the *Akan* tribal groups. That again suggests that any *Akan* who knows the specific origin of this name can take any stranger directly to the *Akan* tribal group from which this name originates, and therefore to the tribe from which Abraham's father acquired this name.

From the discussion and earlier so far, I have established that the ancient *Afrim* people that left Ancient Egypt into the so-called biblical Exodus and later went to Europe to become the Jews and Hebrews were not originally Europeans. They were not originally white. They were not originally Jews, and they were not originally Hebrews. They were originally from the *Akan* and other African tribes that were the Ancient Egyptians in ancient times.

The Afrim people are not Semites either

What is intriguing about the biblical origin of the Jewish people is that Christianity has accepted it as the truth, the absolute truth, and nothing but the truth but most Jewish scholars have refused to accept it because they know or they suspect different. Only Christian Europe has accepted and propagated the biblical version of the origin of the *Afrim* people as the gospel truth. As a result, scholastic speculation as to the origin of modern Jewish people has never been lacking. What is also interesting about these scholastic speculations is that their foundations have also been influenced by the biblical assertion of the origin of the Jewish people into searching for and speculating about people and places in the Middle East and Europe. With the exception *of The Moses Mystery: The African Origin of the Jewish People*, most scholars studying this issue have practically avoided researching into such origins among the African that were the Ancient Egyptians.

In his book, *The Thirteenth Tribe*, Arthur Koestler introduced the Khazars as a "startling discovery of the ancestors of the Jewish people." He wrote:

> One of the most radical propounders of the hypothesis concerning the Khazar origins of Jewry is the Professor of Mediaeval History at Tel Aviv University, A. N. Poliak. His book Khazaria (in Hebrew) was published in 1944, and a second edition in 1951 (1976, p. 16).

Koestler wrote further of Professor Poliak's assertion of the "Khazar Jewry as the nucleus of the large Jewish settlement in Eastern Europe" and that this...

> ... was written before the full extent of the holocaust was known, but that does not alter the fact that the large majority of surviving Jews in the world is of Eastern European – and thus perhaps mainly of Khazar – origin. If so, this would mean that their ancestors came not from Jordan but from the Volga, not from Canaan but from the Caucasus, once believed to be the cradle of the Aryan race; and that genetically they are more closely related to the Hun, Uigur, and Magyar tribes than to the seed of Abraham, Isaac, and Jacob. Should this turn out to be the case, then the term "anti-Semitism" would become void of meaning, based on a misapprehension shared by both the killers and their victims (p. 17).

Note that this assertion is only speculative as the writers points out that "if this is so" then the following conclusions can be made, but it was not so. Most scholars of Jewish history, however, do not recognize the Khazars as the nucleus of the large population of Jews in Eastern

Europe. These scholars write that the Khazars were not even Jews. About these same Khazars, this is what scholars of Jewish history have written:

> Although the Jews were forbidden to engage in missionary activity in Muslim or Christian countries (in both a capital offense), they did not refrain from attempting to spread their faith in the pagan world. In the 8th century, for example, the royal house and the nobility of the Khazar people, who controlled a powerful empire in the lower Volga region, converted to Judaism. The power of the Khazars was broken in the late 12th century, and they disappeared in the 13th. Some of their descendants probably survived among the Crimean Karaites or merged with the Jews of Eastern Europe (1996, p. 76).

From Jewish history, it is clear that the Khazars were not Jews and they could not have been the nucleus of the Jews of Eastern Europe. It is interesting, however, that Koestler makes reference to genetics because twenty three years after his book, the genetics he referred to has shown that the Jewish people were originally black African tribes and not from the Aryan race as perhaps some would have wished to have originated. In terms of genetic evidence, the latest genetic study of the Lemba people in Africa has confirmed this.

Mot scholars who have researched into the biblical origin of the *Afrim* people have found out that the biblical assertion of the origin of the ancient *Afrim* people that became the Jews and Hebrews in Europe is false. As a result, they have been searching for other origins of these people and in the quotation above, Koestler pointed out that if it turns out that modern *Afrim* people originated in Europe then they would not be Semites anymore and the concept of anti-Semitism would be meaningless. Incidentally, the descendants of ancient *Afrim* people that became the Jews and Hebrews in Europe are not Semites, they are Africans.

There is another record cited by Arthur Koestler that seeks to bring out the question of the black racial and ethnic heritage of the *Afrim* people before they supposedly became the Khazar people. Koestler noted that the Arab geographer Istakhri, wrote that:

> The Khazars do not resemble the Turks. They are black-haired, and are of two kinds, one called the Kara-Khazars, [Black Khazars] who are swarthy verging on deep black as if they were some kind of Indian, and a white kind [Ak-Khazars], who are strikingly handsome (p. 20).

From where could the Black Khazars that controlled a powerful empire in the lower Volga have originated? How did black people get to control a powerful empire in the "Caucasus, once believed to be the origin of the Aryan race? Where are these black people now and what then is the Aryan race? Again, the evidence of the original black heritage of the ancient *Afrim* people that became the Jews and Hebrews in Europe is in this quotation and the writing of an Arab scholar, but as usual some scholars have sought ways to deny and reject it. In this particular case, Koestler argued that Istakhri's black-skinned Khazars were based upon "hearsay and legend" because the Turks used to call their rulers the white class and the people they ruled the black class. Perhaps, a very important question that needs to be asked here is who were these people before they became the so-called Khazars?

This question becomes even more pertinent because African tribal, linguistic, and cultural evidence have been found among the people history calls Khazars. According to Koestler, one of the Kings or Kagan of the Khazars was known as King *Busia* (see Arthur Koestler, *The Thirteenth Tribe*, p. 32). Culturally, this reveals that the so-called Khazar people also had a cultural practice of kingship like the Ancient Egyptians. Western historians write the name of this Khazar king as Busir or Bazir. In the *Akan* language, this name is *Busia*, an indigenous *Akan* name. Specifically, the name *Busia* can still be found among the *Brong* branch of the *Akan* group of tribes. This *Brong* branch of the *Akan* group can also be found in Ghana in the *Brong-Ahafo* Region. The name is well known in England as an *Akan* tribal name. How could an *Akan* name be found among supposedly white Khazar kings that were not black or *Akan* people? This should not be difficult to understand because I have already pointed out that the majority of the *Afrim* people that left Ancient Egypt into the so-called Exodus were *Akan* people that spoke the *Akan* language and carried *Akan* cultural names. One of these names was *Busia*. If these so-called Khazars did not originate from the *Akan* tribe and they were not originally black people, where did their king come by the *Akan* royal name, *Busia*? Remember that among these Khazars, the name *Busia* was not just an ordinary name, it was their royal name and therefore central to who they were.

In Khazar history, according to Arthur Koestler, King *Busia* asked his henchmen Papatzes and Balgitres to kill his brother-in-law. *Papatse* is also an African tribal title for a man. Specifically, *Papatse* is a title for a man in the *Ga* language. I introduced the *Ga* people as the biblical Gileadites that used the password "*shiboleth*" in a war with the *Afrim* people.

Also according to Arthur Koestler, in the 13th century, King Andrew of Hungary's custodian of royal revenues was Count *Teka*, "a Jew of Khazar origin." Again, the name of this Count, *Teka*, is an *Akan* word meaning reduce debts. It is interesting that this Count was the custodian of the royal revenues of the King of Hungary and his name was related to reducing debts. What do all these mean? They confirm the African tribal origin of the people that left Ancient Egypt into the Exodus and the *Akan* origin of the majority of these people that became the *Afrim* people. This origin is the reason the ancient *Afrim* people carried *Akan* and other African tribal names and modern Jews and Hebrews have also carried these *Akan* and other African tribal names throughout their history.

The name of Balgitres also sounds like a *Ga* name with a *Tei* suffix. However, that is not all that might link the so-called Khazars to the true origin of the *Afrim* people that left Ancient Egypt into the biblical Exodus. In culture, the Khazars practiced human sacrifice just as it was practiced in Ancient Egypt and also practiced among modern *Akan* people until late into the 20th century. The Khazar people also had rather elaborate funeral rituals just as they were in Ancient Egypt and still are among the *Akan* people in West Africa. A group of people in the geographical region of the Khazars called the Bashkirs worshiped the penis just as it was worshipped in Ancient Egypt and taken into the Canaan by the *Afrim* people that left Ancient Egypt. The Khazar also believed in one supreme god among several gods just as it was in Ancient Egypt. All of these bring the people of Khazar and the people around them closer to Ancient Egypt where the ancient *Afrim* people originated.

Again according to Koestler, in the travelogue of the Arab diplomat Ahmad ibn-Fadlan ibn-al-Abbas, he wrote that he came across a people whose language was like the chatter of starlings. Close by about a day's journey away was a village called *Ardkwa* (see Koestler, p. 37). The name of this village was also derived from the *Akan* name *Adakwa*. This is a variation of my surname name. What is evident in all these is that even in the search for a different origin of the *Afrim* people, the linguistic and cultural evidence of their origin in the *Akan* and other African tribes continues to show. The only problem about this has been that western scholars have not had the linguistic and cultural knowledge to know such evidence.

Before we can confirm who the ancient *Afrim* people that went to Europe to become the Hebrews and Jews in Europe were, we must first find out who they were not. Writing on the mythical racial origin of the Jewish people in *Encyclopaedia Britannica*, Raphael Patai wrote that:

> The findings of physical anthropology show that, contrary to popular view, there is no Jewish race. Anthropometric measurements of Jewish groups in many parts of the world indicate that they differ greatly from one another with respect to all important physical characteristics – stature, weight, skin colour, cephalic index, facial index, blood groups, etc (1973, Vol. XII, p. 1054).

According to Patai, there is great variety in very important characteristics among the Jewish people and that takes us back to the *mixed multitude* of people from the different African tribal groups that went together in the biblical Exodus. Such physical varieties among the ancient *Afrim* people, with the exception of skin color, can still be found among African tribes.

Europeans know that the Jewish people are not originally Europeans. The Jewish people themselves know that they are not Europeans, and it will come as a surprise to many people to find out that though they have claimed to be Semites, the *Afrim* people that went to Europe to become the Jews and Hebrews are not Semites either. The *Afrim* people have sought to identify themselves as Semites only in the past one hundred and seventy years. Who were they before then? That is something they are not revealing. How then did they get to become Semites? The answer is simple. The Semitic racial classification was conferred on them, and since that helped to further conceal their true racial and ethnic identities from Europeans, they accepted it, and have become Semites since.

In 1829, the Anglo-French anthropologist, F. W. Edwards, suggested that because Jewish people are racially different from Europeans, they must belong to a different race that anthropologists have not yet identified. In a private letter to his friend Amedee Thierry, Edwards classified the Jewish people as Semites after the Semitic people that came to occupy the Middle East from where the Bible claims the Jewish people originated. It must be pointed out that once again this private classification was highly influenced by the false biblical narrative on where the Jewish people claim to have originated (see Genesis 11:31, 15:7).

The speculation of Edwards about the hypothetical origin of the Jewish people was made in a private letter that was not supposed to be made public. Amedee Thierry, who was himself a Jew, made it public by asserting that anthropologists have identified the Jewish people to be Semites. Instantly, the Jewish people accepted and began to propagate the idea that anthropologists have found out who they were, and that they were Semites, but it was false. Throughout their history going back over two thousand years, there was no mention of a racial link of the *Afrim* people to any Semitic tribal group anywhere. Modern historical, archaeological, and anthropological research have all failed to discover any evidence that links the Jewish people to any Semitic group in the Middle East. Again, here is an example of how biblical fabrication has influenced western scholastic thinking and perception of world history.

Today, Arabs who are classified to be Semites occupy the geographical area of Ur of the Chaldees. From this, western scholars have simply concluded that if Abraham came from Ur of the Chaldees then he originated from among Semites therefore the Jewish people who claim to be the descendants of Abraham are also Semites. All of these are false assumptions and conclusions. To most western scholars who were raised in the biblical tradition, the Bible says God said the Jews came from Ur of the Chaldees therefore it is the absolute truth. For such western scholars, the question of checking the veracity of this story does not arise because of the fear and reverence for the Bible. However, this is an example of how the Bible has completely influenced western historical thinking and direction into falsehoods. While western research on this issue has failed to provide any evidence in support of the biblical assertion, I have shown that Abraham and his descendants carried *Akan* names. I have also found out the *Akan* tribe in the east from which the patriarch originated.

There is also another biblical link that makes western scholars believe and conclude that the *Afrim* people were Semites. This link comes from the biblical story in which Abraham supposedly slept with his Ancient Egyptian maidservant Haggar and she bore him a son called Ishmael (Genesis 16). Biblical interpretation suggests that the descendants of Ishmael became the Arab people or modern Semites. Again from this, the historical assumption is that Abraham must have been a Semite himself and that is why his descendants became Semites. This analysis is not correct because its basic assumption is false.

I have revealed that the name of Abraham was derived from *Akan* words and these words can be traced to a particular *Akan* tribal group that lived in the Tigris and Euphrates Valley in Babylon in ancient times. An interesting question here is how could the supposed ancestors of Semites come to carry *Akan* and other African tribal names? How could the names of Semites be derived from *Akan* words and language that can be found today in far away Africa? Not only was the name of Abraham derived from the *Akan* language, but also so were the names of his son and grandsons. How could people from the Semitic race get to identify themselves, their God, and the name of their nation not in the Semitic language but in the *Akan* language when the *Akan* people belong to a completely different racial and ethnic classification?

In the discussion of the Exodus, I pointed out that the people that left Ancient Egypt were mostly *Akan* and other African tribal groups. These people can be found today mostly in West Africa. In the discussion of the so-called patriarchal origin of the ancient *Afrim* people, I also pointed out that the names of the patriarchs could be traced to the *Kwahu* tribe that lived in the Tigris and Euphrates valley in ancient times. I pointed out that this tribe could also be found in West Africa. If the descendants of Abraham are modern Jews and Hebrews, then there must be the descendants of the tribe from which Abraham originated somewhere. The question is where is this Semitic tribe from which Abraham was supposed to have originated? How could the so-called descendants of Abraham exist today and the entire tribe from which Abraham supposedly descended be extinct? This Semitic tribe cannot be found anywhere in the Middle East because it never existed. However, the true tribes of the origin of ancient *Afrim* people can be found mostly in West Africa. This simply reveals the falsehood in the biblical origin of the ancient *Afrim* of the Exodus that went to become the Jews and Hebrews in Europe.

The real history of the *Afrim* people even after the Exodus shows that these people worshipped *Akan* gods and called these gods by the same *Akan* names that the *Akan* people of Ancient Egypt called them and still call these gods today. The names of the people that wrote the Old Testament documents are *Akan* names despite their orthographic transpositions and linguistic corruption in numerous languages around the world. The latest genetic evidence discussed above confirms that the people that left Ancient Egypt into the Exodus were African tribes and they were all black people. Moreover, many modern *Afrim* people still carry their *Akan* and other African tribal names. As a result, neither Abraham nor any of his descendants could have been Semites because the *Akan* people and the other African tribes from which the Jewish people originated are not Semites according to modern classification of races.

One major reason that stops western scholars from searching for the origin of the *Afrim* people in Africa is Christian Europe's false interpretation of the so-called Noah's curse. This was also a false interpretation of an aspect of a biblical myth Christian Europe did not understand. Black people in Ancient Egypt created the concept of God, religion, and sacramental practices that became the foundations of the Christian religion, and because the people of the Bible were all black people, Christian Europe's misinterpretation of Noah's curse has no basis. Since the people of the Bible were all black, Europeans could not have originated from Noah's son Japheth for black people to originate from Ham as Christian Europe's interpretation of the biblical Flood asserted. In an earlier discussion, I also showed that this flood narrative was a myth that was not even the myth of the Jewish people as they claimed.

Nevertheless, this false biblical interpretation became the greatest reinforcement in the foundation of the enslavement of black people. It also became the justification for the denigration of the African into sub-humanity. Christian Europe said many uncomplimentary things about black people. As a result, it has been difficult for Christian Europe and western scholars to reveal the truth that the Jewish people that left Ancient Egypt into the so-called biblical Exodus originated from the black people of Ancient Egypt. Such a revelation will not only prove the traditional ignorance of Christian Europe, but it would also shake the foundations of western Europe's conferred superiority on itself. However, if Christian Europe had African historical, linguistic, and cultural backgrounds and could read, see, and understand the Bible, it would know that black people are not the descendants of Ham as it proclaimed, and that black people were not the people that were supposedly cursed by the drunken Noah. The Bible says this plainly in Genesis.

196

Because western historians have not known what we know in Africa, there have been what seem to be several secrets surrounding the story of the origin of the Jewish people. This sometimes frustrates historians and biblical scholars to the extent that most of them do not say or probe much into the racial and ethnic origins of the Jewish people anymore. Some do not want to probe too deeply into it perhaps for fear of even being called anti-Semites.

For example, in *The Story of Civilization: Our Oriental Heritage,* Will Durant simply stated:

Of their racial origin, we can only say *vaguely* that they were Semites (p. 302, emphasis mine).

Why would an eminent historian of the caliber of Will Durant *only say vaguely* that the *Afrim* people were Semites? This is because historians do not really know what the truth is, and more importantly they do know the history behind the Jewish people becoming Semites and they do not believe that they are truly Semites. There are numerous revelations in the biblical story of the origin of the *Afrim* people so let us examine some of them.

The biblical story of the origin of the Afrim people

The biblical story of the origins of the *Afrim* people says that Tera the father of Abraham took his family from Ur of the Chaldees and came to live in *Haran.* What is fascinating here is that the name of Abraham's father, *Tera,* is a transposition of the *Akan* name *Tena.* That itself should confirm the racial and ethnic origin of Abraham and his brothers Nahor and Haran. This should also confirm the racial and ethnic origin of the ancient *Afrim* people that claim descendancy from Abraham. According to the Bible, the name of Abraham's junior brother who supposedly died in Ur of the Chaldees before Abraham left there was Haran. When Tera supposedly left Ur of the Chaldees with his family, the next place they went to settle was also called Haran. The name *Haran* was also derived from the *Akan* word *Haran [Hann]* meaning brightness, radiance, brightened or illuminated by a source of light. Haran must have been a place of settlement before Abraham and his father went there. From this name, it is evident that it must have been a settlement of an *Akan* group of people. It is from this *Akan* word and the belief that the anointed ones are marked, identified, and illuminated by the gods with a bright light around them that the concept of the halo around angels and other Godly beings developed.

The Jewish scholars of the biblical documents must have placed Abraham and his family in Haran to suggest the divine radiance of the place and around Abraham. This name was the most appropriate name to give a place Abraham was supposed to have lived. This is because the scholars of the Bible sought to make Abraham the conduit through which the ancient *Afrim* people found a God outside and different from the Ancient Egyptian gods they had adopted and worshipped in reality. It is interesting also to note that it was in Haran that Abraham supposedly met God. In other words, Abraham went to *Haran,* the illuminated place and met God (see Genesis 11:31-32).

As if Abraham did not know where he came from, the Bible says this God told him that he came from Ur of the Chaldees. Several issues in the history of the *Afrim* people make this suggestion of their origin questionable. In the first place, Abraham did not come from Ur of the Chaldees and I hate to suggest that this God should go back to revise his geography. Abraham came from the east but it was not from Ur of the Chaldees. He came to Ancient Egypt from among the *Akan* tribal group that was the vassal kingdom of the Parthian Empire ruled by the royal family of *Adiabene.* Abraham came from among modern *Kwahu* people and that is how he came to have an *Akan* name because the *Kwahu* people are *Akan.* In a discussion of the *Akan* people and the so-called lost tribes of the ancient *Afrim* people in the next chapter, I will show that the *Kwahu* tribe is one of the so-called lost tribes.

How do we know this? Beside the linguistic and cultural revelations, geographically, the region around the Upper Tigris River is the place Abraham originated because we have identified the African tribal groups that lived in Mesopotamia around the area of Ur of the Chaldees in ancient times. The evidence shows that there were no *Akan* tribes from which Abraham could have originated in Ur of the Chaldees, and therefore have acquired his *Akan* name. It is important to point out also that all the people that have been identified to have lived in Mesopotamia in ancient times were black people that can be found in Africa today. Evidence of the Lemba tribe of Southeast Africa having lived in modern day Yemen confirms this.

Why did the *Afrim* scholars of the Bible in Alexandria seek a distant origin for the *Afrim* people when they actually originated from Ancient Egyptian tribes? The first reason was to disassociate themselves from the Ancient Egyptians so that they could claim that they already knew God and therefore they brought the ideas and documents they were passing on to the Greeks from afar, but that was a lie. Another issue that makes the biblical origin of the *Afrim* people from Ur of the Chaldees even more spurious is the fact that the documents of the Bible were compiled and edited for the Greeks after the **Afrim** people had been dragged into captivity in Babylon and surrounding areas. It was this captivity that must have made the generation of the biblical scholars think they came from Ur of the Chaldees. However, if they claim descent from the line of Abraham then they did not originate from Ur of the Chaldees; they originated from the ancient *Kwahu* tribe of *Adiabene* in the upper Tigris and Euphrates valley.

Could the generation of the Alexandrian biblical scholars have forgotten their true origin? This is not inconceivable because the real history of the *Afrim* people states that when they were taken into captivity, some easily forgot about Jerusalem and their "home" State. This suggests that there were generations of *Afrim* people that only knew of Jerusalem in what would have seemed like a fairy tale. Moreover, the generation that sought to compile and translate the documents of the Bible into Greek was a rather very distant generation that must never have known of the true origin of their ancestors in Ancient Egypt.

In addition to these reasons, the ancient *Afrim* people had gone to intermarry with different peoples in the foreign lands they sojourned for several generations. As a result, the generation of the *Afrim* people that came back to Ancient Egypt was not racially, ethnically, and physically the same as the generation that left in the Exodus. Their racial and ethnic history pointed out that the *Afrim* people tended to take on the physical characteristics of the people among whom they went to live in foreign lands. As a result, the relatively modern generation of *Afrim* descendants that returned to Ancient Egypt could not identify their ancient and original tribal origins among the Ancient Egyptian tribes they met on their return. Consequently, the scholars had to seek another place of origin to suit what they had become and not who their ancestors originally were.

God did not tell Abraham that he originated from Ur of the Chaldees only once. As if Abraham did not hear God the first time, God told him again that he came from Ur of the Chaldees. Why did it become necessary for the Jewish scholars to reiterate the origin of Abraham and this time put into the mouth of God? The answer is because these scholars knew that they were taking the theosophical documents they were passing on to the Greeks from the Ancient Egyptians. From this perspective, the best way for them to claim that these documents were their original documents was to disassociate themselves emphatically from the Ancient Egyptians and seek a different origin from the people from whom they were taking these documents. By claiming that they originated from Ur of the Chaldees, the Jewish scholars of the Bible were seeking to suggest that the biblical documents were their original documents and they did not originate from Ancient Egypt therefore the biblical documents were not Ancient Egyptian. Today, this ancient line of thinking to deceive the Greeks is very transparent. It is clear from this that the Jewish scholars of the Bible knew that they were stealing the biblical documents from the Ancient Egyptians.

Considering the fact that the concept of God originated from human imagination and creation, the idea that God told Abraham that he originated from Ur of the Chaldees is seriously questionable. This is because the original imagined and personified God that the *Afrim* people

198

learned about and adopted in Ancient Egypt could not speak. The God Abraham went to learn about in Ancient Egypt in the priesthood could not speak. The idea that the gods spoke to humans was an ancient magical and mystical concept of deception also invented by the *Akan* people that first imagined the God the *Afrim* people came to know in Ancient Egypt. The *Akan* people still practice this deception in their traditional religion. Unfortunately, this deceptive practice passed into Christianity and became part of the Christian belief in God through the translation of the biblical documents into Greek.

Calculating from the biblical account and assuming that this account were true, Tera and his son Abraham must have left Ur of the Chaldees around 1900 B. C. An extremely important evidence confirming that Tera and his son and family did not originate from Ur of the Chaldees is the fact that we have identified the ancient black African tribal groups that lived in and around Mesopotamia as far back as 2700 B. C. If Tera and his son Abraham ever came out of Ur of the Chaldees in Mesopotamia, they must have come from among one of these tribes. There were no Semites among them, and culturally and linguistically, the *Akan* names *Tena* and *Abre ham* could not have originated from among any of these ancient African tribes in Mesopotamia either.

Modern African tribal groups in the near and Far East in ancient times

The interest of biblical scholars, historians, and archaeologists in finding the place of origin of the Jewish people has been tremendous. As a result, many western historians and archaeologists including Jewish scholars have put a lot of effort in searching for any artifacts that could confirm the biblical origin of the *Afrim* people in Ur of the Chaldees, but they have found nothing because that is not true. It is important to point out at this time that the black people we find in Africa today did not live only in Africa in ancient times, but also they were spread from the center of Africa through the Middle and Far East as far as China and Tibet.

Western historians and archaeologists have found ancient evidence of these black people in the Middle to the Far East but again because they do not have the African linguistic, and cultural backgrounds to identify these people, they have naively interpreted their findings to fit into their beliefs in the biblical narrative and historical assertions. These biblical narrative and beliefs have deceived western historians and archaeologists by making them place Africans only in Africa and denying Africans any historical or archaeological relationship with ideas and artifacts outside Africa. As a result of the historical misdirection from the biblical narrative, most western scholars are also influenced to interpret their historical and archaeological findings in terms of the modern people they find in particular geographical areas today and not the people that lived in these places in ancient times.

For example, in an earlier chapter, I cited the latest genetic study conducted by a group of Chinese scholars suggesting that ancient Chinese people were Africans (see J. Y. Chu et al, *Proceedings of the National Academy of Sciences*, Sept. 29, 1998; review by Robert Lee Holtz, *LA Times*, September 30, 1998). Among the conclusions Chu et al draw is: "It is probably safe to conclude that modern humans that originated in Africa constitute the majority of the current gene pool in East Asia" (see commentary on this article by Cavalli-Sforza, 1998, p. 11501). In the discussion of this study, I also revealed that it is not only genetic evidence that confirms that ancient Chinese people were Africans but my linguistic and cultural research have also confirmed this. There is linguistic and cultural evidence showing that at least ancient *Akan* and *Ga* tribes of modern West Africa were in ancient China. The ancient kings and emperor's list of China confirms this.

How valid and reliable is linguistic and cultural research? Linguistic and cultural studies are part of the sources from which scientists gather information to confirm genetic research. In the Chinese Human Genome Diversity Project, linguistic study was part of the sources of information gathered for the study. In this particular study, the authors used surnames, and in his commentary on the study, Cavilla-Sforza wrote that:

[Surnames] ... are transmitted like Y chromosomes ... Characteristics transmitted patrilinearly tend to be more highly clustered geographically than those transmitted matrilinearly like mtDNA and may be more useful on average than other DNA markers for reconstructing ancient migrations. ... In China surnames are particularly useful, being on average much older than in other parts of the world. ... A China-U.S. team has analyzed surnames from a 1/200 random sample of the Chinese population, by standard techniques of population genetics, and the picture is largely superimposable on the genetic one (*Proceedings of National Academy of Science*, 1998, Vol. 95, p.11501).

In the Human Genome Diversity Project, the results of the linguistic, cultural, and the genetic studies were the same and that means linguistic and cultural research through surnames is as valid and reliable as genetic research. That makes the *Akan* and other African tribal names of modern Jewish people as valid and reliable an evidence of their origin as the genetic study that linked them to the Lemba tribe in Africa. However, there is more.

Modern Japanese people went to the Japanese Islands from China. I have also found out that ancient Japanese rulers had African tribal names and even modern Japanese people still carry mostly *Akan* and *Ewe* tribal names. For example, the Japanese Emperor from 668-6671 A. D. was Emperor Tenchi Tenno. However, I do not think the Japanese people know that the *Akan* name from which the name of this Emperor was derived was *Tachi Tano*. One of my Japanese students stood in awe when I told her that the *Ewe* people in West Africa have the same family name *Ashikaga* as they do have in Japan. In another example, the Japanese lady newsreader called *Sachi Koto* at CNN News in Atlanta is carrying *Akan* names that betray her ancient tribal origin among the *Akan* people. I can tell the specific *Akan* tribal origin of her ancestors from her names. Another African tribal name like *Azuma* can also be found in Japan. There are more Chinese and Japanese names that originated from the names of the African tribes that were in these places in ancient times.

The ancient and modern culture of the *Akan* people who are now in West Africa can still be found among the people of Tibet. What do all these mean? They confirm that black African tribes that are now in Africa lived in places as far as the Far East in ancient times.

Closer to Mesopotamia and the supposed biblical origin of the *Afrim* people, historical, linguistic, and cultural evidence of black people have been found in India. The indigenous people of India originated from the ancient black tribes that lived there, and there are still pockets of black tribes in India. For example, the name of *Manu*, the lawgiver of India is an *Akan* name meaning the second born. What does it mean to the biblical origin of the *Afrim* people? It means if the biblical story of Genesis 11:2 were true and that the people of the Bible were journeying from the east, then these people were all black people and they could have been journeying in the movement that brought them to establish themselves in Ancient Egypt, and later settle in inner Africa.

Ancient Ensiman and Ahanta people in Mesopotamia

Western historians have continued to show that their lack of linguistic and cultural backgrounds have led to gross distortion and misinterpretation of other peoples' histories around the world. For example, when western historians and archaeologists could not identify the people that created the cuneiform writings they found around the Persian Gulf, Oppert arbitrarily gave these unidentified people the hypothetical name *Sumerians* (see Will Durant, *The Story of Civilization: Our Oriental Heritage*, 1935, p. 118). Such arbitrary and speculative approach to writing the history of the *Sumerians* seemed to have concealed the true identities of these great ancient people forever until their story is analyzed and reviewed through linguistic and cultural analysis.

In his discussion of *Sumeria*, Durant wrote:

The early history of Mesopotamia is in one aspect the struggle of *the non-Semitic peoples of Sumeria* to preserve their independence against the expansion and inroads of the Semites from Kish and Agade, and other centers in the north (1936, p. 118; see also footnote, emphasis mine).

This quotation shows that the so-called Sumerians were a non-Semitic race. However, again influenced by the biblical narrative, western historians and archaeologists have succeeded in conferring the Semitic race on the people of Kish and Agade they did not know. The people of ancient Sumeria were not Semites and they were not defending themselves from any Semitic group from Kish or Agade because the people that western historians speculated were Semites were also black tribes that can also be found today in West Africa. Among the earliest major kings of Mesopotamia was Akka [Akaa], king of Kish. Western historians did not know who these people were but that did not stop them from telling these people's story from their speculative imagination. Again, from their speculative imaginations, western historians gave the people of the kingdom of Akka the name *Akkadians* meaning the subjects of Akka, but that was too simplistic and wrong.

The kingdom of Akka was not Akkadia and the people were not Akkadians. Linguistic and cultural evidence shows that a lower king or sub-chief in Akka's kingdom was called an *Ensi* (see H. W. F. Saggs, *Civilization Before Greece and Rome*, 1989, p. 37). The kingdom of Akka was originally called the *Ensiman* meaning the nation of the *Ensi*, where the suffix *"man"* is also *Akan* meaning nation or State. The ancient people of king Akka are the modern *Ensiman* people. These people can be found today on the southwestern corner of Ghana in West Africa. The so-called Sumerians did not simply vanish from the face of the earth as western historians have assumed or their historical accounts have implied. These people moved towards Ancient Egypt and joined the Ancient Egyptian tribes in the Exodus towards inner Africa. These people were black people then, and they are still black people now.

Western historians and Egyptologists do not know that king Akka's people [the hypothetical Akkadians] were the hypothetical Sumerians; and certainly, they do not know that these people are the *Ensiman* people of West Africa. In fact, I believe that most western historians and Egyptologists have never heard of the *Ensiman* people. However, these scholars believe the *Ensiman* people, the hypothetical Sumerians, wrote most of the correspondence they have found between Ancient Egypt and Mesopotamia. Letters in this correspondence became the El Amarna letters supposedly written by the Akkadians. Cultural and linguistic evidence that further confirm that the Akkadians were the *Ensiman* people of today is in the fact that *Akka* [Akaa] is still their most popular royal name. They are known by this name so well that they are also known as the people of Akaa.

Today, the ancient name *Ensiman* is written as *Nziman*. Researchers who would like to go to study or verify this discussion from these people should go to Ghana and ask for the *Nziman* people. Apart from my personal *Nziman* friends, the greatest *Nziman* personality the world may remember was Dr. Kwame Nkrumah, the first President of Ghana. Definitely, Abraham did not come from among the *Ensiman* tribe because in my linguistic and cultural research, I found that the patriarchs of the ancient *Afrim* people carried different tribal names other than the names of the *Ensiman* people or the Akkadians. An *Ensiman* prophet called *Ezeke*, however, was among the people who wrote the documents of the Old Testament. Can you guess what this name has been transposed to in the Bible?

What other linguistic and cultural evidence do we have to confirm that the so-called Akkadians and Sumerians were black people? The *Ensiman* people were not the only tribal group in the so-called Akkadians' or Sumerians' kingdoms. There is evidence that the *Ahanta* people that can also be found today in the same geographical region as the *Ensiman* people were also there. This is confirmed by the fact that the indigenous name of the great god of *Sumeria* was called *Shama* and not *Shamash* as western historians have transposed it. This name takes one directly to the *Ahanta* people now in Ghana because it is most certainly an *Ahanta* name. What is

201

interesting about this name is that in the western region of Ghana where the Ahanta people live, these people have built a city and named it *Shama* after their ancient great god. Further linguistic and cultural analysis shows that the Sumerian king *Uruk* worshipped a virgin goddess whose indigenous *Akan* name was *Anani*. This name refers to the fourth child in the *Akan* language. Western historians orthographically transposed the name of this virgin goddess to *Innini*. What is most remarkable about such western transposition of African tribal names in history and the Bible is that most of the transpositions tend to retain the African phonology and etymology of the words.

Further evidence shows that the indigenous name of the Sumerian sage of *Eridu* was *Adapa* an *Ahanta* derivation of the *Akan* name *Dapaa*. The sage *Adapa* was supposedly initiated into the lore of the goddess called *Yaa*. Western scholars have transposed the name of this goddess as *Ea*. I should point out that *Yaa* was and is still the name of the ancient *Akan* goddess of Thursday. Note the name of this goddess very carefully because the *Afrim* people also worshipped this same goddess after they left Ancient Egypt into the so-called biblical Exodus.

The god of irrigation of the Sumerians was called *Naagyensu* meaning great one here is water. Again, in western historical literature, this god of irrigation was orthographically transposed as *Ningirsu*. From this, it becomes clear that the earliest concept of irrigation among these people was intended to bring water to the gods to help these gods give life to crops. Finally, the quiet sorrowful mother goddess of Sumeria was called *Nimkasa* meaning "one who knows how to speak." Western historians identify this goddess as *Ninkarsag* (see Durant, 1935, p. 127). Linguistically, the *Enziman* and *Ahanta* languages are closely related thus confirming that these two groups of people must have lived together somewhere. These languages also have many cognates in common with the *Akan* language. Perhaps with the right linguistic and cultural backgrounds, scholars who first found the historical existence of the Sumerians would have known that the people they arbitrarily named the *Sumerians* were the *Nzima* and *Ahanta* people who can now be found in the Western Region of Ghana in West Africa. When the *Afrim* people went to live with the Sumerians, these African tribes were the people among whom they went to live.

In an earlier discussion, I revealed that the ancient "international power in north Syria called Kheta" was the *Ewe* people whose story is the biblical story of *Kpotufe* or *Potifar* (see Saggs, 1989, p. 10). I also mentioned that the *Ewe* people were also drawn towards Ancient Egypt. They became Pharaohs and they also joined the rest of the Ancient Egyptian tribes in moving towards inner Africa. They can be found today in the region around the Volta River in Ghana. Abraham certainly did not come from among this tribal group either. However, one fact is established here and that is, if all these people that lived in and around Mesopotamia in ancient times were black people then Adam and Eve coming down to Noah and his son Shem and Abraham and his so-called descendants were all black people (see Genesis 11:11-32).

Beyond all these, the biblical story was not the story of Europeans or English men, it was the story of the black people that lived in the geographical region around Ancient Egypt in ancient times.

Ancient Kwahu people in Mesopotamia

I have already revealed that Abraham came from among the *Kwahu* tribe of the *Akan* people. How could Abraham have come from the *Kwahu* tribe that can be found today in West Africa? The answer is, these people did not live in Africa in ancient times. As late as the 1st century A. D., the Kwahu people were a vassal kingdom in the Upper Tigris region. Western historians believe that this was a vassal kingdom of the Parthian Empire and the *Adiabene* family ruled the kingdom. The word *Adiabene* is a giveaway. It is an *Akan* word that can be traced today to the *Kwahu* people. What is fascinating about this word is that it is so unique that any *Akan* person can tell anyone the tribe from which the word *Adiabene* originates.

202

In the *Akan* language, the word means one has inherited *Abene*, where *Abene* is the city or State. The ancient people whose royal house was at *Adiabene* can also now be found as the modern *Kwahu* people of the eastern region of Ghana. They are *Akan* people and one of the so-called lost tribes of the Jewish people that are not lost.

A major characteristic of the ancient names of places of these African tribes was that they were either named as residences of deities or they were named directly after deities. As a result, these names have not been easily abandoned, and wherever these people went they took the names of their ancient places and deities with them. That is why most of the ancient names and places found in Ancient Egypt and the geographical region of Mesopotamia can also be found in places in modern Africa. The *Kwahu* people have also rebuilt their ancient city *Abene* as their capital city today. Abraham came from this ancient *Akan* tribe. These people were not Semites and they were not Jews. Though western scholars have known for a long time that Abraham was not a Jew, they have never known that his tribe of origin would be somewhere in Africa.

Western historians found all these people in Mesopotamia but because they did not have the linguistic and cultural backgrounds to identify them, they simply told the stories of these people from their speculative imaginations or simply dismissed the people as extinct. All these people are Africans now but they were Mesopotamians and people of other places in the Middle and Far East then. Even the word Mesopotamia is a western name given to that geographical region, but it has an *Akan* prefix *Meso po* meaning *I am carrying the sea*. The suffix "tamia" could be one of those hypothetical names that western historians have haphazardly given to people and places to make their telling of other people's stories possible. The complete word Mesopotamia also has some phonological affinity to the *Guan* language also found in Ghana today. History shows that the *Afrim* people went to live among the Sumerians and even learned the cuneiform writing from these Sumerians. The question is where are these Sumerians now? If the *Afrim* people survived to become Jewish people in Europe, the Sumerians must also be somewhere. The Sumerians also survived to become the *Nzima* and *Ahanta* people of Ghana in West Africa.

A major fact that needs to be established from this discussion is that all the ancient people that have been discussed from ancient China through Tibet to Mesopotamia and Ancient Egypt were black people and they are still black. These people can all be found today in Africa. What this confirms is that if the biblical story claiming that Abraham originally came from the east were true then he came from among a black tribe, an *Akan* tribe and that was the ancient *Kwahu* tribe in the Upper Tigris region. Therefore the search for the origins of the Jewish people should concentrate on black African tribes and not some fictitious Semitic tribes in the Middle East.

The fact that these ancient people were all black people now in Africa should not be difficult to accept because there is evidence in the biblical narrative that the translators of the biblical documents sought to conceal also sought to conceal something. All one has to do is ask one's self what happened to all the tribal groups that lived in the same geographical region of Canaan and interacted with the *Afrim* people in their biblical history? Where are the Amorites, Kenites, Kenizzites, Kadmonites, Hittites, Perizzites, Jebusites, Edomites and all the other groups of people that lived and interacted with the *Afrim* people? How did all these people come to acquire the same "ites" suffix. It is evident that some one was seeking to give these people fictitious names, and that was how they all came to have the same suffix. Who were these people and where are they now? Again, remember that if the *Afrim* people survived living and interacting with these people to go to become the Jewish people in Europe then these people must also have survived and be living somewhere. Considering that all the groups of people the Bible mentions were all black people and not Europeans or Semites, it should not be difficult to figure out where they must be living today.

Where is the evidence to support the Bible story?

For over two thousand years, the biblical account of the origin of the Jewish people has been preached and taught to millions as the absolute truth by people that did not know about any aspect of the history and people behind this Bible. A major aspect of the history of the origin of the Jewish people is the fact that no historical, archaeological, or even anthropological evidence has been found to support any aspect of the biblical story of their origin. This is because they were all lies. In *The Moses Mystery: The African Origins of the Jewish People*, author Gary Greenberg (1996) proclaims emphatically in the title of his work that the Jewish people are Africans. He pointed out the lack of historical and archaeological confirmation of the biblical story of the origin of Jewish people when he stated that:

> How do we know, independent of the Bible, that Israel's presence in Egypt was preceded by an earlier presence in Palestine? Why is there no archaeological record of Israel or the Hebrew people prior to the 13th century B. C.? Why is there no extrabiblical evidence linking any specific Semitic tribes to the Hebrew people? And why did the so-called ten lost tribes disappear from history without an archaeological trace of their existence?" (p. 2).

Apart from the fact that there is no evidence to support the biblical origins of the *Afrim* people in Mesopotamia, scholars have not been able to link these people to any of the modern Semitic people that live in the geographical area around ancient Mesopotamia today. This confirms that the people that lived in ancient Mesopotamia in ancient times were not the same people that live there today. The people that lived in ancient Mesopotamia are the people I have revealed above. These people moved to the only place few western scholars would expect to find the tribal origins of the Jewish people, and that is Africa.

Gary Greenberg went on to point out how incredible the biblical story of the origin of the Jewish people is by stating that:

> "... where a group of people lived in the sixth century B. C., what language it spoke, and what it believed about its historical roots thousands of years earlier, does not without independent corroboration prove where it lived a thousand years earlier, what language it originally spoke, and what took place in its formative years. Certainly, little in the biblical text would have been outside the knowledge of learned Hebrew scribes in the sixth century B. C. Furthermore, the many anachronistic phrases in the early books of the Bible point to a very late editing. This is not to say that in this later time the Hebrews did not speak a Semitic language or strongly identified with Semitic culture" (p. 3)

Another issue that has puzzled historians, geographers, and religious scholars is that at the time the Jewish people claim to have originated from Mesopotamia, human geographical knowledge was not advanced enough for them to be able to point out exactly where they came from. Ur of the Chaldees is a modern English name for the geographical region near the estuary of the Tigris and Euphrates Rivers. What was it called in ancient times when the biblical story claims Abraham was leaving there? Moreover, evidence of the people that lived in Mesopotamia around the time Abraham supposedly left there does not show that the *Afrim* people were a separate group of people. If Abraham ever originated from Mesopotamia, it means he must have originated from a larger group of people. Who are these people and where are they now?

The fact is Abraham and his wife Sarai and their only child Isaac and his twin sons Esau and Jacob could not have been the seed of the entire Jewish nation when these people were not living in their homeland but in foreign lands. As Will Durant pointed out, the greatest snare of thought is the uncritical acceptance of irrational assumptions. Europeans have accepted all these without question for over two thousand years, and they have succeeded in infecting the world to accept them without question too.

204

Ancient Egyptian religious practice of dream interpretation.

The biblical story of the origin and formative years of the Jewish people continues to state that after living in Canaan for a while Jacob and his family of seventy men went to Egypt through a story of sibling hatred in which Joseph was sold to *Potifar*. Again, the name Joseph is a western corruption of the *Akan* name *Osafo* just as his master's name Potifar was a corruption of the *Ewe* name *Kpotufe*. This confirms that the biblical Joseph was an *Akan* and black like the Ancient Egyptians. Not only that, this also reveals that the biblical Joseph and his family were all *Akan* people with a common linguistic and cultural heritage. According to this Ancient Egyptian story adapted by the Jewish scholars of the Bible, Potifar's wife seduced Joseph and accused him of seducing her. He was sent to jail where he interpreted dreams. He was released and brought to the Pharaoh, and he was eventually appointed to the position of viceroy in all Egypt. I have revealed that Egyptologists agree that this story was an original Ancient Egyptian story based upon a myth about the Seventeenth Nome of Middle Egypt (see editorial to the story in *The Literature of Ancient Egypt: An Anthology of Stories, Instructions, and Poetry*, 1972, p. 92).

Because the ancient Jewish people and the *Akan* and other African tribes in Ancient Egypt were the same people, it must have seemed normal to the Jewish scholars of the Bible to take the stories of these tribes and redesign them for the Greeks. Again, the idea of interpreting dreams was an old Ancient Egyptian religious and cultural practice. The *Afrim* scholars of the Bible designed the Joseph story around this ancient religious and cultural practice. Egyptologists have found out that dreams and their interpretations were very important in the religious and cultural lives of the Ancient Egyptians because they believed that dreams were the medium through which the gods sought to communicate and reveal the future. This was the Ancient Egyptian belief from which Jacob supposedly met with God and wrestled with an angel.

The Papyrus Chester Beatty III in the British Museum is a document of dreams and their interpretations. Though the papyrus has been dated to the 13th century B. C., scholars have determined that the dreams and the interpretations in them date back to the Middle Kingdom 2055-1650 B. C. This was almost two thousand years before the Bible was compiled, edited, and translated for the Greeks, and certainly it was longer before the *Afrim* people supposedly went to Ancient Egypt and left there in the Exodus. Before Joseph, Ancient Egyptians had priests whose sole duties were dream interpretations. That makes the portrayal of Joseph as an extraordinary dream interpreter from outside Egypt very doubtful. In any case, scholars have established that the biblical narrative of Joseph was originally an Ancient Egyptian story taken and adapted by the Jewish scholars of the Bible.

The historical record shows that Ancient Egyptians had been interpreting dreams and they had a core of priests that interpreted dreams for thousands of years before Joseph supposedly went there as a slave. There is no record of Joseph's people interpreting dreams or Joseph interpreting dreams wherever they lived before he came to Ancient Egypt and that reveals that again the *Afrim* people simply took an Ancient Egyptian religious and cultural practice and sought to make it their own. Another instance of this was when Abraham went to Egypt and found out that the priests among whom he studied were circumcised. When he wanted his people to be circumcised too, the Bible says God made a covenant with him for all his male descendants to be circumcised. In this case, the idea was that it was not Abraham that wanted his people to practice the Ancient Egyptian cultural practice of circumcision, it was God that wanted the people to do so.

What is also noteworthy about the biblical trip of Joseph to Egypt is that he was appointed to the position of a viceroy in the house of a Pharaoh not long after he got to Egypt. However, the Bible is silent about the linguistic and cultural problems that could have prevented a complete foreigner from a different racial, ethnic, linguistic, and cultural background from being appointed to such a high national office. This shows that *Osafo* and his family were from the same racial, ethnic, linguistic, and cultural backgrounds as the Ancient Egyptians. They were *Akan* and black people.

According to the biblical story, the people of Ancient Egypt received the *Afrim* people warmly at first but later they used them in forced labor. As a result, a hero called Moses was chosen by God to lead the *Afrim* people out of Egypt. The rest of the story is embellished with magic and miracles purported to have been conducted with the power of God. Moses took the *Afrim* people out of Egypt and after wandering for forty years, they finally conquered and settled in Canaan. Again the problem with this story is that there is no shred of evidence outside the Bible's narrative to support it.

According to the Bible, the ancestors of the *Afrim* people lived in Canaan before they moved to Egypt but it was in Egypt that they found a leader. However, this leader was not an *Afrim* himself. Under what credible circumstances would one ethnic group of people peacefully choose their leader from a different ethnic, linguistic, and cultural group? Yet the biblical story of the *Afrim* people states that they accepted to leave Ancient Egypt under a leader who was not an *Afrim*. Does this suggest the sameness of the ethnicity of the Ancient Egyptians and *Afrim* people and if the *Afrim* people were not of the same racial, ethnic, linguistic, and cultural background as the *Akan* people of Ancient Egypt where did they get their *Akan* names of their identity after the Exodus? How did they come by the *Akan* names of the people, places, and things in *Afrim* people's history?

Beyond all that, there has been no independent historical or archaeological record of the *Afrim* people having lived in Canaan before they went to Egypt just as there has been no record of their having originated from Mesopotamia. Again, Greenberg argues that:

> *For Israel's history before the 13th century, we have only the biblical account, but that rests on shaky grounds.* Modern scholars now recognize that the early books of the Bible weren't fully edited until after the 7th century B. C., and perhaps centuries later. ... *The final version attempted to weave a seamless narrative out of diverse collection of contradictory historical claims that reflected clashing political philosophies and opposing doctrines. The resulting compilation indicates numerous compromises of truth* (1996, p. 3, emphasis mine).

From his analyses of the biblical, historical, and archaeological evidence of the origin of the ancient *Afrim* people that went to Europe to become the Jews and Hebrews, Gary Greenberg also concluded in his book that:

1. Israel's appearance in Canaan occurred suddenly in the late 14th or early 13th century B. C., and not after several centuries of evolution from tribes of Semitic-speaking nomads [as the biblical narrative seeks to suggest].

2. The first Israelites spoke Egyptian [*Akan*] and adhered to Egyptian [religious and] cultural practices.

3. No confederation of Semitic tribes preceded the Hebrew monarchy.

4. The "ten" lost tribes disappeared not because of the Assyrian conquest but because they never existed.

Interestingly, all the conclusions that Greenberg makes from his analyses are correct except the last one. No western religious scholars or historians seem to have thought about the fact that the original tribes that the ancient *Afrim* people claim to have lost were Ancient Egyptians, even though the Bible also claims that the people that left Ancient Egypt to become the *Afrim* people lived in Ancient Egypt for over hundreds of years. Greenberg shows in his book that the Jewish people originated from African tribes but he fails to notice that if these people originated from

African tribal groups then the so-called lost tribes of the Jewish people must be Africans, and therefore living somewhere in Africa.

Historical origin of the Afrim people

In *The Moses Mystery: The African Origin of the Jewish People*, Gary Greenberg establishes that modern Jewish people originated from black people and therefore they are Africans. However, his work does not go into detail to reveal the specific tribes from which ancient *Afrim* or modern Jews originated. His work however shows that the Ancient Egyptians are modern Africans and that modern Jews originated from the black tribes of Ancient Egypt. Why haven't western scholars figured this out a long time ago? Greenberg gives a reason for all the shortcomings of western scholarship in this regard and why religious scholars and historians have not considered that the so-called lost tribes could be modern African tribes:

> Until now, studies of pre-Exodus chronology suffered from a form of tunnel vision – the unswerving view that Israel emerged in either Mesopotamia or Canaan. The astonishing surface similarities between the Genesis Flood myth and that of the Babylonians certainly suggested that this was the correct approach, and analyses of Genesis were always based on cross-references of the histories, myths, and cultures of these Asiatic regions. Biblical scholars generally consider the Genesis chronology little more than an imitation of Near Eastern king lists, without any historic validity of its own. ... This view so dominates biblical scholarship that no one seems to have thought to compare the Genesis chronology with [Ancient] Egyptian chronology, even though prior to the Exodus the Israelites allegedly spent hundreds of years in Egypt. Moses' own perspective on the unfolding of history would have been Egyptian, not Canaanite or Mesopotamian (p. 32).

According to Greenberg in this quotation, "Moses' own perspective on the unfolding of history would have been Egyptian, not Canaanite or Mesopotamian." In short, Greenberg was also pointing out that Moses was not a Canaanite or Mesopotamian therefore he would not have perceived history or the world from the point of view of a Canaanite or Mesopotamian. He was an Ancient Egyptian and that was why his perspective of history would have been Ancient Egyptian.

From all the legendary lies in the biblical narrative of the origin of the ancient *Afrim* people, the fact remains that the ancient *Afrim* people that later went to Europe to become the Jews and Hebrews broke away from Ancient Egypt to go to set up their independent kingdoms in Canaan. They set up two kingdoms; one was Israel and the other was Judea. The question is why would a people that left Ancient Egypt as one people perhaps with the same religious, social, and political goals and aspirations break into two kingdoms when evidence in their history shows that they needed to unite for strength? The answer is simple. In the Exodus narrative, there was a "mixed multitude" of people most of who did not come from "the house of Israel". This simply means that the "mixed multitude" was not of *Akan* heritage. At the end of the Exodus, the people from different tribal, linguistic, cultural, and religious perceptions were forced to live together as one nation. However, these differences made it difficult for them to live together so they broke into forming the two nations of Judea and Israel where the *Akan* majority was in Israel and the rest that did not want to be in Israel was in Judea.

Evidence of the various tribal groups that went in the Exodus can be found from three sources. The first evidence is in the various tribal groups whose kings' names can be found alongside the dominant *Akan* names in the Ancient Egyptian Kings' List. The second evidence can be found among these same tribal groups that live together today with the *Akan* people in West Africa. The third evidence can be found in the African tribal names that the Jewish people still carry after over three thousand years of parting from these African tribes into the so-called biblical Exodus.

The real history of the *Afrim* people that left Ancient Egypt into the biblical Exodus shows that people from the various African tribal groups of Ancient Egypt left to go to set up

207

their own kingdoms but unfortunately, they could not defend the kingdoms militarily or even through divine protection. In *The Story of Civilization: Our Oriental Heritage*, Durant points out that despite the effort the *Afrim* people put into making *Yahweh* their supreme deity, *Yahweh* could not defend them from outside invasion in ancient times. For example, when an Ancient Egyptian king and his soldiers sought to pass through Palestine on their way to attacking the Syrians, the *Afrim* king whose indigenous *Akan* name was *Gyasi* counting on the assistance of *Yahweh* refused to let the Ancient Egyptians pass through his land. The Ancient Egyptians attacked Josiah [*Gyasi*], defeated and killed him, and later the Babylonians came to defeat the Egyptians and made Judea a colony of Babylon. *Gyasi* was the indigenous *Akan* name that was transposed into Greek and other European languages as *Jesse, Josiah* and *Joshua* in the Bible.

The successor of Josiah secretly sought to get the help of the Ancient Egyptians to drive away the Babylonians, but the Babylonians heard of this plot and brought their full force of authority on Judea. They captured Jerusalem, took Jehoiakim the successor of Josiah prisoner, and replaced him with Zedekiah. On their way back, the Babylonians took about 10, 000 *Afrim* people into what has been popularly and historically known as the Babylonian Captivity.

Zedekiah also sought the help of the Egyptians against the Babylonians. As a result, the Babylonians returned to recapture Jerusalem. They burned it to the ground, destroyed the Temple of Solomon, killed Zedekiah's sons and his possible successors, and forced the rest of the population of Judea into a second wave of captivity in Babylon (see 2 Kings 25:7). Some of the prophets of Judea interpreted all these as the works of *Yahweh* and that *Yahweh* was using the Babylonians to get back at the *Afrim* people for their sins. Since these names have come up, I must reveal that the name Jehoiakim is a corruption of the indigenous *Akan* name *Yeboa Akim* where *Akim* represents the branch of *Akan* group from which *Yeboa* originated. Note that Zedekiah is also derived from the African tribal name *Zedeki*. Which group of people would carry all these African tribal names if they did not originate from these tribes?

Jeremiah and other prophets continued to condemn the rulers of Judea as fools who could have avoided all these tribulations if only they had listened to the prophets (see Jeremiah 27: 6-8; Ezekiel, 16; 22; 23; 38:2). Ezekiel concluded his condemnation of the captured *Afrim* people with a hopeful Utopian end in which the *Afrim* people would be restored to their old land where they would rebuild the Temple, the priests would be the overlords again, and *Yahweh* would live with the people. From these tribulations in their lives and history, many of the *Afrim* people began returning to Ancient Egypt and those who remained in captivity quickly settled into a life of prosperous captivity. Soon the next generations of the *Afrim* people forgot about Jerusalem. This was the generation that must have been influenced to believe that the place of their captivity was the place of their origin.

While in Babylon, an unknown prophet who also went by the name Isaiah began to predict the liberation of the *Afrim* people from Babylon by the army of King Cyrus of Persia. This second Isaiah also predicted the return of the *Afrim* people to Jerusalem. Eventually, Cyrus attacked and defeated Babylon and freed the *Afrim* people to return to Jerusalem. When some of the *Afrim* people returned to Canaan, they found that other people had taken their former land and they were seen as intruders or even invaders. However, with the help of Zerubbabel, they managed to settle in Jerusalem and began to rebuild the Temple.

Return to Jerusalem

When they returned to Jerusalem and rebuilt the Temple, the *Afrim* people sought to build a new society based upon theocracy, priestly traditions, and the propagation of social laws as divine commands. Durant recorded two important religious events that historians believe were the precursors of the propagation of a common faith of the ancient *Afrim* people. He wrote:

> As the people fell away from the worship of Yahveh to the adoration of alien gods, the priests began to wonder whether the time had not come to make a final stand against the disintegration of

the national faith [in Yahveh]. Taking a leaf from the prophets, who attributed to Yahveh the passionate convictions of their own souls, they resolved to issue to the people a communication from God himself, a code of laws that would reinvigorate the moral life of the nation, and would at the same time attract the support of the Prophets by embodying the less extreme of their ideas. They readily won King Josiah to their plan; and about the eighteenth year of his reign the priest Hilkiah announced to the King that he had "found" in the secret archives of the Temple an astonishing scroll in which the great Moses himself, at the direction of Yahveh, had settled once and for all those problems of history and conduct that were being so hotly debated by prophets and priests. The discovery made a great stir. Josiah called the elders of Judah to the Temple, and there read to them the "Book of the Covenant" in the presence (we are told) of thousands of people. Then he solemnly swore that he would henceforth abide by the laws of this book; and "he caused all that were present to stand for it" (1935, p. 321; see also 2 Kings 22:8; 23:2; 2 Chronicles 34:15, 31-2).

It is important to point out that all these were carefully planned by the priests that felt responsible for saving the drifted souls of the *Afrim* people from the damnation of Yahveh. Notice also that there was a time when the *Afrim* people did not believe in *Yahweh*, the very God they later passed on to the Greeks, Europeans, and into Christianity.

In the biblical fashion of retelling and repeating events and situations, this event is also repeated and retold with new characters in the history of the *Afrim* people. Historians say that around 444 B.'C., a priest called Ezra not Hilkiah or Josiah also assembled the *Afrim* people and read the *Book of the Law of Moses* to them from morning to midday. The priests supposedly read the book to the *Afrim* people for seven days. After these seven days, the priests and people "pledged to accept this *body of legislation* as their constitution and their conscience, and to obey it forever" (Durant, 1935, p. 328; see also Nehemiah 10:23, emphasis mine). Notice that to the ancient *Afrim* people that were seeking to establish a new nation, this book of Moses was a "body of laws, a constitution, and a conscience" not a sacred religious document that must be revered as such. Scholars did not know what the book contained. Nevertheless, according to *Afrim* peoples' history, the content of this book was the Mosaic Law or the Torah that laid the foundation of modern Judaism. The content of this book was supposed to give the *Afrim* people religious, social, and political guidance or direction, and that was why it was known as the Torah meaning guidance or direction. Where did this book come from? According to both the biblical and historical accounts, Moses, the Ancient Egyptian wrote these books.

There is biblical evidence to show that the *Afrim* people that left Ancient Egypt in the Exodus left with malice "aforethought." This is evident in Exodus 3:22 where it states that God told the *Afrim* people to steal gold, silver, and clothes from the Ancient Egyptians and take these along with them in their journey. If this God could tell the people that left Ancient Egypt in the Exodus to steal silver, gold, and clothes from the Ancient Egyptians, and their leader Moses was an Ancient Egyptian priest, then it is not inconceivable that Moses would also take Ancient Egyptian religious documents as the guidance and direction for the journey of the people he was going to lead.

In Exodus 14:5-10, there is an interesting account of horse and chariot races after the *Afrim* people when they left Ancient Egypt. However, the biblical explanation is that the Pharaoh that let the *Afrim* people go into the Exodus changed his mind so his soldiers went after these people to bring them back Egypt. The rest of the story is embellished with Moses parting the Red Sea and killing his own people the Ancient Egyptians to save the lives of their slaves. Modern interpreters of the Bible claim that all of these happened as the will of God. However, again as Will Durant pointed out, the greatest snare of thought is the unquestioned acceptance of illogical ideas. Moses was an Ancient Egyptian and the documents ascribed to him must have all been taken from the theosophical library of Ancient Egyptian priesthood. This shows that none of the biblical documents originally belonged to the *Afrim* people as they later claimed. As Lloyd

Graham put it, the *Afrim* people were nothing but "plagiarists culling mythical ideas they did not understand."

African tribal celebration of the rituals of the [Jewish] Passover

Beyond the myths and the history of the *Afrim* people that went to Europe to become the Jews and Hebrews, there is the real and existing history and culture of the people that were in the story of the Bible. When anyone mentions the Passover, the obvious reference is the Jewish people. The world knows that the only group of people that are associated with the rituals of the Passover is the Jewish people. However, does anyone outside Africa know that African tribes celebrated and continue to celebrate the rituals of the so-called Jewish Passover?

In the research for this book, I spoke to several African tribes including mine. I spoke to people of the *Ga* tribe. Specifically, I spoke to *Ga* people from Labadi in Ghana. I introduced the *Ga* people in the discussion of the Gileadites war with the Israelites in Judges 12. However, I never mentioned that the *Ga* people have a tradition that says they came from Israel. What is believable about this tradition is the fact that the *Ga* people in general and specifically the people I spoke to at Labadi celebrate the rituals of the Passover.

The main festival of all *Ga* people is called *Homowo*, meaning shame to hunger, and a celebration of the first fruits in August. However, before this celebration, the people at Labadi told me that a day is set aside on which their tradition says a spirit would come to pass through their town. These people believe that this spirit would bring a curse on all households that did not perform the rituals of the passing over of this spirit. Among these rituals, there must be no one outside the night this spirit came to pass through. There must no lights in any households and there must be silence. More importantly, the people were required to celebrate the passing of this spirit by killing sacrificial goats and sheep and marking the doors of their households with the blood of these livestock. Households that could not afford sheep and goats by themselves were required to join other households to make it more affordable so that they could share the meat and the blood of the sacrificed livestock they jointly killed. Even today, households that cannot afford sheep and goats perform thus ritual with the sacrificial blood of chicken.

I am not aware that the *Akan* people also used to mark the doors of their households with the blood of livestock but I am aware of the *Akan* folklore of the passing of the *Osaman Tenten*, the tall spirit, through their towns. What these revelations mean is that the rituals of the so-called Jewish Passover were existing rituals of the African tribes from which the Jewish people originated in Ancient Egypt. These rituals existed among these people long before Jewish scholars of the Bible decided to write the fictitious stories surrounding these rituals in the events leading to the so-called biblical Exodus (see Exodus 12). All of these do not only confirm the African origin of the concepts of religion, doctrines, documents, and sacramental practices that the *Afrim* people that went to Europe to become the Jews and Hebrews passed on through the Greeks to entire Europe they also confirm the African origin of the cultural traditions that have long been known to be Jewish traditions in Europe.

Belief and interpretation of the biblical documents

In his discussion of Exodus or Evolution in *Deceptions and Myths of the Bible*, Lloyd Graham noted that in terms of the interpretation of the Bible, "there is no end to the explanations these apologists find to prove the historicity of Hebrew mythology." I mentioned earlier that in Europe, the perception of the Bible has been taken to two major extremes. One extreme believes that the Bible is the word of God and that either God wrote the biblical narratives or he put words in the mouths of divine *Afrim* prophets to write them. What most of these people forget is that the *Afrim* people are the same people the biblical narrative showed that this God would not talk to them even when this God was delivering them from bondage in Ancient Egypt. This God would not even let the *Afrim* people or their herds of animals near the mountain on which Moses went to receive the Ten Commandments. Yet, most people believe that God spoke to *Afrim* prophets and

210

these prophets wrote down the biblical narratives. If this God would not speak to any of the ancient *Afrim* people when he was delivering them from the so-called bondage in Ancient Egypt, what makes it believable that He would later speak to *Afrim* prophets for them to write his "Holy Book?" From the perspective of believers however, the Bible is a holy document.

The other extreme of European and Christian perception of the Bible seeks to "academize" the rational behind the perception. Scholars of this school try to perceive the Bible as history that should be proven, and since neither history nor archaeology has been able to confirm much of the biblical narrative, the Bible to them is nothing but mythology. These scholars argue that the Bible must be mythology because there is no historical proof of anything the Bible has said. Instead, much of what the Bible has said has been found in the folklore and myths of several different groups of people. The problem with this academic approach is that historians have been searching for the context, language, and culture behind the Bible in the wrong places therefore the conclusions of these scholars are also wrong.

The Bible is not holy writ, and it is not mythology. It is the edited and embellished theosophical writings of a people other than the *Afrim* people that introduced the biblical documents to Europeans. This story has a point of view, and it is full of allegory, symbolism, characters, setting, and a plot derived from a disguised attempt to tell history. Biblical narrative is about real people. These people are the *Akan, Afrim,* and other African tribal groups. Discussion in earlier chapters showed that the people that were the people of the Bible had moved after creating their glorious histories in the distant lands Europeans have been searching for the history behind the Bible. The misinterpretation of the Bible in Europe therefore comes from the lack of the necessary linguistic and cultural backgrounds needed to understand the elements through which the book was written.

Throughout this book, I have introduced Ancient Egypt as the setting of biblical thinking and I have introduced the analyses and conclusions of other works to support it. I do not assert this because the Bible was compiled, edited, and translated in Ancient Egypt, but because the biblical documents were Ancient Egyptian documents based upon fundamental Ancient Egyptian thoughts and concepts of religion and Godliness. As I have asserted, the story of religion in this world began from the Ancient Egyptians.

In the course of this discussion, I have repeated in several places that the earliest people of Ancient Egypt were the *Akan* people. This revelation is supported by the fact that the earliest Kings' Lists of Ancient Egypt begin with *Akan* names. In addition to that the most dominant religious deities of Ancient Egyptians were *Akan* deities – *Osoro* and *Asaase*. Incidentally, Christianity acknowledges these ancient religious deities as heaven and earth.

The *Akan* people were the earliest humans to design a socio-political framework of national and societal development based upon religion. What makes these revelations even more credible and fascinating is that the *Akan* people still worship their ancient deities, *Osoro* and *Asaase*. I also showed that in ancient times, these people traveled as far as China to propagate their religious ideas. The *Akan* people in Ancient Egypt were the people the *Afrim* people supposedly went to live with for hundreds of years. All of these were possible because the Ancient Egyptians and the people of *Joseph* that came to live in Egypt had the same racial, ethnic, linguistic, and cultural background and heritage. The *Akan* people were the people from whom the *Afrim* people learned all that they later claimed to have known about religion. They were the religion, sacramental practices, and documents of these people of Ancient Egypt that the *Afrim* people took, edited, translated, and introduced to the Greeks and Europeans.

The irony in all these is that the world has been deceived into believing that the *Afrim* people created the knowledge and concepts of religion in the Bible, but they did not. The credit of this knowledge goes to the *Akan* people of Ancient Egypt and not the *Afrim* people who supposedly went to Ancient Egypt before they ever learned of the concept of religion. What is worse about all of these deceptions is that they have succeeded in making people very ignorant. For example, modern Christian interpretation of the Bible condemns Ancient Egypt, the source from which all the knowledge emanated, and modern African religions that continue to practice the original Ancient Egyptian rituals and sacramental practices of religion as pagan and idolatrous. As Gary Greenberg put it: "biblical scholars consider [Ancient] Egyptian culture alien to the biblical experience" (p. 32) because historians and religious scholars have overlooked the obvious connection between Ancient Egypt and the biblical story of the origin of the ancient *Afrim* people that left Ancient Egypt and later went to become the Jews and Hebrews in Europe.

The fact is modern Christian Europe and Christians around the world have been too far removed from the true origin of the Christian religion. This is because, as I have pointed out, when the early apostolic fathers of Christianity found out that the concepts and documents of Christianity originated from black people in Ancient Egypt, they embarked on a crusade to make sure that this does not become common knowledge in Christendom.

Origin of the Afrim God that became the Christian God

In the discussion of the origin and history of the ancient *Afrim* people, we have not come across any aspect of their history that shows that they imagined or created a God of their own either before they went to Ancient Egypt, or after they left Ancient Egypt in the so-called biblical Exodus. From the biblical narrative, the sense one gets is that the God these people supposedly worshipped was already there and he was the *Afrim* people's God, but that is completely false. This God and other Gods were imagined, created, personified, and worshipped by other people before the *Afrim* people went to know and worship them too.

In *The Story of Civilization: Our Oriental Heritage*, Will Durant introduced the *Afrim* people by stating that:

> As they first entered the historic scene the Jews were nomads Bedouins who feared the djinns of the air, and worshipped rocks, cattle, sheep, and spirits of caves and hills (see 1935, p. 309; J. T. Shotwell, 1931).

The historical claim that the *Afrim* people were Bedouin nomads is also false. After failing to find out where the *Afrim* people came from based upon their biblical narrative, historians resorted to speculating where they must have come from in the same geographical region their ancestry could not be located in the first place. This false claim is heavily influenced by the biblical story of the origin of the *Afrim* people in the Middle East. Most historians have taken the biblical story as the absolute truth. As a result, these scholars' have attempted to design history to confirm what the Bible has said instead of designing history from a verification of what the Bible said. This is an old historical attempt to link the *Afrim* people to some people in the Middle East though history and archaeology have all failed to link them to any group of people of modern times in that geographical area.

Bull worship during and after the Exodus

What is also false is the claim that the *Afrim* people were a religious group of people ostensibly chosen by the Christian God as his children. The Bible states it and Durant points it out truthfully that even the *Afrim* people of the post-Exodus period were pagans who worshipped the cult of the *bull*, *sheep*, and *lamb*. If these people were pagans who worshipped pagan gods even after the Exodus, then the question is what happens to their claim of earlier knowledge of the monotheist Christian God before they went to Ancient Egypt? There are some serious contradictions here between the biblical story and the real history of the *Afrim* people. The biblical story claims that the earliest patriarch of the *Afrim* people knew the *Afrim* people's God before he went to Ancient Egypt though his story shows that Abraham asked his wife to deny their marriage and lie about it so he could join the Ancient Egyptian priesthood and learn about the Ancient Egyptian God.

The biblical narrative also claims that Jacob's family that went to Ancient Egypt knew of religion and had a God before it went to Ancient Egypt and yet, throughout the biblical narrative in Exodus, this God kept asking Moses to keep the *Afrim* people away from him. Even when this God supposedly asked the *Afrim* priests to sanctify themselves to come to see him, He asked Moses not to let the *Afrim* priests come near him "lest he breaketh forth upon them" (Exodus 19, 24). In this narrative, God asked Moses to come up with his brother Aaron and none of the *Afrim* people. Why? According to Durant, the *Afrim* people looked upon Moses and Aaron as magicians and these people patronized professional diviners and sorcerers (p. 309, see also Exodus 7).

The answer to the question as to why this God did not allow the *Afrim* people near him was because this God was an Ancient Egyptian God that knew Moses the Ancient Egyptian priest but He did not know the rest of the *Afrim* people. This God would not even talk to the *Afrim* people except through Moses the Egyptian. How do these contradictory historical and biblical information confirm that the *Afrim* people are the children of God because they knew and had a God before they went to Ancient Egypt? How does this aspect of the biblical narrative also confirm that the so-called God of the *Afrim* people was different from the Ancient Egyptian God?

There is biblical evidence confirming that during and after the Exodus, the *Afrim* people who claim to have known the monotheist Christian God since their patriarch Abraham, worshipped the bull. How could people that supposedly knew and had their own God different from and better than "pagan" gods worship a pagan bull? This was because these *Afrim* did not know of any other god, and they did not have any other god than the god they learned to worship in Ancient Egypt. This Ancient Egyptian god was the bull and that was all they knew.

In Ancient Egypt, from where the *Afrim* people left into the Exodus, the bull was a sacred animal as early as the Predynastic times. The bull was portrayed in Egyptian art and architecture as the symbol of power, strength, manhood, and fertility. In Ancient Egyptian astronomy, the bull was part of the earliest imagery of the solar system. Scholars have found that *Akhenaten* the first monotheist acknowledged the bull because of its astronomical association. Egyptologists have also found out that bulls enjoyed a special status in Ancient Egypt where some bulls were even given human burials when they died. It is the same religious sacredness and reverence for bulls in Ancient Egypt that is now extended to cows in India.

In 1986, P. Behrens wrote a book on the worship of the bull in Ancient Egypt. This article was entitled the *Bull-God* (Stiergotter). W. Helck, E. Otto, and W. Westendorf edited this work. It is evident from these that the *Afrim* people acquired their knowledge of religion and the worship of the bull from Ancient Egyptians. If the *Afrim* people that left Ancient Egypt into the so-called biblical Exodus learned to worship the bull in Ancient Egypt and worshipped the bull during the Exodus then where is the credibility in their biblical assertion that they knew of a monotheist God called *Yahweh* before they went to Ancient Egypt?

The biblical narrative in *Exodus* 32:25-28 tells of how the *Afrim* people danced naked as if possessed before the Golden Calf Aaron made for them during the Exodus. According to the Bible, when Moses came down from the mountain where he supposedly met with God, he supposedly killed three thousand **Afrim** people as punishment for their idolatry and the worship of the bull. Could this be the religious history and fate of people that knew of a monotheist God beside the bull god? The intriguing question is did the killing of three thousand of them deter the *Afrim* people from worshipping Ancient Egyptian and specifically ancient *Akan* Gods? No. They also learned to worship the serpent from Ancient Egypt.

Serpent worship after the Exodus

In *The Story of Civilization Our Oriental Heritage*, Durant points out that the *Afrim* people also worshipped the serpent and that there are numerous images of the worship of the serpent in early *Afrim* history. All of these confirm that the *Afrim* people that left Ancient Egypt into the so-called biblical Exodus had no independent knowledge of religion and they did not have their own gods other than the ones they knew and learned to worship in Ancient Egypt. This is because there is no place in ancient times where the worship of the serpent was so much ingrained into religious, cultural, and superstitious beliefs as Ancient Egypt. Not only did the ancient *Afrim* people learn to worship the bull, lamb, and sheep in Ancient Egypt, but also they learned to worship the serpent from the Egyptians. In Ancient Egypt, the people perceived the serpent as a form of evil to be feared and worshipped at the same time. The Ancient Egyptian god *Apophis* [African name *Akpofe*] was portrayed as a serpent.

In the Pyramid Texts of Ancient Egypt, there is the evidence of the existence of a snake-god going back as early as the 5th and 6th dynasties. Evidence of Ancient Egyptian worship of the serpent can be found in the image of the serpent on the headgear of their rulers The Ancient Egyptians revered serpents because of the snake's ability to renew itself by shedding its skin over and over. In Ancient Egyptian beliefs, serpents were also symbols of resurrection. *The Dictionary of Ancient Egypt* states that in the *Book of the Gates* recovered from the tomb of Seti (1294-1279 B. C.), there was a large winding coil of a snake with the hieroglyphics that translate into the word "lifespan."

Fig. 6: The symbol of the serpent as the object of worship and reverence on King Tutu Ankoma's crown.

This referred to the Ancient Egyptian belief in the cyclical nature of life that developed into the early concept of resurrection and the later concept and belief in reincarnation in some religions of the world.

Cambridge Ancient History reported of the various images of the serpent found in the oldest ruins of the Afrim people (see v. iii, p. 428). There is also the biblical evidence of the brazen serpent that Moses made and Afrim people placed in the Temple and worshipped till the coming of the prophet Hezekiah (see Numbers 21:8-9; 2 Kings 28:4). Biblical evidence of animal worship by ancient Afrim people can also be found in 1 Kings, 12:28 and Ezekiel 8:10. This is the source from where Europeans acquired the God of Christianity and because they did not know that Christianity like all religions began from pagan thoughts and imaginations, they have gone to war, massacred, and burned people of different faiths over the "polished" pagan concept they call Christianity.

It is certain that the people that left in the biblical Exodus did not leave Ancient Egypt under the friendliest and most cordial conditions. Even while they were in Ancient Egypt, these people sought revenge on the Ancient Egyptians by stealing their gold, silver, and clothes. When these people left and met tribulations and woes in Canaan, the group that later returned to Ancient Egypt blamed the Egyptians. As a result, the serpent that brought about the fall of man in the Garden of Eden is a symbolic reference to Ancient Egyptians that kicked these people out to meet such trials and tribulations.

Phallic worship of the ancient Afrim people

The Bible does not tell its believers the true story of the people Christians believe are the children of God and most of these believers have never known that there is any other story about the Bible other than what the Bible itself has told. The Jewish people claim that their patriarchs knew a God that was different from the God of the Ancient Egyptians. Yet, there is no evidence to support this claim and there is no evidence that these people worshipped this God when they supposedly went to Ancient Egypt. Instead, there is all the historical and archaeological evidence that the Jewish people worshipped every Ancient Egyptian God. They worshipped the Ancient Egyptian bull, the serpent, and even the penis. For those who want to know, these were the foundations of what became Christianity in Europe and the most dominant religion of the world.

In the Evolution of the Idea of God, Grant Allen pointed out in 1897 that the Afrim people also practiced phallic worship after the so-called biblical Exodus. In Sex Worship, Cliff Howard (1909) also confirmed that the Afrim people practiced phallic worship. In this brief discussion of the origin of Afrim people's Gods, we have found out that in addition to Yahweh, these people originally worshipped the bull, lamb, sheep, serpent, and the penis. The Afrim scholars of the Bible introduced only Yahweh to Europeans and in their ignorance Europeans thought they have been introduced to the most divine concept of God ever conceived by man. From this ignorant perspective, every other God or form of religion became pagan to Europeans except the one introduced to them. What is sad about all these is that Christian Europe did not even search to find out the origin of the ideas they easily accepted and adopted as their own.

Historians and Egyptologists know that the origin of phallic worship was Ancient Egypt. Ancient Egyptians perceived sexuality and fertility as matters of great importance in their religious and cultural lives. They had a phallic god called Min that was a popular god of sexuality and fertility. Have you heard of this god's dynasty, the Min dynasty in ancient China? In Hathor's Temple at Dendera, Isis [Asaase] is depicted in the form of a kite perched upon the phallus of the mummified Osiris, and in other temple artworks, there are numerous allusions and depictions of sexual acts (see L. Manniche, Sexual life in Ancient Egypt, 1987). Note here that Hathor is a European transposition of the Ewe name Hator. Again, these revelations about the true history of the Jewish people confirm that the Afrim people took all that they knew about religion and religious rituals and practices from the Ancient Egyptians before they went to Europe to become Jews and Hebrews. Will Durant summed it all up when he wrote that:

Just as primitive polytheism survived in [Christianity] as the worship of angels and saints and in the teraphim, or portable idols, that served as household gods, so the magical notions rife in the early cults [of the Jewish people] persisted to a late day despite the protests of prophets and priests (1935, p. 309; see also Reinach: Orpheus: A History of Religions, 1909, 1930).

Akan names of ancient Afrim gods

In the quotation above, Durant uses the *Akan* name of a god but I do not think he knew it or western historians have ever known it. Since the *Akan* name of the ancient household gods of the *Afrim* people has been mentioned here, I would like to reveal that the ancient *Afrim* name for the household gods of Jewish people, *teraphim*, was derived from the *Akan* language. What has long been believed to be the Hebrew word *teraphim* is a corruption of the *Akan* words *tena afim* meaning stay in homes. These gods were the gods of households, and it was the original *Akan* meaning of these words that made these gods household gods. Among ancient *Akan* people, the gods of households were also referred to as the *tena afim* gods. The *tena afim* gods were represented in wooden deities and other three dimensional images. The corruption of these *Akan* words easily became *teraphim*. It is clear that the word *teraphim* is simply an orthographic and not even a semantic corruption of the *Akan* words *tena afim* from which it originates. Here is another example in which the *Akan* word *tena* was transposed in history and the Bible into *tera* as in the name of Abraham's father, Tera..

There is also the name of the angel *Seraphim* that is also a corruption of the *Akan* words *sra afim* meaning visit homes or the visitor of homes. These words are specifically words from the language of a branch of the *Akan* group known as the *Akuapem* people. It was from this *Akan* language version of these people that *Adomea*, the biblical *Edom* and *Idumea* were derived. The *Akuapem* people were the earliest Pharaohs of Ancient Egypt suggesting that they were foundation members of the design and creation of that ancient civilization. The most popular of the *Akuapem* kings in Ancient Egyptian history were the 4th Dynasty king *Akuffu*, and his sons *Okyere Afre* and *Dade Afre* known in western linguistic corruption as *Khuffu, Djedefra, and Chephren.*

Christian Europe would not want to know this and even when it finds out, it certainly would not want Christian masses to know. However, from the historical revelation that the *Afrim* people were worshipping bulls, sheep, lamb, serpents, and the penis after the biblical *Exodus*, it is evident and therefore prudent to conclude that the source of the **Afrim** god that became the Christian God with a capital "G," was definitely an Ancient Egyptian god. This unfortunately is the revelation of a two-thousand-year old secret the *Afrim* people and Christian Europe have never wanted people to know. The following discussion will go into more detail.

The Akan goddess Yah that became the Afrim and Christian God Yahweh

In his discussion of Judea, Durant pointed out that the *Afrim* people took their god *Yahveh* or *Yahweh* from one of the gods of the people that lived in Canaan when they got there. He stated:

Apparently the conquering Jews took one of the gods of Canaan, Yahu, and re-created him in their own image as a stern, warlike, "stiff-necked" deity with almost lovable limitations" (1935, p. 310).

Note here that in the quotation above, there is the revelation that the god *Yah* or *Yahu* that became the Christian God Yahweh was not even an original God of the *Afrim* people that went to Europe to become Jews and Hebrews. This revelation by Durant is extremely important because the *Afrim* people claim that they have had their own God and known this God since their patriarch Abraham. Despite this false biblical claim, the historical evidence shows that these people had taken the worshipping of the bull, lamb, sheep, serpent, penis, and even the *Yah* or *Yahweh* they

216

introduced to Europeans from other people and these people were the Ancient Egyptian tribes from which they originated.

Christianity has never known this and I am rather sorry to reveal it but the god *Yah* or *Yahu* that western historians claim the *Afrim* people took from the people of Canaan was not a god. She was a goddess. The name of this goddess is also presented elsewhere in historical literature as *Yah* or *Ea* in the discussion of other people in the same geographical region of Canaan. For example, in his discussion of the Sumerians, Durant wrote the name of this same goddess as *Ea*, but it is pronounced as *Yah*. She was the goddess of wisdom of the Sumerians. However, she was first and foremost the goddess of the Ancient Egyptians. To the *Akan* people of Ancient Egypt, this goddess was *Yaa*, the goddess of Thursday.

Again, the quotation above confirms that there is no period in the history of the ancient *Afrim* people when they imagined or created their own God or Gods. They always took other people's Gods and simply made them their own. This contradicts the biblical assertion that the *Afrim* people knew the Christian God and had doctrines of religion before they went to Ancient Egypt.

Western historians do not really know where the *Afrim* people took the God *Yah*. The idea that the *Afrim* people took the goddess *Yah* from Canaan was propagated in the New York Times as an archaeological discovery of where the ancient *Afrim* people took this goddess (see May 9, 1931). What is noteworthy about this date is that it was exactly sixty-eight years to the day that the same newspaper published a review of the results of genetic studies confirming that the ancient *Afrim* people that became the Jews and Hebrews in Europe were originally black people.

From the quotation above, it is clear that historians confirm that the God *Yah* was not an original *Afrim* people's God. The history of the *Afrim* people seems to suggest that they did not know this god before they got to Canaan, but that is not true. As it will be shown later *Yah* was an *Akan* goddess but western historians have never known that. This reveals something Christian Europe has never known. Christian Europe has never known that the God the *Afrim* people passed on to Europeans as the Christian God was originally a Goddess. However, the deity that the *Afrim* people passed onto the Greeks and Christian Europe was a God. How did this transformation happen?

Unfortunately, historians have given the modern name of Canaanites to the people that lived in this geographical area in ancient times when the land was not called Canaan. This means the people that lived in the geographical area of Canaan from whom the *Afrim* people supposedly took their god *Yah* were not Canaanites in modern geographical sense of the word. Again, here is an instance in which the real history of the *Afrim* people is being gleaned from their false biblical history, but the two stories do not complement each other.

How do we know that the god the *Afrim* people took from the so-called Canaanites was a goddess? Who were the people from whom the *Afrim* people took the goddess *Yah* and how did this god become *Yahweh*?

In the discussion of the history and religion of the hypothetical Sumerians, Durant stated that a legend of Sumeria told of "how *Adapa*, a sage of Eridu, had been initiated into all lore by *Ea [Yah], goddess of wisdom*, one secret only had been refused him – the knowledge of deathless life (see 1935, p. 128; *Cambridge Ancient History*, v. 1, p. 400). This was the goddess Yah of the *Akan* of Ancient Egypt and the *Nziman* and *Ahanta* people, the hypothetical Sumerians. In the discussion of *Sumerian* religion, the same goddess *Yah* was the goddess that Durant identified as *Ea*, perhaps to make her different from the *Afrim* god *Yah*. This again is one of the results of the traditional biblical influence on western scholarship.

From Yah to Yahveh, Goddess to God

The unique gods and goddesses the *Akan* people created in Ancient Egypt were adopted and worshipped by almost all the people in the entire geographical area of Canaan and beyond.

Even outsiders of this geographical area adopted and worshipped these *Akan* gods and goddesses when they came to know them. In an earlier chapter, I pointed out how the ancient Romans became fascinated with these Ancient Egyptian gods and so-called "cults." A major example was the Greek and Roman adoption of these gods and goddesses. In the same manner, the *Akan* goddess of Thursday known as *Yah,* was adopted and worshipped by almost all the ancient people in the entire geographical area, but she was not a Canaanite goddess as western scholars have asserted. She was an *Akan* goddess that was worshipped by all the *Akan* and other tribal groups that came in contact with the *Akan* people and their religion in ancient times.

How did this goddess come to be? This is a question the modern descendants of the ancient *Afrim* people that came to adopt this goddess as their deity cannot answer. However, we in Africa can reveal how this goddess and other goddesses and gods came to be. The ancient *Akan* people that lived from Ancient Egypt to the region now called Canaan and far beyond, created a deity, a god and a goddess for each day of the week. This concept originated from an ancient *Akan* religious belief that a person born on any particular day comes into the world with the spirit and personality traits of the day. This concept was personified and male and female deities were created and named after the days of the week. The spirit and personality traits of the days were conferred on these deities and soon it was also believed that a person born on any particular day took on the spirit and traits of these gods and goddesses. Consequently, the very first name the ancient *Akan* child received was the spiritual name of the god or goddess of the day on which he or she was born. This ancient religious belief was designed into a permanent religious culture that the *Akan* people in Africa still practice. All *Akan* people still practice giving the names of their ancient gods and goddesses to their children to this day. I have one.

How else do we know that *Yah* was an *Akan* goddess? In the first place, historical evidence has shown that the ancient *Afrim* people took to worshipping all the gods and goddesses they were introduced to in Ancient Egypt. In the second place, the *Akan* people were the most dominant Ancient Egyptians that invented the concept of religion and its attendant gods. The great god and goddess of Ancient Egypt, *Osoro* [Osiris] and Isis [*Asaase*] were the creations of the *Akan* people and they created other lesser gods like the gods and goddesses of the days of the week to serve the great *Osoro* and *Asaase*. Moreover, modern *Akan* people still acknowledge these ancient gods of the days of the week in a more cultural than religious manner. I have already revealed that the Afrim people named their earliest god in the Akan language. *Adonai,* the ancient *Afrim* people's name for God was *Akan* meaning the rare lovable one.

Among the *Akan* people of Ancient Egypt, the goddess of Thursday was called *Yah*. The *Akan* people still call this goddess of Thursday *Yah* and they still believe *Asaase* [Isis] is the major deity of Thursday so they call earth, *Asaase Yah*. It was this goddess that western historians supposedly found among the ancient Sumerians, and it was this same goddess that they believe the *Afrim* people supposedly took from some people in Canaan. The ancient *Afrim* people did not adopt and worship the goddess *Yah* from any Canaanites. They knew and took this goddess from the Ancient Egyptian tribes from which they originated. The worship of this goddess became popular among the ancient *Afrim* people only when they found out that this goddess was revered and worshipped outside Ancient Egypt in far foreign lands.

How then did the *Akan* goddess *Yah* become the Christian God *Yahweh?* The answer is simple, sexist, and it can be confirmed through ancient *Akan* religious beliefs and modern *Akan* religious and cultural practice. Ancient *Akan* religious beliefs and practices considered females spiritually unclean because of menstruation and childbirth. Incidentally, the *Afrim* people of the Exodus also believed in the same sexist ideas about women. This belief was so strong among ancient *Akan* people that even today, *Akan* women in menstruation do not come near the king, cook for him, or even go into a house where a throne is kept. This are some of the reasons I argued that Abraham's wife could not have easily ended up in the house of the pharaoh as the biblical narrative wanted us to believe.

The core of the ancient *Afrim* people that left the *Akan* people in Ancient Egypt knew this. As a result, the all-male religious leaders of the ancient *Afrim* people felt uncomfortable adopting and worshipping a goddess. They simply decided to adopt and worship the male god of Thursday instead of the goddess. The *Akan* name of the male god of Thursday was *Yaw* and it is still *Yaw* among modern *Akan* people. What made this sexist adoption easier was the fact that both god and goddess were deities of the same day so it was simple switching from the female to the male God. *Yah* simply became *Yaw* and then it was later transposed for the Greeks as *Yahweh,* a direct derivation from the *Akan* name *Yaw.*

As far as I am aware, I am the first African, specifically *Akan* scholar to reveal the origin of the Christian God in ancient *Akan* Gods. However, I am not the first scholar to reveal this information. In the 1930s, a European priest who went to live among the *Akan* people in West Africa found close relationship between *Akan* and Hebrew religious thinking, practices, beliefs, and culture. To this priest, the evidence was so overwhelming that it confirmed the origin of the Hebrew God in the *Akan* God. In his book entitled *Hebrewisms of West Africa*, Catholic Father S. J. Williams revealed through linguistic studies that the supposed Hebrew name *Yahweh* originated from the *Akan* word *Nyame*, God. The name of his book is quite revealing. How could *Hebrewisms* be found in as far away a place as in West Africa when Hebrews lived in Canaan in ancient times and in Europe in modern times?

Rev. Dr. Williams did not only find characteristics of Hebrew language, culture, and religious thinking among the *Akan* people in West Africa, but also he even showed that the ancient *Afrim* people and the *Akan* people must have spoken the same language at a point in time. This tends to confirm what Greenberg and I pointed out that the people that left Ancient Egypt in the so-called biblical Exodus spoke Ancient Egyptian language that I revealed to be the *Akan* language. I introduced the evidence that this was the reason these people named themselves, their towns, God, and nation in the *Akan* language.

In Father Williams' linguistic analysis, the *Akan* word for God, *Nyame* was what became *Yahweh,* the Jewish word for God. In English orthography, there is no 'ny' consonant combination. As a result, to Father Williams, the *Akan* word *Nyame* was *Yame*. According to Father Williams therefore, the only difference between the *Akan* word for God and the ancient *Afrim* word for God is in orthographic transposition of one alphabet. He argued that the only change between the two words was that the *M* in the *Akan* word *Nyame* became the *W* in the ancient *Afrim* word *Yahweh*. I have already revealed that it was the *Akan* God of Thursday known as *Yaw* that became the name of the Christian God *Yahweh*. However, the explanation of Rev. Dr. Williams is quite brilliant. It is fascinating to note that through linguistics and the cultural history of the *Akan* people there is evidence that the Jewish word Yahweh originated from an Akan word and concept. The most important point to note here is that my discussion of everything surrounding the Bible is around the *Akan* people of Ancient Egypt. Perhaps to confirm it all a Christian scholar that went to live among modern *Akan* people in West African has also found evidence confirming what I have been revealing in this work.

Rev. Dr. Williams' findings in West Africa is very significant because it confirms the biblical and historical revelations I have made in earlier chapters, and they also confirm the revelations I am going to make in coming chapters. From ancient *Akan* religious and cultural practices, I have shown where the Hebrew God *Yahweh* came from, and from his studies among the *Akan* people Father Williams also confirmed the origin of the Hebrew and therefore the Christian God in the *Akan* language and people. Father Williams assumed, however, that the name *Yahweh* was originally an ancient *Afrim* word, but it originated from the name *Yaw,* the name of the ancient *Akan* male God of Thursday.

Will Durant and many western historians and biblical scholars have suggested that the ancient *Afrim* people took the name of the goddess *Yah* and simply changed it to *Yahweh,* but they have never been able to explain why and how such a change came about. From this discussion, it becomes clear that *the Afrim god that became the Christian Yahweh was the Akan*

God of Thursday taken from the Akan people in Ancient Egypt. This revelation is profound because it means the African God that Christian Europe condemned as pagan was the same God whose name was simply transposed for Europeans. It is even more profound because it also shows that the Catholic Church's and later Protestants' usage of paganism to authorize, support, and propagate the enslavement of Africans was without basis.

It is important that such information comes out at the beginning of this new millennium because religious ignorance and intolerance has led to meaningless squabbles, hatred, bigotry, and prejudice. Such ignorance and intolerance have divided the religious world into warring factions waiting for the opportunity to fight and kill each other because of differing religious perspectives and sacramental practices honoring *the same God.* For example, in the past thousand years, the opposing armies have changed, but people are still fighting the Crusades over the same ignorant religious reasons today and that in my view is senseless and it should stop.

My family and I experienced the worst of religious ignorance when we moved to a new State and city. We were looking for a place to worship and my wife and daughter visited a Baptist Church. They did not know that it was an exclusive white Baptist Church. The day after my family visited this church; two deacons called on us in our home to welcome us into the community. As part of the welcome, they stated that they would love for us to attend their church, but some people in the church do not accept black people that well so it would be better if we looked for another church. The message was plain. Since then, however, what has bothered me is how Europeans would take black people's God, theosophical ideas, documents, and sacramental practices of worshipping and then turn around to claim that black people cannot worship this God with them in their churches for the simple reason that we are black? Only ignorance can lead humans to such a low spiritual level.

Our perception and respect for each other as humans have deteriorated into factors of who, what, where, when, and how we worship *this same God.* I think it is time for all religions to know that the God these religions have fought over as the truest and purest of all Gods is the same God that was imagined, created, personified, and worshipped by the ancient *Akan* people in Egypt for thousands of years before this God was introduced to Europeans and the rest of the world. In another example, if the *Akan* people do not reveal that the *Akan* name *Oboda* meaning creator of the day was what became *Buddha* in the Eastern lands who would ever know? Not only are the images of this religious leader Negroid in features but even today, the priests of Buddha still put on their clothes in the fashion of the ancient *Akan* priests that went to introduce them to religion.

In the hands of Europeans, this God has turned into a God of hatred, prejudice, and bigotry. As Montesquieu pointed out, "There has never been a kingdom inclined to so many civil wars as the kingdom of Christ." Christians have sought to justify every element of their human failures in this God and biblical documents that were not originally intended to be used as such. The original God of the *Akan* people did not hate black and Jewish people because he was black people's God. He did not hate white people because he was a God of all people. He did not hate the so-called sinners because they were all his children. He did not differentiate and hate or kill bi- or homosexuals because they were all "his children." The original God was not designed to be known by only a few people who would turn the whole concept of knowing him into money-making empires either.

I think it is time for the religious world to know that all the perceptions of God in every religion on this earth originated from the same source and imagination. That source and imagination was the *Akan* people of Ancient Egypt. Just giving this God different names in different languages such as **Nyame, God, Allah,** and many others, and interpreting and practicing religion in different ways do not make any one's perception of this God any better, more superior, holier, or different from other peoples' perception of this same God. They all originated from the same imagination, and that was the so-called "pagan" imagination.

220

Modern cultural evidence of the origin of the Christian God in the Akan Gods

The revelation of the origin of the Christian God in the *Akan* God Yahweh can be confirmed in the linguistic and cultural practices of the *Akan* people to this day. This is because the *Akan* people still name their children after these ancient Gods and Goddesses of the days of the week. This can be easily verified from the *Akan* people in Ghana. All *Akan* children have the same names of the Gods of the days on which they were born. Below are the names of modern *Akan* children as they correspond with the names of the ancient *Akan* Gods and Goddesses of the days of the week.

Days	Boys' names	Girls' names
Monday	Kwadjo	Adjoa
Tuesday	Kwabena	Abena
Wednesday	Kwaku	Akua
Thursday	Yaw	Yah
Friday	Kofi	Afua
Saturday	Kwame	Amma
Sunday	Kwasi	Akosua

When I named my daughter who was born on Monday *Adjoa,* I explained to my wife why the child was naturally and spiritually a Goddess of Monday. My wife was baffled and she wondered at the millions of *Akan* girls and women who would be carrying the same name *Adjoa,* and yes millions do. The *Akan* people have not abandoned the reverence of their ancient Gods and Goddesses of the days. Today, the most important *Akan* celebrations and reverence to the Gods of the days are the celebrations of the male Gods of Wednesday – *Wukudae* - and Sunday – *Akwasidae.*

Interestingly, there is historical evidence to show that the worship of these *Akan* Gods and Goddesses were practiced far and wide in the geographical area surrounding Ancient Egypt. Nebuchadnezzar of Babylon also worshipped an *Akan* Goddess of the day. Such evidence is revealed in the fact that King Nebuchadnezzar of Babylon built himself a shrine called the *Shrine of Ekua* at Esagila (see Lloyd Graham, 1995, p. 225). Among the *Akan* gods and goddesses of the days of the week, *Akua* or *Ekua* was the name of the goddess of Wednesday, and it is still the *Akan* name of the girls and women of this Wednesday goddess.

The biblical sequence of the history of the *Afrim* people shows that these people did not take the god Yahweh anywhere but from the *Akan* people in Ancient Egypt. Evidence of this is in the biblical narrative that tells us that *Yahweh* gave the *Afrim* people the *Ten Commandments.* Moses' reception of the *Commandments* was very early in the Exodus and long before the *Afrim* people found a place to settle in Canaan. This means the *Afrim* people knew of *Yahweh,* and this god existed in the lives and imaginations of the *Afrim* people on their way into the Exodus and before they got to Canaan. If the *Afrim* people knew of the God Yahweh early in the Exodus and

221

before they got to Canaan and they were going to Canaan from Ancient Egypt then it is very clear where they learned about and took this God. Moreover, if *Yahweh* was the God that would not let the *Afrim* people near him even when he was supposedly saving them from bondage in Egypt then *Yahweh* as the God of the father of Moses was an Ancient Egyptian God and not an *Afrim* people's God as they later claimed. Consequently, the historical assertion that the *Afrim* people adopted the Canaan god *Yahweh* as their own is false. The *Akan* people of Ancient Egypt worshipped the gods and goddess of the days long before the *Afrim* people went to Egypt. Since the *Afrim* people did not bring this god to Egypt but they knew of him when they were leaving Egypt, the only place they could have become aware and adopted this God was in Ancient Egypt and not Canaan.

Designing Yahweh as a god of the Afrim people

Evidence of other people's myths and folklore in the biblical narrative shows that one thing the ancient *Afrim* scholars of the Bible did quite well was to take other people's Gods, stories, beliefs, and ideas and make them their own. There is biblical and historical evidence that the ancient *Afrim* people went to great lengths to redesign *Yahweh* to their liking and in their own image. If *Yahweh* were an indigenous *Afrim* god, it would not have been necessary for the *Afrim* people to redesign him to suit what the *Afrim* people required in their God. However, the *Afrim* people took this *Akan* God, renamed him *Yahweh*, and personalized him in the image of a God of the *Afrim* people, a God that would fight for the *Afrim* people against all enemies. They needed a fighting God to survive in a belligerent world in those ancient times.

Consequently, as historians and biblical scholars have observed, the *Afrim* people redesigned this Yahweh to make him as human in personification and characterization as humans come in every aspect of our beings. The personification of *Yahweh* into an *Afrim* God with human thoughts, actions, biases, feelings, and humanity can be seen in Genesis 31:11-12; Genesis 28; Exodus 7; Exodus12: 7; Exodus13; 23:19; Exodus 33:23; Exodus 15:3; Exodus 23:27-30; Exodus 14:18; Exodus 20:5-6; Exodus 32:11-14; Exodus 20:5; 34:14; 23:24; 1 Kings 20:23; 2 Samuel 22:35; Leviticus 25:23; Numbers 14:13-18; Deuteronomy 38:16-28). All of these were possible because the concept of God is an imagination so anybody could design a God to suit his or her own whims and whimsicals.

An interesting question that arises with the knowledge of the source of *Afrim* people's God is, was *Yahweh* a monotheist God? No, the *Afrim* people were not monotheists and *Yahweh* was not a monotheist God. It may surprise many Christians to know that *Yahweh* was not the only God of the *Afrim* people, and the cult of *Yahweh* was not the only cult in the lives of the ancient *Afrim* people. Later, the *Afrim* people sought to make *Yahweh* their principal deity but that was not easy because they left Ancient Egypt with several Gods other than *Yahweh*.

Biblical records show that before they got to Canaan, the *Afrim* people had many Gods and *Yahweh* knew that he was not the only God in the lives of the *Afrim* people. The evidence that *Yahweh* was not the only God of the *Afrim* people and that *Yahweh* also knew that he was not the only God in the lives of the *Afrim* people can be seen in *Exodus*. This was the main reason in the first *Commandment Yahweh* supposedly gave to the *Afrim* people, he asked them to abandon all other Gods and put him above all others because he was a jealous God (Exodus 20: 2-5). *Yahweh* asked the ancient *Afrim* people to have no other gods before him. He asked them not to make any other images of any Gods. Yahweh asked the *Afrim* people not to bow down before any other Gods. Yahweh would not have commanded the *Afrim* people not to do all these if he were the only God in the lives of the *Afrim* people. How then can the *Afrim* people claim to have created monotheism, when they were not monotheists themselves?

The concept of *Afrim* people's God that can be gleaned from the first commandment is the same pyramidal polytheist concept of God that was the foundation of Ancient Egyptian polytheism. In this pyramidal polytheist concept of God, there is one supreme God at the top of the pyramid and several other Gods in ascending power and reverence from the base of the pyramid to the top. In Exodus 20:11 and 23:11, the song of Moses acknowledged this pyramidal polytheist perception of God of the ancient *Afrim* people by saying: *Who is like unto thee, O Lord, among the gods?*" Solomon the Temple builder said: Great is our god above all other gods (see 2 Chronicles 2:5). This shows that there were other gods and that reflects the pyramidal polytheist perception of God of the *Afrim* people as they took it from Ancient Egypt.

In *Lectures on the Science of Language*, Max Müller called the recognition of one supreme God while acknowledging other Gods the practice of **henotheism** (see 1866, Vol. 2). The God that is now the Christian *Yahweh* was an *Akan* cult before he became the Canaanite cult of the Afrim people. He was this God that the *Afrim* people introduced to the Greeks and Europeans, and the *Akan* God of Thursday *Yaw* became the Christian God *Yahweh*. Even among the *Afrim* people, *Yahweh* was not superior to other gods though many sought to make him superior, and *Yahweh* himself wanted to be made the superior God. How then is the Christian God different from the original "pagan" God that it had been for thousands of years before Christians knew about him? How is the Christian God from the same imagination and origin superior to the Gods of other lands?

It was from knowledge of all these that in the Preface to the *Deceptions and Myths of the Bible*, Lloyd Graham wrote boldly that:

> There is nothing "holy" about the Bible, nor is it "the word of God." It was not written by God-inspired saints, but by power-seeking priests. Who but priests consider sin the paramount issue? Who but priests write volumes of religious rites and rituals? ... By this intellectual tyranny they sought to gain control, and they achieved it. By 400 B. C. they were the masters of ancient Israel. For so great a project they needed a theme, a framework, and this they found in the Creation lore of more knowledgeable races. ... The Bible is, as we assert, but priest-perverted cosmology (p. 1).

Unfortunately, Graham has also been misled by the biblical assertion of the people that wrote the Bible. These people did not write the documents of the Bible in search of power. They wrote these documents in support of the strong beliefs they had in Ancient Egyptian religion.

The biblical tradition and historians have stated and written a lot about the religion of the *Afrim* people after the Exodus, but there is evidence in these sources to show that much of what the biblical account asserted and historians wrote to support is false. Will Durant pointed out that the *Afrim* people personified *Yahweh* so much that he was more human than a god because he was "greedy, irascible, bloodthirsty, capricious, petulant," and he was not an omniscient God (p. 310). For example, according to the Exodus narrative, this God could not differentiate between the homes of the *Afrim* people from the homes of the Egyptians in the events leading to the Exodus. As a result, he asked that the *Afrim* people mark their homes with the blood of a lamb else he could be mistaken and he might kill the first born of the *Afrim* people while he was seeking to kill the first born of the Ancient Egyptians. This God approved of the most repugnant brutalities as long as it served the good of the *Afrim* people. For example, he ordered Moses to kill many *Afrim* men because they "committed whoredom" with Moabite women. Worse than that, this God supposedly asked Moses to hang the dead bodies of the men he had killed up "before the Lord against the sun" (see Numbers 25:4). In another instance of the brutality of *Yahweh,* it is said that the Ark of the Covenant was not supposed to be touched by any human. However, when the pious Uzzah prevented the Ark from falling into mud he held it momentarily in his hands, and it is said this God supposedly killed him (see 2 Samuel 6:7; 1 Chronicles 6:10).

In the hands of the *Afrim* people, *Yahweh* professed to be merciful to those who loved him and obey his wishes, but he would punish children even for the sins of their fathers, grandfathers, and even great-great-grandfathers. *Yahweh* was personalized to be an unforgiving God. In the events of the Exodus, he thought of destroying all the **Afrim** people for worshipping the Golden Calf. This confirms that the *Afrim* people did not adopt this God when they got to Canaan, instead, they took this God from Ancient Egypt. While pleading for the *Afrim* people before this God, Moses once told *Yahweh* to control his temper and "repent of this evil against thy people" (Exodus 32:11-14). In this instance, it was Moses the human telling this God that it was evil to destroy the *Afrim* people.

When the *Afrim* people rebelled against Moses, *Yahweh* again decided to annihilate all of them. Again Moses pleaded with *Yahweh* to control his temper and change his mind by asking him to think of what other people would say if they heard of such a terrible thing (see Numbers 14:13-18). Abraham also had his opportunity to teach this God mercy and morality when he asked him not to destroy Sodom and Gomorrah if there were even ten good people in these cities. Is this human-designed God not the same as the God the Ancient Egyptians imagined, created, personified, and worshipped for thousands of years before the *Afrim* people supposedly went to Ancient Egypt?

Again Durant pointed out that before Isaiah, the *Afrim* people even never thought of *Yahweh* as the God of all the *Afrim* tribes. In other words, before Isaiah, *Yahweh* was not the God of all the *Afrim* people. They had other gods beside him. Durant wrote:

> Not only was Tammuz accepted as a real god by all but the most educated Jews, but this cult was at one time so popular in Judea that Ezekiel complained that the ritual wailing for Tammuz' death could be heard in the Temple (Ezekiel 8:14, Durant, p. 312).

Which God was *Tammuz* and where did he come from? According to Durant, *Tammuz* was the name of one of the Sumerian kings in the kings' list of the priest–historians of Sumeria. How the king of an ancient civilization became a God of another group of people is unknown. However, Durant continues that the legend of Tammuz "passed down into the pantheon of Babylon and became the Adonis of Greeks" (1935, p. 120). Remember that the name of the Greek god *Adonis* was derived from the *Akan* epithet for God *Adona* that was taken by the *Afrim* people as *Adonai*.

Concerning *Tammuz*, it must be pointed out that the ritual of wailing for *Tammuz* is still a religious practice in Judaism. The object of the wailing must have easily shifted from *Tammuz* to modern *Yahweh* because they were both from the same sources. Nevertheless, there is today a Wailing Wall in Jeruslem and it is considered a holy place.

Even in the time of Jeremiah, many *Afrim* cities and communities had their own Gods as confirmed in "according to the number of thy cities are thy gods, O Judah" and the prophet chastised his people for worshiping even Baal and Moloch (see Jeremiah 2:28; 32:35).

In *Deceptions and Myths of the Bible* , Llyod Graham wrote mordantly about European ignorance and acceptance of religion without questioning its source or who invented it. He wrote:

> Literally, the priestly account of creation is but kindergarten cosmology, yet we [Europeans] have accepted it for two thousand years. This is because western man is incapable of abstract thought. All the metaphysical and cosmological knowledge western man has came to him from the East. The ancient Orientals were capable of such thought but not western man, and this includes the Jews. In his metaphysical incompetence western man puts the stamp of his own ego on everything, including the Creator. Now blinded by his own error, he cannot see that it is only that part of the race incapable of abstract thought that believes in his anthropomorphic creation. That part of him called Christian could not even create a God or religion for itself; it had to borrow these from Middle Eastern Jews. ... In spite of their pretended intimacy with the Creator, the Jews never had knowledge of things cosmic and metaphysical; they were but plagiarists culling mythic artifacts they did not understand (1995, p.2).

How did this God become the God the *Afrim* people introduced to Europeans? The pagan God *Yahweh* had to go through a transformation to become the Christian *Yahweh*. Durant pointed that out too:

The authors of the Pentateuch, to whom religion was an instrument of statesmanship, formed this Vulcan into Mars, so that in their energetic hands Yahveh became predominantly an imperialistic, expansionist God of Hosts, who fights for his people as fiercely as the gods of Iliad (1935, p. 310).

He stated further that:

With the growth of political unity under David and Solomon, and the centering of worship in the Temple at Jerusalem, theology reflected history and politics, and Yahveh became the sole god of the Jews (1935, p. 312).

How monotheist did the *Afrim* religion and people become at this time? Durant answers by stating that:

Beyond this "henotheism" they made no further progress towards monotheism until the Prophets [though Elisha had spoken of one God as early as the 9th century B. C. (see 2 Kings 5:15)]. Even in the Yahvistic stage the Hebraic religion came closer to monotheism than any other pre-Prophetic faith except the ephemeral sun-worship of Ikhnaton [Akan :Akenten] (1935, p. 312).

Major characteristics of the Afrim god

Durant pointed out that virtue and the avoidance of sin was the central tenets of *Afrim* religion at all times. This should not be surprising because virtue and the avoidance of sin were the foundational tenets of Ancient Egyptian religion. The Ancient Egyptian foundation of religion was that the Gods would punish for sins and reward virtue. What is intriguing about these is that the modern descendants of Ancient Egyptians in Africa still believe in these religious practices. In the popular African novel *Things Fall Apart* when Chinua Achebe wrote the phrase: *"Amadiora will break your neck"* he was revealing the beliefs of a people in the responsibilities of their Gods as the protectors of virtue and the castigators of sin. The earliest recorded evidence of the centrality of virtue and avoidance of sin in religion can be found in the *Ancient Egyptian Book of the Dead*.

In ancient *Afrim* religion, there was no Hell as a place of eternal punishment for sins committed in one's lifetime. This is because the concept of heaven and hell are relatively more recent European interpretations and adaptations of the *Ancient Egyptian Book of the Dead*. However, in ancient *Afrim* religion, there was a "land of darkness" where all dead people regardless of sins congregated. In ancient *Afrim* religion, sinners received their punishment in this life and not after death; and there was no reference in any aspect of ancient *Afrim* religion to immortality or life after death. The congregation of the dead in the "land of darkness" was also an Ancient Egyptian belief that can also be found in the *Book of the Dead*. This was the belief that was designed into the story of Jesus and Christians still believe he is coming back from the dead. All of these were taken out of Ancient Egyptian foundations of religion and passed into Christianity.

In ancient *Afrim* religion, sin could be atoned with prayers or sacrifice. In earliest times, this sacrifice or atonement began as actual human sacrifice. In the *Afrim* religion, this sacrifice involved sacrificing and burning one's children as the ultimate plea for atonement from the Gods. This religious ritual of atonement is reflected in Abraham taking his son Isaac into the wilderness to sacrifice him to his God. The subtle hint to change this religious ritual from human sacrifice to the sacrifice of herds was also given in the story of Abraham and his son.

With time, these rituals of atonement changed from human sacrifice to animal sacrifice, and it changed again to simple offering of first fruits of flocks and then to the first fruits of food from the fields. From this stage, the rituals of atonement changed again to become prayer, praise, and the simple request for forgiveness. Again, all these stages of sacrifice and atonement can be traced to the religious history of the *Akan* and other tribal groups now in Africa. Among these people in Africa, the offering of the first fruits of the field is still celebrated in special socio-religious festivals like the *Homowo, Ohum, Kwafie,* and many others.

Among the ancient *Afrim* people, circumcision was seen as the ultimate sacrifice of a part of a man's body. Menstruation and childbirth were perceived as spiritually unclean and that required the sacrificial intervention of priests on behalf of women. All these are still *Akan* cultural and religious beliefs, especially beliefs surrounding modern kingship. From the growth of the complexity of *Afrim* people's religion, a class that was knowledgeable in magic and rituals of the Gods had to arise as the group that was capable of approaching and intervening with the Gods on behalf of humans. This group was the priesthood. Just as it was in Ancient Egypt where the *Afrim* people learned the religious importance of the priesthood, the priests of the *Afrim* people were the custodians of the repository of religious knowledge. They were the only ones who supposedly knew how to pray, sacrifice, and explain the rituals and mysteries of *Afrim* religion properly. They were therefore a very powerful group over the people. Modern *Akan* people still have priests that perform the same roles as the priests of the ancient **Afrim** people. The *Akan* people call their priests *Akomfo.*

According to Durant, despite the emergence and growth of the priesthood and the religious education they gave the *Afrim* people, the people still believed in superstitions and practiced idolatry.

> The hill-tops and groves continued to harbor alien gods and to witness secret rites, a substantial minority of the [Jewish] people prostrated themselves before sacred stones, or worshipped Baal or Astarte, or practiced divination in the Babylonian manner, or setup images and burned incense to them, or knelt before the brazen serpent or the Golden Calf, or filled the Temple with the noise of heathen feasting, or made their children pass through the fires in sacrifice; even some of the kings, like Solomon and Ahab, went 'a-whoring' after foreign gods (see Isaiah 28:7; Judges 8:33; 9:27; 2Kings 17:9-12, 16-17; 23:10-13; Lamentations 2:7; Ezekiel 16:21; 23:37; Isaiah 57:5).

As a result, religious purists like Elijah and Elisha who were not trained priests rose up to speak against *Afrim* people's wanton practice of superstition and idolatry. From this theosophical decadence of the *Afrim* people emerged social decadence in which most *Afrim* people went after riches without any thought to or guidance from morality. The rich among the *Afrim* attained their richness through exploitation, political corruption, money lending, and usury. This soon led to the emergence of two classes of ancient *Afrim* people. These classes were the poor and the rich and that led to the earliest development of slums of poor people among the *Afrim*. It was around this time of social, political, and religious decadence that the earliest of the biblical prophets supposedly emerged.

Who were the biblical prophets?

The prophets Christian Europe believes wrote the biblical documents were nothing more than socio-political consciences that emerged during the decadent periods in the history of the *Afrim* people. These people were not trained priests and they were not known to be part of the cream of scholars of the *Afrim* people. They were mere spokespersons against the moral decadence of the *Afrim* people. The Gods did not inspire the prophets and neither did the Gods put words into their mouths. There is no evidence that they wrote any thesis of their propagations. The consciences that emerged in the form of prophets sought to use religion to appeal to the morality of the *Afrim* people. That is how they became attached to the history of *Afrim* religion.

According to historians, after the death of Solomon, the social, political, and religious differences that emerged among the *Afrim* people was so great that it contributed to the breaking of the then *Afrim* nation into two kingdoms. The Northern Kingdom with Samaria as its capital was originally known as *Ephraim* but this name was later changed to *Israel*. The southern kingdom with the capital in Jerusalem became Judah or Judea. It was in this era of political divisions and social and religious decadence that the prophets emerged. Some of these prophets were fortune-tellers and diviners. According to Durant,

> ...some were fanatics who worked themselves into a frenzy by weird music, strong drink, or devilish-like dances, and spoke, in trances, words which their hearers considered inspired – i.e., breathed into them by some spirit other than their own (see Cambridge Ancient History, v. iii, p. 458-9; see also Sir J. G. Frazer, Adonis, Attis, Osiris, 1907, p. 66).

What is fascinating about such descriptions of the biblical prophets is the fact that I grew up among the *Akan* people and saw all these among the *Akan* people. These fortune-tellers, diviners, moralists, and purists are still among the *Akan* and many other tribes in Africa. Just as modern *Akans* that are converted to Christianity speak of these people with scorn, so did the prophet Jeremiah speak of these so-called prophets with disdain and referred to them as "every man that is mad, and maketh himself a prophet" (see Jeremiah 29:26). Could these people be the deeply religious people that wrote the holy books of the Old Testament?

In *The Passing of the Empires*, Gaston Maspero pointed out that some of these prophets were hermits like Elijah, some lived in schools and monasteries but many were normal people with wives, families, and property (1900, p. 783). From these beginnings, the *Afrim* prophets developed into recognized critics of their times. As Durant warned:

> We misunderstand them if we take them as prophets in the weather sense; their predictions were hopes or threats, or pious interpolations or prognostications after the event; the Prophets themselves did not pretend to foretell, so much as to speak out; they were eloquent members of the Opposition. ... Amos described himself not as a prophet but as a simple village shepherd (1935, p. 316).

From this quotation, it is evident that Amos described himself as a poor village shepherd who might not have had the religious education of even a lay priest. He might not have been even literate, yet the *Afrim* scholars of the Bible attributed one of the books they took from Ancient Egypt to him as the Book of Amos. However, I do not intend to belabor this issue because the very name Amos was derived from an *Akan* name.

The *Afrim* people called these prophets *Nabi* and Durant pointed out that "the men to whom the Hebrew *Nabi* was first applied were not quite of the character that our reverence would associate Amos and Isaiah" (1935, p. 315).

A major characteristic of the prophets and their prophecies was the fact that these prophets knew that the *Afrim* people were not listening to them. As a result, they began putting their words into the mouths of the Gods to give their words credibility and surround this credibility with the aura and perception that their prognostications were not their own words and ideas but the words and ideas of the Gods. In this sense, the Gods did not inspire the *Afrim* prophets; instead the prophets sought to inspire the Gods and beseeched them to act in support of their prognostications.

Most of what the prophets proclaimed was obvious ends that were predictable. Amos predicted the destruction of Israel and it came true (see Amos 5-6; 3:12, 15). Hosea predicted the destruction of Judah and it also came true (see Hosea 8:6-7). Isaiah predicted the fall of the Northern Kingdom (Isaiah 7:8). What most of the prophets spoke about was a futuristic utopiac idealism for which all humans have been striving since the dawn of humanity and we are still striving for these ideals. According to biblical historians, the events these prophets spoke and wrote about came to pass in the destruction of Israel, Judah, and events after the exile. As a result, it is most likely that the compilers and translators of the documents of the Bible must have sought to reinterpret their words and embellish these prophets to make them more than they really were.

Today, we are still striving for this Utopiac idealism so the words of these prophets seem still appropriate. It was from such socio-political perspectives that the biblical prophets

227

supposedly emerged to be perceived as God–inspired preachers whose words must be heeded as the words of the Gods. The question is did these so-called prophets write the Books of the Old Testament, and why did they have mostly *Akan* and other African tribal names?

What actually changed in the passing of the theosophical ideas and sacramental practices of Ancient Egypt into Christianity was the changing of the writing of the name of God from gods to a God with a capital "G."

What has been the legacy of these prophets to modern times? Durant summarizes by saying:

> It was upon the Judaism of post-Exilic days, and upon the world through Judaism and Christianity, that the Prophets left their deepest mark. In Amos and Isaiah is the beginning of both Christianity and socialism, the spring from which has flowed a stream of Utopias wherein no poverty or war shall disturb human brotherhood and peace; they are the source of the early Jewish conception of a Messiah who would seize the government, reestablish the temporal power of the Jews, and inaugurate a dictatorship of the dispossessed among mankind. Isaiah and Amos began, in a military age, the exaltation of those virtues of simplicity and gentleness, of cooperation and friendliness, which Jesus was to make a vital element in his creed. They were the first to undertake the heavy task of reforming the God of Hosts into a God of Love, they conscripted Yahveh for humanitarianism as the radicals of the nineteenth century conscripted Jesus for socialism. It was they who when the Bible was printed in Europe, fired the Germanic mind with a rejuvenated Christianity, and lighted the torch of the Reformation; it was their fierce and intolerant virtue that formed the Puritans (1935, p. 320).

Most of the early prophets of the *Afrim* people supposedly did not leave any records. The authors of the history of the *Afrim* people wrote in the *Britannica* that:

> These early prophets while they were spirited fighters and spokesmen for Yahweh and resolutely combated Israelite idolatry, left behind no writings of their own and are known only from the historical books of the Bible (1996, p. 73).

However, the writings of Amos, Hosea, Micah, and Isaiah who lived in the 8th century B. C. survived and they are part of the biblical documents. The appeal of the prophets to many *Afrim* people of the time was not because they pretended to be the spokespersons of the Gods but because they offered consolation for the poor and a hope of damnation for the rich.

In the discussion in this chapter, I have shown that the biblical origin of the ancient *Afrim* people that became the Jews and Hebrews in Europe is false because there is no historical, archaeological, racial, ethnic, linguistic, or cultural evidence to support it. Instead, there is more than enough evidence of their origin in Ancient Egyptian and *Akan* history, language, and culture.

I pointed out that there are two versions of the history of modern *Afrim* people and none of these versions support each other. Instead, the real history of modern *Afrim* people is derived from their false biblical history. This has turned the biblical and real history of modern *Afrim* people into a form of clever circular reasoning that makes many people think they confirm each other or they are true, but they are not. I introduced readers to modern speculations about the origin of *Afrim* people in the Khazar people. However, the question that still has not been answered is who were the *Afrim* before they supposedly became Khazars?

I also pointed out that the biblical claim that modern *Afrim* people came from the line of one Abraham also supports the fact that these people were black people because this Abraham came from the *Akan* tribe that was at *Adiabene*. I showed that these people are not originally Semites because a speculating anthropologist and his friend conferred that name on them. Finally, I introduced genetic evidence that links modern *Afrim* people to one of the tribes in Africa from which some of modern *Afrim* people originated.

Perhaps more importantly, I have, from the beginning of this work, linked the descendants of ancient *Afrim* people who are the modern Jews and Hebrews to real people and I continue to produce evidence to prove this link. From the beginning of this work, I introduced visual and scholastic evidence to show that the people of the Bible were black people and that Christian Europe has known this for almost as long as Christianity has been introduced to Europe. I linked the ancient *Afrim* people to the Ancient Egyptians. Among the Ancient Egyptians, I introduced the *Akan* people and other African tribes and asserted that these were the people and the tribes from which the ancient *Afrim* people that are the modern Jews and Hebrews originated.

I also pointed out that the majority of the people that left Ancient Egypt into the biblical Exodus were *Akan*. These people created the Ancient Egyptian civilization and religion. In support of this I showed that the people that left in the Exodus identified themselves by the *Akan* name *Afrim*. The name of their God, *Adonai*, was derived from an *Akan* word. The name of the *Essenes* was derived from an *Akan* tribal name. The ancient name of Israel was *Ephraim*, and that was derived from the *Akan* word *Afrim*. The name of modern Israel was also derived from an *Akan* word. Modern *Afrim* people still carry *Akan* and other African tribal names and people of the Bible also carried *Akan* and other African tribal names. The question then is who are the *Akan* people that are in the center of the story of the origin of the ancient *Afrim*, modern Jewish people, and the Bible? That is what the next chapter intends to explore.

6

Who Are The Akan People?

There is no doubt about there being something real behind the churches; unfortunately, it is a long way behind

Don Marquis

By the time the world woke up to claim greatness, the Africans had done all the greatest things.

Introduction

Throughout the discussion in this book, one of the names that have always surfaced alongside the names of the *Afrim* people of the Exodus and the Jewish people of Europe has been the name of the *Akan* people. To answer the question the title of this chapter poses, the *Akan* people were the Ancient Egyptians. The *Akan* people were the tribal group that imagined, created, and developed the Ancient Egyptian civilization. This is deduced from the fact that the earliest names of the kings of the Old Kingdom continuing through almost all the kingdoms of Ancient Egypt were *Akan* names. Not only that, the dynasties of these ancient kingdoms continue to exist among the *Akan* people in West Africa to this day. What is fascinating about these revelations is that the names of the Ancient Egyptian kings of the *Akan* dynasties are still the royal names of the modern kings of these dynasties. For example, one of the earliest names on the Ancient Egyptian kings' list was *Oti*. This name has been transposed to *Iti* and other corrupt variations in Ancient Egyptian literature. The indigenous Akan tribal name of the Ancient Egyptian king *Akenten* has also been transposed to *Akhenaten* in Ancient Egyptian literature. These two names belong to the *Denkyira* Royal Dynasty. Today, the *Denkyirahene* [King of Denkyira] is known as *Oti Akenten* still carrying the name the ancient Greeks transposed to *Iti* and *Akhenaten.*

On February 24, 2000, Pope John Paul II went to modern Egypt and he was reported to have performed a ritual that occurred in the Bible in Ancient Egypt. Most people assumed that the Pope was going to modern Egypt because he was going to visit modern ancestors of Ancient Egyptians, but that was false. The Arabs that live in modern Egypt today are not the modern descendants of the Ancient Egyptians. The Arabs came to live in Egypt and occupy entire North Africa only around 600 A. D. while the history of human civilization created by African tribes in Ancient Egypt began almost six thousand years ago. What is significant about the Pope going to perform a ritual in the Bible in modern Egypt is that it recognizes the central role of the Ancient Egyptians in the Bible. Unfortunately, this biblical ritual does not recognize the ancient role of the *Akan* and other African tribes in the story behind the biblical documents because it is part of the aspects of the history behind the Bible that the early apostolic fathers of Christianity have sought to conceal.

Some scholars have suggested that if humans ever evolved from Africa, the *Akan* people must have been the first. This is because not only did these people imagine and create the greatest civilization when they settled down in Ancient Egypt but also evidence of their ancient presence can be found as far as China, Tibet, and Japan. I have already pointed out and produced the evidence that the *Akan* were the people that invented the concept of religion, its doctrines, and sacramental practices in Ancient Egypt. It was from what he observed mostly about the *Akan* people in West Africa that Reverend Father S. J. Williams wrote the book entitled *Hebrewisms in West Africa.*

From the discussion in Father Williams' book, it is evident that he found the evidence before concluding that the Hebrew people and therefore the Christian concept and name of God originated from the *Akan* people and the *Akan* language. It is important to point out that Father Williams' book confirms my revelation that the *Afrim* people that left Ancient Egypt into the so-called biblical Exodus and later went to Europe to become the Jews and Hebrews originated from the African tribes that were the Ancient Egyptians. That was the reason Father Williams could still see Hebrewisms among the African tribes in West Africa after over three thousand years of separation from the *Afrim* people. That was also the reason I could identify the *Akan* and other African tribal names among modern Jewish people in Europe and America. I would like to point out however, that the title of Father Williams' book reflects the Eurocentric perception of the issue. He saw Hebrewisms among the West Africans and not West Africanisms among the Hebrews. From this perspective, it almost sounds like they are the West Africans that have taken to Hebrewisms and not the Hebrews that took West Africanisms from the black tribes from which they originated in Ancient Egypt.

I have revealed that before the biblical patriarchs of the Jewish people went to Ancient Egypt, they were carrying Akan tribal names. This means these people were Akan people before they went to Ancient Egypt. If ever these patriarchs of the Jewish people went of Ancient Egypt from anywhere, the *Akan* were the people to whom they went in Ancient Egypt. These were the people from whom the majority of the people that left Ancient Egypt into the so-called biblical Exodus originated. The language and culture of the *Akan* people were the tribal elements that the *Afrim* people took into the Exodus. This language and culture in the lives of the people that went into the Exodus confirm this. They were these language and culture of the *Akan* and other African tribes of Ancient Egypt that Father Williams saw and made him conclude that he was seeing the Hebrew people in the West Africans. These Africans were not only central in the foundations of civilization, knowledge, and religion; they were central in the story of the Bible. Linguistic and cultural evidence shows that *Akan* people wrote the documents of the Old Testament and the transposed names of the authors confirm it.

Concealing the name of the Akan people in the history, language, and culture of the Bible

So why haven't modern western scholars found out all these? Beyond European scholars' lack of linguistic and cultural knowledge to know and understand all these there are several reasons they have never found out all these. However, perhaps the most obvious reason is that the biblical narrative is full of several deliberate compromises of historical, religious, and ethnic truths. A careful analysis of these distortions and lies shows that they were design deliberately to deceive the unsuspecting Greeks who must have assumed that they were receiving a more arcane religious knowledge and wisdom from a hitherto unknown group of people from the true "east." However, the greatest lie in the biblical narrative is about the shrouded role of the *Akan* people in the historical and theosophical lives of the *Afrim* people of the Exodus that went on to become the Jews and Hebrews in Europe.

From the centrality of the *Akan* people in Ancient Egypt, civilization, knowledge, and religion, is it possible that the so-called Jewish scholars of the Bible would not know about them in Canaan, and not even in Ancient Egypt? From the centrality of *Akan* people's language and culture among the *Afrim* people that left Ancient Egypt into the so-called biblical Exodus, is it possible that the Jewish scholars of the Bible did not know about them? Why then were the *Akan* people never mentioned in their central role in the biblical documents? Nevertheless, *Akan* is mentioned in the biblical narrative but this name did not receive the special mention it deserved. It was mentioned simply as the name of someone and not as the name of the tribe from which the majority of the *Afrim* people originated.

How could people that originated from the *Akan* tribe and left the *Akan* people in Ancient Egypt not know and mention the *Akan* people in their history? How could people that collectively identified themselves in foreign lands by the *Akan* name *Afrim* not know and mention the *Akan* people in the biblical history? How could people that took their God from the *Akan* people and named him first as *Adonai* and then as *Yahweh* in the *Akan* language not know and mention the *Akan* people in their real or biblical history? How could people that have carried *Akan* and other African tribal names for over three thousand years not know and mention the *Akan* people in their tribal and ethnic history? How could people that gave their earliest nation an *Akan* name and their modern nation still carries an *Akan* name not know and mention the *Akan* people in the biblical history?

Why would people whose prophets that supposedly wrote the Bible carry *Akan* names not know and mention the *Akan* people in the biblical history? Why did the Jewish scholars of the biblical documents not mention the *Akan* people as the people at the center of the biblical narrative? Why would people that supposedly lived in Ancient Egypt for over four hundred years fail to mention the *Akan* people among whom they lived and also fail to mention a single Ancient Egyptian king in the narrative of their history? Why would people that left Ancient Egypt with a mixed multitude of black tribes fail to mention the true name of even one of the tribes throughout the biblical narrative? Why would people that left Ancient Egypt with several black tribes change the original names of these tribes to some strange names that would be easily accepted by the Greeks but would be difficult to recognize by these tribes? So why are the *Akan* people not at the center of the biblical narrative when they were actually at the center of the history, language, and culture of this narrative?

There are two reasons for this. The first reason is the fact that if the *Akan* people and the central role they occupied in the history behind the Bible were acknowledged, the Jewish scholars of the biblical narrative would have given away the source and people from whom they were stealing the documents of the Bible. These scholars of the Bible in Alexandria wanted to claim the glory of the creation of the biblical documents so they decided to conceal the names of the people and the sources from which the documents originated so they could easily claim these documents as theirs. It was for the same reason that these scholars gave tribal groups that left Ancient Egypt into the Exodus fictitious names to make it difficult to identify these tribes later. For example, most readers of the Bible have read and therefore know the names of the Cannanites, Hittites, Amorites, Perizzites, Jebusites, and the numerous tribal groups of "ites," "vites," and "sites" in the biblical narrative. However, they have been made to believe that these people are extinct, but they are not. The names of these tribes were transposed to conceal them in the biblical narrative but the tribes are alive and well in Africa just as the descendants of the ancient *Afrim* people that later became the Jews and Hebrews of Europe are alive.

The second reason the *Akan* and other African tribes were not mentioned overtly is in the Bible. However, Europeans who do not know the history, language, and culture behind the Bible have never known it. This reason is in the part of the biblical narrative where the compilers and translators of the biblical documents made no secret of the fact that they and their people were jealous of their brother's birthright so they found dubious ways to steal it. Do you remember the story of Esau and his jealous twin brother Jacob (see Genesis 27)? The Bible says that the biblical patriarchs of the Jewish people were Abraham, Isaac, and Jacob. According to the Bible, Jacob was the younger twin brother of Esau. How could Jacob have been a patriarch of the Jewish people but his elder twin brother Esau was not? Do you know why Esau was not one of the so-called patriarchs of the *Afrim* people?

The biblical narrative of Esau and Jacob is a true allegory of what the compilers and translators of the biblical documents did to the *Akan* people from whom they stole the religious ideas, doctrines, and documents in Ancient Egypt. Otherwise, how important is the story of a jealous and mendacious Jacob to the biblical narrative? What is intriguing here is that Jacob is the one from whom the Jewish people claim to have originated. How credible is the story that the God of the Jewish people would go to the jealous and mendacious Jacob and not to his elder brother from whom Jacob supposedly stole a birthright and blessing? How could Christianity accept the fact that it was because Jacob stole from his brother Esau that he gained favor in the eyes of God. What message does that send, and I do not ask this for the interpretation of the custodians and protectors of the Bible who do not know the real human story behind this book. How can we reconcile the biblical assertion that this jealous and deceitful Jacob was the one that found God, and which God was this?

Who are the Akan people?

The question in the title of this chapter is who are, and not who were the *Akan* people. This is because the modern descendants of the *Akan* people designed the Ancient Egyptian civilization. They were the people from whom the majority of the people of the so-called biblical Exodus originated. They can be found today in West Africa spread between Ghana and Cote de' Ivoire. What is most revealing about these people is that they are not a people of only one tribe; they are made up of several groups of tribes. Specifically, the *Akan* people are made up of eleven tribal groups. This should not be difficult to accept because in *The Thirteenth Tribe*, Arthur Koestler posited that the Jewish people were no more twelve tribes but they were thirteen tribes. He argued that the Kazar people, the thirteenth tribe, were the original tribe of the ancient *Afrim* people that became the Jews and Hebrews in Europe. However, he failed to explain the issue of the so-called lost ten tribes, how they got lost in the first place, and where they can be found today. These so-called lost ten tribes were not ten, they were more than ten because the *Akan* tribes are made up eleven groups.

The word *Akan* is therefore a generic name used to describe a group of tribes with a common language of minor dialectical difference that has total mutual intelligibility, a common religious belief, and culture. The tribes have a common language and a culture based upon ancient sets of theosophical beliefs, and they believe that all the *Akan* tribes have been the same people from ancient times. These are the people that raised the consciousness of our humanity from the primordial questions of who we are and where we came from to creating the theosophical answers and concepts that sought to explain these issues through religion. They are an ancient world-traveled people. What is least known in the west is that aspects of these people's language can be found in modern European languages especially English and German. These people were the pyramid builders and some *Akan* scholars have even traced this tribe and people to the Stonehenge in England. Today, the *Akan* people can be located mostly in Ghana and in the Cote d'Ivoire in West Africa.

There is something very unique about the *Akan* people that goes farther back than recorded history. As part of the organization of their tribes for the various movements they had to go through in ancient times, the *Akan* people divided themselves into eight clans with eight leaders and identifying insignias to make sure that these leaders took the people wherever they were all going safely. As a result, one major characteristic of the *Akan* people is the various clans to which they belong. Every *Akan* tribal group is made up of members from these eight clans and every *Akan* belongs to one of these clans.

These clans are the *Aduana, Agona, Asene, Asona, Ayoko, Bretuo, Asakyiri,* and *Ekoona.* Every *Akan* community is made up of people from these eight clans. A major cultural significance of these clans is that the *Akan* people believe that members of the same clan have blood ties from ancient times. As a result, members of the same clan never marry each other with the exception of the *Aduana* or *Abrade* clan that has traditionally married within itself. It is from the practice of this clan that Egyptologists concluded that all Ancient Egyptian royal families married within themselves, but that is not generally true. I know this because I am an *Aduana* royalty.

Historical origin of the Akan people

Europeans have told the history of the Akan people and these Europeans began this history from the time they came to the *Akan* people in West Africa. Europeans came to Africa and to the *Akan* people in the 15th century. This suggests that in European scholarship, *Akan* history began only five hundred years ago, but that is false. The childhood of the *Akan* people goes further back than any group of humans on this earth can remember. However, it is only recently that the history of these people has been explored into the beginnings of the past millennium, but it is evident that the childhood of the *Akan* people goes farther back than recorded history.

In the earliest reconstruction of the history of the *Akan* people, European historians went around asking the *Akan* people to tell them who they are, where they came from, and what happened in their history hundreds and perhaps thousands of years ago. Just memory alone has never been adequate in reconstructing a history that is thousands and thousands of years old. As a result, there has never been any deeper study of the history of the *Akan* people and much of what has been said about them has been simply speculative.

For example, most western and African historians know and agree that the *Akan* people were the people of the old Ghana Empire and these people moved to their present locations when the empire was defeated by the Songhai Empire. However, not many scholars have explored where these people came from to build such elegant empires with Universities and centers of learning that far outdated the oldest center of learning in Europe. Is it possible that any people can just get up and suddenly build a magnificent civilization without having the prior knowledge to do so? Where did the *Akan* people come from before they came to build the old Ghana Empire? For the answer, there has been no shortage of attempts at explanations by African scholars and imaginative speculations by western scholars. The answer to this question became a major debate between African and European scholars in the first half of the twentieth century in the Gold Coast [Ghana].

In a book entitled *The Gold Coast Akan*, an *Akan* scholar called Dr. J. B. Danquah asseverated that the *Akan* people migrated from the valley of the Tigris and Euphrates Rivers with other tribes as the Gonja, Bantu, Ewe, and Ga to their present locations in West Africa. Dr. Danquah's assertion is partly confirmed today by my discovery of the *Ewe* tribe, the people of ancient *Kheta* in the Middle East. It is also confirmed by my discovery of the *Nzima* and *Ahanta* tribes as the so-called Sumerians, and also my discovery of the *Kwahu* tribe of ancient *Adiabene* in the Tigris and Euphrates valleys. The genetic discovery of the Lemba tribe, a Bantu-speaking people of Southeastern Africa whose tradition states that a leader named Buba led them out of Judea to southern Africa also confirms that the black people of modern Africa used to live in the Middle East in ancient times. The story of these people also shows that that they lived in Judea in ancient times and in the geographical region of modern day Yemen. I believe it will be redundant to point out that these people were black in ancient times and they are still black people.

Dr. Danquah's attestation of the origin of the *Akan* people does not place them in Ancient Egypt, but today we know that these people were the dominant group of people in Ancient Egypt. According to Dr. Danquah, the migration of the *Akan* people from the valley of the Tigris and Euphrates Rivers took place before 750 BCE. We know that the *Kwahu* tribe, one of the *Akan* tribes, lived in the valley of these Rivers in ancient times. They were the people western historians believe were the vassal kingdom of the Parthian Empire. These people must have been the *Akan* group that moved to Ancient Egypt and then into inner Africa around 750 BCE.

The most remarkable aspect of Dr. Danquah's thesis was that it had major numerous implications for the history and the supposed origination of religion in this region of the world. As a result, most western historians were not prepared to accept or even consider this assertion with equanimity, much less explore it. At the time, most western historians believed that Mesopotamia was the cradle of human civilization and the foundation of their civilization, and at the time not many western scholars were prepared to ever accept that black people in Africa were ever related to the creation of any civilization. In addition to this, Mesopotamia was believed to be the biblical place of origin of the *Afrim* people. From Christianity's point of view, the *Afrim* people originating from black people now in Africa was unacceptable. Moreover, a black African tribe originating from Mesopotamia placed black people rather too close to Ancient Egyptian civilization and the supposed children of Christian Europe's God and that was also unacceptable to Christian Europe and western historians.

Dr. Danquah made his assertion in the 1940s when the Gold Coast was a colony and part of the British Empire. European scholars led by the British historian W. E. Ward vehemently opposed the idea that the *Akan* people ever lived in Mesopotamia in ancient times. He argued using all kinds of "evidence" that the *Akan* people and for that matter all Africans evolved where they live presently, and they have never moved to or from anywhere since. As Charles Kettering said: "A man must have a certain amount of intelligent ignorance to get anywhere."

Fig 7: The (Asesedwa) Ancient Egyptian furniture design of four thousand years ago that modern scholars have found in the Akan Stool design in Ghana.

235

The irony in W. E. Ward's argument against the ancient origin of the *Akan* people in Mesopotamia was that in his own studies of the history of the Gold Coast, he found numerous cultural evidence of Ancient Egypt among the *Akan* people and other African tribes. However, he was much too influenced by European socio-political thinking to even consider the possibility of the *Akan* people having moved to West Africa from somewhere other than Ancient Egypt.

In *A Short History of the Gold Coast*, Mr. Ward wrote that:

"We do not know where the Negro peoples [of West Africa] came from in the first place. We *guess* that they came from somewhere in the east of Africa" (1935, p. 1, emphasis mine).

This was an assumption based upon the late 19th century and early 20th century discovery of the oldest humans in South and East Africa That was the assumption that became the basic knowledge and truth of the origin of the African people in the minds of most western scholars. The rest of Mr. Ward's history of the Gold Coast was based upon this assumption that the Negro people of West Africa came from East Africa.

However, in his travels and interaction with the *Akan* and other tribes of the Gold Coast, Mr. Ward also found a lot of evidence linking these people to Ancient Egyptians so he wrote:

When the Negro peoples moved westwards, they must have known about the civilization of [Ancient]Egypt and learned some of it. It is clear that much of the native civilization of West Africa has been taken from Ancient Egypt: to take an example, the Ashanti stool looks just like a piece of furniture which was used in Egyptian houses four thousand years ago (1935, p. 3-4).

The Stool design Mr. Ward and his colleagues noticed among the Asante people is the design above with only a small variation. The backrest is no more attached to modern Asante Stools. Again, here was a European scholar staring at the evidence of the origin of the Ancient Egyptian civilization in the Africans he was interacting with but he was much too influenced by European socio-political sentiments about Africans to see what was before him.

The fact is what western scholars noticed about the *Asante* Stool design was not just an *Asante* Stool design. It was and still is the Stool design of all the *Akan* people and their kingdoms. The modern names of most of the kings of these Stools can be traced directly to their Ancient Egyptian ancestors on the kings' list (see *Ancient Egypt: The Story Africa Has Never Told*, a manuscript to be soon published by this author).

However, there is an interesting question to be asked in the observation of Mr. Ward. The question is how could people supposedly moving from the east to the west of Africa have known about an Ancient Egyptian civilization far away in the north? How could people that have supposedly never moved from wherever they evolved get to learn the culture of Ancient Egypt so well that they even had similar Ancient Egyptian artifacts dating back to the beginning of Ancient Egyptian civilization over five thousand years ago? It was clear that Mr. Ward and his European colleagues that traveled to West Africa had found the modern descendants of the Ancient Egyptians but they were too knowledgeable to know it. It was also clear that Mr. Ward and his colleagues' opposition to the origin of the *Akan* people in Mesopotamia was intended to be more in support of European denial of the African origin of the Ancient Egyptian civilization than the reality of what these scholars were seeing in West Africa.

Since these discussions in the 1940s, no one has seriously examined the ancient history of the *Akan* people. As a result, we do know the ancient places of settlement and achievements of the *Akan* people but we still do not know where they originated. Today, the arguments and assertions of Mr. Ward and his colleagues have been disproved. These have been disproved by evidence from the *Akan* and other African tribal names of Ancient Egyptian kings, people, and places. They have also been disproved by the genetic evidence and history of the black people that lived in Judea and in the region of Mesopotamia. The genetic studies that found that ancient Chinese people were Africans have also disproved the western hypothesis that Africans had never been anywhere other than where they evolved. It was clear that this hypothesis was merely invented to keep Africans from any relationships they might have had with historical developments around the world.

The linguistic and cultural studies that identified the *Akan, Ga*, and *Ewe* people in ancient near and Far East have confirmed that at least the *Akan, Ga*, and *Ewe* people used to live as far away as China, Japan, and Tibet in ancient times. The revelation of the ancient *Ewe, Kwahu, Nzima*, and *Ahanta* people in Mesopotamia and the upper Tigris and Euphrates valley reinforces the fact that the earliest western historical perceptions of the African in relationship to world civilization especially the Ancient Egyptian civilization and religion were wrong.

Apart from the *Kwahu* people of *Adiabene* having lived in the Euphrates and Tigris Valley in ancient times, there is evidence that *Akan* people lived in Canaan in ancient times. These people lived and named their place of dwelling with the *Akan* name *Adom* meaning providence. This was the ancient *Akan* name that became biblical *Edom*. The land of *Adom* was known as *Adomea* simply meaning a place of *Adom*. This name was what was transposed to *Idumea* in the history of the Jewish people. What is interesting is that from the name of this biblical location, we can identify the specific *Akan* tribe that lived there and named the place. From the name of this place, it is evident to any *Akan* that the *Akuapem* tribe was the *Akan* tribe that lived at ancient *Adomea* in Canaan.

In the earlier discussion story of Esau, I identified the name of   *Osei* belonging to the *Asante* tribe and that raises the number of the black tribes in the region of Canaan in ancient times to nine. In this brief analysis, I have identified nine black tribal groups that lived in the region of Canaan, Babylon, and Mesopotamia in ancient times. The ninth black tribe is the *Lemba* tribe of Southeastern Africa that was identified through genetic studies. I believe that more African tribes can still be identified in the Middle, Near, and Far East since most of the people and places in these regions have retained most of the ancient African tribal names of people and places. In addition to that, there are still black people living from the Middle to the Far East even today. Moreover, there are no other tribal groups anywhere in the world that can claim to have lived in Canaan, Babylon, and Mesopotamia around 2700 B. C. other than black tribal groups.

Biblical origin of the Akan people

The greatest peculiarity of the Bible is that it is so open and yet so confounding that it has opened itself to every imaginable interpretation from historically, linguistically, and culturally false perspectives. That is how Christian Europe has succeeded in falsely interpreting the biblical documents to fit these documents into its own perception of religion, other people, and the world. Speaking on the confounding nature of the Bible, George Bernard Shaw pointed out that: "No public man believes that the Bible means what it says: he is always convinced that it says what *he* means."

There are numerous ethnic, historical, linguistic, and cultural deceptions and fallacies in the biblical narrative. Unfortunately, Christian Europe has never known these. However, if the biblical documents took a hundred years to compile, edit, and translate for the Greeks as Jewish historical tradition suggests then the biblical scholars of Alexandria had a lot of time to plan a lot of deception and cozenage.

One of the greatest deceptions in the biblical narrative is the genealogical chronicle. It is not important to the theosophical intent of the Bible, however, it was important for the foundations of a genealogical deception. Most historians and biblical scholars are aware that the biblical genealogies were fabricated from an unknown source and Gary Greenberg tells us that the source was Ancient Egyptian kings' lists. Almost all historians and biblical scholars know that the Bible's genealogy is a fallacy. As Durant put it: "Even Genesis, if we read it with some understanding of the function of legend, is (*barring its genealogies*) an admirable story…" (1935,

237

p. 339, emphasis mine). Barring its genealogies here refers to the commonly known fallacy of the biblical genealogies.

In *The Moses Mystery: The African Origin of the Jewish People*, Gary Greenberg wrote:

> ... the famous puzzling birth-and-death chronology in Genesis 5 and 11 that provide a continuous chronological link between births and deaths of twenty three generations, beginning with Adam at the dawn of Creation and ending with the birth of Abraham in the early part of the second millennium B. C. generate much controversy. Scholars casually dismiss this chronology as worthless ... (1996, p. 21).

Most scholars find the biblical genealogies worthless but they were not worthless. They were specifically designed to lay the foundations and the support of the deception that followed in the claim of the biblical documents as the original documents of the Jewish people. To claim such a deep philosophy as religion one must have an ancient history of theosophers and that is why the Jewish scholars of the biblical documents created their history and personalities of theosophy, from Ancient Egyptian kings' lists to back up their claim. It is evident from all these that the biblical documents were designed to deceive the Greeks and conceal the truth. It was from this foundation of deception that Christian Europe picked up the Bible, continued to uphold the ancient deceptions, and follow it up with its own deception.

Before I learned that scholars have condemned the biblical genealogies to be worthless, the intriguing question I had was which births and deaths registry was there in the supposed formative years of humanity to record all these from Adam to Abraham? How did the Jewish people record these chronologies even when they did not know how to write and did not have a writing system? Perhaps an even more interesting question is why were such false and deceptive sequences of births and deaths created as part of a supposed religious document for the Greeks?

The false biblical story of the origin of humans was initially based upon a God creating Adam and Eve. However, that did not fit into the intended ideas and stories that were to follow. As a result, the *Afrim* scholars of the biblical documents had to design a second story of the origin of humans. This second story of the origin of humans was based upon a flood wiping out all living things that were before. This gave the *Afrim* biblical scholars a new world to propose and design the earliest theory of human origins. In this second biblical story of human origins, a flood destroyed all humans and animals of the pre-biblical era except Noah, his family, and the pairs of animals he and his family supposedly took into the ark. Even today, we believe in this fable though we know that from the specifications of the ark, pairs of all the supposed animals of the world could never have fitted in it. Perhaps more importantly, from the specifications of the ark and its practically windowless design, the reality of such an event would have wiped out Noah, his descendants, and all the animals in the ark from unhygienic exposure.

In the story of the mythical flood, however, the next group of humans that supposedly developed into modern humans was supposedly peopled from the seeds of Noah through his sons Shem, Ham, and Japtheth (see Genesis 6-10). This false biblical story continues that from the descendants of Shem came Terah who gave birth to Abraham (see Genesis 11: 27). I have already revealed that the *Akan* indigenous name of the father of Abraham was *Tena* and not Terah. This name can b specifically traced to the *Kwahu* people whose royalty used to be at *Adiabene* in the valley of the Tigris and Euphrates Rivers. According to the biblical story, however, Abraham had a son called Isaac (see Genesis 25: 19). Isaac had twin sons Esau and Jacob. The narrative of the birth of Esau and his brother Jacob reveals that the biblical scholars who were editing these narratives were aware of skin color as a mark of human differentiation.

The background to the disassociation of the *Afrim* people that returned to Ancient Egypt from the Exodus from their ancestral black tribes in Ancient Egypt seems a bit understandable. According to *Omane Anto* [*Manetho*], Josephus, Strabo, and Tacitus the ancestors of the *Afrim* people were kicked out Ancient Egypt to stop the plague of leprosy among them from becoming a national plague. However, their descendants could not stay away so they returned to Ancient Egypt. When these descendants returned to Ancient Egypt, they did not fit into the tribal groups from which their ancestors originated anymore. As a result, they had to find ways to disassociate themselves entirely from their ancestral origins and they did that through fabricated history in the biblical documents.

In the post-Exodus era when the *Afrim* people returned to Ancient Egypt and before they went to Europe, they did not fit into their original tribes anymore because they had intermingled with people of other lands. They had lost their original tribal languages and they were beginning to change in skin color. Even those that had not changed physically came with foreign tongues and cultures that made them different from their black ancestral tribal origins. The Alexandrian scholars of the biblical documents were aware of these physical and linguistic changes so they had to design stories and circumstances that would justify their being different and independent from their ancestral black tribes in Ancient Egypt. They found the explanation for their disassociation from their ancestral black tribes in the fabrication of the narrative of the twin brothers, Esau and Jacob.

According to the biblical narrative, these brothers were twins but they were different from each other. The very first difference the scholars of the Bible introduced into this story was the obvious difference in the skin color of the returned *Afrim* people and the Ancient Egyptian tribes from which their ancestors originated. The beginning of this differentiation was designed into the part of the biblical story that stated that while Rebekah was pregnant with twin sons, the children struggled within her. Even a single child struggles in the womb and therefore twins struggling in the womb is not something that should be much of a big deal. However, this was perhaps intended to suggest that these children did not get along from the womb. So Rebekah went to ask the Lord what that meant and the Lord said "*two nations are in thy womb, and two manner of people shall be separated from thy bowels...*" (Genesis 25: 22-23). In other words, Rebekah was going to give birth to twins but they would be different people. This is where the fallacy and the point of separation of the *Afrim* people from the tribes from which they originated in Ancient Egypt began.

The concealed racial and ethnic secret in this story was that the *Akan* and the *Afrim* tribes of the Exodus were originated from the same source but they would separate and become two different people. Today, the people of the black tribes that were the Ancient Egyptians are two different nations. The *Afrim* people that left Ancient Egypt into the so-called Exodus went to Europe to become the Jews and Hebrews and the tribes from which they originated went into inner Africa to become the Africans. This was also another way of making the returned *Afrim* people accept and deal with their differences as a people. The meaning in the symbolism of this story was therefore more relevant to the secret preservation of the racial and ethnic history and heritage of the *Afrim* people that became the Jews and Hebrews in Europe than to any religion in Ancient Egypt or Canaan much less to the Christian religion.

It is evident that the Jewish scholars of the Bible were aware of their physical changes especially the differences in their skin colors and the skin color of the original tribes from which their ancestors originated and they used the biblical narrative of the birth of Esau and Jacob to explain this. This false biblical story continues to say that when Isaac's twin sons were born, "*the first came out red*, all over like an hairy garment; and they called him Esau." After Esau was born, his younger brother also came out holding onto Esau's heel and his name was Jacob (see Genesis 25: 25-26). Jacob's holding of his elder brother's heel in birth seemed to foretell the dependence of Jacob on his brother Esau and he actually depended upon his elder brother for everything including a birthright and even a blessing from their father. The birth narrative of Esau and Jacob seems to suggest that these two brothers were so different that they did not have the same ethnic skin color. As explicit as the biblical scholars were in identifying Esau as being born red, they did not say anything about the color of his younger twin brother. Notice how the silence of the scholars of the biblical documents was intended to suggest here that Esau came out red but his twin brother was nondescript thus almost suggesting that Jacob was the one born with the normal and natural skin color. All of these were designed to help the returned *Afrim* people accept themselves and their changes in skin color.

The redness of Esau from birth also suggests that his skin color would change with growth and that should explain the origin of the skin color of black people while the nondescript skin color of Jacob would explain the other than black skin color of the returned *Afrim* people. It is evident that the story of Esau and Jacob was designed to link Esau to black people from his birth and Jacob to the *Afrim* people and whatever they had become. Why design a story of twins? This was intended to acknowledge the closeness of kinship between the *Akan*, that is black people, and the *Afrim* people that later became the Jews and Hebrews in Europe. This story prognosticated that Esau and his brother would not only be different people but they would not have the same skin color. All of these show that some parts of the biblical documents were carefully designed to deceive and conceal truthful racial, ethnic, and historical information.

What is interesting about this is that later in the biblical narrative, the biblical scholars sought to link the *Akan* people to Esau but that must have seemed too revealing of the source from where they were taking the biblical documents so they confounded it to make it less obvious. It is clear from this however, that the Alexandrian compilers, editors, and translators of the biblical documents were aware that they were stealing *Akan* people's theosophical ideas and stories. I say this because the transposed *Akan* names of the authors of the Old Testament support it. This is also hinted in Genesis 25 where the Bible says that under conditions of extortion, Esau gave his birthright to Jacob for bread and pottage of lentiles.

Jacob's supposed stealing from Esau did not end with the stealing of his birthright. Jacob's envy of his brother and his designs to steal whatever he could from him was evident again in Genesis 27 where Jacob stole Isaac's blessings intended for Esau. In the relationship between the *Afrim* people and their *Akan* tribe of origin, the *Afrim* people returned to Ancient Egypt to steal the theosophical "blessing" and honor due to the *Akan* people for creating the concepts, doctrines, and documents that became the foundations of Christianity. The irony in all these is that in the final analysis, it was Jacob who stole from his brother that found favor with the Jewish people's God. This part of the story led to the silence of the biblical narrative about Esau and his descendants. In other words, Jacob had stolen his brother's birthright and blessings and he was the one the biblical narrative followed because he had the birthright and blessing. That was false.

The biblical story says that the descendants of Jacob became the ancient *Afrim* people when they left Egypt and they eventually went on to become the Jews and Hebrews in Europe. Theirs is the story that is told in the Bible while Esau who originally had the birthright and the intended blessing and his descendants were shoved into obscurity. The question is what happened to Esau and his descendants? No one knows who the descendants of Esau became but there is a clue in the Bible.

Even when Jacob had extorted the birthright and stolen the blessings of Esau from him, the biblical narrative states that Esau was still known as *Edom* (Genesis 25:30). Remember that I have also revealed that Edom was derived from the *Akan* word *Adom*. Just knowing this reveals that Esau was related to the *Akan* people. Specifically, this aspect of the biblical narrative relates Esau to the Akuapem tribe that lived at *Adomea* [*Idumea*] in Canaan in ancient times.

The narrative says that later, Esau took his family and all his possessions and went to live in a country away from his brother Jacob. Esau went to dwell "in mount Seir" in the land of *Edom* and he became the father of the Edomites (Genesis 36, 6-10). What is least known in Christianity is that Esau and his family went to live in the land of *Akan* people and became the father of the *Akan* group that was there. How do we know this? We know this from the revelation that the name of Esau was derived from the *Akan* name *Sau*, and the biblical name of the land *Edom* was derived from the *Akan* word *Adom* meaning providence.

240

The biblical name of the mountain onto which Esau and his family supposedly moved was also derived from the *Akan* name *Sei*. This name is found among modern *Akan* people as *Osei*. It is still the royal and most popular name of the *Asante* people who are one of the so-called lost tribes of the ancient *Afrim* people and modern Jewish people. These names not only reveal that the biblical story was about *Akan* people and therefore black people, but they also hint at the ancient origin of the *Asante* peoples before they went to their present location in Ghana in West Africa. In the discussion above, I pointed out that the *Akuapem* tribe lived in Edom and they might have been the most dominant *Akan* tribe there because the name of the place became *Adomea* and that was definitely derived from the *Akuapem* language.

At least in discussion above, I have shown that the *Akan* people originated from Canaan and the area between the Tigris and Euphrates Rivers. All of these confirm Dr. J. B. Danquah's assertion of the origin of the *Akan* people in the region of Mesopotamia. In fact, I have located the ancient *Fante* people in the region of the Volga around the Caucasus in the area where Aryans claim to have originated.

The Akan people in the Bible

None of the original names of the black tribes that were the Ancient Egyptians and from whom the *Afrim* people originated was mentioned in the biblical documents. The original names of these and other black tribes were the names that were changed into ridiculous names like the Hivite, Hittite, Horite, Amalechite, Levite, Jebusite and other such ridiculous names. The question is who were all these biblical people whose names ended in "sites," "tites," "nites," and "vites?" These names are all similar because they were simply fabricated to conceal the true and original names of these people. Notice how the people of *Adom* became the Edomites in the biblical narrative. The question is how could the *Afrim* people have kept track and recorded their interactions with all these people and never kept track of the ten tribes they claim to have lost? Another important question I have asked elsewhere before is if the *Afrim* people that interacted with these people are still alive and are in Europe then these people must also be alive and should be found somewhere. Where are these biblical people? From the nature of the fabrication of these names it is evident that these people must have been related, and they were. At least they were all black people.

The *Akan* tribe is not mentioned in the Bible as the tribe from which the majority of the *Afrim* people and therefore the Jewish people originated. It was not that the knowledgeable *Afrim* scholars of the biblical documents did not know, but they did not want to tell just as they have refused to reveal who they are and where they originated from for the past two thousand years.

The name *Akan* is in the Bible but it is presented as the name of a person in the false chronologies of the biblical narrative. From the beginning, the name *Akan* was presented in the biblical narrative of the descendants of Esau. However, perhaps as an afterthought, the story of the descendants of Esau was jumbled up and the name *Akan* was cleverly concealed in the confusion of the deceptive biblical style.

The name *Akan* can be found in Genesis 36. Genesis 36:1 begins with: "Now these are the generations of Esau who is Edom." The name *Akan* was mentioned in this chapter that began with this general introduction. However, else where in the chapter, some of the *Afrim* scholars of the Bible must have realized the closeness of this name to the core of the deceptive origin of the biblical narrative. So they had to change the story line to cut off the name *Akan* from direct descendancy in the line of Esau. In doing so, the narrative in the entire chapter was completely confounded. This is one of the clear evidences that the *Afrim* scholars of the biblical documents knew what they were doing and they had plans to deceive the Greeks and claim the concepts they were passing on to the Greeks as their own. This is the reason the chronology of the descendants of Esau as presented in Genesis 36 is full of confusion.

The entire biblical documents were written with a deceptive writing style that has not escaped the notice of scholars. Few historians and biblical scholars have ever had the courage to point out that there are lies and deceptions in the biblical narrative. Even when they find serious fallacies, they tend to conceal the fact that there are suspicions of lies in what they have found through a euphemism. As a result, when biblical scholars found out what was clearly a deceptive biblical writing style, they simply named it *doublets*. Writing on these biblical doublets, Richard Elliot Friedman, the biblical scholar that actually coined this name stated that:

> A doublet is a case of the same story being told twice. Even in translation it is easy to observe that biblical stories often appear with variations in detail in two different places in the Bible (p. 22).

Why would the *Afrim* scholars of the biblical documents adopt such a strange writing style? The answer is simple. It was exactly like a case of telling a lie one day in one place and then being required later to tell the same story another day in another place. There will always be a variation in detail in both stories and that was what happened in the biblical doublets.

Part of the confusion and designs of deception about the *Akan* people in the Bible can be found in the telling of the Esau story itself. In this narrative, the story of the wives of Esau is told in three different settings with different wives. I would like to point out that polygamy was an ancient and continues to be a cultural tradition of the *Akan* people therefore it should not be surprising that the *Akan, Sau,* or the biblical Esau had three wives. In Genesis 26:34, Esau was forty years old when he married "Judith the daughter of Beeri the Hittite, and Bashemath the daughter of Elon, the Hittite" and it caused his brother Isaac and his mother Rebekah a lot of grief. I guess he was too young to marry. In this passage, Esau had to wives. Then in Genesis 28:9, Esau went to Ishmael, Abraham's other son and Esau's uncle, to marry Mahalath, the daughter of Ishmael as his third wife. Esau then had three wives.

However, in Genesis 36:1, the women and their origin in the story of Esau's wives changed. In this chapter, "Esau took his wives of the daughters of Canaan." The first wife was not Judith the daughter of Beeri the Hittite but it became Adah, the daughter of Elon the Hittite. In the earlier story, it was Bashemath who was the daughter of Elon, the Hittite now it was Adah. The second wife was not Bashemath the daughter of Elon the Hittite, but Aholibamah, the daughter of Anah who was in turn the daughter of Zibeon the Hivite. In the earlier story, Esau's third wife was Mahalath the daughter of Ishmael but now she was Bashemath the daughter of Ishmael and sister of Nebajoth. In these short chapters, the women and the stories of Esau's wives changed drastically. Why would a simple story of the wives of Esau be made so confounding? It is clear that the Jewish scholars of the biblical documents wanted to lie and deceive but they were not that good at it. It is also evident that these compilers, editors, and translators of the biblical documents were more intent on concealing something than checking the veracity of the stories they were telling to conceal it. In this chapter, the evidence suggests that they were intent on concealing something about the name and identity of the *Akan* tribe from which their ancestors originated and from whom the scholars of the Bible were stealing the biblical documents.

The deception in this chapter continues as the narrative states further that Esau and his family went to live on mount *Seir* and became the father of the Edomites (Genesis 36:8-9). Until now, *Seir* had been introduced in the chapter as a mountain in Edom. However, in the middle of the presentation of the descendants, sons, and dukes of Esau, the narrative jumped to the introduction of a personality in Edom called *Seir*, the Horite. Seir was no more a mountain; he was a human from the Horite tribe.

What is even more intriguing about this chapter is that where the biblical narrative told us the name of Esau's second wife was "Aholibamah, the daughter of Anah, the daughter of Zibeon," the narrative goes on to say in verse 20 that Anah was no more a female and the daughter of Zibeon. Instead, Anah was the brother of Zibeon and they were the sons of Seir, the Horite. "These are the sons of Seir the Horite, who inhabited the land; Lotan, and Shobal, and Zibeon, and Anah" (36:20). After intense archaeological search, scholars have determined that there is no evidence of any Edomites that were Horites or even known as the Horites. Some scholars have suggested, however, that these people might have been the Hurrians, but again scholars have found no evidence of the Hurrians in Edom either and some scholars reject that suggestion. So what was going on here?

In this confusion and in the course of the chronology of the generations of Esau came the introduction of the name *Akan* supposedly as the child of Ezer (36:27). However, instead of *Akan* becoming the direct descendant of Esau in the biblical narrative, the narrative changes to make the *Akan* the descendant of Seir, the fictitious Horite. The biblical narrative could not state it directly that *Akan* originated from the line of Esau. It passed the origin of *Akan* through a non-existent and fictitious Horite. What do all these tell us? There was a carefully planned deception to conceal all the people around the biblical story leaving only the *Afrim* people that went to Europe to become the Jews and Hebrews.

It is not known whether the biblical narrative intended to suggest that the *Akan* people of Ancient Egypt and West Africa descended from the *Akan* in the generations of Esau. However, that would still be false because historical evidence shows that the *Akan* people existed thousands of years before these fictitious stories were fabricated in the biblical chronology. Otherwise Esau could not have been born to acquire the *Akan* name *Sau* that was transposed to the biblical Esau. However, linking the *Akan* people to Esau in the biblical narrative would have been too direct, and it would have revealed what the biblical scholars of Alexandria were seeking to conceal about the *Akan* people. So the *Afrim* scholars decided to deceive and confuse the introduction of the name *Akan*. To do this, the Jewish scholars of the biblical documents had to change their story line. They therefore restated that Anah the mother of Aholibamah and the daughter of Zibeon was no more a female, and she was no more a Hivite. He was a male called Anah the brother of Zibeon and the sons of *Seir* (Osei) who was a Horite.

Again, why should there be so much confusion in a small narrative less than half page long? It was because the scholars of the Bible were more intent on concealing the secrets they did not want the Greeks to find out than checking the veracity and direction of the stories they were telling. The name *Akan* is therefore mentioned in the biblical narrative but it was not pointed out that it was the name of the tribal group from which the Jewish people originated. It was cleverly hidden in a carefully designed false and deceptive chronology in the discussion of the descendants of Esau.

A pertinent question that might clarify all these deceptions is did the Jewish scholars of the biblical documents in Ancient Egypt know of the *Akan* people in Ancient Egypt? My answer is yes because they showed that they were knowledgeable scholars that supposedly knew of their chronology of origin from Adam to Abraham, Isaac, Jacob, and Joseph, a chronology spanning over two thousand years. At that time, if these scholars knew all the history of these people as they sought to tell in the Bible, they should definitely have known of the Akan and other African tribes from which their ancestors originated. These scholars were so knowledgeable that they could determine the date of Creation and the birth of Adam to be 3761 B. C. As Gary Greenberg pointed out "Adam's birth is placed in 3761 B. C., the date of Creation in Jewish tradition" (p. 40, footnote). How could these scholars have known all these without knowing of the Akan and other tribes from which they originated in Ancient Egypt? How honest and true was the knowledge of the Jewish scholars of the Bible? How could Ancient Egyptian civilization have started around 5000 B. C. and the creation of the world would begin on 3761 B. C.? Could this have been designed to cut off the Ancient Egyptians from the biblical narrative? This mathematical anomaly shows that some one was fabricating a story and unfortunately that story became the biblical story of creation.

Scholars that knew and supposedly had a record of the names and birth dates of all their ancestors supposedly going back to over two thousand years should know about the *Akan* people in Ancient Egypt. They should have known of the *Akan* people because they knew their ancestral history and this history should have told them that their ancestors supposedly went to live among the *Akan* and other black tribes in Ancient Egypt for over four hundred years. Since these scholars purported to know their history so well that they knew the chronology of the beginning of this world from Adam to Joseph, they should have known of the supposed more recent four hundred year span of their ancestors' tarriance in Ancient Egypt among the *Akan* people. They should have known that their ancestors actually originated from the *Akan* and other black tribes of Ancient Egypt and they also should have known that the names of their so-called biblical patriarchs were *Akan* names. They should also have known that when their ancestors left Ancient Egypt in the so-called biblical Exodus, they identified themselves with the collective *Akan* name, *Afrim* and that was why they were known as the *Afrim*.

Since the Jewish scholars of the Bible knew so much from Adam through Abraham to Jacob and Joseph, they should have also known that the earliest nation of their people was named *Ephraim* after the original *Akan* word *Afrim*. The Jewish scholars of the biblical documents in Alexandria were knowledgeable, and they should have known that when the earliest name of this nation was changed, it was changed to Israel, also an *Akan* name. For people that knew their history so well as the Jewish scholars of the biblical documents, they should have known that the names of most of the important personalities in the pre- and post-Exodus history of the Jewish people were *Akan* names. They also should have known that the names of most of the prophets that supposedly wrote the documents of the Old Testament were *Akan* names before they transposed them for the Greeks.

Perhaps, what these scholars should have known above everything else was the fact that the names most of their people carried originated from *Akan* and other African tribal languages and cultures. Even if they did not know that their names were derived from African tribal names, they should have known of their blood relationship with the *Akan* and the black tribes that were the Ancient Egyptians from whom their ancestors originated. At least, the genetic discovery of the Lemba tribe of Southeastern Africa establishes this black blood relationship today.

What is puzzling from all these is why the Jewish scholars of the Bible never mentioned the real names of the *Akan* and other African tribes of Ancient Egypt in their central roles in the creation of the biblical doctrines and documents. It is evident that these scholars knew that the documents they were passing off to the Greeks as theirs were the theosophical documents of the *Akan* people that were Ancient Egyptians. As a result, these biblical scholars had to deliberately conceal and confuse biblical knowledge of the *Akan* and other black tribes of Ancient Egypt so that they would not easily give away the sources and the people from whom they were stealing these documents. It must have been evident to these scholars then that the Greeks and Europeans would never find out the *Akan* and other black tribal connections to the Bible because Europeans did not have the historical, linguistic, and cultural backgrounds to know these. In fact, this is the reason Europeans have never figured out these deceptions for the past two thousand years. Perhaps what the Jewish scholars of the biblical documents did not count on was the discovery and revelation of these deceptions by the *Akan* and other African tribes that were the Ancient Egyptians. Perhaps, these scholars believed that these tribes would never know and therefore their deception was complete.

The *Akan* people were already in Ancient Egypt before the biblical story of Abraham began. If these scholars knew and could remember that far, then they should have known about the people to whom Abraham went in Ancient Egypt. This obvious knowledge shows that the Jewish scholars of the biblical documents already knew about a group of people called the *Akan* before they began to create their false and deceptive story of the peopling of the earth and its subsequent fictitious chronology. The mythical biblical stories of creation, the flood, and deceitful Jacob were all used to push the *Akan* people to the periphery of the biblical narrative instead of the center they originally were.

The biblical revelation of the knowledge of a single person called *Akan* is very significant because the *Akan* people are black and they have always been black people. This suggests that the descendants of this *Akan* could not have been white people. This is not the most powerful evidence that establishes the black identity and heritage of the people of the Bible but it adds to the overwhelming evidence I have presented so far. This seemingly biblical confusion linking Esau to *Edom* [Idumea] and also *Akan* suggests that the descendants of ancient *Afrim* people were as close blood relations to the *Akan* that were in Ancient Egypt just as Esau was the twin brother of Jacob. All of these confirm that the people of the Bible were black and that the Catholic Church was not wrong in its portrayal of the black images of Jesus and his mother in early European Christendom.

To summarize the lives and stories of Esau and Jacob, Esau went to *Adom* to live among *Akan* people in *Adom* and Jacob also went to live among *Akan* people in Ancient Egypt. This should not surprise any historian that knows that these people carried *Akan* tribal names even before they went to the *Akan* people in these various places.

From this biblical analysis, it becomes apparent that *Akan* people were the real reason Esau, the elder twin brother of Jacob, was not part of the so-called biblical patriarchs of the Jewish people. The *Akan* people were the reason the Bible was silent about whatever happened to the descendants of Esau. Remember that the descendants of Esau were the blood relations of the descendants of Jacob, so whatever the descendants of Jacob were so were the descendants of Esau. However, the Jewish scholars of the biblical documents did not want to look that way so they had to design fictitious stories to make these descendants of the same people look different.

The biblical revelation of the knowledge of the name *Akan* is undoubtedly the greatest biblical revelation of the past two thousand years because this revelation snowballs into revealing several other things about history, the Bible, and Christianity. What is most intriguing about the Bible's knowledge of the name *Akan* is that this name is today a generic name for a group of eleven constituent tribes with a common historical, linguistic and cultural heritage. The composition of the modern constituent tribes of the *Akan* people is extremely interesting because the racial and ethnic story of modern Jewish people assert that they have lost ten of their original tribes. What is most interesting about that is the fact that the *Akan* people are made up of eleven constituent tribes, and not ten.

Within the tribal system of belonging, one cannot belong to more than one tribe. Every member of a tribe belongs to one tribe and none else. This means the Jewish people could not and they still cannot belong to ten other tribes that are lost unless these tribal units belonged to a bigger and broader tribal unit of the same historical, linguistic, and cultural heritage. Such individual tribes forming a bigger and broader tribal unit are the *Akan* tribes. From my knowledge of the *Akan* tribe, it is important to point out that for the lost tribes to be the same people racially, ethnically, linguistically, and culturally these lost tribes must have a common racial, ethnic, historical, linguistic, and cultural heritage.

Among the world of tribes, the *Akan* tribe is the only tribe that is designed from a stratification of individual tribes forming a bigger and broader tribal unit with a common racial, ethnic, linguistic, and cultural heritage. These tribes are the only black tribes that lived closest to the biblical story in Ancient Egypt, Canaan, and the Middle East in ancient times. This suggests that if ever the Jewish people have lost any tribes they claim to have belonged to, these are the *Akan* tribes. *Akan* is the only black tribe from whom the names of the Jewish people's patriarchs were derived. What confirms all these is the fact that the Jewish people have carried *Akan* and other African tribal names from their ancient times up to the present. What has made it possible for all of these to remain a secret up to now is that Christian Europe and Europeans have never known the true history behind the Bible and they have not had the linguistic and cultural backgrounds to know any of these plain facts.

From these revelations, it is becoming apparent that there is a lot of historical, racial, ethnic, linguistic, and cultural deception in the Bible. How could God have told Abraham that he originated from Ur of the Chaldees when Abraham was already an *Akan* carrying an *Akan* name before he supposedly went to the *Akan* people in Ancient Egypt (see Genesis 15:7)? Otherwise, which other tribes carried *Akan* linguistic and cultural names in Ur of the Chaldees for Abraham to have acquired his name from them? The most fascinating aspect of this is that there were no

Akan people living in the region of Ur of the Chaldees in ancient times. The *Akan* people that lived closest to Ur of the Chaldees in ancient times lived north in the valley of the Tigris and Euphrates Rivers in what is modern day Iraq. From this background knowledge, is it any wonder that the Jewish people have not revealed who they really were or where they originated before they went to Europe to become Jews and Hebrews? It is clear that someone has been trying to conceal something from Christian Europe, Europeans, and the world. From this point of view, could Jewish historians have deliberately suggested the loss of ten tribes to throw people off the track of searching for eleven? Why did Arthur Koestler write about *The Thirteenth Tribe* when he was only writing about the Kazar people of one tribe? If the Kazar people were part of the Jewish tribes would they not have been part of the so-called twelve tribes and not a thirteenth tribe? What is the secret in Arthur Koestler's number, thirteen?

What is interesting about this number is that with the supposed two tribes of modern Jewish people together and the eleven tribes of the *Akan* people, the number of the tribes rise to exactly thirteen. What does that mean? Th e coincidence in the number of the so-called lost tribes of the Jewish people and the numerous historical, linguistic, and cultural evidence presented so far throughout the chapters confirm the African tribal origin and specifically the *Akan* ethnic majority origin of the original Jewish people that later went to Europe to become the Jews. From this analysis, the biblical story of the coming and going of the Jewish people to and from Ancient Egypt begins to make sense. Again from this revelation, not only is the perennial secret of the ethnic origin of the Jewish people revealed but also some interesting questions about these people can be answered.

Historically, we do not know where the *Akan* people originated before they traveled to all the places from the Near to the Far East. We do know from modern research in human origin that they originated from Africa. We do not know who the most ancient *Akan* people were before they became the *Akan* people in Ancient Egypt and the modern *Akan* people in West Africa. We do know, however, that the *Akan* people were the earliest and the most dominant group in Ancient Egypt. We know that these people designed and laid the foundations of Ancient Egyptian civilization from theosophy. We do know that it was to the *Akan* people that Abraham, Joseph, Jacob and his entire family, and even Jesus Christ supposedly went in Ancient Egypt. We do know that the *Akan* people were black and they are still black people and that suggests that all the people that interacted with the *Akan* people in biblical times were also black people. We also know that the most dominant tribal group that left Ancient Egypt into the so-called biblical Exodus was *Akan*. The question is where did all these people come from for their ancestors to be carrying *Akan* names even before they supposedly went to the *Akan* people Ancient Egypt?

Black people are not the descendants of Ham

I have briefly discussed the issue of black people and the supposed Noah's curse elsewhere but here some more evidence confirming that if ever Noah ever cursed anybody, it could not have been black people because black people did not descend from whoever Noah supposedly cursed. The greatest revelation the discussion in this book and the biblical origin of the Jewish people establish is the fact that *Akan* people and therefore black people were not the descendants of Ham as Christian Europe falsely interpreted the biblical story of Noah and the flood. Black people were not the cursed race of Christian Europe's fictitious interpretation of this biblical episode. Looking at it from a deeper historical point of view, the ancient *Afrim* people that went to Europe to become the Jews and Hebrews were black people. This is because they originated from the black tribes that were the Ancient Egyptians. All the people in the story of the Bible were black people. How then could Noah, who was also a black person curse his fourth grandson to be black when they were already black people? I am asserting that these people in the biblical narratives were all black people from the revelations above and also from the historical and anthropological facts that in biblical times, there were no white people in the geographical region of Canaan, Mesopotamia, the Middle East, or Ancient Egypt. How could the ancient black

246

Afrim people go to Europe to become the Jews and Hebrews and the children of Christian Europe's God, and the black tribes from which they originated be the cursed people of this God in Africa when Noah supposedly cursed all black people according to Christian Europe's fictitious interpretation. This is one of the interpretations of the Bible that shows that Christian Europe has not only be racially prejudiced in its understanding of the Bible, but also it has been totally ignorant of the history and people behind this Bible.

Evidence of the fact that Christian Europe misunderstood the biblical narrative of the flood but interpreted it against black people anyway can be found in the interpretation of the same narrative by the Jewish people. In *The Aryan Myth: A History of Racist and Nationalistic Ideas in Europe,* Leon Poliakov discussed this so-called Noah's curse when he pointed out that:

> It must be remembered that the curse on Ham in the ninth chapter of Genesis, verse 25, is directed against his fourth son, Canaan. In the Jewish exegesis of Rachi, this verse is interpreted as follows: Cursed be Canaan. – "Because of you I shall not have a fourth son to serve me. Cursed be your fourth son therefore, he shall be enslaved to the descendants of his elder brothers on whom falls the duty of serving me." And what was Ham's reason for making him an eunuch? He said to his brothers: "Adam had two sons and one killed the other to inherit the earth, and our father has three sons and desires a fourth!" (1996, p. 347 footnote 15, see also D. C. Allen, *The Legend of Noah.)*

Because the so-called curse of Ham was supposedly against his fourth son, the Jewish people interpreted this to mean that every fourth son is cursed. This clearly shows that Ham was not the one that was supposedly cursed and black people definitely did not descend from Ham's fourth son when all these people were already black people. Jewish people's interpretation of this so-called curse confirms that it was Canaan, the fourth son of Ham that was supposedly cursed. However, the greatest appeal of this curse to Christian Europe and Europeans was that it gave Europeans a fictitious basis to claim that they were also part of the people of the Bible. As part of the interpretation of this fictitious Noah's curse, Christian Europe claimed that Europeans descended from Noah's son Japtheth, but that was categorically false. The biblical story has nothing to do with Europeans. They were only fascinated by it and they forcefully claimed it as their own. What is sad about it is that they never sought to find out to understand what they were fascinated about, and they never sought to find out where the concepts and documents of their fascination came originated so it is understandable for them to make such egregious mistakes in interpretation of these documents..

I have been discussing the biblical documents and their fictitious narratives. It is not that I believe the biblical chronology, but that is all most Christians know and have to go by so I will present my argument from the biblical narrative. As I have discussed above, the biblical story sought to conceal this, however, if the *Akan* people supposedly came from the line of Esau and Esau went to live among the *Akan* people in *Adom,* then we are talking about black people because the *Akan* have been black people since time immemorial. This means Esau was also black and his descendants were black. It also means Esau's younger twin brother Jacob, despite the overt biblical attempt to conceal this was also black. Otherwise, how could Esau have originated from Shem and his descendants would originate from Ham the brother of Shem? It is all too evident that we are dealing with black people because the name of Shem was even derived from the *Akan* name *Sem.*

The people of the Bible were black people and the interpretation of the so-called Noah's curse against these same people is false. However, even if the *Akan* people originated from Ham, that would still not have made them the cursed ones because the ancient *Afrim* people that are the modern Jews and Hebrews in Europe originated from the very black African tribes that Christian Europe believes were cursed. If the Jewish people were not the descendants of Ham then the black tribes from whom they originated could not have been the descendants of Ham either.

According to the fictitious biblical genealogy, *Akan* people are the descendants of Shem (see Genesis 11:10-27). Otherwise, how could the father of Abraham have had the *Akan* name *Tena* [transposed to Tera], and Abraham and his descendants would be carrying *Akan* names? Assuming, however, that the biblical narrative of the origin of the *Afrim* people were true and that they originated from somewhere else and from another tribe as they sought to deceive the world, there is still the question of how their so-called patriarchs came to have *Akan* names. Abraham did not exist before the *Akan* people otherwise he could not have carried an *Akan* name.

Nevertheless, the ignorance of Christian Europe helped it to interpret this biblical episode to mean that black people who were already enslaved in Europe were the descendants of Ham and therefore the ones cursed to be the slaves of white people (see Genesis 9: 20-27). In other words, Christian Europe justified the enslavement of black Africans, as the manifestation of the Christian God's will through Noah's curse. Today, we know that biblical evidence refutes this heinous interpretation of the Bible. It is clear from such ignorant interpretations that it is only people that did not know the racial and ethnic backgrounds, history, language, and culture behind the Bible that would make such erroneous and egregious mistakes in interpretation. Perhaps it is important to point out here that the biblical ideology, doctrines, and documents were all created by black people in the land of black people for black people before part of these people introduced these ideas to the Greeks for it to be taken over by Christian Europe. All the people of the Bible from Abraham through Jesus were black people. The question is were they all cursed too?

What is of both historical and biblical interest is that the enslavement of black people beginning in West Africa began among the *Akan* people. These people are the modern descendants of the people that invented and designed the philosophy of religion, its doctrines, and sacramental practices in Ancient Egypt before the Jewish people passed these ideas on to the Greeks and Europeans.

The Akan people of Adom

How can any historian that knows identify numerous *Akan* names in the history of the ancient *Afrim* people and yet never associate these people with the *Akan*? This could only happen to a historian that did not have the linguistic and cultural backgrounds to know the common linguistic and cultural origin of *Akan* and Jewish people's names, anyway. In the history of the ancient *Afrim* people, historians and religious scholars acknowledge that the place Esau and his descendants went to live was called *Adomea*. This name was also an *Akan* derivative from *Adom* meaning a place of providence. I have also pointed out that in western historical literature, *Adomea* was transposed to *Idumea*. Note here that there seemed to be a pattern in the biblical transposition of *Akan* words into western orthography. In most of the *Akan* words in Jewish history, where the *Akan* word began with an "A," western orthography retained the *Akan* phonology but it began with an "I." That was how *Akan* words like *Afrim* became *Ivrim,* and *Adomea* became *Idumea.*

Apparently, the biblical *Adomea* was an important place in Jewish people's real history. This is because historians state that after Judas Maccabaeus led an uprising and liberated Jerusalem in 164 B. C., Judea became a peaceful independent kingdom for 130 years. During this period when Hasmonean and Herodian dynasties ruled Judea, the country expanded to cover a major part of modern Palestine and *Idumea* – the old Edom (see Jews, *Britannica,* 1996, p. 74). What this piece of Jewish history reveals is that *Idumea* was not originally a part of the geographical area of modern Palestine. Where could it be located today?

According to the biblical narrative, Esau did not just go to live in *Adom.* He went to become the father of the *Adomites.* This suggests that Esau was from the same ethnic, linguistic, and cultural heritage as the Edomites. The *Akan* name of this place also suggests that Esau and his descendants were *Akan* and they spoke the *Akan* language This again confirms the original revelation that the patriarchs of the Jewish people were originally *Akan* people Otherwise, how could Esau have been the father of the *Adomites* and why would any ethnic group give the place they live a name in the language of another ethnic group? The relational implication of this is that Jacob and his descendants could not have originated from a different ethnic group from his twin brother Esau. This deduction is backed by more linguistic evidence of the origin of the ancient *Afrim* people in the *Akan* people. What is linguistically fascinating about modern Jewish names and words that can be traced to *Akan* language and culture is that these words and names are not linguistic cognates, they are the real *Akan* names and words that have merely been transposed into European orthographies. The *Akan* people still use the names and words that I am discussing from Jewish history.

According to western historians and Egyptologists, the *Akan* indigenous name of Ancient Egypt is lost in history. From the above analysis, however, it is most likely that *Adomea* must have been the indigenous *Akan* name of Ancient Egypt before the Greeks came to give it the name *Aegyptus*. This is most likely because Ancient Egypt was created and developed from theosophical ideas and the name *Adomea* is a religious reference to a geographical location. From this analysis also, the centrality of the *Akan* people, their history, language, and culture begins to emerge in both Ancient Egyptian and biblical history.

Akan ethnic origin of the biblical patriarchs

In this work so far, it has not been sufficient for me to show that the people of the Bible were black people or they were Africans. I have endeavored to go deeper into the analysis to reveal specific African tribes to which these people belonged. All of these biblical personalities were *Akan*. Their names and the names of their modern descendants confirm it. Again, the question Nicholas Wade asked in his review of the genetic studies of the Lemba people is pertinent here. How did a [white] Jewish priestly male chromosome come to be found in a black, Bantu-speaking people? The answer is simple, the chromosome originally belonged to the black tribes from whom the *Afrim* people that later went to Europe to become the Jews and Hebrews originated. It was not the Lemba people that changed to black instead it was the *Afrim* people that changed from black to white. Other than that, the *Lemba* people and the part of the *Afrim* people that originated from the *Lemba* tribe were originally the same black people.

The long held belief of Europeans that the *Afrim* people were originally black people is true. Early Europeans that saw the *Afrim* people before they became white knew this. However, modern Europeans who are far removed from the arrival of the *Afrim* people in Europe have never wanted to accept or believe that the people of the Bible were black people, but they were. From this denial and detachment of black people from the center of the Christian religion, it became easy for Christian Europe and Europeans to do the most atrocious and inhuman things to black people throughout their five hundred years of historical interaction.

Linguistic and cultural revelation of the ethnic origins of the Afrim people

In the discussion of the origin of the *Afrim* people, I have shown through various perspectives that they were originally black people. Black people are now the Africans. However, when the *Afrim* people were part of these black tribes, these tribes were not classified as Africans. This is because being African is a modern geographical reference to black people because they live in Africa. However, indigenous black people can be found from the Middle to the Far East. Who would believe that there are indigenous black people even in China?

Today, the *Afrim* people that went to Europe to become the Jews and Hebrews are an amalgamation of several different black African tribes. This is attested to in the biblical story of the Exodus.

> And the children of Israel journeyed from Rameses to Succoth, about six hundred thousand on foot that were men, beside children. And a mixed multitude went up also with them... (see Exodus 12:37-38).

249

The tribal, linguistic, and cultural differences between the *Afrim* people and the mixed multitude that went with them in the Exodus is explained as a multitude that did not belong to the house of Israel. The people of the Exodus that belonged to the house of Israel were the *Akan* majority. That is how they got to name the nation of Israel in the *Akan* language. The linguistic, tribal, and cultural identities the *Afrim* people still carry with them around the world confirms the mixed African tribal multitude that made up ancient *Afrim* people and therefore modern Jewish people. The linguistic and cultural revelation of the origin of the *Afrim* people is therefore a three thousand year old revelation that ties Ancient Egypt, the *Afrim* people, the Bible, Christianity, and Africans, specifically the *Akan* people into a common origin and heritage.

In earlier discussions, I revealed the indigenous *Akan* names of Ancient Egyptian Pharaohs, people, city, and the indigenous *Akan* names of the most important Ancient Egyptian gods. I revealed that the indigenous *Akan* name of the Pharaoh *Psammetichus* I is *Asamaoa Ateko I*, *Akhenaten* is *Akenten*, *Djekara-Isesi* is *Gyakari Asaase*, *Khuffu* is *Akuffu*, *Djedefra* is *Dade Afre*, and *Chephren* is *Okyere [Ochere] Afre*. The indigenous *Akan* name of the most popular Ancient Egyptian sot known in Egyptology as *Djesekaraseneb is Gyasi Kraseneboo*. *Osiris* is *Osoro*, and *Isis* is *Asaase*. The Ancient Egyptian priest *Manetho* who wrote the most credible history of Ancient Egypt is *Omane Anto,* and the *Akan* name of the god *Osiris Khentimentiu* is *Osoro Kantamanto*. The *Akan* name of the most famous Ancient Egyptian city *Memphis* is *Mamfe.* To the modern descendants of the Ancient Egyptians, these names are not extinct. They are still used and they can be found today in *Akan* people's dynasties, names of people, and places.

From the names of the earliest kings of Ancient Egypt beginning from *Omane* [Greek *Menes*], the king who supposedly united the northern and southern kingdoms, it is evident that the *Akan* people created and developed the Ancient Egyptian civilization. This civilization later attracted several other black tribes from the Near, Middle, and Far East and that was how black people came to be concentrated in Africa today.

I have so far stated that the so-called biblical patriarchs of the ancient *Afrim* people that became the Jews and Hebrews of Europe were *Akan*. I have also revealed that the most dominant group of the people that left Ancient Egypt in the biblical Exodus was *Akan*.

Specific Akan tribal origin of the Afrim people

As I pointed out, *Akan* is now a generic name for eleven tribes of the same ethnic, linguistic, and cultural heritage. The biblical story of the origin of the patriarchs of the Jewish people suggesting that they came from somewhere in the east could be partly true. However, they could not have come from Ur of the Chaldees as the Bible claims God told Abraham in Genesis 15:7. After all, nothing in the geographical area of Ur of the Chaldees links Abraham and his descendants to any tribe or group of people in ancient Mesopotamia. However, the names of these patriarchs link them to the *Akan* tribe that lived in the valley of the Euphrates and Tigris in ancient times. *The so – called biblical patriarchs of the ancient Afrim people that became the Jews and Hebrews in Europe originated from among the ancient Kwahu people that lived in the kingdom of Adiabene in the Tigris and Euphrates basin.* How do we know this? The names of the so-called patriarchs are the unique names of the *Kwahu* people. These were the people that had and continue to have *Adiabene* royalty with a modern capital city of *Abene* to match

Once the names of these so-called patriarchs are transposed back from their Greek and European corruption, the *Akan* origin of the names becomes clear, and among the *Akan*, the *Kwahu* origin of the names also becomes very clear.

Beyond the biblical story of the origin of the Jewish people, the linguistic and cultural stories of these people also confirm that they were not originally Hebrews or Jews until they went to Europe over a thousand years after their Exodus from Ancient Egypt. According to the history of the Jewish people, the "ethnic" name *"Jew"* is a relatively modern English name that was supposedly derived from the Greek name *Ioudaios* and the Latin name *Judaeus*. The name

Judaeus, however, originally referred to only the people of the tribe of Judah, but in late biblical times and for reasons that have not been explained, this name was extended to refer to both the people of Israel and Judah (see Esther 2:5; Encyclopedia Britannica, 1997; Alpher, Joseph, [ed.] *Encyclopedia of Jewish History: Facts on File*, 1986; Wigoder, Geoffrey, [ed.] *The New Standard Jewish Encyclopedia: Facts on File*, 1992; *Encyclopedia Judaica*, 1972; Ben-Sasson, Haim H. (ed.), *A History of the Jewish People*, 1976; Kochan, Lionel, *The Jew and his History*, 1985; Patai, Raphael & Patai Jennifer, *The Myth of the Jewish Race*, 1989; Mendes-Flohr, P. R. & Jehuda Reinharz, *The Jew in the Modern World: A Documentary History*, 1980). Even the name *Juda* must have been derived from the *Akan* word *Dwoada* [pronounced *Joada*], referring to Monday, the day of peace in *Akan* culture and traditions.

Lost tribes of Israel

From the point of view of the African tribes from which the ancient *Afrim* people originated, the so-called lost tribes of *Afrim* people are ambiguous. Before we can sort out the ambiguity in the assertion of the lost tribes, we must first seek to explore answers to some questions. The first question is when did the ancient *Afrim* people become tribes and where? How did these people get to belong to and lose ten other tribes? The biblical narrative does not mention any tribe of the Jewish people before they went to Ancient Egypt. Tera, Abraham, Nahor, Haran, and Sarai, the original biblical people that supposedly left Ur of the Chaldees were not a tribe. They were one family, and one family is not a tribe. Isaac did not create a tribe from his family, and so were his sons Esau and Jacob. The seventy men in the family of Jacob that also went to Ancient Egypt were a family and not a tribe. Where then did the ancient *Afrim* people become members of a larger group of people to make it possible for them to be in tribes and lose ten whole tribes?

Some historical and biblical scholars argue that there were no lost ten tribes. However, biblical interpretation suggests that the tribes of Israel originated from the sons of Jacob namely, Ruben, Simon, Levi, Juda, Dan, Naphthali, Gad, Asher, Ishachar, Zebulon, Joseph, and Benjamin. However, this suggestion is false because these people were all members of the same family tribe and therefore members of the same tribe. Belonging to a tribe is acquired through either the mother or father. Whichever way it was, these people belonged to the same tribe. They were twelve children but they could not have been twelve tribes because they already belonged to whatever tribe Jacob belonged. Joseph was already in Ancient Egypt, and Jacob brought the rest of his children and their families also to Ancient Egypt where they all died. Their descendants supposedly became a single tribe and the people of the Exodus. From these people, there were no twelve tribes. So where did the twelve tribes come from and what happened to them?

If the twelve tribes of Israel referred to the loss of the *Akan* people in the Exodus then they had lost some tribes. From this point of view, the twelve tribes were not the tribes from Jacob's children but the tribes of the composition of the *Akan* people.

The next question is how did the ancient *Afrim* people become members of a larger group of tribes to make it possible for them to lose ten of those tribes? Scholars of Jewish history have been searching for and speculating answers to this question. In *The Thirteenth Tribe*, Arthur Koestler tried to answer this question by suggesting that the *Afrim* people became members of numerous tribes by marrying and interacting with different kinds of people. He wrote:

> The prophets may thunder against 'marrying daughters of strange god,' yet the promiscuous Israelites were not deterred, and their leaders were foremost in giving a bad example. Even the first patriarch Abraham, cohabited with Hagar, an Egyptian; Joseph married Asenath, who was not only Egyptian but the daughter of a priest; Moses married a Midianite, Zipporah; Samson, the Jewish hero, was a Philistine; King David's mother was a Moabite, and he married a princess of Geshur; as for King Solomon (whose mother was Hittite), he loved many strange women,

251

including the daughter of Pharaoh, women of the Moabites, Ammonites, Edomites, Zidonians, and Hittites (1976, p. 187, see 1 Kings 11:1).

In normal tribal traditions, people in Israel marrying women from different tribes would not make the whole people of Israel members of the tribes of these foreign wives. In ancient *Akan* tradition, they were the women that married and took their husbands' tribes and not the men. Today, marriage does not change a woman's tribe because tribal affiliation is by blood and that is thicker and stronger than marital affiliation. So this does not answer the question as to how the ancient *Afrim* people become tribes. Koestler, however, goes on to state that:

> Besides, the biblical prohibition of marrying Gentiles exempted female captives in times of war – and there was no shortage of them. The Babylonian exile did not improve racial purity; even members of priestly families married Gentile women. In short, at the beginning of the Diaspora, the Israelites were already a thoroughly hybridized race. ... Another important sources of interbreeding were the vast numbers of people of the most varied races converted to Judaism. Witness to the proselytizing zeal of the Jews of earlier times are the black-skinned Falasha of Abyssinia, the Chinese Jews of Kai-Feng who look like Chinese, the Yemenite Jews with their dark olive complexion, The Jewish Berber tribes of the Sahara who look like Tuaregs, and so on... (p. 187).

There have been numerous attempts to explain the origin of the Jewish people away from the *Akan* and African tribes from which they originated in Ancient Egypt, but all of them have been inadequate. The explanations above are elegant attempts to explain how the ancient *Afrim* people became tribes but they are not adequate. The question these answers do not explain is who were the ancient *Afrim* people before they became the people of Israel and long before they married and or converted all the people whose tribes they took? Again, in tribal traditions, marrying a woman from another tribe does make the man's tribe and people members of the wife's tribe and certainly converting someone into one's religious beliefs does not make one and one's people part of the tribe of the converted.

I have already revealed that the people that left Ancient Egypt into the biblical Exodus to go to create Israel were mostly from *Akan* and other African tribal groups. This is how the ancient *Afrim* or modern Jewish people became tribes. The lost tribes of modern Jewish people therefore do not refer to the tribes of the consorts of Abraham, Joseph, Moses, David or Solomon. These lost tribes do not refer to the Moabites, Ammonites, Edomites, Zidonians, or Hittites, and certainly they do not refer to tribes the Jewish people met in the Babylonian captivity, the Falasha in Ethiopia or the Chinese and Yemenite Jews they converted. The lost tribes of modern *Afrim* people refer to the *Akan* and mixed multitude of tribes that left Ancient Egypt into the so-called biblical Exodus. This is where the tribal origin of the Jewish people began and modern Jewish people have carried the linguistic and cultural evidence to confirm this to this day.

What is intriguing about the tribal origin of the Jewish people is that it was after these people had left Ancient Egypt that they became tribes. This should tell anyone that they became tribes from the existing tribes that were the Ancient Egyptians, especially since they did not go to Ancient Egypt as even s single tribe. Interestingly, the *Akan* people are made up of eleven tribes. These modern *Akan* tribes *are Akuapem, Akwamu, Akyem, Asante, Assini, Bono, Fante, Kwahu, Sefwi,* and *Wassa* and *Denkyira.* Out of these tribes, I have discussed the ancient *Akuapem* tribe that lived at *Adomea [Idumea]* in Canaan. I have also discussed Osei of Seir Mountain in Edom. I have also revealed that m embers of the *Assini* tribe, the kin tribe of John the Baptist and Jesus, were in Judea. Beyond all these, there were several other tribes that were not *Akan*, and people from all these tribes were part of the so-called biblical Exodus.

There is also this issue to examine. To be a tribal group, constituent tribes must have a common historical, linguistic and cultural heritage. These tribes must also have a common theosophical belief. Where else on earth do we have eleven tribal units of the same people forming a common linguistic and cultural group, and also having a common history that goes back to Ancient Egypt and the geographical area around Canaan? All of these confirm that the *Akan* tribes are the so-called lost tribes of the ancient *Afrim* people that became the Jews and Hebrews in Europe. That was how the *Essenes* became a tribal and political group in Judea. In the *Deceptions and Myths of the Bible*, Lloyd Graham quotes Eusebius as saying of the *Essenes*: "These ancient Therapeutae [Essenes] were Christians and their writings are our Gospels and Epistles" (1995, p. 281).

Graham wrote further that:

Believers in the Christian origin of morality might also read Josephus' account of the Essenes, whom he called "the most virtuous men on earth," and whose cult, according to Pliny existed for ages before the time of Christ (p. 434).

The story of the *Akan* and Jewish people is therefore the story of the same racial and ethnic people some of whom went north to Europe and the rest went south into inner Africa. The larger group of the *Assini* people went south to inner Africa in the Exodus of the *Akan* and other African tribes from Ancient Egypt. This confirms that the so-called lost tribes of the Jewish people are not lost. They are the eleven tribal groups of the *Akan* people, and there is even more historical, linguistic, and cultural evidence to confirm this.

The *Encyclopedia Britannica* states that "*both John the Baptist and Jesus had affinities with the Essenes* (1996, p. 74). The greatest revelation in the discussion of the *Assini* tribe is the fact that I do not just assert that Jesus was a black man just as early Catholic Church portrayed him and his mother in early European Churches. I reveal here that he was an *Akan* from the *Assini* tribe.

Ancient *Afrim* characteristics in the *Akan* people

Throughout the discussion, I have hinted, more than once, of the evidence of the *Akan* names that modern descendants of the ancient *Afrim* people still carry after parting from the *Akan* people for over three thousand years. I have introduced evidence of the *Akan* people in Ancient Egypt, and biblical narrative has also confirmed the supposed tarriance of the Jewish people in Ancient Egypt for almost half of a thousand years. I have also introduced evidence linking the *Akan* and the ancient *Afrim* people in Canaan and the geographical region surrounding it. To confirm all these and make the entire discussion more rounded, comprehensive, and complete, it is important that some evidence of the relationship of the *Akan* and Jewish also be found among modern *Akan* people in West Africa.

The discussion so far has been seeking historical, linguistic, and cultural evidence from among the Jewish people and linking them to the *Akan* people in Africa. I have been trying to reveal the *Akanness* in the Jewish people and the Bible. However, if the Jewish people really originated from the *Akan* and other tribes of Ancient Egypt, there must be some evidence of "Jewishness" in these *Akan* and other African tribes too. After all, the Jewish people still carry the names of these African tribes therefore these African tribes must also have something that could relate them to the Jewish people too. The questions therefore are, are there any modern *Akan* and other African tribal characteristics that can be found in modern Jewish people in Europe? Are there any modern Jewish characteristics in modern *Akan* and other tribes in West Africa? To the first question, I say yes, modern Jewish people still carry *Akan* and other African tribal names, and to the second question I say let us explore the scholarship on this issue.

Numerous European scholars have stumbled upon evidence of the relationship among the *Akan*, ancient Jewish people, and the Bible. However, the scholastic relationship of the ancient Jewish people to Africans has seemed so inane and preposterous to western religious and scholastic minds that when an African scholar pointed it out in the middle of the 20th century, the idea was only good for European laugh. In *The Akan Doctrine of God: A Fragment of Gold Coast [Ghana] Ethics and Religion*, Dr. J. B. Danquah wrote:

> With the possible exception of Sir A. B. Ellis, in his *Tshi-Speaking Peoples of the Gold Coast*, no one who seriously studied the products of Akan thought ever doubted that they have had a definite conception of the true nature of God or what it ought to be (1944, p. 1).

In this quotation, Dr. Danquah asserted emphatically that the *Akan* people "have a definite conception of the true nature of God or what it ought to be." This is simply stating that the concept of God as presented in Christianity and other religions around the world is the same concept that the *Akan* people have in West Africa. From what I have revealed about the *Akan* people in Ancient Egypt and in the Near and Far East, this statement confirms the centrality of the *Akan* people in world religions, and this has major implications and revelations.

Who was Sir A. B. Ellis? He was a British army major in the 1st West India Regiment stationed in the Gold Coast [Ghana] in West Africa. Ellis and his people were the ones that recruited and trained West African soldiers for the Second World War. What is most noteworthy about the book of Sir A. B Ellis is that the table of contents read like the table of contents of modern Egyptology. In other words, he found almost everything that modern Egyptologists have written about Ancient Egypt among the modern *Akan* people in West Africa. The *Tshi* [*Twi*] speaking people are *Akan* and in this book, Sir Ellis discussed *Akan* Religion, Manners, Customs, Laws, Language etc. Specifically, he discussed the religious beliefs, general deities, local deities, *samantin* and *sabonsam* (ghosts and devil), tutelary deities of individuals [the teraphims], priesthood, psycholatry and human sacrifice, fetishism, oaths, ordeals, omens, family divisions and animal worship, and modes of reckoning time. He also discussed religious ceremonies and festivals, ceremonies at birth, marriage and death, State ceremonies, system of government, laws, language, music, and traditions and folklore of the *Akan* people.

Scholars that read Sir Ellis' book alongside a modern book about Ancient Egypt would think the modern book was derived from this older book. However, this is scholastic evidence revealing that European scholars have found the modern descendants of the Ancient Egyptians, but they could not see them.

Around the beginning of the 20th century, the curiosity of some European scholars about the authenticity and origin of biblical literature and culture did not end in Europe. Some European scholars went to Africa in search of a long suspected relationship between biblical literature and culture and the African people. What is most interesting about these Europeans is that most of them went to the *Akan* people in the Gold Coast [Ghana]. Some of these Europeans went to Africa in the service of colonial governments. Others went to Africa as religious missionaries going to propagate the Christian Gospel to "pagan" Africans. However, most of these missionaries ended up very surprised by the striking similarities they found between African and biblical theosophy, language, and culture.

European missionaries who went to live and work in Africa specifically in Ghana among the *Akan* people found very strong similarities between the language and rhetoric of the *Akan* people and the biblical *Proverbs*. This is extremely significant because Egyptologists have found that the biblical Proverbs must have originated from Ancient Egyptian literature. Western scholars that went to Africa to propagate the Christian gospel to Africans also found a strong relationship between biblical literature and the language and rhetoric of the *Akan* people that were the Ancient Egyptians. This is the very first time evidence from Europe and Africa is introduced in support of Ancient Egyptian and specifically *Akan* origin of the biblical documents.

A missionary from the former Basel Missionary Society, a German-Swiss called Reverend J. G. Christaller, lived in the Gold Coast at the beginning of the twentieth century. Ironically, he lived among the *Akuapem* people, the people that lived in the biblical Edom and gave ancient *Adomea* its name. Rev. Christaller was so fascinated with the similarities between the everyday admonitions and teachings of *Akan* proverbs and the Proverbs in the Bible that he studied *Akan* proverbs very well. He found that the logic and rhetoric in the *Akan* and biblical proverbs were exactly the same. From this and other studies, Rev. Christaller concluded that *Akan* proverbs must have been the original source of the biblical Proverbs. Rev. Christaller therefore collected, translated, and published 3600 *Akan* proverbs for the information and study of Christian communities in Europe (see Foreword to *Twi Mmebusem*, 1962, by C. A. Akrofi).

In his *Preface* to the *Akan* proverbs, Dr. C. A. Akrofi noted that:

> Proverbs play a very important part in the everyday language of Twi-speaking [Akan] people. They adorn the speech and make it rich and flavoursome. They point up the crux of an idea with vivid clarity. Indeed, in Akan society, skill in the use of proverbs is a hallmark of good breeding.

From Dr. Akrofi's quotation, it is evident that proverbs and knowledge of them have long been designed into *Akan* cultural traditions. Such a design of an aspect of a people's lives into a cultural tradition does not happen overnight. It takes several generations over a long period of time. This confirms that *Akan* people dealt with proverbs in their ancient past.

Rev. Christaller was a Presbyterian minister who had control over the Presbyterian schools of the Gold Coast. He became such an authority on *Akan* proverbs in the Gold Coast that he was the first to recommend that proverbs should be taught in all *Akan* schools, and he also suggested how they should be taught.

In his analysis of *Akan* proverbs, Christaller found that *Akan* proverbs and sayings covered every aspect of their lives. He found proverbs about God, fetishes, soothsayers, and wizards just as the *Akan* beliefs were in Ancient Egypt. He found proverbs that spoke about man's general state, condition, fate and destiny. He found *Akan* proverbs dealing with the physical man – his head, face, eye, ear etc. There were proverbs through which *Akan* thoughts about plants, animals, minerals, land, water, rain, wind, sun, moon, and stars were expressed. He also found *Akan* proverbs about time reflected in days, nights, years, seasons, and other aspects of nature. Rev. Christaller found proverbs that referred to the domestic, social, economic, and political conditions of the *Akan* people. He found proverbs that dealt with *Akan* thoughts on the intellectual conditions and faculties of man as reflected in wisdom, foolishness, learning, rudeness, reason, and prudence, etc. What fascinated Rev. Christaller most was the fact that he found proverbs about *Akan* morality that were so similar to the admonitions of the Ten Commandments that he asked that these proverbs "may be arranged according to the *Ten Commandments*, at least the fifth to the tenth, under respective virtues and vices" (see Akrofi, *Twi Mmebusem*, p. vii).

In fact, proverbs had been such an ordinary part of the everyday language of the *Akan* people that not many indigenous *Akan* scholars thought much about them until European missionaries and scholars that came to live among the *Akan* in West Africa saw *Akan* proverbs as the true and original source of the biblical Proverbs. As a result, the earliest and most notable collections of *Akan* proverbs in print were by Rev Riis, Rev. Christaller, and Captain Charles Rattray, all Europeans who knew the importance of their discovery of *Akan* proverbs and their relationship to the biblical Proverbs. What makes these findings and revelations among the *Akan* people in West Africa even more fascinating is the fact that Rev. Riis and Rev. Christaller were all ordained ministers of the Presbyterian faith. They had studied and learned to believe the Bible, and that gave a lot of credibility to what they found among the *Akan* in West Africa.

In the Bible, we have been told that Israelite King David wrote the biblical Proverbs. Not only do we find here that David did not create the Proverbs as Jewish scholars of the biblical documents claimed, but also we have found the people whose daily sayings, admonitions, philosophy, concepts, and morality were the Proverbs in the Bible. Western scholars that have studied Ancient Egypt have also found that the biblical Proverbs originated from Ancient Egyptian literature. In *The Wisdom of Ancient Egypt*, Joseph Kaster wrote:

The most important of the "wisdom-books," and the longest, is Amenemope. *It has often been compared to the Biblical Proverbs, with which it has many points of contact both in thought and in actual phraseology:* In reading Amenemope, even the reader who has but a nodding acquaintance with Proverbs will note the remarkable similarity in phrasing to Proverbs 22:17-24. Another important point of similarity is the religious tone and attitude, which permeates Amenemope (1968, p. 179, emphasis mine).

We now know that the biblical Proverbs were African tribal proverbs in Ancient Egypt. To some scholars, 900 B. C. has been the date conferred on the papyrus from which Egyptologists discovered Amenemope's proverbs. Other scholars point out that this papyrus was copied from an earlier text that dates as far back as between 1580-1320 B. C. Historians and biblical scholars have debated as to whether the proverbs of Amenemope influenced the biblical proverbs or the other way round. Naturally scholars who have first been influenced by biblical thinking would not see anything influencing the Bible though these scholars also know that Amenemope's proverbs were written almost a thousand years before the biblical documents were compiled, and they were compiled in Ancient Egypt where Amenemope first wrote down his proverbs.

A British Army officer in the Gold Coast called Captain Charles Rattray also observed the very close similarities between *Akan* religious thoughts and concepts and Christian thoughts and concepts. He was so fascinated with this observation that he suspected a link. As a result, he asked the British Government that was ruling the Gold Coast at the time to appoint him the British Government's Anthropologist in the Gold Coast to enable him study the suspected relationship between the *Akan* and Jewish people specifically, *Akan* religious thoughts and concepts.

Captain Rattray was appointed the British Government's Anthropologist in the Gold Coast and his work on this observation was so significant that it eventually earned him an honorary Doctorate Degree from Oxford University. Captain (Dr.) Rattray who studied *Akan* thoughts and concepts through the collection of *Asante* proverbs and the study of the *Asante* people pointed out that the *Asante Nyame [Asante* God] is the same as Yahweh of the Israelites. It is of interest to point out again that the *Asante* people are a tribal group of the *Akan people.* Readers will remember that the *Seir* Mountain in biblical Edom where Esau and his family moved was derived from Sei or *Osei* and that is a typical *Asante* name.

Is it not ironic and a major evidence of Christian Europe's ignorance that in Europe Christianity pronounces African religion as pagan religion and in Africa, scholars that have studied the African religious concepts, doctrines, and language proclaim that the foundations of Christian religion, concept, and doctrines originated from African religion.

In his work, Captain (Dr.) Rattray also confirmed that the *Akan* God was the same as the Christian God that was introduced to Europeans by the *Afrim* people that went to Europe to become the Jews and Hebrews. Considering that the *Akan* and the *Afrim* people lived together in Ancient Egypt before the *Afrim* people left to go to become the Israelites, this is a major confirmation of the revelation I have made concerning these two people.

What is also interesting and worth mentioning about the works of these early European scholars in Africa among the *Akan* people is that most of the works are either carefully tucked away in the archives of European Universities or they are hidden in private collections of special works. It is as if someone is carefully monitoring what information about Africa should get out to the European masses and what should not. This was all because around this period, no western scholar, Christian, or colonial politician was willing to entertain the idea that the *Akan* people and other tribes of West Africa were remotely related to the ancient *Afrim* people that became the Jews and Hebrews in Europe, in anyway. European scholars were not ready for the idea that Africans were the Ancient Egyptians much less accept that the Africans were the people of the

Bible. Some are still not ready for these ideas today not because they are not true but because of their personal socio-political sentiments.

Perhaps, the most prolific among the European scholars that saw and propagated the relationship between African and Christian thoughts and concepts was a German professor from the University of Berlin. His name was Dr. Diedrich Westermann. His work on *Akan* and other African tribes was so popular that in his day, European colonial governments and institutions consulted him in the design of their colonial policies because of his knowledge and ideas about African people. His views were instrumental in drawing Africans into what was then called the Christian community of Europe. His works can be found in what was called the *Duff Lectures* he delivered in Scotland in 1935. The Oxford University Press published these lectures in 1937 under the title *Africa and Christianity*. Basically, the title of these works simply suggested that scholars have found Africanisms in Christianity. However, who was willing to believe or propagate such an idea considering that the thought of Africans as pagans had been the dominant European perception of Africans for centuries, and it is still the dominant European religious perception of Africans?

Numerous European scholars followed the study of the similarities between African tribal thoughts and concepts and biblical thoughts and concepts. They all arrived at several conclusions that are not known to many in the west. In *Religion and Medicine of the Ga People*, Dr. M. J. Field showed in 1937 that the Supreme Being of the Ga people is certainly a sky god. Dr. Field analyzed the *Ga* word for God and pointed out the sameness between *Nyonmo*, the Ga word for God, and the Hebrew *Yahweh*. From the discussion of the African linguistic origin of the name *Yahweh*, we have found out that Rev. Father Williams found the linguistic origin of *Yahweh* in the *Akan* name *Nyame*, and Dr. M. J. Field also found the linguistic origin of *Yahweh* in the *Ga* name *Nyonmo*. The *Ga* name for God was derived from the *Akan* name *Nyame*. However, it is important to point out here that all these scholars were convinced of their findings through linguistic and cultural analysis. Again, here was a western scholar who knew from simple comparative linguistic analysis that *Ga* people's word for God in West Africa was the same as the Hebrew *Yahweh*. The only mistake he made here is the fact that *Yahweh* was not originally Hebrew, as I have pointed out in the origin of the Christian God. Yahweh was derived from the name of the God *Yaw*, the ancient *Akan* name for the God of Thursday.

Among European scholars that found similarities between Africans and Jewish people, perhaps the most serious was Father S. J. Williams. Father S. J. Williams was so much convinced of the similarities of thought and concepts between the *Akan* and Jewish people that he wrote a book entitled *Hebrewisms in West Africa*. The title of this book said it all. In addition to all his analysis in this work, Dr. Williams suggested that the *M* in the *Akan* word *Nyame* (God) is the old *W* in the Hebrew *Yahweh*. That would change the Hebrew word *Yahweh* to *Yahmeh*, closer to the *Akan* word for God. I would like to point out that all these scholars interpreted their findings in Africa from the foundation that the biblical documents were created by the Jewish people but that was false. The question is why did these Europeans scholars find the concepts, rhetoric, and language of the Bible so similar to African tribal concepts, doctrines, and language? The reason these scholars found such striking similarities between *Akan* and other African tribal thoughts, concepts, doctrines of religion and rhetoric and the Bible was because the biblical documents were original *Akan* and other African tribal documents in Ancient Egypt. Jewish scholars simply translated these Ancient Egyptian documents for the Greeks. This is also the reason no evidence of these biblical documents have been found in Israel or Judea. Beyond the revelation of the African tribal names of the authors of the Old Testament that I am going to reveal in the next chapter, here is important evidence that confirms that the Africans wrote the documents of the Bible. It is important to note that this evidence takes us to the tribes from which the authors of the biblical documents originated.

In Dr. Williams' analysis, the Hebrew word *Yahweh* came from the *Akan* word *Nyame*. In other words, Dr. Williams was practically confirming that *Hebrews* and *Akans* must have been related in some linguistic way. Anyone who goes to live among *Akan* and other African tribes in West Africa would find evidence revealing the relationship between these people and the ancient *Afrim* people that went to Europe to become the Jews and Hebrews without even looking. Where else in the world do people eat *matzo* other than modern Jewish people in Europe? Did Dr. Williams find out something in his studies that he refused to tell? This was possible because again, who was willing to believe or propagate such an idea considering that the thought of Africans as pagans had been the dominant European perception of Africans for centuries? The most important point here is that the revelations in this work surround the *Akan* people, and Father Williams' findings among the same *Akan* and other African tribes confirm the veracity of his and this work.

Western scholars did not just study the *Akan* people and the tribes surrounding them in West Africa. Some went to East Africa and also found linguistic similarities between references to God in some East African languages and the *Akan* word for *Nyame*. Among East African tribes, Edwin Smith found that their words for God – *Nyambi* and *Nzambi* were similar to the *Akan Nyame*. From all these studies, Father (Dr.) Williams pointed out that the Hebrew Tetragrammaton JHWH, NZMB, and NYNM are none other than *Akan* and other African tribal names for God. These early Europeans did not know that their works were basically establishing the long lost relationship between the *Akan* and the ancient *Afrim* people that went to Europe to become the Jews and Hebrews.

All of these confirm what St. Augustine wrote hundreds of years ago:

> That which is known as the Christian religion existed among the ancients, and never did not exist; from the very beginning of the human race until the time when Christ came in the flesh at which time *the true religion, which already existed, began to be called Christianity* (Lloyd Graham, p. 280-1, emphasis mine).

Notice that Christianity understandably influenced St. Augustine. However, he acknowledged that the concepts, doctrines, and philosophy of Christianity existed long before Christianity. The people in whose minds and imaginations this concept, doctrine and philosophy first existed and originated were the *Akan* and other African tribes that were the Ancient Egyptians. All of these explain why the Classical and Biblical traditions have long conspired to distort and destroy Ancient Egyptian history.

Another early Christian, Eusebius also stated the same idea when he pointed out:

> That the religion published by Jesus Christ to all nations is neither new nor strange. For though, without controversy, *we are of late and the name of Christians is indeed new; yet our manner of life and the principles of our religion have not lately been devised by us, but were instituted and observed, if I may say so, from the beginning of the world* (Graham, p. 281, emphasis mine).

Again in this quotation, the ancients among whom religion existed from the beginning of human race were the Ancient Egyptians who are now the *Akan* and other African tribes. These were the people that devised our modern manners and principles of religious life and observed and instituted it from ancient times. There is something in the quotation from Eusebius that must be pointed out. Europeans have claimed the concepts, manners of life, and principles of religion as their but as "they are of late." They have named these as Christianity but that is only a new name for what had existed among Africans since time immemorial.

In the works of European scholars and missionaries in Africa they found similarities between Ancient Egyptian and biblical literature. More than anything else, these people specifically identified the *Akan* people as having the same linguistic, thought, and rhetorical patterns as the *Afrim* people that went to Europe to become the Jews and Hebrews. This relationship directly takes the African tribes to the biblical documents and the Bible. In terms of religion, the evidence now confirms that long before Christianity, the thoughts and concepts used in creating the Bible and Christianity were African religious thoughts and concepts. The irony in all these is that, while Christians in Europe were proclaiming Africans as pagans, European missionaries and scholars in Africa were discovering what they believed were the foundations of Christian thought and doctrine among *Akan* and other African tribes.

Since I have already established that the *Akan* and other African tribes were the Ancient Egyptians, the findings of European scholars in Africa among the *Akan* people further confirm the origin of the concepts of Christianity in Ancient Egypt and the *Akan* people. The works of western scholars both in Europe and Africa have all confirmed a strong relationship between the *Akan* and ancient *Afrim* people. However, there are still unrevealed linguistic and cultural evidence that shows even closer relationships amongst the *Akan*, other African tribes, and the ancient *Afrim* people who are the modern Hebrews and Jews in Europe.

The Akan language Family

Since much of this work is based upon language and culture, it is important that I introduce the *Akan* language family for interested scholars to study and confirm or disprove what I have asserted and revealed in this work. In the study of the linguistic family of the *Akan* and all African languages, western scholars have been very much influenced by the false biblical interpretation that black people originated from the lineage of Noah's son, Ham.

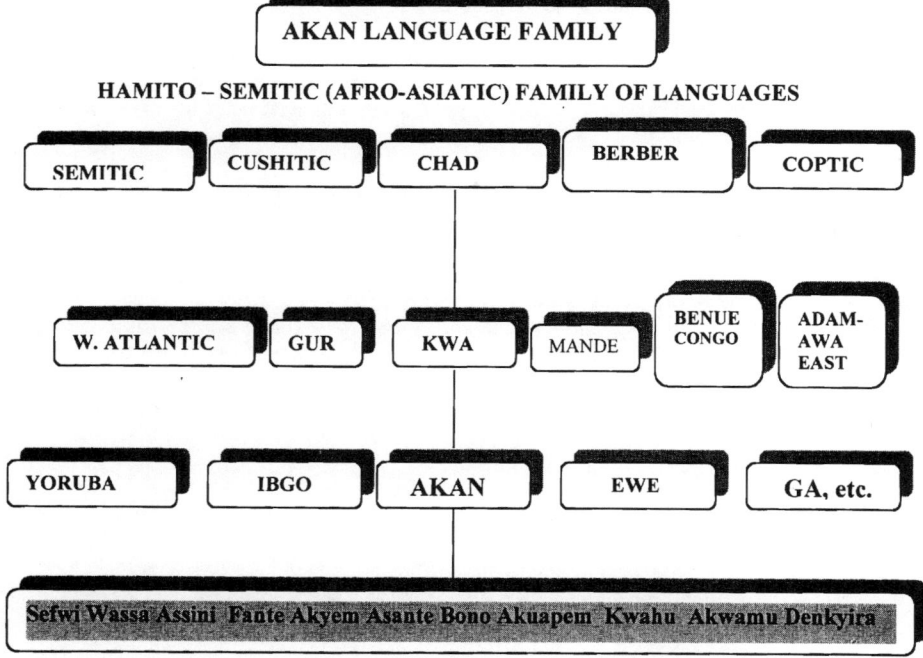

Fig. 8: Akan tribal family, the so-called lost tribes of modern Jewish people.

As a result, though African languages have been found to belong to the same origin and family as most Asiatic languages, African languages are erroneously known as Hamitic languages in western scholarship; that is the language of the descendants of Ham.

From this false perception, German Egyptologist Karl Richard Lepsius coined the name Hamito-Semitic or Semito-Hamitic to classify African and Asian family of languages. The name Hamito-Semitic, however, tends to link African and Semitic languages. That name in turn tends to suggest some form of linguistic and perhaps cultural origin and relationship between African and Semitic tribes and languages, including the Jewish people's language. The name Hamito-Semitic was therefore too close to what the Jewish people have never wanted to reveal for over two thousand years. As a result, in 1950, Joseph Greenberg, an American linguist and a modern *Afrim* coined the name Afro-Asiatic family of languages cutting off the name of Semites that supposedly include Jewish people from African languages. This was ostensibly to cut off the language of the supposed children of Ham from the language of the supposed children of God and lead western scholars off the trail of the suggested linguistic relationship between African and Semitic languages. All of these were also based upon the false idea that the Jewish people are Semites, which they are not.

Today, some scholars still use the names Hamito-Semitic or Semito-Hamitic to classify the African and Asian family of genetically related languages, while others prefer Afro-Asiatic to cut off any Semitic connection to African languages. I prefer the Afro-Asiatic family of languages because Christian Europe's biblical interpretation of the origin of black people from Noah's son Ham is false, and the classification of the Jewish people as Semites is also false. Moreover, the Jewish people have never been linked to any linguistic or tribal group of people among the Semites because they did not become Semites by blood, language, or even culture. They became Semites by someone conferring it on them, as I pointed out in the last chapter.

The *Akan* family of languages begins as an Afro-Asiatic family of genetically related languages. Linguists believe this family of languages is made up of five main languages that originated from an original parent language. These linguistic offshoots from the parent language are Semitic, Berber, Cushitic, Chadic, and Egypto-Coptic, a defunct language of Ancient Egypt. Scholars believe that the next level of African languages known as the Niger-Kordofanian languages emerged from the Chadic languages.

Above is a diagram of the *Akan* family of languages as western scholars have classified them. Again, I must point out that these classifications were designed from historical knowledge that was heavily doped by biblical influence. The veracity of this knowledge and assumptions are slowly falling to pieces as genetic studies continue to reveal the ultimate truths as to what history really was and not what early historians and religious scholars said or wished it were.

The eleven *Akan* linguistic and cultural groups shown here are the tribes the Jewish people claim to have lost for over two thousand years. They have never been found till now because they are in Africa and no western scholar, no matter how open-minded, would remotely search near Africa to look for information about modern Jewish people. Christianity would not even allow that.

African linguistic and cultural identities of Afrim people

Though the biblical line of Shem that supposedly ended in the formation of the Jewish people begins with Arphaxad who was born two years after the supposed biblical flood, the story of the origin of the Jewish people begins from Abraham about twelve generations later. The question is who were the generations before Abraham and what happened to them? They were all black people and they can be found in the many tribes of Africa.

Because western scholars do not have the linguistic and cultural backgrounds to trace the people of the Bible to wherever they are today, most history and religious scholars have concluded that the Jewish patriarchal story beginning with Abraham is false. These scholars have concluded that Abraham was only a mythical figure imagined in designing the fictitious biblical story. In *Deceptions and Myths of the Bible*, Lloyd Graham wrote:

Today Jewish scholars freely admit that the accounts of Adam, Cain, and Noah belong in the realm of mythology; in other words, the Bible is mythology until, as they say, "we come to the historical Abraham, the father of the Jewish race" Now why should a book of mythology suddenly become history with Abraham? (p. 110).

From this point of view, most western scholars tend to suggest that the entire biblical story is fictitious. However, these scholars miss a point and that point is the concept of God is a belief and not literature. It was a belief in humans long before we learned to write, therefore it is not about the biblical documents, it is about believing in something you think is greater than yourself.

In *The Moses Mystery: The African Origin of the Jewish People*, Gary Greenberg also reiterated what most western historians and biblical scholars believe by stating categorically that:

> There is so much personality in these stories that many scholars find it hard to believe that these patriarchal families were made up of whole cloth. ... Nevertheless, the patriarchal story is false (p. 17).

As the title of his book proclaims, Greenberg showed that the *Afrim* people originated from among the black people of Ancient Egypt and modern Africa but because he did not have the African linguistic or cultural knowledge, he also had to conclude that the patriarchal personalities were fictitious. Whether it was false or not, the names of the so-called biblical patriarchs can all be traced to the *Akan* language. It only requires *Akan* linguistic and cultural knowledge to identify these so-called biblical patriarchs.

Abraham

In the biblical introduction of the patriarchs, this personality was first called Abram perhaps the shortened version of Abraham. What is interesting and at the same confusing about this biblical character is that he was a religious and mythical figure in the legend and folklore of many lands and among many people before he became the Christian Abraham. As a result, it has been difficult for scholars to find out who he really was. In the works of western historians and religious scholars, the Hindus knew him as Brama or Brahma, the Hindu Creator. The Persians knew him as Abriman or Ahriman, the evil ruler of darkness. The Babylonians knew him as Abarama a mythical farmer, and the Moslems claim him as Ibrahim, the spiritual father of the Moslem religion and the one who produced the Kaaba, the sacred stone at Mecca.

What has been wrong with the search of this biblical personage in history and religion is that scholars have been misdirected and therefore misinformed in their search. Western historians and religious scholars who have been influenced by the false biblical origin of the ancient *Afrim* people in Mesopotamia, and have also been influenced by the Indo-European Hypothesis, look to the East for answers to biblical mysteries, but the answers are in Africa via Ancient Egypt. What these misdirected scholars do not know is the fact that Ancient Egyptians [mostly *Akan*] priests went to all these areas in the East to propagate their religion before there was religion in these places. The answers are in Africa and that is the reason they have not found any evidence that confirms the history of the ancient *Afrim* people in the Bible or in the Middle East.

Anthropologists, historians, and religious scholars have not been able to link the name of Abraham or his travels to any tribal group in the Middle East because the name Abraham did not originate from any of the languages in modern Middle East. The name of the biblical Abraham was not a real name. It was a symbolic name derived from two *Akan* words. This name was created from the *Akan* words, *Abre ham,* meaning tired of wandering or roaming. The two *Akan* words *Abre ham* put together became *Abreham* from which the European name Abraham was derived. Remember that the name of the father of *Abre ham* was *Tena* also an *Akan* name. The name of *Abre ham* was chosen carefully by the Jewish scholars of the Bible because it was the most fitting name for the supposed patriarch of a people whose entire history has been nothing but wandering on deserts and in other people's lands.

The biblical story of this patriarch himself was a story of wandering in which *Abreham* supposedly came with his father Tena from Ur of the Chaldees to Haran and Canaan and then to Ancient Egypt before he went back to settle in Canaan. The wandering must have skipped a generation because Abraham's son Isaac did not do much wandering. However, *Abreham's* grandson Jacob and his family also wandered into Ancient Egypt where they supposedly lived for almost half a thousand years and then left to become the ancient *Afrim* people. These people left Ancient Egypt and for forty years they could not find where they were going though they were supposed to be led by God. Forty years is a long and difficult time of wandering anywhere much less in a desert.

Even after the *Afrim* people found a place to settle, other people would not let them settle in peace. They were conquered and taken into several foreign lands for centuries. There is no group of people whose history is made up of so much wandering from place to place as the ancient and modern *Afrim* people; and *Abre ham* referring to a wanderer were the most perfect words for the name of the patriarch of a wandering people. Note that the name is *Akan* confirming that the earliest *Afrim* people and the people of the Bible were mostly *Akan*, and they were all black people.

I would, however, like to point out again that *Abreham* did not come from the south in Ur of the Chaldees. He came from among the people of the vassal kingdom of the Parthian Empire that was ruled by the *Adiabene* family in the Upper Tigris region. These people were the *Kwahu* tribe of the *Akan* group of tribes. Moreover, we have identified and discussed the people that lived in the lower region of the Tigris and Euphrates Rivers from around 2700 B. C., and we found that linguistically, *Abreham* could not have originated from among them. In addition to that the Upper Tigris region is closer to the ancient geographical region of Haran and Canaan. Therefore it is the most likely source from where a family would have traveled to Canaan than from Mesopotamia in the south that is hundreds of miles away from Canaan.

Sarah

Another confirmation of the derivation of *Abreham's* name from the *Akan* language is the fact that according to the biblical narrative, *Abreham* married a woman who also had an *Akan* name. Within the biblical narrative, this woman has been known as Sarai and Sarah. The *Akan* name from which this name was derived was *Saara*. Among the *Akan* today, this is a unique name found mostly among the *Agona* people, a division of the Fante group of *Akan*. I personally do have distant relations that are known *as Saara* at *Agona Nsaba* in the central region of Ghana.

Isaac

By his wife *Saara*, *Abreham* eventually had a son known among the patriarchs as Isaac (see Genesis 21:3-4). He was the son *Abreham* was going to sacrifice to God (see Genesis 22). This biblical narrative confirms the ancient religious practice of human sacrifice among the *Afrim* people that left Ancient Egypt to go to live in Canaan because it was also the practice in Ancient Egypt. Modern *Akan* people from Ancient Egypt practiced this religious ritual of human sacrifice late into the twentieth century. Some scholars argue that this practice is not abandoned but it has been made more covert. This was a practice the *Afrim* people took from the *Akan* in Ancient Egypt. British historians would confirm that human sacrifice was an open religious ritual practiced among the *Akan* in the Gold Coast until the end of the first half of the 20th century. The name of Isaac was the first real *Akan* name of the patriarchs. The original *Akan* name from which the biblical Isaac was derived was *Sakyi* [pronounced *Sachi*]. Because this was a real name, there is orthographic evidence that it was deliberately transposed to conceal its origin. It was the *Akan* name *Sakyi* that was transposed to Saki [Sachi] and then further transposed to *Isak* by removing

262

the "I" from the end to the beginning to make it *Isach*. The final alphabet "k" changed to "c" in European orthography.

Esau

The biblical story of the patriarchs continues with *Sakyi* having twin sons by his wife Rebekah. The older son was called Esau and the younger was called Jacob. As I have pointed a couple of times before, the name of Esau was derived from the *Akan* name *Sau* [pronounced with a nasalized "au"], and the *Akan* phonology and etymology of the name is still discernible. Among the *Akan* people, this name can be traced directly to the ancient *Kwahu* people at *Adiabene*, the ancient vassal kingdom of the Parthian Empire that lived in the upper Tigris region. These people were just across from Haran, the biblical country of *Abreham* and his family.

There is an interesting story about the ancient *Kwahu* and the *Afrim* people. Though the *Afrim* people were not supposed to do so and they were almost forbidden to propagate Judaism in foreign lands, they went to the royal house of *Adiabene* and succeeded in converting the people of *Adiabene* to Judaism. Unfortunately, the royal house of *Adiabene* and their people converted to Christianity in the 2nd century. This should not have been much of an important historical occurrence but for some unknown reason, the conversion of the ancient people of *Adiabene* and their reconversion to Christianity has been so important that it is now part of Jewish history (see Jews in the Diaspora, *Encyclopaedia Britannica*, 1996, p. 75). The *Akan* name *Sau* was transposed into Greek as Esau where the prefix "E" was just added to try to conceal its ethnic origin and identity.

Jacob

The younger twin son of *Sakyi* was Jacob. This name was also a derivation from the *Akan* word **Gyakabo** [*Jakabo*]. In the *Akan* language, the word *Gyakabo* is not a real name; it is a nickname for a lazy never-do-well; someone who does not do anything but sits around like the rock. The Bible sought to reveal the meaning of this name in Genesis 25: 27 when it said:

> And the boys grew: and Esau was a cunning hunter, a man of the field; and Jacob was a plain man, dwelling in tents.

The *Akan* word *Gyakabo* literally means when everyone leaves the rock is the only thing left behind because a rock does not go anywhere. In other words *Gyakabo* was the rock that went nowhere and did nothing. It was this *Akan* nickname that was transposed into European languages as Jacob, a direct derivation from *Gyakabo* [*Jakabo*]. The symbolism of how the group that left Ancient Egypt in the biblical Exodus stole the wealth and philosophy of religion from the *Akan* people of Ancient Egypt is told in the story of Esau and Jacob beginning from Genesis Chapter 27.

There is a biblical verse that summarizes what the Jewish scholars of the Bible did to the *Akan* people of Ancient Egypt. Genesis 27:22 states what Isaac said: The voice is Jacob's voice, but the hands are the hands of Esau." Hands do the work while voices can simply claim what does not belong to them. The hands of Esau are symbolic of the brains and wisdom of the *Akan* people, and the voice of Jacob is symbolic of the theft and false claim of ownership of the work of the *Akan* people in foreign lands. We should not forget however that this same voice told us that Jacob was a "deceiver, a thief, and a scoundrel." Unfortunately, the biblical narrative tells us that it was to Jacob that the Jewish God revealed himself. It was therefore easy for this God to be given to Jacob the scoundrel than to Esau the cheated but chaste.

From the perspective of the *Akan* tribal origin of the *Afrim* people, the biblical patriarchs were:

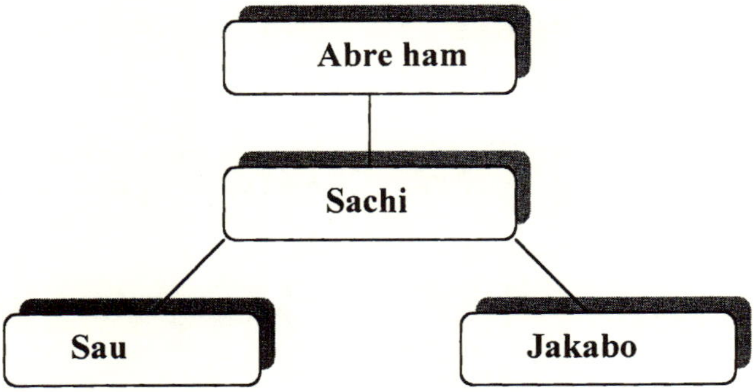
Abre ham
Sachi
Sau
Jakabo

Fig. 9: Original Akan names of the biblical patriarchs

Israel

Beyond the *Akan* names of the so-called patriarchs of the *Afrim* people that went to Europe to become the Jews and Hebrews, there was another important *Akan* name in the lives of these people before they went to become Jews. Among the *Afrim* people, the name of the most popular place of all places on earth is Israel. It is a name of self- identification of Jewish people. To the Christian world, Israel is the holiest place on earth, the supposed chosen place of the residence of God. To modern Jewish people, Israel is the ancient and spiritual home of their origin. The question is from which language did the word Israel originate and what did it mean? Most scholars have taken it for granted that the word Israel was Hebrew and so they have never asked such a question. It may come as the greatest surprise to Christians and perhaps some modern Jewish people to know that the name Israel was derived from an *Akan* word. The earliest name of modern Israel was *Afrim*, after the collective *Akan* name by which the people of the Exodus identified themselves to foreigners. This was the name that was transposed to *Ephraim*.

According to the biblical narrative that introduced this name, Jacob wrestled throughout the night with a man who did not want to be seen during the day (Genesis 32:24-30). As day was breaking, this man touched a vital point on Jacob's thigh and threw it out of joint. This was supposed to disable Jacob so the man could escape but Jacob held onto this man and would not let him go. Jacob was up to his extortion tricks again when he asked this man to bless him before he would let him to go. The Bible says this man changed the name of Jacob to *Asrae*. In the *Akan* language the word *Asrae* in this context means *the visited one*. Notice how this *Akan* word and its meaning fit perfectly into the biblical narrative and the consequent proclamation of Jacob as the divine and visited one. Jacob did not see the man he wrestled and this man would not even tell Jacob his name yet, Jacob proclaimed to have seen God face to face so he called the place Peniel. This visitation was the first to be given the *Akan* name *Asrae*. This preamble set the stage for the name of Jacob to be changed to *Asrae*, meaning the visited one.

In the typical fashion of biblical doublets, this story was told again in the Bible with differences in place names. Perhaps, to suggest that the wrestler that first changed the name of Jacob to *Asrae* was not the real God, the "real" God supposedly appeared unto Jacob and asked him to go to Bethel where Jacob supposedly dreamed of another man on a ladder. As Jacob was going to Bethel, God supposedly appeared unto him at Padanaram. This God also changed the name of Jacob again to *Asrae* by saying: "Thy name is Jacob: thy name shall not be called any more Jacob, but *Asrae*, but *Asrae* shall be thy name: and he called his name *Asrae*" (Genesis 35:10). All of these references and emphasis were meant to suggest that someone had visited Jacob. Was this someone God? Apart from believing it without question, how do we know that this someone was God? From our knowledge of the origin and creation of this God, that was impossible but the Bible says it happened and people that do not know the story behind the Bible have believed it for over two thousand years.

As in most *Akan* words in the Bible and other western historical accounts, the *Akan* phonology in *Asrae* was retained in the western orthography of Israel. However, in western orthography, the *Akan* "A" was transposed to a long "I" to retain the original *Akan* phonology. Moreover, the circumstances and the narrative for changing the name of Jacob to *Asrae* [Israel] is told twice to emphasize that God visited Jacob, thus making him the *Asrae* or the visited one.

Later, the *Afrim* people conferred the new name of Jacob onto their nation thus changing it from *Ephraim* [*Afrim*] to *Asrae* [Israel]. In this change, the name meant the visited placed. The name of modern *Asrae* in the original *Akan* language from which it was derived means the visited place. This was the ancient and original linguistic meaning of *Asrae*. However, modern *Afrim* scholars must have conferred a different meaning onto it to throw Europeans off their ancient and ethnic linguistic trail just as they simply claimed that they have lost their earliest language now known as classical Hebrew. How could a language be lost when the people that speak it are still living? The people of the so-called biblical Exodus spoke Akan and named their nation in the *Akan* language. I have asserted elsewhere that the lost Classical Hebrew was the *Akan* language, and the name of *Asrae* [Israel] is part of the evidence.

If the *Afrim* people that left Ancient Egypt in the Exodus were not *Akan* people, then the biggest question is how did they get to take their identity, name themselves, and name their nation in the *Akan* language? Which group of people would give their nation a name from the language of an ethnic group they do not belong and why? Again, this was not a linguistic coincidence, the *Afrim* people were originally *Akan* people, and the Bible reveals the common origin of the *Akan* and *Afrim* people in the allegorical blood ties of Esau and Jacob.

Akan and African tribal names of personalities in ancient Jewish history

Beyond the patriarchal names that can be traced to their ethnic origin in the *Akan* people, the *Afrim* people's real history also contains names of personalities that can also be traced to their tribal origin among the *Akan* and other African tribes. I have already pointed out that after Antigonus, the last of the Hasmonean kings was overthrown in 37 B. C., the *Afrim* people broke into tribal, religious, and political sects. Among these groups was the *Assini* tribal and political group. How could an *Akan* tribal group be found among the *Afrim* people as early as 37 B. C., if these people were not *Akan*?

In 132 A. D., a Jewish leader called *Simeon Bar Kokhba* led a Jewish revolt against the Romans for three years. He was supported by Rabbi *Akiba*. These two names are African tribal names. The name *Simeon* or *Simon* was derived from the *Akan* name *Siamon* meaning one that buries alive. This name was originally an appellation for a powerful person, a king; that is, this person had enough power to bury alive. This was a popular *Akan* royal name the Jewish people had encountered because the name can also be found in the Kings' Lists of Ancient Egypt. *Siamon* ruled Ancient Egypt from 978-959 B. C.

The name *Bar Kokhba* is also derived from the *Akan* words *Baako ba* meaning the child of one. The original *Akan* names that were transposed to *Simeon Bar Kokhba* were *Siamon Baakoba*. *Siamon Baakoba* was supported in his revolt by Rabbi *Akiba*. The name *Akiba* is not a derivation. It is the actual modern name of the *Nzima* and *Ahanta* people. In an earlier discussion, I pointed out that these were the people of *Akka* that were misidentified as the Akkadians and Sumerians.

After the defeat of *Baakoba*, Galilee became the center of Jewish congregation. Among the talmudic academies of Galilee was one at *Sepphoris*. This city must have been named after a leader or a great warrior of the Jewish people in the various encounters in wars in their history. This is because the name of this city was derived from the *Akan* name *Safori* meaning *Ofori the Warrior*. *Safori* is still a royal name that can be found among the *Akyem* branch of the *Akan* tribes. There was also a rabbi *Ha Nasi* in Palestine. This name was derived from the *Akan* name

Anansi meaning the spider. There are modern *Akan* people also named *Anansi*. All of these names can still be found among the descendants of the tribes from which the *Afrim* people originated. These were the tribes that carried these names in Ancient Egypt before the *Afrim* people took them to Canaan.

Akan and African tribal names of modern Afrim people

I have asserted throughout this book that the people that left Ancient Egypt into the so-called biblical Exodus were Ancient Egyptians that were black people. I have produced evidence throughout the book to show that the so-called people of the Bible were all black people. This means they were Africans but that is rather generic. I have produced specific historical, linguistic, and cultural evidence to show that the people that left Ancient Egypt in the so-called biblical Exodus were from *Akan* and other African tribes. The greatest evidence confirming that the people of the biblical Exodus were *Akan* and other African tribal groups are in the *Akan* and other African tribal names these people have carried with them after over three thousands of years of separation from these African tribes.

People in Europe that do not know African tribal names have heard, seen, and read many Jewish names and assumed that these names are Jewish or Hebrew, but they are not. They are African. African tribal names are unique to specific tribes and that means from the African names of Jewish people that still carry them, we can identify the specific tribes from which their ancient ancestors originated.

For some unknown reason, in my travels and stay in Europe, I seemed to have attracted Jewish friends with African names. In Russia, my friend was called *Anuchin*, a European transposition and corruption of the *Akan* name *Anokye* [pronounced *Anochi*]. In Italy, I met a friend called *Cuoko,* another European transposition and corruption of the *Akan* name *Akuoko*. There were more of my Jewish friends with African tribal names in Germany than I could count. However, my most chilling experience in my encounter with Jewish people with African tribal names was in Denver in Colorado. I met a lady called *Nimmo* working at a bank teller. With a big chill in my spine and goose bumps all over me, I went to speak to her. I have relatives and friends called *Nimo* back in Ghana. As I was talking to her, I felt like I was seeing through her and what has happened in her life and the life of her ancient ancestors was slowly unfolding and glowing towards me. Then it suddenly flashed through my mind that this woman could have been one of my relatives called *Nimo* in Ghana. Even in her white skin she still looked like a *Nimo* I know.

This is where my courage and curiosity to do this work on African tribal names of Jewish people originated. Most modern Jewish people still carry their ancient African tribal names. This is extremely remarkable because throughout their history, Jewish people have shown that they are willing to shed their names, racial, and ethnic identities so that they would fit into whichever linguistic and cultural societies they found themselves. As the scholars of *Britannica* wrote, "In every country in which the Jews lived for a considerable time, their physical traits came to approximate those of the indigenous people" (1996, p. 71).

Evidence in the history of Jewish people also shows that just as they have been willing to change their physical traits, so have they been willing to change their names or adapt them to fit into the linguistic environments they find themselves. When they got to Europe, they dropped their collective ethnic name *Afrim* and took the names Jews and Hebrews to fit into European societies. When the Anglo-French anthropologist Edwards classified them as Semites in 1829, they simply accepted it and they have been Semites since. That is why it is very remarkable that thousands and perhaps millions of Jewish people still carry their African tribal names as marks of their true racial and ethnic heritage.

While the Jewish people have failed to tell the world who they are, where they came from, and what language they spoke in their formative years, biblical, historical, linguistic, cultural, genetic, and scholastic evidence link them more to the Africans and specifically to the *Akan* people than any other group of people on this earth. To a great extent, this work has not turned out to be only the revelation of the Africans who wrote the Bible but also, it has turned out to be a revelation of the ancestral origin of the Jewish people and also a revelation of their specific tribal roots. This is a secret that has not been known for over three thousand years, and I do not think modern Jewish people remember it either.

Many of the Jewish people's African tribal names have been completely Europeanized through western orthography but their African phonologies, etymologies, and meanings can still be discerned. For example, the name of the last Israeli Prime Minister who was defeated by Ehud Barak in 1999, Mr. *Benjamin Netanyahu*, is an Europeanized version of an African tribal name, and this name has retained its etymology and phonology. The African name Netanyahu originates from the *Ga-Adangme* tribe and language, and it is a combination of two tribal names. The original tribal names from which *Netanyahu* was derived are *Netey* and *Nyaho* combined and Europeanized to Neteynyaho and spelled *Netanyahu*. These are names the *Ga-Adangme* people still carry and Mr. *Netanyahu* can find his heritage among them. The name of his successor Barak is also African. The indigenous African tribal name from which Barak was derived is Baraka.

Other African tribal names of the Jewish people have been Europeanized by adaptation, that is, by adding suffixes to make them fit into the linguistic, cultural, and geographical regions these people found themselves. For example, the name of the notorious "son of Sam" is *Berkowitz*. The indigenous African tribal name of this man is *Akan*, and it is originally *Berko* referring to one who was born during the war. Usually, children born during wars and conflicts are given this name. It is this name that the owner added "witz" to make it fit into the linguistic and cultural naming patterns of Eastern Europe.

I have already pointed out that the biblical name *Joseph* and the historical name *Josephus* were derived from the *Akan* name *Osafo*. What is most interesting about the indigenous *Akan* name *Osafo* is that there are modern *Afrim* people that still carry this original name. For example, at the *California Institute for the Future*, there is an eminent scholar known as *Paul Saffo*. *Saffo* is an *Akan* name derived from the full name *Osafo*. What makes the name *Osafo* or *Saffo* even more interesting to biblical discussion is the fact that the name *Osafo* among the children of *Jakabo* confirmed the *Akan* heritage of the children and family of Jacob even before they went to Ancient Egypt.

In other parts of Europe as in Germany, Austria, and Switzerland the most popular suffix used by the Jewish people was "man." While many Jewish people have retained their indigenous African tribal names, many more had to change their names entirely as a way of shedding the Jewish identities Europeans hated. This is because beyond their physical characteristics and religious practices, the African tribal names of Jewish people have been unique and different from European names so they were easily identifiable from their names, and there came a time when that was dangerous to their lives.

Among the linguistic and cultural evidence of their origins, Jewish people still carry *Akan* and other African tribal names like these:

Alberdi – an adaptation of the *Akan* name *Abedi.*

Arkoff – a European adaptation of the Akan name *Arkofo*

Ackom – an adaptation of the *Akan* name *Akom.*

Breman – an *Akan* name spelled and pronounced just as it is in *Akan.*

Adjemian – an adaptation of the *Akan* name *Agyeman* [pronounced *Adjeman*].

Cornu – an adaptation of the *Ga-Adangme* name *Konu.*

Danchi/Danchev – an Eastern European adaptation of the *Akan* name *Danchi.*

Domina - an Akan name meaning lover of the grave.

Dewaele – an adaptation of the *Yoruba* name *Adewale.*

Baars/Bahr/Barr – an adaptation of the *Akan* name *Baah*

Sahene – *Akan* meaning warlord.

Berko - *Akan* name meaning born during a war.

Berkowitz - an Eastern European adaptation of the *Akan* name *Berko*

Belko - orthographic variation of the name *Berko.*

Darko - *Akan* name meaning relies on war.

Diakun - a Europeanized adaptation of *Darko*

Darkowitz - and eastern European adaptation of *Darko*

Odom – Akan meaning benefactor, also a European adaptation of the *Akan* name *Odum.*

Sowa - *Ga-Adangme* name

Seih - European adaptation of the *Akan* name *Osei,* an *Akan* name, and an *Asante* name.

Atta - Akan name for a male twin.

Addair - European adaptation of the *Akan* name Adae, also the name of the ancient fortieth day celebration traditionally observed on Sundays - *Akwasidae.*

Tzachor – orthographic variation of the *Ewe* name *Tsakor.*

Koerner – European orthographic variation of the *Akan* name *Kona* or *Kone.*

Corder – an adaptation of the *Akan* name *Koda* or *Okoda.*

Adamo – an African tribal name.

Bioardi – Europeanized variation of the *Akan* name *Boadi.*

Lauteh – original name is *Larteh*; today the name of a people and a city.

Bauer – Europeanized adaptation of Hausa name Bawa. Spelling is German meaning builder.

Meara – from the *Akan* words *Me Ara* meaning only me. The Irish adds a prefix "O" to make it *O'meara.* The Irish have also been carrying some African tribal names like McAdo, McAidoo, etc.

Mantei – an adaptation of the *Akan* name *Mantey.*

Aponte – original Akan name is *Aponti*

Ankney - *Ankani*, Akan name.

Sakas - Saka, Akan name.

Moye - Moye, a Nigerian name possibly *Yoruba.*

Kersey/Kessel - a European adaptation of the *Akan* name *Kesse* meaning big.

Hazo - an adaptation of an *Ewe* name spelled Hazor today.

Boutwell - Europeanized adaptation of the *Akan* name *Botwe.*

Chiri - European adaptation of the *Akan* name *Okyere.*

Benoit - French adaptation of the *Akan* name *Benoa*, mostly carried by the *Kwahu* people.

Briffault – French adaptation of the *Akan* name *Brefo*

Boeheim - European adaptation of *Akan* name *Boahen.*

Tamberelli – an African tribal name.

Toobin - European adaptation of *Toben* meaning well roasted. Name said to be the legendary appellation of medicine men.

Pienemann – an adaptation of the *Akan* name *Pinaman.*

Menteer/Minter – original *Akan* name is *Minta.*

Kradin - *Akan* name meaning spiritual name.

Boni - European adaptation of the *Akan* name *Bonin.*

Kuehne - European adaptation of the *Akan* name *Kune.* Name also sometimes shortened as Kuhn.

Viau - adaptation of the *Ewe* name *Viawu.*

Tamburri - name found among the *Mosi* people north of Ghana.

Ancona - European adaptation of the *Akan* name *Ankoma.*

Ancoma – another European adaptation of *Ankoma.*

Hankamer – an adaptation of *Ankama* a variation of *Ankoma.*

Bornez - Eastern European adaptation of the *Akan* name *Bona.*

Buehlman - European adaptation of the *Akan* name *Boama*.

Arkow - European adaptation of *Akan* name *Arko*.

Quammen - European adaptation of Akan birth name *Kwame*, name for a boy born on Saturday as in *Kwame Nkrumah*.

Azulay - European adaptation of the Frafra name, *Azule*. This was the tribe that lived on the Frafra oasis near Ancient Egypt in ancient times. Others spell it *Azure*.

Zuniga – African tribal name *Zuniga*.

Debra – is the *Akan* name *Debra*.

Eiges - European adaptation of the *Akan* name *Agyei*.

Ilou/Alou - European adaptation of the Yoruba name *Alu*

Ahi - adaptation of the *Akan* name *Arhin*.

Farquahr - European adaptation of the *Akan* name *Farkwa*.

Tabikman – Eastern Europeanized adaptation of *Akan* name *Tabi*.

Kaikko - European adaptation of the *Akan* name *Kwaku* for a boy born on Wednesday.

Ebow - a European adaptation of the Akan name *Ebo*, Fanti name for a boy born on Thursday.

Boyardee - European adaptation of the *Akan* name *Boadi*.

Sotolongo - a name currently found among the tribes of the West African Sahel region.

Malben – European adaptation of the *Akan* name *Amoaben*.

Manevitz- an adaptation of the *Akan* name *Omane* or *'Mane*

Tumen - European adaptation of the *Akan* name *Tumi*.

Arnow - a European adaptation of the *Akan* name *Anno*.

Kuby/Kubie - European adaptation of the *Akan* appellation *Kubi* for the Akan name Appiah.

Paglia – West African, name currently found in the Sahel region.

Sapon - from the original *Akan* name *Sapon*.

Amateau/Amato - European adaptation of Fante name for a posthumous child.

Juman - European adaptation of the *Akan* name *Dwuma*, pronounced *Juma*.

Boam - a shortened form of the *Akan* name *Boama*.

Teboe – original *Akan* name is *Tibu*, also an Ewe name.

Bauman/Baumert - a Germanized adaptation of the *Akan* name *Boama*.

Baer/ Bayer - a Germanized adaptation of the *Akan* name *Baye*

Fehr - European adaptation of *Ofei*, an *Akuapem* name.

Danson - European adaptation of the *Akan* name *Danso*.

Arye/Ayers/Ayre - European adaptation of the *Akan* name *Aye*.

Pankow/ Pankov- European adaptation of the *Akan* name *Panko*.

Ashikaga - *Ewe* name. Can also be found among the Japanese from ancient *Ewe* people's presence on that island in ancient times.

Azarri – adaptation of the *Akan* name *Asare*.

Pelinka – African tribal name.

Kanka - *Akan* name, also shortened version of the *Akan* name *Kankam*.

Kato - *Akan* name, also the name of a town in the Brong Ahafo region of Ghana.

Ziga - Ewe name.

Tottori – an adaptation of the African tribal name *Totori*.

Conconi – an adaptation of the *Akan* name *Konkoni*.

Fodor – an adaptation of the *Akan* name *Fodwuor*.

Assante – an *Akan* tribal name.

Duer – an adaptation of the *Akan* name *Dua*.

Oure – an adaptation of the *Akan* name *Oware*.

Benes – an adaptation of the *Akan* name *Benneh*.

Fafara – an adaptation of the tribal name *Farafara*, the tribe that lived on the oasis by the same name near Ancient Egypt in ancient tines.

Sakai – an adaptation of the *Akan* name *Sakyi [Sachi]*. This was the name that was transposed to Isaac.

Kronman – an adaptation of the *Akan* name *Nkrumah*.

Amaker – an adaptation of *Igbo* name *Amaka*.

Kete – an ancient *Akan* name spelled *Khety* in Egyptology as in the name of *Dua Khety.*

Kasay/ Kessel/Kisseh – adapatations of the *Akan* name *Kesse.*

Zinsser – an adaptation of the *Ewe* name *Azinse.*

Eddo – an adaptation of the *Akan* name *Addo.*

Ocko – an adaptation of the *Ga* name *Oko.*

Cantey – an adaptation of the *Akan* names *Okai Anti*

Amanpour – an *Akan* name spelled and pronounced just as it is in *Akan.*

Boahim – an adaptation of the *Akan* name *Boahen.*

Labonte – a *Ga-Adangme* name spelled and pronounced just as it is in *Ga.*

Foley – an adaptation of the *Akan* name *Ofori.*

Parkow – an adaptation of the *Akan* name *Apako.*

Ramsey – an adaptation of the *Yoruba* name *Ramisi.*

Brambilla – an African tribal name.

Barbuor – an adaptation of the Akan name *Barfuor.*

Zewe – an African tribal name.

Mamman – an adaptation of the African tribal name *Marma.*

Tigar – an adaptation of the *Ewe* name *Tsigar* or *Ziga.*

Beauman – a French adaptation of the *Akan* name *Boama.*

Affron – an adaptation of the *Igbo* tribal name *Effron.*

Dombi – an adaptation of the *Akan* name *Dombie.*

Dapar – an adaptation of the *Akan* name *Dapaa*, an appelation for a boy born on Saturday.

Corey – an adaptation of the *Akan* name *Okore.*

Nemo/Nimoy – an adapatation of the *Akan* name *Nimo.*

Ober – an adaptation of the *Yoruba* title *Oba.*

Dades - an adaptation of the *Akan* name *Dade.*

Zaremba – an African tribal name.

Timko – an African tribal name.

Zanardy – an adaptation of the African tribal name *Zanadi*.

Alkow – an adaptation of the *Akan* tribal name *Arko*.

Grumet – an adaptation of the African tribal name *Grumah*.

Gerhke – an adaptation of the *Ewe Gerke*.

Hennig – an adaptation of the *Akan* name *Hinneh*.

Sotsu – an adaptation of the *Ewe* name *Sossu*.

Deico – an adaptation of the *Akan* name *Darko*.

Okuda – an adaptation of the *Akan* name *Okoda*.

Jase/Jesse/ Jersey - European adaptation of the *Akan* name *Gyas*i [*Jasi*]. This name can also be found in Ancient Egypt in names as Djeserkaraseneb.

Brodfeuhr - a German adaptation of the *Akan* name *Brefo*.

Kander – African tribal name, mostly probably a *Ga-Adangme* name. Also name of a suburb of Accra, capital city of Ghana.

Kabrin - an African tribal name, most probably Hausa.

Auletta - from the African tribal name *Awuleta*, most probably *Yoruba* in origin.

Daigler - Europeanized adaptation of the African tribal name *Daglia*.

D'Abo – African tribal name *Adabo* found among the *Akans* and also among *Yorubas*.

Bota - from the *Akan* name Bota, Europeanized to Botha in the Netherlands.

Adubato - African name, most propably found among the people of *Dahomey* and the *Ewe* tribe. Can also be found among the *Akans* and *Yorubas*.

Becker - adapted to fit the German orthography as a German name, originates from the *Akan* name *Abeka*.

Pinker – an adaptation of the *Akan* name *Pinka*.

Fenton - from the *Akan* name *Fenten*

Foree - Europeanized adaptation of the *Akan* name *Ofori*.

Kuerten/Querten - European adaptation of the *Akan* name *Kwarten*.

Benanti - *Akan* name found in the Brong Ahafo region where it would simply mean walking.

Herschong - from the *Akan* name *Ashun* or *Eshun*.

Tafoya - from the *Akan* name *Tafowa*.

Bouchey/ Boaicchi - European adaptation of the *Akan* name *Boakye [Boachi]*.

Gedemer - European adaptation of the *Ewe* name *Gedema* or *Gbedema*.

Danko - the original *Akan* name from which *Darko* became the corruption.

Bennewitz - eastern European adaptation of the *Akan* name *Benneh*.

Boehnen/Bonner - eastern European adaptation of the *Akan* name *Bonnah*, meaning dig graves.

Wode/Wade – adaptation of the *Akan* name *Wade*.

Mansaeu - European adaptation of the *Akan* name *Manso*.

Susser – European adaptation of the *Ewe* name *Suza*.

Sasso – an adaptation of *Sasu*, an *Akan* name, specifically a *Kwahu* name.

Annen – European adaptation of the original *Ga-Adangme* name *Annan*

Muzila - African tribal name.

Debayo - adaptation of the *Yoruba* name *Adebayo*.

Ojala – African tribal name.

Ojeman - adaptation of the *Akan* royal name *Agyeman [Ajeman]*.

Coussey - European adaptation of the *Akan* name *Kusi*

Sekih/Satcher – European adaptation of the *Akan* name *Sakyi*. Transposed to *Isaac* in patriarchal times.

Sokolik – an adaptation of the *African* tribal name *Sokoli*.

Daiber - European adaptation of the *Ga-Adangme* name *Dzaba/Djaba*.

Nadeau - an adaptation of the *Akan* name *Naadu* possibly a contraction from the two Akan names *Nana Adu*.

Dano – *Akan* name meaning that day.

Vargyas – adaptation of African tribal name *Varga*, mostly found among the *Frafra* people.

Knode - adaptation of the *Akan* name *Konadu.*

Anson - *Akan* name, unchanged in orthography.

Browar - European adaptation of the *Akan* name *Bruwa.*

Eike – European adaptation of the *Yoruba* name *Ake.*

Gerigh – European adaptation of the *Akan* name *Agyare.*

Genna – from the *Akan* name *Ajena*

Turchie – Europeanized adaptation of the *Akan* name *Takyi.*

Osias – adaptatiopn of the *Akan* name *Osei*

Curran – adaptation of the *Akan* name *Korang*

Lemenu – *Ewe* name

Dibiase – *Akans* share this name with *Ewes.*

Kasich – A derivation from the *Ewe* name *Akasi* and also *Kesse*

Dansich – a derivation from the *Akan* name *Adansi*

Zapor – an *Ewe* and other African tribal name.

Beddoe – from the *Akan* name *Badu* meaning the tenth born.

Labadie – from the *Ga-Adangme* word *Labadi.*

Pieneman – from the *Akan* name *Pinaman.*

Cote – derived from the *Ga–Adangme* name *Kotei*

Zamprogna – a European adaptation of the African name *Zamprona.*

Basoa – an exact *Akan* name.

Dench/Denchi – a European derivation of the *Akan* name *Danchi.*

Akron - An *Akan* name from the *Akuapem* tribe.

As Edwin Schrock of Illinois put it so profoundly: "it's been many and many a year since you and I were one person." It's been many and many a year since the *Akan* and other African tribal groups of Ancient Egypt and the *Afrim* people that eventually went to become the Jews and Hebrews in Europe were one people. These are only a small sample of the millions of modern Jewish people that still carry African tribal names as the true marks of their racial and ethnic identities. Perhaps, I should explore writing another book with these names However, the fact that this small number consists of numerous different African tribal names confirms the true origin of the ancient *Afrim* people that left Ancient Egypt to go to live in Canaan and then move on to Europe. If these people were not from these African tribes, where, when, why, and how did they come by these names?

The idea that the *Afrim* people that left Ancient Egypt into the biblical Exodus must have been Ancient Egyptians, as I have revealed in detail, is slowly gaining acceptance among biblical scholars. A major effort toward propagating this idea is the 1996 work of Gary Greenberg, *The Moses Mystery: The African Origin of the Jewish People*. However, some scholars can still not bring themselves to accept the fact that the ancient *Afrim* people that are the modern Jews and Hebrews were actually Africans. Perhaps in anticipation of someone like me coming out to reveal such overwhelming evidence of the Ancient Egyptian and therefore the African origin of modern Jewish people, some scholars have began exploring the idea and speculating only a minor link of the Jewish people to Ancient Egypt. As Richard Elliot Friedman pointed out in *Who Wrote The Bible*?

> Some investigators doing research on early Israelite history have concluded that, historically, only a small portion of the ancient Israelites was actually slave in Egypt. Perhaps, it was only the Levites. It is among the Levites, after all, that we find people with Egyptian names. The Levite names Moses, Hophni, and Phinehas are Egyptian, and not Hebrew. ... These investigators suggest that the group that was in Egypt and then in Sinai worshiped the God Yahweh. Then they arrived in Israel, where they met Israelite tribes who worshiped the God El. Instead of fighting over whose God was the true God the two groups accepted the belief that Yahweh and El were the same God. The Levites became the official priests of the united religion, perhaps by force or perhaps by influence 1987, p. 82).

These scholars point out some Ancient Egyptian names among modern Jewish people to argue that perhaps only the Levites were slaves in Ancient Egypt because they carried Ancient Egyptian names. Friedman goes on to say however that: "This [speculation] is in the realm of hypothesis, and we must be very cautious about it" (p. 83). The names of Levites above could not have been Ancient Egyptian because these names are not *Akan* or other African tribal names. However, if the three names of Levites point to the fact that they might be Ancient Egyptians, then the *Akan* and other African tribal names that millions of modern Jewish people still carry is more than conclusive

It was from their original African tribal roots that the Jewish people got these African tribal names and they have retained them for thousands of years. That might perhaps mean that the names still have some secret and special significance for the people that carry them.

From all these, the ultimate conclusion supporting the thesis of this book is simply that the people of the Bible were black people and this confirms the veracity of the early black image of *Ayesu*, [Jesus], and his mother in early Catholic Churches in Europe.

From the discussion so far, it has also become clear that the biblical documents the Jewish scholars passed on to the Greeks were not original Jewish documents but they took them from the theosophical repository of the Ancient Egyptians. This Ancient Egyptian theosophical repository was of course *Akan* people's theosophical library. How do we know this? We know this from the fact that most of the transposed names of the supposed authors of the Old Testament were *Akan* names. From these foundations, it is now time to reveal the names of The Africans Who Wrote The Bible.

7

The Africans Who Wrote The Bible

Ye shall know the truth, and the truth shall make you mad.
Aldous Huxley

Between truth and the search for truth, I choose the second.
Bernard Berenson

Truth makes many appeals; not the least of it is its power to shock
Jules Renard

Introduction

Did God write the Bible or did this God inspire his prophets to write it? Is the Bible a document of man's attempts to accept and imagine a power greater than he in his quest to explain things he did not understand, or there is a God somewhere that asked that his words be written for humans? In an Arts and Entertainment Network Documentary on *Who Wrote The Bible?* one of the biblical scholars expressing the general scholastic view of how the Bible has been made to be more than it actually is simply said, "You cannot establish the authority of a book better than saying God wrote it." This God is portrayed to be the greater power over human lives and deaths and certainly one cannot confer any greater power on a book than saying it is the book of the one that has power over our lives and after-life. This is the foundation in the fallacy of many people's perception of the Bible today. In the quest for the acceptance of the documents of the Bible and the people that supposedly wrote these documents for the Greeks, these documents were first presented as having been written by God himself. When this view was questioned in the events leading to the Reformation, the story of the authorship of the biblical documents was slowly changed to the Bible having been written by prophets inspired by God.

The Bible has been received in Europe and promoted under the banner of Christianity as the most glorious book ever written by man. Eminent European scholars of the past and present contend that the most remarkable quality of the Bible is the fact that it is a formula for societal design, religion, law, history, poetry, education, morality, and philosophy of life all designed into one tome. This in itself shows that the content and complexity of the work are above what the short and turbulent history of the ancient *Afrim* people that left Ancient Egypt into the so-called biblical Exodus would justify. In other words, the quality of the work is not the kind a people that were on the move, harassed by their neighbors, conquered here, and dragged into captivity there could have written. The quality of the work reflects the thinking, religious, and world perception of a people that had lived in peace over a long period of time and such were not the *Afrim* people that went to Europe to become the Jewish people. They were the Ancient Egyptians. These were the people that had observed nature, designed, and practiced religion for thousands of years before the *Afrim* people supposedly went to them.

As a result of its deep philosophical and theosophical content however, whichever way one perceives the Bible, one can find something in it to explain and interpret any situation. In short, it is an excellent book. At the same time, historians and even biblical scholars have found many illogical assertions, deficiencies and inconsistencies within the Bible. These scholars have specifically found out that the Bible is full of "primitive legend," "pious fraud," "historical inaccuracies," "unnecessary repetitions," and some parts seem to have been hastily put together without much literary or philosophical planning. Nevertheless, as Will Durant puts it in *The Story of Civilization: Our Oriental Heritage*:

... this is the first recorded effort of man to reduce the multiplicity of past events to a measure of unity seeking in them some pervading purpose of significance, some law of sequence and causation, some illumination for the present and future (1935, p. 340).

According to Durant, "there is nothing more perfect in the realm of prose than the story of Ruth," and the Psalms. Durant, however, acknowledges that the Psalms seem not to be the work of David, and that it might have been influenced by the writings of Ancient Egyptian pharaoh *Akenten* [Greek *Akhenaten*]. Nevertheless, literary and biblical scholars still contend that the Bible is the best of the world's lyric poetry.

The *Afrim* people that left Ancient Egypt into the so-called biblical Exodus and later went to Europe to become the Jews and Hebrews claim that their priests, prophets, and scholars wrote the biblical documents. Yet, these people can not to tell with certainty who the authors of these documents were. In the words of the biblical scholar Richard Elliot Friedman quoted earlier from his book entitled *Who Wrote The Bible*?, he pointed out that:

> It is a strange fact that *we have never known with certainty* who produced the book that has played such a central role in our civilization. There are traditions concerning who wrote each of the biblical books – the Five Books of Moses are supposed to be by Moses, the book of Lamentations by the prophet Jeremiah, half the Psalms by King David – but how is one to know if these traditional ascriptions are correct? (1987, p. 15, emphasis mine).

I would say without reservation that Friedman is one of the well-respected biblical scholars in the field. The revelation in his quotation therefore represents the state of the knowledge of scholars in this field. His usage of the pronoun "we" confirms this.

What is most disturbing in Friedman's revelation of the state of the knowledge of biblical scholars about the authors of the biblical documents is the fact that the Jewish scholars that compiled, edited, and translated the documents for the Greeks assigned names to each document. These are the names around which the Christian religion was developed in the formative years of Christianity. Why then would biblical scholars point out that they do not know for sure who wrote the documents of the Bible? It is apparent that these scholars know more about the documents of the Bible than lay readers and believers. Part of the knowledge they have is the fact that these scholars have begun to discover that the authors the Jewish scholars of the biblical documents assigned to certain documents were false. These authors are not the real authors of these biblical documents. What then was going on here?

This is therefore evidence to suggest that even in the assignment of authors to the biblical documents, there was some calculated deception. What made it necessary for the Jewish scholars of the Bible to deceive readers and believers about the people that wrote these documents? Could it be that the foundation of deception from which the Bible was designed was the reason the real names of the authors of the New Testament documents also had to be concealed? If the Jewish scholars of the Bible would deceive readers and believers about the authors that wrote these documents, how difficult could it be for these scholars to steal the documents from other people? Wouldn't that be the reason they would assign fictitious authors to these documents in the first place? That is what I have been saying all along that the documents of the Bible were not the original documents of the *Afrim* people that later went to Europe to become the Jews and Hebrews.

Nevertheless, the *Afrim* people have claimed that their God-inspired prophets wrote the biblical documents but after almost two thousand years of searching, western historians and biblical scholars have still not found the true source and the real authors of these documents or any evidence that Jewish prophets wrote them. The flaw in the search of these western scholars however is in the fact that few of them have been willing to consider with equanimity that

Ancient Egypt was the source of the biblical documents and black people from the black tribes of Ancient Egypt were the authors. Most Egyptologists, however, know that Ancient Egypt was the source of the biblical documents but they are also not willing to be the bearers of the news that exposes Christian Europe to "pious fraud" and theosophical embarrassment. What these scholars do not know in the west is the fact that the names of the authors of the Old Testament documents are transposed African tribal names that can still be discerned by those who know these African names.

Jewish people have long claimed in Europe and in the Christian world that their priests, prophets, and scholars wrote the Bible. However, modern scholars of the Bible most of who are Jewish have also found that ancient Jewish scholars of the Bible deceived us in their assignment of authors to documents of the Bible. This is very significant and the fact that these scholars have not found any external evidence to support the claims of the Bible about who wrote these documents is also very significant. From all these, any evidence showing that even one biblical document was not an original Jewish document is also very significant. The question is why would the Jewish scholars of the Bible assign false authors to the documents of the Bible? What would make such a gross deception of the ancient Greeks and later Europeans and the Christian world necessary? Even the necessity to ask these questions confirm what I have revealed and discussed that the documents of the Bible were not Jewish people's documents and that Jewish scholars of the Bible simply took these documents from the Ancient Egyptians. In the discussions in the preceding chapters, I showed that historians, Egyptologists, and biblical scholars have found numerous documents of the Bible that were not original documents of the Jewish people and these documents have been traced instead to Ancient Egyptian theosophical literature.

The Jewish people's historical account of the creation of the biblical documents

Despite the fact that the documents of the Bible were not created by the Jewish people, their biblical scholars and historians have succeeded in creating Jewish history from the Bible to support their claim of this book. Jewish history tells a story about how Jewish priests found the documents of the Bible from nowhere. It is important to note that in Jewish history, there is no evidence of Jewish prophets and priests writing the documents of the Bible anywhere. There is no evidence of a store of written documents from which the biblical documents could have been a part.

According to the history of the Jewish people, mostly written by their scholars and taken up by Christian Europe and European scholars, the greatest religious threat to the social order of the ancient *Afrim* people before they went to Europe to become Jews and Hebrews was their movement away from worshipping *Yahweh* to worshipping alien gods.

What is interesting about this reason as the foundation for the creation of the biblical documents is that these were the same reasons the Ancient Egyptians wrote their numerous social and religious documents most of which are found in the Bible today. In *The Story of Civilization: Our Oriental Heritage*, Will Durant pointed out that Ancient Egyptians lamented the social decay of their society and therefore:

> Another sage, Ipuwer, bemoans the disorder, violence, famine, and decay that attended the passing of the Old Kingdom; he tells skeptics who "would make offerings if" they "knew where the god is," he comments upon increasing suicide, and adds like another Schopenhauer: "Would that there might be an end of men, that there might be no conception, no birth. If the land would but cease from noise and strife be no more" (pp. 194-5)

It is evident from this quotation that the Ancient Egyptians also had the same reason of societal decay and straying from their religion to write the documents that the Jewish people have claimed their people wrote. Durant noted that " in the end, he [Ipuwer] dreams of a philosopher-king who will redeem men from chaos and injustice." From this it is prudent to deduce that the concept and the need for a king that would come to redeem men was already expressed in Ancient Egypt before some unknown scholars designed their stories to make Jesus the philosopher-king that supposedly came to deliver humans.

From the *Wisdom of the Ancient Egyptians*, Durant quoted the lamentation of Ipuwer. Commenting upon Ipuwer's lamentations, Durant wrote that:

> This is already the voice of the prophets; the lines are cast into strophic form, like the prophetic writings of the Jews; and Breasted properly acclaims these "Admonitions" as "the earliest emergence of social idealism which among the Hebrews we call 'Messianism' (p. 195).

Durant points out here that the voice of Ipuwer sounded exactly like the supposed later voices of the Jewish prophets. James Henry Breasted pointed out that these writings were the earliest records of the emergence of social idealism. According to Breasted, this Ancient Egyptian social idealism became Messianism for the Jews. In other words, Breasted pointed out that they were the Ancient Egyptians and not the Jewish people that created the earliest record and concept of the emergence of the kind of social idealism that is found today in biblical documents. What is important to note about the similarities western scholars have found in Ancient Egyptian and biblical literature is that the Bible and the claims of the Jewish people had already influenced these scholars. As a result, though these scholars knew that there existed Ancient Egyptian records before Jewish scholars went to Ancient Egypt to translate these documents for the Greeks, none had the courage to question Jewish people's claims of the creation of the Bible.

Nevertheless, the history of the Jewish people states that as the people continued to "stray" into alien gods, religious ideas, and practices, the social, religious, and political positions of the Jewish priestly order were threatened. The priests decided to find a way to regain control of the social order over which they were once the overlords. Before this period, Jewish priests were mostly like the Ancient Egyptian priests from whom they learned the practices of priesthood. These priests were not social politicians, propagandists, or the spokespersons of any gods. When the social and moral order of the Jewish people supposedly broke down, the history of the Jewish people says that the priests found out that they needed some heavenly help to get the attention of their people. As a result, the priests decided to change their traditional roles and follow the same communication strategies and approaches in which the prophets attributed whatever they said to the gods. It is clear from this part of the history that ancient *Afrim* priests were originally not the spokespersons of the gods, but the prophets that purported to be spokespersons of some gods were more successful in getting the attention of their people. So the priests also decided to adopt this rhetoric style and the foundation of what has become a two thousand-year old pious fraud was laid.

The priests decided to bring back the strayed ***Afrim*** people with what they would call a direct message and communication from God. To do so, the priests had to win over the prophets to their cause. So they decided to issue a code of religious laws that would appeal to the prophets and at the same time help win back the rotting soul of the *Afrim* nation. At this point, nobody knows what had happened to the *Ten Commandments* of morality the *Afrim* people supposedly received from this same God in the desert. However, it is clear from their history that the *Afrim* people did not perceive these Commandments to be as sacred as Christians have made them today.

To make their strategy of winning back the strayed souls of the *Afrim* people work, the priests first had to win the support of their king, King Josiah, who agreed to the secret plan of deception by the priests. As it can be seen from the story of how the *Afrim* people claim they came to acquire the foundations of the biblical documents, it was through fraud and "priest-perverted deception." Will Durant narrated the fraudulent plot of the *Afrim* priests when he wrote:

... and about the eighteenth year of his reign *the priest Hilkiah announced to the King that he had "found" in the secret archives of the Temple an astonishing scroll in which the great Moses himself, at the direct dictation of Yahweh,* had settled once and for all those problems of history and conduct that were being so hotly debated by prophets and priests. The discovery made a great stir. Josiah called the elders of Judah to the Temple, and there read to them the "Book of the Covenant" in the presence (we are told) of thousands of people. Then he solemnly swore that he would henceforth abide by the laws of this book; and "he caused all that were present to stand to it" (Durant, 1935, 320-1; see also 2 Kings 22:8; 23:2; 2 Chronicles 34:15, 31-2, emphasis mine).

There is no greater way toward establishing the authority of a book than saying that it is the book of God. Note how the priest Hilkiah supposedly told King Josiah that he had found a book that Yahweh directly dictated to Moses to write down. How did the priest Hilkiah know this and why hadn't anyone known this before in the entire history of the *Afrim* people? From this we begin to see how the foundational lies behind Christianity developed. Note also that the priests and prophets were debating the quest for a new history for the *Afrim* people after the Exodus and before they went to Europe to become the Jews and Hebrews. This history was supposedly hundreds of years before Jewish scholars returned to Ancient Egypt to translate the biblical documents for the Greeks. From this point of view, these scholars' creation of the fictitious story of Esau and Jacob as two nations in their mother's womb begins to make sense. As I have pointed out, this story was used to separate the *Afrim* people of the Exodus from their tribal origins in Ancient Egyptian tribes.

Above everything else, note also that in this quotation from Jewish people's real history, the "discovery" of the so-called "Book of Covenant" was a strategically planned deception of the Jewish people themselves by their priests. From what is known today, it is evident that all these were fabrications. However, it is also clear that the Jewish people's own story of the supposed creation of the foundation documents of the Bible was carefully planned to deceive the Jewish people themselves. Since then, this deceived the Greeks, later entire Europe, and millions around the world. Even in their own history, Jewish people do not deny that their so-called foundation documents of the Bible began from pious fraud. Why would Jewish historians and biblical scholars admit to creating such a deception in claiming that the biblical documents were their original documents? This was because this deception was the better of the choices to cover up a bigger deception. Either the Jewish historians and biblical scholars had to create such a deception in their history to help them claim the documents of the Bible or they had to admit that these documents were Ancient Egyptian in origin.

What makes their story of the creation of these documents even more spurious is the fact that the priests claimed that *Yahweh* directly dictated the content of the Book of Covenant to Moses and therefore it was the word of God. This was the story the *Afrim* scholars of the biblical documents told to claim the origin of the first five books of the Bible as theirs. From this foundation, the first five books of the Bible were attributed to Moses but it was all a lie as biblical scholars have found out today.

Early European scholars could not separate the real history of the Jewish people from their biblical history. As a result, it was not after the Reformation that some scholars had the nerve to analyze and question the source, content, and authorship of the biblical narrative attributed to Moses. Among the earliest scholars to show that Moses did not write the first five books of the Bible was the 16th century British philosopher Thomas Hobbes. The views of Hobbes opened the door for other scholars who had similar views to speak their minds and write books about the fallacies they had found in different parts of the Bible. Dutch philosopher Spinoza and the French Calvinist Isaac de la Peyrere all published their views on this ideas confirming that Moses did not write these books.

Among the most revealing evidence these scholars introduced to support their claim was the fact that the text supposedly written by Moses described his death and place of burial (see

Deuteronomy 34:6). How could a person who had died and been buried write about his own death and burial? To scholars, this showed that Moses did not write "all" the books attributed to him. Someone wrote "some" of the Books of Moses after his death and attributed those also to him. If Moses did not write these five books who then wrote them? How do we know that Moses even wrote some of these Books attributed to him? Why would ancient *Afrim* scholars of the biblical documents claim that Moses wrote these books when he did not write them? Again, we do have evidence of another fictitious attribution of the authorship of a biblical document and that suggests that these documents could not have been original *Afrim* people's documents. That is enough evidence to suggest that these documents were definitely stolen from somewhere, and the evidence shows that they were Ancient Egyptian documents. Otherwise, why would Jewish scholars claim that their prophets and priests wrote these documents and then attribute the documents to some fictitious authors that did not write them?

Some scholars of African descent have suggested that the documents in the so-called *Book of Covenant* were part of the religious documents the people that went into the biblical Exodus took from Ancient Egypt. These scholars introduce two arguments in support of their assertion. First, the Bible confirms that the people of the Exodus were capable of deceiving stealing gold, silver, and clothes from their Ancient Egyptian neighbors. However, it does not mention and it is not inconceivable that these people also took religious documents from Ancient Egypt. The second argument is that Moses is now known not to have been a Jew but an Ancient Egyptian priest. Therefore, he could have taken these documents from the Ancient Egyptian priesthood and still that does not make these Jewish documents.

Modern scholastic evidence of the origin of the sources of the biblical documents

The deception in Jewish people's claims of the authorship of the documents of the Bible is further exposed by the fact that modern scholars have been discovering evidence of literary editing and authorship that is not consistent with something that would have been done if the documents were originally written by ancient *Afrim* prophets as the Bible claims. In *Who Wrote The Bible*? Richard Elliot Friedman wrote:

> The critical analysis of authorship has also extended beyond the Five Books of Moses and has touched every book of the Bible. *For example, the book of Isaiah was traditionally ascribed to the prophet Isaiah, who lived in the eighth century B. C. Most of the first half of the book fits with such tradition. But chapters 40 through 66 of the book of Isaiah appear to be by someone living about two centuries later.* Even the book of Obadiah, which is only one page long, has been thought to be a combination of pieces by two authors (p. 29, emphasis mine).

In summary, Friedman points out that the book of Isaiah believed to have been written by Isaiah was not written by him because parts of the content of the book reflects a later period after Isaiah. All of these confirm that the biblical documents were not the original works of *Afrim* prophets or scholars. In effect, the Jewish people have claimed these documents of the Bible for the past two thousand years but our emerging knowledge shows that these were not their documents. This was the foundation history of the documents that early Christians and later followers of the Christianity have come to believe it is the book of God.

As usual, western scholars who are mostly influenced by the biblical tradition have believed the biblical story, and they have based much of their scholarship upon it. These scholars have not been able to determine what the "Book of the Covenant" contained. However, they have speculated that its content must have been a restatement of the laws, decrees, demands, and admonishing of the temple priests and the prophets. Some scholars have even speculated that this book was *Exodus* chapters 22 and 23 or it might have been *Deuteronomy*.

Despite all these, the biblical story says that the people who heard directly from the reading of this document and those who heard of it elsewhere were pleased. The narrative in

Nehemiah 10:29 states that "the people pledged to accept this body of legislation as their constitution and their conscience, and to obey it forever" (see Durant, p. 328). What is interesting about this historical narrative is that there is no mention of the time, place, and manner in which Moses or the so-called *Afrim* prophets and priests wrote these documents. There is no mention of the divine origin of these documents and how they were to be taken as holy writ. Finally, there is no mention of anyone's name except the priest Hilkiah who supposedly found the documents. How could it be said that the biblical documents including the first five books of Moses were the documents of the entire Jewish people if only one person knew of the existence of the Book of the Covenant? How could it be said that the concept of religion initiated from the Book of Covenant was the religious concept of the Jewish people if only Hilkiah knew of the existence of such a concept and documents? These are all parts of the legendary lying lore that the revelation of the Africans who wrote the documents of the Bible is about to dispel.

I am trying to reveal through a variety of sources that the documents of the Bible were not the original documents of the *Afrim* people whose scholars supposedly compiled, edited, and translated these documents for the Greeks. However, another scholar has already revealed much of the scholastic evidence confirming that the biblical documents were Ancient Egyptian in origin.

In *The Moses Mystery: The African Origin of the Jewish People*, Gary Greenberg assembled evidence to show that the *Afrim* scholars of the biblical documents in Alexandria took Ancient Egyptian documents and redesigned them as their own for the unsuspecting Greeks and later Europeans. Writing about the biblical chronology in Genesis, for example, Greenberg stated:

> Scholars casually dismiss this [Genesis 5 & 11] chronology as worthless, but in later chapters I will show that it provides a highly accurate record of Egyptian dynastic history (1996, p. 21).

In this book, Greenberg showed that the Genesis chronology was designed from the chronology of Ancient Egyptian kings now known in Egyptology as the Kings' Lists. He elaborated this by further stating that:

> The evidence shows that the Genesis birth and death dates derive from Egyptian king lists and provide an exact one-to-one correlation with the starting dates for Egyptian dynasties and several important Egyptian kings. These correlations begin with the foundation of the First Dynasty (c. 3100 B. C.) and end with the start of the Eighteenth Dynasty, over 1500 years later (p. 21-2).

The foundation of the entire biblical story is based upon the premise that there were some ancient *Afrim* people that developed the religious concepts, doctrines, and documents that the *Afrim* scholars passed into Europe as the foundations of Christianity. If such a claim was fraudulent and the fabrication of these ancestors was based upon existing Ancient Egyptian documents then the entire biblical narrative and the claim of these so-called ancestors rests on very shaky grounds. Why would the *Afrim* scholars of the Bible design their fictitious ancestry from Ancient Egyptian Kings' lists? Was it because they originated from the *Akan* and the other African tribes that were the Ancient Egyptians? Did this origin make it alright in the minds of the Jewish scholars of the Bible to use the stories of their true tribal ancestors of Ancient Egypt to create a fictitious story of origin for themselves? Did the Jewish scholars of the Bible do this to conceal a story of their origin that they did not want the Greeks to know but they did not want the Jewish people to forget? One thing that becomes clear here is that using Ancient Egyptian Kings' Lists to create their fictitious history of origin was the needed foundation upon which these scholars could claim the Ancient Egyptian stories they were plagiarizing to make it all fit in perfectly and look authentic.

I have pointed this out several times over and this also clearly confirms that the   *Afrim* scholars of the biblical documents did not only compile, edit, rewrite, and translate the biblical documents in Ancient Egypt, but also they actually took Ancient Egyptian historical and theosophical records and tried to make these records their own. As a matter of fact, the *Afrim* people have succeeded in telling the world that these documents were their creations for over two thousand years.

In his discussion of the date of the Exodus, Greenberg wrote that:

> My analysis places the Exodus in 1315 B. C., during the co-regency of Rameses I and Setho I. Such a date means Moses and Akhenaten were children together, raised, and educated at the same time in the royal household of King Amenhotep III (p. 22).

Again, the revelation by Greenberg that Moses and *Akenten* [Akhenaten] grew up and were raised and educated together in the same household is important because *Afrim* scholars later argued that their ancestors created what they call universal monotheism. However, Ancient Egyptian history shows that it was the pharaoh *Akenten* that invented the concept of monotheism. The analysis above shows that Moses knew *Akenten* and that Moses took the idea he introduced to the *Afrim* people as monotheism from *Akenten*, the original monotheist. Again, this confirms that *Afrim* scholars' modern claims of their ancestral creation of monotheism are also false.

For an in-depth research and analysis of the Exodus, Greenberg delved into Ancient Egyptian texts and the writings of several classical historians. He noted that:

> The [Ancient] Egyptian materials parallel the biblical story [of the Exodus] in many areas but reverse the role of Moses and the pharaoh, making Moses the cruel ruler and Pharaoh the young child who was hidden away and later returned to liberate his people. Reducing the parallel themes to their essential elements, we learn how Egyptian mythological and literary motifs helped shape the biblical story of Moses (p. 22).

Notice how Greenberg puts it that Ancient Egyptian documents "parallel" the Exodus narrative in many areas except that the roles of Moses and pharaoh are reversed in the biblical narrative. They are not the Ancient Egyptian documents that "parallel" the Exodus narrative instead it is the Exodus narrative that "parallels" Ancient Egyptian documents. From the fact that the Ancient Egyptian documents existed before the biblical narrative was written, and from the fact that the biblical narrative was written in Ancient Egypt, it becomes clear from this perspective where the Jewish scholars of the biblical documents took the story of the Exodus.

Notice also how the same Ancient Egyptian leitmotif of a young child that was hidden away from an evil ruler and later returned to free his people was used to design the story of Jesus Christ. In this discussion, Greenberg was wrong in one respect. Ancient Egyptian myths and literary motifs did not help shape the biblical story in any way. The simple truth is that the Jewish scholars of the Bible simply took Ancient Egyptian documents and edited them to make these documents their own. That was how Ancient Egyptian texts and biblical stories came to parallel each other, and it was also the same reason other scholars found similarities between Ancient Egyptian and biblical literature. They were the same Ancient Egyptian texts simply edited, translated into Greek, and assigned to fictitious Jewish authors.

In his analysis of the biblical patriarchs, Greenberg again found an Ancient Egyptian connection. He wrote:

> The evidence shows how the early Israelites [the Afrim people] adapted [Ancient] Egyptian myths about the god Osiris and his family and transformed them into stories about distant human ancestors, removing them from the magical realm of Egyptian religion and placing them in the hands of the one and only God of Israel (p. 22).

In this quotation, Greenberg also pointed out Jewish people's creation of fictitious distant ancestors to try to authenticate their plagiarism. Again, Greenberg showed that the biblical patriarchal history was derived from Ancient Egyptian mythology and that the patriarchs were simply imagined. However, my linguistic and cultural analysis has shown that there must have been patriarchs that originated from among the *Akan* tribe that was the vassal kingdom of the Parthian Empire in the Tigris and Euphrates region. This is because these patriarchs carried names from *Akan* words and names. In other words, the patriarchs that supposedly went to Ancient Egypt were *Akan* people that went to other *Akan* people in Ancient Egypt.

The most important point in Greenberg's book is that the *Afrim* people that later went to Europe to become the Jews and Hebrews originated from the black African tribes of Ancient Egypt and that the biblical documents were taken from Ancient Egyptian sources. The Ancient Egyptians are modern Africans and Greenberg concludes that it was from these Africans that the ancient *Afrim* people or modern Jews and Hebrews of Europe originated. All I did in support of this work was reveal the specific African tribes from which the ancient *Afrim* people originated through tribal, linguistic, and cultural evidence.

It is not only Greenberg that has asserted that the biblical documents originated from Ancient Egyptian sources. In E. F. Wente's *The Contendings of Horus and Set,* he showed that the biblical story of Esau and Jacob right from their births to the purchase of Esau' birthright, the role of their mother, and many other details originated from the Ancient Egyptian story of *Horus* and *Set.* It is interesting to point out here that the name of this author *Wente* is an African tribal name. Specifically, it is a *Guan* tribal name.

These were the foundations and sources of the documents and beliefs that eventually became Christian documents and beliefs in Europe. With Europeans far removed from the veracity of the biblical story, and from the strategy of the early apostolic fathers not to reveal any of these to the Christian masses, Europeans took the ancient pagan worship of the *Akan* and *Afrim* people and called it Christianity. However, they first converted the names in these concepts and doctrines into European names, gave the stories new characters with fictitious and transposed names, and simply called it Christianity.

The rise of Yahweh to supreme deity

The story of how Yahweh became the supreme deity of the Jewish people is also very interesting. The continued history of the Jewish people states that the period after the reading of the so-called Book of Covenant to the *Afrim* people was the time their priests decided to make *Yahweh,* the supreme and sole god of the *Afrim* people. Seeing it as a way of consolidating his political and religious power among his people, King Josiah took advantage of the mood of his people during this period to raid the altars of *Yahweh's* rival gods in Judah. Josiah cast:

> "out of the temple of the Lord [Yahveh] all the vessels that were made for Baal, he put down the idolatrous priests, and "them also that burned incense unto Baal, to the sun, and to the moon, and to the planets; he defiled Topheth, ... that no man might make his son or his daughter to pass through the fire to Molech; and he smashed the altars that Solomon had built for the Chemosh, Milcom, and Astarte (Durant, 1935, p. 321; see also 2 Kings 23:2. 4, 10, 13).

It is important to note in this quotation the various deities that the *Afrim* people that went to Europe to become the Jews and Hebrews worshipped and held sacred. According to the historical account that has been designed to make *Afrim* people the inventors of monotheism, Josiah's raid of these various deities paved the way for *Yahweh* to become the leading deity of the *Afrim* people. The story goes on to say that nevertheless, the *Afrim* people never stopped or abandoned the worshipping of their communal, private, individual, and sometimes even outside deities. This *Yahweh* is still the deity the *Afrim* people worship today, and he was the deity the *Afrim* scholars of the Bible introduced to the Greeks for him to become the *Yahveh* or Jehovah of Christianity.

It is also important to note that the various names the *Afrim* people later gave this deity also deceived Europeans. When one hears of *Adonai, Yahveh, Jehovah, Lord, God, Lord God,* and other names and epithets describing God, one would think this God is a newfound, special, and different God from the God of the Ancient Egyptians that first imagined and personified this concept. He was the same God from the cults of *Yaa* and *Yaw* of the *Akan* people. He was the God of the cult of the *Afrim* people before he became the God of the cult of European Christianity.

The brief history above was what *Afrim* historians and biblical scholars told Europeans and made them believe in the legendary lying lore of Christianity for over two thousand years. This was the lore that has shaped European world-view and scholastic perception of every discipline for almost a thousand years. The organization and development of European societal foundations were based upon this lore of deception and pious fraud that became the Christian religion.

The story of Ancient Egypt, Akan, and Afrim in the foundations of the Bible

This book is the about the Ancient Egyptians, the Africans, the Jewish people, the Bible, and European Christianity. It is the related history of all these that I have been trying to present throughout the book and now that I am about to reveal the indigenous African tribal names of the authors of the Bible, I feel it is important to go over a summary of this story to freshen the foundations for the coming revelations. It is a very serious theosophical problem to find out that the Christian God *Yahveh* was the ancient *Akan* God of Thursday. It is even worse to find out that Moses did not write the five biblical Books of Moses and that Isaiah also did not write the biblical book attributed to him either. The revelation that the Genesis chronology was based upon Ancient Egyptian Kings' Lists does not help matters. Further revelation that the story of Esau and Jacob was adapted from the Ancient Egyptian story of *Horus* and *Set* effectively erodes the foundational beliefs we have had in the biblical documents since childhood.

In an earlier discussion, we found out that the biblical story of *Osafo* [Joseph] was taken from an Ancient Egyptian story. We even found out that this story was an ancient *Ewe* story. All of these go to show that the biblical documents that *Afrim* scholars claim were created by their people were actually created by the Ancient Egyptians. Perhaps, the greatest evidence of this is in the *Akan* and other African tribal names [not Jewish names] of the authors of the Old Testament documents.

Throughout the book, I have revealed evidence of the racial, ethnic, linguistic, and cultural origin of the *Afrim* people that went to Europe to become the Jews and Hebrews in the African tribes that were in Ancient Egypt. These were the tribes from which the *Afrim* people broke away before they could identify themselves to foreigners as *Afrim* people. From all these, it would be prudent for any reader to assume that if the Jewish people were originally Africans as I have established then they must be the Africans who wrote the Bible, but that would be false. The people that wrote the documents of the Old Testament were not Jews.

In the preceding chapters of this book, I have been introducing the foundations upon which I am going to reveal the Africans who wrote the documents of the Old Testament Bible. I pointed out that in the beginning of it all was Ancient Egypt. This was the geographical setting and the birthplace of theosophy or the philosophy of religion and its sacramental practices. Ancient Egypt was also the birthplace of the myths, legends, concepts, and stories that found their way into the biblical narrative. The Ancient Egyptians created the concept of religion complete with the gods and sacramental practices with which to interact with these gods. In my discussion of Ancient Egypt, I revealed that the earliest people of Ancient Egypt that created religion and developed the magnificent civilization based upon religion were the *Akan*. I introduced evidence from Ancient Egyptian history and religion to show that the *Akan* people created and developed the earliest religion and human civilization.

286

Perhaps the greatest revelation in this work is not the revelation of the Africans who wrote the biblical documents but the revelation of the humans that created and developed the Ancient Egyptian civilization and religion. This is because this revelation elevates the Ancient Egyptian story from the story of an extinct group of ancient people to the continuing story of real humans of modern times. This revelation makes the Ancient Egyptian story come alive and it actually humanizes not only the developmental foundations of our humanity on this earth, but also the people in the biblical narrative.

The biblical narrative states that Abraham went to Ancient Egypt with his wife Sarah. I have already revealed that Abraham and his father originated from among the *Kwahu* tribe that was then a vassal kingdom of the Parthian Empire. The *Kwahu* people were and they are still *Akan* people. Abraham and his father *Tena* [Tera] came from among these *Akan* people in the east to the *Akan* people that were in Ancient Egypt. Another revelation here is that in the *Akan* language, the name of Abraham's father was *Tena* and not Tera as the Jewish scholars of the Bible transposed this name for the Greeks and Europeans. The names of *Abre ham*, his father *Tena*, his son *Sachi*, and grandsons *Sau* and *Jakabo* were all *Akan* names that were transposed into European languages. This simply means that these so-called biblical patriarchs were *Akan* people and not Jews or Hebrews.

The biblical narrative continues that *Jakabo's* son *Osafo* [Joseph] was sold to Ishmaelites and Midianites but he ended up in the house of *Kpotufe* in Ancient Egypt. Through *Osafo*, the family of *Jakabo* made up of seventy men went to live and die in Ancient Egypt. After almost four and half centuries, the biblical narrative states that *Jakabo's* family that supposedly went to Ancient Egypt left in an Exodus without knowing where it was going or with any particular destination in mind. What is intriguing about this Exodus was that seventy men supposedly went to Ancient Egypt but six hundred men left Egypt into the biblical Exodus. Mathematically, it does not take much to realize that the people that left Ancient Egypt in the so-called biblical Exodus were Ancient Egyptians. Since we have identified the *Akan* and other black African tribes to be the Ancient Egyptians, it is evident that the people of the Exodus were nothing but black people. This is even more obvious from the fact that the ancestry of the *Afrim* people that became the Jews and Hebrews in Europe has been genetically traced to an African tribe and no other group of people anywhere on this earth.

As usual, numerous western scholars have speculated about what made the people leave in the Exodus. It is evident, however, that the people that left Ancient Egypt in the biblical Exodus did not leave under cordial relations. This is evident because the generation of the *Afrim* people that returned to Ancient Egypt blamed the Ancient Egyptians for their ordeals. This is shown clearly in the Genesis story where the serpent, the symbol of Ancient Egyptian royalty, was made the cause of the fall of "man" in the Bible. The serpent in the biblical story of Creation is therefore a symbolism referring to the Ancient Egyptians.

However, some western scholars who do not have much to go on to prove the historical occurrence of the Exodus have argued that without independent confirmation outside the Bible, there is no evidence that the Exodus even occurred. The most recent and perhaps the most interesting hypothesis and speculation can be found in *The Moses Mystery: The African Origin of the Jewish People* by Gary Greenberg. He stated that:

> Outside the Bible there is no evidence that the Exodus even occurred. It is only because of the fervency with which ancient Israel proclaimed such a demeaning origin that historians give any credit at all to the biblical account (1996, p. 8).

The linguistic and cultural evidence I have presented in this work in the names of people, places, and cultural practices show that the Exodus actually occurred. What happened to cause the movement of such a large group of people away from Ancient Egypt is not known and there has never been a shortage of conflicting speculations.

287

This is the chapter for the revelation of the Africans who wrote the Bible. From the beginning of the book, this revelation has been based upon some foundational revelations. The most important point in these foundational revelations is that the group of people that left Ancient Egypt in the biblical Exodus was composed of *Akan* and other African tribes. What evidence do we have to prove this? I have provided the evidence throughout the book. However, since this is new information that seems to question the veracity of the two thousand year old lore and belief in the biblical narrative, it would help to remind readers of the major ideas upon which these revelations were made so that they can better piece these ideas together. Moreover, the revelations in the book are based upon a different language and culture hitherto unknown in Europe therefore it would be prudent to recount them.

1. The so-called patriarchs of the people that left Ancient Egypt in the biblical Exodus came from an *Akan* tribe, the *Kwahu* tribe of ancient *Adiabene* to be exact.

2. These patriarchs carried *Akan* names – *Tena, Abre ham, Sakyi, Sau,* and *Jakabo.*

3. From these names, it is evident that these people were *Akan* and therefore black people. The fact that these people were black is supported by the important genetic discovery of the *Lemba* tribe that lived in Judea in biblical times before part of these people went to Europe to become the Jews and Hebrews.

4. I have revealed that the so-called patriarchs of the *Afrim* people that left Ancient Egypt into the Exodus were *Akan* people because they carried *Akan* names. It was because of their *Akan* origin that the group that left Ancient Egypt into the biblical Exodus identified themselves to foreigners as the *Afrim* people. This is an *Akan* word meaning people who have broken away from their tribal origin or larger group. Their taking of the *Akan* collective name *Afrim* confirms that these people were truly *Akan* people.

5. These people spoke the *Akan* language and the earliest name of their god *Adonai* was derived from the *Akan* epithet for God, *Adona*, meaning the rare and loveable one.

6. Another name of the God of the people of the Exodus was *Yahveh*. This name was also derived from the *Akan* name of the male God of Thursday. Before then, these people worshiped *Yaa* or *Ea*, the *Akan* name of the female God of Thursday.

7. The earliest name of the nation of the Exodus was *Ephraim*. This name was derived from the collective *Akan* name *Afrim*. Notice how the same word *Afrim* is here transposed into a completely different orthography.

8. When the ancient name of the nation of these people was changed from *Ephraim*, it was changed to *Asrae.* The name *Asrae* is also derived from *Akan,* and it means the visited one. This name was supposedly given to *Jakabo* by a wrestler that visited him one night. The *Akan* name *Asrae* was what was orthographically and phonologically transposed to Israel.

9. In support of all these, I showed that it was not only the *Akan* people that lived in the geographical area of the biblical Canaan. There were also the *Nzima, Ahanta, Ewe,* and *Ga* people in the geographical area of the biblical setting. All these ancient people live today with the *Akan* people in Ghana in West Africa.

10. The greatest evidence and confirmation of the occurrence of the Exodus and the fact that the people that left into the Exodus were *Akan* and other African tribes can be found in the *Akan* and other African tribal names that modern Jewish people have carried up to today. This is profound because modern Jews left Ancient Egypt over three thousand years ago. These names are also the greatest testimony and confirmation of the fact that the Ancient Egyptians from whom the people of the biblical Exodus acquired their names were the *Akan* and other African tribes.

11. Using mostly linguistic and cultural evidence, I have also shown throughout this book that Ancient Egypt was the geographical setting of the biblical documents. It is not because the documents of the Bible were compiled, edited, and translated into Greek in Ancient Egypt but because the biblical documents contain numerous Ancient Egyptian myths, legends, stories, thoughts, and concepts of religion and Godliness. Modern historical, archaeological, and biblical scholarship have confirmed this.

12. Western historians, archaeologists, and Egyptologists have all confirmed that the stories of the Creation, Tower of Babel, Flood, Joseph, and Moses were derived from Ancient Egyptian myths and folktales and the myths and folktales of the surrounding lands of Ancient Egypt.

13. These scholars have also found out that the biblical Psalms and Proverbs were also taken from Ancient Egyptian sources. The fact is these narratives were the foundations upon which the biblical concept was designed. If these were all taken from Ancient Egyptian mythical and literary sources then it is evident and therefore prudent to conclude that the rest of the biblical narratives were also taken from Ancient Egyptian sources.

14. I also pointed out that in terms of culture, the biblical claims of circumcision as an original Jewish religious and cultural tradition is false. *Abre ham* and the ancient *Afrim* people took this cultural and religious practice from the Ancient Egyptians. In another discussion, I revealed that the *Ga* people in Ghana in particular still practice the rituals that are practiced today in the Jewish Passover. If African tribes practice the rituals of the "Jewish" Passover then the tradition was not originally Jewish because the *Afrim* people that later became the Jewish people were the ones that supposedly went to live with the African tribes in Ancient Egypt, and not these African tribes that went to live with the *Afrim* people in Canaan. As a result, any direction of religious and cultural transfer would be from the African tribes to the *Afrim* people and not the other way round. This is also supported by the fact that there is no evidence that the *Afrim* people went to Ancient Egypt from anywhere. This means the *Afrim* people that later went to Europe to become the Jews and Hebrews were originally Ancient Egyptians before they accepted being called Jews or Hebrews in Europe.

15. Even the adoption of the cross as a sacred Christian symbol was derived from the Ancient Egyptian religious and sacred symbol *NKWA*. For a very strange and unknown reason, European scholars have the meaning of this symbol right, but the name for it is wrong. The *Akan* people whose ancient religious and sacred symbol it was called it *Nkwa*, meaning *Life.* The name of this symbol is one of the Ancient Egyptian evidence confirming that the *Akan* people created the concepts, symbols, and sacramental practices of the religion that the *Afrim* people sought to make their own. It is also evidence showing that the theosophical concepts and documents that the *Afrim* scholars of the Bible gave to the Greeks and later all Europeans in the biblical narratives were Ancient Egyptian in origin.

16. What makes European scholars' findings of Ancient Egyptian sources in the Bible even more credible is the fact that western scholars that went to Africa did not only confirm Ancient

Egyptian sources in the Bible, they found the people that were the Ancient Egyptians. They were these people whose stories, theosophical concepts, and documents became the source documents of the Christian Bible.

17. W. E. Ward found cultural evidence of Ancient Egypt in the *Akan* people through what he believed to be a very important Ancient Egyptian artifact that the *Akan* and other African tribes still used in West Africa.

18. The Basel Missionary minister Reverend J. G. Christaller confirmed the Ancient Egyptian origin of the biblical Proverbs in his discovery of the origin of the Proverbs of *Akan* and other African tribes. Rev. Riis, another Basel Missionary also collected *Akan* proverbs because of their supposed biblical similarities and importance.

19. Captain Charles Rattray studied the similarities between *Akan* and Christian religious thoughts, concepts, and practices. He also studied *Akan* proverbs. This was not a minor study because it earned him an honorary doctorate degree at Oxford University. It would not have brought him such an honor if the findings were trivial and false. Rattray concluded that the *Akan Nyame* [God] in West Africa was the same as the Hebrew *Yahweh*.

20. Dr. M. J. Field who studied the *Ga* people that live with the *Akan* in the same country also found out that the *Ga Nyomo* [God] was the same as the Hebrew *Yahweh*. Remember that the *Ga* people were the people that fought the ancient *Afrim* people in the biblical story found in Judges 12:4-6.

21. Father [Dr.] S. J. Williams also found out that the *Akan Nyame* was the same as the Hebrew *Yahweh*. The only orthographic difference between these two names, according to Father Williams, was that the *Akan* "M" was transposed to become the Hebrew "W." His study is extremely important because he directly and linguistically linked the *Akan* people of West Africa to the ancient *Afrim* people in Canaan and modern Jewish people in Europe.

22. The biblical narratives are samples of ancient wisdom and several scholars have doubted the claim that the Jewish people created these documents in their short history of having their own nation. Gary Greenberg, himself a Jew, argued that the ancient *Afrim* people that became the Jews and Hebrews in Europe did not have an ancient tradition of writing that would have made it possible for them to produce the biblical documents they claim to have produced in distant ancient times. He wrote:

> Even if we assume that the Bible is derived from earlier sources yet to be discovered, it still describes events that occurred more than a thousand years before its completion, and in those ancient times few peoples had a strong tradition of historical writing and perspective. ... Though several nations had written records in the second, third, and fourth millennia B. C. from which modern historians can draw conclusions, there is no evidence that Israel was among them (p. 3).

The greatest irony

The greatest irony in all these is that the world has been deceived into believing that the *Afrim* people that went to Europe to become the Jews and Hebrews created the biblical knowledge and concepts of religion that became European Christianity. The fact is the *Afrim* people did not create the knowledge they passed on to the Greeks through the biblical documents. They took this knowledge from the larger group of black tribes from which they originated. The credit of the creation of this knowledge therefore goes to the *Akan* and other African tribal groups of Ancient Egypt and modern West Africa. What is worse about all of these deceptions is that they have succeeded in making people comfortably ignorant of the truth. For example, modern Christian interpretation of the Bible condemns Ancient Egypt, the source from which all the knowledge emanated as a pagan and idolatrous society that must be condemned by Christianity. European ignorance also condemns modern African religions that continue to practice the original ancient rituals and sacramental practices of Ancient Egypt, from which Christianity emerged. That is wrong. It will be grievously wrong for any group of scholars to compile, edit, rewrite, and translate Shakespeare into another language and for another culture and then claim that they originally created those literary materials. This was what happened with the biblical documents.

I have tried not to blame modern Christians for being so easily deceived and misled. The fact is modern Christianity is too far removed from the origin of the Christian religion. This is because when the early apostolic fathers of Christianity found out that the concepts and documents of Christianity originated from black people in Ancient Egypt they embarked on a crusade to make sure that this information does not become common knowledge in Christendom, and it has been all lies since. When the Catholic Church found out all these, it began religious intolerance, persecution, and massacres in Ancient Egypt and that later turned out to become the foundations of European Inquisition.

Modern Jew's dilemma

Do modern Jewish people know of all these deceptions? I believe some do. However, the dilemma of these people is that their ancient scholars have bequeathed them with a huge lie before the whole world. What should they do? One good lie requires another. As George Bernard Shaw pointed out, "A man comes to believe in the end the lies he tells about himself" and so there have been a series of lies all intended to uphold the lies their ancient scholars told in the biblical narrative. The dilemma therefore is should modern Jews tell the truth and betray the Bible that millions of people have come to believe in, or be quiet and sustain the lie and the beliefs of millions around the world? This is the reason Jewish people have been quite on the most important issues that could betray them and their ancient scholars.

Perhaps, the most important of these issues is where they actually came from beside the biblical lie. So for over two thousand years, the ancient *Afrim* people that are now the Jews and Hebrews in Europe have failed to reveal their racial and ethnic origin, where they came from, or what language they spoke in the land from where they originated. To prevent others from researching their background and finding out who they really were, they came with the story that they have lost ten tribes and the reason and circumstances of this loss are simply ludicrous. In the opinion of some African scholars, Jewish people do not know where they came from anymore.

The Africans who wrote the Bible

For over five hundred years, Christian Europe and European scholars have slowly been burying the evidence of the African origin of the concepts of Christianity in false explanations, interpretations, and theoretical hypotheses. Since Renaissance scholars drew attention to human differences through skin color, Christian Europe and Europeans have been deceived into believing that changing the skin color of the people of the Bible from black to white would finally bury the truth. So the Catholic Church and its supporters were the first to change the original skin color in their ancient portrayals of the people of the Bible. What these people failed to do was seek to destroy the real human elements of the biblical story, the linguistic and cultural elements that could lead the so-called people of the Bible back to Ancient Egypt and to the African tribes of their origin. The only reason Christian Europe and European scholars have not been able to destroy the linguistic and cultural evidence I have introduced in this work is because they have not known that such powerful evidence exists.

It is for this single most important reason for Europeans that the names of people, things, and places in Ancient Egyptian history has been so grossly distorted. For example, western scholars present the names of Ancient Egyptian kings from three different sources. Some write the history of Ancient Egypt from the *Manetho* list, other use the *Africanus* list, and still others use the *Eusebius* list. All of these lists have different transpositions of the names of the same Ancient kings. As if that is not enough confusion, modern scholars have also created four lists of Ancient Egyptian kings from what they unearthed in their archaeological quests. Under Ancient Egyptian kings' lists, modern scholars have the Abydos list; they also have the Sakkara list. There is also the Turin Canon, and finally the Palermo Stone list.

Beyond all these confusions that have almost practically cut off the Africans from their Ancient Egyptian heritage, some modern scholars of Egyptology have found out that the African names of Ancient Egyptian kings can be still discerned by African tribes. So these scholars have designed a strategy to further change the orthographic representation of Ancient Egyptian names of people and places. This is to help further distort and conceal any linguistic and cultural links these names might have to African tribes.

For example in Egyptology today, the indigenous *Akan* tribal name *Dade Afre*, the son of *Akuffu*, the fourth dynasty king, was originally transposed into Greek as *Djedefra*. Some modern Egyptologists that are seeking to further distort and destroy the Ancient Egyptian story beyond the recognition of the African tribes that were the Ancient Egyptians have most recently further transposed this name to *Radjedef*. A careful analysis of this transposition shows that these scholars simply took the last letters of the name and placed them in front so as to create a name that has no linguistic or cultural link to any languages or names in Africa. The indigenous *Akan* name of the brother of *Dade Afre* is *Okyere Afre*. This name was traditionally transposed into Greek as *Chephren*, and sometimes some scholars presented it as *Kafra*. In more recent times, some scholars have further transposed it to *Rakhaef*. All of these are intended to show that if historians and biblical scholars knew of the African names of the authors of the Old Testament Bible that I am about to reveal, they would have done something to conceal these names a long time ago.

In the discussion of this chapter, I pointed out how Jewish scholars of the Bible falsely assigned authors to most of the biblical documents because they took these documents from Ancient Egyptian sources and tried to make them their own. This is the single most important reason several documents in the biblical narrative do not have names of authors. It is also the reason modern historians, Egyptologists, and biblical scholars have been discovering the sources from where the biblical documents originated.

Another major evidence that confirms that ancient Jewish priests and prophets did not create the biblical documents their scholars later claimed is the fact that none of their early prophets wrote anything. As the scholars of Jewish history in the *Britannica* wrote:

> These early prophets, while they were spirited fighters and spokesmen for Yahweh and resolutely combated Israelite idolatry, left behind no writings of their own and are known only from the historical books of the Bible (p. 1996, p. 73).

The truth is none of the so-called prophets left behind any writings. The Jewish scholars of the biblical documents could simply not assign the documents they had found to these early scholars. They decided to assign the Ancient Egyptian documents they had found to later prophets and design the hitherto nonexistent history of the Jewish people around them. What is most interesting is that most of the prophets to whom the scholars assigned biblical books had *Akan* and other African tribal names. As a result, anybody who is familiar with *Akan* and other African tribal names can easily discern the original African names that were transposed to fit them into European tongues.

One important reminder in the revelation of these names is that the names have been transposed and rendered into Greek and other foreign tongues in ways that seemed intended to conceal the ethnic identities of the people who wrote these biblical documents. These names were originally first translated into Greek and as Joseph Kaster pointed out in *The Wisdom of Ancient Egypt:*

> ... The Greeks had a cavalier attitude to all foreign names and absolutely *"murdered"* them (emphasis mine). Thus the name of the Egyptian deity who was the scribe of the gods and the patron of learning, which reads, in Egyptian, something like Djehwty, the Greeks rendered variously as Thoth, Thouth, Thout, and in theophoric (god-bearing) names introduced further corruption plus the ornament of a Greek ending, with the result that in the name of a king such as Djehwty-ms, "Born of the god Djehwty," we get such specimens of wild renderings as Tethmosis and Thmosis" (1993, pp. xiii-xiv).

Documents of the Old Testament:

Creation

There are three very disturbing issues about the documents of the Bible. Not only do we find specific Ancient Egyptian records in these biblical documents, but also as we have discussed, we find that the authors that were assigned to certain documents in the Bible are false. The third issue is that none of the modern scholastic search for the sources of the biblical documents remotely links the Jewish people to these documents despite the stories their early scholars created around these documents. If the biblical documents truly belonged to the Jewish people and if their prophets truly wrote these documents, there would not be Ancient Egyptian documents in them and there would not be false authors assigned to them. The evidence shows that these two major issues about the Bible could happen only under plagiarism. For example, we have already discussed that the biblical narrative begins in the Old Testament with the story that Moses wrote the first five Books of Moses. We have been taught this and millions have believed it for over two thousand years but today, no biblical scholar believes that Moses wrote the first five books of the Bible. As a way to save some of the legendary lying lore of the past two thousand years, some scholars suggest that at least Moses must have written some of these books but not all. One thing I have noticed about defenders of the biblical tradition today is that they are very flexible and they tend to modify their stories based upon what researchers have found to contradict the claims of the Bible.

The documents of the Bible begin with the Creation story. In an earlier discussion, I pointed out that Gerald Massey showed in his work that the transposed names Adam and Eve were definitely African in origin. The biblical home of *Adam* and *Eve* was *Eden*. In the discussion of the work of Gerald Massey, I revealed that the name *Eden* is a European corruption and orthographic transposition of the *Akan* word *Edan*, meaning a house or home. From these revelations, it is clear that the creation story in the beginning of the Bible was derived from an Akan version of this story. Otherwise, the biblical story would not have contained the *Akan* names of the major characters and elements in the story.

What is most intriguing about the beginning of the Bible with the Creation story is that Ancient Egyptians already had a Creation myth that turned out to be very identical to the biblical Creation myth. The Ancient Egyptians even had a better Creation story because they began with the imagination and personification of God and then continued with this God creating everything else including humans. That makes more sense than the biblical story that begins with a God from no where creating things and humans on this earth.

Some scholars of Ancient Egyptian history have already pointed out that the biblical Creation myth was taken from Ancient Egyptian religious documents. In *Egyptian Religion*, the British Egyptologist, Sir Wallis Budge pointed out that the Creation story and its references to one God must have been taken from Ancient Egyptian literature. In support of this assertion, Sir Wallis Budge presented several examples of excerpts from Ancient Egyptian religious literature that exactly "parallel" some of the thoughts and rhetoric of the biblical story of Creation. For example, he quoted the most fundamental Ancient Egyptian religious concept in the creation of God as follows:

1. God is One and alone, and none other existeth with Him; God is the One, the One Who hath made all things.

2. *God is from the beginning*, and *He hath been from the beginning*; He hath existed from old and was when nothing had being. He existed when nothing else had existed, and what existeth He created after He had come into being. *He is the father of beginnings*. (Notice these italicized ideas and the biblical foundation of creation that also states: "In the beginning …")

3. God is the eternal One, He is eternal and infinite; and endureth for ever and aye; He hath endured for countless ages, and he shall endure all eternity.

4. God is life, and through Him only man liveth. He giveth life to man, and he breatheth the breath of life into his nostrils. (In the Ancient Egyptian version, God breathed into the nostrils of man to give him life and in the biblical version, God "breathed into his nostrils the breath of life …" Genesis 2:7).

5. God himself is existence, He liveth in all things and liveth upon all things. He endureth without increase or diminution, He multiplieth Himself millions of times, and he possesseth multitudes of forms and multitudes of members.

6. God hath made the universe, and he hath created all that therein is: He is the Creator of what is in this world, of what was, of what is, and of what shall be. He is the Creator of the world and it was He who fashioned it with His hands before there was any beginning; and he established it with that which went forth from Him. He is the Creator of the heavens, and the earth, and the deep, and the waters, and the mountains. God had stretched out the heavens and founded the earth. What His heart conceived came to pass straightway, and when He had spoken His words came to pass, and it shall endure for ever (pp. 37-40). This is the basic Ancient Egyptian concept of God and Creation that was expanded in the rewriting of Genesis 1& 2: 7.

Do the ideas above sound Ancient Egyptian or biblical in origin? To Egyptologists who have seen and read these Ancient Egyptian religious documents, these ideas are definitely Ancient Egyptian in origin. However, to Christians who do not know or have any sources of religious knowledge other than the biblical sources, these documents would sound biblical. Perhaps, the greatest evidence against Jewish people's claims of the origin of these religious concepts is the fact that the biblical documents were compiled, edited and translated into Greek in Ancient Egypt. Anyone reading *Egyptian Religion* today would think these excerpts are biblical writings, but they are from earlier Ancient Egyptian religious records on Creation.

Western scholars, most of who have been raised in the biblical tradition, can never bring themselves to assert that these were the Ancient Egyptian documents from which the Jewish scholars of the Bible designed the story of Creation. Compare this Ancient Egyptian literature to the biblical literature (Genesis 1), and you will see that the two concepts and rhetoric are too similar to be a coincidence. These quotations also reveal the monotheist God that existed in Ancient Egypt before the Jewish people supposedly went to Egypt and left there.

Beyond all these, I also pointed out that Moses was not a Jew. He was an Ancient Egyptian, and if he supposedly wrote the biblical account of Creation, then he definitely must have acquired and therefore taken his ideas from what he already knew from Ancient Egypt. The Bible also confirms that Moses acquired all his wisdom from Ancient Egypt.

Biblical tradition states that Moses had some scrolls with him during the Exodus thus suggesting that he took Ancient Egyptian religious documents with him in the Exodus. Richard Friedman pointed out in *Who Wrote the Bible*, that the evidence shows that Moses did not write the first five books of the Bible. As Greenberg put it:

> The claim that the Five Books of Moses were assembled from earlier source documents is referred to by scholars as the Documentary Hypothesis. Today, hardly a biblical scholar in the world actively working on the problem would claim that Moses or any other single individual wrote the Torah (p. 28).

From all these, especially the striking similarities between Ancient Egyptian and biblical literature, it is evident that the biblical story of Creation was created from Ancient Egyptian concept of God, religious thoughts, and rhetoric. The question here is if it became necessary for the Jewish scholars of the Bible to use Ancient Egyptian documents right from the beginning of the compilation of the biblical documents, how can we present and defend the Bible as original Jewish religious concepts and documents? If it became necessary for the Jewish scholars of the Bible to design a false chronology of their ancestry based upon Ancient Egyptian kings' lists, how can we defend the Bible as original Jewish people's document? These are the reasons the Bible conspired with the classical tradition to destroy and distort Ancient Egyptian history, religion, and literature so that Christians would never find out that biblical concepts, stories, and narratives originated from Ancient Egyptian sources.

In addition to these, I have already discussed that George Smith of the British Department of Oriental Antiquity found clay tablets with stories of the creation and the fall of man as they were narrated in the Bible. Smith and his colleagues also found the myths of Paradise, the Flood, and the Tower of Babel in the folklore of Ancient Egypt and several other places. However, since the biblical documents were compiled in Ancient Egypt, it is prudent to conclude that the Jewish biblical scholars took the Ancient Egyptian versions of these stories. The question here is why have scholars never found any documents with the creation story in Israel?

Beyond it all, not many western scholars would come out directly to reveal that the biblical documents were Ancient Egyptian in origin because Ancient Egyptians are known in the back of the minds of most western scholars as modern Africans. Revealing that the biblical documents are Ancient Egyptian in origin is basically acknowledging that Africans created and wrote these documents. This is itself enough to divert the course of scholastic truth concerning Ancient Egypt and the Bible to wild scholastic speculations ostensibly intended to exclude the Ancient Egyptians and therefore the *Akan* and other African tribes that actually created these concepts and practices.

The Flood

As I pointed out above, George Smith and his western colleagues were searching for the sources of the biblical documents in the Middle East. I pointed out that the greatest flaw in western scholastic search for the origins and sources of biblical myths has been the fact that these scholars have been deceived and therefore blinded by the unswerving idea that the ancient *Afrim* people that left Egypt into the Exodus originated from Mesopotamia when they actually originated from Ancient Egypt. As a result these scholars have always searched for the sources of biblical narratives everywhere except Ancient Egypt where the biblical documents were compiled, edited, rewritten, and translated for the unsuspecting Greeks.

Another ancient mythology that ended up in the Old Testament as the words and actions of God was the biblical Flood. Historians, archaeologists, and biblical scholars have found that many ancient peoples including Ancient Egyptians had stories about a flood. Greenberg wrote:

> Mesopotamians also believed in a worldwide flood, … Because Noah was the tenth generation in Genesis, scholars generally agree that the Genesis and Mesopotamia flood myths derived from a common source (p. 66).

However, western scholars chose to search in Babylon and they claim to have found astonishingly striking similarities between the narrative of the biblical Flood myth and Babylonian flood myth. In an earlier discussion, I showed that Professor Wolley went to excavate the area around Ur of the Chaldees and found evidence of a catastrophic overflow of the Euphrates River and that lingered in the memories of the people around as the flood. Notice how Professor Wolley was also deceived by the biblical narrative to go to search for the origin of the flood myth in Mesopotamia. However, in the conclusions of Professor Wolley, there was no flood anywhere on the magnitude that scholars of the biblical documents created. It is important to point out that no historical or archaeological record of the biblical flood has attributed this myth to Israel or the Jewish people. As George Smith and his colleagues pointed out, the Ancient Egyptians also had a flood myth most probably already written down. Again, since the documents of the Bible were compiled, edited, rewritten, and translated for the Greeks in Egypt, it is prudent to conclude that the Jewish scholars of the Bible took the Ancient Egyptian version of the flood myth and made it the biblical version.

Every linguistic and cultural analysis of the central characters in the biblical myth of the Flood does not point to the characters as Jewish people or even as the people that created the flood myth. In *Deceptions and Myths of the Bible*, Lloyd Graham stated that the name Noah originated from the Chaldean name "*Nuah*, the third person in the Chaldean Trinity, and also the third sign in the Chaldean zodiac (p. 87). This undoubtedly helped to lead western scholars to search for the origin of the myth of the biblical flood among the Chaldeans. However, if the word *Nuah* was Chaldean then the Chaldeans must have also spoken the *Akan* language or a language similar to it. This is because the word *Nuah* is an *Akan* word of neutral gender for sibling. It is clear that even in their search among the Chaldeans, western scholars found some linguistic evidence that linked the flood myth to the Ancient Egyptians. However, because these scholars did not have the linguistic and cultural backgrounds to realize that the evidence they had found related to the *Akan* people of Ancient Egypt, they assumed the origin of the biblical flood must have been in the lore of the Chaldeans.

Graham also pointed out an Ancient Egyptian connection in the Flood myth when he stated that "the word *ark* is Egyptian and it means a chest or box for preserving sacred things" (p. 90). How could a myth that was supposedly created by the Jewish people and also told in Chaldea name the most important artifact in this myth in an Ancient Egyptian language and not Jewish or Chaldean language ? In the mythology of the flood, the biblical *ark* served as a chest or box for preserving the sacredness of life on earth.

In my search for the possible linguistic origin of the word *ark* among the African tribes that were the Ancient Egyptians, I could not find one language that said *ark* to refer to a box. In the *Akan* language, however, I know the word *adaka* meaning a chest or box for preserving things, not necessarily sacred things. It is most likely that it was the *Akan* word *adaka* that these scholars transposed to the biblical word *ark*, just as they have done with several Ancient Egyptian names of gods, people, places, and words. This linguistic analysis gives even more credibility to Ancient Egyptian connection to the biblical flood myth. What makes all these even more interesting is the fact that the *Akan* people of Ancient Egypt also had the names *Anoah* and *Ano*, both of which could have been easily transposed to Noah. It is most likely that the biblical flood was the Ancient Egyptian version of the flood using *Anoa* or *Ano* as the central character.

296

Another evidence in the story that links the flood myth to the *Akan* people in Ancient Egypt is that the biblical son of *Anoa* was *Sem*, the indigenous *Akan* name that was transposed to *Shem*, the son of Noah.

Taking the Chaldean and the Ancient Egyptian connections together, a question arises. How could a man supposedly with the Chaldean name *Nuah* come to be in a myth that was compiled and translated in Ancient Egypt with the Ancient Egyptian word *ark* as the central artifact in the story? This myth must have been told in many lands surrounding Ancient Egypt, but the geographical and linguistic evidence suggests that the Jewish scholars of the Bible in Alexandria took the Ancient Egyptian version of this myth, transposed the name *Anoah* to Noah, and also transposed the Ancient Egyptian word *adaka* to *ark*.

Beyond all these, scholars have pointed out that the ark and the story surrounding it was a myth. This was because no ark of the size given in the Bible could have taken in all that it supposedly took in for all the animals and humans to survive after the supposed length of the rains. In his criticism of the incredulity in the mathematical figures given for the design of the ark, Lloyd Graham wrote:

> According to some, the Hebrew cubit was only 18 inches, others say 20. Even with the latter, the ark would be only 500 feet. Into this Noah put eight people, two or seven of every animal species, and sufficient provisions for one hundred fifty days; another account says one year. And for ventilation there was only one little window twenty inches square. The absurdity here is so great, I suspect it was meant as a hint for us to do a little thinking (p. 89).

Not only did the myth of the biblical flood not originate from the Jewish people but in this discussion, I have shown that the central character, name, and version of the story that was included in the biblical documents originated from Ancient Egypt.

The Genesis Chronology

Gary Greenberg pointed out that biblical narratives have fooled many western scholars until now. He noted:

> As recently as the seventeenth century, as brilliant a scientist as Isaac Newton devoted much of his energy to writing The Chronology of Ancient Kingdoms Amended, in which he attempted to conform the histories of different nations to the chronological claims of Genesis. While it is understandable that early students of the Bible, such as the Hellenistic Jew Demetrius, might carefully comb it for every chronological clue to world history, scientists such as Newton doing so strikes an odd note in today's society. However, in Newton's time geology and archaeology had not yet advanced into disciplined sciences and two hundred years separated Newton from Darwin's theory of evolution. Then, belief in Creation and the Flood did not require any suspension of scientific understanding (p. 26).

Again, in the search for the origin of the Genesis chronology, early western scholars were deceived by biblical narratives into believing that Ancient Egypt had nothing to do with biblical myths. Nevertheless, all these scholars also knew that the documents of the Bible were compiled, edited, rewritten, and translated in Ancient Egypt. These scholars were actually blinded by the false belief that " Ancient Egyptian culture was alien to the biblical experience." We have found that the biblical creation story was Ancient Egyptian in origin, and the flood was also Ancient Egyptian in origin. In the latest study of the biblical chronology, Gary Greenberg noted that:

> Another nineteenth century challenge to the Genesis chronology came through the emergence of archaeology as a scientific discipline. Because of their interest in biblical studies, archaeologists devoted much of their attention to the lands mentioned in the Bible. This led to the discovery of evidence that often contradicted biblical claims.

The convergence of these academic streams overflowed the banks of fundamentalist biblical inerrancy, consigning much of Genesis to the realm of myth, including the Genesis chronology. Ironically, recent advances in Egyptian archaeology enable us to demonstrate that the Genesis chronology is derived from a historically accurate chronology of Egyptian dynasties (p. 30).

What makes this revelation even more significant is the fact that the Jewish scholars of the Bible had access practically to every Ancient Egyptian document. In an Arts & Entertainment documentary on *Who Wrote The Bible*, scholars suggested that Ptolemy the Greek ruler of Ancient Egypt asked that the Jewish scholars to translate the biblical documents into Greek for the Alexandrian library. This confirms that the *Afrim* scholars of the Bible had access to all the Ancient Egyptian names and documents that appear in the Bible. From this, it is not inconceivable that they would want to design the biblical chronology from existing Ancient Egyptian kings' lists as Greenberg has asserted. These scholars also had the motivation to do so because they wanted to separate themselves from the Ancient Egyptian tribes of their origin and that meant they needed to create a new historical heritage. For this, they had to design a false chronology of their people from Egyptian kings' lists. As Greenberg put it:

> ... the Genesis birth and death dates, counting from the year of Creation, unquestionably derive from Egyptian kings' lists and were intended to mark off a chronological history of the world from the Creation to the Exodus as the Egyptians knew it (p. 32).

All these references to Ancient Egyptians of course refer to the *Akan* and other African tribes that were the Ancient Egyptians who originally developed and wrote down all these ideas. It must also not be forgotten that these were the black tribes from which the *Afrim* people that later went to Europe to become the Jews and Hebrews originated. The question is how could people that did not have any writing system in the second millennium have written down their ancestral chronology going back to the fourth millennium? The only way they could have done this was to design a false ancestral chronology going back that far alongside the existing Ancient Egyptian chronology of kings. Another question is how did people whose origin, religion, and history began with the Exodus around 13th B. C. have had ancestors going back thousands of years before the Exodus?

The Tower of Babel

In the search for the source of the myth of the biblical Tower of Babel, again, western scholars were directed past Ancient Egypt. As George Smith and his colleagues have pointed out, Ancient Egypt also had a myth of the Tower of Babel most probably already written down long before the compilation of the biblical document. Lloyd Graham pointed out that the name *Babel* meaning the Gate of God came from the Akkadian-Sumerian *Babili* about 3900 B. C. I have identified the Akkadians and the Sumerians elsewhere as the *Nzima* and *Ahanta* tribes that lived in these places in ancient times. I do not profess to know the language of these people that well however, I do not think *Babili* is a word that can be found in any of these people's modern languages.

Again, what makes this biblical narrative interesting is the fact that in the language of the *Akan* that were in Ancient Egypt, the word *baabaa* is used to refer to confounded speech. This could easily have been transposed to the biblical Babel. I have already revealed that the majority of the people that left Ancient Egypt into the Exodus were *Akan*. They therefore spoke the *Akan* language and that the *Akan* words we are discovering in the biblical narrative should be linguistically normal from the descendants of a people that spoke the *Akan* language. It is fascinating that there was and still is an *Akan* word *baabaa* that refers to confounded speech and there is also the biblical narrative of the Tower of Babel [*Baabaa*] that is also about the foundations of confounded speech. Scholars have never known this linguistic relationship so they have never considered searching for the biblical source of this myth in Ancient Egypt and among the modern descendants of the Ancient Egyptians in Africa.

The Exodus

I have discussed earlier in this chapter that some western scholars do not think the actual movement of humans that became the so-called biblical Exodus even occurred because there is no extra-biblical evidence to support such movement of a large group of people. However, there is an Ancient Egyptian account that closely parallels the biblical account of the Exodus. There is also a very interesting discussion entitled *Exodus: The Egyptian Version* in Greenberg's book *The Moses Mystery: The African Origin of the Jewish People*. In this chapter, Greenberg showed that the Exodus account must have originated from Ancient Egyptian historical documents because Ancient Egyptian documents and the Exodus narrative are very similar in many ways except that the roles of Moses and the pharaoh were reversed. In the Egyptian narrative, Moses was the evil king and the subjugated pharaoh later returned to take back his throne and liberate his people. Greenberg wrote:

> The biblical and Egyptian accounts of the Exodus each combine a mixture of fact and fiction, but one can now be easily separated from the other. Reading the two versions side-by-side and placing them in chronological and historical context, we can recover the nature and origins of the Exodus (p. 204).

The real problem with a discussion like this is that only a few scholars know of the supporting and revealing Ancient Egyptian documents while the entire world knows about the biblical documents that were derived from these Ancient Egyptian documents. As a result, most people have never heard that there is an Ancient Egyptian version of the biblical Exodus. Scholars now believe that the biblical version originated from the Ancient Egyptian version and that this biblical version was embellished and fictionalized to make it the Jewish version.

Within the Exodus narrative, there is also the story of the creation of the Mosaic Law and the conferring of divine origin onto it. Again, here is evidence from surrounding myths and documents showing that the biblical narrative surrounding supposed *Afrim* people's reception of the Ten Commandments on Mt. Sinai was not an original Jewish people's idea. In Chapter three, I introduced evidence to show that the story of Moses going onto Mount Sinai to receive laws from God was not an original story and document of the Jewish people. It was an existing documented myth in Ancient Egypt, in surrounding nations, and among several peoples. Here is part of the evidence. In Ancient Egypt, the god *Thoth* gave the people the *Laws.* The sun god *Shamash* gave the *Hammurabi Code*. King Minos of Crete received laws from a deity on Mt. Dicta, and in Greece, Dionysius was the Lawgiver with two tablets of stone on which the laws were written like Mose's tablets. Persians also had a myth of how they received their laws on a mountain amid thunder and lightening (see Durant, p. 331, see also Diodorus Silicus I xciv, p. 1-2, Doane, T. W., *Bible Myths and their Parallels in other Religions,* 1882, pp. 59-60).

It is important to note in all these discussions that no historical or archaeological record remotely links the Jewish people to the creation of these biblical myths. The evidence therefore suggests that the Jewish scholars of the Bible simply took the Ancient Egyptian version of this story, edited, rewrote it to make it their own, and translated it into the biblical document for the Greeks.

The biblical story of Joseph

Not only do scholars know that the biblical story of Joseph is not an original Jewish story but these scholars have found the exact Ancient Egyptian source from which the story originated. Egyptologists have found that the Ancient Egyptian source from where the story of Joseph originated was the story known as the *Tale of Two Brothers*. For the comparison of the original Ancient Egyptian story and the biblical story of Joseph see Simpson, Faulkner, & Kelly, *The Literature of Ancient Egypt: An anthology of stories, instructions, and poetry*, 1972, pp. 92-107; Joseph Kaster, *The Wisdom of Ancient Egypt: Writings from the time of the Pharaohs*, 1968, pp. 270-281).

The biblical story of Joseph is designed around his supposed par excellence ability to interpret dreams. Joseph Kaster showed that the interpretation of dreams was an original Ancient Egyptian religious and cultural practice and that "the entire [Joseph] episode has a completely authentic Egyptian background, and is shot through with Egyptianisms – literal translations into Hebrew" (p. 153). In other words, the biblical episode of Joseph is authentically an Ancient Egyptian story. Kaster shows that even the rhetoric of the story is Egyptian and that the biblical narrative shows that this story was literally translated into the Hebrew language. Joseph Kaster is himself a Jewish scholar that has studied Egyptology. If the biblical story of Joseph was not originally a Hebrew story but one literally translated from another language into Hebrew, he must know. Much of the discussion in this and previous chapters have shown that the *Afrim* scholars of the Bible took Ancient Egyptian myths, stories, and doctrines and claimed that they created them. Here is a scholar who pointed out clearly that the story of Joseph was definitely Ancient Egyptian and that it was literally translated into Hebrew.

In the discussion of this story, I also revealed the African tribe whose original story the story of Joseph was. I revealed that the indigenous African tribal name *Kpotufe* was what was transposed to the biblical *Potifar*.

Biblical Psalms

Even where western scholars have found direct evidence linking Ancient Egyptian theosophical documents to the biblical documents, they have sought ways and reasons to deny, distort, or reject the evidence they themselves have discovered. Archaeologists working in modern Egypt have found an Ancient Egyptian papyri whose exact contents can be found in biblical Psalm 104. These scholars believe that the papyri were part of the pharaoh *Akenten's* [Akhenaten's] *Hymn of Aten*. In The Dictionary of Ancient Egypt, Ian Shaw and Paul Nicholson wrote:

> Akhenaten's hymn to the Aten has been shown to have strong similarities with Psalm 104, but this is probably only an indication that the two compositions belong to a common literary heritage or perhaps even derive from a common Near Eastern original (p. 54).

Note that in this quotation, scholars no where remotely suggest that this Psalm is the original creation of the Jewish people who have claimed it for over two thousand years. It is clear that scholars have found that the biblical Psalms are Ancient Egyptian in origin, however, acknowledging this would also be acknowledging that Africans wrote the documents of the Bible. So some scholars seek strange and sometimes illogical reasons to deny Ancient Egypt and her modern descendants, the Africans, of the historical honor that is theirs. Otherwise, how could Akhenaten's *Hymn of Aten* and Psalm 104 have a common literary heritage when they were over a thousand years apart? How could they have originated from a common Near Eastern original source when biblical tradition claims the Psalms are the original religious documents of the Jewish people? How could these documents have originated from a third source outside Ancient Egypt when there is no historical or archaeological evidence of such a source anywhere in the Near East?

Still the defense of some scholars is that there are one hundred and fifty Psalms in the Bible and the fact that scholars have found only one Ancient Egyptian document that is exactly like a biblical Psalm does not mean that the entire biblical Psalms were all originally Ancient Egyptian documents. This line of thinking seeks to present the argument that until Ancient

Egyptian documents containing all the biblical Psalms have been found, these scholars will never accept the fact that the Psalms originated from Ancient Egyptian writings, and most probably from *Akenten*, the monotheist's Hymns. Ancient Egyptian papyri documents are very rare and the fact that the only one found exactly matches a biblical Psalm shows that all the Psalms must have originated from Ancient Egyptian sources.

In an earlier discussion, I also pointed out that historians and biblical scholars have now found out that King David did not write the biblical Psalms. It is becoming the tradition in biblical scholarship that when new evidence contradicting the assertions of the Bible are discovered, some biblical scholars change or even bend their stories to accommodate the new discovery. For over two thousand years, biblical tradition has asserted that King David wrote the Psalms. When new evidence contradicting this was discovered, the story was modified. In Elliott Friedman's *Who Wrote The Bible*, he pointed that scholars believe that David wrote only "half of the Psalms" (1987, p. 15).

The questions biblical scholars have failed to answer are which half of the biblical Psalms did King David write, and which half was written by someone else? Who wrote the other half of the Psalms King David did not write and from where did that other half originate? Why did the biblical tradition claim for the past two thousand years that King David wrote the Psalms when he did not write them? The answer is because when these biblical assertions were made knowledge was not this advanced and no one remotely anticipated that thousands of years later, future generations would easily discover the lies. Moreover, during this long period no one ever thought that the evidence contradicting this claim would ever come out. Doesn't this confirm that the Jewish scholars of the biblical documents in Ancient Egypt were not dealing with their own documents but the documents of other people? Again, if it became necessary for the Jewish scholars of the Bible to include even one Ancient Egyptian document in the biblical Psalms, what would have prevented them from taking the entire Psalms from the same source? Couldn't that be the reason scholars have now found out that King David did not write the Psalms, at least half of them?

Scholastic discoveries and revelations contradicting the two thousand-year claims of the Bible are astounding. What has been even more psychologically traumatizing for historians, believers, and biblical scholars has been the courage to accept these scholastic discoveries and revelations. From this brief discussion of the origin of the Psalms, it is again clear that the biblical Psalms were also Ancient Egyptian religious documents.

The biblical Proverbs

The one biblical document for which western scholars have found evidence of its origin both in Ancient Egypt and among the modern descendants of the Ancient Egyptians in Africa is the Proverbs. Biblical tradition however has asserted for the past two thousand years that King Solomon (965-928 B. C.) wrote these biblical Proverbs. In the Song of Solomon, he tells in 1:5 that he is black and handsome thus confirming that even if he wrote the biblical Proverbs, they originated from the minds and imaginations of black people. We know, however, that Solomon did not write the biblical Proverbs. In more modern times, Egyptologists have found that the Proverbs are identical to a Late Period Ancient Egyptian wisdom text known as *Instruction of Amenemipet son of Kanakht*. On this, the above-cited authors of *The Dictionary of Ancient Egypt* wrote:

> The same reason is usually given for the very close parallels that have been observed between a Late Period wisdom text known as *Instruction of Amenemipet son of Kanakht* and the Biblical book of Proverbs, although it has been suggested by some scholars that the writers of Proverbs may have been influenced by a text of the *Instruction of Amenemipet* itself (p. 54).

In this quotation, not only have scholars found out that the biblical Proverbs must have originated from the work of Amenemipet's son, but some have even suggested that the Proverbs must have originated from the work of the father, Amenemipet himself. Apart from that there is no Jewish document of the compilation of Proverbs by any of their ancient ancestors. The use of Proverbs is also a linguistic and cultural tradition that leaves its mark in the language and thinking of the people that use them. If Proverbs were that important in the Hebrew language and thinking for the Jewish scholars to include them in the biblical documents then there must be a Jewish record of it in the Jewish language or literature, but there is none. There is no such mark in modern Hebrew language as it is in the *Akan* and the other African tribal languages that were in Ancient Egypt.

Why would Egyptologists believe that the *Instruction of Amenemipet son of Kanakht* influenced the biblical Proverbs? It is because the biblical Proverbs are styled exactly as the *Instruction of Amenemipet son of Kanakht*. For example, the *Instruction of Amenemipet son of Kanakht* begins with the title of the work, the name of the author and whose son he was. The biblical Proverbs also begin with the work, the author, and whose son he was: "The Proverbs of Solomon the son of David...(see Proverbs 1)." Why would scholars seriously believe that the *Instruction of Amenemipet* influenced the content of the biblical Proverbs? This is because Amenemipet wrote his instructions for his son and the biblical Proverbs were also supposedly written for an unknown son.

In addition to the two Ancient Egyptian sources of the biblical Proverbs, there is a third source known as *The Instruction of a Man for His Son*. A line in this *Instruction* directed to a son says, "Listen to my voice. Do not pass by my words, do not be indifferent about what I shall say to you." The biblical version says, "My son, hear the instruction of thy father...." That was very good editing Europeans did it. Will Durant pointed out emphatically that " the Proverbs, of course, are not the work of Solomon, though several of them may have come from him; they owe something to Egyptian literature and Greek philosophy" (p. 342).

Again, notice how the two thousand-year-old legendary lying lore is changing. First, biblical tradition claimed that Solomon wrote all the Proverbs. When evidence contradicting this assertion emerged, the story changed to "though several of them may have come from him." Scholars cannot tell as usual what Solomon may have written and what he may not have written. Note that acknowledging that all the Proverbs are original Ancient Egyptian documents is also an open acknowledgement of the centrality of the Africans in the Bible. As a result, even though the evidence is overwhelming, not many scholars have the courage to point out the lies they have found to prove the legendary lying lore in Christianity.

What is noteworthy here is that no part of the scholastic discussion of the biblical Proverbs attributes them to the *Afrim* people as they have claimed for the past two thousand years. On the other hand, I have already revealed the works of Basel Missionaries, Reverends Riis and J. G. Christaller and their discoveries of the origin of the Proverbs in the *Akan* and other tribes of West Africa. I also discussed the work of Captain Charles Rattray on the similarities of *Akan* and Christian religious thoughts, concepts, rhetoric, and practices. In the case of the biblical Proverbs, not only do we know that the Jewish scholars of the Bible took the Proverbs from Ancient Egyptians, but we also know the descendants of the Ancient Egyptians from who they took these Proverbs.

Songs of Solomon

Just as scholars have found out that Solomon did not write the Proverbs so have they also found out that he did not even write the *Song of Solomon*. Durant pointed out that the source of the Song of Solomon "is an open field of surmise." Today, historians and biblical scholars have found out that it was a lie to attribute the *Song of Solomon* to King Solomon. This is a very serious example of the plagiarism that Lloyd Graham accused the Jewish people in *Deceptions and Myths of the Bible* when he wrote:

In spite of their pretended intimacy with the Creator, the Jews never had great knowledge of things cosmic and metaphysical; they were but plagiarists culling mythic artifacts they did not understand (1995, p. 2).

Though scholars have found that King Solomon did not write the *Songs of Solomon*, they still do not know the source and the author(s) of these Songs. As a result, they also speculate that these songs must have originated from Babylon, or they may have been Greek in origin because of some Greek words found in them. We know that the concepts of these songs and the original language from which they were translated into Greek were not Hebrew. If they were Hebrew, historians and biblical scholars would have pointed it out. Instead, they claim it must have been Babylonian or Greek. Why should we be surprised that the *Songs of Solomon* had some Greek words in them? The *Songs* and the entire biblical documents were originally translated into Greek so there must be Greek words in them, but that does not mean Greeks created these Songs. Still other scholars think, "it may be a flower of Alexandrian Jewry, plucked by some quite emancipated soul from the banks of the Nile" in Ancient Egypt. Durant wonders "what winking- or hood-winking- of the theologians did these songs of lusty passion find room between Isaiah and the Preacher" (p. 341).

It is true that the *Songs of Solomon* are not religious songs; they are songs of pure lust yet they found their way into what has been considered the most sacred religious documents ever written. The reason is simple; it was not by winking or hoodwinking of the ancient theologians that the seemingly "pornographic" *Songs of Solomon* got to be part of the biblical documents. Its presence in the Bible is evidence of the fact that the Jewish scholars of the Bible perceived every Ancient Egyptian writing as inspired by the Gods and so they were willing to take and include anything and everything they could lay hands on from the Egyptians. The Songs they attributed to Solomon were one of such documents they laid their hands upon and as long as these Songs came from the repositories of the Ancient Egyptian priesthood, they were deemed proper to be included in the compilation of a religious book.

Somewhere in its history, Christianity accused the Ancient Egyptians of being sexually promiscuous yet when sexually promiscuous documents as the *Songs of Solomon* found their way into the biblical documents no one dared to trace them to the promiscuous Ancient Egyptians. Neither Solomon, ancient Jewish priests, prophets, nor scholars wrote *the Songs of Solomon*. Ancient Egyptians wrote the biblical *Songs* attributed to Solomon. In an earlier discussion of this *Song*, I cited two evidence within the *Songs* itself. In Solomon 1:5-6, the writer tried to explain why he was black by using the Ancient Egyptian argument originally propounded by Herodotus of Halicarnassus. In this earlier discussion, I also pointed out that this hypothetical explanation, albeit false, was first propounded by Herodotus to explain the blackness of the people he came to meet in Ancient Egypt. Only an Ancient Egyptian writer would have known and used this explanation to explain his blackness because this explanation was pertinent only to Ancient Egyptians at the time.

I have also revealed that in the *Song of Solomon*, evidence of the Ancient Egyptian origin and authorship of this *Song* is in Solomon 1:9 where the author compares the beauty of his women to "a company of horses in Pharaoh's chariots." Only and Ancient Egyptian would have made such a comparison as this because only an Ancient Egyptian would have known the beauty of the horses in Pharaoh's chariots and not a King of the Jewish people in far away Canaan. Why would a foreign king compare the beauty of his women to the horses of another king when he could have had such beautiful horses himself? How could the women of Israel whose beauties were supposedly being praised in Canaan know and appreciate the symbolism in the comparison of their beauties to horses they had never seen and could never imagine from the stables of a far away King in a far away land they must have only heard about?

What is also least known in the search for the origin of the Songs of Solomon is the fact that Ancient Egyptian kings had a tradition of having songs written for them. For example, there is the *Cycle of Songs in Honor of Senwosre Kakari III* (see *The Literature of Ancient Egypt: An Anthology of Stories, Instructions, and Poetry* by Kelly Simpson (ed.), p. 279). The indigenous *Akan* name of this king who reigned Ancient Egypt from 1874-1855 B. C. was what was transposed to *Senusret Khakaura III*. It is therefore prudent to conclude that Solomon did not write the biblical songs attributed to him just as scholars have found out that most of the supposed authors of Israel to whom the Jewish scholars of the Bible attributed the Books of the Bible did not write them. Again, these scholars of the biblical documents simply took and rewrote Ancient Egyptian songs and attributed them to their king to make it all look like their kings also had songs written for them.

Another fact that western scholars have never known is that the name Solomon originated from the African tribal name *Salome*. The linguistic corruption of this name under foreign tongues from *Salome* to *Solome* and then to *Solomon* in European languages is evident. This name is specifically an *Ewe* traditional name.

The Book of Job

Another mysterious story that should not have found its way into the biblical documents because it was against the foundational belief in Yahweh was the Book of Job. Thomas Carlyle (1795-1881), British essayist, historian, and philosopher wrote that the Book of Job is " one of the grandest things ever written with a pen. ... A noble book, all men's book! It is our first, oldest statement of the never-ending problem – man's destiny, and God's ways with him here on this earth. ... There is nothing written, I think, in the Bible or out of it, of equal literary merit" (see Complete Works of Thomas Carlyle, Vol. I, Durant, p. 343). Nevertheless, other scholars have also found that the Book of Job is so much anti-God that it might not have been intended to be part of the documents that espouse this God.

In his work entitled *The Book of Job*, Morris Jastrow, Jr. pointed out that the Book of Job "is corrupt even beyond the custom of sacred scriptures" and that it is full of "edifying emendations" for which he suspects numerous interpolations and mistranslations (vii, p. 9-10, see also Durant, p. 343). The "numerous interpolations and mistranslations" could have been the result of attempts at editing and rewriting a foreign story to make it one's own. This, however, is another evidence of the attempt by the Jewish scholars of the Bible to redesign stories that were not theirs to make them their own. Another evidence that the intent and direction of the Book of Job was redesigned to fit into Jewish history of tribulations is in the fact that in this book, the wicked prospers and the righteous suffers. *Yahweh* allows Satan to shower Job with all kinds of adversities and tribulations. The content of this work was a great affront to the Jewish God *Yahweh*. This is because the story of Job seems to deny any rewards in worshipping this God and it seeks to overturn whatever this God had been proclaimed to be.

Most scholars agree that the Book seems to question the truth and sense of judgement and fairness of *Yahweh*. Durant wrote:

> All Israel has worshipped Yahveh (fitfully), as Job had done; Babylon had ignored and blasphemed Yahveh; and yet Babylon flourished, and Israel ate the dust and wore the sackcloth of desolation and captivity. What could one say of such a god? (p. 344).

In the story, Job becomes skeptical of *Yahveh* but a prologue in which Satan tells this *Yahveh* that Job is a righteous man seeks to save the direction of thought of this Book from propagating the opposite of what the biblical documents were intended to do. How could Satan have known that Job was a righteous man and *Yahweh* did not know?

Ecclesiastes

Another evidence showing that the religious documents that the Jewish scholars of the Bible passed on to the Greeks were not original Jewish people's documents can be found in

Ecclesiastes. If it is true that Jewish priests, religious scholars, or prophets wrote this document, the scholars of the Bible would have known the author. However, because Jewish people did not write this document, scholars of the Bible did not know who to attribute this document. There is evidence that they tried to attribute this document to someone but even then it became a confusion in the biblical account. As Durant points out in his footnote, "the author calls himself by a confusing literary fiction, both 'Koheleth' and 'the son of David, king of Jerusalem' – i.e., Solomon" (see Eccles. 1:1, Durant, p. 346). How credible is it that the documents of *Ecclesiastes* would be the original documents of the Jewish people, but their scholars would not know who wrote them? How credible is it that in their attempts to assign this document to an author, the scholars of the biblical documents could not even assign them to a particular credible author? Under what circumstances would it be credible for the Jewish scholars of the Bible to assign a document they supposedly wrote to a fictitious author or authors?

In explanation of this, some Jewish biblical scholars have argued that it was the tradition of Jewish scholars to concentrate on the name of the work and not the name of the author. I have already pointed out the dilemma of these scholars in upholding the *legendary lying lore* their ancestors left them. Beyond all these, there is evidence that there were Ancient Egyptian documents that parallel the biblical *Ecclesiastes* (see Brian Brown, *Wisdom of the Egyptians*, Breasted, *Dawn of Conscience*).

The Book of Lamentations

Biblical tradition has ascribed the biblical *Lamentations* to Jeremiah but again many Jewish biblical scholars have argued that Jeremiah did not write them. According to Durant:

> In his old age, says orthodox tradition, he wrote his "Lamentations," the most eloquent of all the books of the Old Testament (p. 324).

However, in the Jewish *Encyclopaedia*, vol. vii, p. 598, Jewish scholars have argued against Jeremiah's authorship of the *Lamentations*.

Does any Christian know that the Ancient Egyptians also had *Lamentations*? There are *The Lamentations of Kwaku Pra Sebe* (see Kelly Simpson, p. 230). Again, the *Akan* names of the Ancient Egyptian author of these *Lamentations* confirm that the biblical Lamentations were also Ancient Egyptian in origin. The Ancient Egyptian *Lamentations* are part of the documents found in *Papyrus Chester Beatty IV* now in the British Museum. Note that it was the indigenous *Akan* name *of Kwaku Pra Sebe* that was transposed into Greek and ended up in Egyptology as *Khakheperre- sonbe*.

Again, from all these discussions, it is clear that the Jewish scholars of the Bible that translated the documents that became the contents of the Christian Bible actually edited, rewrote, and translated Ancient Egyptian documents as their own. No biblical scholar has been able to establish with authority any aspect of the Bible that was originally created and written by Jewish prophets or priests. Even, the documents the Bible claims that the Jewish people had in their history, the same Bible also states that Jewish priests simply found them. There is a major difference between finding some documents somewhere and claiming later that one originally wrote these documents. There is also a major difference between translating some documents for other people and later claiming that one wrote these documents.

Otherwise, how could the biblical story of creation be that identical to the Ancient Egyptian version of creation for which there were documents long before the biblical version was translated into Greek in Ancient Egypt? How could the name of the central character in the biblical myth of the flood be identical to the ancient *Akan* name of *Anoa* and the ark seem to have been derived from the *Akan* word *adaka* with the same meaning? How could the *Song of Solomon* supposedly written by King Solomon in Canaan between (965-928 B. C.) be based upon Ancient Egyptian symbolism of beauty? How could Ancient Egyptian documents of instruction be found

305

in the biblical Proverbs? How could missionaries and scholars in Africa come to believe that the biblical Proverbs originated from the *Akan* and other African tribes among whom they went to live in West Africa? How could an Ancient Egyptian document end up in the biblical Psalms? How could modern scholars link most of the biblical documents to Ancient Egyptians and not the Jewish people that have claimed these documents for over two thousand years?

Voltaire said "Truth is a fruit, which should not be plucked until it is ripe," and this is the time. Despite all these inconsistencies, pious fraud, and scholastic plagiarism and inaccuracies, the biblical documents have been accepted in Europe as the greatest religious documents man has ever written. Christian Europe is the champion in defense of these inconsistencies, pious fraud, scholastic plagiarism, and historical inaccuracies because they have never known half of the racial, ethnic, linguistic, and cultural story behind the Bible. Christian Europe simply accepted and believed in these documents without knowing anything about them and without checking their history or veracity. Unfortunately, the Bible itself has succeeded in determining the scope and sequence of what Europeans historians can find out.

In his discussion of Exodus or Evolution in the *Deceptions and Myths of the Bible,* Lloyd Graham noted that in terms of the perception and interpretation of the Bible, "there is no end to the explanations apologists find to prove the historicity of Hebrew mythology." The greatest flaw in Christianity is that Christian Europe has sought to cover up the biblical inconsistencies, pious fraud, scholastic, and historical inaccuracies with false explanations and interpretations. However, the racial, ethnic, linguistic evidence showing that Africans wrote the biblical documents of the Old Testament are very plain. Discussion of the content of the biblical narratives above has shown that the Jewish people did not write the documents of the Bible. If they did, the Bible would not be full of Ancient Egyptian documents and names.

The Africans who wrote the Bible

I have practically devoted the entire discussion in this book to revealing the *Akan* and other African tribal origin of the Jewish people that went to Europe to become the Jews and Hebrews. As a result, it would be prudent for any reader to assume and conclude by now that the Jewish people must have been the Africans that wrote the Bible, but that would be false. Early Jewish scholars propagated the idea that their ancestral prophets wrote the documents of the Old Testament. Ignorantly, Christian Europe accepted and propagated this around the world through Christianity. Modern biblical scholars have had no choice but to accept the false idea that ancient Jewish prophets wrote the documents of the Old Testament, but there is no evidence to support this. The evidence, on the other hand, shows that even accepting what they claim they were the Jewish people did not have any form of writing in the ancient times their ancestors were supposed to have written these biblical documents.

I cited this evidence earlier, but it is again pertinent here. Gary Greenberg wrote in *The Moses Mystery: The African Origin of the Jewish People* that:

> Even if we assume that the Bible is derived from earlier sources yet to be discovered, it still describes events that occurred more than a thousand years before its completion, and in those ancient times few peoples had a strong tradition of historical writing and perspective (p. 3).

Greenberg continued that:

> *Though several nations had written records in the second, third, and fourth millennia B. C. from which modern historians can draw conclusions, there is no evidence that Israel was among them (p. 3, emphasis mine).*

While the historical evidence shows that few ancient people had a strong tradition of writing, Michael Grant pointed out in *The Ancient Historians* that Herodotus of Halicarnassus showed that the Ancient Egyptians had a strong tradition of writing, record keeping, and history:

> The Egyptians who live in the cultivated part of the country, by their practice of keeping records of the past, have made themselves much the best historians of any nation of which I have had experience. In the very earliest times of a united Egypt, or even just before (c. 3200 B. C.), the deeds of kings were already sculptured upon reliefs. Khufu [*Akufu*] and Khafre [*Okyere Afre*] of the Fourth Dynasty are shown by inscriptions of the twenty-sixth century to have possessed libraries, and at least as early as the Fifth Dynasty, there were written records comprising annals and kings lists going back to the fourth millennium B. C. (see Grant, 1994, p. 3; Herodotus, Bk. II, p. 77).

This piece of evidence confirms that between the Jewish people and Ancient Egyptians, the most likely people to have written the biblical documents were the Ancient Egyptians and that explains why there are numerous Ancient Egyptian writings in the Bible.

In addition to these, the historical evidence [albeit cleverly designed] further shows that there were no Jews and there was no Judaism in the ancient times modern Jewish people claim their ancestors wrote their religious documents. They did not have any religion then. The evidence again shows that at least it was after 200 A. D. that the Jewish people began to compile the documents that led to the development of Judaism just as the biblical documents had led to the development of Christianity.

The greatest false belief in Christianity therefore has been based upon the assumption that the Jewish people wrote the documents of the Bible therefore the names of the people and places in these documents and their assigned authors were all Jewish names. One of the most important evidence that debunks the Jewish people's two thousand-year claim that they wrote the Bible is the transposed *Akan* and other African tribal names of the authors of the Old Testament documents.

All the discussions and revelations in this book have been designed to reveal the Africans who wrote the Bible. At this point, I would like to reiterate some ideas I have said and repeated throughout the book. Historians and biblical scholars agree that the so-called biblical Exodus occurred in the 13th century B. C. These historians and biblical scholars also agree that the Jewish people did not go to Europe until around the 2nd century B. C. As scholars of Jewish history wrote in the *Encyclopaedia Britannica*:

> By the 2nd century B. C., Jewish settlements were founded in Cyrene, west of Egypt, as well as in Greece and Rome, Gaul (France), and other Roman colonies (1996, p. 75).

In the history of when and how the Jewish people went to Europe to become Jews and Hebrews, scholars of Jewish history point out that the word Jew is an English term, the word Hebraeus was Latin, and the word Hebreu or Ebreu was Old French. From these emerged the English words Jew and Hebrew. The date the Jewish people went to Europe to become Jews and Hebrews is very important to establishing the foundation for the revelation of the Africans who wrote the Bible. The importance of this foundation is in the fact that the people that left Ancient Egypt in the 13th century B. C. into the Exodus were not Jews and they were not Hebrews, at least not until after the 2nd century B. C. I have already revealed that these people originated from the *Akan* and other African tribal groups that were the Ancient Egyptians.

From this foundation, it is also clear that the people that went to Canaan to set up the State of *Asrae* [Israel] were not Jews, and they were not Hebrews. They were black people from *Akan* and other African tribal groups. Collectively, these people identified themselves with the *Akan* word *Afrim*. This was not a Hebrew word; it was an *Akan* word and the corruption of this word to *Ivrim* did not make it a Hebrew word either because the people of the Exodus were not Hebrews.

The people of the Exodus that identified their God with the *Akan* word *Adona* [transposed to *Adonai*] were not Jews and they were not Hebrews either. They were still from *Akan* and other African tribes. The people that worshipped the goddess *Yaa* in Canaan and later changed her name to *Yaw* from which *Yahweh* was derived were not Jews and they were not Hebrews. In short, the people that left Ancient Egypt in the Exodus were *Afrim* people. These people were originally from African tribes and they were known as *Afrim* from the 13th century to the 2nd century B. C when Europeans gave them the new name, Jew. The fact that Europeans gave the Jewish people that went to Europe the name Jews and Hebrews does not make the people of the *Akan* and other African tribal groups from which they originated Jews and Hebrews. A major revelation in this piece of historical information is that there were no Jews and Hebrews anywhere in this world until after the 2nd century B. C. when the *Afrim* people appeared in Europe.

So how did Europeans get to claim that the people of the Bible were Jews and Hebrews? The answer is simple. Part of the *Afrim* people that went to Europe with the biblical documents became the first Jews and Hebrews. These people then turned around to claim that since they were then known to be Jews and Hebrews in Europe, the rest of the *Akan* and other African tribes that composed the *Afrim* people of the Exodus were also Jews and Hebrews, but that was wrong. Otherwise, the *Akan* and other African tribes from which the *Afrim* people originated before they became Jews and Hebrews would also have been Jews and Hebrews, but they are not. Ignorant of the true situation, Europeans also assumed that the people of the Bible were known as Jews and Hebrews so the Bible was translated into European languages using the new and assumed names of the *Afrim* people. Without knowing it, the Bible has been basically propagating that the people of the *Akan* and other African tribes of the so-called biblical Exodus were Jews and Hebrews, and that is also wrong. These people were from *Akan* and other African tribal groups and my revelation of their modern names confirm it all.

It is needless to point it out that the biblical story was and still is the story of black people because the *Akan* and other African tribes whose story is the biblical story are not white. These biblical stories were the stories of the *Akan* and other African tribal groups that were the Ancient Egyptians and not the group from these people that went to become the Jews or Hebrews in Europe. The people that wrote the biblical documents assigned to them in the Bible were therefore not Jews or Hebrews. They were from *Akan* and other African tribes and their *Akan* and other African tribal names confirm it. Just as most modern Jewish people have retained their indigenous *Akan* and other African tribal names up to today, so did the Jewish scholars that compiled, edited, and translated the biblical documents for the Greeks also retain the indigenous African tribal names of the authors of the Old Testament documents. These African tribal names of the authors of the Old Testament are still discernible despite their transposition through numerous European languages over a couple of millennia.

There is a lot of evidence that the Jewish scholars of the biblical documents went to great lengths to conceal information about other people. Why then would the Jewish scholars use the exact African tribal names of these authors? Perhaps, they assumed that transposing these names into Greek, a completely different language would render the names indiscernible even to the Africans whose names these were and still are. Or perhaps, they assumed that these documents were going into a foreign land where the people whose documents and names they were would never be to find them out. One thing is clear, however, and that is these scholars never anticipated that knowledge and a religion from these documents and names would grow and spread to every corner of the earth.

People in Europe that do not know African tribal names have heard, seen, and read their Bibles for hundreds of years and assumed that the names of the authors of the Old Testament are Jewish or Hebrew names, but they are not. They are African tribal names. As I have already pointed out, African tribal names are so unique that from the names of these authors of the Old Testament, we can identify the specific African tribes from which their ancient ancestors originated.

However, from the description of how the Greeks "murdered" the *Akan* and African tribal names they met in Ancient Egypt, and from how modern Jewish people have transposed their ethnic *Akan* and African tribal names, it is prudent for the reader to expect that the Greeks and other European languages have also "murdered" the names of the Africans who wrote the Bible. These names have been rendered in Greek and various European linguistic corruptions and orthographic transpositions. Despite all these, the *Akan* and African tribal phonologies and etymologies in these names are always discernible because most of the names are so unique and different that they cannot be linguistically distorted beyond recognition. The ability to identify these names only requires knowledge of the language and culture of the *Akan* and African tribes involved and that has been my advantage. A major revelation here is that the *Akan* and other African tribes from which all the names I have revealed in this book originated still carry and use these names just as the Jewish people have carried and still use them. This means it is easy to verify these revelations from the African tribes. The most important point to remember, however, is that these people were not Jews or Hebrews.

Amos

In the Old Testament, there is the ***Book of Amo*** [pronounced *Ahmo*]. The name *Amo* was and it still is an indigenous *Akan* name. *Amo* was a royal name in the New Kingdom of Ancient Egypt. The first of the 18th Dynasty kings of Ancient Egypt was called *Amo*. He ruled from c.1575-1550. In the various versions of the transposition of Ancient Egyptian kings' names into Greek, Africanus called this king *Amos* and Eusebius called him *Amosis*, In other renderings, he is known as *Ahmose*. This name was therefore Ancient Egyptian and *Akan* and not a Jewish name. It was the document of this *Amo* in Ancient Egypt that the Jewish scholars of the Bible took and conferred onto a fictitious *Amo* in Israel and then wrote the history of Israel around him to make this plagiarism more authentic.

As this name was transposed into the Greek language, the scholars simply added the Greek ornamental suffix "s" to it and it has since become *Amos* to the Greeks, Europeans, and the world. From English phonology, this name is pronounced with a long "A." However, I have heard and noticed that some Jewish people and even biblical scholars pronounce this name with a short "A" just as it is pronounced in *Akan*. In their pronunciation therefore, *Amos* is pronounced *Ahmos*. Take off the suffix "s" and the pronunciation of this name becomes exactly as it was in the ancient *Akan* language of Egypt and continues to be today in Africa. Nevertheless, *Amo* is an African name, and the name of this author originated from an African tribe. Scholars that are interested in checking out the veracity of this revelation and the origin of this name should go to the *Akan* people in Ghana.

Isaiah

There is also the ***Book of Asa*** in the Old Testament. A major revelation in the transposition of the names of the *Akan* and other African tribal authors of the Old Testament documents is that most of the names were simply transposed by adding the suffix "iah," just as the scholars of the Bible added "ites" to the names of almost every other group of people in the Bible. From this formula, the indigenous *Akan* name *Asa* was transposed to *Asaiah* in the Greek Bible. The transposed name *Asaiah* was further transposed into Western European tongues as *Isaiah*. In the transposition of this name into European orthography, specifically English orthography, the short "A" as in "Ah" in the *Akan* pronunciation of *Asa* was transposed to a long "I" in European transposition to retain the initial *Akan* initial pronunciation of the "Ah" sound. As a result, I have never heard anyone pronounce the word *Isaiah* with a short "I." From the name of

Asa, I would even venture to suggest that this author originated from among the *Akuapem* tribe. Remember this was one of the *Akan* tribes that lived in biblical *Adom [Edom]*. They were the earliest *Edomites* but they were also Ancient Egyptians. Their kings were among the earliest kings of Ancient Egypt. Scholars that are interested in checking out this name should go to the Eastern Region of Ghana and ask of the *Akuapem* people.

Jeremiah

There is also the ***Book of Kyereme*** [pronounced *Chereme*] in the Old Testament. This was the indigenous *Akan* name that was first simply transposed to *Cheremiah* and then further transposed to Jeremiah in Western European tongues. In the transposition of this name, notice how the consonant combination "*Ch*" sound in *Cheremiah* easily became the "J" sound in *Jeremiah*. What makes it easy to discern most of these African names that were transposed into European orthographies is that the transpositions distorted the orthographies of these names but they sought to retain as much of the phonologies as possible. As a result, most of these names were transposed according to how Europeans heard them pronounced. In English orthography, this name is pronounced as ***Chereme*** with a "*Ch*" pronunciation as in chair. In European ears however, the "*Ch*" sound in the name sounded like a "J." We have lived with Europeans in Ghana for more than a century and we know how they hear our names. The *Akan* name *Chereme* is still *Jereme* in European ears and orthography. However, it was this *Akan* name *Kyereme* that was transposed to *Cheremiah* and it became *Jeremiah* under foreign tongues and orthography.

Zechariah

There is also the *Book of Sekyere* in the Old Testament. In English phonology, this indigenous *Akan* name is pronounced *Sechere*. In the initial transposition of this name, it became *Secheriah* with the normal "iah" suffix. However, in English phonology the alphabet "S" has a "Z" phonological property as in the pronunciation of "cease" and "resistance." In foreign ears and under European tongues, the initial "S" in *Sechariah* became a "Z" and the name became *Zechariah*. One interesting aspect of the pronunciation of this name is that most people pronounce it as "*Zachariah*" but it is never written with an "a" in the Bible. The orthography of this name has retained the original "e" after the "S" though the pronunciation is different. It was the indigenous *Akan* name *Sechere* that was transposed into Greek and other European tongues as Zechariah. The etymology of this name is not Hebrew.

Obadiah

There is also the ***Book of Oboadee*** in the Old Testament. This is also an indigenous *Akan* name meaning the Creator. It was the *Akan* name ***Oboadee*** that was transposed to *Obadiah* in European ears, phonology, and orthography. Note how the transposition here is only a slight change in phonology and orthography – the original *Akan Oboadee* became *Obadee* in European ears and then *Obadiah* in European languages and orthography.

Joshua

There is also the ***Book of Gyasi*** in the Old Testament. In European phonology, this name is pronounced *Jasi*. This is an indigenous *Akan* name that was common in Ancient Egypt. The Greeks transposed this name in Ancient Egyptian history to *Djoser, Djeser*, and other European orthographic variations. Among the famous Ancient Egyptians with this name was *Gyasi Kraseneboo*, the famous ancient sot. It was this indigenous *Akan* name that was transposed into the Bible as *Joshua*. Evidence of the indigenous *Akan* origin of the transposed name *Joshua* and the process of the transposition of this name can be found in the Catholic Bible. In 405 A. D. when St. Jerome translated the Greek Bible into Latin, he came across and copied some names that were closer to their original African phonologies and etymologies. Among these names was the name **Gyasi**. As a result, in the Douai-Confraternity Version of the Catholic Bible, the name **Gyasi** [pronounced *Jasi*] was transposed into Latin as **Josue** closer to its **Akan** phonology and etymology (see the Table of Contents of the Catholic Old Testament in Chpt. 3). As a result, the Book of Joshua in the Protestant Bible is the Book of *Josue* in the Catholic Bible. Since the Catholic Bible is older and was corrupted by only Latin and Greek languages, and since the rest of the Bibles originated from the Catholic Bible, it is evident that the original name that was later transposed to Joshua in Western Europe was the name *Josue* [*Josu*] from the Catholic Bible. This was the name closest to the original *Akan* name *Gyasi* [*Jasi*]. The *Book of Joshua* was therefore the *Book of Gyasi* [*Jasi*] that was transposed to *Josue* and finally Joshua under the rubble of foreign European tongues.

Haggai

There is also the **_Book of Agyei_** in the Old Testament. In English phonology, this name is pronounced *Ajei*. The earliest Greek and Catholic Bibles were closer to the original phonologies and etymologies of the names of the Africans who wrote the Bible. This is because the Greeks and Romans were closer to the history of the creation of the Bible and they must have been exposed to original documents that had names closer to original African etymologies and phonologies. Also in the name of religious purity, early Greek and Roman writers tried to maintain as much of the original phonologies and etymologies in the names of the Bible as possible. The name *Agyei* is also *Akan*. In the Catholic Bible this name was Latinized to *Aggeus* where the ornamental Latin suffix "us" was simply added to the *Akan* "*Agge*" for it to become *Aggeus* (see chapt. 3). In foreign ears and under Western European tongues, the name *Agyei* was orthographically transposed to **Agai** and it was pronounced "*Agai*," closer to its original *Akan* phonology. A German missionary who was my teacher used to pronounce this name "Aggai" with a short "a" on the first vowel and a long "a" on the second vowel. He therefore pronounced it closely to the *Akan* name *Ajei*. In English phonology, the alphabet "g' also has a "j" phonological property as in words like "gem, giant, gentleman." As a result, "Aggai" was also pronounced *Ajei*. However, in further European orthography of this name, a silent prefix "H" was added to make it *Haggai* and that also changed the pronunciation. Originally, the initial "H" was silent but in later pronunciations it became pronounced. However, if the "H" is not pronounced and the first vowel is pronounced short and the second long, it becomes exactly the original *Akan* phonology of this name.

Hosea

There is also the **_Book of Osee_** in the Old Testament. *Osee* is an *Akan* and therefore an African tribal name; specifically it is a popular *Asante* name. We met this name in our discussion of Esau [*Sau*] and the movement of his family to go to live on the Seir [*Osee*] mountain in Edom [*Akan Adom*]. This *Akan* name was originally transposed in Europe to **Osea**. That was still close to its *Akan* phonology and orthography. However, in other European orthographies, the name *Osea* was further transposed and given a silent prefix "H" just as *Aggai* was given a silent prefix "H." The name *Osea* then became *Hosea* with the initial silent "H" not pronounced. However, in modern times, the silent "H" is pronounced. Evidence of the *Akan* origin of the name *Osee* and the process of its transposition and transformation to Hosea can also be seen in the Catholic Bible where the name is still written as **Osee** closer to its *Akan* phonology and orthography as possible. Today, most people that carry this name in Ghana have also sought to Europeanize it. They do not write it as *Osee* anymore, they write it as **Osei**.

Samuel

There is also the **_Book of Asamoa_** in the Old Testament. *Asamoa* is also an indigenous *Akan* name. This was the *Akan* name that became **Samuel** in the Bible. The direction of the

311

phonological and orthographic transposition of this name began from *Asamoa* to dropping the initial "A" for it to become *Samoa*. In foreign ears and under stranger European tongues, the ending "a' in *Samoa* was pronounced long and it began to sound like *Samoe*. The orthography of named followed this wrong phonology and the name finally became *Samuel* with an ending "l" in the modern Bible.

Daniel

There is the Book of Daani in the Old Testament. This name is also *Akan*. The process of the transposition and transformation of this name simply added the suffix "el," and it became *Daani-el*, Daniel. What is interesting about the transpositions of these names is that the patterns of transposition are also evident in the patterns of transposition of the African tribal names of modern Jewish people. For example, the *Akan* name *Tumi* can be found among modern Jewish people as *Toumy*, and *Mante* can be found as *Mantei*. The *Akan* name *Abedi* can also be found among them as *Alberdi.*

Jonah

There is the ***Book of Ajena*** in the Old Testament. This is also an indigenous *Akan* name. The transposition of this name began with the dropping of the initial "A." The name then became *Jena*. In foreign ears and under further European tongues it began to sound *Jona* and it finally became Jonah with an ending "h" in the European orthography.

Ezekiel

There is also the ***Book of Ezeke*** in the Old Testament. *Ezeke*, is a Nzima name and it is pronounced *Ezeke* and not *Ezeki* as it might be pronounced in English phonology. We met the *Nzima* people when we discussed King Akka whose people were supposedly the Akkadians. In English phonology, this foreign name was pronounced *Ezeki*, and adding a suffix "el" simply transposed it to ***Ezekiel***. Remember that I mentioned that the people that went into the so-called biblical Exodus were *Akan* and other African tribes. Here is one of the tribes of these people. The Jewish scholars of the biblical documents found all these documents in Ancient Egypt. The ancestors the people of the Exodus left behind in Ancient Egypt wrote these documents.

Ezra

There is also the ***Book of Ezra*** in the Old Testament. This is also derived from a *Nzima* name. The indigenous Nzima tribal name I know of is *Azra*, and it is not difficult to see the direction of the transposition of this name. European pronunciation of *Azra* with an initial long "A" simply transformed the name to Ezra. There is an orthographic variation of this name in the Apocrypha.

Habakkuk

There is the ***Book of Baako*** in the Old Testament. *Baako* is also an *Akan* name. We first met this name in the revelation of the African names of Simeon Bar Kokhba as *Siamon Baakoba*. This Jewish historical personality was the one that led a revolt of the Jewish people against the Romans for three years. It was after the defeat of *Baakoba* and the destruction of Jerusalem that the Romans built the city Aelia Capitolina on top of the ruins of Jerusalem. We have seen how a silent prefix "H" was added to the transformation and orthography of some names of the authors of the Old Testament. The name *Baako* easily became *Baaku* in European ears. The prefix *Ha* was also a common prefix in the names of some personalities in Jewish history. For example, Rabbi Judah Ha-Nasi, the patriarch of Palestinian Jewry also had that *Ha* prefix in his name. I have already mentioned that Ha-Nasi's name was derived from the *Akan* name *Anansi*. In the process of the transposition of this name the prefix *Ha* was simply added and the name *Ha –Baako* became Ha Bakku and then Habakkuk. It was the indigenous *Akan* name *Baako* that was transposed to *Bakku* and then later given the prefix "Ha" and a suffix "k" for it to become *Habakkuk* under for tongues.

Nahum

There is also the ***Book of Nana [Naa] Afum*** in the Bible. This is also an *Akan* name. Among the *Akan, Nana* is a prefix to a name as an appellation of respect for royalty, old age, or some achievement that benefited the people as a whole. Even today, this name is pronounced with a contraction and a glide over the second "na." However, the first "na" is pronounced long for it to sound like *Naafum*. In European ears and under countless foreign tongues *Naafum* began to sound like *Naahum* and it eventually was written *Nahum*. I would like to go further into the origin of this name to suggest that *Naafum* can be found today among the *Akuapem* people that lived in ancient *Adomea* [*Idumea* or biblical *Edom*].

Nahemi

There is also the *Book of Nahemi* in the Bible. This is an African tribal name. I heard this name in the Volta Region of Ghana. However, I believe the Ga-Adangme people also have a name like that. This is the indigenous African tribal name that was transposed with the traditional "iah" suffix for to be become Nahemiah. In English phonology and orthography this name easily became Nehemiah where the first "a' was pronounced long and later written as "e."

Zephaniah

There is also the *Book of Sapanin* in the Bible. This is an indigenous *Akan* name. It means the oldest war. This was the name the biblical scholars transposed to *Sapaniah* with the traditional "iah" suffix. In the Greek language, the "P" acquired the property of "F" and the name was then written in Greek as *Saphaniah*. Under further European tongues and orthographies, the initial "S" in *Saphaniah* acquired the "Z" property of an "S" and became Zephaniah.

Malachi

There is the *Book of Malachi* in the Bible. This name has not gone through much transposition. It is pronounced *Malachi* in the African language from which it originates. It is pronounced with the last "chi" syllable pronounced as we pronounce "chi" in chisel in English.

How did these people get to write the books assigned to them in the Old Testament? The Jewish scholars of the biblical documents found these books among Ancient Egyptian documents. They took these documents and their *Akan* and other African tribal names and began to write the hitherto non-existent history of the Jewish people around these people just as they took the Ancient Egyptian kings' lists and designed their false ancestral chronology from them. They then claimed these people as their ancient prophets. Even if we accept the false assumption that the Jewish people wrote these documents, the reader should remember that in the period these documents were supposedly written, the *Afrim* people were not Jews and they were not Hebrews. In the supposed historical times of these authors, there were no Jews and Hebrews, at least not until hundreds of years later yet.

Some African names in the New Testament documents

The Old Testament story is closer to the original *Akan* and other African tribal groups that left in the so-called biblical Exodus than the New Testament. As a result, there are more *Akan* and other African tribal names in the Old Testament than the New. While the Old Testament is full of identifiable *Akan* names, the New Testament was based upon a deliberate

313

attempt to conceal the names of the writers and the characters within. The main reason for the deliberate concealment of the authors of the New Testament was that the Old Testament had the supposed credibility of having been written by Jewish prophets, centuries before and therefor it was more credible.

Early Christians perceived the Jewish prophets that supposedly wrote the biblical documents as having had some intimacy with God therefore their works were more pristine and true. They believed God inspired these prophets to write his words, so the Old Testament to them was truly God's words. On the other hand, these early Christians were also aware that none of the modern Christians was yet inspired by God to do such a work therefore the works of such inspired writers were not acceptable as worthy of inclusion in the book of God's truth. The New Testament did not have the honor of having been written by "inspired-prophets," so the best way to protect its honor was to try conceal the contemporary names of its authors and characters hoping to create an aura of "inspired" mystery around the authors and the documents.

As a result, most of the scholars whose works were selected for the New Testament and many others whose works were not selected had to write anonymously or pseudonymously. In *Who Wrote the New Testament: The Making of the Christian Myth*, Burton Mack explained it this way:

> "... most of the writings in the New Testament were either written anonymously and later assigned to a person of the past or written later as a pseudonym for some person thought to have been important for the earliest period. Striking examples of the latter are the two letters said to have been written by Peter, both of which are clearly second century creations. Thus over the course of the second and third centuries, centrist Christians were able to create the impression of a singular, monolinear history of the Christian Church. They did so by carefully selecting, collecting, and arranging anonymous and pseudonymous writings assigned to figures at the beginning of the Christian time" (1989, p. 7).

What this means is that even in the New Testament, there was form of "pious fraud" just as there was in the creation of the Old Testament. The names of Matthew, Mark, Luke, and John, the "apostles" that Christians have believed wrote the New Testament were not the true names of the authors of these four gospels. These are the names later Christians gave to these "anonymous" writers.

Apart from the four gospels of the New Testament, there are other works that are earlier collections of the teachings about Jesus. Even these supposed earlier works were all written anonymously or pseudonymously. Some of these earlier works of the teachings of Jesus were the **Sayings Gospel Q, the Gospel of Thomas**, and other pieces of early writings.

Despite all these, the central characters in the biblical documents that became the New Testament also had *Akan* and other African tribal names.

From Apau to Paul

There is the name of *Apau* in the New Testament. This is an indigenous *Akan* name. The transposition of this name began with the dropping of the initial "A." The name then became *Pau,* and from this further European transposition sought to Europeanize it by adding the suffix "l." It then became the Paul we have in the Bible today but it is pronounced with the short "o" sound. In the New Testament therefore, *the Akan* name *Apau* was what was transposed into European tongues as *Paul*, a direct derivation from *Pau.*

From Gyemi to James

There is the indigenous *Akan* name **Gyemi** in the New Testament. In English phonology, this name is pronounced *Jemi*. In European transposition, a long "a' replaced the original *Akan*

314

"e" and it initially became *Jame* and then it was given the usual Greek ornamental suffix "s" for it to become *Jemis* and then *James*.

From Apete to Peter

There is the indigenous African tribal name *Apete* in the New Testament. This is a *Ga-Adangme* name. Do you remember the former Prime Minister of Israel, Netanyahu, got his name from the *Ga-Adangme* people. I introduced the *Ga-Adangme* people in their war with the Jewish people in Judges 12. The *Ga-Adangme* people were part of the African tribal groups that left Ancient Egypt into the so-called biblical Exodus. The direction of the transposition of this name is quite evident. Again, the initial "A" in the indigenous name *Apete* was dropped and it became *Pete*, and in European orthography a suffix "r" was added for it to become *Peter*. The African tribal name from which the European and biblical name *Peter* was derived was *Apete*. The picture of the image of St. Peter elsewhere in the book confirms the African origin of this biblical personality and his name.

From Gyadu [Jadu] to Jude

There is the indigenous *Akan* tribal name of *Gyadu* in the New Testament. In English phonology, this name is pronounced as *Jadu*. The direction of the transposition of this name is evident. It began as a phonological corruption of *Jadu* and ended up under the rubble of foreign tongues as *Judu* and then Jude with a final silent "e." The biblical name of *Jude* was Europeanized from the *Akan* name *Gyadu [Jadu]*. Some *Akan* scholars and friends of mine have suggested that the biblical name of *Juda* must have been transposed from this same *Akan* name *Gyadu* just as the name of Israel was derived from the *Akan* word *Asrae*.

From Ayesu to Jesus

In an earlier discussion, I revealed that the name of the tribal, political, and religious group to which John the Baptist and Jesus belonged was *Assin*. *Assin* is one of the tribal groups of the *Akan* people. *Assin* was the name that was transposed to *Essene* in the history of the Jewish people and pronounced as *Essen* under European tongues.

The direction of the transposition of the indigenous *Akan* name *Ayesu* into European orthography and phonology is evident. It began with the dropping of the initial "A." The name was transposed into Greek as *Yesu* and then given an ornamental suffix "s" for it to become *Yesus*. What is noteworthy about this name is that Western Europeans call him Jesus from Greek orthography. However, the Catholics call him *Yesu* [Jesu] closer to the original *Akan* phonology of this name. How then did the "Y" in *Yesus* become a "J" in *Jesus*?

In the early period of the development of the English alphabets, there was no "Y". The alphabet "j" was written with a small "v" on top and pronounced as "y" (see A Companion to Baugh and Cable's *History Of the English Language*, 2nd ed., p. 2). It was from the alphabet "j" with a small "v" on top that the alphabet "Y" with a "v" on top was derived. This is the reason modern alphabet "Y" carries a 'V' on a horizontal bar. The bar was originally part of the lower half of the letter "J." The etymology of the name of *Yesu* is not only *Akan* because the *Ewe* people also have a variation of the name as *Adzesu*. Some of my colleagues think the *Ewe* variation is even closer to the European name of *Jesus*. Whichever way one wants to take it, the name *Jesus* was derived from an African name. Elsewhere in this book, I also revealed that the indigenous *Akan* name that became *Josephus* in Latin and *Joseph* in English was *Osafo* and I will never be surprised if further research reveals that the indigenous name of the mother of Jesus was *Omari*, also an *Akan* name. Otherwise, how did a non-European come by the indigenous name Mary?

What is most interesting about these revelations is that the *Akan* names that were transposed and corrupted in foreign tongues are still the names of modern descendants of the ancient *Akan* and other African tribes from whom the *Afrim* people broke away into the Exodus.

315

All these names can therefore be verified from the *Akan* and the other African tribes that were the Ancient Egyptians in Africa.

The Africans in the Apocrypha

Not many Christians know about the *Apocrypha*, though some must have heard of it. Early Christian communities found out very early that some of the documents purported to have been written with the ordination of God were downright fictitious and fraudulent. Among such documents were the writings that were compiled into what was called the **Apocrypha**. The documents of the *Apocrypha* used to be part of the Old Testament but they were removed when early apostolic fathers of Christian communities found out that some fictitious documents were being passed around as God's words. This was the reason these documents were given the Greek name *Apocrypha*. In the *Apocrypha* too, some of the main characters also have *Akan* names.

From Asare to Azariah

There is the indigenous *Akan* name *Asare* in the *Apocrypha*. This was the name that was transposed first to *Asari* and then the "s" took on the phonological property of a "z" under foreign European tongues, and it became *Azari*. The suffix "a" was added to make it *Azaria* and then a silent "h" was eventually added to its orthography. What is interesting about this is that the *Hausa* people in Northern Nigeria also have the name *Zaria* as the name of one of their cities.. The *Hausa* people were also in Ancient Egypt. They were also part of the people that left into the Exodus. They left the word *Sereki* meaning king in Ancient Egyptian history. This is the word that was transposed in Egyptology as *Serekh*.

From Saara to Sirach

There is also the name of **Saara** in the *Apocryphal* documents. *In The Wisdom of Jesus the Son of Sirach*, or the *Ecclesiasticus*, the *Akan* name *Saarah* was Europeanized to *Sirach* with the "i" pronounced long. When **Sirach** is pronounced with a long "I," the phonology approximates the original *Akan* phonology of this name.

From Nana Sei to Nanasseh and then Manasseh

In the *Apocrypha*, The Prayer of **Manasseh** was written by **Nana Sei**. The *Akan* name *Nanasei* became Manasseh in foreign ears and under foreign European tongues. In the Old Testament, there is evidence of another **Osei** writing one of the documents of the Bible. I have pointed out that the name of this *Osei* name was what was transposed to **Hosea** with a silent prefix "H."

Maccabees

Finally, the name of the *Maccabees* in the *Apocrypha* is derived from the *Akan* words *Maka Bi* referring to a group that had also had its say. *Maka bi* in the Akan language means I have also had my say.

Conclusion

From the discussions and revelations throughout the book, it is clear that:

1. The people that left Ancient Egypt into the so-called biblical Exodus were Ancient Egyptians, specifically, they were mostly *Akan* people joined by other African tribes. However, the Jewish scholars of the Bible deliberately sought to conceal the racial and ethnic origin of the Jewish people and the source of the biblical documents in Ancient Egypt by stating that the Jewish people went to Ancient Egypt from Ur of the Chaldees in Mesopotamia. None of the

revelations in this book that tie the Jewish people to the *Akan* and other African tribes that were the Ancient Egyptians tie them to any group of people in ancient Mesopotamia.

2. It is clear today that the biblical assertion that the *Afrim* people that went to Europe to become the Jews and Hebrews originated from Ur of the Chaldees was false. This is because intense modern historical, archaeological, anthropological, and even genetic research have all failed to link the Jewish people to any group of people that lived in Mesopotamia in ancient times or live there in modern times. I have quoted Gary Greenberg in support of this discussion else where in the book but permit me to quote it again:

> How do we know, independent of the Bible, that Israel's presence in Egypt was preceded by an earlier presence in Palestine? Why is there no archaeological record of Israel or the Hebrew people prior to the thirteenth century B. C.? Why is there no extra-biblical evidence linking any specific Semitic tribes to the Hebrew people? And why did the so-called ten lost tribes disappear from history without an archaeological trace of their existence? For Israel's history before the thirteenth century we have only the biblical account, but that rests on a shaky ground. Modern scholars now recognize that the early books of the Bible weren't fully edited until after the seventh century B. C., and perhaps centuries later. ... The final version attempted to weave a seamless narrative out of a diverse collection of contradictory historical claims that reflected clashing political philosophies and opposing religious doctrines. The resulting compilation indicates numerous compromises of truth (The Moses Mystery: The African Origin of the Jewish People, pp. 2-3).

There has been no extra-biblical evidence linking the Jewish people to any group of Semitic tribes in the Middle East yet there has been genetic evidence linking them to an African tribe. What does that mean? Western scholarship or the Jewish people themselves have never been able to answer these questions because the fundamental claims that prompted these questions are all lies. However, Africa's story in this book answers all these questions and more.

3. The scholars of the Bible could not deny the origin and relationship of the *Afrim* people to the Ancient Egyptians so they stated that the *Afrim* people went to live in Ancient Egypt for only 430 years. Again, after intense research, there has been no evidence beside the biblical fabrication to confirm that the Jewish people went to Ancient Egypt from anywhere outside Ancient Egypt. The only evidence that I have confirmed through linguistic and cultural analysis is the fact that these people left Ancient Egypt and went to Canaan. If there is no extra-biblical evidence of their coming to Ancient Egypt but there is biblical, historical, linguistic, and cultural evidence of their leaving Ancient Egypt, then the people that left Egypt in the Exodus did not come from anywhere, they were originally Ancient Egyptians. Specifically, they were from the *Akan* and other African tribes that were the Ancient Egyptians.

4. To further disassociate the ethnic origin of the *Afrim* people and the origin of the biblical documents from Ancient Egypt, the *Afrim* scholars of the Bible further stated that the *Afrim* people were slaves in Ancient Egypt. This was to suggest that these people were not in mainstream Ancient Egyptian life to be exposed to Ancient Egyptian religious ideas or documents, but that was false. The *Afrim* people and their leader Moses learned everything they claim to have known about religion from Ancient Egypt. The Bible itself says so.

5. Again, modern scholastic research has found out that the biblical claim that the *Afrim* people were slaves in Ancient Egypt was also another biblical falsehood. In an essay entitled *Go Down into Egypt: The Dawn of American Egyptology* in *The American Discovery of Ancient Egypt* (1995), Gerry D. Scott III noted that George Sandys published his travelogue to Egypt in 1615 and pointed out the "erroneous notion that these monuments [the pyramids] were

constructed by Hebrew slaves (p. 37). (For the work of George Sandys itself see Warren R. Dawson & Eric P. Uphill (1972) *Who was Who in Egyptology*, 2nd rev. ed., Egypt Exploration Society, London).

6. Modern historians, Egyptologists, and biblical scholars all agree that the Hebrews were not slaves in Ancient Egypt. Some scholars have agreed that the *Afrim* people were not slaves in Ancient Egypt. These scholars have even hypothesized that if ever the *Afrim* people were slaves in Ancient Egypt, they must have been only the Levites because they carried Ancient Egyptian names. Asa matter of clarification, I have not yet found the names of the Levites among any African tribal names.

7. Every aspect of the origin of the *Afrim* people, their ancient language, culture, religion, and the origin of the biblical documents go back to Ancient Egypt, specifically to the *Akan* and other African tribes that were the Ancient Egyptians. These are the reasons the Jewish people have failed to reveal who they are, where they came from, what language they spoke in their earliest times and the people they left behind where they originated.

8. From this background, it becomes clear why Christian Europe has never wanted the true story of Ancient Egypt to be told. It also becomes clear why Christian Europe has influenced and encouraged western scholars to refuse to acknowledge and even deny that the Ancient Egyptians were black people and their modern descendants are the black Africans. Going back to the beginning of the book, it becomes clear why early the Catholic Church first displayed the black images of Jesus and his mother and later changed them to white images.

Beyond these, there are not many conclusions to be drawn at the end of a work like this. The book set out to reveal the Africans who wrote the Bible and it has done just that. Along the way, the book revealed a lot of things that historians, Christian Europe, and many Christians around the world have never known. Among the revelations in this book is the fact that Ancient Egyptians were black people and their modern descendants are the modern black people of Africa. Within the black people in Africa, the book went on to reveal that the *Akan* people are the specific tribal groups that created and developed the ancient civilization before it became the attraction and nucleus of all other black tribes.

The *Akan* were in Ancient Egypt before the *Afrim* people supposedly went there. The *Akan* lived at the biblical *Idumea* [Edom] before the documents of the Bible were put together. The majority of the people that left Ancient Egypt into the biblical Exodus was *Akan* and yet, the biblical chronology sought to present the *Akan* people in a way that would lead no one to suspect that they were central to the biblical story. The book revealed that the *Akan* were the people that invented the concept of religion. They imagined, created, personified, and worshipped a God for thousands of years before the *Afrim* people supposedly went to Egypt and even longer before this concept of God was introduced to Europeans. It is no wonder that these are the people to whom the ancient *Afrim* people supposedly went to learn about religion and the worship of God as the biblical narrative reveals.

I introduced a genetic study that confirmed that the ancient *Afrim* people that became the Jews and Hebrews in Europe originated from the black people that became the Africans. The book also revealed that the biblical *Abre ham* originally came from the *Akan* tribe that was at ancient *Adiabene*. This group was the *Kwahu* people that can be found today in the Eastern Region of Ghana. In support of this, I revealed that the names of the biblical patriarchs, cities, and many modern Jewish people originated from *Akan* and other African tribal languages and names. For example, I revealed that the original *Akan* name of Israel was *Asrae* and I showed the biblical evidence in support of the linguistic meaning of this name.

In this discussion so far, the biblical, historical, linguistic, cultural, and scholastic presence of the *Akan* peoples in *Afrim* and biblical history has been established beyond doubt. The evidence presented here is so overwhelming that there is no doubt that the origin of religion and Christinaity is in the *Akan* people who are found today in West Africa, and not in the branch of the Africans that went to become the Jews and Hebrews in Europe. This is not a truth most Europeans would want to know after being deceived into believing the *legendary lying lore* in their religion for over two thousand years. This is not a truth many people would like to know after designing their lives and livelihood around this *legendary lying lore.* This is not a truth Christian Europe would like to know after feeling secure in the lies of its religion for over two thousand years. Nevertheless, the story must be told and this is it.

This story has been the greatest secret kept in Christendom and the possibility of such a revelation has been the greatest fear of Christian Europe for over two thousand years. The Jewish scholars of the Bible did not want the Greeks to know the source of what they were passing on to them. However, the Greeks were the first to find out that they had been deceived. When the Greeks found out, they first denied it and then sought to sooth their consciences by naming their religion the Orthodox or True Church so as to differentiate their Church from the so-called "pagan" source they did not want to be found associated with or even want their people to know. This became even more important to the Greeks when the foundations of Christianity became a competition between them and the Roman Catholic Church in Rome. When the Catholic Church found out the true source of Christianity in Ancient Egypt, it went after this "pagan" source and made sure that the rest of Europe never found out this information. When the rest of Europe found out, it did a lot of things including changing the black images of Jesus and his mother to white images to make sure that the Africans never found out, but now the Africans have also found out the truth, and they know.

Some western historians have argued that the sources of the biblical documents are not important. According to Durant, the most important thing is the fact that the biblical documents are among the finest laws, history, poetry, and philosophy in the world and that is all that matters. To Europeans, the origin of the biblical documents may not be important because they can never claim it as theirs. They would if they could. However, the revelation of the origin of the sources of the biblical documents is important to the *Akan* and the African tribes that gave the greatest gifts of thought and perception to this world and yet the world does not know them or would not want to acknowledge them. Humanity and this world rose to this height from the depths of the thoughts and imagination of these people and the world should know this. What is worse in all these is that Europeans designed the foundations of their development from all the knowledge the ancient Africans had created and then they turned round to claim that the Africans that created all that they have used in their development were inferior, subhuman, and uncivilized. The ancient Africans long showed humanity that being superior, human, and civilized is not in simply claiming to be all these but in doing what would reflect these.

Despite Durant's awareness that the biblical authors that were assigned to books in the Old Testament were not the people that wrote them, he still wrote that Hebrew theology and Greek philosophy came together to form the foundations of European intellect. However, I believe he knew he was wrong. This is because he attributed the foundation of European intellect to Hebrew theology but the documents the Jewish scholars passed on to the Greeks were not Jewish documents. They were Ancient Egyptian and therefore the documents of the Akan and other tribes that were the Ancient Egyptians. Moreover, the theology that the *Afrim* people passed on to Europeans was not the theology of Hebrew people. When this theology was being passed on to the Greeks, there were no Jews or Hebrews anywhere in this world. It was after this theology had been passed on to the Greeks and Europeans that a group of *Afrim* people went to Europe to be known as Jews and Hebrews. The theology that the *Afrim* scholars of Alexandria passed on to the Greeks and Europeans was Ancient Egyptian and therefore *Akan* theosophy and theology. The works of scholars that went to live and work among the *Akan* people in West Africa confirm this.

319

Durant also attributed the philosophy that became the foundation of European intellect to the Greeks. However, I believe he was saying what every European scholar would say but he did not believe it. He knew the origin of philosophy was in the *Akan* and the Ancient Egyptians and Durant acknowledged this himself. In his discussion of Philosophy, he wrote that:

> Historians of philosophy have been wont to begin their story with the Greeks. The Hindus who believe that they invented philosophy, and the Chinese, who believe that they perfected it, smile at our provincialism. It may be that we are all mistaken; for among the most ancient fragments left to us by the Egyptians are writings that belong, however loosely and untechnically, under the rubric of moral philosophy. The wisdom of the Egyptians was a proverb with the Greeks, who felt themselves children beside this ancient race (1935, p. 193; see also Plato, *Timaeus*, 22B).

In this book, I have established that the *Afrim* people took what they claim as their theology from the *Akan* people in Ancient Egypt. If the Greeks were children beside the ancient wisdom of the Egyptians then it was not Hebrew theology and Greek philosophy that came together to form European intellect. Rather, it was *Akan* theosophy, theology, and philosophy that went to Europe through the Jewish people and the Greeks to become the foundations of European intellect.

In *Africa: The Face Behind The Mask*, Basil Davidson, the most eminent British historian on Africa wrote:

> Whether in the range of history, archaeology, social anthropology, or the arts, we are in the presence of a major shift in attitude toward the depth and scope of humanity's enterprise in Africa. ... Today it is increasingly seen and written that the truth about old Africa was seldom or never like this ... One by one our old fixations about Africa go quietly to pieces.
>
> Quietly, no doubt. For none of this has been much noticed in the world at large or, where it has been, readily welcomed and accepted. There is nothing surprising in this reluctance: what other peoples have thought and often still think about Africans must drag along with it a heavy weight of ancient and accustomed prejudice. The stereotype of "savage Africa" was cast in Elizabethan times, if not earlier, and the mold has grown rock-hard since then (*The Light of the Past: A Treasury of Horizon*, 1967, p. 192).

There is a major challenge in this quotation for Christianity. Most Christians do not know this but modern Christianity is false in many ways. For example, modern European portrayals of Jesus, his mother, and the people of the Bible as white people are false. Even the name *Jehovah* that Renaissance scholars and Christian Europe gave to *Yahweh* is false. The challenge therefore is for Christianity to break the rock-hard mold of racial and prejudicial sentiments against the worshipping of the true black Jesus, his mother, and the people of the Bible just as Christian Europe used to do before racial prejudice against black people got into Christianity. Christians should go back to portraying Jesus, his mother, and people of the Bible as the black people they originally were. On Christmas and Easter, Christians should be honest with themselves in the name of religious purity. They should portray and celebrate the birth and the death of *Ayesu* [Jesus] as the black person he was.

Bibliography

Acosta, Jose de (1606) *Histoire naturelle et morale des Indes*, Paris.

Adams, W. Y. (1977) *Nubia: Corridor to Africa*, Princeton University Press, Princeton.

Addis, W. E (1892) *Documents of the Hexateuch*, London.

Akrofi, C. A. (1962) *Twi Mmebusem (Twi Proverbs)* Macmillan & Co Ltd. London.

Albright, William Foxwell (1963). *The Biblical Period from Abraham to Ezra,* Harper, New York.

Aldred, Cyril (1988) *Akhenaten: King of Egypt*, Thames & Hudson, London.

Allen, Don Cameron (1949) *The Legend of Noah*, Urbana-Champagne University Press, Illinois.

Allen, Grant (1897) *Evolution of the Idea of God*, New York.

Allen, J. P. (1989) *Religion and philosophy in ancient Egypt*, Yale University Press, New Haven.

Allen, J. P. (1988*) Genesis in Egypt: The Philosophy of Ancient Egyptian Creation Accounts*, Yale Egyptological Series, 2, New Haven, Yale University Press.

Allen, J. P. Assman, J, et al., (1989) *Religion and Philosophy in Ancient Egypt*, Yale Egyptological Series, 3, New haven, Yale University Press.

Alpher, Joseph (1986) ed. *Encyclopaedia of Jewish History* (Facts on File).

Alt, Albrecht (1966) *Essays on Old Testament History and Religion*, Double Day, Garden City, New York.

Alter, Robert (1996) *Genesis: Translation and Commentary*, Norton & Co. New York.

Altizer, Thomas, J. J. (1966) *The Gospel of Christian Atheism*, The Westminster Press, Philadelphia.

Assman, J. (1984) *Agypten: Theologie und Frommigkeit einer fruhen Hochkultur,* Stuttgart Germany.

Bacon, Benjamin (1892) *The Genesis of the Genesis*, Hartford, Conn.

Bardis, O. (1967) Circumcision in ancient Egypt, *Indiana Journal for the History of Medicine*, Vol. 12 #1, pp. 22-3.

Baron, Salo W. (1952-80*) A Social and Religious History of the Jews*, 2nd rev. ed., 18vols. Columbia University Press, Columbia.

Barr, James (1987) *Biblical Chronology: Legend or Science*, University of London, London.

Baugh, Albert C. & Cable, Thomas (1993) *A History of the English Language,* Prentice Hall, Englewood Cliffs, NJ.

Beddoe, J. (1885) *The Races of Britain, A Contribution to the Anthropology of Western Europe*, Bristol, England.

Ben-Sasson, Haim H. ed. (1976) A History of the Jewish People, Harvard University Press.

Boaz, Noel T (1997) *Eco Homo: How the Human Being Emerged from the Cataclysmic History Of the Earth*, Basic Books, HarperCollins Publishing, Inc., New York.

Boyd, Paul C (1991) *The African Origin of Christianity*, Vol. II, Karia Press, London.

Breasted, James Henry (1967) *Ancient Times: A history of the Ancient World*, Vol. 1, Ancient Near East, Ginn & Company, Boston, Mass.

Breasted, James Henry (1933) *The Dawn of Conscience*, New York.

Breasted, James Henry (1912). *The Development of Religion and Thought in Ancient Egypt*, New York.

Breasted, James Henry (1909) *A History of Egypt; From The Earliest Times to the Persian Conquest*, Charles Scribner & Sons, New York.

Breasted James Henry (1906) *Ancient Records of Egypt*, Vols. 1-5, Chicago.

Briffault, R. (1927) *The Mothers,* Vol. 3. p. 205, New York.

Bright, John (1981). *A History of Israel*, 3rd. ed. Westminster, Philadelphia.

Brodie, F. M. (1945) *No Man Knows My History: The Life of Joseph Smith, the Mormon Prophet*, Knopf Books, New York.

321

Brown, B. (1923) *Wisdom of the Egyptians*, New York.

Bruno, Giordano (1584) *Spaccio della bestia triofante*, London.

Budge, Wallis E. A. (1967) *The Ancient Egyptian Book of The Dead, The Papyrus of Ani (Egyptian Text Transliteratioin and Translation*, Dover Publications, Inc., New York.

Budge Wallis E. A. (1988) *From Fetish to God in Ancient Egypt*, Dover Publications, Inc., New York.

Budge, Wallis E. A. (1988) *The Gods of the Egyptians*, Dover Publications, New York.

Budge, Wallis E. A. (1988) *Osiris and the Egyptian Resurrection,* Vols. I & II Dover Publications, New York.

Budge, Wallis E. A. (1959) *Egyptian Religion*, Bell, New York.

Cambridge Ancient History, Vols. 1- 6, 1924, New York.

Cambridge Ancient History, 1924, Vol. 1, p. 456.

Cambridge Ancient History, 1924, Vol. 5, iii, p. 428.

Cameron, Ron (ed.) (1982) *The Other Gospels: Non-Canonical Gospel Texts*, Westminster Press, Philadelphia.

Campenhausen, Han von (1977) *The Formation of the Christian Bible*, Fortress Press Philadelphia.

Carpenter E, (1920) *Pagan and Christian Creeds*, Harcourt, Brace & Co, New York.

Carus, P. (1900). *The History of the Devil and the Idea of Evil from the Earliest Times to the Present Day*, Open Court Publishing Co., Chicago.

Catholic Jerusalem Bible.

Cavalli-Sforza, Luca. L (1998) *The Chinese Human Genome Project*, in the Proceedings of the Academy of Sciences of the United States of America, Vol. 95 # 20.

Cheyne, T. K. (1893) *Founders of Old Testament Criticism*, Methuen, London.

Churchward, A. (1924). *The Origin and Evolution of Religion*, George Allen & Unwin, London.

Clements, R. E. (1967). *Abraham and David*, SCM, London.

Colenso, John William (1863) *The Pentateuch and the Book of Joshua Critically Examined*, Vol. I, pp. 171-3.

Cook, H. (1931) *Osiris: A Study in Myths, Mysteries and Religion*, C. W. Daniel Co., London.

Cowan, A. R. (1914) *Master Clues in History*, London.

Crossan, Dominic (1973) *In Parables: The Challenge of the Historical Jesus*, Harper and Row, New York.

Curtin, Philip D. (1965) *The Image of Africa, British Ideas and Actions, 1780-1850,* London.

Danquah, J. B. (1944) *The Akan Doctrine Of God: A Fragment of Gold Coast Ethics and Religion*, Lutterworth Press, London.

Davidson, Basil (1991) *African History*, Simon & Schuster, New York.

Davidson, Basil (1987) *The Lost Cities of Africa*, Little, Brown & Co, Boston, Mass.

Davidson, Basil (1967) *Africa: The Face Behind The Mask*, in The Light of The Past: A Treasury of Horizon, Simon & Schuster, Inc., New York.

Dawson, W. R. & Uphill, E. P. (1972) *Who Was Who in Egyptology,* Egypt Exploration Society, London, pp. 259-60.

Diamond, Jared (1997) *Guns, Germs, and Steel: The Fates of Human Societies,* Norton & Co, New York.

Diop, Cheikh Anta (1974) *The African Origin of Civilization: Myth or Reality*, Lawrence Hill Books, Chicago, Illinois.

Doane, T. W. (1882) *Bible Myths and their Parallels in Other Religions*, Truth Seeker Co., New York.

Dodson, Aidan (1995) *Monarchs of the Nile*, Rubicon Press, London.

Driver, S. R. (1972) *Introduction to the Literature of the Old Testament,* Peter Smith , Gloucester.

Duff, Archibald (1910) *History of Old Testament Criticism*, Watts, London.

Duling, Dennis C. & Perrin N. (1994) *The New Testament: Proclammation and Parenesis, Myth and History*, 3rd ed. Harcourt Brace, New York.

Durant, Will (1935) *The History of Civilization: Our Oriental Heritage*, MJF Books, New York.

Emerton, J. A. *The origin of the Promises to the Patriarchs in the Older Sources of the Book of Genesis*, Vetus Testamentum 32:14-32.

Encyclopaedia Britannica, 1996.

Encyclopaedia Britannica, 11th ed. P. 15.

Encyclopaedia Britannica, 1997.

Encyclopaedia Judaica, 1972, Keter Publishing House.

Ellis, A. B. Sir (1887) *The Tshi-Speaking Peoples of the Gold Coast of West Africa*, Chapman and Hall Ltd., London.

Erman, Adolf (1971) *Life in Ancient Egypt*, Dover Publications, Inc, New York.

Eusebius (1981) *Preparation for the Gospel*, Trans. Gifford, E. H., Baker Book House, Michigan.

Fage, J. D. (1967) A History of West Africa: An Introductory Survey, Macmillan, London.

Field, M. J. (1937) *Religion and Medicine of the Ga People*, cited in Akan Doctrine of God, J. B. Danquah located at George Padmore Library of African Affairs, Accra Ghana.

Fishberg, M (1911) *The Jews – A Study of Race and Environment*, London & Felling-on-Tyne.

Frankfort, H. (1948) *Kingship and the Gods; A Study of Ancient Near Eastern Religion as the Integration of Society and Nature*, University of Chicago Press, Chicago.

Frazer, James Sir (1918) *Folklore in the Old Testament*, Vols. I, II, III, Macmillan & Co, London.

Frazer, James, Sir (1926) *The Worship of Nature*, Macmillan & co, New York.

Frazer, J. G. (1907) *Adonis, Attis, Osiris*, London.

Friedman, Richard Elliot (1987) *Who Wrote The Bible?* Summit Books, New York.

Gardiner, Alan, Sir (1961) *Egypt of the Pharaohs*, Oxford University Press, Oxford.

Gibbon, E. (1923) *History of Christianity*, Peter Eckler Publishing, New York.

Gilbert, Martin ed. (1990) *The Illustrated Atlas of Jewish Civilization: 4000 years of Jewish History*, Macmilan, London.

Graham, Lloyd, M (1995*) Deceptions and Myths of the Bible*, A Citadel Press Book, Carol Publishing Group, NJ.

Grant, Michael (1994) *The Ancient Historians*, Barnes & Noble, New York.

Grant, Robert (1948) *Short History of the Interpretation of the Bible*, Macmillan, New York.

Graves, Kersey (1875) *The World's Sixteen Crucified Saviors*, London.

Graves, Robert & Patai, Ralphael (1966) *Hebrew Myths: The Book of Genesis*, McGraw-Hill, New York.

Gray, Edward M (1923) *Old Testament Criticism*, Harper, New York.

Greenberg, Gary (1996) *The Moses Mystery: The African Origin of the Jewish People*, A Birch Lane Press Book, Carol Publishing, New Jersey.

Grimal, Nicolas (1992) *Histoire de l' Egypte ancienne (A History of Ancient Egypt*, translation by Ian Shaw) Blackwell Publishers, Cambridge, Mass.

Groll, S. (1985) *Pharaonic Egypt, the Bible, and Christianity*, Jerusalem, cited in the Dictionary of Ancient Egypt.

Habel, Norman (1971) *Literary Criticism of the Old Testament*, Fortress, Philadelphia.

Halpern, Baruch (1983) *The Emergence of Israel in Canaan*, Society of Biblical Literature Monographs, Scholars Press, Decatur, GA.

Harnack, Adolf von (1990) *Marcion: The Gospel of an Alien God*, Trans. John Steely & Lyle Bierma, Labyrinth Press, Durham, NC.

Harris, J. R. (1971) *The Legacy of Egypt*, 2nd ed. Oxford University press.

Herder, Johann-Gottfried von (1774-1803) *Outlines of Philosophy of the History of Mankind*, Book VI.

Herodotus, *The Histories*, Vols. 1-8, Trans. Aubrey de Selincourt, Penguin Books, Middlesex, England.

Higgins, Godfrey Sir (1836*) The Anacylpsis, or an Inquiry into the Origin of Languages, Nations,* *and Religions,* Vols. 1 & II, Longman, Green & Co, London.

Hillers, Delbert (1969) *Covenant: The History of a Biblical Idea,* John Hopkins, Baltimore.

Hitler, Adolf (1939) *Mein Kampf,* Trans. James Murphy, London.

Hoffman, Michael A (1993) *Egypt Before The Pharaohs,* Barnes & Noble, New York.

Holtz, Robert Lee (1998*) Early Chines from Africa, Study Confirms,* Los Angeles Times Review of the Chinese Human genome Diversity Project, September 30.

Hopfner, Thomas (1922-5) *Fontes Historiae Religionis Aegyptiacae,* Vols. 1-5, 1923, pp. 281-4, Bonn, Germany.

Hornius, Georgius (1666) *Arca Noae, sive historia imperiorum et regnorum* ...cited in Adalbert Klemm, 1960, p. 113, Gottingen, Germany.

Hornung, E. (1983) *Conceptions of god in Ancient Egypt; the one and the many,* London, cited in the Dictionary of Ancient Egypt.

Howard, Cliff (1897*) Sex Worship,* New York.

Humboldt, Alexander von (1848) *Cosmos,* trans. Otte, London, p. 368.

Hyatt, J. P. (1941) *Torah in the Book of Jeremiah, Journal of Biblical Literature,* 60: 381-96. Irwin, John, *American Hieroglyphics.*

Jackson, J. G. (1933) *Was Jesus Christ A Negro? & The African Origin of The Myths and Legends of the Garden of Eden,* Curtis Alexander (ed.), 1987, ECA Associates, Chesapeake, Virginia.

Jackson, John J. (1994) *Introduction to African Civilizations,* A Citadel Press Book, Carol Publishing Group.

James, E. O. (1965) *Christian Myth and Ritual: A Historical Study,* The World Publishing Co., Cleveland, New York.

Jean-Jacques Rousseau (1755). *Discours sur l'origine de l'inegalite parmi les hommes,* section j, Paris France.

Jewish Encyclopaedia vol. vii, p. 88.

Jonckheere, F. (1951) *La circoncision des anciens Egyptiens, Centaurus,* Vol. I, p. 212-34.

Jordan, Winthrop D. (1968) *White over Black: American Attitudes Toward the Negro, 1550-1812,* University of North Carolina Press.

Josephus, Flavius (1976) *Against Apion,* Trans. Thackeray, H. St. J., Harvard University Press, Cambridge, Mass.

Josephus, Flavius, *Works,* Vols. I & II, trans. Whitson, Boston, Mass.

Kaster, Joseph (1993) *The Wisdom of Ancient Egypt,* Barnes and Noble, New York.

Kersten, Holger & Gruber, Elmar R. (1995) *The Jesus Conspiracy,* Barnes & Noble, New York.

Kochan, Lionel (1985) *The Jew and His History,* Scholars Press.

Koestler, Arthur (1976) *The Thirteenth Tribe,* Omni Publications, Palmdale, CA.

Leibniz, Wilhelm Gottfried (1507) *New Essays Concerning Human Understanding,* Book I, II, p. 20.

Levenson, Jon (1975) Who Inserted the Book of the Torah? *Harvard Theological Review,* 68: 203-33.

Locke, John (1490) *An Essay Concerning Human Understanding,* Book IV, Chpt VII, p. 16 – Instance in Man, London.

Loewen, James W (1995) *Lies My Teacher Told Me,* Simon & Schuster, New York.

Lurker, Manfred (1980) *The Gods and Symbols of Ancient Egypt,* Trans. Barbara Cummings, Thames and Hudson, London.

Mack, Burton L. (1995). *Who Wrote The New Testament: The Making of the Christian Myth,* HarperCollins Publishers, San Francisco.

Mack, Burton L. (1993) *The Lost Gospel: The Book of Q and Christian Origins,* HarperSanFrancisco, San Francisco.

Mack, Burton L. (1988) *A Myth of Innocence: Mark and Christian Origins,* Fortress Press, Philadelphia.

Mackenzie, Donald A (1980) *Egyptian Myths and Legends*, Gramercy Books, New York.

Manniche, L. (1987). *Sexual life in Ancient Egypt,* London.

Martinengo, Lorenzo (1994) *Egypt: Gift of the Nile*, Passport Books, NTC Publishing, Illinois.

Maspero, Gaston (1900) *The Passing of the Empires*, London.

Massey, Gerald (1883) *The Natural Genesis* (A Book of The Beginnings...) Vols. I & II, reprint 1998, Black Classic Press, Baltimore, MD.

Mauperituis, Pierre-Louis (1757) *Dissertation physique a l'occasion du Negre Blanc*, Chpt VI, Paris France.

Mbiti, John S. (1990) *African Religions and Philosophy*,2nd ed., Heinemann Publications, New Hampshire.

McCabe, J. (1929). *The Story of Religious Controversy*, The Stratford Co., Boston.

McCabe, J. (1935) *The Social Record of Christianity*, Watts & Co., London.

McDonald, Lee M. (1989) *The Formation of the Christian Biblical Canon*, Abingdon Press, Nashville.

McLean, Bradley (1995) On the Gospel of Thomas and Q. In *The Gospel Behind the Gospels: Current Studies on Q*, (ed.) Ron Piper.

Mendes-Flohr, Paul. R., & Reinharz Jehuda (1980). *The Jew in the Modern World: A Documentary History*, Oxford University Press.

Meyer, Marvin (1992) *The Gospel of Thomas: The Hidden Sayings of Jesus*, HarperSanFrancisco, San Francisco.

Milgrom, Jacob (1976) *Cult and Conscience*, Brill, Leiden.

Monet, P. (1968) *Egypt and the Bible*, Philadelphia, cited in the Dictionary of Ancient Egypt.

Montagu, Ashley (1943) *Edward Tyson, M. D., F. R. S*, Philadelphia.

Morenz, Siegfried (1973) *Egyptian Religion*, Ithaca: Cornell University Press, New York.

Moret, Alexandre (1912) *Kings and Gods of Ancient Egypt*, G. P. Putnam & Sons, New York.

Moyers Bill (1996) *Genesis: A Living Conversation*, Doubleday Publishing, New York.

Muller, Max (1866). *Lectures on the Science of Language*, 2vols. New York.

Neil, W. (1975) *Harper's Bible Commentary*, Harper and Row, New York.

New English Bible.

New America Bible

Nkansa Kyeremateng, K (1996) *The Akans of Ghana: Their History and Culture*, Sebewie Publishers, Accra, Ghana.

Noth, Martin (1962) *Exodus*, Westminster, Philadelphia.

Oesterley, W. O. E. (1927) *The Wisdom of Egypt and the Old Testament*, London.

Patai, Raphael & Patai Jennifer (1989) *The Myth of the Jewish Race,* rev. ed. Wayne State University Press.

Peet, T. E. (1922) *Egypt and the Old Testament*, Liverpool University press, Liverpool.

Plato: *Dialogues.* Trans Jowett, Vols. I-IV, New York.

Poe, Edgar, Alan (1845) Some Words with a Mummy.

Poliakov, Leon (1974), *The Aryan Myth: A History of Racist and Nationalistic Ideas in Europe,* Barnes & Noble, New York.

Pritchard, James B. (ed.) (1995*). Ancient Near Eastern Texts Relating to the Old Testament,* Princeton University Press, Princeton.

Propp, William H (1987) The Skin of Moses' Face – Transfigured or Disfigured, *Catholic Biblical Quarterly.*

Quirke, S. (1992) *Ancient Egyptian religion,* London, British Museum Press.

Ragland, L. (1936). *The Origins of Religion*, Watts & Co., London.

Rainey, A. F. (1987) *Egypt, Israel, Sinai – archaeological and historical relationship in the Biblical period,* Tel Aviv, cited in the Dictionary of Ancient Egypt.

Raven, Charles E. (1958) *Natural Religion and Christian Theology*, Vols. I & II, Cambridge.

Redford, Donald B. (1984) *Akhenaten: The Heretic King*, Princeton University Press, Princeton.

Redford, D. B. (1970) *A Study of the Biblical story of Joseph (Genesis 37 – 50)*, Leiden, cited in the Dictionary of Ancient Egypt.

Redford, D. B. (1992). *Egypt, Canaan, and Israel in ancient times*, Princeton University Press, Princeton.

Reinach, S. (1909, 1930) *Orpheus: A History of Religions*, New York.

Robertson, J. M. (1936) *Christianity and Mythology,* Watts & Co., London.

Robertson, J. M. (1928) *Pagan Christs*, 2nd edition, Watts & Co., London.

Rogers, J. A. (1975) *World's Great Men of Color*, Vols. I & II, Simon Schuster, New York.

Rousseau, Jean-Jacques (1755*) Discours sur l'origine et les fondements de l'inegalite parmi les hommes*, Paris.

Rylands, L. G. (1940) *The Beginnings of Ghostic Christianity*, Watts & Co., London.

Sachar, Howard (1986). *The Course of Modern Jewish History*, rev. ed. Dell Books.

Saggs, H. W. F. (1989) *Civilization Before Greece and Rome*, Yale University Press, New Haven.

Sauneron, S (1960*) The priests of ancient Egypt*, London, cited in the Dictionary of Ancient Egypt.

Save-Soderbergh, Torgny (1996) *Pharaohs and Mortals*, Barnes & Noble, New York.

Scott, III, Gerry D. (1995) Go Down into Egypt: The Dawn of American Egyptology, in *The American Discovery of Ancient Egypt*, Los Angeles County Museum of Art, Los Angeles.

Seeley, David (1994) *Jesus' Death in Q*. New Testament Studies #38, p. 222-34.

Sharpe, Samuel (1863*) Egyptian Mythology and Egyptian Christianity*, Watts & Co., London.

Shotwell, J. (1913) *The Religious Revolution of Today*, Boston.

Siculus, Diodorus (1948) *Diodorus Siculus,* 12 vols. Trans. C. H. Oldfather, reprint Loeb Classical Library, 1968).

Simpson, William Kelly (1972, Ed.) *The Literature of Ancient Egypt: An Anthology Stories, Instructions, and Poetry*, Yale University Press, New Haven.

Spence, Lewis (1990) *Ancient Egyptian Myths and Legends*, Dover Publications, New York.

Stanton, William R (1960) *The Leopard's Spots: Scientific Attitudes toward Race in America, 1815-59*, University of Chicago Press, Chicago.

Starr, Chester G (1991) *A History of the Ancient World*, Oxford University Press, New York.

St. Clair, G. (1898) *Creation Records Discovered in Egypt: Studies in the Book of the Dead*, David Nutt Co., London.

Steinberg, Meir (1991) Double Cave, Double Talk: The Indirections of Biblical Dialogue. In *Not in Heaven: Coherence and Complexity in Biblical Narrative*, Jason Rosenblatt & Joseph Sitterson (eds.), Indiana University Press, Bloomington, Ind.

Steindorf George & Seele, Keith C. (1957) *When Egypt Ruled The East,* University of Chicago Press, Chicago.

Strabo: *Geography*, Vols. 1-8, Loeb Classical Library, New York, 1917-32.

Stringer, Christopher & McKie, Robin (1997) *African Exodus: The Origins of Modern Humanity* Henry Holt Company , Inc., New York.

Strouhal, E. (1992) *Life in Ancient Egypt,* Cambridge University Press, Cambridge, pp. 28-29.

Tacitus (1964) *The Histories*, Penguin Books, New York.

Taschen, Benedikt (1994) *Description de l'Egypte: Publiee par les ordres de Napoleon Bonaparte*, Benedikt Taschen Verlag GmBH, Koln, Germany.

The Holy Bible, King James Version, A Regency Bible, Thomas Nelson Publishing.

The Holy Bible, Revised Standard Version.

The Holy Bible, New Revised Standard Version.

The Apostolic Fathers. Trans. Kirsopp Lake, Harvard University Press, Cambridge. Loeb Classical Library.

Time Magazine – *Who was Moses?* Vol. 152 # 24, December 14, 1998.

Tod, Jas, Lt. Col. (1894) *Annals and Antiquities of Rajasthan*, 2 Vols. Calcutta, India.

Trigger, Bruce G. (1995) Egyptology, Ancient Egypt, and the American Imagination, in *The American Discovery of Ancient Egypt*, Los Angeles County Museum, Los Angeles.

van Seters, J. (1975) *Abraham in History and Tradition*, Yale University Press, New Haven.

von Humboldt , Alexander (1848) *Cosmos, A Sketch Description of the Universe*, Vol. 1, trans. by. E. C. Otte, London.

Von Herder, Johann-Gottfried (1774-1803) *Outlines of a Philosophy of the History of Mankind*, Berlin, Germany.

Wade, Nicholas (1999) *Group in Africa Has Jewish Roots, DNA indicates*, New York Times Review, May 9, 10..

Walton, John (1981) The Antediluvian Section of the Sumerian King List and Genesis 5, *Biblical Archaeologist*, Fall.

Ward, C. O. (1907) The Ancient Lowly, Vol. 2, p. 76, Chicago.

Ward, W. E. F. (1991) *My Africa*, Ghana Universities Press, Accra, Ghana.

Ward. W. E. (1960) *Short History of Ghana*, Longmans, Green & Co, London.

Wente, E. F. (1972) The Contendings of Horus and Set, In *The Literature of Ancient Egypt*, Simpson, William Kelly (ed.) Yale University press, New Haven.

Westerman, Diedrich (1937) *Africa and Christianity*, from Duff Lectures, Scotland, 1935, Oxford University Press, Oxford.

Westfall, Richard S (1958) *Science and Religion in 17th Century England*, Cambridge University Press, New Haven.

Wigoder, Geoffrey ed. (1992) *The New Standard Jewish Encyclopaedia* (Facts of File).

Williams, S. J. (1930) *Hebrewisms in West Africa*, cited in *The Akan Doctrine of God*, J. B. Danquah located at George Padmore Library of African Affairs, Accra, Ghana.

Wilson, John A (1956) The Culture of Ancient Egypt, University of Chicago Press, Chicago.

Wooley, Leonard C (1965) *The Sumerians*, Norton Books, New York.

Made in the USA
Middletown, DE
11 April 2025

74145084R00217